THE ENGLISH MILITIA IN
THE EIGHTEENTH CENTURY

STUDIES IN POLITICAL HISTORY

Editor: Michael Hurst
Fellow of St. John's College, Oxford

THE
ENGLISH MILITIA
in the Eighteenth Century

The Story of a Political Issue
1660 – 1802

by
J. R. WESTERN

LONDON: Routledge & Kegan Paul
TORONTO: University of Toronto Press
1965

First published 1965
in Great Britain by
Routledge & Kegan Paul Ltd
and in Canada by
University of Toronto Press

Printed in Great Britain by
Richard Clay (The Chaucer Press) Ltd
Bungay, Suffolk

CONTENTS

v

PLATES

*Photographs reproduced by permission of the
British Museum*

PREFACE

THIS book began as an attempt to write a supplementary volume to the Webbs' great work on *English Local Government from the Revolution to the Municipal Corporations Act*. The militia then represented the harnessing of the machinery of local government to the raising of a military force. The amount of trouble it gave to local officials, if nothing else, fully entitles it to the same amount of attention that histories of local government commonly bestow on poor relief or road repairs. My work on the subject soon showed me that it was in fact entitled to more attention and of a rather different kind. For unlike other aspects of local government in the eighteenth century, the militia never ceased to figure as an issue in national politics. The study of it therefore led me, as Edward Gibbon was led by service in it, "to feel the characters of our leading men, the state of parties, the forms of office, and the operations of our civil and military system".[1] To these wider themes I have sought to give pride of place.

This then is not a work of military history but a study in English politics and local government. The military interest of a force that seldom fired a shot in anger is small. However, its history does raise certain purely military problems. What, for instance, was the value of irregular forces at that time? What was the value of local levies that were mobilised in wartime only and served under amateur officers? Did their sketchy peacetime training fit them to take over the defence of the country when they were called out? These questions cannot be answered at all adequately but I have done my best.

It may be thought strange that this book begins just *after* the Civil War and ends just *before* the main struggle with Napoleon. I have given my reasons for this in the Introduction but would add, in favour of stopping in 1802 (*a*) that the amount of material for the next decade is very great: my guess is that it is equal in volume to the whole of the material for the previous 140 years available for writing this book; (*b*) the subject is already covered by J. W. Fortescue, *The County Lieutenancies and the Army, 1803–1814* (London, 1909). The author himself calls attention to the limitations of this work at

[1] G. B. Hill (ed.), *The Memoirs of the Life of Edward Gibbon* (London, 1900), p. 138.

the beginning of his preface. But I think it could only be superseded by another book devoted entirely to this decade and doing fuller justice to the wealth of material available.

I am very conscious that I have by no means exhausted the material available even for the subject that I have tackled. I have, moreover, been obliged to leave out parts of the story in order to confine the whole to a reasonable length. I would have liked to include a full history of the militia in Scotland, which presents a most illuminating contrast to that of England. The story of the militia is not fully intelligible without thorough study of the constitutional history of the army, but to this I have only had space for passing references. It may well be thought that I should have confined myself to a more detailed study of a narrower period. But I feel that this is a subject so completely unexplored, with every question answered raising a dozen fresh ones, that a pioneering essay and the erecting of a few signposts will be more useful. I hope in the future to go on to cover a little more of the ground and I hope also that the various subjects which I have touched on will receive more attention from historians in general than they commonly have in the past.

Among the many who have helped me, I am particularly grateful to the late Richard Pares and to Mr T. H. McGuffie, who guided my first attempts to investigate eighteenth-century military matters. The late Sir Lewis Namier kindly allowed me to see Sir Roger Newdigate's diary and the correspondence of the fourth Duke of Bedford while they were in his care for use in the writing of the *History of Parliament*. I have received valuable hints from him and Mr John Brooke, as also from Miss Gladys Scott Thomson. I am grateful to Mr P. H. Williams and Professor G. E. Aylmer for reading the first draft of my opening chapters. Dr W. R. Ward has been good enough to read and comment on the whole work. My wife has shared the laborious task of reading the proofs. The many mistakes that remain in this book are of course the fault of the author, not of his valued helpers.

I gratefully acknowledge the permission of the Trustees of the Fitzwilliam estate to use the Wentworth Woodhouse muniments in the Sheffield City Library; of the Trustees of the British Museum to reproduce the illustrations in this book; and of the Controller of Her Majesty's Stationery Office to publish transcripts of Crown-copyright material in the Public Record Office.

J. R. WESTERN

January, 1965.

NOTE ON ABBREVIATIONS AND
THE METHOD OF DESCRIBING SOURCES

1. In most cases I have referred to books in the footnotes, after the first occasion, by the name of the author or editor (in the case of some of the parliamentary reports, the publisher). When I have used several works by the same author, or works by authors with the same name, I have added a short title in the references. Anonymous pamphlets are referred to by a short title after the first mention and so are most of the MSS. collections not located in the British Museum or the Public Record Office. MSS. in county record offices identified only by a number are normally from the lieutenancy records of the county concerned.

2. Letters in unfoliated collections of MSS. are referred to by the writer and date. Old Style dates have not been altered but the year has been taken to begin on January 1. Spelling and punctuation have as a rule been modernised.

3. Abbreviations and standard short references:

(*a*) BM = British Museum, London.
   Add. = Additional MSS.
   Eg. = Egerton MSS.

Key to numbers:

    Add. 6839. Letters to Sir A. Mitchell.
        21048. Earl of Suffolk, correspondence with Lord Cornwallis, 1661–4.
        21922. Sir R. Norton, deputy lieutenant, Hants, letter book, 1640–62.
        21947–8. Duke of Richmond, correspondence, 1660–73.
        27411. Calverley papers.
        27447–8. Paston correspondence, 1570–1701.
        27918–28088 and Eg. 3425–3505. Godolphin and Osborne papers.
        28230. Lady Seaforth, correspondence, 1716–18.
        29551. Finch-Hatton correspondence.
        29599. Carews of Beddington, Surrey, correspondence, 1585–1815.

29913, 30012. Jervis papers.

30867. John Wilkes, correspondence.

32163. Earl of Carlisle, estate accounts, 1662–7.

32324. Seymour, Barons Troubridge, correspondence.

32526. Essays by Roger North.

32702–33129. MSS. of the Duke of Newcastle, other members of the Pelham family, etc.

33574, 33582. Hale of King's Walden, Herts., MSS.

34167–8. Sir R. and Sir W. Twysden, accounts.

34222. Earl of Westmorland, joint lord lieutenant of Northamptonshire, letter book, 1660–5.

34303. Forest subdivision, Berkshire, minutes of meetings, 1786–95.

34306. John Milward, deputy lieutenant, Derbyshire, letter book, 1660–6.

35351–36250. Hardwicke papers.

36913, 36922. Aston papers.

37721. Westmorland, extracts from rate-books, etc.

37842, 37874. Windham papers.

38213. Liverpool papers.

39246. Wodehouse papers: Suffolk lieutenancy letter book, 1664–76.

40102, 43770. Melville papers.

41142. Townshend papers.

41254. Viscount Fauconberg, lord lieutenant of North Riding, letter book, 1665–84.

41851, 41854, 42058. Thomas Grenville, 1755–1846, papers.

Stowe 263. Letters to Sir Charles Hanbury Williams, 1755–7.

Eg. 1719. Lady A. Egerton to Count Bentinck, 1752–63.

2043. Col. B. Reames, diary of proceedings in the house of commons, 1661–2.

2136. Sir Francis Dashwood, papers.

2537, 2542. Sir Edward Nicholas, secretary of state to 1662, papers.

2717. Gawdy, of West Harling, Norfolk, correspondence.

(N.B. The above key is intended only to identify volumes of MSS. cited in this book and it does not list all the volumes in each of the collections referred to.)

(*b*) Public Record Office, London:

The following are the classes of records referred to:

WO.1	Secretary at War, in-letters.
WO.3	Commander in Chief, out-letters.
WO.4	Secretary at War, out-letters.
WO.6	Secretary of State, out-letters.
WO.17	Monthly returns.
WO.25	Registers, various.
WO.27	Inspection returns.
WO.34	Amherst papers.
WO.68	Records of disbanded militia regiments.
SP.41	State Papers: in-letters, domestic.
SP.44	State Papers: entry books, domestic.
HO.42	Home Office: in-letters, domestic.
HO.43	Home Office: entry books, domestic.
HO.50	Home Office: in-letters, military.
HO.51	Home Office: entry books, military.
PRO 30/8	Chatham correspondence.
PRO 30/24	Shaftesbury papers.

(c) Other Abbreviations:

CJ	=	Journals of the House of Commons.
CSPD	=	Calendar of State Papers, Domestic Series.
CTB	=	Calendar of Treasury Books.
DNB	=	Dictionary of National Biography.
HMC	=	Historical Manuscripts Commission, reports (followed by the number of the report or name of collection reported on).
LJ	=	Journals of the House of Lords.
RO	=	Record Office.

(Frequently cited are:

Northamptonshire RO: X.266–70. Lieutenancy minute books and other papers.

Lancashire RO: LC. Lieutenancy correspondence.
LM. Lieutenancy minutes.

East Sussex RO: LCG/EW. Lieutenancy minutes, county

LLE; LLM. Lewes subdivision, minutes and papers.

LPM. Pevensey subdivision, minutes.)

Wentworth Woodhouse = Wentworth Woodhouse MSS., Sheffield City Library.

4. From 1758 the pay and clothing of the unembodied militia were provided by annual acts. Where mention is made of a provision of these acts, the reference usually given is to the first act in which it appears.

INTRODUCTION

THIS book attempts, through the study of one controversial institution, to say something about the general content of eighteenth-century politics—the formation of public opinion, the processes by which it influenced legislation and the limitations placed on the power and efficiency of government by the state of public feeling. The conditions of the time make it necessary to tell the story largely in terms of local interests and private quarrels. But fragmented though the life of the nation then was, there did exist some consciousness of common, national interests. On this the power of the state depended: without it, the government of the United Kingdom would have suffered the same decline as did the Polish Republic or, less spectacularly, that of the Dutch. What Englishmen took to be the general interest and the obligations of the citizen resulting therefrom are the main subject of this book.

Military administration in this period is a neglected subject but one well suited to a study such as the present. The seventeenth century saw the emergence of standing armed forces in this country and politics thereafter were deeply influenced by the potential increase of state power which this represented. At the same time in the century after the Restoration the interference of the central government in local administration and religious affairs was greatly reduced. As a result, the defence of the nation and of its interests abroad became the main business of the central executive and of parliament also, in so far as it dealt with national rather than local affairs. Military questions therefore had a central position in politics, and though they seem to have a more restricted significance than the religious concerns of the seventeenth century or the social and economic ones of the nineteenth, this was not really so. The interest in them was at least as much political as technical. The armed forces were seen as a means by which the ruler could dominate society and remould it to his will. Every group seeking political power wished to control them. For all concerned with preserving parliamentary institutions, what constituted control was a perennial problem. The executive had to be given the means to keep up in the arms race, and yet the domestic power which the armed forces gave it—either directly or through the workings of the patronage system—had to be kept within bounds.

The militia had only a subordinate part in military organisation from the end of the Civil Wars onward, for it was restricted to service at home and saw little fighting. For a study of the present kind it has however two great advantages. It had close connections with local administration and so with the all-important local as well as with national political life. It was, moreover, a live political issue—though often only just alive—for a very long time. Indeed, the climax of the story comes in just those middle years of the eighteenth century when most political issues were as good as dead. A history of the militia therefore has something to contribute to the study of political conditions in all parts of the century and to the bridging of the rather featureless gap between the periods of excitement at its two ends. The account begins—as is very often the case with an eighteenth-century institution—at the Restoration. The immediate reason for this is that the Restoration militia acts and the measures of the Interregnum from which they largely derived were the first comprehensive legislation on the subject and the acts of 1660–2 were in force till 1757. There are deeper reasons both military and political. The Civil War period saw the first emergence of an English standing army, and in consequence the emergence of the militia in the sense in which the term is used in this book—namely, something different from a standing army—and all the consequential questions of whether the nation should rely on one or the other or both and what the relationship between them should be. It was also from the time of the Civil War that the problem of the relations between crown and parliament began to assume the form characteristic of the eighteenth century. Government came to depend on their continuous co-opera-tion. Attempts to dispense with one or the other or both during the Interregnum did not succeed; nor did subsequent attempts to rule without parliament. Legislative power passed steadily out of the king's hands but the king remained powerful because the legislature was not so constituted that it could exercise complete and continuous control over the executive. An appropriate division of labour between king and parliament had therefore to be painstakingly worked out, and this was the political setting for the narrower military questions.

In the first part of this book, the making of the Restoration militia settlement and the clash of tendencies which it represented are first described; then the working of the settlement and the strengths and weaknesses which resulted from the way in which it was made. The second part describes the agitations for reform, at length successful, which themselves stemmed from those strengths and weaknesses. The last part deals with the workings of the new system, seeking as before to pinpoint the after-effects of its political origins. The story of its growth and modification is carried, in the last two parts, down to 1802—to the consolidating militia act passed after the Peace of Amiens. The system established in 1757 lasted like its predecessor for almost a century—until 1852.[1] But the 'Napoleonic' decade after 1802 saw a very great expansion of military activity and the growth of a very complicated system involving several different kinds of force: the militia formed a part of this and can no longer be studied independently. The political interest of the militia question, at any rate in its traditional form, was moreover almost at an end by the turn of the century. These are some of the reasons which have prompted the ending of this book in 1802. In a final chapter an attempt is made to return to the themes outlined above and point the moral of a story inevitably diffuse but not, I hope, without point.

[1] J. W. Fortescue, *A History of the British Army* (London, 1899–1930), vol. xiii, pp. 22–3. But cf. vol. xi, p. 448.

In loving memory of my Mother

ELISABETH WESTERN

PART ONE
The Militia of the Restoration

I

THE ORIGINS AND CHARACTER
OF THE RESTORATION
MILITIA ACTS

T HE militia of the Restoration, like the whole political settlement of that time, was created by the coming together of
groups and policies more commonly and naturally found in opposition to one another. To this is due both the character of the force
and its eventual decay. The deepest and most enduring factor at work
in its making was the national dislike of standing armies. It was
the formation of the New Model Army and the beginning soon
afterwards of its interference in affairs of state which turned anti-
army sentiment into an active political force. But the thing itself
seems already to have been well established. A pamphlet published
in August 1648 already contained in outline all the arguments
against standing armies which were to be endlessly reiterated for
more than a century thereafter. Standing armies were represented as
unnecessary, inefficient and dangerous: unnecessary for England
because she was an island and did not therefore need to maintain
troops in time of peace; inefficient because the discipline of an army
deteriorated during the enforced idleness of peacetime and so it
became useless; and dangerous because an army was bound to have,
and to fight for, an interest of its own distinct from that of the nation.
The history of both the Roman and the Ottoman empires was held
to show that where there was a standing army there would also be
arbitrary government.[1]

Dislike of armies did not, however, constitute the sole reason for
having a militia; there were other reasons quite different and just as
important. These arose from the fact that the people at large were

[1] *The Peaceable Militia, or the Cause and Cure of the late and present War*,
pp. 2–4. For the date of publication see G. K. Fortescue (ed.), *Catalogue of the
Pamphlets . . . Collected by George Thomason* (London, 1908), vol. i, p. 663.

still in possession of arms. It is common knowledge that gentlemen long continued to wear swords. It was equally the case that householders commonly kept arms to protect themselves against thieves.[1] For some years after 1660 the existence of dumps left over from the Civil Wars, and of disbanded soldiers well able to use them, was a constant source of alarm. Until 1670, proclamations periodically called on soldiers of the disbanded army to leave the capital.[2] Towards the end of 1661 the town of Exeter surrendered 937 old musket barrels to the Ordnance, despite which a store of arms was soon afterwards reported to be hidden in the Guildhall there. A correspondent of Sir Edward Seymour drew the conclusion that this and no doubt other cities were planning a rebellion.[3] In October 1660 a prebendary of Bristol reported that the stables of a house where his predecessors had lived were now full of cannon-balls.[4] In December of that year a barrel of gunpowder was intercepted on its way to a 'Commonwealths man'.[5] These are three examples from a great number. The danger was increased by the existence of towns and even houses with fortifications able to stand a siege. To such places armed bands might retire and defy the government. In 1668 a spy reported that some persons were planning to seize Raby Castle in county Durham as a place of refuge to be occupied if there was ever an attempt to massacre them. It was thought that 100 men might hold it against 10,000.[6] To anyone who recalls the Huguenot cities of refuge in earlier times this report will not seem implausible.

Arms continued to be kept above all by those animated by what it is for once correct to call a feudal spirit—at least a bastard-feudal spirit. When Ormond passed through the midlands to Chester in July 1662, on his way to take charge of Ireland, he was received en route not only by the militia of the different counties but also by 'the peaceable gentry with their formal livery cloaks'.[7] On great public occasions, like the election of county members or the 'progresses' of great public figures, the more opulent landowners expected to appear at the head of a body of dependents. These men were commonly armed[8] and were intended at need to make a more than ceremonial appearance. Large country houses commonly contained a store of arms to equip them. Nobody perhaps could rival

---

[1] Cf. the remarks of Sir Robert Atkyns, CSPD, July–September 1683, pp. 402–3.,

[2] R. Steele (ed.), *Tudor and Stuart Proclamations* (2 vols., Oxford, 1910) nos. 3296, 3339, 3361, 3396, 3403, 3425, 3533.

[3] HMC, *Exeter City*, p. 216; HMC, *Leyborne-Popham*, p. 193; HMC, *Somerset*, p. 93.

[4] CSPD, 1660–1, p. 311.   [5] *Ibid.*, p. 412.   [6] CSPD, 1667–8, p. 437.

[7] HMC, *Ailesbury*, p. 163.

[8] See, e.g., descriptions of Monmouth's progress in the north midlands in the CSPD, 1682, pp. 389–90, 423.

the Duke of Beaufort, who even in 1718 was found to have three field guns and a 'pateire', 84 muskets, 22 other guns, a dozen swords, a barrel of gunpowder and another of musket-balls newly cast.[1] But in 1683 the Earl of Macclesfield had 49 muskets and various other weapons and two of his Cheshire friends, members of the Legh clan, had 14 and 9 muskets respectively.[2] In Shropshire a Mr Forrester and his son were found in the same year to have about 30 muskets and other guns, and also confessed to having had 50 pikes which they had burnt.[3] At Blickling Hall in Norfolk there were found 34 bills, clubs, javelins and the like, besides a brace of pistols, four larger guns, a quantity of armour and six old swords.[4] Sir Christopher Calthorp in the same county in 1689 had 12 muskets, a snaphance, a brass musketoon and some pistols, about 40 javelins and halberds, eleven old rusty swords and some old armour.[5] Again, a great many more examples could be given; and for every verified case there were many reports unverified or untrue of such arsenals.

A civil population in arms represented a constant threat of disorder if not of worse. For financial and administrative no less than for political reasons it was impossible to maintain a standing force strong enough to disarm or entirely overawe the nation.[6] The only alternative was to arm and organise the friends of government as a sort of amateur gendarmerie to counterbalance the malcontents. If there was a rising, the loyalists were to come together and beat it down. At other times they were to try and anticipate trouble by searching for and confiscating the arms of likely troublemakers and more generally to discourage the disaffected by 'showing the flag' and making it seem that force was on the side of the authorities.

It followed that once a standing army was in being, a militia could be wanted for either of two contrasting purposes: to supplant the army or to assist it by taking over work that it would otherwise have had to leave undone because of its insufficient numbers. This contrast will appear in different forms all through this book and it was already to be seen in the development of the militia question between the formation of the New Model and the passing of the militia acts of the Restoration. The first attempt to use the militia to supplant, or at any rate counterbalance, the army came at the climax of the struggle between the New Model and the Long Parliament, at the end of 1648. On December 2, while the party hostile to the army was

[1] HMC, 4th Report, Appendix, p. 366.   [2] HMC, *Kilmorey*, p. 364.
[3] CSPD, July–September 1683, pp. 82, 137, 149, 162–3 167–8, 175–6, 186.
[4] HMC, *Lothian (Blickling)*, p. 130.   [5] HMC, *Le Strange*, p. 109.
[6] Sir William Darcy did propose to Secretary Nicholas after the Restoration that the whole population be disarmed. Good subjects would then not have to fear that 'reconciled' enemies would be able to plot to 'rob us of peace church and sovereign'. BM, Eg. 2542, ff. 526–7.

still in control, parliament passed a Militia Ordinance which was the true parent of all subsequent militia legislation. It was the first time that all the law and custom relating to the subject was reduced into a single measure of reform and codification. A day or two later the army put its friends in control of parliament by means of Pride's Purge and one of the first acts of the new majority was to rescind the Militia Ordinance.[1] That the Ordinance was a weapon against the army seems the only reasonable conclusion from this sequence of events. The parliament which met in 1654 according to the Instrument of Government returned to the charge and sought to establish a militia under parliamentary and local civil control, while reducing the army by almost half.[2] For this reason among others the Protector hastened to dissolve it. Similarly, the officers of the army got rid of the revived Rump for a second time in 1659 in part because of suspicions aroused by its passing a militia ordinance.[3] When in 1660 Monk again restored the Rump and brought back into it the members who had been 'secluded' in 1648, their last act, along with the ordering of free elections, was the establishment of a militia controlled by their own friends. So suspicious did this seem to the army that Monk at one point tried to dissuade them from it and had difficulty in preventing some of his officers from stopping it by force. This militia was duly established and was in arms at the time of the Restoration.[4] Such were the first attempts to use the militia against the army. It will be seen that they were made by parliamentarians. The militia is traditionally regarded as a tory cause but its strongest and sincerest supporters were always to be on the parliamentary or whig side. In 1660, however, the cavaliers were not wanting in enthusiasm for a force that might protect them against the remains of the New Model.[5]

Against the anti-army militia plans must be set those in the same interregnal years which were designed to help the army. The friends of the army in the Rump, having rescinded the Militia Ordinance of 1648 as soon as they got control, passed an ordinance of their own in 1650 that was very similar except in giving control of the force to

[1] C. S. Firth and R. S. Rait (ed.), *Acts and Ordinances of the Interregnum* (London, 1911), vol. i, pp. 1248–52.

[2] S. R. Gardiner, *History of the Commonwealth and Protectorate* (London, 1894–1903), vol. iii, pp. 51, 65–6, 89–91.

[3] G. Davies, *The Restoration of Charles II* (San Marino and London, 1955), pp. 114–15.

[4] Davies, pp. 298–300. Firth and Rait, vol. ii, pp. 1450–5. HMC, 7th Report, Appendix, pp. 462–3. Richard Ellsworth asked later for a reward for warning. Monk of this officers' plot (CSPD, 1660–1, pp. 155, 508). For the work of the militia thus settled see, e.g., HMC, 5th Report, Appendix, p. 361.

[5] But the Earl of Peterborough thought the militia dangerous. It taught the use of arms to the disaffected. CSPD, 1663–4, p. 300.

members of their own 'party organisation'. In March 1651 they were warned to be ready to combat risings expected in various parts of the country in conjunction with a royalist invasion from Scotland. When the invasion did take place, they stood ready in the several counties to overawe the conspirators; some of them were even sent to join the army, and served with some distinction at Worcester.[1] In 1655 Cromwell revived the militia to combat the widespread conspiracy of that year, and it was militia of a sort, not ordinary troops, that were placed at the disposal of that epitome of military rule, the Major Generals.[2] In 1659, when the restored Rump passed an ordinance similar to that of 1650, its aim seems to have been the suppression of rebellion rather than of its own army. There was another very ambitious royalist conspiracy at this time and it was quite largely due to the militia that in the end only an isolated group of the conspirators got as far as action.[3] The restored royal government hastened to establish a militia to frustrate plots and preside over the dissolution of the old army. At first the plan was to have no other force.[4] But it was soon found expedient to have a few standing troops as well and the royal government was destined increasingly to regard the militia as auxiliaries of the army.

Thus by 1660 there was coming into being an oppositional or 'country' view of the militia and also a governmental or 'court' view. They did not necessarily conflict but they were different, and this is reflected in differing opinions about the sort of force that the militia ought to be. The model most in favour was that of the old trained bands. These had a double origin. From the ancient obligation on each man to keep arms according to his social rank had evolved an obligation on all property owners to supply and equip soldiers (or to serve in person) for home defence. Large proprietors supplied more than one soldier and small ones were combined in groups, each of which had to find and equip a man. At the same time the practice grew up of selecting a proportion of the able-bodied manhood of each county to receive a certain amount of military training for some days each year at the common expense. These two bodies tended to be identical and there was also a tendency to think that they ought to be different in character from the troops hired to fight abroad.[5] Sir Robert Cotton told the privy council in 1627

---

[1] Gardiner, vol. i, pp. 298–9, 404, 407, 441–2, 445–6. The phrase quoted is his.
[2] *Ibid.*, vol. iii, pp. 128, 146–9, 171–2. For the Major-Generals, chap. xl and the supplementary chapter.
[3] 'Sir George Booth's business' in Cheshire. Davies, pp. 131–5. Firth and Rait, vol. ii, pp. 397–402, 1336–42, for the Rump's ordinances. [4] LJ, vol. xi, p. 237.
[5] W. B. Willcox, *Gloucestershire, a Study in Local Gvernment*, 1590–1640 (New Haven, 1940), pp. 79–92. J. Wake (ed.), *Papers Relating to Musters, Beacons, Subsidies, etc. . . . in the County of Northampton*, A.D. 1586–1623 (Northampton

for the land forces, if it were for an offensive war, the men of less livelihood were the best spared; and we used formerly to make such war
Purgamenta Reipub[licae] if we made no further purchase by it. But
for the safety of a Commonwealth, the wisdom of all times did never
intrust the Public Cause to any other than to such as had a portion in
the Publick Adventure.[1]

When the temporary levies of men of 'less livelihood' evolved into a
standing army, there was all the more reason to believe that the social
order might be in danger unless home defence was in the hands of
men of property. The parliamentary militia ordinances of 1648–60 all
took the trained bands as their starting point. They rescued them
temporarily from inanition,[2] fixed the obligations by which they were
levied and kept in being, and saw to it that the right people were in
control. The militia acts of 1661–3 were to follow this example.

There was, however, another pattern in being. The militia which
Cromwell had entrusted to his Major Generals in 1655 was quite
unlike the trained bands. It consisted of volunteers who were paid
£8 a year in return for attendance at quarterly musters and whenever
needed. It was financed by a tax on the wealthier of the 'malignants'
whom it existed to keep in check. Numbering 6020 horse and a mere
200 foot, it was under a tenth of the size of the trained bands. But,
unlike them, it was compact and simple in its organisation and could
do a good deal of service without enormous expense.[3] This was the
type of force most in line with the 'court' view of the militia, the
trained bands being more akin to the 'country' view. There are signs
that after the Restoration ministers were attracted by the Cromwellian example. A paper supposed to be in Clarendon's hand records
the details of a strikingly similar plan. Sixty-two troops of horse
totalling 7213 officers and men were to be maintained out of the
proceeds of a single month's assessment of £70,000 each year—a
significant figure as will later be seen. They were to be divided among
the counties in proportion to the amount at which each was assessed.
The lowness of their pay—the privates again got £8 a year—suggests
that they were not to be on permanent duty.[4] During the 1660s the
government will often be found trying to alter the traditional militia
system along these lines—attempts that were always unpopular be
cause they amounted to making the militia more like a standing army.

Record Society, 1926), Introduction, pp. liv–xcvi, civ–cxii. BM, Harl. 6844, reproduced in F. Grose, *Military Antiquities* (2nd ed., London, 1801), vol. i,
pp. 79–96.
    [1] J. Rushworth, *Historical Collections* (London 1659), Part i, vol. i, p. 469.
    [2] They were all temporary measures.
    [3] As p. 7, n. 2. For the strength of the trained bands, below p. 23. This militia
had in the outcome to be kept always embodied like the army and so did not save
money as planned.   [4] BM, Add. 37425, ff. 47–53.

Behind this division of opinion stood the much older and deeper controversy about the extent of the military prerogatives of the crown. This had been one of the causes of war in 1642, and the need to end it was the immediate cause of the Restoration militia acts. In 1642 parliament had challenged the king's exclusive right to control the armed forces and successive parliaments maintained this challenge against both Charles and Cromwell. By contrast Charles II was allowed to take control of the forces in 1660 without any dispute. By way of compensation there was determined resistance to the prerogative powers of exacting men, arms and money for military purposes.

These powers, deriving from the common law obligation to serve in defence of the realm, were an old source of grievance. Statutes of the fourteenth century had provided that nobody was to be obliged to provide soldiers, save in consequence of feudal obligations or a parliamentary grant; also that nobody was to be forced to serve in person outside his own county (save during an invasion) or to keep arms in excess of what had been obligatory in former times.[1] The last restriction was given point by the existence of the Statute of Winchester (1285), which laid down exactly each man's obligation to keep arms according to his social class. Under Tudors and Stuarts these restrictions were almost forgotten. Men were pressed for foreign service, and an act of Philip and Mary's reign[2] enforcing attendance at musters could only help, not hinder the government. The obsolete requirements of the Statute of Winchester as to weapons were slightly modernised by another act of the same year,[3] but this again was no impediment to the government; in any case it was repealed at the beginning of James I's reign,[4] and the obligation to provide arms, if the country was not to revert to the conditions of the thirteenth century, had of necessity to be reinterpreted at the discretion of the royal officials. In practice, the propertied classes were not compelled to serve abroad in person and their home defence obligations were to some extent fixed by custom.[5] But in these matters and still more over billeting and local taxes to supply the needs of the soldiers they were much at the mercy of a 'forward policy' by the government or its agents.

[1] W. Stubbs, *Constitutional History of England* (library ed., Oxford, 1880), vol. ii, pp. 588–93. *Statutes of the Realm*, vol. i, pp. 255, 321; vol. ii, p. 137.
[2] 4 & 5 Phil. & Mar., cap. 3.   [3] 4 & 5 Phil. & Mar., cap. 2.
[4] I Jac. I, cap. 25, s. 7.
[5] The temporary militia act of 1661 was to be without prejudice to the future rights of places charged by its sanction with men and arms 'beyond the ancient proportion' (13 Car. II, cap. 6, s. 3). On military obligations on the subject before the Civil Wars see the works cited in p. 7, n. 5; also C. G. Cruickshank, *Elizabeth's Army* (London, 1946).

Parliament before the Civil Wars wished therefore to reduce and fix the military obligations of the subject by statute. The Petition of Right made a start by declaring the billeting of soldiers in private houses to be illegal.[1] In December 1640 the commons set up a committee to enquire into the misdeeds of the county lieutenancies and the levying of military taxes contrary to law and to bring in a bill to regulate the conduct of the lieutenancies and the 'rating, levying and assessing of the arms of the kingdom'.[2] The Militia Ordinance of 1648 and its successors did just that and represent not only an aspect of the struggle between parliament and the army but a move towards fulfilling an old parliamentary aspiration.

It seems to have been the pamphlet of 1648 already referred to which first linked this question with that of control. It was written to advocate legislation fixing the military obligations of the subject as an alternative to direct parliamentary control of the militia. The author thought that it would be safer for control of the sword and control of the purse to be in different hands.[3] This closely foreshadows the provisions of the Restoration militia acts.

In 1660 the restored royal government tried to re-establish a militia under royal control by the use of the prerogative as before 1642.[4] However, not only was it no longer practicable to restore the organisation which had then existed,[5] but the legality of the orders given was often questioned. In Montgomeryshire there were refusals to pay a charge of 32s. per soldier imposed for the replacement of worn-out arms. The king's right to levy men and weapons was contested. The musters were much hindered and several persons had to be imprisoned.[6] In Lancashire in 1661 it was impossible to pay some of the soldiers who were mustered because the constables refused to collect the assessment made by the lieutenancy for the purpose, claiming that they had no power to make such a levy.[7] At the end of

---

[1] Martial law was also declared illegal and so, vaguely, were charges imposed by the lieutenancies. S. R. Gardiner (ed.), *Constitutional Documents of the Puritan Revolution, 1628–1660* (Oxford, 1889), pp. 2–4.

[2] CJ, vol. ii, p. 50. I am indebted for this reference to a Manchester B.A. thesis by Mr J. T. Goodfellow, 'the Organisation of the Militia under the Early Stuarts' (1956).   [3] *Peaceable Militia, passim.*

[4] But to some extent it took the ordinance of the restored secluded members as its guide to the system. CSPD, 1660–1, p. 150; cf. p. 459, where the rates specified for charging horse and foot are the same as in the ordinance.

[5] Assessments of liability to provide troops made before 1642 had been made out of date by changes in landownership. BM, Eg. 2542, ff. 526–7; BM, Add. 21922, ff. 247–8. In Yorkshire few of those who had formerly managed the militia and knew how it was done were still alive. HMC, 5th Report, Appendix, p. 195: Thos. Gower to John Langley, 31 October 1660.   [6] CSPD, 1660–1, p. 462.

[7] CSPD, 1661–2, pp. 156, 181. This was in November when a temporary militia act had already been passed.

1660 the privy council had to issue a general order for the putting into force of the act of Philip and Mary for attendance at musters against the many people who were avoiding the service of the trained bands on frivolous grounds.[1] The legality of the militia's police activities—searching houses, seizing suspects and so on—was also questioned. Henry Coker, who was engaged on this work in Wiltshire, was threatened with litigation by some of his victims despite his commission and his instructions from the lieutenancy and the privy council. He believed that he was only saved by the militia act of 1661.[2] There is indeed no doubt that the militia acts of 1661-3 were all required in the first instance as measures of indemnification. Protection was given by them to all those concerned in hunting down 'fanaticks' whose loyalty was in doubt, from the time of the return of the secluded members onwards; to local civil officers helping the lieutenancy; and to those who had demolished fortifications. The militia organisation which the royal authorities had brought into being was legalised and confirmed in existence first until 25 March 1662 and later until 25 March 1663.[3] The corollary of an indemnity was that a proper statutory basis should be given to the activities of the militia in future. Therefore, although the king secured the prerogative of command, it proved possible to deprive him of the other prerogative powers hitherto the effective basis of the military strength of the crown.

II

With the foregoing in mind, some sense can be made of the scanty reports of militia proposals and debates in the Restoration parliaments. A militia bill was introduced in the commons in November 1660, but did not even reach the lords before the Convention Parliament was dissolved. It was violently attacked as setting up martial law and 'entrenching on the Subject's privilege'. Bamfield claimed that parts of it were taken from the bill for perpetuating the system of Major Generals that had been rejected by the Cromwellian parliament in 1656.[4] Complaints were made, notably by Prynne, of oppressive behaviour by the new lieutenancies in the exercise of their police functions. It would seem that at this stage the police powers intended to be given to the militia authorities for the harassing of the disaffected were as much a cause of complaint as the character of the force.[5]

[1] BM, Add. 21922, f. 244. [2] BM, Add. 32324, f. 131.
[3] 13 Car. II, cap. 6, ss. 1, 2. 13 and 14 Car. II, cap. 3, ss. 15, 20. 15 Car. II, cap. 4, ss. 16, 18.
[4] For which see C. H. Firth, *The Last Years of the Protectorate* (London, 1909) vol. i, chap. iv.
[5] W. Sandby (pub.), *The Parliamentary or Constitutional History of England from the Earliest Times to the Dissolution of the Convention Parliament*, etc.

The ordering of a militia bill was one of the first acts of the commons when the Cavalier Parliament met in the spring of 1661. It was Sir Heneage Finch, the Solicitor General, who with Serjeant Charlton was instructed to bring it in. Despite these signs of concern by the government's friends in the house, the bill stuck fast in a 'committee of the whole' of which Finch was chairman and it was clear that it could not be passed before the summer recess.[1] A temporary act was therefore hastily passed, declaring that the command of all military forces and forts belonged to the king and neither house of parliament might pretend to it. As noted earlier, it also continued the existing militia organisation until the spring and indemnified certain persons concerned in it. Two clauses were added in committee calculated to preserve the rights of the subject. The bill was not to be prejudicial to districts at present charged above their 'ancient proportion'; and soldiers were not to be obliged by virtue of it to march out of the kingdom, otherwise than as the laws allowed.[2]

It was only in the spring of 1662, nearly a year after its first introduction, that the 'permanent' militia bill became law. The parliamentary session had been adjourned, not terminated, for the summer recess: the friends of the bill were thus able to revive it at the committee stage, where it lay dormant. It rather seems as if they had now become more skilled in parliamentary tactics. On 3 December 1661 Sir Roger Bradshaigh told the commons of a plot to kidnap three deputy lieutenants in Lancashire, Sir Philip Musgrave spoke of dangers threatening the garrison of Carlisle which he commanded, and there were several other reports of the same kind. The house sent some of its members to inform the king and ask him to prepare to put down an insurrection. At the same time a very large committee, including all who were or had been commissioned officers of the king or his father, was set up to bring in a militia bill 'suitable to the present condition of this kingdom'. Soon afterwards the king communicated to both houses details of a huge plot in which all the enemies of the cavaliers from anabaptists to purchasers of crown lands and presbyterians were included.[3] All this seems very like a warming up of the house to produce action.

The commons' committee favoured a plan of the Cromwellian type. A 'temporary' standing force of 1200 horse was to be raised, apparently from the existing militia and for service until the danger

(London, 1751–61), vol. xxiii, pp. 2, 14–15, 22–4 (cf. pp. 51–3). CJ, vol. viii, pp. 175, 184, 187–8, 207–8. A bill to raise a militia tax in London also failed to pass, *ibid.*, pp. 192, 206–7, 231.

[1] *Ibid.*, pp. 249, 254, 257–8, 264, 267, 273–5, 280, 284.

[2] *Ibid.*, pp. 303–4. LJ, vol. xi, pp. 313–14, 317, 330–1. 13 Car. II, cap. 6.

[3] CJ, vol. viii, p. 324. BM, Eg. 2043, ff. 23, 29–31. He later denied that it was done to induce them to vote a standing force. HMC, *Beaufort*, p. 51.

from the plot was over. A bill on these lines seems to have been considered, without having gone through a first and second reading, by a committee of the whole house, and after long debate the central feature of it was accepted on January 14.[1] But at the next meeting of the committee the Solicitor General replaced Sir Robert Atkyns in the chair and 'the Old Bill for the militia' was considered.[2] This must have been the bill of the previous summer revived. Why this change took place I do not know.

Such was the atmosphere in the commons that the Old Bill passed its remaining stages there and an addition was made to it of crucial importance if the views of court and parliament were to be kept in harmony. On February 22 a proviso was approved by which the king was empowered to raise up to £70,000 a year for three years—in the same way as a month's assessment for that amount—for the payment of any militia he might find it necessary to employ on active service.[3] This was something taken from the Rump ordinances of 1650 and 1659—that is, the main legislative attempts during the interregnum to adapt the trained bands to serve the needs of the executive government.[4] The great point of it after the Restoration was that the government received money enough to make fairly ambitious use of the militia for some time without having to ask for supply from parliament. There is one hint that an attempt to include a provision of this kind (perhaps a more ambitious one) earlier on had been the cause of the bill sticking in the previous summer.[5] The importance of the subject was shown clearly at the end of the session. In his speech to the king, the Speaker referred at length to the extra revenue granted in the bill, and the royal assent was pronounced in the form usual for money bills.[6] As in other parts of the Restoration settlement, the government was consenting to the limitation of its powers to exact money and services in return for a somewhat inadequate grant of revenue.[7]

Having survived the commons' suspicions of the executive, the

[1] BM. Eg. 2043, ff. 36-7. HMC, *Finch*, vol. i, p. 173: Nicholas to Winchelsea, December 5. CJ, vol. viii, pp. 343-5. Members were asked to supply the preparatory committee with details of the number of militia men then found by their respective counties. No doubt this would have been the basis for apportioning the new levy. *Ibid.*, p. 326. BM, Eg. 2043, f. 24. What looks like the reply of the Yorkshire members is in CSPD, 1661-2, p. 182.
[2] BM, Eg. 2043, f. 38. CJ, vol. viii, p. 347 (cf. p. 344).
[3] CJ, vol. viii, p. 371.
[4] See below, p. 19. The ordinances granted one sum only, by the same method: £35,000 in 1650 and £90,000 in 1659.
[5] HMC, 5th Report, Appendix p. 171; Charlton to Leveson, 25 May 1661.
[6] LJ, vol. xi, pp. 471-2.
[7] Provisos were also accepted saving the privileges of London and other towns and protecting the militia from being sent abroad. CJ, vol. viii, pp. 381, 386.

bill ran into fresh danger because of disagreement between the two houses. The lords amended the bill in such a way as to give the lord lieutenants[1] complete authority in the main branches of militia organisation—appointment of officers, command and the levy of money and men. The commons on the other hand wished that in the appointment and dismissal of colonels, lieutenant-colonels and captains the lord lieutenant should act only subject to royal approval. In the levying of men, money and fines they wished him only to act in conjunction with his deputies. They said that powers were granted in the bill such as had never been granted by parliament before (for instance, those for leading men out of their county and for raising money). It would be wrong to entrust these powers to a few powerful individuals. They also thought that the charge of the militia would be more willingly borne and more fairly distributed if the assessing was done by the gentlemen of the county.[2] The lords persisted in giving the lord lieutenant power to appoint officers but subject to overriding royal control. They agreed that the deputy lieutenants, whose appointment was to be subject to royal approval, should be joined with him in the levying of soldiers and taxes. These terms proved acceptable to both houses; but the lords continued to insist that the lord lieutenant, acting alone, should have power to fine defaulters and this the commons could not accept. [3]

An equally intractable disagreement concerned the privileges of the peers as a body. From the time that it was restored to life in 1660, the house of lords claimed that its members and their servants could not be obliged to contribute to the militia.[4] They now offered to bear militia charges like anyone else, but demanded a special tribunal of five privy councillors (all to be peers) to assess them. The commons did not reject this outright, but it proved hard to find a formula on which the houses could agree.[5] The lords had taken a month to get

[1] The lords also proposed to give official recognition to this term, which then as now was the one in common use. The commons objected because it looked like an attempt to restrict the office to peers. The lords withdrew, although they claimed that they had only wished to show respect to commoners holding this high office (CJ, vol. viii, p. 418. LJ, vol. xi, pp. 454, 457, 459). There was evidently much suspicion between the houses. 'Lieutenant' was and remains the proper legal term for this office: only peers holding it can properly be called 'lord lieutenants'. But this book follows common usage.

[2] LJ, vol. xi, pp. 454–5. CJ, vol. viii, pp. 418–9.

[3] *Ibid.*, pp. 431 (where 'finding' should surely be 'fining'), 432–3. LJ, vol. xi, pp. 457, 463. Cf. 13 and 14 Car. II, cap. 3, s. 2.

[4] LJ, vol. xi, pp. 15, 19, 21, 213, 233; cf. p. 345.

[5] *Ibid.*, pp. 431, 456. CJ, vol. viii, pp. 423, 424. The lords did not fail to note that the commons objected to peers assessing commoners but not to commoners assessing peers. The lords also wished that their houses should not be liable to search save by special order from the king but on this they gave way. *Ibid.*, p. 421. LJ, vol. xi, pp. 455, 457.

through the bill, the houses quarrelled about it for another month and it was now May. The king was impatient. On the 15th he sent a message asking the houses to speed the passing of this and other bills so that he could give his assent to them before going to Portsmouth.[1] The time had come for a strong effort at compromise and Finch reappeared on the scene, reporting from a committee to examine the lords' latest proposal about their own assessment. This was now to be done by twelve commissioners, but the lieutenancies were to have power to distrain on peers in default. The commons insisted on exempting the special tax of £70,000 from the privilege and the lords agreed. Even then it was only by 91 votes to 89 that the commons decided, after Finch had explained the position to them, to accept this as a final settlement of the question. On the other issue of the fines they stood firm and the lords gave way. At last a settlement had been reached. The commons caused it to be recorded in their journal that they were not convinced of the lords' right to special treatment in the matter of assessments but had given way out of concern for public safety, because the end of the session was approaching. Two days later (May 19) the bill received the royal assent and the session closed.[2]

The government seems to have made one more attempt at this time to make the militia the basis of a small standing force. In February 1663 the commons appointed a committee to look into the deficiencies in the act of uniformity and almost at once referred to it several other acts, including that on the militia. On March 16 there came a royal message in answer to an address on religious toleration which had included a promise of help in the preservation of the peace. It asked that the kingdom might be put in a posture of defence.[3] An act resulted by which the lieutenancies were enabled to keep part of the militia permanently embodied for the maintenance of order and to keep any insurrection in check until the rest of the militia could be assembled. Each militia unit could when necessary be called on for fourteen days' guard duty a year in lieu of the twelve days' training required by the act of 1662.[4] With this small move in the crown's favour the Restoration militia settlement was at last complete. The story of its making illustrates to perfection how the independence and power of parliament no less than of the monarchy was restored in 1660. An unusually royalist house of commons proved as tenacious as any in defence of the rights of its order and

[1] CJ, vol. viii, p. 429.
[2] LJ, vol. xi, pp. 457-8, 463-4, 466, 472. CJ, vol. viii, pp. 431-3.
[3] CJ, vol. viii, pp. 437, 439, 451.
[4] 15 Car. II, cap. 4. For its passage, CJ, vol. viii, pp. 464, 469, 480, 484, 492, 495, 516, 518, 523-5, 529, 531; LJ, vol. xi, pp. 563-4, 567, 572.

judicially temperate, to say the least, in satisfying the wants of the crown.

III

The militia system established by the acts of 1661–3 gave the king the shadow but only a little of the substance of power. On the one hand his sole right to command the forces was affirmed and they were controlled entirely by his nominees. He appointed the lord lieutenants and if he wished might appoint the deputy lieutenants and officers too; he might at any time displace any of them. More normally it was the lord lieutenant who appointed the officers and, subject to royal approval, his deputies also. The lord lieutenant was empowered to arm and array the forces to be raised under the acts, to lead them wherever he was ordered and to train them; the last might be done in his absence or by his delegation by two of his deputies. The important magisterial powers needed to make the militia work belonged however to the lieutenancy[1] as a whole, two or three of them being the number required to perform an act, according to the matter in question. The lieutenancy assessed and imposed the various charges on the subject by means of which the militia was raised.[2] In addition they or the 'chief officers on the place' might, during invasion or rebellion, impress carts for transport, paying sixpence a mile for the use of a cart with six horses or five oxen and a penny a mile for a horse. They were to appoint one or more treasurers and clerks to receive the militia funds, who were to account to them on oath every six months.[3] They could hear evidence on oath as to the ability of persons to bear the militia charges. They could impose up to five days' imprisonment on soldiers failing to appear when summoned, as well as a fine of £1 for a horseman or 10s. for a foot soldier. They could levy all fines and penalties under the act by distraint on their own authority.[4]

The lieutenancy was a valuable prop of royal authority in the counties. The deputies were much more numerous than they had been under Elizabeth. Most of the lists which survive show between ten and twenty names per county, and though some counties had fewer than ten, a few reached the forties.[5] The number of justices of the peace in England and Wales, however, was 2500 in 1650 and is

---

[1] The lord lieutenant and the deputy lieutenants.

[2] 13 and 14 Car. II, cap. 3, especially ss. 1, 2, 13, 15.

[3] *Ibid.*, ss. 8, 12. Cf. Firth and Rait, vol. ii, pp. 401, 1338, 1451, on carts; pp. 1339, 1452 on accounting. These were innovations of the Rump in 1650 and 1659 respectively.

[4] 13 and 14 Car. II, cap. 3, ss. 10–11. Cf. Firth and Rait, vol.i, pp. 1248, 1250; vol. ii, pp. 1337–9, 1451–2.

[5] E.g. CSPD, 1700–2, pp. 30–1, 225 (Middlesex and the West Riding).

estimated to have reached 3000 by 1689[1]—an average of over fifty per county. The deputy lieutenants were a select body by comparison and there is little doubt that they were meant to be a sort of inner circle, exercising a general oversight over county administration in the interest of the crown.[2] In 1668 Arlington told the Duke of Richmond that the king was displeased at his proposing the appointment of so many deputies in his county of Kent. He found that their being numerous lessened their activity and would prefer to see the existing numbers reduced and none appointed who had a lesser commission in the militia than lieutenant-colonel of foot or captain of horse.[3]

On the other hand the lieutenancies, though put firmly under royal control, were not empowered to exact very much from the subject. Owners of property, whether real or personal, had to provide soldiers and equipment according to their means, the poorer supplying the infantry. Those who had not property enough to supply a whole horse or foot soldier were to be joined in groups, each of which provided a man. The ordinances of 1648–60 had provided lower limits below which proprietors were not obliged to contribute at all, but the act of 1662 specified only that lesser proprietors were not to be charged with horse. It was thus harder on the poor, but on the other hand the scale of charges was lower and there were more explicit safeguards of the rights of the subject. The charges imposed by the successive enactments are shown in the following table.

Amounts of Annual Income from Land or of Personal Property Charged with One Soldier by the Ordinances of 1648–60 and the Act of 1662

	Horse		Dragoon		Foot		
1648	£154	p.a. or 2400	£50 p.a. or 500		£20‡ p.a. or 200¶		
1650	200*	„ „ 2000	*133. 6s. 8d. or 333. 6s. 8d.		20‡	„ „	200¶
1659	300*	„ „ 4000	*200 or 3000		20‡	„ „	300¶
1660	500*	„ „ 6000	—		40§	„ „	500¶
1662	500*	„ „ 6000†	—		50	„ „	600

* Minimum £100.   † Minimum £1200.   ‡ Minimum £10.
§ Minimum £15.   ¶ Minimum £200.

Developing the ground opened by the removal of the lower limit of liability for foot service, the act of 1663 permitted the lieutenancies to require petty constables to raise foot soldiers in respect of all the estates in their parishes liable to find less than one man and recover the cost by a rate. This was in fact the common practice already. There were thus three sources of men: individual contributors,

[1] S. and B. Webb, *English Local Government from the Revolution to the Municipal Corporations Act*, vol. i, *The Parish and the County* (London, 1906), pp. 320–1.
[2] The lord lieutenant was often a minister or courtier, mostly absent.
[3] CSPD, 1667–8, p. 398.

contributors in groups and the parishes.[1] A further source lay in the use of the fines charged on defaulters (which settled down at a maximum of £20 for a horse and £5 for a foot soldier) for recruiting. In 1662 the government instructed the lieutenancies to accept £10 a year from anyone willing to pay it in lieu of finding a man and horse. The ordinance of 1659 had permitted this, but when the lords sought to introduce such a provision into the bill of 1662 it had been specifically rejected by the commons.[2]

No great outlay seems to have been required to meet these obligations. The equipment which a militia man had to have was given statutory definition in 1662. A horse soldier was to have armour, namely, 'back, breast and pot', of which the last two were to be pistol-proof. His horse was to have a saddle, bit and bridle of a specified kind and his weapons were to be a sword and a case of pistols with barrels at least 14 inches long. Pikemen were also to have armour and their pikes were to be of ash and 16 feet long; existing 15-foot ones, however, were to be allowed. The musketeer's weapon had to have a barrel at least 3 feet long and a bore to take bullets weighing twelve to the pound; existing muskets made to take bullets weighing fourteen to the pound were to be accepted. Musketeers were to have a 'collar of bandoliers' for their ammunition and all the foot were to have swords.[3] All this cannot easily be translated into money terms—time, place and the strictness or otherwise of the local militia authorities would obviously introduce variations. But some random figures will indicate the order of magnitude of the charge. The articles of armour required cost 14s. 6d. in the civil war period.[4] The price of pikes for the Ordnance in 1657 was 3s. 4d.[5] An estimate, probably optimistic, of prices which regular soldiers would have to pay about 1696 shows the weapons of a cavalryman costing up to £1. 14s., infantry swords 5s., and a fusil and bandoliers 17s. 6d.[6] It would appear from these figures that the cost of equipping either sort

---

[1] The ordinances further empowered the lieutenancies to arm the well affected and in 1648 even to order a general call-up. After 1648 the forming of groups of contributors was specifically mentioned, but the ordinance of 1648 only said that no-one shall be obliged to find a 'whole' foot soldier who has not . . ., etc. 13 and 14 Car. II, cap. 3, ss. 3–5. 15 Car. II, cap. 4, s. 4. Firth and Rait, vol. i, pp. 1248, 1249; vol. ii, pp. 399, 400, 1336, 1337, 1449, 1450. 15 Car. II, cap. 4, s. 19 laid down that those with over £200 p.a. or £2400 were not to be charged with foot.

[2] CSPD, 1661–2, p. 442. Cf. LJ, vol. xi, pp. 456, 458. For the fines, 13 and 14 Car. II, cap. 3, ss. 9, 32; 15 Car. II, cap. 4, ss. 3, 5. Cf. Firth and Rait, vol. i, pp. 1249–50; vol. ii, pp. 401, 1341, 1451.

[3] 13 and 14 Car. II, cap. 3, s. 21.

[4] Grose, vol. ii, p. 335 (footman's armour).

[5] C. H. Firth, *Cromwell's Army* (2nd ed., London, 1912), p. 73.

[6] C. Walton, *History of the British Standing Army, 1660–1700* (London, 1894), pp. 357, 808.

of infantryman would have been in the neighbourhood of £1. 3s. This may be compared with the £1. 12s. charged for the replacement of foot arms by the lieutenancy of Montgomeryshire in 1660, which no doubt included an addition for the cost of transport to that remote county, and may have included items not specified in the act.[1] For a cavalryman the cost might vary greatly according to whether the provider kept a horse suitable for his use. The New Model paid £7. 10s. and upwards for its cavalry horses,[2] and in 1715 a horse with its furnishings was bought for £6. 13s. 9d.[3] Taking into account the prices for equipment quoted above, it would seem that to provide a cavalryman might cost anything from £10 (if a special horse had to be bought) to under two (if that was not the case). Comparison with the amounts of landed income or personal property liable to the charge of one horse or one foot soldier suggests that the 'capital outlay' involved in either case was not onerous. The burden was further reduced by failures to renew worn-out equipment promptly.

The 'running costs' likewise were not large. When the men were called out, those who supplied them had to furnish them with powder—½ lb. for a musketeer and ¼ lb. for a cavalryman. When they were exercised, the 'finders' had likewise to pay them for each day, so spent: 2s. (raised in 1663 to 2s. 6d.) for a horseman and 1s. for a foot soldier. For further expenses, such as the provision of extra ammunition, drums, colours, etc., the lieutenancy could impose each year a 'week's tax', that is, one-quarter of the amount contributed by their area when parliament voted one month's assessment of £70,000 from the whole country. Besides this permanent levy, the king was further empowered, as noted above, to order the raising of an annual 'month's tax' of £70,000 for militia purposes for three years only. If the militia was called out on active service the 'finders' could be ordered to advance up to a month's pay to the men, but this was to be repaid and nobody was to advance a second month's pay before this had been done. The last two provisions originated in the ordinances of 1650 and 1659 and between them were the means of getting the unwieldy force effectively mobilised.[4] Neglecting for the moment the extra charges that fell on certain areas the 'week's tax' can be

---

[1] CSPD, 1660–1, p. 462.   [2] As note p. 18, n. 5.

[3] HMC, 5th Report, Appendix, p. 404. But in 1691 the Lancashire lieutenancy demanded horses worth £13. Cheetham Society publications, 1st series, vol. ix: *Norris Papers*, p. 24.

[4] These ordinances also charged the same sums on 'finders' for days of absence from musters as the rates of daily pay which were the same as those laid down in the act of 1662. 13 and 14 Car. II, cap. 3, ss. 6, 7, 23; Firth and Rait, vol. ii, pp. 400–1, 1338; cf. p. 1450, and 15 Car. II cap. 4, s. 2 which also ordered pay for days spent going to and from musters; s. 7 ordered musketeers to bring ½ lb. of bullets and if they had a matchlock, 3 yards of match.

said to have been £17,500 a year for the whole country and the burden of pay on the 'finders' as follows:

	Horse	Foot
Pay for exercise, maximum allowed p.a.	30s.	12s.
14 days' service in place of musters, when required, p.a.	32s. 6d.	14s.
Month's pay advanced, when required.	70s.	28s.

This was chicken-feed compared even with the exiguous revenues of Charles II's first years—one of the first taxes voted, for instance, was an *eleven month's* assessment at the rate of £70,000 a month. In any case, we shall soon find reason to doubt if the full amount of the routine charges was often called for.[1]

Sometimes the 'finders' hired equipment for their men as occasion required, or came to some similar arrangement in which capital and current costs were amalgamated. Surviving specimens of payments of this kind again give the impression of cheapness. In 1670 Lord Roos and Lady Chaworth paid the following for a soldier serving for them, apparently in London:

1 day's muster: pay 2s., powder 6d., a sword 6d.
To go to the General's (?Albemarle's) funeral: pay 2s. 6d., hire of buff coat, 2s. 6d., sword and powder 1s.
To go out 2 days 'about conventicles': pay 5s., powder, muster master and hire of sword 2s. 6d.

In 1674 a further payment of £5 to a Mr Hilton for 'showing horse' in the Lincolnshire militia for one year is recorded.[2] Lord Carlisle's bailiff in Yorkshire in the two years ending Michaelmas 1676 paid £8 for two-fifths of a militia horse in the North Riding and £1. 17s. 6d. for four foot soldiers in the East Riding.[3] In 1685 a man was found

---

[1] For the number of days' service ordinarily required in a year, cf. pp. 15, 26–28. Recorded payments of militia charges are always small. Sir Roger Twysden in Kent put down the 'month's taxes' at 2d. in the £ and the 'week's tax' at ½d. In 1663 lands whose half-yearly rents were respectively £22 and £34. 5s. paid 5s. 2d. and 9s. (BM, Add. 34167, ff. 51–3; Add. 34168, ff. 16, 19, 34, 41, 46, 66). Rowland Hale, a Hertfordshire gentleman, had to allow his farmers much larger sums for taxes than those for militia expenses. For instance (BM, Add. 33582, ff. 82–3):
John Finch and his widow: gross rent £40 p.a.; allowed in:
1664: 5 days' training, 12s. 6d. Pay for musters and storing (borrowed) arms 7s.
1669: 8 days' training £1. *Taxes £5. 7s.*
?1670: 5 days' training 12s. 6d. Mending arms 3s. *Three months' tax £1. 6s. 9d.*
'Ni. Honor' (f. 93) was allowed the following in his half-yearly settlements: the first figure is the net sum he paid:
July 1664. £21. 6s. 8d. 1 month's and 1 week's tax, 5s.
June 1665. £20. 16s. 8d. 1 month's tax, militia, 3s. 6d. *Royal Aid, 11s. 6d.*
Jan. 1666. £20. 19s. 4d. 1 week's tax, 2s. *Royal Aid, 12s. 4d.*
Jan. 1667. £19. 10s. 10d. 1 week's tax, 1s. 10d. *Taxes, etc., £2.*
[2] HMC, *Rutland*, vol. iv, pp. 547–8, 551.
[3] BM, Add. 32163, f. 46.

ready to contract for satisfying the charge of one horse falling on part of the Earl of Danby's estate for £5 a year.[1]

Under the Restoration system the subject had only two real grievances. One was that the burden was unequally distributed. The acts of 1662-3 specifically laid extra obligations on certain areas. The lieutenancy of the City of London was to have power to raise each year a tax not exceeding the City's share of a month's assessment of £70,000—in other words they were granted the 'month's tax' in perpetuity. Their special responsibility for the safety of the king's person and government and the contribution of their forces to the Restoration were the reasons included in the act for this special grant, and it was so far justified that the City militia often needed to levy this tax to pay off its debts.[2] The Cinque Ports had a militia of their own, and this was to be maintained at its customary strength unless the lieutenancy found cause to reduce it. This involved the inhabitants in a greater liability than they would otherwise have faced, and they were therefore exempt from militia charges in respect of lands lying outside the Ports. The corporate towns which had a separate militia were to continue to provide the number of men customary in the past, and the traditional organisation was also preserved in the Isle of Wight and the Stanneries. This might result in the inhabitants contributing less than the average, but at Barnstaple at least it was held to mean that they paid more.[3] Likewise, in the Isle of Wight it was said that estates worth only £10 a year or even less were charged with a whole foot soldier.[4]

Assessments for the provision of soldiers were often complained of as unfair. In 1668 and 1682 lieutenancy meetings were held in the North Riding specifically because of complaints among those charged.[5] George Jeffreys in Northamptonshire was aggrieved at being charged with half a horse in 1667, because his estate was worth less than £100 a year and he had heard that gentlemen with estates worth over £500 a year were charged no more than he. Two years before he had appealed against the charge and been told that he would hear no more of it. Nevertheless, his contribution was suddenly demanded with only a day's notice given and he had once again to appeal.[6] It was his partner in the charge of one horse who had passed on the summons, and as one would expect the system of

---

[1] BM, Add. 28051, ff. 201, 204.

[2] 13 and 14 Car. II, cap. 3, s. 27. The lieutenancy always asked the king's leave to raise the tax, though the act did not oblige them to. See, e.g., CSPD, 1679-80, p. 97; CSPD, 1680-1, pp. 582, 590.

[3] 13 and 14 Car. II, cap. 3, ss. 26, 28, 30. 15 Car. II, cap. 4, s. 20. Cf. HMC, 9th Report, Appendix, p. 216.

[4] BM, Add. 46501, f. 40.   [5] BM, Add. 41254, f. 20.

[6] BM, Add. 29551, f. 325.

partnerships in the finding of men was a great source of real or supposed injustice. In 1716, for instance, Lord Lonsdale was told that the 'principals' of cavalry in Cumberland and Westmorland who had provided horse to oppose the rising in the previous year had in many cases received nothing from the 'bearers' who were supposed to share the charge. It was twenty-three years since the militia obligations had last been fixed and in the interval many 'bearers' had died, leaving the 'principal' to bear the burden, while in other cases the 'principal' had died and a 'bearer' had stepped into his place without first getting authority to exact contributions from the other 'bearers'.[1] It was only in 1697 that the lieutenancies were given power, in default of private agreement among the partners, to fix who was to be the 'principal' and what the others were to contribute.[2] No doubt enforcement of these shared obligations before then was not easy.

The other grievance was occasional illegal exactions. In 1691 some inhabitants of the parish of St James', Westminster, petitioned the king against an abuse committed by the local captains of militia. They summoned the poorer inhabitants to appear when their companies were called out and fined them 2s. 6d. if they did not, converting the money to their own use.[3] When a system of permanent militia guards was instituted in 1663, the lieutenancy of Devon asked Exeter corporation to erect four guard houses and four sentry houses for them and promised to pay the county's share of the charge. The work was done but the city was still seeking payment in 1665.[4] The provisions of the law regarding equipment must often have been departed from because they soon became obsolete. The law was eventually changed in 1715, when pikes and armour were done away with and all the infantry were given a standard armament of a musket with a barrel 5 feet long, a bayonet, a cartouche box and a sword. The cavalry similarly were henceforth to have carbines, and the design of their swords and pistols was altered.[5] But there is reason to believe that some of these changes had already been made illegally: in particular, that armour had been given up. In 1690 the armourers of London

---

[1] BM, Add. 37721, f. 43.

[2] 7 and 8 Wil. III, cap. 16, s. 2. Cf. 9 Wil. III, cap. 31, s. 3; 10 Wil. III, cap. 18, s. 3; 1 Ann. stat. 2, cap. 15, s. 2.

[3] The petition was simply referred to the lord lieutenant. As they claimed that persons with less than £50 p.a. in land or £600 in personal estate were not liable to serve, they may simply have been in the wrong. CSPD, 1690–1, pp. 14–15.

[4] HMC, *Exeter City*, pp. 217–18.

[5] *Broad* swords and pistols 12 inches long instead of 14 inches. Muskets the same bore as before. 1 Geo. I, stat. 2, cap. 14, s. 3. In 1722, with doubtful wisdom, the lieutenancies were empowered to vary the length and calibre of muskets: in some places it was said to be easier to get muskets of other patterns than the statutory one. 9 Geo. I, cap. 8, s. 7.

complained to the commons that for want of execution of that part of the militia laws their trade was likely to be ruined.[1]

Changes in weapons probably did not increase the expense to those charged,[2] but the abandonment of armour was accompanied by the introduction of uniforms. A guide to the militia laws published in 1684 said that captains might allow buff coats and belts for cavalry and cloth coats of one colour and buff belts for infantry in place of armour. Anyone who objected to the substitution might be brought to reason by being made to wear his armour throughout the time he was on duty![3] In Lancashire, in 1689, order was given that the staff officers and soldiers were to have new blue hats, coats, breeches and stockings, with new belts, scabbards and sashes.[4] In 1691 the Earl of Macclesfield wrote to his deputies in Herefordshire that the militia in other counties was being 'clothed' and he hoped they were doing the same.[5] The provision of uniforms had no legal sanction and was calculated to increase expenses, especially for musketeers, who had not been obliged to have armour. In 1668 the Duke of Richmond caused quite an upset in Kent, where he acted as lieutenant in the absence of the Earl of Winchelsea on a foreign embassy. He ordered that armour was to be dispensed with and the men were to have red coats lined with black down to the knees 'as is the custom of soldiers' (with the exception of his own regiment which was to wear yellow). Captains were to report to the lieutenancy any 'finders' who failed to supply their men accordingly. Sir Roger Twysden, who thirty years before had refused to pay ship-money, now refused to join with the other deputies in giving out the order about the uniforms and in consequence was dismissed from the lieutenancy. He rightly observed that the law 'provides for conduct money but no whit for coating the soldier'. He remembered 'coat and conduct money to have been [one] of the first things layd hold on to make the late good Prince odious' and he did not wish to 'tread in the same steps [that] exposed so good a King, and that so fresh in memory too, unto so great envy'.[6]

The force raised on the basis described above was large but not very efficient. It seems to have amounted to some 90,000 at most, of which 6000 were horse and the rest foot.[7] Surviving muster rolls give the

[1] CJ, vol. x, p. 466.

[2] See Walton's tables, cited above p. 18, n. 6.

[3] *A Method for Executing the Powers Relating to the Militia and Trained Bands According to the Acts of Parliament since the Happy Restoration of . . . Charles the II* (London, 1684), pp. 24–5.

[4] HMC, *Le Fleming*, p. 248.   [5] HMC, *Portland*, vol. iii, pp. 469–70.

[6] BM, Add. 34176, f. 80. HMC, *Finch*, vol. i, pp. 509–10.

[7] A list in CSPD, 1690–1, p. 214, shows 92,668 of both arms in England and Wales. Returns to the house of commons in 1697 show 446 officers and 6426 men

impression of a force containing both a middle-class and a lower-class element. Soldiers provided by townships were marked off from those supplied by individuals (whether singly or in partnerships). In the West Riding the two categories were referred to respectively as 'common' and 'private' soldiers;[1] in Derbyshire as 'trained and private foot';[2] in Cheshire as 'trained and freehold bands'.[3] The term 'trained bands' was often confined to the soldiers supplied by townships, those provided by individuals being apparently regarded as joining on a sort of freelance basis. There was much variation in the ratio between the different types of soldier. In some musters at Pontefract and Rotherham in January 1661, the numbers of 'common' and private soldiers were fairly equal.[4]

Wapentake	No. of Townships	'Common' Muskets	Corselets	'Private' Muskets	Corselets
Tickhill } Strafforth }	77	162	118	161	91
Osgodcrosse	50	72	50	69	57
Staincrosse	39	60	22	50	32

Major Hale's Hertfordshire company on the other hand came from a richer area. The number of men per township was larger and all of them were provided not by the townships but by individuals or partnerships. In 1667 thirteen townships yielded sixty musketeers and thirty-five pikemen. Ten of each were supplied by individuals; the remainder by groups of two to five persons.[5] In Northamptonshire the foot in 1663 were mainly supplied by the townships, their contributions being mostly very small. A few individuals were separately assessed, mostly clergymen. In the hundred of Nobottlegrove, for instance, five ministers contributed four musketeers, thirteen towns twenty-four musketeers and ten pikemen, and three individuals associated with two towns in two partnerships were charged with two musketeers.[6]

The cavalry was the contribution of the wealthier class and the townships were not concerned with it. In 1663 the Cheshire horse numbered 113. Six persons furnished three horse each and four others each supplied two. Two pairs each furnished three horse jointly and another, two (as did a group of three). Forty-three persons

in the horse, and 2331 officers and 74,775 men in the foot (Camden Miscellany, vol. xx, pp. 8–10 of the *Minute Book of James Courthope*). The trained bands amounted in 1638 to 93,718 foot and 5239 horse (CSPD, 1638–9, p. 277. This reference, too, I owe to Mr Goodfellow). The figure of 200,000 in Chamberlayne's *Angliae Notitia* appears to be without foundation.

[1] BM, Add. 28082, ff. 15–34.   [2] BM, Add. 34306, f. 15.
[3] BM, Add. 36922, ff. 46–7.   [4] As note 3. Corselets are pikemen.
[5] BM, Add. 33574, ff. 112–22.   [6] BM, Add. 34222, ff. 57–75.

furnished one horse each, twenty-two pairs and sixteen larger groups the same.[1] In the same year 174 horse were supplied by commoners in Northamptonshire and 40 by peers (the infantry of the county numbered 833). The peers of course had been assessed separately and they were evidently organised on their own. The commons' horse were apportioned like the foot among the hundreds; the peers' were not.[2]

The hint of participation by men of property which the form of the muster rolls gives must not be made much of. Sir William Darcy told Secretary Nicholas soon after the Restoration that freeholders and their sons had ceased to serve in the militia because it had so often been sent far away from home. Persons without property had taken their place, who would probably side with the troublemakers in any disturbance: it had 'long been the principle of the vulgar, the injustice of their superiors to lord it over them and in all parts of the kingdom by some yet inculcated into them'[3] [sic.] Muster rolls show a certain number of contributors serving in person. In Hale's company there were in 1667 seven doing so (six as 'bearers' for a partnership) and seven more who each appear to have been related to one of the partners for whom they served. In 1676 there were still seven of the former sort and three of the latter.[4] If a proprietor of an estate lived outside the county where it lay, his steward or two of his most substantial tenants were made responsible for discharging the militia obligation upon it at the owner's expense.[5] They sometimes did so by appearing in person, thus adding to the better-class element in the ranks. Thomas Millner was suddenly and unprecedentedly (perhaps illegally) called on in 1680 to supply two horse in respect of some of the Earl of Danby's land. He attended the muster in person, together with someone he describes as the Keeper.[6] But the act of 1662 specifically laid down that nobody was to be obliged to serve in person,[7] and there is no evidence that more than a very few contributors did so.

To the ordinary militia soldiers were sometimes added volunteers. These might be recruited in the same way as the militia proper, only on a voluntary basis. A number of persons in Manchester offered to raise a force of volunteers to fight against Monmouth's rebellion, but only ten intended to serve themselves; the rest were to find men to serve for them and pay their expenses. One man offered to supply two horse and two foot; by contrast, ten foot were to be provided by

---

[1] BM, Add. 36922, ff. 30–2. The Bishop, the Dean and Chapter, and some clergymen each contributed one.
[2] As p. 24, n. 6.   [3] BM, Eg. 2542, ff. 526–7.
[4] BM, Add. 33574, ff. 112–22, 129–35.   [5] 13 and 14 Car. II, cap. 3, ss. 16–17, 29.
[6] BM, Add. 28051, f. 66.   [7] 13 and 14 Car. II, cap. 3, s. 25.

twenty people joined in pairs.[1] Organised bodies of volunteers were popular at the time of the Restoration, when the peace of the country was not secured and the militia sometimes disorganised. There were occasions, however, when a sudden emergency gave no time for organisation. Those who would serve and had arms were then tacked on to the militia without more ado. This often happened during the second Dutch war. In June 1667 the enemy suddenly appeared off Deal and 160 of the townsmen turned out in two hours to help the embodied militia company.[2] A false alarm in Cornwall in the previous year had caused 10,000 men to assemble in three hours. Hugh Acland admitted 117 to his volunteer company out of three times that number offering to join.[3] In July 1666, orders were given in the North Riding that on an alarm everyone willing to serve was to go to the militia rendezvous, where they would be given officers. Preparations were made to arm them, from private stocks if need be. Constables were ordered to make a list of the reserve stocks of 'common arms' and of all other arms whatever. A list was then prepared of the persons into whose hands the arms were to be put.[4]

When it came to training, the legal provision was hopelessly inadequate. If guard duty was not done instead, each regiment of militia was supposed to be mustered once a year for four days, *inclusive* of the time taken by the men in travelling to and from home. In addition, the separate companies might be ordered to muster up to four times a year for not more than two days at a time.[5] Much of the exiguous time thus allowed for training was consumed in checking the muster rolls, inspecting the arms and settling disputes about the provision of men. Sometimes a little more was attempted, especially by making the musters fewer and longer. No doubt under the pressure of the Dutch war, musters of the Suffolk foot companies lasting seven days were ordered for April and May 1665.[6] The Duke of Monmouth ordered in 1677 that in Staffordshire there should not only be an annual muster of the whole county force in May but that each captain of a company or troop should hold local musters as often as he conveniently could.[7] (Each company would normally come from one district within the county.) A little was done to supply professional instruction. Most of the officers were, of course, ordinary country gentlemen, but the muster master in each county had a salary and was supposed to be a professional soldier.[8] There were

[1] HMC, *Kenyon*, pp. 181–3. Over 100 men were to be raised.
[2] CSPD, 1667, pp. 225–6.   [3] CSPD, 1665–6, p. 470.
[4] BM, Add. 41254, ff. 3–5.   [5] 13 and 14 Car. II, cap. 3, s. 21.
[6] BM, Add. 39246, f. 5.   [7] CSPD, 1677–8, p. 91.
[8] By 15 Car. II, cap. 4, s. 6, he was to get not more than 1s. from each horse and 6d. from each foot soldier. In 1665 the two lord lieutenants of Northamptonshire asked their deputies to recommend someone for the post 'of Civill Carriage

sensible provisions in the act of 1662 to ensure that the men supplied for the militia were fit, and that they would stay in the service for a fair time and not consist of a perpetual succession of raw recruits. The men hired by those on whom the charge fell had to be approved by the captain of the company in which they were to serve. An appeal could be made from his decision to the lord lieutenant or two deputy lieutenants. The captain's consent was likewise needed (again subject to appeal) before a hired man could leave the service and the penalty for doing so without a discharge was a fine of £20 or three months imprisonment.[1] There is no knowing how far the law was kept to or how long the men served. In Major Hale's company, sixty-seven out of ninety-five men serving in 1667 appear to have been still serving in 1676.[2]

Even supposing the law and best custom on all the foregoing points to have been faithfully observed, the militia could hardly have become a well-trained force. The amount of activity was bound to be very limited, because the funds which the law provided were so small.[3] But even the low standard of efficiency that was attainable was in practice not often reached. There can be no doubt that the militia suffered severely from the long decline in central interference in local administration that set in after the Restoration. Musters were often not held for years on end, even in the coastal counties much exposed in wartime. By the 1670s there were complaints that the North Riding militia had not met for two, three or four years at a time.[4] In Suffolk the lord lieutenant had to 'iterate' his orders for the settlement of the militia more than once in the early '60s. His county was behind the rest, he was frequently called on for a report of progress and he even feared that parliament might complain. After a burst of activity during the second Dutch war there was total decay. In 1671 Lord Suffolk ordered his deputies to put the 'trayned force' in order, not knowing when the king might order a muster and fearing that they were in a bad state. In 1674 he was still complaining of the long discontinuance of musters.[5] Cumberland was another county where an efficient militia was much to be desired, owing to the turbulent state of Scotland. But the county militia did not

and Souldier Sufficient to undertake it'. (BM, Add. 34222, f. 54). In 1674 Captain Jack Tonge of the Coldstream Guards was given the post in Cumberland and Westmorland, but he was seconded to Virginia in 1676! (CSPD, 1676–7, p. 407. HMC, *Le Fleming*, pp. 111, 165).

[1] 13 and 14 Car. II, cap. 3, ss. 25, 32. The Wiltshire lieutenancy issued similar regulations on their own authority in 1661, and even forbade the selling of trained *horses* without permission. BM, Add. 32324, f. 79.

[2] BM, Add. 33574, ff. 112–22, 129–35.

[3] Further explained in chap. ii.   [4] BM, Add. 41254, ff. 21–2.

[5] BM, Add. 21048, ff. 1, 16. Add. 39246, ff. 22, 24–7.

assemble between 1676 and 1679 and in 1677 the governor of Carlisle reported them very ill-trained.[1]

Besides neglecting the musters, the lieutenancies constantly failed to exact the full amount of what was due from the contributors in support of the militia. The act of 1662 seems at first to have increased the size of the force considerably,[2] but even in 1662–3 the lord lieutenants of Northamptonshire complained of slowness in settling the militia charge there.[3] As early as 1666 the government thought it necessary to instruct the lieutenancies to replace men formerly supplied by persons who had left the county or were dead.[4] During the third Dutch war the militia on the coast of Suffolk was reported short of men through the neglect of the deputies, and short of officers because of 'death' 'sulking' and 'fear'.[5] The Cheshire lieutenancy in 1696 was in trouble because the schedule of the existing assessment for the militia had been lost. Unless it was replaced there would be no legal remedy against anyone refusing service. But if a new one was made, the peers could not be charged since the lieutenancy had not power to assess them. If the old assessment was simply confirmed, changes that had taken place in the ownership of land might make it inoperative. Already a peer had refused to bear the charge on some land that he had inherited from a commoner.[6] The special machinery for assessing peers seems indeed never to have been set going except in 1662.[7] By the end of the century many of them seem to have been evading their obligations, on part of their lands at least.[8]

The lieutenancies were often reluctant to levy the 'week's tax' for the expenses of the militia not met by those who found the men. In the North Riding none seems to have been levied in the years 1671–5.[9] In 1674 the Cheshire deputies told the lord lieutenant that they had

[1] HMC, *Le Fleming*, p. 159 no. 2180. CSPD, 1677–8, p. 468.

[2] Cf. the figures for the 'old' and 'new' assessment in Northamptonshire, BM, Add. 34222, ff. 36–7, 55.

[3] *Ibid.*, ff. 36, 40.   [4] BM, Add. 39246, f. 16.   [5] BM, Add. 39246, ff. 24, 27.

[6] BM, Add. 36913, f. 293. Add. 36922, ff. 28–9.

[7] Attempts to revive it were made in 1679 and 1693. CSPD, 1661–2, p. 442, CSPD, 1679–80, p. 83, and 1693, p. 202. The commissioners of 1662 improperly told the lieutenancies to assess bishops themselves: HMC, *Le Fleming*, p. 30; cf. 13 and 14 Car. II, cap. 3, s. 33.

[8] See the examples in the long report on the militia in 1697 reproduced in Sir G. J. Hay, *An Epitomized History of the Militia (the 'Constitutional Force')*, London, ?1906, pp. 114–35. This also gives several instances of laxness in revising the assessments and shows that in some places the clergy were not charged. (The only statutory exemption was of militia officers, for the first £500 p.a. in land or £6000 personal property: 15 Car. II, cap. 4, s. 10.) In 1715 the peers who should have contributed in Nottinghamshire appear to have done so voluntarily. BM, Add. 32686, ff. 61, 79, 80. Add. 33060, ff. 38, 54–5.

[9] BM, Add. 41254, f. 2.

not hitherto raised the tax because they considered that the county raised an unduly large number of militia in proportion to its size. They were accordingly reluctant to pay their clerk a regular salary.[1] A similar unworthy economy was proposed in Middlesex in 1690: new colours were to be paid for by stoppages out of the officers' next year's pay.[2] In the same year Shrewsbury had to press his deputies in Hertfordshire to raise the tax, for which he understood there was an urgent need.[3] In 1700 the Duke of Newcastle said that for some years he had neither raised the tax nor held musters in his two counties.[4]

The slackness of the lieutenancies could only encourage default by those assessed. In Kent there were complaints that the various troops and companies had never been mustered simultaneously, so that the same men could appear in several of them, serving for different people, and make the force appear more complete than it was.[5] In 1674 the villagers of Dalton were in arrears with their militia tax, and a special meeting of deputies was proposed to deal with them. Two years later they seem still to have been putting off the evil day by appeals to the lord lieutenant.[6] In 1674 most of the Lancashire foot arms were found to be defective, and the constables of Coniston were ordered to provide each man with the equipment laid down in the act. The old arms were to be handed in when the new ones were received. In 1689 many of the muskets of the Lancashire militia were ordered to be replaced, to the great charge of the county. In 1690 the militia arms *throughout England* were found so defective that the king ordered a special report on the subject,[7] with no apparent result.

The militia of the Restoration was thus a force which even on paper had serious deficiencies. In practice, despite bursts of activity in times of crisis, it was foredoomed to waste steadily away into inanition.

[1] BM, Add. 36922, ff. 35–6. It is not clear if the deputies meant that they had *never* raised the 'week's tax'. 13 and 14 Car. II, cap. 3, s. 12, ordered the appointment by each lieutenancy of a treasurer and a clerk, but did not say what they were to be paid. On the excessive charge on Cheshire, cf. Hay, p. 115.
[2] HMC, *Portland*, vol. ii, p. 163.
[3] CSPD, 1689–90, p. 424.
[4] BM, Add. 33084, f. 165.
[5] CTB, 1660–7, p. 716: early entry book xiii, p. 180.
[6] HMC, *Le Fleming*, p. 112 no. 1544; p. 125, no. 1717.
[7] *Ibid.*, pp. 112, 248, 267.

II

TRIUMPHS AND REVERSES
1660 – 70

FOR a few years after the Restoration the militia was fairly successful, despite its shortcomings. Its only task was the maintenance of internal security and that was always what it did best. With the second Dutch war, however, there appeared new problems and tasks which revealed its defects and the need for reform. This in turn led to differences of opinion between king and parliament which for the time being ended in deadlock. In all these developments the militia was simply sharing the fate of the Restoration settlement as a whole.

The first duty of the militia was to secure the permanence of the Restoration by the frustration of plots and the repression of disloyalty. That was what the government had wanted a militia for, and because of the enthusiasm felt for the restored king there was zeal enough in the execution of the militia laws to make the system effective. This widespread loyalty should not make us suppose that the services of the militia at this time were not important. The royalists in 1660 clearly enjoyed much more support than any government for a long time before, but much of it was based on highly fallacious expectations, such as that all taxes would be abolished. Like the royalists during the Interregnum, the republicans could go into hiding or exile, plan for better days, even claim to be the legitimate government. In October 1662 it was being said that a council of six was in charge of the current plot and that it based its authority on an ordinance of the Rump.[1]

The republicans were by no means in a hopeless position. The soldiers of the disbanded army were the best and largest reserve of trained fighting men in the country and were not without other advantages. It was said that in the area of Stafford and Lichfield there were many old soldiers living near to one another, while the soldiers

[1] HMC, 7th Report, Appendix, p. 463.

30

of the militia lived far apart. If the former were the first to take up arms, it would be impossible to assemble a force to disperse them.[1] The officers of the old army living in the north were said to have better horses than the cavaliers.[2] Some of the old soldiers were to be found in the standing forces still in royal pay, and Lord Fauconberg thought that the garrison of Tynemouth in 1662 could not be depended on.[3] The corporations might also be expected to give some help. Even when purged of interregnal nominees, they still contained many who were lenient towards the government's enemies, no doubt because of the bias of the towns towards dissent. Major (and sheriff) Streamer with his men of the Bristol militia were violently obstructed in the imprisoning of some Quakers in 1664 by a rich citizen named Knight. To his indignation, the mayor would do no more than bind over both men to keep the peace.[4] The congregations of dissenters from the established church might themselves afford a convenient nucleus of republican activity. Their opposition to the established order was often non-violent and not overtly political; the Quakers who marched naked through north country towns crying 'woe to Yorkshire'[5] did not need to be opposed by an armed force. But in 1662 the burgesses of Beverley, for instance, tried to put a seditious preacher of their choice in possession of the minster, despite the opposition of the mayor. The county troop of militia and the deputies had to be called in to stop the riot.[6] In 1664 there was a complaint that the election of churchwardens at Newbury had been riotously interrupted and a guard of Reading militia was asked for, to be quartered in the houses of the rioters.[7] It is not surprising to find the deputies in Norwich in November 1663 ordering a search for arms at a dissenters' meeting place.[8]

The militia's activity against the republicans was in part preventive —the seizure of their arms and the breaking up of their organisation—and in part defensive—the keeping available of enough force to crush any rising that might occur. The republicans strove to achieve concerted action, whether for rebellion or more peaceful purposes, and the government tried to keep them in an invertebrate condition. A connected story could be made of the fight between the government and the sectaries in the years 1660–6, divided into campaigns like a regular war.[9] All that will be done here will be to indicate the methods used by the militia in their part of the struggle.

The disarming of the disaffected was ordered by the royal govern-

[1] CSPD, 1663–4, p. 155.   [2] CSPD, 1664–5, p. 246.   [3] CSPD, 1661–2, p. 441.
[4] CSPD, 1663–4, p. 428.   [5] CSPD, 1660–1, p. 472.   [6] CSPD, 1661–2, p. 379.
[7] CSPD, 1663–4, pp. 553–4.   [8] Ibid., p. 333.
[9] This has in part been done in a useful article by the Rev. Henry Gee, 'the Derwentdale Plot, 1663', Transactions of the Royal Historical Society, 3rd series, vol. xi (1917), pp. 125–42.

ment in its first instructions to the lieutenancies in 1660 and repeated with greater force in those issued in January 1661 in consequence of Venner's rising in London. By 1666 it was thought sufficient to order a special watch on those of the disaffected who had horses or arms above their station, which were to be taken from them.[1] This with the breaking up of conventicles was the main routine work of the militia and many examples could be quoted. In August 1661 the deputies of Essex ordered a search at the house of Thomas Cooke, sometimes called Colonel. Much powder and bullet was found, though at first Cooke said there was none on the premises; afterwards he claimed not to know how it had got there. Sir Martin Lumley with part of his troop conducted the search and took security of the Colonel to appear before the deputies, which he duly did.[2] In February 1666, on the interception of some treasonable correspondence, the Dorset deputies ordered a captain to search the houses of some who did not go to church, besides arresting three or four nonconformist ministers.[3] In Derbyshire a former captain suffered, so he said, by having had the care of some gentlemen's arms which Lambert had ordered to be confiscated. These arms had since been reclaimed, but not it seems before someone had used their presence in the captain's house to incriminate him. His premises had been searched nine times in one week to the great terror of his wife, though he swore that all the arms he had himself were one small rapier and a fowling-piece and asked God to forgive his accusers.[4]

Towns as well as men were disarmed in cases where they were especially suspect. The government's main weapon against them was the Corporation Act of 1662 which set up a commission in each county to remove from the corporations all whose loyalty was suspect and replace them with reliable men.[5] In certain cases this was not thought enough, and the independence of the town was further sapped by the destruction of its fortifications. On 30 June 1662 the government gave orders for this to be done in the case of Northampton, Coventry, Gloucester and Taunton. The reason given was that the good fortifications of the towns were a standing temptation to revolt and that as it would be too expensive to maintain garrisons there to keep order they were to be 'slighted'. The lord lieutenant of the county was ordered in each case to go in person with a body of the county forces to the town and inform the corporation of what

[1] CSPD, 1660–1, p. 150. CTB, 1660–7, pp. 184, 191. CSPD, 1665–6, p. 538. By 13 and 14 Car. II, cap. 3, s. 14, any two deputies were empowered to order a search for arms.

[2] HMC, *Round*, p. 280. [3] CSPD, 1665–6, p. 273.

[4] BM, Add. 34306, f. 12.

[5] J. H. Sacret, 'The Restoration Government and Municipal Corporations', *English Historical Review*, vol. xlv (1930), pp. 232–59.

was to be done. He was then to destroy the gates, walls and other fortifications.[1]

In Northamptonshire the Earls of Westmorland and Exeter, joint lord lieutenants, fixed July 10 as their day of entry into the county town. They told their deputies to occupy it with the trained bands of the surrounding area as soon as they could and seize all the arms there. Although the hay harvest made it difficult to collect any men, the deputies were able to report on the 9th that they were in occupation. Two hundred muskets had been found in the town hall and a few in the vestry of the great church and these were under guard. Next day the two earls arrived and sent for the mayor and other dignitaries, who obeyed the orders that they were given 'yet we dare not say with what countenance of satisfaction because we could not pierce into their hearts'. Demolition then began. The king had originally promised £50 towards the work in each town but this proved insufficient. The cost at Northampton was almost £136.[2] The government paid £600 for the work at Coventry.[3] At Gloucester the total cost was expected to be £1200, for ramparts 15 yards wide had to be removed.[4]

In addition to disarming them, the government sought to curtail the activities of those whom they suspected by confining the leaders and preventing their followers from assembling. The first instructions to the lieutenancies in 1660 were to watch the disaffected and not allow them to meet, to put down risings and suppress vagrants.[5] In December 1660 (and again later) the officers and soldiers of the disbanded army were ordered to leave the capital:[6] an order which foreshadows the removal of dissenting preachers from the corporate towns by the Five Mile Act. Venner's rising produced more drastic orders. The oaths of allegiance and supremacy were to be tendered to the disaffected and those refusing them were to be secured. Seditious meetings professedly for religion were to be interrupted.[7] This last order began the active persecution of dissenters and gave the reason for it. The cavaliers, with some justice, considered conventicles to be the local party headquarters of their most violent opponents.

Mass arrests were the first result of these orders, but they did not go on long. In March 1661 the release of Quakers held only on suspicion was ordered, the danger having passed and many petitions for leniency having come in.[8] The Hampshire deputies asked Trea-

[1] CSPD, 1661–2, pp. 423–4. BM, Add. 34222, f. 23.
[2] *Ibid.*, ff. 22–7. CSPD, 1661–2, pp. 434, 443. On the £50, cf. p. 431.
[3] *Ibid.*, p. 477.   [4] *Ibid.*, p. 447.
[5] CSPD, 1660–1, p. 150.   [6] *Ibid.*, p. 415.
[7] CTB, 1660–7, pp. 184, 191. F. Bate, *The Declaration of Indulgence* (London, 1908), p. 16.
[8] BM, Add. 34222, f. 18.

surer Southampton if they were to confine persons assembling for worship who called themselves 'Quakers, Anabaptists and Fifth Monarchy Men as a mark of distinction and separation and may be subject to take fire on any encouragement from their bloody confederates above'. They were expected to refuse the oaths if asked to take them; there seemed nothing to do but put them in the common gaol, though the expense would be great and the gaol would soon be full. Southampton in reply declared that they were dealing with 'irrational and contumacious' people who gloried in punishment, 'supporting one another in prisons, which they so clog that they seem to impose the necessity of releasing them'. He thought it best to 'clap up' only some of the ringleaders and perhaps make the 'rabble unquiet and uneasy' and disturb their meetings.[1] In July 1662 the government issued fresh orders. Disturbances were to be put down, the vagrant and seditious punished. The republicans were to be watched, for they were thought to be plotting, but they were too numerous to imprison. The leaders only were to be secured; the rest were to find security. This was henceforth the system.[2]

The activity of the Hampshire deputies in 1661–2 shows the sort of way in which these orders were interpreted. One Herbert of Monmouth they thought fit to confine 'until the storms were over'. He had been in charge of the Marquess of Worcester's sequestered estates and had become so unpopular that he had had to leave his own county and live in retirement, mixing only with his own kind. So at least he said; the deputies clearly thought worse of him. At Andover, all those who had given the bailiff cause for suspicion were examined. 'Those of inferior quality' had all been 'engaged in the late unhappy distemper' and might 'take fire again on any encouragement'; the 'better sort' on the other hand were 'more likely to be active with their purses and their wishes than their hands' and had lately been very 'conformable' to the church. It was therefore thought enough to take bond for their good behaviour. In response to the orders of July 1662 the deputies only arrested six persons in the first instance, being unwilling to make a disturbance in the county. A preacher named Ellis fled to the Isle of Purbeck and at their request was hunted for and caught by the lieutenancy of Dorset. One prisoner was interesting enough to be sent for to London, but he was too ill to travel.[3]

As for the conventicles, as soon as the first orders to disperse them were given the Quaker meetings were beset by the militia at Oxford, Abingdon and other places round about.[4] From then on, the pres-

---

[1] BM, Add. 21922, f. 245. CTB, 1660–7, p. 282.
[2] CSPD, 1661–2, p. 442. Cf. CSPD, 1665–6, p. 518.
[3] BM, Add. 21922, ff. 250–9.   [4] CSPD, 1660–1, p. 473.

sure was continuous. At the end of October 1662, Secretary Bennet told the Berkshire lieutenancy to suppress all dangerous meetings and especially to take up all the teachers—the civil and military powers to act together.[1] Viscount Conway was told in June 1664 that the militia in one district was out each Sunday to suppress meetings.[2] In January 1664 Lord Brereton reported that he had taken some presbyterians at a conventicle, but let them go when they promised to desist and paid the wages of the soldiers.[3] In October 1664 Lord Colepeper interrupted a large meeting of Quakers in the Isle of Wight and made numerous arrests. The two leaders were strangers to the island and Colonel Slingsby sent them a copy of the Koran in English to read in prison. Should they be led to turn Turk, he said, it would be a great blow to the whole sect.[4]

Although some effort had been made to prevent it, there gradually grew from these activities a wretched population of prisoners and of others whose freedom was transitory. John Miller declared in 1665 that he had spent a year in Windsor Castle, had been a month at liberty on bail and then had been arrested again on a warrant from the deputies of Bedfordshire; he was confined thereafter in Bedford gaol. He asked to be charged or liberated, and attributed his misfortunes to the displeasure of an eminent person.[5] In April 1666 four men said in a petition that they had been committed two and a half years before by the lord lieutenant of Nottinghamshire and had not yet been tried.[6] Four prisoners in the Wiltshire gaol in 1661 petitioned for release. They said that they had only been worshipping God peacefully according to their way because they had heard that indulgence was shown to their sect by the authorities in the capital. They had been singled out as more dangerous and disaffected than the rest. Confined among sufferers from contagious diseases and without hope of release, they were likely to die and their families to starve. The lieutenancy took care to assemble evidence against these men and particularly to show that one, Blare Allen a 'phisitian', had told those arresting them that 'Captain Long would not be so harsh unto them[;] it was his day now but might be theirs another time'.[7]

Of defensive, as distinct from preventive, measures the most important was the setting up of a standing guard in accordance with the act of 1663. In August of that year a circular ordered that one-twentieth of the militia was always to be on duty, successive detachments serving for fourteen days at a time.[8] The same orders were given in December 1664 when the militia had all done a first year's

[1] CSPD, 1661–2, p. 531.　　　　[2] CSPD, 1663–4 p. 603.
[3] CSPD, 1663–4, pp. 435–6.　　[4] CSPD, 1664–5, pp. 108–9.
[5] CSPD, 1665–6, p. 126.　　　　[6] Ibid., p. 373.
[7] BM, Add. 32324, ff. 107–9.　[8] CSPD, 1663–4, p. 231.

service in this way, and in the following May they were told to do a third year's service on completion of the second.[1] To make this possible, money had to be available. The levy of the first 'month's tax' had been ordered already in December 1662, and the second and third were ordered to be raised in January 1664 and May 1665. The men were paid by the 'finders'; the sergeants, corporals and drummers were ordered to be paid out of the 'week's tax', supplemented if need be by the proceeds of fines on defaulters. Latterly, however, the commissioned officers also received pay and for this and for more extensive mobilisation, if for nothing else, the 'month's tax' was necessary.[2] The Devonshire deputies used the 'week's tax' to pay the non-commissioned officers and advanced pay to the commissioned officers which they asked should be defrayed from the 'month's tax'.[3] Bristol repeatedly asked for the proceeds of its 'month's tax' to be released to pay the militia there. The lieutenancy complained on one occasion that the officers had received no pay that year, and on another that the 'week's tax' did not yield a sixth of what was wanted for the NCOs.[4] But the government was chary of allowing the lieutenancies to use up the 'month's tax', with what result will later be seen.

The guard was not always too enthusiastically mounted. In Northamptonshire the 'soldier's duty' prescribed in the royal letter of January 1664 was deferred by order of the lord lieutenants until better weather and better times for the husbandmen.[5] Cumberland and Westmorland had only 600 militia each, so it was pointless to keep up a permanent guard of one-twentieth of the whole force; it would have been too small. It was apparently decided that the foot companies should serve in turn for fourteen days for as long as that would take and that close contact should be maintained with the adjoining counties.[6] Derbyshire decided for similar reasons against maintaining guards, and in January 1665 was given official permission not to.[7]

In a few places the guards were helped by the survival in good repair of a castle well placed for keeping rebellious territory in awe. Garrisoned by a few regular soldiers and commanded by a member of the local lieutenancy, they functioned as part of the militia system. Lord Herbert said that Chepstow Castle was the key to four Welsh

[1] CSPD, 1664–5, pp. 125, 348.
[2] CSPD, 1661–2, p. 603; 1663–4, p. 458; BM, Add. 39246, f. 2; and as n. 1 and p. 35, n. 8. Daily rates of pay were: Captains 10s. (horse), 8s. (foot); Lieutenants 5s. or 4s.; Quartermasters 4s.; Ensigns 3s.; Sergeants 2s. 6d.; Corporals and Drummers 2s.
[3] CSPD, 1663–4, p. 252.   [4] Ibid., pp. 301, 486; 1664–5, p. 250.
[5] BM, Add. 34222, f. 46.   [6] CSPD, 1663–4, pp. 258, 263.
[7] BM, Add. 34306, ff. 31, 43–4.

counties and a bridle on the disaffected, who were very numerous. The militia on the other hand were very few—Monmouthshire could not maintain fifteen men on constant duty—and there was no other garrison near. He apparently secured the continuance of a garrison there, reduced from 100 to 60 men to save money.[1] Lord Newport was anxious to control Ludlow Castle because it was in his lieutenancy of Shropshire, and for a time succeeded.[2] Later, however, it was Lord Carbery, Lord President of Wales, who established a small garrison there: he commanded the militia throughout the Principality and all the Welsh militia money was stored in the castle.[3] Chester castle was in a position of great strategic importance and the only fortified place in a large area full of dispossessed clergy and malcontent presbyterian gentry.[4] The deputies of Cheshire asked that a local man, Sir Geoffrey Shakerley, be appointed governor because of the need to act in concert with the loyal gentry:[5] this was done. Later the castle was repaired at their request, the money being advanced from militia funds and repaid from the revenues of the palatinate.[6] Carlisle again, under the locally important Sir Philip Musgrave, was the real headquarters of the militia of the Lake District. It will be seen that castles received attention particularly in the wilder areas.

In certain coast towns where there was a regular garrison, the officer commanding it also controlled the militia. The large militia of the Cinque Ports was thus largely organised by the governors of the castles there. Until he was disabled by the Test Act, the Duke of York was Lord Warden and supervised them; afterwards, ministers seem to have done this instead. In 1683 a lengthy muster of the force was supervised by the governor of Deal and Colonel Rooke.[7] In all these cases the defence of the coast rather than police work was the main preoccupation; but the governor of York, a place of great internal importance, likewise commanded the militia there.[8]

In certain places there were other special arrangements for the command of the militia calculated to ensure prompt and co-ordinated action in an emergency. The capital was the most important case.

[1] CSPD, 1663–4, p. 359; cf. 1661–2, p. 591. This Lord Herbert was the son of the Marquess of Worcester who eventually became Duke of Beaufort and Lord President of Wales. Cf. below, pp. 38, 82.

[2] BM, Eg. 2537, f. 229.   [3] CSPD, 1663–4, p. 399; 1664–5, pp. 169, 363.

[4] CSPD, 1661–2, p. 452. HMC, *Kilmorey*, p. 372.   [5] CSPD, 1663–4, p. 205.

[6] CSPD, 1665–6, pp. 58, 110, 331; cf. 1666–7, p. 530; 1667, pp. 37, 51, 201, 210, 441.

[7] CSPD, July–Sept. 1683, p. 410. The government's interest is shown by many references to the appointment of officers in CSPD; e.g. in 1680–1, pp. 459, 479. Cf. the situation in Newcastle, CSPD, 1671–2, p. 310.

[8] See, e.g., CSPD, 1667, p. 209; 1670, p. 204.

The body of commissioners who controlled the City militia were of necessity mainly civic worthies. But the militia of the Tower Hamlets was controlled by the Governor of the Tower as lieutenant. For many years after 1660 this post was held by Sir John Robinson. He had taken an important part in organising the City forces before and during the Restoration,[1] and continued to be the live wire of the City lieutenancy as well as that of the Hamlets. Under Charles II Middlesex always had a professional soldier as lord lieutenant: at first Albemarle and then the Earl of Craven.[2] The borough of Southwark was put under their command although it was in Surrey and its civil administration belonged largely to the City.[3] Thus the City was almost surrounded by the area they controlled. In times of special emergency when the king was absent, Craven was made lieutenant-general of all the forces in London and Westminster.[4]

Some instances occur of one person holding the lieutenancies of several counties,[5] and though this might only reflect their social or political importance it sometimes had administrative significance also. In particular, the shadow of Tudor conciliar government was kept in being thereby in the remoter areas. In 1665 the Duke of York was sent to reside in that city, partly to escape the plague but also 'to secure the peace of those parts'. The government feared that the outbreak of war with the Dutch would encourage plotting. They sent special orders to the lieutenancies and the Duke reiterated these to the northern counties, received reports and gave further orders of his own.[6] In 1667 the Earl of Carlisle and Lord Ogle were made lieutenants-general of Cumberland, Westmorland, Northumberland and Durham and Lord Berkeley of Stratton the same for Suffolk, Cambridgeshire and the Isle of Ely.[7] These were wartime appointments. But as already noticed, the Lord President of the Council of Wales commanded the whole militia of the principality. When the Marquess of Worcester (later Duke of Beaufort) held the office, he combined it with the lieutenancies of Gloucestershire, Herefordshire and Monmouthshire.[8] When the Council of Wales was abolished in 1689 the centralised control of the militia survived for a time. Sir George Treby, the Attorney-General, thought that it should be given to a secretary of state.[9] Instead, all the counties which Beaufort had

---

[1] CSPD, 1671, p. 386. On the Tower Hamlets, 13 and 14 Car. II, cap. 3, s. 21. On Robinson, below chap. iii, pp. 18, 24.

[2] The son of a Lord Mayor (*Complete Peerage*.)

[3] CSPD, 1671–2, p. 427. [4] E.g. CSPD, 1682, p. 177.

[5] E.g. the Duke of Bedford received Middlesex, Cambridgeshire and Bedfordshire in 1701. CSPD, 1700–2, p. 445.

[6] HMC, *Various*, vol. ii, p. 119; *Le Fleming*, p. 38. CSPD, 1664–5, p. 514.

[7] CSPD, 1667, pp. 208, 214, 277. [8] *Complete Peerage*.

[9] CSPD, 1689–90, pp. 383–4.

controlled were given to the Earl of Macclesfield, who had commanded the Prince of Orange's bodyguard on his landing in 1688.[1] After his death in 1694 Wales was divided into a northern and a southern lieutenancy, the former being held for two years by Secretary Shrewsbury.[2]

Such were the measures intended to make the militia respond promptly to the stimulus of danger. There was, of course, a further need, to know promptly when danger was at hand. This involved the deputies in a good deal of detective work which, fascinating though it is, would take too long to describe here. When danger seemed to be on the way, the militia was got ready for more extensive action. It seems to have been in the autumn of 1663 that plotting reached its zenith.[3] Militia activity increased accordingly. In Somerset the meetings of the disaffected were very private, but one man reported that he had been told that a rising was in prospect and it was said that Ludlow was in the area. Early in October a guard was mounted in the larger centres of population in the county to examine all travellers.[4] The Lancashire militia had just been dismissed at the beginning of October when new information led to its reassembly; orders were also given for the seizure of weapons. The militia apparently remained assembled for some time, but any troublemakers there were kept in hiding.[5] In November Atkinson, a plotter who had escaped from custody, was reported to have told friends that he would release the prisoners in Appleby gaol and take revenge on certain persons could he but gather twenty horse. The militia of the area was in a bad way—some companies without arms, some without officers, some untrained —but some of the Westmorland foot were raised and the gentry privately collected fifty horse. Twenty persons were arrested and after three days it was thought safe to dismiss the troops. In Cumberland the loyal gentry gathered at Cockermouth, which much intimidated the Quakers.[6]

The West Riding was the centre of the plot, and on October 9 Sir Thomas Gower, sheriff of Yorkshire, reported extensive precautions there. The chief 'fanatics' had been seized. Though there was probably no danger, the trained bands were to be raised. Little could be done against a sudden rising, but two troops could be got ready before the rest and signals had been arranged which would enable them to assemble in ten hours. Some populous boroughs had been told to provide mounted musketeers, and to save the expense of the

[1] *Complete Peerage.*
[2] CSPD, 1694-5, pp. 119, 122; 1696, p. 61.
[3] Gee, pp. 134-9.   [4] CSPD, 1663-4, p. 296.
[5] CSPD, 1663-4, pp. 281, 291, 294, 299, 346.
[6] *Ibid.*, pp. 318, 332, 340. HMC, *Le Fleming*, p. 31.

trained bands trusty gentlemen were watching the roads.[1] On the 10th the trained bands assembled and on the 14th 1500 foot and 500 horse were collected at Pomfret under the command of the Duke of Buckingham,[2] lord lieutenant, who had been sent down by the king to take charge. In the East Riding 1000 foot and 300 horse were ready to march if the West needed help, and in the North Riding the trained bands were mustered on the 13th, and 300 foot were ready to assemble on the slightest warning.[3]

The performance of the militia on this occasion was not everywhere flawless and it was harshly criticised. The Dean of Carlisle said that in Durham it was so scattered that thirty good horse could seize the deputies and other chief gentry and thus crush it at a blow.[4] Sir John Goderich and Sir Solomon Swale found that the rebels expected half the West Riding militia to join them, while in the eastern half of Sussex there was said to be no militia at all.[5] But Atkinson the plotter claimed that he had not joined in any attempt to rise because the king controlled the militia and would have been able to crush it. He also deposed (more convincingly) that Major Greathead had said that the trained bands being quartered round Leeds would discourage his men, but that he would raise 1000 on their removal.[6] Gower thought that the danger in the West Riding had passed once the rebels saw that the country was 'forward' to take up arms. Once the militia had assembled they were at a loss.[7] It was above all the moral effect of the militia that counted. Its operations showed that the authorities were vigilant and that they enjoyed the powerful and enthusiastic support of the gentry. In closing the first session of the Cavalier Parliament the king urged his hearers

> so to settle the Militia [i.e. in their several counties when they got home], that all seditious insurrections may not only be prevented, to which the minds of too many are inclined, but that the People may be without reasonable apprehension of such insecurity.[8]

This task the militia really seems to have accomplished. By 1666, doubts about the permanence of the Restoration had disappeared, and the fear of republican plots gave place to fears of other kinds. One cause of this was surely the conspicuous advertising by the militia of who was now master in the wielding of armed force. By ceaselessly tormenting the members of the party once dominant, by always taking the offensive against them and never permitting them to rally and recover their political cohesion, they broke their spirit and made them cease to appear formidable.

[1] CSPD, 1663–4, p. 293.   [2] Ibid., pp. 295, 299.
[3] HMC, Portland, vol. ii, p. 144.   [4] CSPD, 1663–4, p. 381.
[5] Ibid., pp. 294, 299.   [6] Ibid., pp. 485, 592.
[7] Ibid., p. 296.   [8] LJ, vol. xi, p. 474.

II

The second Dutch war now supervened and subjected the militia to the test of participation in serious fighting. The result was devastating. It is important to stress, however, that the devastation did not occur primarily in the military field. The tasks assigned to the militia were modest and it did not perform them too badly. Although the Dutch fleet was then the equal of the English, it never enjoyed mastery of the sea long enough to make possible a full-scale invasion. An ostentatious display of force to discourage raids in the periods of enemy ascendancy at sea was all that was required of the militia, and this was not beyond its powers.

Thus, in 1666 the English fleet was defeated in the Four Day's Battle at the beginning of June, and so at the end of the month the militia were ordered to be ready to assemble at agreed rendezvous in case of alarm. The warning beacons on the sea coast were to be carefully watched.[1] Orders were further given for a quarter of the cavalry of the inland counties to be raised and concentrated at St Albans, Maidenhead and Northampton.[2] On July 15 orders were given that the forces of the coastal counties were to attack the enemy if they landed, as they several times had done, and give no quarter.[3] Later in the month the people of the Isle of Wight were heartened by the arrival of three well-equipped companies from Berkshire.[4] There was at least some degree of alacrity in response to these orders. The whole of the Gloucestershire horse (well equipped with buff coats, carbines and pistols) had been anxious to be chosen to go out of the county and so had that of Lancashire. The Warwickshire horse went cheerfully, and well-appointed troops from Staffordshire and Shropshire passed through Coventry.[5] Lord Bath inspected the Exeter militia, which he found in good order, with good officers and plenty of ammunition. He then spent some time organising the Devon militia and left it in a 'hopeful' way. The Cornish militia he thought good because he had seen it well settled the year before.[6] A meeting was held at Bodmin which was reported to have provided for a 'full and noble' appearance on invasion. There was a full and willing muster despite the harvest, and the deputies were very diligent, putting the companies on duty and getting in twelve barrels of powder.[7] Such exertions were as much as was required. On July 25 the English defeated the Dutch in 'St James' Fight'. On August 6 the horse were ordered home because of the victory.[8] The emergency had lasted

---

[1] CSPD, 1665–6, p. 466.
[2] *Ibid.*, p. 504. Cf. n. 5 and 8.
[3] *Ibid.*, p. 538.
[4] *Ibid.*, pp. 533–4, 568.
[5] *Ibid.*, pp. 546, 551, 556.
[6] *Ibid.*, pp. 507, 541, 566.
[7] *Ibid.*, pp. 569, 578, 593.
[8] CSPD, 1666–7, p. 16.

little more than a month, and few had been on service that long.

In 1667 there was another brief emergency. The English had decided to lay up their fleet; at the end of May the Dutch decided to undertake an expedition against the Thames. By way of compensating for their naval weakness, the English authorities on May 29 ordered the militia of the fourteen maritime counties to assemble. The beacons were again to be carefully watched, and if the enemy appeared they were to be discouraged from landing by assembling as large a body of men as possible, especially of horse, and even including men unfit for real service.[1] On June 10, the Dutch having reached the Thames, orders were given for a concentration of force. Half the militia of Essex and Surrey were to go to Barnet and Southwark respectively, the remainder staying at home for local defence; such of the Essex forces as were not required around Harwich were to go to Leigh, more or less opposite Chatham, following the motions of the Dutch.[2] Some at least of them, under Lord Oxford the lord lieutenant, seem to have joined in the defence of Chatham.[3] Wiltshire and Berkshire had each to send three companies of foot and a troop of horse to the Isle of Wight. Five or six hundred Hampshire men went to the Portsmouth area and three or four Dorset companies to Weymouth and Portland.[4] It appears that the other counties had orders from the Council to have their forces ready to march to a rendezvous to oppose an enemy landing, and that some attempt was made to plan marching routes for concentrating them at certain points.[5]

The main events of this campaign took place on the coast and not at sea; the militia accordingly participated in them. The disgrace of Chatham was no great battle honour for them, but the detachments of Kent and Essex militia that were there[6] did not constitute the main body of the defenders. On the opposite side of the Thames estuary, which was also threatened by the Dutch, the militia bore the main responsibility and did rather better. The regiment that was duly sent towards Leigh led the Dutch, who had been burning houses on Canvey Island, to retreat towards the Nore. By June 18, when forty Dutch sail were seen off the coast, the Suffolk militia were rather belatedly being drawn thither and Harwich was well garrisoned. The militia were in good spirits, and many gentlemen had come in attendance on the Duke of Monmouth.[7] On the afternoon of July 2

---

[1] CSPD, 1667, p. 130.   [2] Ibid., p. 167.
[3] See ibid., p. 244.   [4] Ibid., pp. 167–8.
[5] CSPD, 1667–8, p. 151. HMC, various, vol. ii, p. 124.
[6] See CSPD, 1667, pp. 170–71, 176, 205, 207, 277–8.
[7] CSPD, 1667, pp. 171–2, 186–7, 207, 217. See, too, pp. 249, 252, 258.

the Dutch landed near Landguard Fort, across the river from Harwich in Suffolk, and attacked it. Their covering force, well protected by a tract of enclosures, held off the militia under Lord Suffolk, but the assault on the fort failed and the Dutch retired under heavy pressure.[1] They appeared more than once off the Suffolk coast, but were gone by July 25[2] and thereafter confined themselves to local attacks, further to hasten the peace. Again, therefore, the militia were called on for only one month's intense activity (say June 11–July 11).

At other times the militia had often to deal with small raids by privateers and the like, which in the days of sail the British fleet, however strong it might be, was never mobile enough to prevent altogether. Dorset and Yorkshire were the main trouble spots, though other places all along the coast were plagued. In the summer of 1666 the trained bands were in arms at Whitby to help some colliers chased in there, while hostile ships were driven from Bridlington by the guns of the fort and the mobilising of the local men.[3] The country folk in arms rescued three colliers chased ashore near King's Lynn, and a French ship abandoned a vessel it had forced ashore at Torbay when the trained bands arrived.[4] In the following year the Pembrokeshire militia saved two ships from a privateer, and in both seasons a more or less permanent guard was kept up at Lyme Regis.[5] Of even more importance was the continuance of the repressive work of the militia, to prevent co-operation between the enemy without and the malcontents at home. The government thought that the war would greatly encourage the disaffected, and with some reason. When the Dutch landed at Chatham a great conventicle opened in Somerset. Elsewhere the militia had to be kept together after the alarm to cool the courage of the Presbyterians, who boasted that the Dutch would not rest until they could preach freely.[6] In its various circulars the government did not fail to remind the lieutenancies of the need for vigilance in this direction and called for the continuance of the system of standing guards in 1666. Forces were twice concentrated in the Isle of Ely, which was clearly felt to be a likely meeting place of invaders and insurgents.[7] For this sort of ancillary task the militia was well enough suited, as has been shown.

The militia, therefore, did not entirely fall down on the job in the

[1] *Ibid.*, pp. 259, 263, 266.
[2] See *ibid.*, pp. 266–7, 270–1, 285–6, 289, 296, 308, 325, 329–30.
[3] CSPD, 1665–6, p. 556; 1666–7, pp. 116, 124.
[4] CSPD, 1665–6, p. 542; 1666–7, p. 30.
[5] CSPD, 1665–6, pp. 497, 508; 1667, p. 284. BM, Add. 21947, f. 105.
[6] CSPD, 1666–7, pp. 218, 244.
[7] CSPD, 1665–6, p. 25; 1667, pp. 195, 220, 251.

second Dutch war; but it became painfully obvious that the rather small job it was given was the largest which it was capable of doing. It was not impossibly inefficient, and there are signs that the discipline of the men improved enormously if they were kept together for a fair time on service. The Yarmouth companies called out in the alarm of 1667 were reported to have become very proficient by daily drill, though at first they had scarcely known right from left.[1] But it was now that the weak financial foundation of the force became painfully apparent. It was always unpopular and soon became impossible to assemble so many men for any length of time. In January 1666 Albemarle told Arlington that the trained bands would do well if the lord lieutenants were ordered to have them ready and the officers took pains to exercise them on holidays but that it would be too 'chargeable' to the country to draw them together. (Some militia were in fact called out at this time, but soon sent home because of the expense.)[2] In May the government was reluctant to assemble the militia because it would clash with the harvest. Captains of troops and companies were instead to enquire into deficiencies of men and equipment.[3] In July Albemarle said that it would be well to have the trained bands ready, but large new forces might 'break up all' for want of money. He disapproved of the order to assemble the Kent militia with a month's pay: the king would have to repay this before they could be so charged again.[4] Treasurer Southampton was most severe with his deputies in Kent about the poor state of their forces in 1665–6, but he did not fail to say that the militia was to be got ready with the least trouble to the inhabitants.[5] The one month's emergencies of 1666 and 1667 represented the longest spell of duty that the militia could be paid for; in any more serious emergency they were likely to be useless.

Inevitably, the government returned to the plan of remodelling the militia into a smaller force that could be kept on foot longer. On 2 July 1666 lord lieutenants were told that the privy council had decided that three regiments of horse each of 500 men were to be raised. They were to be paid out of the unspent balances of the 'month's taxes' levied for the militia; each county was to send its balance, and an account of what it had spent, to Sir Stephen Fox, the Paymaster-General. The reason given for the levy was that the enemy might attempt a landing if he saw no increase in strength.[6] An infantry regiment and seventeen independent cavalry troops, subsequently to be regimented, were ordered to be raised at almost

[1] CSPD, 1667, p. 262. [2] CSPD, 1665–6, pp. 199, 219, 231–2.
[3] BM, Add. 39246, f. 16. [4] CSPD, 1665–6, pp. 485, 506, 513.
[5] CTB, 1660–7, p. 642; cf. pp. 696, 716.
[6] CSPD, 1665–6, p. 489.

the same time.[1] These units were intended to be what the Duke of Richmond's regiment is once called—'select militia'.[2] Raised by influential personages, they were intended to serve during emergencies and then be dismissed subject to recall. The commissions to raise the original three regiments had been issued some time before the order was given to proceed with the work, and apparently they already existed as cadres.[3] The force was dismissed in September 1666,[4] but it seems that the units continued to exist as cadres for when the attack on Chatham in 1667 led to another levy of the same kind, those who had raised troops in 1666 were simply ordered to re-embody them. The seriousness of the situation made a larger force than before seem desirable, amounting to 12,000 foot and 3200 horse. Twelve regiments of infantry were ordered.[5] The whole remained embodied until August.[6]

It is possible that this expedient might have been the making of the militia had not the war made the government desperately short of money. This led it to weaken the position of the militia both administratively and politically by the fraudulent conversion of the balance of the 'month's taxes' appropriated to militia use by act of parliament. Already, in May and June 1665, the counties were being coaxed, on the plea of security, to send their balances for safe keeping in the Tower.[7] The deputies of Somersetshire regarded this with great suspicion, but were mollified by being allowed to entrust their money to the Governor of Portsmouth instead.[8] Much of the money requested for the 'select militia' in 1666 was thus already in royal hands and was sent for direct from its custodians.[9] It was no less easy in this situation to divert the money from its proper use. In July 1665 orders were given to pay £20,000 from the Tower to the Treasurer of the Navy, Sir George Carteret. Other sums had already been diverted to the Ordnance.[10] When the money had remained under local control the government continued to walk warily. In November

---

[1] June 30–July 9. The orders to the raisers of the first three regiments were dated June 23. *Ibid.*, pp. 454 (misdated Jan.), 475–6, 489.

[2] *Ibid.*, p. 561. It was formed from the independent troops.

[3] *Ibid.*, p. 454. The *replacing* of dead or insufficient officers is there mentioned.

[4] CSPD, 1666–7, pp. 166–7, 176.

[5] CSPD, 1667, pp. 172, 179–83, 189.

[6] See *ibid.*, pp. 386, 396, 399, 426.

[7] CSPD, 1664–5, pp. 395–6, 409, 438, 448–9, 478. In December 1664 the lieutenancies had been told if possible to keep their money in the nearest royal fortress, but they were to retain the keys of the chest in which it was stored (BM, Add. 39246, f. 2. CSPD, 1664–5, pp. 125–6). The king promised to use the money for purposes specified in the act.

[8] *Ibid.*, p. 520.

[9] CSPD, 1665–6, p. 495. Including some local fortress commanders.

[10] CSPD, 1664–5, p. 492.

1665 it asked for a large sum of Devon and Cornwall money (lodged at Plymouth) for recruiting and the repair of fortifications. Repayment was promised and the excuse was made that the plague made movements of cash inconvenient.[1]

In all the government succeeded in laying hands on militia money to the amount of £72,541. 8s. 11½d., which was disposed of thus:

To Col. Wm. Legge, Ordnance	£37,169. 16s. 5½d.
To Sir George Carteret, Navy	12,060. 0. 0.
To Sir S. Fox for the 'standing militia'	23,311. 12. 6.

Thus only a third of the money went to the militia, and of this the campaign of 1666 consumed £20,139. 4s. 10d. The residue was then applied to the fortification of Plymouth.[2] The result was that even the 'select militia' had difficulty in getting pay,[3] while in 1667 the militia proper came to a dead stop for want of money. The government had kept it going in July 1666 by allowing it to retain enough money for a fortnight's pay,[4] and thereafter made occasional payments to it out of central funds.[5] But in June 1667 a privy council circular said that, with invasion actually taking place, the king had money neither to raise an army to release the militia from constant duty nor to pay the militia itself. The justices were ordered to meet and consider how to keep the militia on foot. There was a somewhat naïve promise that the king would meet all charges and a strong appeal to 'patriotts'.[6] By the end of the month the hope was being expressed that no more service would be needed,[7] and the Essex deputies said bluntly that they could not keep their men together unless they received the means to pay them; the mutiny of an Essex company at Chatham is perhaps to be explained by lack of pay.[8] The authorities thought it best to order some detachments to go home.[9] The special fund which had been created to strengthen the militia in 1662 was gone beyond recall, and it is probably fair to say that from this blow the militia never recovered.

The foregoing events were all the graver in that they led to disagreements between king and parliament which were fatal to the

[1] CSPD, 1665–6, pp. 59, 64, 77. Cf. p. 271.

[2] CSPD, 1668–9, pp. 341, 349. BM, Add. 30999 ff. 1–3, cited in CTB, 1667–8, Introduction, p. lvii. They do not quite tally. I assume the money paid to Legge and Carteret was for the departments in which they held office.

[3] CSPD, 1666–7, p. 166; 1667, p. 336.

[4] CSPD, 1665–6, p. 538.

[5] Notably when it had done more than the twenty-eight days' service for which the 'bearers' had to advance pay. CSPD, 1666–7, p. 55; 1670, pp. 547–8.

[6] BM, Add. 41254, f. 17. In August 1667 the Cornish lieutenancy met to deal with defaulting 'bearers' and raise money for the militia. CSPD, 1667, pp. 398–9.

[7] Ibid., p. 237.   [8] Ibid., p. 244.

[9] Ibid., pp. 244, 332. Cf. HMC, Le Fleming, p. 50.

prospects of militia reform. The commons were hostile to the 'select militia', perhaps because some officers of the old parliamentary army had been invited to take part in it.[1] When, because of the emergency, the houses met for a few days at the end of July 1667, they asked the king for the dissolution of the standing forces. Charles replied in a very injured tone and explained that the forces in question were purely temporary in character.[2] The commons were not satisfied; at the head of the charges which they later put forward against Clarendon came that of advising the king to create a standing army.[3]

The commons likewise resisted the embezzlement of the militia money. According to Arlington, its removal into royal hands in 1666 was everywhere unpopular; the West Riding deputies were especially indignant because they had just been setting on foot a voluntary contribution of £2000 to supplement existing militia funds.[4] In some counties the lieutenancy seems to have refused to hand the money over.[5] The commons were determined that there should be a proper account of the whole. In February 1667 they rejected some amendments offered by the lords to the bill for taking an account of the money spent on the war. Their reason was that they wanted an enquiry into a number of funds which the amendments would have excluded, and the militia money was among these.[6] In December 1667 it was resolved to set up a committee in the New Year to consider both the auditing of militia expenditure and the wider question of amending the militia laws.[7] This was eventually done, and on 8 May 1668 Sir Thomas Meres on the committee's behalf advised the house to secure a proper account of the three 'month's taxes' from the sheriffs and other receivers of it; also, to desire the king to reimburse those who had advanced pay to the soldiers serving for them in the previous year, as required by law.[8] From the time of the embezzlement and the 'select militia' there was unending suspicion between king and commons in militia matters.

The outcome of the demand for an account of the embezzled money was curious. The commission finally established to audit the war expenditure duly went into the question and found that, as

[1] Cf. CSPD, 1667, pp. 198–9.

[2] CSPD, 1667, pp. 342–3. C. Robbins (ed.), *The Diary of John Milward* (Cambridge, 1938), pp. 82–4. D. Ogg, *England in the Reign of Charless II* (2nd ed., Oxford, 1956), vol. i, p. 313.

[3] *Milward*, pp. 99, 113–14. Ogg, p. 315.

[4] Each area was given a quota to be raised by the constables like a tax. HMC, *Various*, vol. ii, pp. 122–3. CSPD, 1665–6, p. 512.

[5] Lincolnshire had paid nothing by the end of 1666, and the North Riding still had £900 in July 1667. CSPD, 1666–7, p. 320; 1667, pp. 281, 286.

[6] *Milward*, p. 81.

[7] *Ibid.*, p. 175. CJ, vol. ix, p. 41.

[8] *Ibid.*, pp. 74, 96–7.

already noticed, some of the money remained in local hands.[1] In 1671–2, when the king was trying to govern without parliament, attempts were made to get in the money,[2] and the Ordnance accounts show £1284. 13s. received from that source between November 1670 and March 1672.[3] The commons again complained of the misuse of militia money in 1675, though now it criticised the local rather than the central authorities.[4] In 1683 the government again tried to lay hands on the remaining local balances,[5] and seem to have been encouraged by the outcome to think of trying also to appropriate the 'week's tax', which of course continued to be levied each year. In January 1685 the law officers were asked to report on the legality of a plan to use this as a fund to finance Chelsea Hospital, then just founded.[6] In other words, the commons tried to get the remaining money applied for the benefit of the taxpayer; the crown, when it felt safe from parliamentary interference, tried to seize the balances for its own use.

III

Another trend emerged after the second Dutch war which damaged both the efficiency and the popularity of the militia. Its work in repressing dissent and disloyalty began to seem odious. No doubt this was a consequence both of the eclipse of republicanism and of the revival of more moderate opposition because of the mismanagement of the war. In April 1668 there were lively complaints in the commons of the militia's interference with the liberties of the subject. Deputy lieutenants were illegally committing people to the custody of the Provost Marshalls. The son of the late speaker Lenthall had twice been so treated. A candidate for the mayoralty of Bath who was a captain in the militia had imprisoned many citizens who had intended to vote against him. Sir Thomas Clifford called attention to the unrepealed act of Philip and Mary which empowered the pressing of men by lieutenancies under severe penalties for disobedience.[7] When it was proposed that all deputy lieutenants sitting in the house

---

[1] CTB, 1681–5, pp. 812–31. This subject is further discussed in the next chapter.

[2] CTB, 1669–72, pp. 951, 976, 988, 1050, 1074; cf. Warrants not for Money, vol. iii, pp. 17, 19 (ibid., pp. 1245–6).

[3] Ibid., Introduction, p. xix. Daniel Fleming suggested that the penalties for not going to church and like offences should be properly enforced and the proceeds diverted from the poor to the navy and militia. CSPD, 1670, p. 60.

[4] A. Grey, Debates of the House of Commons (1667–94) (London, 1763), vol. iii, p. 23.

[5] CTB, 1681–5, p. 993. Cf. pp. 1014, 1018, 1022, 1039, 1043, 1078.

[6] The idea seems to have been that the king should allow each county to keep a part of its tax for militia use. CTB, 1681–5, p. 1505. For a later plan to appropriate local balances unaccounted for see CTB, 1685–9, pp. 1545–6, 1717.

[7] See above, pp. 9, 11.

should be members of a committee to consider the militia, the motion was defeated—apparently by the hostility of the many members who were justices but not deputies.[1] Just before this a debate on a proposal for religious toleration revealed the house in two minds about the whole policy with which the militia was connected. Colonel Sandys and Sir John Denham argued that where there was toleration only a standing army would be strong enough to keep order. France and Holland, whose commercial prosperity was being used as an argument for toleration, were only kept in order by this means. Sir Thomas Littleton replied that Poland enjoyed toleration but had no standing army. Sir John Birkenhead, however, contended that the Polish militia was unusually well organised and capable both of defending the country from attack and keeping order despite a proliferation of heresies.[2]

As doubts about the policy of intolerance spread through the country, the militia became less efficient in the work of repression. In 1668 Sir Edmund Wyndham complained in the commons that many deputies were remiss in the discharge of their duties, and some actually favoured the dissenters. He called for a purge of the lieutenancies and an improvement in militia efficiency, to force the 'assembling people' to 'be quiet'.[3] The dissenters seem to have sensed a change of atmosphere and become bolder in resistance. In 1670 there was passed the last important measure against them, the Conventicle Act. The London dissenters (reinforced, it was suspected, by friends from elsewhere) forcibly obstructed its execution. The first attempt to enforce the act in the capital by disturbing meetings was on Sunday, May 1. Even by doubling the watch, however, this could not be done. On Sunday the 15th some militia were in action, but the number of those resisting the law appears to have risen. The various metropolitan militia authorities thereupon established a systematic organisation of guards, at the suggestion of Sir John Robinson. But on the following Sunday the Lord Mayor estimated that 12,000 persons attended at eight meeting houses. The doors of three of them were guarded by over 3000 men and it was impossible to arrest the preachers. In any case, the trained bands were disinclined to use the necessary force.

The Duke of York now came to town—the court was at Dover for the conclusion of the notorious Secret Treaty with France—and exceptional powers were given to the City lieutenancy. It was autho-

---

[1] Grey, vol. i, pp. 123–4. *Milward*, p. 243. The Mr Lenthall said to have been arrested at Oxford would most probably have been the speaker's son, high sheriff of the county in 1672.

[2] Grey, vol. i, pp. 110–15. *Milward*, pp. 215–20.

[3] Grey, vol. i, p. 103.

rised, as it had been at the time of Venner's rising, to lead the militia against the king's enemies and fight, kill and execute them. On Sunday, May 29, the militia succeeded in breaking the furniture of one meeting house and locking it up. But at Doolittle's meeting the congregation prevented them from arresting the old man who was preaching. In Bishopsgate Street a man who was addressing an audience of several thousands was rescued by them when he was seized. Some onlookers said that they loved the liturgy but not this way—a most significant remark. Already Secretary Trevor had declared with horror that either the law or the peace must be broken. The way seemed open for a struggle of doubtful outcome between an enraged populace and a force neither very efficient nor enthusiastic for the cause.

The authorities did eventually gain ground by numerous arrests of their leading opponents, and by sending guards to seize the meeting houses on Saturdays and keep the congregations from getting in.[1] The commons were still hostile to the cause of toleration, and when they met in the autumn they were very rough with two of the arrested men who had ventured to plead habeas corpus and prosecute those who had arrested them.[2] But it is significant that they also set up a committee to consider both the militia and the conventicle acts.[3] Thinking men must have been coming to realise that it was becoming increasingly difficult to enforce repressive laws by the means at the crown's disposal. The Declaration of Indulgence in 1672 and even Charles II's long reluctance to break with the Exclusionists may well be partly due to this episode.

In the decade after the Restoration the militia showed itself useful in what we would call auxiliary or paramilitary functions, but unfit for anything more important. Henceforth, the government's main reliance was placed on the building up of standing forces. Since parliament showed itself as averse to plans for making the militia efficient as it was to a standing army, there was no incentive for the government to go on with them.[4] A chance was thus lost of giving the nascent regular army a basis in the traditional military institutions of the country, founded however remotely on the principle that military service was an obligation of every subject of the crown. The

[1] For the whole affair see CSPD, 1670, pp. 226, 229, 233–7, 239–40, 243–4, 254, 259, 267–8, 275–6, 283, 343, 545; HMC, *Le Fleming*, p. 71. Grey, vol. i, pp. 295–7.

[2] Grey, vol. i, pp. 294–300, 303–10.

[3] Renewed in March 1671. CJ, vol. ix, pp. 168, 175, 215. I think that the commons might have produced a plan for reforming the militia after the second Dutch war if they had sat more continuously.

[4] They seem to have created some sort of 'select militia' in 1673 (CSPD, 1673, pp. 5, 293–4). Forces of the same kind were also raised on later occasions as we shall see, but only in an auxiliary role.

government continued to use and to value the militia in its auxiliary capacity, but the enthusiasm which had given the force its vigour in the first years of the Restoration was now on the wane and in its place there was a growing feeling that important parts of the militia's work were undesirable. Thus the militia was both deprived of the possibility of growth and also threatened with decay through the growing reluctance of those responsible to make the system work. It took the best part of a century to throw off this double incubus.

III

EIGHTY YEARS DECAY
(*c.* 1670 – 1757)

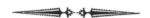

T HE militia as established at the Restoration remained theoreti-
cally in existence until 1757. But, if the volume of the surviving
evidence is any criterion, there was more militia activity in the first
fifteen years or so after the Restoration (down to the end of the third
Dutch war in 1674) than there was in the eighty years thereafter. This
was not more than marginally because the government was unwilling
to use the militia. Whenever there was a serious danger of invasion or
rebellion, it was either called out or told to get ready. This happened
as late as 1745. On such occasions ministers would also encourage
minor legislation to make the force more usable. An act of 1715,
besides modernising its equipment in the way already described,
suspended the obligation of reimbursing pay advanced by the
'bearers' before they could be called on for more. It empowered the
lieutenancies to draw out any part of the militia with a month's pay,
which was to be repaid within six months by a rate levied in the same
manner as the land tax. The act was to be in force for five years.[1] In
1722, when the government was very unpopular and a jacobite
plot was in the wind, it was revived and renewed for seven years.[2] In
1734, when Walpole had the excise crisis behind him and an uncertain
general election in prospect, it was again revived, until 24 June 1735.[3]
A similar measure was passed in 1745,[4] and Newcastle was considering doing the same in 1756.[5] Internal decay, not governmental

---

[1] 1 Geo. I, stat. 2, cap. 14. That it was a ministerial measure is suggested by its
introduction by Lord Coningsby and Col. Bladen, two 'court whigs'. Also, Lord
William Powlett, at one time a leading representative of the Junto in the commons, was a teller for the noes on a motion to adjourn the debate on first reading.
CJ, vol. xviii, pp. 234, 240. Cf. DNB and R. Walcott, *English Politics in the Early
Eighteenth Century* (Oxford, 1956), index s.v. Coningsby, Powlett.
[2] 9 Geo. I, cap. 8, ss. 6, 7. See CJ, vol. xx, pp. 83, 113.
[3] 7 Geo. II, cap. 23. See CJ, vol. xxii, pp. 293, 296.
[4] CJ, vol. xxv, pp. 12–9. 19 Geo. II, cap. 2. [5] BM, Add. 32996, ff. 357–8.

hostility, was what caused the gradual ending of militia activity. The general reasons for the decay have already been mentioned. This chapter attempts to give, not a comprehensive account of all that the militia did in its declining years, but a more precise demonstration of why and when the decline occurred.

I

The poor military performance of the militia, though it was always getting worse, was not the main factor in its decline. The militia always looked ridiculous whenever it took the field, and this may certainly have convinced many people of the need for a standing army. But the tasks which it had to do were so humble that it was usually equal to them. When invasion threatened its main job, as in 1666–7, was simply to make a show of force ashore in order to discourage improvised raids during brief periods of enemy ascendancy at sea. In May 1672, at the opening of the third Dutch war, the Earl of Winchelsea, lord lieutenant of Kent, pointed out that there would be a short period of great danger until our fleet could get out and be sure of intercepting the Dutch if they came. He rapidly set up guards along the coast and got his whole force ready to march at an hour's warning. He hoped that the regular troops would be instructed to obey him.[1] In May 1673, likewise, a Hampshire regiment was sent to guard Portsmouth, while Harwich, Landguard and Yarmouth were reinforced by regiments from Essex, Suffolk and Norfolk respectively. Kent and Northumberland, too, had each to supply two regiments, their destinations being Tynemouth, Berwick, Chatham and Gravesend.[2] After the battle of Beachy Head in June 1690 the whole militia was drawn out for a month.[3] Near Portsmouth a camp of 20,000 men was formed, including the militias of Wiltshire, Hampshire and Berkshire. Eight thousand regulars and militia were concentrated on the Isle of Wight. The Queen held a great review of the City militia, totalling 10,000 men, in Hyde Park.[4] Round Torbay, whither the French had sailed, some 40,000 militia and posse gathered, and were said to be very cheerful but in extreme want of good officers to discipline the raw though faithful countrymen.[5] All the same the French did not attempt more in face of them than the sack of Teignmouth and soon showed signs of departing. By August 6 it was possible to order the foot to be dismissed at the end of a month's service to prevent a deficiency of labourers at the harvest.[6]

---

[1] CSPD, 1671–2, pp. 487, 607.   [2] CSPD, 1673, pp. 270, 293.
[3] HMC, *Portland*, vol. ii, p. 163. BM, Add. 38861, f. 41.
[4] The king was in Ireland. HMC, *Le Fleming*, pp. 279–81, 283. HMC, *Downshire*, vol. i, part i, p. 357.
[5] As n. 4. HMC, *Fitzherbert*, pp. 28–9.   [6] HMC, *Portland*, vol. ii, p. 164.

On such occasions, whether mobilised or not, the militia continued to be relied on for the important though inconspicuous work of holding down those who might be tempted to rebel and call in the enemy. When French fleets appeared off the coast in 1708 and 1744 for instance, orders were given for seizing the horses and arms of papists and other disaffected persons. In 1708 those in the northern counties had to be taken into custody.[1]

In time of rebellion, similarly, the militia often disgraced itself when called upon to fight the rebels, yet performed the same sort of invaluable auxiliary service for the army that in time of invasion it performed for the navy. Monmouth in 1685 had no difficulty in brushing aside the militia who first opposed his progress. On June 15, four days after his landing at Lyme Regis, he marched north and met the Devon militia at Axminster. Four thousand of them had been at a muster and so been able to march against him at once. But because he did not trust his troops, Albemarle the lord lieutenant retreated. Intensifying what it was meant to cure, this caused the troops to flee, abandoning much equipment. One regiment retreated as far as Wellington, 22 miles away.[2] Two regiments of the Somerset militia had meanwhile reached Chard, and part had moved to join Albemarle. But when they got near Axminster some country people told them that Monmouth was there. An old soldier cried that they were betrayed, whereat the soldiers threw down their arms and fled, leaving their officers and colours behind. Half at once went over to the rebels, and the county force was reduced to one troop and one regiment which could not be trusted because 'the others had shown them the way to run'.[3] The minute regular force which Feversham brought to put down the rebels was joined by some militia, but he soon sent away three Hampshire regiments reported to be in great disorder. He was less worried about his lack of infantry than fearful of the militia mutinying in the face of the enemy and said 'je ne conte rien sur la milice que pour dire qu'elle marche'.[4]

In spite of all this, the militia made an important contribution to the success of the royal forces. Firstly, it lay across the several routes which the rebels might take, making it impossible for them to march quickly round the flank of Feversham's army. Their way out to the north was blocked by the Gloucestershire militia at Bristol. Worsted

[1] HMC, *House of Lords*, 1708–10, pp. 108–10. BM, Add. 32702, f. 87.
[2] T. B. Macaulay, *The History of England from the Accession of James II* (C. H. Firth ed., London 1913–15), vol. ii, p. 570. W. R. Emerson, *Monmouth's Rebellion* (New Haven, 1951), pp. 54–5 and p. 93, n. 50.
[3] HMC, 3rd Report, Appendix, p. 99. HMC, *Stopford Sackville*, vol. i, pp. 1–3. Mostly cited in Emerson, *loc. cit.*
[4] HMC, *Stopford Sackville*, vol. i, pp. 10–12.

in a tiny engagement outside it, Monmouth turned eastward towards Bath.[1] Here there was a garrison of 500 militia from Oxfordshire, Wiltshire and Somerset. He sent a summons to the town to let part of his force march through it, which was refused. A rebel soldier in bravado called on the town to surrender and was shot dead.[2] Monmouth turned south but his object was to turn east again, into Wiltshire. To prevent this, the Wiltshire militia was kept marching up and down the county boundary while the main royal force tried to sit on Monmouth's tail. While thus engaged, Lord Pembroke, the lord lieutenant of Wiltshire, learned that Monmouth had been proclaimed king at Frome, towards which the rebels were now marching. He quickly marched there himself, defeated the body of peasants (said to number 1000) that had risen, and disarmed them. The proclamation was torn down and the constable who had made it was arrested. When Monmouth reached Frome he thus found his supporters without out arms and was himself unable to arm them. It was then that he gave up the attempt to break out across country and retreated westward, whence he had come.[3] The militia had headed him off.

Secondly, as the last incident shows, the militia as usual prevented trouble from spreading by holding down and disarming those who might rise in support of the enemy. Even in Somerset the lord lieutenant had at first been confident that the common people, who would rise if they could, could not assemble because of the good watch kept. (In actual fact there are signs that the watchers let everyone through.)[4] In Wiltshire one Coleman, a rich inhabitant of Devizes, was imprisoned for 'entertaining' some men well mounted and armed for, it was thought, the rebel service. These men had escaped arrest, but others were caught making arms.[5] As early as May 19 the lieutenancies had been warned to be on the alert, and on June 20 they were told to arrest all persons likely to be disaffected and keep them in custody in certain suitable towns—those of Somerset, for instance, in Bristol and those in the East Riding in Hull. After the rebels had been defeated at Sedgemoor, the lieutenancies were urged to take great care in placing guards, securing unknown travellers, searching

---

[1] HMC, 3rd Report, Appendix, pp. 97–8. Emerson, pp. 56–8. Macaulay, vol. ii, pp. 586–8.

[2] HMC, *Stopford Sackville*, vol. i, pp. 4, 5. HMC, *Ormond*, NS., vol. vii, pp. 343, 344. Cf. HMC, 3rd Report, Appendix, pp. 98–9.

[3] 'Iter Bellicosum . . . the Heroick March of . . . Colonell John Windham Esqre. with his Regiment of Foote into the Western Parts of England' by Adam Wheeler 'one of the Drums of his Honors owne Company', ed. H. E. Malden, *Camden Miscellany*, vol. xii, pp. 160–1. Macaulay, vol. ii, pp. 589–90.

[4] HMC, *Stopford Sackville*, vol. i, p. 2. Emerson, p. 92, n. 18.

[5] Letter in BM, Add. 38012, printed by G. Davies in *English Historical Review*, vol xliii (1928), pp. 604–5.

for fugitives and preventing disorder; almost at once, however, it was felt safe to let most of the prisoners go. In this way the rebellion was hamstrung everywhere save in its original seat. The main plotters outside that area were Wildman and his friends in London and Lords Delamere and Macclesfield in Cheshire. Wildman, perhaps, had never meant to stir, but Delamere had boasted that he had 'fixed the militia of this county' and hoped to raise 20,000 men. He made a number of semi-secret journeys between London and Cheshire which he had great difficulty in explaining away afterwards. But special measures were taken to secure him, and Cheshire did not stir.[1]

The last important service of the militia in 1685 was to prevent the effective occupation by the rebels of the territory through which they passed. The Dorset militia had managed to head Monmouth off Bridport and were heartened by being joined by Churchill and a few regulars. Under his command the Dorset men closely followed Monmouth throughout his march until they fell in with Feversham. They were by then completely exhausted and he sent them home to keep the peace in their own county.[2] On June 23, two days after Monmouth had marched off towards Bristol, the Devon militia reoccupied Taunton and by the 26th was also garrisoning Lyme Regis, the starting point of the rebels.[3] Nowhere did the latter succeed in interrupting royal authority for long, thanks to the militia, which gave to the magistracy a combative character enabling them to hold their own.

The militia was sometimes able to perform similar services in later rebellions. In 1715, for instance, the Cumberland and Westmorland militia had to face a jacobite invasion. Their attempts to resist it were futile. The seven companies of foot were not concentrated against the enemy but were quartered in six different places; in any case, they do not seem to have been well enough armed for battle. The posse did concentrate, assembling at Penrith and Appleby on November 2 and 3, but it was at once dispersed by the advancing rebels.[4] What the militia could do, however, was to prevent an effective enemy occupation of their territory. When the rebels marched through, Lord Lonsdale and some other gentlemen took refuge in Appleby castle.

[1] HMC, 3rd Report, Appendix, pp. 96–7, 99, 270. HMC, *Rutland*, vol. ii, pp. 91–2. HMC, *Le Fleming*, p. 197. Emerson, pp. 16–18, 27, 29–32.

[2] Macaulay, vol. ii, pp. 566, 568. HMC, 3rd Report, Appendix, p. 97. HMC, *Stopford Sackville*, vol. i, p. 11.

[3] HMC, *Stopford Sackville*, vol. i, pp. 5, 6. E. F. Ward, *Christopher Monk, Duke of Albemarle* (London, 1915), p. 208.

[4] HMC, *Carlisle*, pp. 16–18. BM, Add. 37721, ff. 38–9. R. C. Jarvis (ed.), *The Jacobite Risings of 1715 and 1745* (Cumberland County Council Record Series, vol. i: Carlisle, 1954), pp. 19–23, 149–65. Jarvis points out (pp. 98–100) that contemporary jacobite sources mainly speak of the force at Penrith as the posse. I do not see why he goes on to argue that the militia were there as well. The evidence all points to one company only having been present.

As soon as they were past, orders were given for four companies to assemble at Penrith, while to judge by the amount of pay ordered for them the two companies at Carlisle served for thirty-six and twenty-five days respectively, and that at Cockermouth for twenty-eight days.[1] The authority of the government in the area was not interrupted save when the rebels were marching through. As the rebels outnumbered the local militia, no more could have been achieved, even if the militia had been more efficient.[2]

The fact is that the inefficiency of the militia was the result rather than the cause of decay. The militia was not bound to be bad. That of Lancashire fought creditably beside the regulars in the destruction of the small jacobite force at Preston in 1715.[3] Feversham spoke well of some units in 1685 and others improved after a shaky start. One Wiltshire regiment was surprised on a night march and 'could not unite in a body' till it reached its destination—clearly the men had scattered in panic. But a little later, when they were called from their camp to take part in the battle of Sedgemoor, they came in good order and made great haste.[4] Lord Pembroke the lord lieutenant was said to have

> behaved himself very well and was the cause that the militia under him in Wiltshire did their duty too in this last business here in the West.[5]

Even the remnant of the Somersets that were left after the initial rout behaved well thereafter.[6] The system would work if it was made to work but it was not. As explained already, the trouble arose partly from the drying up of the funds. The initial disgrace of the Somersets seems to have arisen from the demoralisation of the men through lack of pay.[7] But support was lacking in other ways too.

II

The real trouble with the militia was not its inefficiency but its growing distaste for its function of repression. This increased steadily

---

[1] Jarvis, pp. 93, 167–8, 171–2. HMC, *Le Fleming*, p. 355.

[2] Jarvis, p. 23: the rebels supposed to have numbered 1500, the militia seven companies and one or two troops. A company was normally *c.* 100 strong.

[3] R. J. T. Williamson, *History of The Old County Regiment of Lancashire Militia* (London, 1888) pp. 17–21.

[4] HMC, *Stopford Sackville*, vol. i, pp. 11, 19. Wheeler, pp. 160, 162.

[5] Rochester to the Prince of Orange, asking on the king's behalf for Pembroke to be made a general in the Dutch service. E. Japikse, *Correspondentie van Willem III en Hans Willem Bentinck* (The Hague, 1927–37), part ii, vol. ii, pp. 708–9.

[6] HMC, 3rd Report, Appendix, p. 98.

[7] *Ibid.* The letters here are undated, but I think there can be no doubt of the period to which they refer.

with the growth of opposition movements (whig before 1689, tory-jacobite after) strong in numbers and social respectability. The militia remained useful as long and as far as the government succeeded in counterbalancing this decline in zeal.

The obvious way to do this was to give the militia something of a party political character. There is evidence from the start that lieutenancies tried, by means of their power to object to recruits, to give the force the right political colour. A Northamptonshire warrant of October 1660 directed all 'towns and persons' charged with finding foot soldiers to take care to array none that had been in arms against the king.[1] Lord Newport reported about this time that his officers and soldiers in Shropshire were all loyal to the present and had been to the former king. If any were found to be otherwise, they would be cashiered, as several had been already.[2] In 1696 the lieutenancies were empowered themselves to appoint men to serve for papists and nonjurors charged with finding soldiers.[3] If the lieutenancy itself was of the right political complexion the militia could be made the same.

It was at the height of the exclusion crisis that there came the first important attempt to remodel the command of the militia on party lines. The government was urged by Henry Layton in 1678 not to put any in command of the militia who were not royal and episcopal in inclination, at least without a great number of those who were so, to counterbalance them. He suggested that a list be made of those who had paid upwards of £400 in composition for their sequestered estates during the Interregnum. These sufferers for the cavalier cause and their descendants were the fittest people to command the militia.[4] The king did nothing on these lines for some time; he probably had not resolved to break with the commons and in militia appointments he was even willing to take parliamentary advice.[5] By the end of 1680, however, parliament was complaining of undesirables being placed in the lieutenancies, and in 1681–2 there was a wholesale removal from them of members and supporters of the parliamentary opposition. In January and February 1681, Suffolk, Manchester and Essex were deprived of their lord lieutenancies, and a direct royal order was sent to remove Grimstone and Titus from being deputies in Hertfordshire and appoint four others in their place.[6] Other orders of the same sort followed, and in June there was a general order to put out of the lieutenancies all who had lately been turned out of the commission of

[1] BM, Add. 34222, f. 11.   [2] BM, Eg. 2537, f. 266.
[3] The deputies were to receive £8 per horse and 30s. per foot soldier from those charged. 7 and 8 Gul. III, cap. 16, s. 3. Continued by 9 Gul. III, cap. 31, s. 2; 10 Gul. III, cap. 18, s. 2; 1 Ann. stat. 2, cap. 15, s. 3.
[4] CSPD, 1678, pp. 562–4.   [5] See below, p. 61.
[6] CSPD, 1680–1, pp. 149, 173, 182, 190. Cf. a newsletter, pp. 184–6: the king began 'what has been so talked of . . .'. See p. 82.

the peace.[1] The Marquess of Worcester commented on the list which he had sent in of persons to be removed in his counties, that he had left in all those 'tolerable and possible to be reclaimed' as he understood that it was not intended to make a 'thorough reformation'.[2] On the other hand Lord Lindsey sent a list of justices and deputies who had refused to thank the king for his declaration (after the last exclusion parliament) promising to govern according to law. He said that he hoped it was now realised that the policy of courting 'Presbytery' was a mistake. Unless the persons on the list were put out, people would not believe that he enjoyed the king's confidence and he could not answer for the militia. Though he hoped that force would never have to be used, it would be 'an ill time to model it when the enemy is in the field!'[3] It is well known that James II purged the lieutenancies along with the other local authorities in 1687–8, removing those who refused to assist his plans for abolishing religious tests and replacing them with catholics and dissenters.[4] It is well to note that James was here reversing another purge, begun in his brother's time.

The Revolution brought a violent reaction against this sort of thing. Under the threat of invasion, James undid his own purge and restored those whom he had turned out.[5] In 1689 recommendations of the appointments of justices and lord lieutenants were submitted by the existing lord lieutenants and the MPs for each county;[6] the latter, elected after the Revolution, would balance the tory tendency of the former. But partisan appointments soon began again. In 1690 there were changes in favour of the tories[7] and in 1696 the whigs had their revenge at last. In consequence of the discovery of plans for a jacobite coup in conjunction with a French invasion, they secured an act obliging all office-holders to sign the association that had been formed for the protection of the king's person and government. In the form of subscription the king was described as 'rightful and lawful' and so the stricter tories, who would not obey him save as king *de facto*, were excluded from office.[8]

At the accession of Anne there was again a reaction and the government tried to give the lieutenancies a non-party character. The Earl of Berkeley was sent a list of persons mentioned to the queen as fit to be deputies in Gloucestershire and also told to reinstate John Howe as lieutenant-colonel. He evidently objected that it was for him as lord lieutenant to make such proposals. Secretary Nottingham

---

[1] CSPD, 1680–1, p. 302.   [2] *Ibid.*, p. 319.   [3] *Ibid.*, p. 409.
[4] F. C. Turner, *James II* (London, 1948), pp. 322, 328–32.
[5] *Ibid.*, p. 419.   [6] HMC, *Kenyon*, p. 219.
[7] Macaulay, vol. iv, pp. 1806–8.
[8] The privy council saw to the removal of deputies. 7 and 8 Gul. III, cap. 27. HMC, *Portland*, vol. ii, p. 177. HMC, *Rutland*, vol. ii, p. 161.

blandly replied that that was why he had sent him the list. Any objection he might make would be faithfully reported to the queen, but he could hardly think it reasonable that she should be deprived of the services of those against whom no real objection could be made.[1] The Earl of Rutland gave offence by sending in a list of proposed deputies for Leicestershire from which nine persons recommended to the queen were omitted—including some MPs. His son-in-law, John Leveson-Gower, warned him that Anne 'will be queen of all her subjects and would have all the parties and distinctions of former reigns ended'.[2] But once again there was a change and partisan appointments were common during the last fifty years of the life of the Restoration militia.[3]

It was, however, impossible to give the militia very much of a party character without running counter to the sentiments of the gentry and destroying the prestige which the lieutenancy needed to have among them if it was to do its work. There was a feeling that deputies and officers must be men of substance in their county. It was only the militia ordinance of 1648 that included a property qualification—an interesting sign of the oligarchic tendencies of the presbyterians. Their militia commissioners were to have estates at least of the value to be charged with the finding of one horse soldier.[4] Later enactments provided only for an oath or oaths of loyalty to the government, whatever that might be.[5] But the principle of a qualification had, nevertheless, to be respected. In 1681 Sir Henry Palmer, a man of great 'interest', was appointed to command a regiment in Kent in place of Sir Thomas Peyton who had sold all his estates in the county.[6] In 1700 Richard Hewett was asked by Lord Burlington to find two qualified gentlemen to command troops in the West Riding, the commanders of which had resigned.[7] In 1680 the Earl of Yarmouth ordered a Norfolk officer worth only £4 a year to be turned out, the deputies to replace him.[8]

Certain families were represented in the lieutenancy almost as of right, son succeeding father as a deputy.[9] Sir John Holland resolved to make Sir William Gawdy major of his Norfolk regiment, his father having been so. He refused to respect the pretensions of seniority

---

[1] CSPD, 1702–3, pp. 104–5, 114–15.

[2] Leveson-Gower was then Chancellor of the Duchy of Lancaster. Rutland resigned but returned in 1706. *Ibid.*, p. 339. HMC, *Rutland*, vol. ii, pp. 173, 184–5.

[3] Note especially the importance attached to lieutenancy changes after the return of Harley in 1710, below p. 63, n. 2.

[4] Firth and Rait, vol. i, p. 1251.

[5] The most important were 13 and 14 Car. II, cap. 3, ss. 18–19; 1 Gul. and Mar. sess. 1, cap. 8, s. 11.

[6] CSPD, 1680–1, p. 200.   [7] BM, Add. 27411, ff. 231–2.   [8] BM, Add. 27448, f. 7.

[9] E.g. CSPD, 1682, p. 350 (vol. 420: 26).

among the captains and when he had appointed the father his attitude had been just the same.[1] Some noble families had an acknowledged hereditary right to the lieutenancies of certain counties; when the headship of such a house devolved on a minor, someone else was given the lieutenancy explicitly for the duration of the minority only.[2] All this meant that the government could alter the composition of the lieutenancies only to a certain extent. If lists of lord lieutenants and deputies at different dates are compared, the continuity is more striking than the changes.[3] It followed that in local administration, as in eighteenth-century ministries, the party men had to be combined with moderates whose only loyalty was to the crown as such.

The crown was hampered in various ways by this feature of the militia system. A lieutenancy might be incapacitated by party quarrels. A mysterious dispute arose in Cumberland between the Earl of Carlisle, lord lieutenant, and Sir George Fletcher. Fletcher was ordered by the king in September 1680 to desist from acting as a deputy and resign his colonelcy. This seems to have been taken as a sop to the party then dominant in parliament; Daniel Fleming wrote that neither Fletcher's father nor his own could be charged with being papists, traitors or fanatics (Carlisle's father was an adherent of Cromwell) and the local cavaliers supported his cause warmly. When the political wind changed he was restored, but Carlisle seems to have refused to reinstate him. The Musgraves pressed his cause at court. At length the king personally heard representatives of both sides and ordered that Fletcher should be restored but should apologise to Carlisle. Those in 'prime stations' of service, said Charles, must live in good understanding. Carlisle was none too pleased with this but was mollified by the tone of Fletcher's apology.[4]

'Hereditary' lord lieutenants could be a nuisance in several ways. They might be too young or inexperienced to function without careful watching. In 1672 the new Duke of Somerset had to be restrained from turning Thomas Thynne out of the lieutenancy of Wiltshire and

[1] BM, Eg. 2717, f. 190.

[2] E.g., Lord Conway in Warwickshire (1681) vice Lord Northampton (CSPD, 1680–1, p. 638); Henry Boyle in the West Riding (1704) vice Lord Burlington (BM, Add. 28040, f. 66.)

[3] E.g. BM, Add. 28088, f. 3 (date, 1675); CSPD, 1689–90, pp. 20–2, 26–7; CSPD, 1700–2, pp. 248–57; CSPD, 1702–3, pp. 389–97. The last two include deputies and cover the important changes at the beginning of Anne's reign in twenty-one counties. In fourteen of them the lord lieutenant was the same and in nine of these two-thirds or more of the new list of deputies were reappointments. In five of the seven where the lord lieutenant was changed, a third or more of the new deputies were reappointments. Only in Oxfordshire was there an almost complete change of deputies.

[4] HMC, *Le Fleming*, pp. 170, 181, 191, etc. CSPD, January–June 1683, pp. 177, 192, 202–3, etc.

Thomas Littleton out of the muster-mastership of Somerset.[1] In 1675 the young Duke of Albemarle was told to confirm in office the existing militia officers and the clerk of the peace.[2] Worse still, they might be politically unreliable and yet impossible to get rid of. This was the case of the ninth Earl of Derby in Lancashire and Cheshire, doubly irremovable in Charles II's reign because he was married to the granddaughter of the first Duke of Ormond, the most distinguished survivor of the old cavaliers. In the exclusion crisis he was uneasily neutral, supporting opposition candidates in parliamentary elections but opposing the signing of petitions which they got up. In October 1681 he angered the king by appointing Lord Colchester colonel of militia. Already in September he had feared he would be 'eased' of his lieutenancies and Ormond saw to it that suitable representations were made to the king. In May 1682 a loyal address which he sent up from Lancashire was not very graciously received; it spoke of the *king's influence over his successor* being the main security for the future against popery, schism and arbitrary government.

Later that year the Duke of Monmouth reached Cheshire in one of his progresses. Ormond warned Derby to have nothing to do with him and received a foolish reply, saying that it was rumoured that Monmouth was reconciled to the court. Dr Fowler, rector of Whitchurch, warned Secretary Jenkins that there were the makings here of a revolt. The gentry were mainly loyal but the Delamere interest, on the other side, was stronger than theirs among the populace. If in addition the lord lieutenant was unfaithful, the militia might be surprised and the loyal gentry disarmed. In vain the loyalists begged Derby to raise the militia. All that they could do themselves was to match the biggest opposition demonstration with one of their own. On September 12 Monmouth was entertained at a great race and sports meeting at Wallasey. On the same day the loyalists, assisted by friends from Staffordshire, held a great meeting of their own in the Forest of Delamere at which 80 gentlemen and 2000 others were said to have been present. This was really a private and surreptitious mobilisation of the militia. Had the other meeting been used to inaugurate a rebellion, the loyalists would have been ready to fight.

The gentry complained bitterly to the government of Derby's laxness, but they received nothing but thanks for their zeal and a promise that he would be spoken to.[3] Nobody, high or low, dared to challenge the Earl. In 1683 his deputies thought of promoting a loyal

[1] CSPD, 1672–3, pp. 101, 108, 232.   [2] CSPD, 1675–6, p. 450.

[3] At their request Ormond ordered that troops in Ireland be ready to go over if there was trouble. Derby was also accused of not securing the county gunpowder. HMC, *Ormond*, NS., vol. vi, pp. 151, 159, 362–3, 369–70, 428, 436–7, 444–5, 453, 455. HMC, *Kenyon*, pp. 139–41. CSPD, 1680–1, p. 488. CSPD, 1682, pp. 313–14, 342–3, 389–91, 393, 421–2, 431–2, 460–1.

address and presenting it to Derby only after the militia officers had signed it, so that he would have no chance to make it sound like the one from Lancashire. But they dared not do this without the approval of higher authority, and they were told that the king did not wish them to try it as he hoped to win Derby by kindness.[1]

But it might fairly be argued that cases like this were too unusual to count. The more general limitation on the government's power to use the militia which resulted from the character of the lieutenancies was that what the militia was ordered to do had to be reasonably acceptable to moderate opinion. The militia could be given something of a party colour, but the extremists alone could not make it work.

III

The consequence was that the militia could be used against invasion or rebellion, but it did not prove possible in the long run to keep it active against more moderate forms of opposition. As such repression was its staple task, the decay of this inevitably meant the decay of the militia as an organisation, until it almost ceased to exist in the long periods when there was no invasion or rebellion afoot.

The only constant exceptions to this rule were parliamentary and other elections, where the militia could be used because rough stuff was the order of the day in any case. The lieutenancies were always thought to be important in general elections[2] and in 1685 James II tried to use them systematically to control the choice of members. The lord lieutenants were told to attend the county elections and as many of the borough elections as they could get to, prevent intrigues and disorders by the disaffected, and see that only loyal persons were chosen.[3] But the influence of the lieutenancy was largely due to the social eminence of those who were in it and the fact that their appointment showed them to enjoy governmental favour. It might have nothing to do with the militia, still less with any improper use of it. The Duke of Norfolk in 1685 ordered his deputies in the three counties of which he was lord lieutenant to get the gentry to agree on two candidates for the county, whom he would pledge himself to support. At a meeting of the Surrey gentry which he attended, three names were put forward. He thereupon caused the meeting to choose two of them by secret ballot and to these he gave his support.[4] The Earl of Rutland seems likewise to have given his support as lord

---

[1] Derby was again weak-kneed at the time of the Rye House Plot. CSPD, January–June 1683, pp. 285–6, 308, 312. HMC, *Ormond*, NS., vol. vii, p. 59.

[2] E.g. in 1710: HMC, *Portland*, vol. iv, pp. 546, 563, 608, 611, 693–4. But cf. vol. vii, p. 23 cited in W. R. Ward, *Georgian Oxford* (Oxford, 1958), p. 38.

[3] HMC, *Rutland*, vol. ii, p. 86.   [4] HMC, *Le Strange*, pp. 105–6.

lieutenant to candidates in Leicester town and county chosen freely by the gentry.[1] These must surely be the freest unfree elections ever held.

But there were many cases in which it was specifically the militia which interfered. Sir Thomas Littleton told the commons in 1678 that every man commanding the militia was a 'Bashaw' in his own county.[2] In 1671 the commons rebuked the lieutenancy of Devonshire for trying to influence an election by means of warrants to the high constables giving instructions to the freeholders.[3] The conduct of Lord Townshend in Norfolk provoked in 1675 an address against the long continuance of lord lieutenants and their deputies in office. This was said to make it possible for them to terrify and enforce obedience from poor countrymen, and increase their influence by appointing only their own friends to civil and military office. This was against the interests of prince and people alike and was the cause of party divisions in parliament. Lord lieutenants should resign after so many years' service and the duration of parliaments should be reduced.[4] As it happened, Townshend was soon afterwards removed from his post, and after the next county election it was the turn of his friends to complain of the undue influence of the militia.[5]

This influence was felt not only in violent ways but in the field of patronage. In 1660 the deputies of Hampshire asked that some of their number be allowed to be colonels of regiments because the gentlemen who were not deputies were either inexperienced or politically unsound. Treasurer Southampton, the lord lieutenant, granted this request but said that the government's general intention was that deputies were not also to be officers 'from the intent of engaging the more persons by the more plenty of employments, other Countries abounding with persons of quality, whose interests were all fit to be engaged'.[6] It was an honour to be included in the command of the militia and it could give one a handle against local enemies. In 1666 Lord Fanshawe selected for mobilisation those of the Hertfordshire cavalry who had voted the wrong way in the previous election.[7] There was also a chance of financial profit. The three 'month's taxes' levied after 1662 were very imperfectly accounted for and a good deal stuck to the hands both of the civil officials who collected and the militia officials who received it. The accounts taken by the commission set up after the second Dutch war show £731. 19s. 3d. unaccounted for in the hands of Lord Newport in Shropshire, £1043. 9s. 2d. due by Sir Hugh Smith as sheriff of Somer-

---

[1] HMC, *Rutland*, vol. ii, pp. 86–7.
[2] Grey, vol. v, p. 323.   [3] Grey, vol. i, pp. 353–5.
[4] BM, Add. 27447, f. 353. See Ogg, *Charles II*, vol. ii, pp. 474–6.
[5] CJ, vol. ix, pp. 568, 599, 600.   [6] BM, Add. 21922, f. 243.
[7] HMC, *Verulam*, p. 70.

set, £439. 9s. 7½d. for which Colonel Strode was answerable in Kent, and so on.[1] This money did not prove easy to recover. Two officers entrusted with the task in Dorset asked a collector for £230 and were plainly told that he had made use of it in his trade and could not pay. Another collector they imprisoned, some refused to appear at all and a good many they feared to be either disloyal or near bankrupt.[2] In 1683 nothing could be found of £283. 5s. debited to Lord Loughborough, nor of another £1088. 17s. 8d. which he had received.[3]

The lesser posts in the militia were actively sought after and it was accordingly valuable to have them to bestow. Robert Boune in 1671 asked the Duke of Richmond to get Lord Ashley, who was to succeed him as lord lieutenant of Dorset, to continue him as muster-master, from which employment he got most of his income.[4] In the same year two applicants asked the king to intervene in the appointment of a muster-master in the City[5] and in 1672 he intervened in the appointment of a lieutenancy clerk there.[6] Sir John Bramston tried a bit later to get Lord Oxford to give the muster-mastership of Essex to a relative[7] and Sir William Frankland similarly approached Lord Fauconberg in the North Riding.[8] (In both cases the job had been promised elsewhere.) This sort of situation contained the makings of an electoral 'interest', which seems duly to have appeared. In a petition to the commons by a candidate defeated at Leicester in 1706 it was claimed that a Sergeant Mason in the militia had been threatened with dismissal if he did not vote the right way.[9] In 1677 there had certainly been interference in a Leicester election by the militia of the county. Lord Roos, son of the lord lieutenant, the Earl of Rutland, sent out a circular to all holding commissions or having any 'dependence' on them in the militia and who had votes in the borough to vote for his uncle. A little later an election at Grantham was won by an alliance of Rutland and the Earl of Lindsey, his opposite number in Lincolnshire. The defeated candidates petitioned the commons, claiming improper interference by the militia. Lindsey warned Roos that several members who sat for places in his lieuten-

---

[1] CTB, 1681–5, pp. 826, 828–9. The accounts are on pp. 812–31: note that *uncollected* arrears are entered separately.

[2] BM, Add. 21948, ff. 78, 116, 120.

[3] CTB, 1681–5, p. 869. Of course the fault was not always with the person immediately accountable. The sheriff of Wiltshire in 1663 was asking a decade later to be excused £570 because of his services to the crown and the absconding of his deputy. CTB, 1672–5, p. 25. CTB, 1676–9, pp. 576, 1343–4. CTB, 1679–80, pp. 86, 552, 799; cf. CSPD, 1676–7, pp. 111, 118–19, 154.

[4] BM, Add. 21948, ff. 168–9.   [5] CSPD, 1671, pp. 226, 357.

[6] CSPD, 1671–2, pp. 146, 151.

[7] Camden Society, 1st series, vol. xxxii: *Autobiography of Sir John Bramston*, pp. 332-3.

[8] HMC, *Frankland–Russell–Astley*, p. 90.   [9] CJ, vol. xv, p. 136.

ancy would vote against them on this issue unless he came to town.[1]

The use of force by the militia could be important in constituencies where the electorate was large and a contested election was likely in any case to turn into a free fight. It was alleged that in Norfolk in 1676 the lieutenancy, officers and justices collected a mass of voters by their 'power and terrour, industry & art' to vote 'contrary to their own Judgments & Inclinations as they themselves publicly and generally declared'. The lord lieutenant himself was 'the chief instrument' at one booth during the poll, while the booth of the candidate he was opposing was molested by sheriff's men and halberdiers. Things do not seem to have altered by 1710 when Lord Townshend was informed that a sergeant named Wells was expected to bring thirty voters from Bury. But it should be borne in mind that the candidate whom the lieutenancy were opposing in 1676 was escorted into Norwich by 4000 horse.[2]

In boroughs with a large electorate the militia was especially likely to be important because it could be used as a counterweight to a corporation hostile to the crown. Even if a town had a lieutenancy of its own, this seems commonly to have been kept out of the hands of the corporation. In Barnstaple the corporation always had a commission from the lord lieutenant of Devon to muster and train their militia. Nevertheless, the Duke of Albemarle insisted on appointing the captain himself, and in addition gave virtual control over the force to a deputy of the county living nearby. The corporation long protested against this and in 1690 were trying to secure parliamentary guarantee of their privilege, inclusive of the right to elect their captain.[3] In 1682 the government was anxious that the young Earl of Northampton, who was due to 'inherit' the lord lieutenancy of Warwickshire when he came of age, should be elected to the recordership of Coventry which had likewise been in his family for generations. Despite the influence of the mayor, the dissenters succeeded in carrying the election of Lord Brooke. It was then suggested that Lord Northampton should be made captain of a company of volunteers which it had been proposed to form in the town. If he was to be lord lieutenant as well, he would soon make himself popular, teach the town better manners and be a leading card in the election of 'honest' parliament men.[4]

In the City of London the militia and the lieutenancy were particularly important. The latter consisted of a body of commissioners who might number over a hundred. Though they included the Lord

[1] HMC, *Rutland*, vol. ii, pp. 35, 44, 48, 50–1.
[2] BM, Add. 27447, ff. 344–5, cited in Ogg, *Charles II*, vol. ii, pp. 474–6.
[3] HMC, 9th Report, Appendix, pp. 215–16. CJ, vol. x, p. 344.
[4] CSPD, 1682, pp. 19, 35–6.

Mayor, Recorder, and most at least of the aldermen, they were royal nominees and care was taken to make them as reliable as possible. In 1681 there was a purge here as elsewhere, and the purged lieutenancy purged the officers, removing those who were not true members of the established church.[1] In 1690 and 1710, to give only two examples, there were important changes in the lieutenancy in the tory interest at the time of a general election; the former provoked strong parliamentary protest.[2] In 1713 a letter reporting the progress of a poll in the City said that in view of the influence of the magistrates, common council and lieutenancy, it was surprising that the whigs had done so well.[3] Here as elsewhere, the lieutenancy was in part no more than a sort of party caucus. Sir John Robinson, long its leading member, was a sort of government election agent: in October 1676, for instance, he one day met the 'honest' common council men and exhorted them to attend on the morrow, apparently at the election of the Lord Mayor.[4] Presenting loyal addresses at strategic moments was an important task of the City as of all lieutenancies. In May 1681 the City corporation presented an address to the throne praying for the frequent sitting of parliaments. The lieutenancies of the City and the Tower Hamlets replied with an address of thanks to the king for his promise to govern according to law. Both were presented at a meeting of the privy council, the Lord Mayor and some aldermen attending and dissociating themselves from the address of the corporation. The Lord Chancellor thereupon rebuked the latter for its impertinence.[5]

But the City lieutenancy used more violent means also, the best documented case being the election by the citizens in September 1682 of two sheriffs, North and Rich, who were supporters of the court. This was of vital importance because the sheriffs empanelled the juries for trials in the City. Hitherto whigs had been chosen and so the City was a safe refuge for opposition leaders whom the government wished to bring to trial. The new sheriffs and their successors were the means of destroying this sanctuary and making the power of the government feared in the City. It seems fairly clear that the militia played an important part in this royal reconquest of the capital. The election was fought hard and irregularly on both sides and the poll on September 28 took place after a previous, very tumultuous, election in June had been quashed by the government. The whigs

[1] CSPD, 1680–1, pp. 166, 228–9, 236–7, 239, 260, 307, 524.
[2] For 1690: W. Cobbett (ed.), *Parliamentary History of England* (London, 1806–20), vol. v, pp. 590–4; LJ, vol. xiv, pp. 481, 483–4, 486, 488, 491–3, 500–1, 505; vol. xv, pp. 236, 238–40. For 1710: BM, Add. 31143, ff. 554, 588; HMC, *Dartmouth*, vol. i, p. 299.
[3] HMC, *Lonsdale*, p. 247.   [4] CSPD, 1676–7, p. 375.
[5] HMC *Ormond*, N.S., vol. vi, pp. 66–7.

contested the validity of this and evidently made enough hubbub on the morning of the poll to give the lieutenancy a plausible ground for acting. Lt.-Col. Quiney had already been posted with a guard at the Guildhall to keep order. He was now ordered to keep everyone off the hustings who was not permitted to be there by the Lord Mayor. Leaving a guard under Captain Edwards outside, he advanced with a company into the hall. The aldermen of the opposite party were roughly thrust into a corner and threatened with 'military discipline' if they did not keep quiet. Papillon and Dubois, the whig candidates whose election had been annulled, were not allowed to come on to the hustings and those expected to vote for them were turned off and in some cases at least thrown out of the hall with considerable violence. The lieutenancy congratulated Quiney on what he had done and promised to help him defend himself from any molestation. Thus the trained bands of London, which had defended parliament against Charles I, conquered the City for Charles II.[1]

Elections apart, however, the last real success of the militia as a stamper out of opposition seems to have been at this very time— against the exclusionists from 1681 onwards. It was by the executive action of the state that they were deprived of their commanding hold over the commons and the public and reduced to a helpless and suffering minority. The share of the militia in this will not be discussed at length here because the methods used were the same as those by which the republicans were harried after 1660. Arms were searched for, suspicious persons arrested, the assembling of conspirators anticipated by mobilisation and conventicles broken up.[2] On the discovery of the Rye House plot in June 1683 there was a nation-wide alert on these lines,[3] and the militia was alerted again on the death of Charles II.[4] How it helped to defend James against Monmouth and secure him a docile parliament has already been told.[5]

The exclusionists could be treated in this way because a large part of the governing class regarded them as no better than rebels. But even so, the social eminence of some of them must have been embarrassing to the authorities. In 1683 the houses of two peers, Lords

---

[1] HMC, *House of Lords*, 1690–1, no. 267. This is the evidence brought by the whigs in 1690 against those in the new commission of lieutenancy to whom they took exception (cf. p. 67 and n. 2.) In assessing it, it should be borne in mind that the tories were again in power and so there was no incentive for anyone not a militant whig to testify against them. Some like Mr Knightley and Sir John Lawrence were clearly not anxious to speak. Cf. CSPD, 1682, p. 478.

[2] CSPD, vols. for 1681–5, *passim*.

[3] CSPD, January–June 1683, pp. 339–40 and onwards. CSPD, July–September 1683, pp. 89–91, 93 and *passim*.

[4] CSPD, 1684–5, pp. 307–8.

[5] Above, pp. 54–6, 63–4.

Stamford and Macclesfield, had to be searched for arms.[1] So did the house of Arthur Onslow, head of an eminent Surrey family, who was further bound over to keep the peace.[2] Sir Robert Atkyns, a judge whose sympathy with the opposition had led him to retire, complained that his arms had been taken from him after a search, though they were not concealed and would have been surrendered on request. He felt both dishonoured and defenceless. His career as a judge had left him, unfairly as he thought, with enemies, and he was afraid to leave his house.[3] At the time of Monmouth's rebellion not only non-conformist ministers but also those who had served in arms against the king's father and brother were ordered to be arrested. In consequence of this outrageous and unprecedented command, the eminently respectable Sir Edward Harley was confined for a month in Hereford. He records that he was civilly treated and not put in prison as his like were elsewhere.[4]

This social factor was an impossible handicap to the militia when it came to disarming Roman Catholics. Under Charles II this only happened occasionally, under parliamentary pressure: after the Great Fire of London for instance,[5] or at the time of the Popish Plot.[6] But from 1689 onwards the main repressive task to be done was against papists and non-jurors.[7] Not only had they to be watched and disarmed, but papists were now forbidden to own horses of more than a certain value. Something like spoliation resulted. Beasts were seized and either kept by or sold for the profit of the crown or granted to the person who had seized them.[8] When the militia searched the house of a Cheshire papist named Massey, some regular soldiers apparently joined in and started to plunder, thinking that this was the purpose of the search and that they ought to have a share. For this they were punished.[9]

Still more than the exclusionists, the papists and jacobites were a party of the gentry, and their fellow-gentry in charge of the militia found it repugnant to treat them with the vigour which they used towards mere dissenters. What could they answer to a papist like Nathaniel West who in 1666 pointed out to Daniel Fleming that none

[1] CSPD, July–September 1683, p. 93.
[2] HMC, 7th Report, Appendix, p. 680.
[3] CSPD, July–September 1683, pp. 402–3.
[4] HMC, *Portland*, vol. iii, pp. 384–5. HMC, 3rd Report, Appendix, p. 97.
[5] CSPD, 1666–7, pp. 250, 258, 287.
[6] CSPD, 1678, pp. 580–1. Also in 1671, 1673 and 1675. Steele, nos. 3545, 3579, 3584, 3608.
[7] Steele lists proclamations calling for action against them annually in 1689–92 and 1699–1702 and in 1696, 1710, 1711 and 1714.
[8] E.g. CSPD, 1689–90, p. 159; CSPD, 1690–1, p. 73.
[9] CSPD, 1689–90, p. 165. Cf. Addenda, 1689–95, p. 342.

were as loyal as they and slyly remarked that he was not so well furnished with arms as he had been when he had risen for the king in 'Sir George Booth's business'?[1] Lord Cullen was most puzzled how to act towards his catholic neighbours in 1666, especially towards Lord Peterborough's old aunt from whose house five or six persons had been seen to go out at night armed with *portmanteaus*. He duly took part in the search of papists' houses and found that his neighbour Pulton had two birding guns and a sword, besides militia arms. He asked leave to restore the guns—Pulton was so fond of shooting![2]

The attitude of the Cheshire lieutenancy in 1696 is most instructive. It was decidedly whig in colour[3] and it was required to take action because there was a serious prospect of invasion and rebellion. Lord Rivers the lord lieutenant said that 'since they are pleased to be in earnest, 'tis time to leave off complimenting our neighbours'.[4] But when it came to seizing suspects the deputies made difficulties. The governor of Chester castle would not admit them without a special order, it was not 'convenient' to send persons of quality to the common gaol, and house-arrest would be expensive for the county.[5] Eventually it was decided to arrest a certain number and the militia was sent out after them. The victims tried to submit with dignity and pathos. Lord Gerard had already declared that he would prefer to surrender rather than give anyone the trouble of taking him. Sir Rowland Belasyse said that his health was too bad to allow him either to walk or travel by coach; he had not worn boots for several years. He asked leave to stay at home, from which he promised not to stir. Sir Rowland Stanley offered any security he could afford and hoped that he would not be blamed for trying to avoid a spell in prison that would certainly injure his health.[6] Moved no doubt by these appeals, the deputies released everyone on parole. Only two gentlemen found themselves in Chester castle, because they had chosen to surrender to the governor instead of to the lieutenancy. But Lord Rivers urged that instead the 'better sort' be sent to the castle and the rest to the common gaol. Fresh orders also came down from the government, and reports of continued preparations for invasion. Sir Willoughby Aston, one of the deputies, remarked that they had been too lenient. All those on parole were called on to surrender and at length twenty-three went to prison for a time.[7]

---

[1] HMC, *Le Fleming*, p. 44. Papists in Lancashire protested to the privy council. CSPD, 1666–7, p. 128.

[2] *Ibid.*, pp. 174, 337.

[3] Sir W. Aston, for instance, had formerly been put out of it as an exclusionist. BM, Add. 36922, f. 43.

[4] BM, Add. 36913, f. 213.   [5] BM, Add. 36922, f. 44.

[6] BM, Add. 36913, ff. 232, 235–6, 238, 242.

[7] *Ibid.*, ff. 255–6, 258, 260, 280. BM Add. 36922, f. 45.

The growth of tolerant attitudes in religious matters reinforced the reluctance to act against papists. In 1744 the Duke of Newcastle was successfully applied to by his friend White to interpose in favour of one in Northumberland named Errington, whose horses had been seized. 'I am sure', White wrote 'acts of severity on account of religion are not countenanced by your friends and mine.' Lord Tankerville, the lord lieutenant, pointed out that Errington, though very old and reckoned a good sort of man, had been a rebel in 1715.[1] But he was all for leniency and pointed out that little had been done about the papists anywhere else and he had no wish to make enemies for the king by what he did.[2] In 1745 it was with the greatest distaste that Newcastle's cronies in Sussex impounded, on orders from above, the horses and arms of John Caryll. John Page told him that he would restore the arms 'with a thousand times the satisfaction [with which] I received them'. He and his two colleagues on the bench joined 'in compliments to you, and in saying, they have not gone thro' a more disagreeable task [in] a long while . . . You behaved with great propriety and politeness; if you really think we did so on our parts, it will be a future satisfaction to them' [sic].[3]

Behind this growth of humane feeling there lay something no less fatal to the militia—the disappearance of the particular danger it was especially qualified to guard against. The civil population ceased to have arms and ceased therefore to be readily able to rise against the government. Already in 1666 there was a complaint that the Dorset coast was dangerously open to attack because of the lack of local supplies of arms and ammunition. Before the civil wars each county had had a magazine and all the nobility and gentry had kept arms and horses. There were now no arms except those of the trained bands.[4] From now on there was something of a drive against arms-keeping. In 1684 the government ordered that the arms seized everywhere after the discovery of the Rye House plot were not to be returned to their owners as usual but either kept for the use of the militia or handed over to the Master General of the Ordnance.[5] In 1671 the first of a series of game laws greatly reduced the number of persons authorised to hunt, empowered the lord of every manor to appoint a gamekeeper, and empowered gamekeepers to search houses for, and confiscate, sporting gear belonging to unauthorised persons. This included guns.[6] In 1715 the impotence of the posse of

[1] BM, Add. 32703, ff. 50–1, White to Forbes; f. 90.
[2] BM, Add. 32703, f. 40.　　[3] BM, Add. 28230, ff. 303, 310.
[4] CSPD, 1665–6, p. 487.　　[5] CSPD, 1684–5, pp. 26–8, 83–4.
[6] The qualification for being allowed to take game was henceforth a freehold of £100 p.a. or a long leasehold of £150 or being the son and heir of an esquire or having a special franchise. The previous figures had been £40 freehold, £80 in leasehold for life or £400 worth of personal estate. C. Kirby, 'The English Game

Westmorland in the face of the rebels is ascribed in one source to the 'late disarming of the people by our wise game laws'.[1] Be that as it may, searches in the eighteenth century showed the papists to have virtually no arms in their possession any longer.[2] Not that it can ever have been easy for a sensible man to be frightened of the catholics; in 1693 it was computed that those of them able to bear arms totalled 4940.[3] The menace to government of a numerous and disaffected arms-bearing population was increasingly localised in the Highlands of Scotland.

In its place came the rather different problem of the evasion and defiance of the high taxes and customs duties which resulted from the struggles with France. Disturbances increasingly resulted from these or from other economic grievances. At first the militia was the main standby against them,[4] but it was never at all good in this field. In 1666 the Hereford town militia had to be purged of a number of men who had joined in resistance to distraint for the recovery of hearth tax. Even the members of the company who did not take the wrong side at first resisted the disarming of those who had.[5] In 1675 the London weavers rose in protest against the introduction of 'broad' or 'engine looms' from France, and went about smashing them. The ministers thought that the civic authorities could easily have put down these disturbances, but, in fact, they went on for three days and had to be suppressed by the Duke of Monmouth with some regular troops. Not only did the militia behave so badly that some arrests were made of men who were said to have encouraged the rioters but the redoubtable Sir John Robinson disgraced himself by refusing to allow the militia of the Tower Hamlets to go to the help of the civil power. He was severely reprimanded and was in danger of losing his post.[6]

By 1738 ministerial spokesmen in parliament were making law-enforcement one of their main grounds for retaining a standing army. Walpole was sure that if called on to suppress smuggling, protect the turnpikes or enforce the gin act, the militia would take the wrong side. The riots provoked by parliament's attempt to restrain the excessive drinking of spirits gave courtiers a fine chance to hold forth on the

Law System', *American Historical Review*, vol. xxxviii (1932–3), pp. 241–2; C. and Mrs E. Kirby, 'The Stuart Game Prerogative', *English Historical Review*, vol. xlvi (1931), pp. 241, 251–2.

[1] BM, Add. 37721, f. 39.

[2] See, e.g., reports from the counties in 1705 in HMC, *House of Lords 1704–6*, no. 2249 annexe (b).

[3] CSPD, 1693, pp. 448–50.

[4] See M. Beloff, *Public Order and Popular Disturbances, 1660–1714* (London, 1938), index, s.v. militia.

[5] CSPD, 1666–7, p. 321.   [6] CSPD, 1675–6, pp. 250, 252–63, 265, 475–6.

terrible depravity of the common people and the need of standing forces to hold them in awe. Lord Hinton reiterated Walpole's examples in the lords and said that the militia was composed of a low sort of people who would side with their like. He rejected the argument that if the laws were milder the militia could enforce them. He pointed out that nobody liked paying taxes and no law could be more enlightened than the gin act. The Lord Chancellor, Hardwicke, said that since King William's time there had been a great growth of sedition and immorality.[1] The courtiers clearly had much reason on their side. A citizen army might fight against enemies, at home and abroad, who were fairly generally unpopular. It was much less likely to fight well on the other side, upholding the government when its interests clashed with the desires of the citizens or protecting an unpopular minority like the importers of broadlooms.

The militia then was rendered unfit by the changing political climate for the repression of political movements hostile to the government, and it did not prove suitable for the increasing task of ordinary law-enforcement. It was probably never so useful to the government after 1685 as it was down to Monmouth's rebellion. James II disorganised it by his purge. The suppression of the catholics after the Revolution was so unpopular that regular troops had to be called in on an appreciable scale to do it.[2] In the sleepy Walpole era the whole organisation seems to have sunk into inanition. In 1745, even in 1715 and to some extent in the invasion scare of 1690, it seems to have been as easy in most places to raise a body of volunteers from scratch from among the friends of the government as to call out the militia. The Liverpool Blues, raised by the spontaneous efforts of the townspeople, was of some service in 1745; the Lancashire militia, which had received no training since King William's time except when called out in 1715, could do hardly anything.[3] In December 1745, when a French landing was hourly expected in Kent, the deputies simply asked all willing to fight to assemble with whatever arms they had.[4] The militia had really lost the advantage that could be set against its military inefficiency—namely, that it was a force always in being.[5]

[1] Cobbett, vol. x, pp. 405, 524–36, 555–61. Lord Bathurst (p. 549) was for leaving the people their gin if only an army could take it from them.

[2] Lumley said that this had been unavoidable in Northumberland and lamented the poor choice of persons to be deputies and justices. The government hinted that justices should investigate carefully when a protestant claimed to own a papist's horse. CSPD, 1689–90, pp. 153, 154, 179; and see pp. 131–2, 144–5.

[3] Except for a company which joined the Blues. Williamson, chap. iii.

[4] J. Bonhote, *Historical Records of the West Kent Militia* (London, 1909), pp. 79, 80. They had tried to make the militia ready, cf. pp. 77–8.

[5] On 1745 see further below, pp. 112–13. In 1715 an attempt was made in Warwickshire and Staffordshire to build up a force on the basis of the posse:

Yet we should not copy the politicians of the time who lamented the passing of the old militia. Its spirit is well conveyed in a letter about the suppression of disturbances in 1715 which speaks of 'an end of tory mobbing here for the whig mob, being headed by officers and gentlemen, has quite silenced them'.[1] Never did an institution better deserve to be called a relic of the bad old days. Its passing was a step towards taking the gun out of politics and bringing civilisation and humanity into our political life.

Calendar of Treasury Papers, 1714–19, pp. 123–4, 130, 159–60, 210 on Warwickshire; pp. 126, 260 on Staffordshire. In 1690 the City had raised, besides its militia, 6000 auxiliary infantry, 400 horse and 1000 dragoons: HMC, *Finch*, vol. ii, pp. 354–5; HMC, *Le Fleming*, pp. 279–83, 285; CSPD, 1690–1, pp. 65–6.

[1] HMC, *Lennard*, p. 366.

PART TWO

The Restoration of the Militia

IV

THE MILITIA AND PARTY POLITICS (FROM SHAFTESBURY TO WALPOLE)

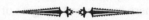

DEMANDS for the reform of the militia arose originally because both the development of a standing army and the continued use of the militia for purposes of repression were unpopular. The opposition to the growth of the army is an important subject in its own right but its contribution to militia reform was so negative that it is only briefly treated here.[1] It followed a regular pattern. After every war or crisis there was a demand in parliament for the disbanding of all or most of the forces which had been raised to meet the danger. Usually this clashed with governmental demands that a considerable number be kept in pay. In 1673 when the third Dutch war was ending, the commons voted a standing army a grievance.[2] When war with France was averted in 1678 they pressed eagerly for the disbanding of the forces newly raised to protect the Dutch.[3] Even King James' unprecedentedly 'loyal' parliament was unwilling to support his building up of the army once Monmouth's rising was over.[4] After the peace of Ryswick, King William fared no better.[5] After the peace of Utrecht and the death of Louis XIV the campaign against the army was resumed.

Essentially it was a straightforward campaign for disarmament.

---

[1] E. Arnold Miller, 'Some Arguments used by English Pamphleteers, 1697–1700, Concerning a Standing Army', *Jol. of Modern History*, vol. xviii (1946), pp. 306–13, gives a good idea of the arguments used on both sides from first to last.

[2] Cobbett vol. iv pp. 604–8.

[3] Ogg, *Charles II*, vol. ii, p. 574. He is wrong in thinking that the militia bill of 1678 provided for the disbanding of the army.

[4] Ogg, *England in the Reign of James II and William III* (Oxford, 1955), pp. 158–62. Macaulay, vol. ii, pp. 685–9. Cobbett, vol. iv., pp. 1369–82.

[5] As note 1. See, too, Macaulay, vol. vi, pp. 2736–42.

Much was made of the abuses committed by, and to be expected from, the army. But the main argument was that the danger at home or abroad was being exaggerated and elaborate precautions against it were not necessary.[1] Alternatively, it was argued that an invasion of this country was impossible without lengthy preparations, which would always be discovered in time to allow defensive forces to be raised from scratch before the attack came.[2] Such arguments led naturally to the conclusion that the existing militia, despite its faults, was good enough for the nation's needs.

This conclusion was unfortunately strengthened by the tendency of government supporters to run down the militia. They hardly needed to do this, for they could usually show that in spite of the appearance of calm there were grave dangers of aggression or rebellion to be guarded against.[3] They might also argue that a surprise attack was not impossible, especially because in a despotic state military preparations could be kept secret.[4] But although governments continued to use the militia, government spokesmen dwelt tactlessly on its inefficiency. Secretary Coventry in 1673 said that since the 'business of Landguard point' the Dutch knew how worthless the militia were.[5] In the commons in 1685 the affair at Chatham was likewise rather unwarrantably used to discredit it.[6] Supporters of the militia complained that courtiers were constantly ridiculing it.[7] Dryden's mockery of the force was long remembered:[8]

[1] I think that before the Revolution the stress was on the licentiousness of armies; later, on the absence of danger. On the latter point see *An Argument Showing that a Standing Army is Inconsistent with a Free Government and Absolutely Destructive to the Constitution of the English Monarchy* (London, 1697), pp. 26–7. *A Letter from the Author of the Argument against a Standing Army to the Author of the Balancing Letter* (London, 1697), p. 4. *A Short History of Standing Armies* (London, 1698), pp. 39–42, 45.

[2] See, e.g., Roger North's unpublished essay, BM, Add. 32526, f. 77.

[3] And that the army was not as black as it had been painted. *Some Reflections on a Pamphlet lately Published, Entitled an Argument*, etc. (London, 1697), pp. 21–5. *A Brief Reply to the History of Standing Armies in England* (London, 1698), pp. 5, 7–10. *The Case of a Standing Army Fairly and Impartially Stated* (London, 1698), pp. 14, 24–5. *Some Queries Concerning the Disbanding of the Army Humbly Offered to Public Consideration* (London, 1698), pp. 2, 3, 9, 10. *The Case of Disbanding the Army at Present Briefly and Impartially Considered* (London, 1698), p. 3. *Reflections on the Short History of Standing Armies* (London, 1699), pp. 9–13, 15, 19, 22. Cf. the debates in 1685 (p. 77, n. 4.)

[4] *A Letter Balancing the Necessity of Keeping a Land Force in Time of Peace with the Dangers that may Follow on it* (London, 1697), pp. 4–6. *Reflections on a Pamphlet*, pp. 17–20. *Brief Reply*, pp. 12–13.

[5] Cobbett, vol. iv, p. 605.

[6] Cobbett, vol. iv, p. 1372.

[7] See, e.g., *The Argument against a Standing Army Rectified and the Reflections and Remarks upon it in Several Pamphlets Considered* (London, 1697), p. 14.

[8] Cf. below, p. 148, n. 2.

Mouths without hands, maintained at vast expense,
In peace a charge, in war a weak defence:
Stout once a month they march, a blustering band,
And ever but in times of need at hand . . .
The cowards would have fled, but that they knew
Themselves so many, and their foes so few.
But crowding on, the last the first impel
Till overborne with weight the Cyprians fell.[1]

It was only natural therefore that the argument was often heard that the existing militia was adequate or that its shortcomings were due to courtly sabotage.[2] In 1673 Mr Powle told the commons that he had discovered a plot to make the militia useless by demoralising the officers. They were given 'chargeable employments' when on service, but when money or honour was to be gained they were not allowed to command. Many in consequence had resigned.[3] In 1685 Sir Thomas Clarges said that the militia had done considerable service against the rebels and could have crushed them had a certain great nobleman been properly supported. Sir Hugh Cholmondeley said that it had kept Monmouth from Bristol and Exeter and was as good a force as any that could be raised at home.[4] In 1723 both the Duke of Wharton and Lord Strafford said that the militia had served well during the 'fifteen', even in disaffected areas.[5] This was a splendid excuse for doing nothing to reform the militia and the commons usually did nothing, save perhaps appoint a committee of enquiry.[6] To some extent this was an impasse caused by its being both true and untrue to say that the militia was a useful force. Only in 1678 and after 1697 (and in different circumstances in 1689) did a really serious move for reform take place and this was because of the other factor at work.

The repressive activities of the militia were naturally always resented by the opposition of the day and it was here that there was a real incentive to reform militia organisation. Greater efficiency was not the object however. Instead there was a challenge to the power of the crown over the armed forces, in the same spirit as in 1642. Traces of this can be found as early as 1675 when Powle opposed the setting up by the commons of a committe to investigate the militia. He said that the trained bands were in danger of degenerating into a standing

---

[1] See *Cymon and Iphigenia*, lines 399–413. But this was a translation and not published till 1700.
[2] The courtiers were also accused of sabotaging the navy. *An Argument showing*, pp. 18–19, 23. *The Second Part of an Argument Showing that a Standing Army*, etc. (London, 1697), pp. 20–2. *Letter from the Author of the Argument*, p. 10.
[3] Cobbett, vol. iv, p. 607.   [4] Cobbett, vol. iv, pp. 1372–3.
[5] Cobbett, vol. viii, pp. 387–8, 391.
[6] E.g. in 1675 (CJ, vol. ix, p. 321) and at the end of the debates in 1685, p. 77, n. 4.

army and that until the Cavalier Parliament had 'declared it' they had always been 'kept as a secret how to be employed'.[1] He evidently feared that the reform of the militia might increase the power of the crown.

The real attack on the crown's control of the militia began with the exclusion crisis. The revelation of the Popish Plot in 1678 made the commons desire the protection of a mobilised militia. They asked for London, Westminster, Southwark and the suburbs to be guarded by the militia during the session and the king agreed.[2] When the revelations of Bedloe were debated there was a demand for the seizure of papists' horses and reports that they were secretly raising a military force. Sir Gilbert Gerrard, indeed, thought that the opportunity for seizing the horses had already passed and suggested asking the king to have at least half the militia kept in readiness until the security of the nation was assured. Mr Bennet said that the government would never employ the militia while they had guards and so demanded the dismissal of the army.[3]

Later in the long debate, Powle brought attention back to the need to 'countenance the legal force' and proposed that a third of the militia should always be in readiness to serve. The house welcomed the idea but Sir Thomas Lee pointed out that, apart from the statutory days of exercise, the militia could only be summoned by special royal order. The 'bearers', too, could not be made to advance any pay if they had formerly advanced a month's pay and not been reimbursed. Like the king at other times, the commons were unable to use the militia because there was no fund to pay it.

Their response was somewhat confused. Sir Thomas Meres had claimed, oddly and symptomatically, that king, lords and commons could pass an Ordinance to get round the difficulty of pay until the law could be altered. Powle claimed that what the king did by the advice of the two houses had the force of law. At length it was resolved (November 18) to ask the king to have a third of the militia raised for a fortnight to secure the peace of the kingdom. A committee was appointed both to draw up the address and bring in a bill to make the militia more useful.[4] On November 22 the commons adopted an address requesting that the whole militia serve in rotation, a third at a time, and that all suspicious persons be arrested. The lords were asked to concur in this. Having also discovered the financial obstacle,

[1] Grey, vol. iii, pp. 23–4.
[2] CJ, vol. ix, pp. 520–2, 530–1. They had made a similar request in 1674 (*ibid.*, p. 292.)
[3] He subsequently revived an idea of 1674 that the king should be guarded by the militia, who would thus learn their duty. Cf. Grey, vol. ii, p. 392.
[4] Grey, vol. vi, pp. 211–16. CJ., vol. ix, p. 541. The alerting of the posse in each county was also to be asked for.

they replied next day that they would do so as far as they legally could. On the same day a bill was introduced in the commons to accomplish what the address could not do.[1]

The bill provided that within forty-two days from December 10 all the forces raised under the 'late Acts' were to be mustered and exercised in such a way that a third was always on duty during that time and none served for more than fourteen days, those not on duty being kept in a state of readiness. By November 27 it had passed both houses. On November 30 the king vetoed it, not, he said,

> for the dislike of the matter, but the manner, because it puts out of his power the militia for so many days. If it had been but for half an hour, he would not have consented to it, because of the ill consequences it may have hereafter, the militia being wholly in the Crown.

It was only the second time in his reign that he had vetoed a public bill.[2]

The king was conciliatory. He said that if he was supplied with money he would 'employ such of' the militia as 'are necessary for the safety of himself and the kingdom'. He later promised his assent to any bill that did not interfere with his power over the militia.[3] The commons, nevertheless, were indignant. The veto was said to be part of a plot to prevent the disbanding of the army. Sir John Birkenhead angered members by saying that what they were doing reminded him of the militia ordinance of 1642.[4] But if other aspects of the commons' activity during the years 1678–81 are considered, the king's fears can be seen to have been not ill-founded.

The leaders of the opposition desired to have the command of the militia bestowed on persons friendly to themselves. In a debate late in 1678 on a motion to declare standing armies illegal, Sir Henry Capel urged that the great men about the king should advise him to appoint the nobility and gentry to places of trust and remind him that he could not have the people's purses without their hearts. This demand he elucidated by complaining of the 'new doctrine' of dismissing lord lieutenants and justices who were honest men and had served both the king and his father. Would the king but 'exercise

---

[1] LJ., vol. xiii, pp. 370, 372–3. CJ., vol. ix, pp. 544–5. Cf. Grey, vol. vi, pp. 270–1.

[2] HMC, *House of Lords, 1678–88*, pp. 64, 67. Grey, vol. vi, pp. 270–1, 273–4, 300–1. CJ., vol. ix, pp. 546–8. LJ., vol. xiii, p. 394, Cf. Ogg, *Charles II*, vol. ii, p. 456, citing C. E. Fryer, 'The Royal Veto under Charles II', *English Historical Review*, vol. xxxii (1917), pp. 103–11. Ogg is wrong about what the bill contained. See, too, M. A. Thomson, *Constitutional History of England, 1642–1801* (London, 1938), pp. 158–9.

[3] LJ., vol. xiii, p. 394. CJ., vol. ix, p. 552. Grey, vol. vi, pp. 300–1, 316.

[4] Grey, vol. vi, pp. 301–14, 316–20. Cf. HMC, *Ormond*, vol. iv, p. 486; CSPD, 1678, pp. 562–4, Layton to Williamson.

his own thoughts', the nation would be united in war and questions in parliament would cease to be decided by small majorities. The misery of the nation he attributed to those who kept king and parliament from good understanding.[1] In other words he wanted the king to stop building up a party of his own in commons and nation and make a present of local office and influence to opposition leaders.

In the next parliament the commons took up the same theme when they debated the defence of the nation on a motion by Sir Gilbert Gerrard (14 April 1679) that the militia be made more useful. It was argued that unless it was put in better hands, to strengthen it would be to weaken their own position. Many complaints were made against individual lord lieutenants, deputies and officers. The navy was also considered and some wished for the removal of all officers appointed by the Duke of York, whether in the navy or in the militia of the Cinque Ports, of which he had been Lord Warden.[2] In the second exclusion parliament, the commons did more. In the debate before the first resolution to adopt the exclusion policy, Trenchard declared that the militia was in the hands of the Duke's party, which made them tremble.[3] Later that month (November 1680) the lords asked for a list of all the lord lieutenants, deputies and militia officers. When it was received, a motion for a committee to examine it to see if any persons listed or their wives were papists was lost.[4] In the commons on 18 December, Hampden called for the purging of the lieutenancies and Sir William Jones mentioned the Marquess of Worcester in particular as having too many counties under his control.[5] On the 20th an address to the king complained that several deputies and justices properly qualified had been removed in favour of others who favoured popery and tyranny. It asked that lord lieutenants should be 'persons of integrity and known affection to the protestant religion' and that deputies and justices should be all this and also 'men of ability, of estates and interest in their country'.[6]

A more direct attack was also made on the military powers of the crown by demanding a general arming of the people against the papists. This happened first in a most interesting debate in December

[1] Grey, vol. vi, p. 281.

[2] The Test Act had, of course, deprived the Duke of this post and that of Lord High Admiral. For the debate see Grey, vol. vii, pp. 107–14; HMC, *Ormond*, N.S., vol. v, pp. 48–9. In April the king proposed that if a papist came to the throne lieutenancy appointments should be vested in parliament. LJ, vol. xiii, p. 547.

[3] Grey, vol. vii, p. 413, cf. vol. viii, pp. 17–18.

[4] HMC, *House of Lords, 1678–88*, pp. 199–201. LJ, vol. xiii, pp. 679–80.

[5] Grey, vol. viii, pp. 187–8, 190. HMC, *Ormond*, N.S., vol. v, p. 530, Jenkins to Ormond. Cf. HMC, *Beaufort*, pp. 74–5, 81, 114. (Worcester became Duke of Beaufort in 1682.)

[6] CJ, vol. ix, p. 685.

1678 on the instructions to be given to a committee on a bill for the easier and speedier conviction of recusants. Sacheverell caused the discussion to take a military turn by proposing that it should be a felony for a papist to ride armed, even though he held the king's commission, and that any protestant might disarm or resist him. Sir Thomas Lee said that the country ought to be able to rise against such people, even if they were duly commissioned. Sir Harbottle Grimstone, the Master of the Rolls, agreed and said that it would not be inconsistent with the royal power over the militia. Sir Charles Wheeler objected that the power of the sword belongs to God and his deputies alone, and Sir William Coventry said that such a proposal would allow forty thousand to rise, which surely no law could justify. Sir Robert Sawyer replied that the intention was only to provide for the arrest of felons, which was legal, and that in this way it would become dangerous for a papist to take a commission or bear arms. Grimstone intervened to say that he had not meant to suggest giving power to the nation to rise but only to each locality to arrest papists found in arms.

Sacheverell now let the cat out of the bag. He asked the house to allow the committee to frame a measure repealing the clauses in the militia and corporation' acts imposing 'the non-resisting oath'—that is, an oath never to oppose forces whose commanders bore the king's commission. He wanted those about the king who would not suffer resistance to papists to reveal themselves. Sir Thomas Meres urged that this was a matter to be left to 'the magistrate', but the Speaker had to rebuke members for hissing. Later on, Sacheverell made an even more dramatic proposal. He asked for the Act of Association of 1585[1] to be read. This had been passed to enable the nobility and gentry to form an association for self-defence in the event of the queen being murdered by papists. They were to avenge her death and ensure that control of the country remained in protestant hands. He then asked for a 'non-obstante' to the obnoxious oaths to enable protestants to act in defence of their king and religion. Secretary Coventry intervened to suggest a relatively harmless way of doing this: commissions held by papists were to be deemed no commissions and resistance would therefore be legal. It was resolved that a clause on these lines be put in the bill and also one for any convicted papist taking a commission or appearing in arms to be seized as a felon.[2]

What all this pointed to was a sort of private army in rivalry with

[1] 27 Eliz. I, cap. 1.
[2] Grey, vol. vi, pp. 328–35. Cf. vol. vii, p. 151; vol. viii, pp. 134–5, 167–8. What Coventry proposed was what the framers of the 1662 militia act seem to have intended it to mean. Cf. E. Timberland (pub.), *History and Proceedings of the House of Lords* (London, 1742), vol. i, pp. 41–3.

the militia—or more probably, consisting of a part of the militia itself under opposition command. To this plan the parliamentary leaders constantly recurred—next to exclusion it was perhaps their main hope. In a debate on the succession in April 1679, Bennet desired a law empowering the people to arm themselves against a king seeking to introduce popery.[1] In the debate on the first exclusion bill in May, Colonel Birch lamented that the existing militia law prevented them from fighting against anyone commissioned by a popish king.[2] In December 1680 the commons had a debate in committee on how to secure the kingdom against popery and arbitrary government. It was decided to bring in bills for banishing all important papists and for a protestant association. The address of December 20 which asked for a purge of the lieutenancies also asked for royal assent to an association bill.[3]

Thus the king's veto of the militia bill of 1678 was a not unreasonable response to parliamentary designs. It was Burnet who, according to himself, first made the king aware of those designs. Noting how

the nation was now so much alarmed that all people were furnishing themselves with arms, which heightened the jealously of the court

he says regarding the opposition and the militia bill:

I found some of them hoped, when the bill passed into a law, they would be more masters, and that the militia would not separate till all the demands of the two houses should be granted. I gave the king notice of the consequences of that bill, and of the effects it might have. He rejected the bill when offered to him for his assent, and thanked me for the advice I sent him.[4]

Once Charles was alert to the danger, he was able to meet it very effectively with his veto. The opposition did not dare to repeat the experiment of the militia ordinance of 1642, and the debate of 1680 on the means of defence against popery has in consequence an air of despair about it. The opposition scored only one success, of a defensive kind. The Habeas Corpus Act obstructed the repressive activity of the militia by making it harder to imprison people without trial. Secretary Jenkins told a magistrate in 1680 that since the passage of the act it was impossible simply to arrest anyone for anything less than

[1] Cobbett, vol. iv, p. 1125.

[2] *Ibid.*, p. 1132.

[3] *Ibid.*, pp. 1234–50. CJ, vol. ix, p. 685.

[4] G. Burnet, *History of My Own Time*, ed. O. Airy (Oxford, 1900), part i, vol. ii, p. 178. Burnet had been under Grimstone's protection, which he lost because of this incident (T. E. S. Clarke and H. C. Foxcroft, *Life of Burnet* (Cambridge, 1907), pp. 139, 156–7.) On the whole matter see K. G. Feiling, *A History of The Tory Party, 1640–1714* (Oxford, 1924), pp. 177–8, to which I am indebted for the last reference.

actual words of high treason. He told Bevil Skelton that the act, along with hostile juries, manacled the government.[1]

II

In 1689 the amendment of the militia laws was attempted again under happier auspices. The dangers threatening the Revolution at home and abroad made everyone, including the new king, wish for an efficient militia. Danger also made the whigs a little more respectful than of old of the royal prerogative. The mutiny of Dumbarton's regiment to which we owe the first mutiny act not unnaturally produced a demand in parliament for the raising of the militia. Colonel Mildmay said that they numbered 150,000, were loyal and cost the central government nothing.[2] In April there was an address asking the king to have the militia put in order, especially in London, Middlesex and the coastal counties.[3] In a debate in June occasioned by the discovery of some treasonable papers, Hampden urged that the militia be put in good order. Sir William Williams thought the need to use it against the papists so urgent that reform would have to be postponed.[4] Later that month the king urged the two houses to finish their business and adjourn so that (among other things) the members could go to their counties and reorganise the militia. This was exactly the language used by Charles II in 1662.[5] As at that time, the situation was ripe for a measure both safeguarding the rights of the subject and seeking to improve the efficiency of the militia.

Part of the old exclusionist military programme got into the Bill of Rights. Not only was a standing army in time of peace declared to be illegal but protestant subjects were declared to have the right to keep arms for their own defence. The declarations were cagily drafted. A peacetime army was illegal 'except by consent of parliament'; subjects were only to possess arms 'suitable to their condition and allowed by law'.[6] On the other hand there was a far more unequivocal provision in another act, by which the non-resisting oath in the militia act of 1662 was done away with.[7]

The commons, however, wanted a militia act as well. In April 1689 a committee was set up to prepare a bill, and Sacheverell—to whom were later added Garraway, Somers and Sir Christopher Musgrave —was especially asked to take care of it. Its sponsors were thus two prominent old whigs, one prominent young one and a notable old

[1] CSPD, 1679–80, pp. 587, 600.
[2] Cobbett, vol. v, pp. 179–82. Macaulay, vol. iii, p. 1348.
[3] CJ, vol. x, p. 112.   [4] Cobbett, vol. v, pp. 341–5.
[5] LJ, vol. xiv, p. 259. In 1690 he ordered an inspection of all militia arms, see p. 29 above. Cf. p. 40.
[6] 1 W. and M., sess. 2, cap. 2.   [7] 1 W. and M., cap. 8, s. 11.

tory. The bill was introduced in the commons in June and reached the lords in July. It took the form of a general act to replace the acts of 1661–3 and it retained the main features of the Restoration system. Some of the alterations were designed to redress grievances and others to promote efficiency.[1]

The former included firstly an attempt to pay off old scores by clipping the wings of the lieutenancies. At the start of the year Sir Henry Capel had said: 'this assembly has been chosen with freedom. There has not been a better election a great while, without force of the lord lieutenants.'[2] It was desirable to preserve this happy state of affairs. The power that individual magnates might gain from the militia was lessened by providing that nobody was to be lord lieutenant of more than two counties.[3] Central control was diminished by denying the king the power of appointing and dismissing officers and deputies without reference to the lord lieutenant. The repeal of the existing militia acts and the silence of the new measure on the subject removed the lieutenancies' powers of searching for and confiscating the arms of suspects.[4] The commons favoured the disarming only of certain carefully defined categories of persons like papists;[5] even in the debates before the settlement of the crown the complaint was heard that the militia act had been used to disarm all England.[6] Complementary to the absence of disarming provisions in the militia bill was a clause indemnifying all those who had taken up arms for the Prince of Orange.

There were also clauses to check financial abuses and thus both relieve the subject and curtail a source of political corruption. Treasurers or receivers of militia money were henceforth to be bound to give security and to account for all money received. Anyone who refused to render an account could be distrained on for the debt and committed if he could not pay. As before, the accounts received by the deputies were to be laid before quarter sessions. But the justices

---

[1] For the bill's career, CJ, vol. x, pp. 102–3, 112, 137, 163, 169, 186, 192, 197, 199, 207, 212, 214, 223, 235; LJ, vol. xiv, pp. 284, 287, 302–3. For its contents, HMC, *House of Lords, 1689–90*, pp. 206–17.

[2] Grey, vol. ix, p. 4.

[3] The lords seem to have rejected this proposal. Cf. HMC, *Le Fleming*, p. 247, no. 3549.

[4] The repeal clause was offered in the commons on report and adopted after consideration by a committee headed by the Attorney-General. CJ, vol. x, pp. 212, 214.

[5] It was in this bill that it was first provided that when a papist or reputed papist was liable to provide a soldier for the militia, the man was to be chosen by the lieutenancy. In partnerships of several contributors to provide a man, the 'bearer' was always to be a protestant (*ibid.*, p. 212.)

[6] Sir Richard Temple, echoed by Boscawen. Grey, vol. ix, pp. 31–2. Cf. Sir William Williams, *ibid.*, p. 30.

were now specifically obliged to examine them and raise objections if they saw cause.[1] The imposing by militia officers of charges not sanctioned by the lieutenancy was specifically made illegal. A few of the charges which the law did recognise were reduced, notably those in respect of the pressing of carts.

At least half the changes in the law incorporated in the bill were designed not to relieve the subject but to promote efficiency. One clause had revolutionary implications. If those liable declined to provide soldiers, the lieutenancy was empowered to order the constable and two inhabitants of each parish to make a list of the persons there able to bear arms. From these the deputies were to choose men to serve. Had this provision been widely resorted to, it would have meant compulsory training for a definite proportion of the able-bodied male population. This would have anticipated the reforms at length achieved in the elder Pitt's day, given point to the subject's newly recognised right to bear arms, and more than either pointed the way towards a system of compulsory military service.

The equipment of the militia was to be modernised. Armour was abolished for the infantry, and each man was to have a uniform cloak or coat. Pikes were to be shorter and the cavalry were to have carbines as well as pistols. Lieutenancies were empowered to purchase small field-guns. By a proviso inserted in the lords, the Welsh and some remote English counties[2] were allowed to convert their cavalry into dragoons—that is, mounted infantry especially suited to operations in rough country. The amount of training which the force was to receive was increased. The quarterly company musters were to last three days instead of two and the annual general muster in each county six days—no longer inclusive of travelling time—instead of four. More important was the provision that in 1689 only there was to be a general meeting lasting twelve days, beginning on July 24. A penalty was introduced for failing to keep arms in repair. In short, there was a real effort to rescue the militia from decay and make it equal to the perils now facing the country.

This statesmanlike measure was destroyed by the quarrel between the king and the more militant whigs which ended the life of the Convention Parliament. Having stuck for some reason at the report stage in the lords, the bill was killed by the prorogation of October 1689, revived by the commons when they met again, and finally extinguished by the dissolution of January 1690.[3] The new parliament

[1] In Suffolk in 1675 it was found that accounts were not being presented to quarter sessions. (Cf. Grey, vol. iii, p. 23 and BM, Add. 39246, f. 29.) Herefordshire quarter sessions were unable to understand the accounts of the 'month's tax' presented in 1668. (HMC, *Portland*, vol. iii, p. 307.)

[2] Cornwall, Cumberland, Westmorland and Northumberland.

[3] As p. 86, n. 1. Also CJ, vol. x, pp. 279, 282, 302, 324, 328, 335.

had a decidedly tory colouring and showed little enthusiasm for militia reform, although some action was forced on it by events. In April 1690 the commons discussed in committee how to secure the government against the adherents of the late king. Heads of a bill were adopted which included the confining of papists to their places of residence and a power to the lieutenancies to assemble the militia whenever necessary. Pay was to be advanced to the soldiers by those who had provided them, even though the pay which they had formerly advanced had not been repaid. This was in effect the expedient embodied in the bill of 1678. But the resulting bill did not get beyond a first reading.[1] The whig historian Somerville accuses the tories of supporting its introduction only to divert attention from their refusal to take the Oath of Abjuration.[2]

The invasion scare that summer which followed the defeat of the Anglo-Dutch fleet at Beachy Head forced parliament to do more. As noted earlier, the militia had to be called out, and at such a time no account could be taken of the failure to refund pay previously advanced—the providers had to be called on for more. This meant that as in 1660 the lieutenancies were in danger of having their orders questioned or resisted as illegal.[3] Accordingly, in December 1690 the lords sent to the commons a bill to prevent vexatious suits against those taking action for the defence of the kingdom. The commons had already ordered the introduction of a general militia bill, which was awaiting its first reading. This seems now to have been abandoned. On the same day that they received the lords' bill, the commons ordered one to be brought in to enable the militia to be raised in the current year, although the month's pay formerly advanced had not been repaid. This bill was rapidly enacted and made it lawful for the militia to be raised by royal order and for the providers to be charged with a further month's pay, any time down to the end of 1691.[4]

This was the first of a series of acts passed each year till they were superseded by the ministerial measure of 1715 already noticed. In effect, they created an extra militia tax of a month's pay, to be levied or not as the situation required. Occasionally a provision from the

[1] Cobbett, vol. v, pp. 611–12. Cf. pp. 638–47. CJ, vol. x, pp. 392–4, 401.

[2] Quoted by Cobbett, vol. v, p. 612. But the session ended 23 May.

[3] Thirteen Welsh justices refused to pay the militia tax or send horses. The muster-master who was witness to this was arrested by bailiffs to prevent his giving evidence and the Lord Chief Baron refused him protection. BM, Add. 28088, f. 50.

[4] CJ, vol. x, pp. 433, 440, 442, 459, 472–3, 488, 490, 506, 514, 524, 529–32, 536. 2 W. and M., sess. 2, cap. 12. The lords' bill (HMC, *House of Lords, 1690–1*, pp. 187–8) apparently dropped and the commons refused (CJ, vol. x, p. 530) to accept an indemnity clause in their bill. In November 1689 the previous house of commons had ordered a bill to protect those helping to bring in the new sovereigns from private prosecutions. Grey, vol. ix, p. 461.

bill of 1689 would be inserted into one of them and become law.[1] Proposals for better accounting in particular seem to have been favoured by the tories as a means of 'smearing' their rivals.[2] Clauses on this subject were carried on several occasions, and the act of 1715 required treasurers to give security and render accounts to quarter sessions within the year.[3] But all proposals of a radical character were rejected. When the first of the temporary bills reached the report stage in the commons, some radical amendments were offered. The lieutenancies were to be able to hire soldiers, at the statutory rate of pay, for all those charged who were unable to find them. The militia was to pay no more for its quarters than the regular troops had to under the mutiny act. All those who had taken the new oaths of allegiance and supremacy were to have the right to arm themselves in time of invasion or rebellion. But the parliament elected in 1690 would have no truck with the schemes of the Convention.[4] Such was the disappointing end to the efforts to reform the militia at the time of the Revolution. Another chance had been lost of attempting to create some sort of citizen army to balance the growing regular forces.

III

After the peace of Ryswick the extremer whigs made a supreme effort to carry their militia programme by exploiting the powerful pressure which then arose for disarmament. They were defeated and no serious effort at militia reform was made thereafter for fifty years. But they rendered an essential service to the cause. Because of the lapsing of the censorship they were able to urge their views in pamphlets, numbers of which appared in 1697–9. Their opponents replied in kind, and thus the conflicting opinions regarding militias and standing armies which were held in seventeenth-century England[5] were systematically set down in print and related to the general

[1] As noted above, pp. 22, 58.

[2] In 1695 a clause was offered making the levy of the 'trophy tax' conditional on the submission of accounts to quarter sessions for the previous three years. This was amended to ten years, i.e. bringing in periods of tory ascendancy, and the clause was lost. CJ, vol. xi, p. 304. In 1705 the lords blocked a clause requiring accounts for money raised in Dorset at the time of the Revolution but they let it through in 1712 after the tory creation of peers. LJ, vol. xvii, pp. 693, 696, 698. CJ, vol. xiv, pp. 534, 557, 565–6, 568, 576. Cf. 10 Ann., cap. 33, s. 3.

[3] 11 W. III, cap. 14, s. 2. 1 Ann., stat. 2, cap. 15, s. 4. 4 and 5 Ann., cap. 10, ss. 2–3. 6 Ann., cap. 28, ss. 2–3. 10 Ann., cap. 33, s. 4. 1 Geo I, stat. 2, cap. 14, ss. 4–6.

[4] CJ, vol. x, p. 530.

[5] Opinions long in existence, cf. *The Peaceable Militia* (1648) described at the start of part i, chap. i. A later precursor is John Hampden, *Some Short Considerations Concerning the State of the Nation* (1692), reproduced by Cobbett, vol. v, appendix, pp. lxxvii–viii.

political ideas of the time. From this body of pamphlet literature were drawn the opinions current on both sides of the question for most of the eighteenth century.[1] Thus the tradition of militia reform was preserved from oblivion until it could again become politically important.

The case made by pamphleteers for militia reform is accordingly of importance to us. They based it on political views which curiously combined the appeal to ancient usage beloved of radicals in the seventeenth century with the reliance on reason and experiment more characteristic of radicals later on.[2] Accused of being Socinians and republicans, they included some like John Toland[3] who were decidedly unorthodox in religion and many whose general outlook exemplifies the trend towards rationalism. Andrew Fletcher of Saltoun complained that 'it is become almost everywhere a crime to reason about matters of government' and that men 'think study and knowledge necessary in everything they go about, except in the noblest and most useful of all applications, the Art of Government'.[4] Reason was to be applied to political problems and what seemed to result was a theory of society derived from the laws of mechanics. This is best seen in the preface to John Trenchard's *Short History of Standing Armies*—the classic and best-remembered work on this side of the question.

> We have not only our own Experience, but the Example of all Times, to prove that Men in the same Circumstances will do the same things, call them by what names of distinction you please. A Government is a mere piece of Clockwork, and having such Springs and Wheels, must act after such a manner: and therefore the Art is to constitute it so that it must move to the public Advantage. It is certain that every Man will act for his own Interest; and all wise Governments are founded upon that Principle: so that this whole Mystery is only to make the interest of the Governors and Governed the same.

[1] The better pamphlets were often reprinted and pilfered from. *Reasons Against a Standing Army* (London, 1717) consists entirely of pilferings; only references to current events are altered. Cf. p. 117, n. 1.

[2] For the men and their ideas see C. Robbins, *The Eighteenth-Century Commonwealthsman* (Harvard, 1959).

[3] His *Christianity Not Mysterious* had appeared in 1696 and was condemned as heretical by the Irish parliament. For the writing of the pamphlets see further above p. 77, n. 1, 5. For their authorship see Miller's article there cited (footnotes to pp. 306-7 and p. 310, n. 34) summarising S. Halkett and J. Laing, *Dictionary of Anonymous and Pseudonymous Literature* (new ed., 7 vols., Edinburgh and London, 1926-34); D. Wing, *Short Title Catalogue of Books Printed in . . . 1641–1700* (New York, 1945-51) and the DNB.

[4] *A Discourse of Government with Relation to Militias* (Edinburgh, 1698), pp. 4–5. This is an expanded version of *A Discourse Concerning Militias and Standing Armies* which appeared in London in 1697.

If that were done 'our Government would act mechanically, and a Rogue will as naturally be hang'd as a Clock strike twelve when the Hour is com'.[1] The way to achieve it was by establishing a balance of power in the constitution. Trenchard thought that

> All Title arises upon an equal distribution of Power; and he that gets an overbalance of Power (for you and I are balancing) takes away the Title from the rest, and leaves them a Possession without a Right, which is a Tenure at the Will of the Lord. [2]

The object should be 'as much as possible to keep the Legislative and Executive Parts asunder, that they may be a check upon one another.'[3]

All this advanced thinking led however to very old-fashioned conclusions. True, the pamphleteers had republican leanings. They were much influenced by republican authors, such as Harrington and Machiavelli.[4] Trenchard denounced both Cromwell and the Stuarts but was full of praise for the Rump.[5] He and Walter Moyle once suggested that a standing army might be safe in a republic but otherwise a people was only free if it had no army. A list of 'free' peoples drawn up on this basis consisted mainly of republics.[6] But the real ideal of the group was found in the 'gothic constitutions' of medieval Europe, monarchical but dominated by the feudal nobility and representative Estates.[7] They thought that 'all Europe was in a manner a free country till very lately'[8], and their great desire was to preserve the ancient English constitution

> in this unhappy Age, when an universal Deluge of Tyranny has overspread the face of the whole Earth; so that this is the Ark out of which if the Dove be sent forth, she will find no resting place till her Return.[9]

There was thus nothing incongruous in the presence among them of Samuel Johnson, unlike his famous namesake a whig but also a true

---

[1] *Short History*, pp. iii, iv.

[2] *Letter from the Author of the Argument*, pp. 14–15.

[3] *Short History*, p. vii.

[4] *Argument Showing*, pp. 23–4. But Bacon is also mentioned. Toland published Harrington's works, and Neville, another radical, had translated Machiavelli, Robbins, p. 32.

[5] *Short History*, p. 8.

[6] Poland, Biscay, the Swiss, Venice, Genoa, the Dutch, the German cities, Ragusa, Algiers, Tunis, and England and Scotland before the late reigns. *Argument Showing*, pp. 10–12.

[7] Robbins, pp. 34–5, 38–9, 45.

[8] Robert Molesworth, *An Account of Denmark as it was in the Year 1692* (3rd ed., London, 1694), preface, p. 21. Molesworth was influential in radical circles and published this work to call attention to the spread of despotism. Robbins, pp. 88–109.

[9] *Argument Showing*, p. 2.

precursor of Colonel Blimp for whom the English constitution owed nothing to 'Aristotle or Plato or any of those Platform Men' but 'consists of downright Honesty and deep Thought'.[1]

The militia plans resulting from these ambivalent ideas were at once backward-looking and subversive. From the mechanical view of society came the notion that arms and property must be in the same hands. Only if the armed forces of the state consisted of men of property—or at least of their immediate dependents—was property itself safe.[2] If arms were given to men of slender means, if those bearing arms were but a small minority of the population, then the interest of the warriors would be different from that of the nation. They would have both the inclination and the ability to take possession of all property and political power. History rather than abstract argument was invoked to prove this, but it was an unhistorical, rationalist history in which the same causes were always producing the same effects. A huge list of instances was compiled to show that mercenary armies always sought to seize power and destroy free institutions and usually succeeded. The examples came mainly from ancient Greece, Rome and Carthage; from France, Italy and the Ottoman Empire in later times; and from English history, beginning with Richard II's archers and ending with Cromwell and James II.[3]

The decay of 'gothic' institutions was seen as the cause of the trouble in modern times. Fletcher explained that a political revolution had taken place throughout Europe about 1500. Before that time the system of military tenures had meant that army and people were one and kings had no force with which to oppress their subjects. But the revival of learning and the invention of printing and the compass caused an increase in luxury. To pay for this the baronage commuted the military service of their tenants for money and in turn paid taxes to the king instead of fighting for him in person. Thus kings acquired mercenary troops and a monopoly of military force and were able to turn themselves into despots.[4]

The remedy was to replace mercenary forces by a militia. But not the existing militia under royal control: to Fletcher this was simply the first step away from the safe balance of the feudal system and towards military despotism. He insisted that only if the officers were popularly elected and the soldiers paid by those obliged to provide

---

[1] He was against 'Outlandish frippery and foreign Knacks' and for prohibiting immigration. *A Confutation of a Late Pamphlet Entitled A Letter Balancing*, etc. (London, 1698), pp. 22–31. For his career see DNB.

[2] *Argument Showing*, pp. 4, 22.

[3] *Argument Showing*, pp. 8–10, 14–15. *Second Part of an Argument*, pp. 5–15. *Short History*, pp. 1–19.

[4] *Discourse Concerning Militias*, pp. 5–11. *Discourse of Government*, pp. 5–19. Cited by Robbins, pp. 181–2.

them would liberty be safe.[1] This was republicanism (not to say anarchy) brought in by the back door; and though the other writers were not as blunt as Fletcher, they all agree with him in substance.

Moyle and Trenchard indicated only briefly the line to be followed. The ancient laws obliging the manhood of the nation to practise at shooting with the bow were to be amended and made to refer to firearms. Each parish was to have a stock of arms and ammunition and organise regular target practice, encouraging it by offering prizes. Various suggestions were made which would enable an effective force to be drawn from a nation thus recalled to arms. The militia was to be cut to 60,000, of which a third was always to be on duty. The men and horses were to serve in it till formally discharged by their masters. The 'inferior officers' and privates of the disbanded army were as far as possible to be incorporated in the militia.[2] This pointed towards the old governmental plan of a 'select militia', and to that extent was useful.

Fletcher and Toland produced more elaborate plans. Toland wanted compulsory drill once a week in each parish for all men between the ages of 16 and 40. The men of each hundred would assemble for training three or four times a year. The country would be divided in three and these divisions would take it in turns to provide 20,000 men for an annual camp for advanced training. Although everyone was to attend the parochial drills, only freeholders were to have their own arms and serve in the militia proper. The rest were to serve abroad or in emergencies. By contrast Moyle and Trenchard[3] thought that it was safe to arm freeholders' servants because they would be loyal to their masters.

Toland wanted a property qualification for officers, who were to serve for three years and then be replaced in a constant rotation. This was to prevent a single party gaining control. Appointments were vested in the crown during King William's lifetime but thereafter were to be elective.[4]

Fletcher's plan may be described as a modernised variant of Toland's. Training was to begin in the great camps (Fletcher added a fourth for Scotland), which were to be permanently in being but always on the move. On reaching the age of 22 every man was to spend one or two years in camp. Thereafter they were all to attend a

---

[1] *Discourse Concerning Militias*, pp. 19, 22. Cf. Lord Bathurst's speech in 1738, Cobbett, vol. x, pp. 545–6.

[2] *Argument Showing*, p. 21.   [3] *Argument Showing*, p. 22.

[4] *The Militia Reformed, or an Easy Scheme of Furnishing England with a Constant Land-Force* (London, 1698), pp. 26–55. Lord lieutenants remained a crown appointment without restriction. London was to have an annual camp of its own. Each hundred was to have a field-gun and each parish a disbanded regular NCO with half-pay for a year and leave to practise any trade.

parish drill once a week and go to camp for a short time each year. The big camps were to be officered by professional soldiers, imported if necessary from abroad, until the system had itself produced men equal to the task. For the reserve of trained men, Fletcher did not think a permanent organisation under officers necessary.[1]

Toland and Fletcher both saw that a great change of attitude was needed before the freeholders would undertake a heavy burden of public service; but they welcomed the possibility of making military training a great school of public virtue. Fletcher thought the older men of quality too far gone to be redeemed and proposed at first to apply his scheme only to the young. In the permanent camps they were to live a life of the greatest austerity. Those who came from the educated classes were to study fortification, gunnery and the like. All were to read some military history and those suitably gifted were to learn how to make stirring speeches to the troops. Some were likewise to be entrusted with religious instruction in the camp, for no clergy were to be allowed there. Sunday was always to be strictly devoted to prayer and study. Toland thought that reluctance to serve in the militia would disappear once it had ceased to be composed of hirelings from the lower classes. To encourage this development he proposed that, except for those already over 18, nobody might hold government office who had not served two campaigns on land or at sea. He thought that this (especially service at sea) would raise the deplorably low level of education in the upper class, encouraging the study of mathematics, geography, astronomy and history. He saw such service as complementary to the Grand Tour. By uniting the profession of arms with those of the arts in the same persons, it would be possible to avoid an otherwise inevitable division of mankind into cowards and barbarians.[2]

The first reason why these plans came to naught was that the danger from France had caused many of the moderate whigs to rally to the 'court' view that a standing army was essential. It was they who were the main defenders of that view in the pamphlet war. For them the question was simply which was more dangerous—'to trust King William or King Lewis'.[3] The arguments which they deployed in defence of King William's cause deserve study again because of their influence on later thinking. The opponents of the court claimed

---

[1] *Discourse of Government*, pp. 51–7. Camping the militia to make them serviceable was proposed in the commons by Colonel Birch in 1678. Grey, vol. v, pp. 104, 121, 152–3.

[2] *Discourse of Government*, pp. 50, 52–5, 60. *Militia Reformed*, pp. 45–6, 55–60, 74–5.

[3] *Case of a Standing Army*, p. 28. *Some Queries*, p. 5. *An Argument Proving that a Small Number of Regulated Forces . . . Cannot Damage our Present Happy Establishment* (London, 1698), p. 5.

that the danger from the army was mathematically certain, while that from invasion was at worst only contingent.[1] The court whigs had to show that the danger from the army was also no more than contingent. They did this by attacking their opponents' mechanical view of history and politics. Daniel Defoe denied outright that like causes in history always produce like effects. He said that the aims and circumstances of Henry VIII and James II were much the same though the results of their actions were very different.[2] Another writer more mildly said that historical examples were only relevant when it had been shown that the circumstances were exactly the same.[3] Another, while agreeing with the *Short History* that the interests of ruler and ruled were properly speaking identical, criticised it for not allowing for the depravity of human nature. This often made men unable to see what their true interests were and so government could never go like clockwork.[4] Another pamphlet, attacking the notion that like causes produce like effects, said roundly that happiness comes from the virtue of princes and misery from the wickedness of the tories.[5] Attempts were made to meet the historical case against standing armies and find respectable English precedent for them.[6] These were mostly misguided, but Defoe was on strong ground in pointing out that James I and Charles I had managed to govern despotically for a time without a standing army and James II had failed to do more with one.[7] Another writer tried to argue that the English army had consistently been on the side of liberty since 1660, the threat thereto having formerly come from the radical extremists.[8]

The conclusion that was supposed to follow from all this was that a standing army could be tolerated if there was adequate parliamentary control. It was Lord Somers' *Balancing Letter*—the enduring classic on this side of the controversy as the *Short History* was on the other—which put the case best. The annual parliamentary review made necessary by the consideration of the mutiny bill and the voting of the estimates would make possible a constant scrutiny of army administration. An army could only be dangerous to liberty after an extensive purge of unreliable elements—according to Somers this had taken Julius Caesar ten years—and so parliament would receive timely warning of any danger and could insist on redress. This argu-

---

[1] *Letter from the Author of the Argument*, p. 12. *Second Part of an Argument*, p. 17. *Discourse Concerning Militias*, p. 21.

[2] *Reflections on a Pamphlet*, pp. 3, 4.

[3] *The Case of Disbanding*, pp. 1, 2.

[4] *Reflections on the Short History*, pp. 1, 2.

[5] *A True Account of Land-Forces in England*, etc. (London, 1699), pp. 5, 6.

[6] See particularly *A True Account of Land-Forces*, pp. 18–47.

[7] *Brief Reply*, p. 5. Cf. *A True Account*, pp. 16, 47–8.

[8] *Some Queries*, pp. 9–10.

ment was not as conclusive as is sometimes made out. It could be very fairly said that the Stop of the Exchequer or Cromwell's dissolution of the Rump showed how a determined executive could break through limitations on its power.[1] But this was but to confirm Somers' concluding argument, that constitutional checks in the last resort were no use and

> we must trust *England* to a *House of Commons*, that is to itself. When ever the fatal Time comes, that this Nation grows weary of Liberty, and has neither the Virtue, the Wisdom nor the Force to preserve its Constitution, it will deliver all up; let all the Laws possible and all the Bars imaginable, be put in the way to it. . . . I would not have us venture upon present and certain Ruine, because that which must preserve us now from it, may at some time hereafter have ill Effects on our Liberty. They cannot be considerable as long as *England* is true to itself.[2]

The second reason for the failure of the militia reform plans was that their feasibility was doubted even by many of those who had no cause to love an army. Anyone wishing to abolish this had of course to meet the argument that only highly trained professionals could hope to succeed in a modern war. Defoe said that to make a new army from scratch took three years and 30,000 lives; and elsewhere that the English were 'the worst raw men in the world and the best when once got over it'.[3] The champions of the militia thought that they had an answer to this. They argued that it was only the technical aspects of war such as engineering that had come to require professional training. They claimed that professional troops rapidly became useless in peacetime through living in demoralising idleness. As explained earlier, a note of complacency crept in with the claim that the existing militia was inefficient because of courtly sabotage. This had made men of quality reluctant to appear in arms and display their military ignorance.[4] But freeholders with something worth fighting for would surely fight better than hired ragamuffins kept in order by the lash.[5] Toland and Fletcher even thought that they could be made to serve abroad by turns, ending a dearth of soldiers that

[1] *Argument Showing*, p. 17. *Second Part of an Argument*, pp. 15–16.

[2] *Balancing Letter*, pp. 14–16.

[3] *Reflections on a Pamphlet*, pp. 16, 21. *Brief Reply*, pp. 11, 14. Cf. *Case of a Standing Army*, pp. 18–20. *Balancing Letter*, pp. 7, 8, 11.

[4] *Argument Showing*, pp. 20, 24, 25. *Discourse Concerning Militias*, p. 23. *Short History*, p. 42. *Discourse of Government*, pp. 31–2, 47–9. North's essay, BM, Add. 32526, ff. 75–9. Cf. above, pp. 1–2; part i, chap. ii, p. 25. One conclusion drawn was that the militia could not be made efficient till the army was abolished: only then would court sabotage stop. In 1673 Sir Nicholas Carew said that the regular troops then were new levies and so no better than militia. Grey, vol. ii, p. 220. Cf. *Argument Showing*, p. 23.

[5] *Ibid.*, p. 20.

caused battle to be shunned for fear of casualties.[1] At home a very large militia could be maintained at the same cost as a small standing force[2] and so any invader would be overwhelmed by superior numbers. Johnson thought that living in a free society had made all Englishmen brave, whereas on the continent only the nobility were so. Invasion could easily be met and there was little need for training in advance.[3] The great exploits of militia-type forces in the past were dwelt on[4] and so was the prowess of the militias still flourishing in Switzerland, Poland, the English colonies and the Channel Islands. Much was made of the recent valour of Londonderry and Enniskillen. Moyle noted also—and this seems a better point—that the ill-organised Catholic Irish had held out for a long time against the regular troops of King William.[5]

The court whigs were unconvinced. The examples, past and present, of successful irregular forces were disposed of by saying that they only had to face other troops of their own kind or that they had special geographical advantages.[6] The more general arguments were dismissed on the ground that the propertied class could never be induced to devote any substantial amount of time to war. One writer remarked that this could only happen if there was a return to conditions in Saxon times, with no trade and a different distribution of property. A militia that really did work would have to be so like an army that it would not diminish but undesirably increase the power of the crown. This, it was suggested, was what had happened in Sweden.[7]

What was particularly important was that these arguments found an echo among the tories and jacobites. It was these groups who now made up the bulk of the opposition, compensation for the defection of the moderate whigs. The Association of 1696 had lessened their share of local office[8] and given them the same interest as the exclu-

---

[1] *Militia Reformed*, pp. 67, 73. *Discourse of Government*, p. 58.

[2] *Argument Showing*, p. 23. *Short History*, p. 41. Fletcher (*Discourse of Government*, p. 46) inclined to think that an inefficient militia would do for home defence. The great purpose of having an efficient one was to preserve liberty.

[3] *Confutation*, pp. 2, 18–21.

[4] Down to the Armada and Civil Wars. *Argument Showing*, p. 25. *Letter from the Author*, pp. 8–9. *Discourse Concerning Militias*, pp. 23–4. *Short History*, p. 8.

[5] The Epiriots, Hungarians and Catalans were also cited. *Argument Showing*, pp. 20–1. *Letter from the Author*, p. 10. *Second Part of an Argument*, p. 21.

[6] *Reflections on a Pamphlet*, pp. 22–3. *Balancing Letter*, pp. 12–13. *Brief Reply*, p. 13. *Case of a Standing Army*, pp. 13–14.

[7] *Reflections*, p. 18. *Case of a Standing Army*, pp. 18–20, points out that soldiers were mostly unmarried ex-vagabonds. *True Account*, p. 23 on the Saxons. Cf. *Balancing Letter*, pp. 9–10, that Rome and Sparta were warrior republics and their experience was no guide. For the views of an experienced general on the whole matter see the Duke of Argyle's speech in 1733, Cobbett, vol viii, pp. 1241–9.

[8] See above, p. 59.

sionists earlier in 'reforming' the militia in order to gain control of it. The court whigs did not fail to point out the opportunities which an indiscriminate arming would give to disloyal elements.[1] But support from this quarter was lukewarm—one bill was even said to have failed because the jacobites withdrew their support.[2]

The tories seem to have felt the embarrassment of a party long accustomed to the sobering responsibilities of office when forced to voice the wilder cries of opposition. They kept pretty silent on the army question but wrote enough to make it fairly clear what their views were. Roger North's unpublished essay sets out the main arguments current against the standing army. But the militia is also condemned. Its loyalty to the government could never be relied on in a civil conflict in which the country was at all evenly divided. Since 'it is the humour of the English to be warm and zealous by fits', there would be no concern for its efficiency, save in time of danger; 'in a short time, like all other English institutions, it would grow into desuetude and perfunctory if not ridiculous practice.' North placed his reliance on bodies of volunteers raised by noblemen and gentlemen who were firm supporters of the government. He pointed to the example of Oliver Cromwell who had found that only 'preaching zealots were a match for the high spirited cavaliers'.[3] This was a typical court view and so was that of a treatise of Queen Anne's reign, whose author was certainly a tory. He had been a militia officer for nearly thirty years, beginning at the Restoration. His father had been ruined in 'fortune and person' by the Civil War and had never been compensated. He had found that Church of England men seldom grumbled at militia service without due cause and most complaints came from dissenters. Against their appeals to Magna Charta he had been wont to argue (mistakenly) that the militia was liable for foreign service. The examples by which his plan of reform was inspired were those of the Swedish and French militias—both essentially authoritarian expedients for raising an army.

He proposed that the militia should be a source of recruits for the army and itself send contingents on short expeditions to the coast of France. The men were still to be found by the landowners, but to help them they were to have power to impress vagabonds. On the other hand, they were to care for their men in sickness or disablement and help them when they left the service. The militia was to be reduced to 50,000 men. A quarter of them were to assemble for a month's training each year at (he suggested) Hounslow Heath. They

---

[1] E.g. *True Account*, pp. 49, 64–5. Cf. Miller's article, p. 308.

[2] *Reflections on the Short History*, p. 8. Cf. *Short History*, p. 41.

[3] BM, Add. 32526, ff. 75–9. It was written after the Revolution, to which it refers, but I do not know when.

were to have their own uniforms but borrow arms, tents and other equipment from the Tower. To encourage respectable men to enter the ranks the superior officers were to be gentlemen. But the lieutenant of each company was to be a professional soldier in permanent pay, responsible for training. Young freeholders who had done good service in the ranks and become sergeants were to be made lieutenants and given a chance later to enter the army.[1] Despite some points of agreement with Toland and Fletcher, this plan irresistibly recalls the court whigs' warning that a really efficient militia would increase the power of the crown. Its author would have found it hard to work harmoniously with the anti-army party.

Thus neither of the 'court' parties could patronise the sort of reform which the extreme whigs wanted. In any case neither was eager to do so for fear of losing the chance of royal favour. There were rumours that the tories were plotting to win the favour of the king by offering to support him over the army question. In 1697 Lord Mulgrave and his friends were said to be planning to do this, with the additional object of making the king unpopular.[2] Moyle and Trenchard thought that many whigs had failed to support them because they feared that if they did, their leaders would be turned out and replaced by tories.[3] Thus Toland could write that while some said the tories would never pass an effective militia bill, others declared that the whigs were against it.[4]

The last and most important reason for the failure of the reform plans was that the majority of the commons were interested only in cutting defence costs and regarded militia bills as a mere gesture to show that they were not indifferent to national security. This seems to be the inescapable conclusion from a study of the proceedings in parliament. In December 1697 (despite much cajoling of members before the session began),[5] the commons voted to return to the establishment of 1680—say 10,000 men.[6] At the same time it was decided to bring in a bill to reform the militia. The country gentlemen were

---

[1] *Observations Upon the Subject Matter Relating to the Militia* (1711), *Some Private Thoughts Humbly Propos'd for Making the Militia of South Britain More Useful* (1712). These are substantially the same, and on p. 3 of the earlier one are mentioned earlier editions in 1707 and 1709. The author says he had several times testified before parliament on the subject, it is not clear in what way.

[2] HMC, *Portland*, vol. iii, p. 593.

[3] *Argument Showing*, p. 5. *Short History*, p. 23.

[4] *Militia Reformed*, pp. 6, 7.

[5] *Short History*, p. 23.

[6] The total establishment of the three kingdoms at the end of the war was about 87,000 (Walton, p. 497.) Even when the English establishment was cut to 7000 in 1699, the grand total remained as high as 24,500. See G. Davies, 'The Reduction of the Army after the Peace of Ryswick', *Jol. of the Soc. of Army Historical Research*, vol. xxviii (1950), pp. 15–28.

enthusiastic for this and seem to have thought that if the navy and militia did their part, the reduced establishment would be enough.[1] Efforts continued to get more money for the army,[2] and eventually enough was voted for 3000 marines. Also, for financial reasons and because the king of Spain threatened to die, the commons let the king choose his own time and method for reducing his forces. He was able to save some by sending them to Ireland, and he reduced the size rather than the numbers of his regiments, thus facilitating re-expansion.[3]

The militia bill, meanwhile, had done badly. Its history is obscure. The commons appointed a committee to draw it up and asked for a return of the strength of the existing militia. In February 1698 it was decided that the existing militia laws should be repealed and the new bill was then brought in. It was only a skeleton. There was a proposal that the deputies and most of the officers should have a property qualification and that all were to have a residence qualification. But the amounts of the qualifications, the size of the force, the amount of its duty each year and the financial provision for it had all been left blank. The bill was brought in by Sir Richard Onslow, an important whig county member.[4] It was read a second time in March but at the committee stage there were strong signs of lassitude. The first sitting was twice postponed and it was said that some had grown so indifferent that they did not care if no day was assigned. When the sitting did take place many objections were raised and so few attended that it looked as if nobody intended the bill to pass. After two more such sittings no more was heard of the bill.[5] Perhaps as the commons relented a little over the army they felt less need to reform the militia.

The next session saw the army in graver danger than before. The efforts which the government had made to slow down disbandment seem to have aroused suspicion. Even before parliament dispersed for the summer and the elections, Jack How seems to have come to town specially to stir up the question, and an address asking for an account of what had been done was pushed through by Musgrave.[6] The elections of 1698 greatly strengthened the body in the commons

---

[1] CSPD, 1697, pp. 505–6, 513. The commons had appointed a committee to overhaul the militia laws in 1695. CJ, vol. xi, p. 194.

[2] CSPD, 1697, pp. 516–7, 528–9. G. P. R. James, ed., Letters ... to the Duke of Shrewsbury ... by James Vernon (London, 1841), vol. i, pp. 442, 460. Short History, pp. 23–5.

[3] Vernon, vol. i, pp. 463–5, 482; vol. ii, pp. 1, 2, 179–81. Cf. E. Japikse, ed., Correspondentie van Willem III en Van Hans William Bentinck (The Hague, 1927–37), part i, vol. i, p. 221.

[4] CJ, vol. xii, pp. 12, 37, 45–6, 127, 132. CSPD, 1698, pp. 114–15.

[5] CJ, vol. xii, pp. 147, 162, 169, 177, 178, 192, 197, 206, 243. CSPD, 1698, pp. 154, 160, 197. Vernon, vol. ii, p. 35.

[6] Vernon, vol. ii, pp. 85, 94. CJ, vol. xii, p. 295. On Howe and Musgrave, DNB.

that was 'whiggish without being ministerial'.[1] When parliament met again its feelings were so clear that the ministers and their friends made no attempt to oppose disbandment. As in the previous session Robert Harley took the lead, and at his behest the commons cut the army to 7000 men and put their decision into a disbanding bill which could not be evaded. The king was mortified to the point of considering abdication. He thought, however, that there were many in the commons who would respond to a lead on the army question, and since his ministers hung back he resolved to give it himself. In assenting to the disbanding bill he solemnly warned parliament that they were endangering national security.[2]

The commons at once assured the king of their resolve to give him all necessary support and a few days later took his speech into consideration; when, Vernon says,

> Mr. Harley was pretty quick in proposing, that for a further security of the nation, a bill should be brought in for better regulating the militia, which was readily closed with, as if it were a good deliverance from a debate, that was perhaps apprehended on all sides.[3]

Thus the unofficial leader of the house had taken up the subject; and when a militia bill duly appeared it was Harley's friend Foley who presented it. Moreover his father, old Sir Edward Harley who had sat in the Long Parliament and incurred the hostility of the army by his opposition to them in 1648, appears to have been concerned in framing the bill. But notwithstanding its distinguished sponsors, it disappeared after the second reading.[4]

After 1699 the commons made no further significant efforts to reduce the army or reform the militia. Probably they realised that no money would be saved. Under-Secretary Ellis remarked of the bill of 1699 that an effective militia would be very like a standing army and be very expensive.[5] On the second reading of the earlier bill Sir William Williams, the only speaker who opposed it, said that it would introduce a great and permanent tax and a standing army that must be dangerous either to king or people.[6] Those who wanted militia reform in order to curb the power of the crown looked elsewhere. In the session of 1699–1700 the commons took up the cause of those

---

[1] Macaulay, vol. vi, pp. 2845–6.

[2] *Vernon*, vol. ii, pp. 230, 235–7, 239–42, 246–8, 253–9. Cf. Macaulay, chaps. xxiii–xxiv. Vernon seems to have agreed with the king's view of the commons.

[3] Vernon, vol. ii, p. 263.

[4] CJ, vol. xii, pp. 484, 491, 540, 548, 586, 609, 613, 623, 626, 640, 656, 665. Feiling, *Tory Party*, p. 332, says the bill reached the lords but gives no reference. The life of Robert Harley by his brother says (HMC, *Portland*, vol. v, p. 645, note) that Sir Edward brought in a militia bill at the end of William's reign. There is no sign of this in CJ, but it seems plausible to connect him with this one.

[5] CSPD, 1699–1700, p. 49.   [6] CSPD, 1698, pp. 134–5.

excluded from local office by the Association. A committee investigated the commissions of the peace and the personnel of the lieutenancies. Its report resulted in an address in the style of 1680, asking that gentlemen of quality and good estates be put into both. An amendment to add 'restored' to 'put in' was carried by 119 votes to 113 and one to add 'who are well affected to his Majesty' was defeated by 120 to 112; this shows the real sense of the measure.[1] The king politely assented to the address, but next year the suspicious commons ordered lists of justices and deputies to see if anything had been done. This led to an abortive bill for establishing a property qualification for holders of these offices.[2]

Also in the spirit of 1680 were some attempts to get arms into the hands of the people. In April 1701 a last militia bill was introduced in the commons by Paget, a follower of Harley.[3] It did not get beyond a second reading but seems to have prompted a letter to Harley from Dr Francis Lloyd, proposing that all able-bodied men be obliged to furnish themselves with arms.[4] In February 1702 a bill on these lines was presented to the house of lords. It provided that persons taking the oaths of allegiance and supremacy and having lands or revenues of a certain amount (left blank) might keep *one* musket each, for target practice by their sons, their servants and themselves. This bill, too, stuck at the second reading.[5] The controversy may be said to have ended for the time being with the renewal of the war with France.

The reform plans described in this chapter stand condemned for the same reason as the then existing militia itself. They were an undesirable anachronism, looking backward to barbarous anarchy, not forward to ordered liberty. They were popular only because they were expected to cost nothing. Such proposals as had some military value stood no chance of adoption. They cost money and were so bizarre as to entrust control of the forces to the executive.[6] They could

[1] CJ, vol. xiii, pp. 8, 39, 236, 264, 301–2.

[2] CJ, vol. xiii, pp. 308, 314, 378, 390, 398, 491, 731, 752, 758, 776, 778. Cf. an earlier abortive bill in 1699. CJ, vol. xii, p. 527.

[3] CJ, vol. xiii, pp. 343, 466, 476, 487, 489. For Paget, see references in Walcott. (I assume he is the same as the CJ's Pagitt.)

[4] HMC, *Portland*, vol. iv, p. 16, cited by Ogg, *James II and William III*, p. 482. He is wrong in identifying this scheme with the next to be mentioned.

[5] HMC, *House of Lords, 1699–1702*, pp. 487–8. LJ, vol. xvii, pp. 48, 55, 57, 60.

[6] A few plans should here be mentioned which tried to approach military problems without party bias or even to do justice to the case both for and against the army, in the manner of later plans considered in the next chapter: *Essay for Better Regulating the Militia* (London, 1701); *An Argument Showing that a Standing Army with Consent of Parliament is not Inconsistent with a Free Government* (London, 1698); *The Argument Against a Standing Army Rectified and the Reflections and Remarks upon it in Several Pamphlets Considered* (London, 1697).

not therefore be popular and they were less attractive to the court than a standing army. It was in building this up and finding, in the mutiny acts and otherwise, a balance between king and people like that in the Restoration militia acts, that the military achievement of the Revolution lay. This is not to say that those who opposed the growth of the army were fools. They were right in thinking it a great potential danger to constitutional liberty. They were also right in thinking that it would become so inefficient in peacetime as almost to nullify the advantage of having it in being.[1] But they failed to see that these objections cancel out. The army was inefficient because its officers, recruited by purchase, were commonly men of property and even of parliamentary influence who could not be properly disciplined. This represented an approximation to the principle that arms and political power should be in the same hands. At the same time the power of the crown over the army was at any rate greater than its authority in local government and so the army did not collapse as thoroughly as the militia. A balance however precarious between liberty and efficiency had come into being.

[1] See, e.g., J. W. Fortescue, *History of the British Army* (London, 1899–1930), vol. ii, pp. 14–36, on this point and what follows.

V

NEW TRENDS IN STRATEGY
AND POLITICS, 1739-57

WHEN at length the rebirth of the militia took place it was because the public had become seriously and sincerely worried about national defence. This in turn was due to a worsening of Britain's strategic position. In the wars of William and Anne, Britain had been part of an increasingly successful coalition. In the eighteenth-century wars from 1739 onward she found herself increasingly isolated in face of a hostile Europe. The Dutch and Austrians, at first rather feeble allies, eventually became enemies. Spain was a fairly constant foe, and the revival of her strength that took place under Bourbon rule was thus to Britain's disadvantage. Attempts to make a friend of Russia came to nothing. The brilliant alliance with Prussia lasted only for a single war. The powers were jealous of British supremacy at sea and expansion overseas. France had their sympathy in opposing Britain instead of the other way round. After the French Revolution this gradually changed, but it was a slow process which French aggrandisement long did more to hinder than to help.

Events early called attention to the resulting threat to British security. Early in 1744 the French signalised—or rather anticipated— their entry into the war between Britain and Spain by a surprise naval concentration against the English coast, which caused the greatest alarm. In 1745 the Young Pretender, though ill-supported by the French, achieved remarkable successes. The British army had to be withdrawn from the continent and there was a financial crisis in London.[1] A memorandum in the Newcastle papers explained the situation. In Queen Anne's day the defence of Britain was said to

---

[1] On which see Miss L. S. Sutherland, 'Sampson Gideon and the Reduction of the Interest', *Economic History Review*, 1st series, vol. xvi (1946), pp. 15–29. There seems to have been no such thing in 1744, see P. Yorke's journal quoted in Cobbett, vol. xiii, p. 645.

have required only 6000 men, but at that time Paris itself was threatened by the allies. The European powers now viewed French preparations against Britain with indifference. The navy had not force enough to guard against simultaneous invasion preparations both in Brest and in Dunkirk. A handful of invaders had been able to raise a large rebel army and draw supplies from France in defiance of our navy. Twice the country had been saved by a favourable wind, which in 1744 interfered with the French concentration and in 1745 brought the British troops swiftly home. The French had ample resources to spare, and at little expense could strike a blow which at the very least would seriously injure both commerce and credit. The navy would be diverted from the protection of trade and the general alarm would make money scarce and dear: Britain's war potential would be diminished.[1] The arguments of this memorandum were finally driven home by the events of 1756. By merely preparing an invasion of Britain, the French prevented the British from adequately strengthening their Mediterranean forces and so were able to take Minorca. Britain further suffered the humiliation of seeing her own defence entrusted for some months mainly to foreign troops.

There accordingly arose an agitation for the reform of the militia, beginning in 1745, reaching a climax in 1756 and finally victorious in 1757. The great new feature of the arguments used in its support, both in pamphlet and parliament, was their military relevance. It was not merely that they made the most of the dangers facing the nation, taking over arguments formerly the property of the defenders of the standing army.[2] The wars now in prospect were for Britain colonial rather than continental and were therefore more popular than those against Louis XIV. There was a strong wish for offensive action and this the advocates of the militia were eager to further by relieving the army and navy of the burden of home defence. They said that with a strong militia in being the fleet would be free to act against the enemy's coast;[3] and that had the militia been able to defend Britain in 1745 the army need not have left Flanders and the navy could have been set to conquering the French possessions in the East and West Indies, then in a bad state of defence.[4] In 1756

---

[1] BM, Add. 33048, ff. 387–8.

[2] *A Scheme for Establishing a Constitutional Militia* (Eton, 1747; London, 1756), pp. 5, 6: *A Proposal for a Regular and Useful Militia* (Edinburgh, 1745), pp. 1–2.

[3] *A Plan for Establishing and Disciplining a National Militia* (London, 1745), p. xxxiii.

[4] *A Seasonable Letter to the Author of Seasonable and Affecting Considerations on the Mutiny Bill* (London, 1751), pp. 40–1. Cf. *The Counterpoise* . . . by W[illiam] T[hornton] Esq., 2nd ed. (London, 1753), p. 16; Oglethorpe's speech in 1750, Cobbett, vol. xiv, p. 760.

Earl Temple told the lords that it was the want of a militia that had prevented reinforcements being sent to America.[1]

Of course the desired object might have been achieved by augmenting the army, but those who favoured the militia said that this was beyond the country's means. Samuel Martin wrote that even the existing army was more than the nation could afford.[2] Thomas Pitt told the commons in 1750 that the militia had been neglected and the navy starved in order to pay for an army that would not be strong enough to protect us if the depleted fleet lost command of the sea.[3] In 1756 Lord Stanhope said that if the French had command of the sea for only a few weeks they could land 100,000 men. To maintain regular forces of the same strength to oppose them would cost £3 million a year and even then there would be no trained reserve to replace casualties.[4]

It was therefore proposed that a large body of men should be given at least some rudimentary military training but kept in civil employment until the moment of danger, when alone the nation would be at the expense of calling them into pay. William Thornton, the first important champion of the cause in parliament, claimed that an efficient militia would cost only £100,000 a year on a peace footing. Had it existed in 1745 he thought that the country would have saved £3 million, and because it would make the enemy think twice about attempting invasion it might not be required to fight more than once in thirty years.[5] It was a pamphleteer of 1756 who perhaps put the case best. He argued that now that Britain had lost her allies the contest with France had become one of endurance. We had to fight a long war, husbanding our resources while trying to destroy those of the enemy. A cheap militia for home defence had an obvious part to play here. There were then about 100,000 troops in pay of which 40,000 were available for home defence. If the navy was to be freed for the offensive that number must be doubled. New regular troops on that scale could only be paid for by cutting down the navy and would be wasteful because their function would be defensive and they would mostly do nothing. It would be far better to revive the militia and train the whole male population by rotation. If there was an invasion those being trained could be used to oppose it and the rest would form a reserve.[6]

[1] Cobbett, vol. xv, p. 767.   [2] *Plan*, p. xxix.

[3] The opposition, with some support from William Pitt, pressed for a larger naval establishment. Cobbett, vol. xiv, p. 736; cf. pp. 909–10, etc.

[4] Cobbett, vol. xv, pp. 709–10.

[5] *Counterpoise*, Appendix, pp. 4–6; cf. p. 47.

[6] *An Enquiry Concerning the Nature and End of a National Militia* (London, 1756), pp. 36–48. Expecting a long war, the author was able (p. 59) to meet the objection that peace would come before a militia could be organised. Cf. p. 57.

Such views were encouraged by continental trends towards conscript armies of the modern type. The much admired Prussian army now consisted largely of conscripts, who in peacetime served only two months in the year with the colours. France had developed a militia into which part of the nation's manhood, chosen by lot, was obliged to enter. In peacetime it met for occasional training. Embodied on the outbreak of war, it was used mainly for garrison duties and for supplying the regular army with large numbers of trained recruits. These examples showed that reserve formations, whose members did not spend their whole lives under arms, could nevertheless be useful. Other cases seemed to show that patriotic enthusiasm could sometimes make a civilian in arms a match for a professional soldier. When the Hungarian diet warmly espoused the cause of Maria Theresa it became possible to levy large bodies of Hussars in that country. They and the Croatian Pandours brought to the west the techniques of guerrilla warfare first used against the Turks. This led to a vogue for 'light troops' and doubts about the reigning system of tactics based on rigid mechanical drill. The successes of irregular troops in America pointed the same way—notably the capture of Louisburg by British colonists in 1745 and the defeat of Braddock by the French and their Indian allies in 1755. In both of these engagements the regulars showed up badly.[1]

All this enabled advocates of the militia to speak with more conviction of the prowess of citizen armies. Thornton laid most stress on the French militia, which he thought might even be important in protecting the French king from his own regular troops. He pointed both to Prussian and Austrian experience in support of his case, along with the inevitable Swiss and one or two more.[2] One Bonell sent the elder Pitt a militia plan directly based on the French system.[3] The success of the Americans was frequently mentioned.[4] But what drove the lesson home was the experience of 'the '45'. The Highlanders were pointed to as a militia—a ragged and unruly one at that—which had ranged through the country unchecked and inflicted several defeats on regular troops. At the same time the zeal

[1] For this paragraph see W. O. Shanahan, *Prussian Military Reforms, 1786–1813* (New York, 1945); J. Gebelin, *Histoire des Milices Provinciales, 1689–1791* (Paris, 1882); J. F. C. Fuller, *British Light Infantry in the Eighteenth Century* (London [1925]). On the Hungarians, cf. above p. 97, n. 5.

[2] Genoese, Corsicans, Poles. *Counterpoise*, pp. 2, 3, 19, 20, 37, 49–51, Appendix, p. 12. But Martin refused explicitly to follow the continental example because he saw its remoteness from the old militia ideal. *Plan*, p. xxviii.

[3] PRO, 30/8, vol. 77, ff. 149–52. Cf. BM, Add. 33048, f. 388.

[4] T. Whiston (ed.), J. Christian, *A Political Discourse Upon the Different Kinds of Militia* (London, 1757), p. 17. *A Letter to the People of England on the Present Situation and Conduct of National Affairs* (London, 1756), p. 48. *Counterpoise*, pp. 31–2. Beckford's speech in Cobbett, vol. xiv, p. 1108.

and exploits of those who had taken up arms for the government were good evidence that the materials for a militia were at hand. From their ranks came several of the militia's parliamentary champions. William Thornton and James Oglethorpe had both raised volunteers in Yorkshire and joined the regulars in pursuit of the rebels. In asking leave to bring in a militia bill, Thornton could remark that he had been first in the field at the time of the late rebellion and had himself commanded a militia of sorts. The silent contrast with the theoreticians and sedition-mongers who had been the foremost patrons of the cause hitherto is obvious. In his pamphlet, Thornton praises both Oglethorpe and the volunteers and militia fighting for the government in Scotland. They were believed in particular to have shown up much better than the regulars in the reverse at Falkirk.[1] The regiments raised by some English noblemen at this time were also used—though not all agreed with this as we shall see— as evidence of popular military enthusiasm.[2]

Of the many arguments put forward against militia reform at this time the only ones effectively challenging the principle of the thing were economic. Accordingly, they figured much more prominently in the controversy than they had done fifty years before. It was claimed that a militia, though not always in pay, would nevertheless be more costly than the same number of regular troops. This was because military training always made men unfit and unwilling to earn their living by honest work. The working-class, as every recruiting officer knew, formed their ideas of military life from the soldiers' vices—idleness, drunkenness and debauchery. If they were trained to arms they would consider themselves entitled to imitate those vices—with disastrous consequences for Britain's competitive position in world markets. Nations like the Swiss, with whom military training was universal, had no industries: war was their profession. The King of Prussia cared both for arms and for manufactures, but did not attempt to combine them in the same persons.[3] War was thought a fit occupation only for backward peoples engaged in subsistence farming. William Lyttelton told parliament that a warlike spirit was incompatible with the spirit of industry and that the

[1] *Counterpoise*, pp. 23–5, 32–40, Appendix, p. 1. On the Highlanders cf. BM, Add. 33048, f. 388; *A Proposal for Arming and Disciplining the People of Great Britain, etc.* (London, 1746), pp. 1–5, 21–5. On Falkirk and kindred subjects, cf. the Scottish pamphlets cited below, p. 163.

[2] Sir J. Hinde Cotton in Cobbett, vol. xiv, p. 1090.

[3] *A Word in Time to Both Houses of Parliament . . . By a Member of Neither House* (London, 1757), pp. 5, 6, 27–30. *Further Objections to the Establishment of a Constitutional Militia* (London, 1757), pp. 33–4. *The Nature and Use of Subsidiary Forces Fully Considered* (London, 1755), pp. 39, 40. It was indeed only the Prussian peasants who were conscripted. Skilled workers were exempt. Cf. Shanahan, pp. 41–3, 47–8.

progress of civilisation had consequently destroyed the military power of the Greek city states.[1] 'Since the reign of Queen Elizabeth,' Lord Hardwicke told the lords,

> more especially since the Restoration, when military tenures were totally abolished, the people of this kingdom have been gradually weaned from arms, and formed, and habituated to trade, manufactures, and arts. From hence as from one great source, have flowed your commerce, your colonies, your riches, your real strength; which has enabled you ... to balance the power of your neighbours; some of whom have far outgone you in national military force.
>
> ... It is a self-evident proposition, and must be admitted to me, that the being educated and trained to arms, gives a habit, and a love of that kind of life. Amongst the common people, it induces a love of idleness, of sports, and at last of plunder.

For proof they had only to look to the Scottish Highlands.[2]

The alternative to a reformed militia favoured by those who argued in this way was the temporary importation of foreign mercenaries resorted to in 1745 and 1756. Militia supporters said that this would be more expensive[3] and that it would put a strain on the balance of payments, while money spent on the militia would stay at home.[4] The reply was that the export of bullion would be less damaging than the burden of a militia. If the struggle between France and Britain was to be one of endurance, the object must be to make France spend more than ourselves. For this, attacks on her seaborne trade would not suffice: there must also be pressure on her land frontier. Foreign mercenaries were needed for this work and as much money as possible should be spent on them. If instead we concentrated on a militia for home defence we would exhaust ourselves without making France pay anything at all.[5]

Foreign mercenaries, however, were open to serious military and political objections. There was the wound to national pride by the entrusting of national defence to foreigners. One writer said that public indignation on this account was the whole cause of the militia

---

[1] Cobbett, vol. xiv, p. 1094.

[2] Cobbett, vol. xv, pp. 734–6. P. C. Yorke, *The Life and Correspondence of Philip Yorke, Earl of Hardwicke* (Cambridge, 1913), vol. ii, p. 264.

[3] *Counterpoise*, pp. 20, 24. *A Discourse on the Establishment of a National and Constitutional Force in England* (London, 1757), p. 73. This was by Charles Jenkinson.

[4] *A Second Letter to the People of England on Foreign Subsidies, Subsidiary Armies and their Consequences to this Nation* (3rd ed., London, 1756), p. 48, cf. pp. 31–48.

[5] *The Important Question Concerning Invasions, a Sea War, Raising the Militia, and Paying Subsidies for Foreign Troops ... First Published in the Evening Advertiser* (London, 1755), pp. 13–20, 38–62. *The Nature* etc., pp. 42–53; cf. pp. 28–32, that foreign mercenaries less dangerous to liberty than native ones.

agitation.[1] Mercenaries, anyway, might not be available at the right time[2] and they might betray their employers. If the trials of Carthage on this score seem remote,[3] there was a recent instance to hand; in 1745 some troops transferred from the Dutch service refused to fight against the rebels because a French contingent was serving with the Pretender and they were bound by the terms of a recent capitulation not to serve against the French.[4] Home defence needed a solider base than this, if only to inspire confidence. Charles Jenkinson wrote in 1757

> We ... stand singly against a powerful neighbour who alone has frequently baffled the united force of Europe, and whose numerous and unemployed troops are now ready to take every opportunity that may offer to invade our country; ... any person ... would wish ... that some internal constitutional defence was established: which might preserve us not only from the evil, but from (what in a commercial kingdom especially is of no small consequence) the frequent terrors of it.

Instead

> Sudden, temporary and eventually destructive expedients have been the whole of our ministerial conduct. [5]

Thornton said that the French had planned invasion in 1744–5 largely because of the tempting lack of militia and fortifications. He thought that the increase of the national debt resulting from the hire of foreign troops would cause other nations to despise us: France and Spain would believe that our finances were so encumbered that we could not fight and would treat us accordingly. He claimed that this fate had already overtaken the Dutch.[6]

Militia supporters did not of course admit that soldiering always had bad economic effects. Thornton said that less labour would be lost by 200,000 militiamen drilling part of their time and then returning to work than by 20,000 regular troops who thought of themselves as 'Gentlemen Soldiers' and not obliged to work at all.[7] Another writer thought that if everyone received military training, bearing arms would no longer be thought of as entitling a man to the vices of a gentleman.[8] But even if the opposite were admitted, it seems clear that there was a need to sacrifice a little opulence to the needs

[1] *Gentle Reflections upon the Short but Serious Reasons for a National Militia* (London, 1757), pp. 5, 6.

[2] Whiston, pp. 81–2.   [3] *Ibid.*, p. 27. Cf. *Plan*, p. xxi.

[4] *Counterpoise*, pp. 20–1. Cf. F. H. Skrine, *Fontenoy and the War of the Austrian Succession, 1741–1748* (London, 1906), pp. 295–6.

[5] *A Discourse*, pp. 11–12. Cf. pp. 41–7.

[6] *Counterpoise*, pp. 50–1, Appendix, pp. 7, 8, 13. He thought (*ibid.*, p. ii) that English party divisions also encouraged invasion.

[7] *Ibid.*, Appendix, p. 6.   [8] *An Enquiry*, pp. 57–9.

of defence. Foes of the militia did not usually venture to oppose out-right the building up of native forces[1] and it is probable that almost everyone came to agree with the writer who said that the French had learned from us how to build up trade and colonies 'in aid of their military power' and we must learn from them to 'mix the military spirit with our civil and commercial policy'.[2]

II

New strategic thinking was not, however, the only reason for the rebirth of the militia. Those who sought to revive it, however sincere their interest in national defence, wished also as a rule to resuscitate the old agitation against the standing army and the executive govern-ment already described. True, they no longer aimed at abolishing the army. This would have been inconsistent with their concern for the empire. Thornton wished to retain the army for the defence of the colonies and for holding down Ireland and the Scottish Highlands. He was also for continuing the regiments of Guards. Something like this was said by them all.[3] For many years even ministers had pre-tended to believe that the standing army might one day be abolished. Now even their opponents acknowledged that it could never be.[4] Lord Temple said in 1756 that this had cleared the air. He thought that the government had formerly neglected the militia so as to have an excuse for maintaining an army and also because of the dispute about the extent of the crown's powers over it. Now that these old controversies had died, the reform of the militia would in no way lessen the power of the crown.[5]

This was not entirely true. The army was still greatly feared—less now as a source of *coups d'état* than as a source of political patronage. For this reason the increase in its size made necessary by war from

---

[1] On this and the previous point see Lord Temple's speech in Cobbett, vol. xv, pp. 759-60, 762.

[2] *Reflections Previous to the Establishment of a Militia* (London, 1756), p. 3.

[3] *Counterpoise*, p. 42, Appendix, p. 6. Cf. *Plan*, p. 78; C. S. (i.e. Charles Sack-ville, Lord Middlesex), *A Treatise Concerning the Militia* (London, 1752), pp. vi, 6-8, 43-4; *An Enquiry*, pp. 15-17; *A Modest Defence of the Army by a Soldier* (London, 1753), pp. 4, 5; BM, Add. 33048, f. 387.

[4] See Cobbett, vol. xiv, pp. 431, 451. The decisive moment was perhaps at the passing of an act (1735) to prevent army interference in elections. See Cobbett, vol. ix, pp. 891-2.

[5] Cobbett, vol. xv, pp. 760-1. Cf. Horace Walpole, *Memoires of the Last Ten Years of the Reign of George II* (London, 1822), vol. i, p. 447. Jenkinson said that unfortunately the militia system dated from the Restoration, which was much inferior to the Revolution as a constitutional settlement. The failure to reform it at the Revolution he suggested was due to the extensiveness of disloyalty and the fact that France was too busy elsewhere to invade us. Neither reason applied any more. (*A Discourse*, pp. 7-11.)

1739 seemed likely to increase the power of the crown. Corbyn Morris, an important ministerial publicist, recognised the change in the character of the fears which the army aroused in a famous pamphlet with which he made his debut in 1741. Much of it is taken up with an attempt to refute Bolingbroke's thesis that the proportion of the national income controlled by the government was increasing.[1] Against the power of the army, whatever form it took, the militia could be, in Thornton's words, *the Counterpoise*. This argument had two variants. On the one hand it was claimed that if the people were trained to arms the army would no longer be dangerous and might even be a bit larger than would otherwise be safe.[2] On the other hand there was the argument that a standing army would be dangerous if it grew beyond a certain size. The financial burden would become intolerable and the army would be strong enough to dominate the state in some way or other. Thornton claimed the authority of Sir Robert Walpole for the view that the state would be lost if the army rose above 12,000 men. If the militia was revived the size of the army could be kept within safe limits.[3]

The militia agitation was thus a movement of political opposition, championed by those out of office and resisted until 1756 by the ministers. This political factor contributed greatly to the success of the movement, but also made the plans associated with it less sound from a military point of view than they might have been.

A sensible approach to militia reform already existed in the traditional expedients of a 'select militia'[4] and temporary levies of volunteers. Ministers always tried something like this in emergencies just as they always tried to raise the old militia: they thought both useful in a limited way and both gave an impression of activity. As already noted, volunteers had been raised both in 1715 and in the invasion scare of 1690.[5] In 1745 the main measures were the local associations and the noblemen's regiments. The former were companies of volunteers for local service raised under the auspices of the lieutenancies and financed by local subscriptions.[6] Like the old militia they were valued chiefly for police work. They were further regarded as a means of keeping up morale, giving work to the unemployed and (by

---

[1] *A Letter from a By-stander to a Member of Parliament: Wherein is Examined What Necessity There is for the Maintenance of a Large Regular Land-Force in this Island*, etc. (London, 1741), pp. 28–114. For Morris see DNB. On the electoral dangers of a large army, see *A Discourse*, pp. 67–8.

[2] *A Discourse*, pp. 75–6. Cf. *An Enquiry*, pp. 12–14. Jenkinson said the army was to be the royal force, the militia that of parliament.

[3] *Counterpoise*, pp. 1, 3–5, 52. *A Discourse*, pp. 66–7. *A Treatise*, p. 6, 7. These arguments are not mutually exclusive though they appear so at first sight.

[4] Above, pp. 44–5.   [5] Above, part i, p. 73, n. 5.

[6] See, e.g., HMC, *Ancaster*, pp. 443–6.

preserving tranquillity) supporting the government's financial credit.[1] The fifteen regiments raised by noblemen were on the same basis as the regular army save that the men were only enlisted for a short term. County subscriptions assisted their levy,[2] so to that extent they, too, could claim kinship with the militia. Though they too were largely a moral gesture,[3] they were potentially a means of strengthening the army. When the emergency was over there were attempts to use both types of force more directly for this purpose by trying to get recruits from them for the line.[4] In 1756 levies by noblemen were again proposed, this time mainly of cavalry. [5]

After 1745 ministers occasionally thought of creating permanent institutions on similar lines. In reply to Thomas Pitt's plan of 1750 described below, Lord Barrington urged that both for political and economic reasons it was not desirable to train the masses to arms. On the other hand it would be a good thing if the propertied classes— down as far as the shopkeepers and farmers—received some military training. Colonel Conway, in support, wanted to reorganise the militia so that it could give military training to men of means. The command should be given to gentlemen of 'fortune and martial character' and all disreputable elements excluded.[6] Morris produced a militia plan at Hardwicke's suggestion, shortly before the fall of Newcastle in 1756. The whole male population was to be divided into four classes—nobility, gentry, yeomanry and commonalty. The upper classes were to arm themselves mainly it seems to keep the rest in order. From the younger members of the commonalty there was to be drawn by ballot a force of 100,000 men, who were to train for a month each year. From them, in turn, recruits were to be drawn by ballot who were to serve five years in the army.[7] The ministers were feeling their way towards the classic nineteenth century pattern of bodies of volunteers for local and temporary service plus a reserve[8] from which the army could at need be augmented.

This was true of opposition plans also, but they were a good deal more remote from the objective of a coherent military system. Some,

---

[1] BM, Add. 35889, f. 64; Add. 35588, ff. 133–4; Add. 33048, f. 387.

[2] See, e.g., HMC, *Lothian*, p. 151.

[3] So Lord Hardwicke thought. BM, Add. 35351, ff. 82–3.

[4] See, e.g., BM, Add. 32705, f. 460; HMC, *Buccleuch and Queensberry (Montagu House)*, vol. i, p. 409.

[5] See below, pp. 121–2.

[6] Their speeches are in Cobbett, vol. xiv, pp. 723–9, 754–8. Barrington had himself produced a militia plan in 1745 before joining the ministry. S. Barrington, *Political Life of William Wildman, Viscount Barrington* (London, 1815), p. 8.

[7] BM, Add. 35880, ff. 294–301. I take it to be in reply to ff. 302–4. Cf. Charles Yorke's belief in the necessity of an auxiliary force in 1757, Add. 35353, ff. 227–8.

[8] Cf. suggestions by Chesterfield in 1739 and William Lyttelton in 1751. Cobbett, vol. x, pp. 514–15; vol. xiv, p. 1098.

indeed, were clearly inspired by the works of Trenchard and his friends. Writers like Martin or Lord Middlesex wanted a general arming of the people, especially of the propertied classes, and a diminution of royal control over the resulting force.[1] Thornton—disappointingly in view of his military experience—raised the old cry that the existing militia would work well enough if it was not for the hostility of the court. Let property qualifications be introduced for deputy lieutenants and officers and let them be under a legal obligation to execute the powers they had for training the militia and all would be well. These and a slight increase in the amount of drill that the militia had to do were almost all the proposals that Thornton made.[2]

Much more to the point were what might be called the opposition versions of the 'select militia' idea. A plan of 1745 envisaged the voluntary enlistment of some 50,000 men, each county in Britain to contribute a suitable number. They were to be formed into regiments and given a uniform. They were to assemble for six field days a year and also were to be drilled in their spare time by Chelsea pensioners. They were to be unpaid unless called on for more service than this but were to get a 'premium' when they had reached a certain standard of efficiency. Embodied for service whenever required, they were not to be removed from Great Britain. The advantage claimed for the plan over simple augmentation of the army in time of need was that the men would be available much sooner; it was not claimed that they would be more efficient. They were also expected to be a valuable nursery of recruits for the regulars.[3] Another plan first published in 1747 proposed the enlisting of 18,000 men, the lieutenancy of each county being assigned a quota to raise. They were to be formed into regiments and paid £2. 5s. a year as a sort of retaining fee. Liable to embodiment when required for service, they were not to receive any training before that time, nor were the junior regimental officers to be appointed till then. Intensive training on embodiment was held to be sufficient. But the lieutenancies were to have power to exercise the men locally if they wished.[4]

---

[1] *Plan, passim. Treatise*, pp. 31–42. Martin wanted the officers to be popularly elected. Middlesex favoured appointment by the lord lieutenant but was nevertheless accused of reviving 'the old doctrine of [1641]: a standing army but the King not to be trusted with it'. *A Modest Defence*, pp. 7, 53.

[2] *Counterpoise*, pp. 57–66. See, too, summary in *Gentleman's Magazine*, vol. xxii (1752), p. 441. A plan in the Shaftesbury Papers (PRO 30/24, bundle 30, no. 43) looks a bit like a compromise between Thornton's ideas and the more visionary plans for a general arming.

[3] *A Proposal for a Regular and Useful Militia* (Edinburgh, 1745). The publisher remarks in the preface that it seemed to have been written before the war.

[4] *A Scheme*, 8–27. (I have seen the 2nd ed., 1756.)

Plans like these were sometimes the work of ministerialists, breathed hostility to the militia and sought rather to strengthen the army.[1] But usually their authors had all the characteristic aspirations of the militia enthusiast, tempered only by a wish to find an embodiment for them that was really practical. They were willing to seek their ends by a reform of the army. In 1750 Thomas Pitt proposed that regular enlistments should be for a term of years instead of for life. He believed that this would induce young men of the middle and even of the upper class to enlist. On leaving the army these citizen soldiers would enter the militia and so revive it. The general diffusion of military training would make the nation secure against both domestic tyranny and foreign enemies. Lord Strange, who echoed these arguments, added that if soldiers had the prospect of regaining liberty they would not be willing to help in its overthrow.[2] Here the militia's supporters sought their customary ends by indirect means. It was this moderate approach which found expression in the militia bill of 1746[3]—the first to be put before parliament—and also in the bill that was at length carried in 1757.

The opposition plans were not really so unlike those evolving in ministerial circles at the same time. The second type could provide an army of reserve. The more old-fashioned type had more affinities with bodies of volunteers for local service. This comes out very clearly if the views of their authors are considered more closely. They were against making personal service compulsory. Thornton bitterly opposed a bill for instituting a census of population devised by Corbyn Morris in 1753 because it was meant as a first step towards conscription. He thought this fit only for slaves.[4] On the other hand they were eager to see personal service come as the fruit of patriotic

---

[1] It is not always easy to tell if a pamphlet is for or obliquely against the militia. That in p. 114, n. 3 says (p. 3) that the rich would not fight for the state because they had too much to lose and the poor for the opposite reason. *Proposals for Carrying on the War with Vigour, Raising the Supplies Within the Year, and Forming a National Militia* (London, 1757), pp. 40-4, and *A Proposal for Arming and Disciplining the People of Great Britain* (London, 1746) are essentially plans for an army reserve.

[2] Barrington and Conway replied that only those would enter the army who were predestined for it by their dislike of honest work. These included the Highlanders, who must never be allowed to leave the army once in, lest they enlisted for the Pretender. The debate is in Cobbett, vol. xiv, pp. 723-58.

[3] Apparently: see *Gentleman's Magazine*, vol. xvi (1746), p. 237. Cf., too, *An Essay on the Expediency of a National Militia* (London, 1757), which proposed a body of men in constant pay who would be soldiers in wartime and work on the roads in peacetime. On Strange, cf. below, p. 120.

[4] Cobbett, vol. xiv, pp. 1317-20, 1323-4, 1357-8, cf. Grenville's and Hillsborough's comments, pp. 1351, 1363-4; *Counterpoise*, p. 40; above p. 113, n. 7. Cf. Middlesex's view, *Treatise*, pp. 33-4, 40, commented on in *A Modest Defence*, pp. 49-52.

zeal and the means of moral regeneration. They would all have agreed with the writer who complained that

> We would turn this nation into a company of manufacturers, where each is confined to a particular branch, and sunk into the habits and peculiarities of his trade. In this we consult the success of manufacture; but slight the honours of the human nature: we furnish good work; but educate men, gross, sordid, void of sentiment and manners, who may be pillaged, insulted and trod upon by the enemies of their Country.[1]

What their views pointed to was the encouragement of voluntary military service among the civil population and this was precisely what Thornton and Samuel Martin[2] had been doing in 1745.

But in two important respects all government plans differed from all opposition ones. Firstly, the government envisaged only a force of secondary importance, under the control of the army and serving its needs. The opposition wanted a force of equal importance with the army and some degree of independence from it.[3] Secondly, the government naturally wanted the crown to control the force and appoint its officers. The opposition always envisaged some dilution of that control.[4] Therefore the plans of the government were preferable from the military point of view but were liable to be passed over in favour of those of the opposition because they tended to increase the power and patronage of the crown.

This was not the only reason why it was an opposition plan that became law in 1757—when some of its supporters had won office—rather than one associated with the Pelhamite ministers. The latter's preference was for regulars and foreign mercenaries. They showed interest in reviving the militia only in sudden crises and under pressure, and so their plans were not taken very seriously. Those who criticised the opposition plans, moreover, did not always do so effectively. What they mainly did was to revive the arguments of fifty years before: that any militia would be a disorderly rabble drawn from the lowest class and that whether efficient or not it would be more dangerous politically than the army.[5] These arguments were applied to all opposition plans indiscriminately. This was a fair

---

[1] *Reflections Previous*, p. 12. [2] BM, Add. 35588, ff. 123–5.

[3] But note that both Martin (*Plan*, p. xxxv) and Middlesex (*Treatise*, pp. vi, 7, 43–51) wanted to use the militia to recruit the regular or other offensive forces.

[4] But Thornton said—indeed stressed—that militia patronage would be useful to the government. *Counterpoise*, pp. 45–6.

[5] The last either by increasing or destroying the crown's power. See the splendid, ironical *Short But Serious Reasons for a National Militia* (London, 1757) by Soame Jenyns, reprinted in his *Works* (Dublin, 1790), vol. ii, pp. 149–61. Cf. *A Word in Time*, pp. 7–26; *Further Objections*, pp. 22–9; *The Important Question*, pp. 23–9; Lord Sandys in Cobbett, vol. xv, pp. 756–7; and above, p. 114, n. 1 and p. 115, n. 4.

approach because so much of what was said by militia enthusiasts likewise derived from the previous century. The whole debate has an infuriatingly repetitive and backward-looking character.[1] But some of the militia plans were of a new kind, and militia supporters in general paid more attention to problems of discipline[2] and mostly conceded that on active service the militia should be under martial law. The political danger of arming the people had, moreover, lessened. One writer pointed out that enemies of the ministry were no longer thought foes of the constitution and the light of truth had made the whigs abandon 'fanaticism' and 'democracy' and the tories 'ius divinum and passive obedience'.[3] Only one new and favourite argument of the militia's friends was rebutted by their critics: that the defence of the country was best entrusted to a force spread over it in small detachments.[4]

III

Yet even if the Pelhams and their associates had striven harder and more skilfully, it is doubtful if their ideas on defence could have prevailed. Suspicion of the executive was still a great force in politics. Military reformers could accomplish nothing in its despite and little without actively winning it to their side. This can be clearly seen from the first ten years of the renewed militia agitation. The story begins in 1745 when the ministers' emergency plans for new defensive forces encountered strong political hostility. The subscriptions and associations in the counties were said to have been got up by those anxious to win ministerial favour for selfish reasons. The subscriptions were denounced as an illegal tax: nobody would dare not to subscribe for fear of being thought disloyal.[5] This objection was often to be heard on similar occasions later on. Thornton claimed later that the associations began too late to be of any great service.[6] The deputies of Durham were so hostile to the association there that they asked (successfully) for the horse militia to be raised instead.[7] The regiments

---

[1] A good example is the debate on the army estimates in December 1751 (Cobbett, vol. xiv, pp. 1086–1127).

[2] E.g. *Plan*, pp. 46–64. Moreover, Martin (pp. xvi, 22, 40–5) wanted to put disbanded army officers and soldiers into the militia to train it. He, Thornton and Middlesex hoped that militia training would be good discipline for the poor and reduce crime, idleness and tippling. *Plan*, p. 4. *Counterpoise*, p. 21; *Treatise*, pp. 63–8. The rich were to be brought to co-operate by making the militia fashionable: Thornton hoped the king would take the lead. *Counterpoise*, pp. 17–19; cf. pp. 12–15, 30. *Plan*, p. 19.

[3] *A Seasonable Letter*, pp. 30–40.   [4] See Note at end of chapter.

[5] Sydenham in Cobbett, vol. xiii, p. 1352. Cf. below, pp. 210, 219.

[6] *Counterpoise*, pp. 5, 6.

[7] C. I. A. Ritchie, 'The Durham Association Regiment, 1745'. *Jol. of the Society for Army Historical Research*, vol. xxxiv (1956), pp. 106–119.

raised by noblemen were very vulnerable to the same sort of attack. Although they were avowedly temporary, the officers were to be entitled to half-pay on reduction. This seems to have been an after-thought, to which the king only reluctantly consented and which was violently opposed in parliament. The new officers were represented as incapable novices who were likely to gain rapid promotion by the influence of their noble patrons, to the discouragement of the more deserving. Against this the rather lame excuse was urged that the need was great and the royal word pledged. Had the regiments been quickly raised and useful, all might have been forgiven. But this was notoriously not so: Henry Fox, who had been in opposition on this issue though connected with the ministry, later said that he would not trust those to raise a regiment who could not raise half a crown.[1] The whole episode left a very bad taste, which Sir Charles Hanbury Williams preserved in a satirical poem.

> Of all the Jobs that e'er have past
> Our House since times of jobbing
> Sure none was ever like the last
> E'en in the days of Robin.
> For he himself had blushed for shame
> At this polluted Cluster
> Of fifteen Nobles of great fame
> All bribed by one false Muster. . . .
>
> Three Regiments one Duke contents
> With two more places you know.
> Since his Bath Knights his Grace delights
> In tria juncta in uno.
> Now Bolton comes with beat of Drums
> Tho' fighting be his loathing.
> He much dislikes both Guns and Pikes
> But relishes the Clothing. . . .
>
> And now dear Gower thou man of Power
> And comprehensive Noddle
> Tho' you've the Gout yet as you're stout
> Why won't you place in Saddle
> When you might ride to either Side
> Choose which K——g you'd serve under?
> But dear Dragoon change not too soon
> For fear of th' other Blunder.

[1] Lord John Russell (ed.), *Correspondence of John, Fourth Duke of Bedford* (London, 1842–6), vol. ii, p. 180. Cobbett, vol. xiii, p. 1382–91. *A Letter to William Pitt, Esq., Concerning the Fifteen New Regiments Lately Voted by Parliament* (London, 1746). Lord Ilchester, *Henry Fox, First Lord Holland* (London, 1920), vol. i, pp. 116–19, 126–7. J. B. Owen, *The Rise of the Pelhams* (London, 1957), pp. 287–9.

> This faithful Band shall ever stand
> Defend our faith's Defender
> Shall keep us free from Popery
> The French and the Pretender.
> Now God bless all our M——y
> May they the Crown inviron
> And hold in Chains whate'er Prince reigns
> And rule with Links of Iron.[1]

It is interesting that William Pitt, who defended the regiments in the commons, had just made a bill to exclude from that house all army officers below the rank of lieutenant-colonel a part of his price for joining the ministry.[2]

There was a tinge of class conflict reinforcing opposition to the courtiers on this issue. It was a grievance against the nobles' regiments that they were the preserve of the nobility alone. An Essex gentlemen named Olmius, an old and staunch ministerialist whose object in life was a peerage, offered in 1745 to raise a corps of 500 men. As a result he fell foul of his lord lieutenant, Lord Fitzwalter, who told him in a rage that such offers did not become private gentlemen but only lord lieutenants and the very prime of the nobility, and tried to punish him by having him made sheriff.[3] Thornton in the first edition of his pamphlet[4] contrasted the generous disposition of the middle ranks of society with the selfishness of the upper class.[5] This trend of thought was encouraged in the years that followed by the link now seen to exist between the militia question and the game laws. It was these which had brought to an end the acquaintance of the people with firearms and the cultivation of marksmanship as a popular country sport. Their repeal was a necessary step in any general revival of military prowess. Sometimes they were regarded as a sinister ministerial design to put the people at the mercy of a standing army. It was asked whether the nobility and gentry valued the safety of their partridges and hares above that of their country. The formation in 1752 of an association for preserving game—a national offshoot of various local associa-

---

[1] 'The Heroes', tune, 'Sally in our Alley'. W. E. Manners, *Some Account of the . . . Life of the Right Hon. John Manners, Marquis of Granby* (London 1899), pp. 27–9. In some places I have followed the version in BM, Add. 29913, f. 20. 'Robin' is Walpole.

[2] Owen, p. 285.

[3] BM, Add. 32874, ff. 209–10.

[4] *The Counterpoise*, etc. (London, 1752), preface.

[5] One Yorkshireman thought that even the 'mad general' Oglethorpe and his 'bucks' had made more 'noise' than they deserved. The soberer people who had served at home under old officers in associated companies had done more good. He praised the officers for serving without reward and not exploiting public distress. HMC, *Du Cane*, p. 77.

119

tions for enforcing the game laws—brought the subject very much to the fore and added a curious reinforcement to the militia agitation.[1]

Positive action to reform the militia resulted from the events of 1745. In the commons Lord Strange at once called for militia reform, and a bill was duly brought in in 1746. But by then the revolt was subsiding and the bill never even reached the lords.[2] That the agitation was kept alive ready for the next favourable crisis was due to a further political factor and one, moreover, of the personal kind so characteristic of the eighteenth century. This was the rise of the Duke of Cumberland. Second son of the king and from 1745 commander-in-chief of the army, he was by virtue of the military patronage at his disposal the predestined leader of a political faction. In the course of the 1750s it duly appeared, with Henry Fox as its chief parliamentary ornament.[3] What made Cumberland so important in politics, however, was the death of Frederick, Prince of Wales in 1751. This made it likely that Prince George, the next heir, would come to the throne while still a minor. In that case Cumberland could hardly be prevented from being the leading figure in a regency. This expectation was worth much present power to him.

Those to whom the rise of Cumberland was unwelcome naturally attacked him under the guise of attacking the dangerous political influence of the army. Cumberland played into their hands by his attempts to improve military efficiency after the peace of 1748. At his suggestion some of the provisions of the mutiny bill were made stricter. In particular, officers on half-pay were made subject to martial law and commanding officers were empowered to 'revise' the sentences of courts-martial held by their authority: that is, to order the court to reconsider any sentence which seemed insufficiently severe. The cry was raised, especially by the Prince of Wales' party,[4] that this was an attempt to make the army more docile and so more likely to be the willing tool of a would-be despot. The ministers at first stood their ground but at length were obliged to remove or alter

[1] Kirby in *American Historical Review*, vol. xxxviii, pages 253–6. *A Third Letter to the People of England on Liberty, Taxes and the Application of Public Money* (London, 1756), pages 12–22. *A Fifth Letter . . . on the Subversion of the Constitution and the Necessity of its Being Restored* (London, 1757), pages 34–5. *The Gentleman's Magazine*, vol. xxvi (1756), pages 384–5. Cf above, pages 71–2.

[2] Cobbett, vol. xiii, p. 1362. CJ, vol. xxv, pages 12, 61, 86, 112, 115, 118, 128, 132, 134, 151, 161, 165, 166, 172–4, 226. (There were, in fact, bills in two succeeding sessions, no doubt the same, cf. page 226.)

[3] L. B. Namier, *The Structure of Politics at the Accession of George III*, 2nd ed. (London, 1957), pages 25–6.

[4] A. N. Newman, 'Leicester House Politics, 1748–1751', *English Historical Review*, vol. lxxvi (1961), pages 580, 582.

the offending clauses.[1] The death of the Prince ended the agitation and dissolved his party. The ensuing Regency Act was no triumph for Cumberland because he was so generally distrusted. In the event of a minority he was to be no more than president of a council to advise the titular regent, the dowager Princess of Wales. But there remained a widespread fear—already voiced by the Prince's followers before his death—that the Duke might use his control of the army to seize the throne for himself.[2] In this connection the militia question again attracted attention.

Already, in 1747, the Prince had pledged himself to support a militia bill on coming to the throne. This and a number of other promises were intended to win tory support for his candidates in the ensuing general election.[3] No doubt it accounts for the production of a militia plan by Lord Middlesex, a leading follower of the Prince whose wife had been the Prince's mistress.[4] Middlesex claimed in his *Treatise* that he had often discussed the subject with the Prince, who had approved his plan. In 1752, the year after the Prince's death, Thornton and Oglethorpe brought forward a militia bill in the commons. The first editions of both *the Counterpoise* and Middlesex's *Treatise* were brought out in a great hurry to win support for it. The bill was killed at the committee stage by prorogation. In 1753 there were second editions of both pamphlets and the bill was reintroduced but was thrown out at the second reading.[5] Timing and circumstances suggest that it was the political situation just described which produced this peacetime recrudescence of the militia agitation.

Cumberland did other involuntary services to the cause of the militia. His and his father's hostility were one reason why the ministers failed to adopt an effective policy of their own for home defence. The proposal for noblemen to raise cavalry in 1756 was dropped because, said Newcastle, 'as you know, *we* love nothing but Regular Troops'. A plan agreed between Cumberland and Lord Gower was adopted instead by which the nobility and gentry in each

[1] For the opposition view see *Seasonable and Affecting Observations on the Mutiny Bill, Articles of War and Use and Abuse of a Standing Army* (London, 1750); *A Seasonable Letter*; for the other side, *The Ancient and Present State of the Military Law in Great Britain Considered* (London, 1749); *A Modest Defence*, pp. 65–74.

[2] *Seasonable and Affecting Observations*, pp. 58–60. R. Sedgwick (ed.), *Letters From George III to Lord Bute, 1756–66* (London, 1939), pp. xx, xxi, xlviii–ix.

[3] Owen, pp. 312–13.

[4] According to Horace Walpole, *George II*, vol. i, pp. 65–6 and note.

[5] *Treatise*, pp. vii, viii, *Counterpoise*, 1st ed., pp. 58–60; 2nd ed., p. ii. CJ, vol. xxvi, pp. 405, 408, 422, 499, 504, 513, 549, 620, 659. Thornton says the first edition of *The Counterpoise* was published in the spring of 1752 but the *Monthly Review* notices both that and the *Treatise* in the February number. The bill was introduced in January.

county were to come together and use their influence to raise men for new regular regiments. Enlistments were to be for three years or the duration of the war.[1] Newcastle and his friends worked hard to make this scheme succeed.[2] But the military authorities again sabotaged their efforts by refusing to honour the promise given to some of the recruits that they would not be sent abroad. In particular, the men raised for Lord Digby in Somerset and Dorset were put on board transports more or less by force. This caused much resentment, not least among those who had helped to raise the men.[3] Henry Fox, who was Digby's uncle and Cumberland's leading friend in the ministry, said in 1765 that he had 'begged, lamented and do to this moment lament it'.[4] Sir George Savile complained bitterly to Rockingham that 'it was employing gentlemen to do a job which none but gentlemen were able to do, and at the same time using them in a manner no gentleman ought to bear'. The gentry were willing to help in home defence but not to do the work of army recruiting sergeants.[5]

Cumberland also helpfully quarrelled with some intelligent army officers and drove them into opposition. Oglethorpe was court-martialled on account of a reverse he suffered in pursuit of the Pretender and ended his military service under a cloud.[6] He was not, properly speaking, a professional soldier; but George Townshend had served not only against the Pretender but in all the continental campaigns of the British army during the Austrian war. By now a colonel, he was destined to take an important, though disputed, part in the capture of Quebec and later to rise to the highest military rank and hold high ministerial office. He appears to have fallen foul of Cumberland for two reasons: he was supposed to be the author of a pamphlet criticising Cumberland's generalship in Flanders and he had made the Duke a target for his notable talents as a caricaturist, doing somewhat ample justice to His Royal Highness's rotundity of figure. Heir of a great whig family and grandson of Sir Robert

---

[1] BM, Add. 32863, f. 215. Cf. BM, Eg. 3426, ff. 122–6; Add. 32862, ff. 446–7. For terms of service, MSS. of 4th Duke of Bedford, vol. xxxii, ff. 6, 12; Shaftesbury papers, PRO. 30/24, bundle 28, f. 82. It was a common belief, attributed to the great Duke of Marlborough, that cavalry was the key to home defence because the enemy would not be able to bring horses. *Plan*, p. 7. *Essay on the Expediency*, p. 42.

[2] BM, Add. 32863–4, *passim*.

[3] See Walpole, *George II*, vol. ii, pp. 46–7; *Fourth Letter to the People of England* (2nd ed., London, 1756), p. 103, note.

[4] Ilchester, vol. i, pp. 305–6. It does not appear that the government officially sanctioned the promises thus made by its close friends, cf. Bedford MS cited in n. 1.

[5] Wentworth Woodhouse, R.1–81.

[6] A. A. Ettinger, *James Edward Oglethorpe, Imperial Idealist* (Oxford, 1936), pp. 266–70.

Walpole's sometime associate, he was supposed to inherit his politics from his mother, who was reputed a jacobite. With influence in the important county of Norfolk and affinities with what was left of both whig and tory sentiment, he was well placed to champion a popular cause. His military knowledge made him well suited for the militia question. In 1750 he retired from the army and identified himself with the anti-military agitation. He helped to pilot the militia bills of 1752-3 through the commons.[1] The bill of 1756, carried at length in 1757, was his work.

Cumberland had his share in providing the militia cause with a still more eminent champion. It was because Fox (with Cumberland behind him) was given a leading place in the ministry in the autumn of 1755 that Pitt went into wholehearted opposition. He enthusiastically supported Townshend's bill, and it was to be of vital importance that his support was not withdrawn when he returned to office.

IV

An attempt has now been made to indicate the more general causes of the revival of the militia during the Seven Years' War. Although it somewhat anticipates the detailed description of that revival, this chapter can best be ended with an indication of the elements from which the mass of militia supporters were drawn. Those who supported the cause in parliament held periodic meetings to decide on their line of action. One such meeting was held in April 1759 and George Onslow sent Newcastle a list (which survives)[2] of those who attended. The members of parliament present numbered forty-five, whom Onslow classified as twenty-three tories and twenty-two whigs. Sixteen were county members[3] and nine others came from 'popular' constituencies with sizeable electorates.[4] The proportion of tories and of representatives of counties and 'popular' constituencies was very much higher than in the commons as a whole.[5] On the other

---

[1] DNB. CJ, vol. xxvi, pp. 408, 549. For the hostility of Cumberland towards the Townshends see the instance quoted in C. V. F. Townshend, *The Military Life of Field-Marshal George, First Marquess Townshend, 1724–1807* (London, 1901), pp. 129–31. For other officers not favoured, see *A Seasonable Letter*, p. iii.

[2] BM, Add. 32889, ff. 400–1. See Appendix C.

[3] From Anglesey, Berkshire (2), Buckinghamshire (2), Dorset, Essex, Gloucestershire, Hampshire, Kent, Lincolnshire, Middlesex, Somerset, Surrey, Wiltshire.

[4] Colchester, Exeter, Newcastle, Nottingham, York (electorates over 1000) Beverley (electorate almost 1000); Grantham, Maldon, Oxford University (electorate 500 or more). See Namier, pp. 80–1; W. R. Ward, *Georgian Oxford* (Oxford, 1958), p. 235.

[5] Larger boroughs returned 112 members and counties 92 out of 513 for England and Wales (Namier, pp. 62, 80–1). Namier lists 113 members returned as tories at the elections of 1761 (*England in the Age of the American Revolution* (2nd. ed. London, 1961), pp. 419–21).

hand the number of whigs and of representatives from small boroughs was not negligible. The group seems to consist mainly of 'independent' members whose main animus, whether they were nominally whig or tory, was against the 'court'. To these, however, were joined certain 'courtiers' and the like, brought in no doubt by rivalries like that concerning Cumberland, or because their constituents expected it of them, or to spy.[1]

The amount of support which the militia enjoyed in each county can be gauged by the speed with which the acts of 1757–8 were put into execution.[2] It is at once apparent that the counties on the south and east coasts were almost all to the fore, and so were most of the counties of southern and eastern England adjoining the coastal counties. No doubt this reflects mainly the greater consciousness which these areas had of the dangers of invasion. It was also the case that this area included most of the populous counties where popular causes were often strongly supported.[3] From Yorkshire, Norfolk and Devon and less strongly from Kent and Gloucestershire (to name no more) the militia won such support. Important leaders of the cause, too, came from the area. Yorkshire, aroused already by the jacobite invasion, had sent forth Thornton and Lord Rockingham and Sir George Savile were also important militia enthusiasts, though with little sympathy for the political side of the movement.[4] The tory Vyners in Lincolnshire, the young Townshends and Walpoles in Norfolk, the young Duke of Grafton in Suffolk, Lord Shaftesbury in Dorset were others who figured largely in the proceedings both in parliament and in the country. The Sackvilles in Kent, Pitt's brother-in-law, Lord Temple, in Buckinghamshire, and the Duke of Bedford were others involved, mainly perhaps because they were opponents of Newcastle.[5] It does not seem, however, that counties allowed their opinions on the militia to be formed for them by the local notables. Bedford's lieutenancy of Devon was much more forward than his other county, Bedfordshire.[6] Lord Cholmondeley was able to raise the militia in Cheshire and Flint but not in the other Welsh counties of which he was lieutenant: he accordingly offered to

[1] Onslow himself, member for Surrey, or Fairfax, member for Kent, for whom Newcastle was at that moment trying to get a pension (Namier, *Structure*, p. 413) no doubt comes into one of the last two categories.

[2] Appendix A.

[3] The use of the old militia at election time may perhaps have created a special animus against royal control of it.

[4] For Rockingham's enthusiasm and eagerness to take personal command, see his letters of 25 June and 29 August 1759 in SP. 41/30.

[5] For all these see the next chapter; for Rockingham and Savile see particularly chap. v.

[6] *Bedford, Correspondence*, vol. ii, p. 383.

resign.[1] Despite the enthusiasm of Lord Strange, Lancashire was slow off the mark.[2] It would seem at first sight that the backwardness of the coastal county of Sussex and the democratic county of Middlesex could only be due to the local influence of Newcastle; but reasons will be forthcoming for doubting this.

In contrast to the activity of the coastal belt of the south and east the midlands and Wales were an area of fairly solid apathy,[3] broken only by one instance of great activity in Warwickshire and one or two creditable performances in Wales. This should be one more warning against the view common then and since that the militia was chiefly a tory movement. If toryism be equated with the nostalgic near-jacobitism to be found in the midlands, then the militia had little to do with it. The cause was strongest in the more seaward-looking areas, more conscious alike of foreign military dangers and advanced political thinking. Such in brief was the character of the only serious political movement surviving in England in the middle years of the eighteenth century.

Note

One new strategic argument in favour of reviving the militia was effectively dealt with by the other side in the controversy. This was that the forces for home defence needed to be not only larger but more dispersed than before. Lord Westmorland told the lords in October 1745 that an efficient militia would be more use against invasion or rebellion than a standing army because it would be spread all over the country and so able to nip any trouble in the bud. He also thought that the disarming of the Highlands had encouraged rebellion. Friends as well as foes had been deprived of their arms, but no force of regulars had been left to secure the country.[4] These arguments were widely echoed. Thornton called for a force 'more local and more impartial' than the army, which he claimed could never protect the coast against buccaneers and smugglers nor yet concentrate even 6000 men to defend the capital. For these purposes and for police work in general he thought that the 160,000 men which he mistakenly believed to be the strength of the old militia would be required.[5] Counter arguments were both economic and military. It was absurd to have a force that was

---

[1] But he had no property in Wales save in Flint. His other counties were Anglesey, Caernarvon, Merioneth and Montgomery. He and his son were both at the meeting of April 1759 just mentioned. See PRO. 30/8, vol. 26, ff. 163-4; cf. his letter of 7 June 1759 in SP. 41/30.

[2] SP. 41/30, Lord Strange, 12 June 1759.

[3] E.g. Derbyshire, Herefordshire, Northamptonshire, Shropshire, Worcestershire. SP. 41/30: Duke of Devonshire, 10 June; Lord Bateman, 9 June; Lord Halifax, 15 June; Lord Powis, 8 June; Lord Coventry, 8 June, all 1759. Cf. n. 1.

[4] Cobbett, vol. xiii, p. 1321; cf. Oswald, pp. 1364-72, and Barnard, pp. 1377-82.

[5] *Counterpoise*, pp. 41-2, Appendix, pp. 6, 7. Cf. *Plan*, pp. xxx-xxxi, and Preface, p. 6; *Treatise*, pp. 8, 9, 11, 63-8; *Proposal for Arming*, pp. 1-5, 21-5; Cobbett, vol. xiii, p. 1429.

virtually unable to concentrate at a threatened point. Enormous armies were not required: the best authorities such as Turenne preferred them to be small and composed of volunteers. A huge militia would at most be a useful police force. The general arming of the people needed to create it would be very costly and not always lay the burden fairly.[1] The existing militia law was useful as a means of calling a large body of civilians to arms in the very rare and extreme emergencies when every man counted and nothing better could be done.[2] Any more ambitious plan would be superfluous. Of course it was the old-fashioned militia plans that were especially hit by this argument, although it was not only the old-fashioned authors who desired a dispersed force.

[1] *Modest Defence*, pp. 22–6, 36–41, 44–9, 54–63.
[2] *The Nature and use of Subsidiary Forces*, pp. 37–40.

VI

THE MAKING OF THE NEW MILITIA, 1755-9

IN the summer of 1755 hostilities began between Britain and France, and that autumn Pitt opened his attack on the ministry. It was now that the militia agitation (to judge from the surviving evidence) became continuous instead of episodic. The early disasters of the war sufficed to bring Pitt into office and carry a militia bill through parliament. But it proved so difficult to bring the new militia into being that the thing might never have been done but for the stimulus of a new invasion scare in 1759. Such in outline is the story told in this chapter.

(I) THE BILL OF 1756 AND ITS ENACTMENT

On 8 December 1755, after there had been a good deal of criticism of government military measures, George Townshend moved in the commons for a committee of the whole house to consider the state of the militia laws. Pitt seconded him. The committee duly sat and reported on 21 January 1756, whereupon it was resolved that the militia laws were ineffectual and leave was given for a bill to reform them. This bill completed its passage through the commons on 10 May. It was the subject of very lengthy deliberations in committee, the house at one stage ordering its recommittal and at another its printing with all the amendments to date.[1] To this extent it was a very well considered measure. But according to Horace Walpole the business was too exhausting for most members, and attendance sank to a bare dozen. Apart from Pitt and Townshend, the members who concerned themselves most with the bill were Speaker Onslow and

---

[1] Walpole, *George II*, vol. i, pp. 447–51. CJ, vol. xxvii, pp. 331, 395, 396, 523, 535, 553, 555, 565, 573, 577, 595, 600. For the length of the sittings cf. Sir Roger Newdigate's diary in Warwickshire R.O.: Newdigate of Arbury, Box 1, sub. 5, 7, 8 April, etc.

Lord George Sackville, the last an army officer of some distinction who had formerly opposed the militia but had changed sides since then politically.[1] The bill was thus the work of men with military and governmental experience rather than inveterate government-haters. Its acceptance by the commons owed much to the success of the French in convincing the ministers that they intended an invasion. The ministerial response (in March 1756) was to send for German troops—a decision that caused even their friends to feel alarm and shame. Lord Walpole[2] told Hardwicke that

> the tories in general, although some few are engaged in the conduct of it [the militia bill], do not approve it extremely; but the considerable persons who moved and earnestly supported the questions for bringing over the Hessians and Hanoverians expressed themselves as looking upon our calling in foreign strength to be indeed a necessary but a temporary support ... until a more natural and national defence, against all dangerous emergencies to the public, could be formed and made serviceable.[3]

Lord Downe, member for Yorkshire, was a case in point—supporting the ministers yet 'inveighing against trusting our defence to foreigners, complaining nobility, gentry not armed etc'.[4] Supporting the militia bill gave suitable expression to such feelings, but Murray[5] thought that many who did this dreaded its passing.[6]

The militia bill that finally reached the lords was an ingenious compromise between the military needs of the situation and the political desires of the country gentlemen.[7] Very roughly, it may be said that the parts relating to the men and their training satisfied the former and those concerning the command and control of the force had more relation to the latter. The force to be raised was to number about 60,000 men and each county was given a specific

[1] Walpole, *George II*, vol. i, pp. 445, 451. On Sackville cf. Cobbett, vol. xiii, pp. 739–45.

[2] Sir Robert Walpole's brother 'old Horace', who received a peerage just at this time.

[3] BM, Add. 35594, ff. 40–1, quoted in W. Coxe, *Memoirs of Horatio, Lord Walpole* (London, 1808), vol. ii, p. 424.

[4] Wentworth Woodhouse, R. 1–72, Murray to Rockingham, 23 March 1756; R. 1–73, Downe to Rockingham, 25 March 1756.

[5] Another chief ministerial spokesman in the commons, about to be made Lord Mansfield.

[6] BM, Add. 32865, f. 105.

[7] For the content of the bill see *A Bill for the Better Ordering of the Militia Forces in the Several Counties of that Part of Great Britain Called England. Absolutely Necessary to be Perused by All People at this Juncture* (London, 1756). The process of amendment can be followed in the printed copies of the bill at various stages preserved in the Hardwicke Papers, BM, Add. 35877, ff 249, 259, 277 ff.; Add. 35880, f. 188 ff.

number to levy. The new militia was thus to be two-thirds the size of the old (and we should remember that most people thought that the old was much bigger). The levy was to be made by taking a census of all able-bodied men between the ages of 18 and 50 and selecting a proper proportion of them in each parish by drawing lots. Those chosen were to serve for three years and then be replaced in the same way. They had, however, the options of finding a substitute or paying a fine of £10; in the latter case they would be appointed to serve again on the next occasion. Thus there was no question of a general arming of the people. There was provision, as the supporters of the scheme emphasised, for their general *training*, by rotation in service; but as there was no insistence on personal service, even this principle was put in doubt.

The men of each county were to be formed into companies and regiments and were to drill every Sunday from February to October. As far as possible this was to be in their own villages, but one Sunday in four they were to meet in half-companies and in Whit-week each regiment was to assemble for a few days' drill. A minimum of military efficiency was ensured by requiring the adjutant in each regiment and most of the sergeants to be appointed from the regular army by the crown. Discipline was to be enforced by fines and imprisonment, the penalties to be imposed by the civil magistrate. The crown was authorised to call the militia out whenever it saw fit in time of 'actual or imminent danger'. They were then to receive the same pay as the army, to be under the command of its generals and to be subject to martial law.

The plan owed something to foreign example. George Townshend's papers contain memoranda on the Spanish, Piedmontese, Swiss and Swedish militias, with notes showing his interest in France, Prussia and other places also. The Spanish and Piedmontese systems are reminiscent of that adopted in England, although the former provided only for voluntary enlistment, the latter for outright conscription. The Swiss and Swedish systems were something very different but from the former seems to have come the idea of experienced regular officers superintending the training.[1] Events were to show that the bill provided an adequate starting-point for the creation of a reserve force, able to take over the defence of Great Britain. Its weakest part was that relating to training,[2] but this was destined not to matter.

[1] John Rylands Library, Manchester: English MSS., no. 939, items 38–40. Cf. Jenkinson, who also quoted Saxe in favour of rotation. *A Discourse*, pp. 54–6, 60–1.

[2] Lord Temple claimed that there would always be warning enough of invasion to intensify the training; also that the first steps, like getting used to the noise of firing, were the hardest. Cobbett, vol. xv, pp. 762–4. Opponents of the bill thought the amount of drill entirely insufficient and that the new force would never be ready in time for service in the current war (the bill had been intended to come

Owing to the long duration of the war, the militia was to be trained by protracted service.

Of the provisions of the bill with political overtones the most important was the establishment of a scale of property qualifications for the deputy lieutenants and different commissioned ranks of militia officer. They were to be appointed by the lord lieutenants and the king was empowered to order their removal.[1] But the lord lieutenants were obliged to appoint at least twenty deputies in each county from among those with the necessary qualification. Also, the business done by the deputies—of which the levying of the men was the most important item—could if necessary be done by deputies in conjunction with land tax commissioners, and with the latter in the majority. These commissioners had the rare distinction of being officials of the national government who were not appointed by the crown. They were named by the house of commons in the annual land tax act.[2] As for the militia officers, it was provided that every five years one field officer[3] in each regiment and up to half the officers in each of the lower ranks had to retire if persons duly qualified offered to serve in their stead. Such persons were to have a legal right to be appointed. Clearly all this represented an attack both on the royal prerogative and on the prevailing system of patronage. Each member of a defined propertied class was to have a right to share in an important branch of local administration and military command. The royal choice could modify this right but so too could the choice of the house of commons. No set of men obnoxious to the court could be indefinitely proscribed. In a suitably toned-down form this was a return to the anarchical aspirations of the previous century.[4]

Another feature of the scheme perhaps appealed even more to the country gentlemen. The old militia had been based entirely on various charges on the land. All these were swept away. The money needed to pay, clothe and arm the militia was to be voted each year by parliament and found out of general taxation. Townshend did not fail to point out that this meant relief to the landed interest. Of course the low cost of the militia when unembodied was a vital point

into force in September 1756). *A Word in Time*, pp. 44–6. *An Impartial View of the Conduct of the Ministry* (London, 1756), pp. 32–9, which last thought that the principle of rotation meant a diffusion of military training noxious to industry.

[1] He could no longer make appointments directly.

[2] See W. R. Ward, *The English Land Tax in the Eighteenth Century* (London, 1953). Many commissioners were rather poor (Ward, p. 88), and an amendment was suggested at one point to require a higher qualification from those doing militia business. BM, Add. 35877, f. 265.

[3] Colonel, lieutenant-colonel or major.

[4] Cf. *Enquiry Concerning the Nature*, etc., pp. 47–8, 53–7. The Prince of Wales in 1747 had promised the tories to support a similar measure: anyone with £300 a year in land was to be a J.P. as of right. Owen, p. 313.

anyway. Townshend claimed that to keep the force fit for service would cost £175,000 a year, whereas regular troops to the same number would cost a million and a half: over eight times as much for the same result.[1] Of course parliament's control of the purse, which had balanced the king's exclusive control of the old militia, became more absolute than ever. This was recognised by obliging the king to notify parliament if he called out the militia for service. If parliament was not sitting he was to declare his intention in council.[2] To complete this brief survey of the bill, we should note that certain classes of people were entirely exempt from service, that in Wales and in some small English counties the qualifications were to be lower, that in the City and the Cinque Ports the old system was continued, and that such rights to a separate lieutenancy as were possessed by the Tower Hamlets and various corporate towns were preserved.

The design of the bill was calculated to make it popular with all shades of opinion, patriotic or subversive. It was difficult for ministers to oppose it and in the commons they did not try. Fox was sceptical but not unfriendly.[3] Lyttleton the Chancellor of the Exchequer was rather feebly in favour of it.[4] The lords, however, were called upon to play their traditional role of barring popular measures embarrassing to the court. It was on the third reading there (24 May 1756) that the main debate on the bill took place. It was strongly condemned by two of the country's most eminent elder statesmen in office, Lord Chancellor Hardwicke and Lord President Granville,[5] as well as by one less eminent, Lord Sandys. It was taken to a division and thrown out by 59 votes to 23.[6] In one of his most famous speeches, Hardwicke argued that the bill upset the constitutional balance established at the Restoration by obliging the king to inform parliament when the militia was called out and by entrusting extensive powers to the land tax commissioners.

> The scale of power, in this government, has long been growing heavier on the democratical side. I think this would throw a great deal of weight into it. What I contend for, is to preserve the limited monarchy entire; and nothing can do that but to preserve the counterpoise.

[1] Rylands' English MSS., no. 939, items 23, 25. These are clearly 'briefs' for Townshend's use in the commons. He makes the following comparisons with ordinary levies then being made:

10 new foot regiments, 7000 men, p.a.	£152,591. 10s. 0d.
6544 Hessians, for 306 days, f.o.b.	£163,357. 9s. 9d.
Militia, officers and men, 67,077, p.a. ...	£175,197. 10s. 0d.
Same no. at the rate of the 7000 above, p.a.	£1,549,610. 0s. 0d.

[2] Cf. below p. 138, n. 5.   [3] Walpole, *George II*, vol. i, p. 441.
[4] *Ibid.*, p. 451. BM, Add. 32864, f. 499.   [5] Formerly Carteret.
[6] Walpole, *George II*, vol. ii, pp. 44-5. Cobbett, vol. xv, pp. 706-69. LJ, vol. xxviii, pp. 595, 605-6, 611-12.

The absence from the bill of permanent provision for the pay of the force had the same tendency.[1] He admitted that a case could be made for the bill's having actually increased royal power, but this only showed that its tendency was unsettling. It was calculated to revive the contention between king and parliament that had formerly caused the civil war. He further thought that the act could never be executed and would cause boundless trouble and confusion.[2]

Hardwicke seems to have been alone in unravelling the constitutional aspects of the measure enough to supply chapter and verse. Granville and Sandys both concentrated on the difficulty of executing the act. They argued that it was similar in its administrative character to the existing law and so would suffer the same fate. Granville shrewdly said that in former ages the

> general military spirit did not so much proceed from any express law, as from the fashion and humour of the times. Every one of our great barons was himself bred up from his infancy in the practice of all sorts of military exercises; and they did not value themselves ... so much upon the yearly revenue ... as upon the number of brave and expert soldiers they could upon any occasion bring into the field.

Without such a spirit, militia laws were useless. Sandys tried to show that the old act provided for more drill than the new plan and pointed out that the new plan was the harder on the poor man. He, too, took up the proposition that the measure might undesirably strengthen instead of weakening the power of the crown.[3] Ministers were keen to have it both ways.

But though at last they had ventured firmly to resist the bill, ministers were already thinking of further retreat. On the very day of the last debate in the lords Murray told Newcastle that if the bill proved popular in the country it would certainly pass the commons again next year. The sting of the agitation could only be drawn by accepting militia reform in principle and concentrating on detailed criticism and amendment.[4] Lord Walpole was against the rejection of the bill by the lords. People would say that it should have been given a trial and suspect ulterior motives for the ministers' hostility. If the bill was passed and proved ill-contrived it would do its authors

[1] It may have been unintentional. Lord Temple (Cobbett, vol. xv, p. 764) said that no financial provisions were inserted so that the lords would not be prevented from offering amendments by its being a money bill. But annual voting of the funds was insisted on ever afterwards. Hardwicke made the inclusion of permanent financial provision a condition of his support for a militia bill.

[2] The speech was printed for private circulation. Yorke, vol. ii, pp. 262–5. Cobbett, vol. xv, pp. 724–46 (p. 731 for the quotation).

[3] *Ibid.*, pp. 714–19, 752–9. Cf. *An Essay on the Nature and Use of the Militia* (London, 1757) on the last point.

[4] BM, Add. 32865, ff. 104–6.

harm instead. He wanted the ministers to propose amendments and in public was for passing the bill to give it a fair trial while opposing its use for factious purposes.[1]

The weight and moderation of the bill's supporters in the lords were also calculated to make the ministers cautious. The most important peer to speak for the bill was the Duke of Bedford. He had been some years a minister and was the chief begetter of the noblemen's regiments of 1745 and the raiser of one of the more reputable of them. He commended the bill as the nearest they could get to compulsory military service. By passing it the legislature would give a lead in the revival of a military spirit that it would be for the gentry to take up. If they failed to co-operate in the execution of the act, they at least might be made the object of further compulsion.[2] Lord Temple similarly stressed the value of the measure in providing a reserve of trained men. Owing to the system of rotation, these would become available for recruitment by the army.[3] It was the military value of the bill that was stressed in the debate: its political side was soft-pedalled. Temple's main political point was that the proposed militia could never be the tool of despotism. Too many illegal acts were required to make it subservient, and those who had been trained in it would be well prepared to resist.[4] True, Lord Stanhope said (and Bedford hinted) that liberty could not endure if only regular troops had arms. Lord Talbot even hoped to see such a revival of military enthusiasm that elections would be won, as in ancient Rome, by the best and bravest officers.[5] But both Stanhope and Talbot were careful to note the need for caution and experiment.[6]

In this situation even Hardwicke did not venture to oppose the reform of the militia outright. He told the lords that he was in favour of it in principle, and that if a bill was brought in next session providing for a militia of half the size now proposed and more strictly under royal or army control he would support it.[7] In August Newcastle

---

[1] BM, Add. 35594, ff. 40–1, 49–50, quoted in W. Coxe, *Memoirs of Horatio Lord Walpole*, vol. ii, pp. 424–8. [2] Cobbett, vol. xv, pp. 719–24.

[3] Cf. *An Enquiry Concerning the Nature*, pp. 47–8, 53–7. But this writer (pp. 42–3) indignantly rejects the idea of recruiting for the army from the militia.

[4] Cobbett, vol. xv, pp. 766–7.

[5] Cobbett, vol. xv, pp. 706, 710–11, 719–21, 746–9. Bedford said that regular soldiers should not be enlisted for life. Pitt had been careful to say in December 1755 that he wanted a strong army as well as a militia (Walpole, *George II*, vol. i, p. 449). [6] Cobbett, vol. xv, pp. 707–8, 750.

[7] Yorke, vol. ii, p. 265. Cf. *A Modest Address to the Commons of Great Britain and in Particular to the Citizens of London: Occasioned by the Ill Success of our Present Naval War with France, and the Want of a Militia Bill* (London, 1756), p. 28, which claims that the bill would have led to a general arming but Hardwicke's proposal to halve the size of the projected force would turn it into a 'crown army'.

asked Hardwicke whom they should employ to draft such a bill.[1] Thus even before Newcastle's fall the battle for militia reform was in large measure won.

But victory was finally assured by the fall of Minorca on 28 June 1756. In the great outburst of fury against the ministers which followed the militia question played an important part. George Townshend sent a copy of the rejected bill to (apparently) all the principal towns represented in parliament, with a circular asking them to consider it and, if they saw fit, petition the commons in its favour. He urged that the loss of Minorca and the sending for foreign troops made the bill more desirable than ever and he entered into the comparative costs of a militia and of regular troops.[2] A stream of petitions to the throne and instructions to members from their constituents duly materialised from both boroughs and counties, the City of London in the lead. The need for a reform of the militia was there put beside demands for enquiry into past misfortunes and the punishment of offenders.[3] It mattered little that the friends of the ministry were active on the other side, and some inveterates of the opposition, such as Lord Shaftesbury and Sir John Barnard, refused to join in.[4] That autumn Pitt returned to office and brought other friends of the militia with him. The king's speech at the opening of parliament announced that the foreign troops brought over by the previous ministry were to be sent home and recommended that a militia bill be passed. Two days later, on 4 December 1756, the commons set up a committee to bring one in[5] and this produced a bill substantially the same as that of the previous year.

However, the outgoing ministers did not suffer a complete defeat. They had a numerous parliamentary following which was strongly represented in the new ministry. They abandoned neither the struggle for power nor their opposition to the militia bill. In the latter case, all they were in doubt about was the method. Lord Barrington thought in October that they should let Townshend bring in his bill again and

[1] BM, Add. 32997, ff. 22, 25.

[2] *HMC, Lothian (Blickling)*, p. 238. BM, Add. 32866, f. 376. Cf. Add. 35351, ff. 343–4; Add. 35594, f. 167; Add. 32867, ff. 72–3.

[3] E.g. *Gentleman's Magazine*, vol. xxvi (1756), pp. 408 (London), 496–7 (Yorkshire), 545–6 (Ipswich).

[4] BM, Add. 32866, ff. 401–2, 492, 496–7. Newcastle stirred up his Sussex friends, f. 431. Lord Chief Justice Willes found universal discontent on his midland circuit, but addresses had been prevented, Add. 32867, ff. 5–7. The Bristol tories promoted an address but moderate men would not sign; a counter-address was got up, *ibid.*, ff. 99–101, 153–7, 193–200, 270–5. In Surrey Speaker Onslow refused to present the address and the important tories mostly would not sign, *ibid.*, ff. 332–3. Lord Walpole dissuaded Norwich Corporation from petitioning by arguing against its constitutional propriety, *ibid.*, ff. 166–8, 262–3, 453, 482–3.

[5] CJ, vol. xxvii, pp. 621, 627, 650.

offer amendments in the lords. So few people knew what the existing bill contained that it could be transformed without anyone noticing. Hardwicke objected that it would be most invidious for the lords to have to alter drastically a bill approved by the commons two years running, especially as some of the contentious points made it akin to a money bill. Even friendly peers would resent their house being given such an unpleasant task. Hardwicke wanted any scheme that was put forward to make its first appearance not there but in the commons.[1] Accordingly, it was there that a plan was finally proposed, the work of H. S. Conway. Its main feature was the raising of some 30,000 men in the larger towns, each town being allotted a quota. They were to have officers with a property qualification and professional adjutants and NCOs, were to meet regularly for drill and in emergencies were to be embodied and act like regular troops. The point of the scheme was that a militia raised only in the towns would be permanently concentrated into largish bodies instead of being widely scattered. It could meet more easily for drill than a country militia. There would be no disorderly marches to and from the places of exercise and no scattering of arms among the parishes—two things of which Conway was much afraid. Each town would have a proper magazine under the eye of the adjutant. So that the towns should not seem overburdened, Conway annexed a plan, which we have met before,[2] for a body of reservists to be enlisted in each county, liable to be incorporated in the army in emergencies. They were to be roughly equal in number to the town militia and were to receive a pension but no training.[3]

On 26 January 1757 George Townshend presented to the commons the bill drawn up by its committee.[4] Conway thereupon outlined his rival plan, which was at once attacked by two militia stalwarts, Lord Strange and Beckford. Fox supported Conway and suggested that the house should choose between the two plans by a vote taken on the first amendment in committee. The debate suggests that nobody knew quite what to do or how far to go. Townshend's bill had received three important changes, to which he drew attention in introducing it. Although he did not say so, they were obviously a response to some of Hardwicke's criticisms in the lords the previous year. Hardwicke had said that the property qualifications were fixed too high and so the requisite number of officers and deputies would be

[1] BM, Add. 35594, ff. 263–5, 296–7. Barrington wanted a straight army reserve which Hardwicke said would be unpopular but Barrington said was like continental militias.

[2] It seems to be roughly the same as *A Scheme*, etc.: see above, p. 114.

[3] BM, Add. 33048, ff. 401–6. That this refers to Conway's plan appears from comparison with Add. 35351, ff. 360–1; Newdigate, Box 2, item B 2539/22.

[4] CI, vol. xxvii, p. 667.

hard to find. The amounts of almost all the qualifications were now reduced by anything up to a half.[1] Hardwicke, like Conway, had feared that the arms left in the hands of the churchwardens might be seized by rioters. The other two changes met this point: the arms were now to be in the care of the sergeants and the lord lieutenants were to have power to order their removal to a safe place in any emergency.

Of the new ministers and their friends, George Townshend's brother the brilliant Charles[2] spoke warmly against the bill's opponents in the lords in the previous session and took the rabble-rousing line that a militia was needed as a counterweight to the army. Lord George Sackville, however, though equally firm against the lords, repudiated the counterweight argument and supported the bill as an additional security to the nation. Legge, now Chancellor of the Exchequer, saw much the same objections to both the militia plans, preferred the existing bill but would support either. George Grenville[3] spoke against Conway and the lords, but temperately. On the other side, Fox spoke of the danger that the lords might reject Townshend's bill but said he had been for it the previous year and was quite ready to support it again. Hardwicke and Newcastle had failed to decide whether to back Conway's plan or press for amendments to Townshend's. Consequently, Hume Campbell who had some amendments ready reflecting their views, did nothing.[4]

Conway apparently adopted a suggestion of Fox and tried to get his plan incorporated in the bill at the committee stage. It was passed over without a division.[5] The notes survive of a speech by George Townshend attacking it. He said that the scheme was hopelessly vague: the size of the quotas, the method of levying, paying and clothing the men and the times of exercise were not precisely expressed. It was far more open than had been the existing bill in the previous session to the charges of being unknown to the nation and unapproved by it, and of taking a long time to perfect. The force which Conway proposed was, in any case, too small. With the existing bill they might hope to go faster than in the previous year: it

[1] Only that of lieutenants was virtually unchanged. Cf. 30 Geo. II, cap. 25, s. 3, and BM, Add. 35877, ff. 259–60. Hardwicke's criticisms are at Cobbett, vol. xv, pp. 736–7, 739.

[2] Treasurer of the Chamber.

[3] Treasurer of the Navy.

[4] This debate is reported at length by Lord Dupplin to Newcastle, BM, Add. 32870, ff. 115–6. Cf. Walpole, *George II*, vol. ii, pp. 132–3. Both Sackville and Legge said that arms would be more in danger from riots in the towns than in the country.

[5] Newdigate's diary, 22 February 1757. CJ, vol. xxvii, p. 726.

could come into force on 1 May and the men could start drill in September.[1]

After three sessions in committee and two on report, the commons gave the bill its third reading on 25 March.[2] Newcastle and his friends may have been trying to get it amended. The borough of Nottingham where they had influence presented a petition asking for the preservation of its privileges under the existing militia law: this was the only borough that bothered to do so.[3] But the only important defeat for the sponsors of the bill was over drill on Sundays. This was another thing that Hardwicke had objected to in the lords the previous year[4] and he had been widely followed. Soame Jenyns could say that the bill had benefited religion by uniting clergy and dissenters—that is, in opposing drill on Sundays.[5] The observance of Sunday was declared to be the true sign of the strength of 'serious religion' in a nation. Sunday drill would be 'excluding the *almighty* from our politics . . . bidding defiance to him, by a solemn repeal of one of his laws, and signing and sealing to the downfall of our country'. It was suggested that the defeats already suffered in the war might be due to the decline of Sunday observance. Drill should be on weekdays: the smallness of the numbers involved meant that trade would hardly suffer.[6] When the bill again appeared in the commons in 1757 there were several petitions to this effect.[7] When the question was debated it was carried in the negative without a division,[8] and amendments were adopted providing for drills by half companies on the first Monday and by whole companies on the third Monday of each month. Drills were thus to be fewer but in larger bodies, which was some compensation.[9]

The situation which Hardwicke had feared had now come to pass. If the bill was to be substantially altered, the lords would have to do it. The lords gave the bill its first reading and ordered it to be printed

[1] Rylands' English MSS. no. 939, item 30 (undated). Townshend asked Pitt to attend and prevent the destruction of his bill 'under the pretence of substituting another plan they have not prepared and never mean'. W. S. Taylor and J. H. Pringle (ed.), *Correspondence of William Pitt, Earl of Chatham* (London, 1838–40), vol. i, pp. 222–3, quoted in Townshend, pp. 131–2.

[2] CJ, vol. xxvii, pp. 674, 726, 733, 741, 756, 787, 816.

[3] CJ, vol. xxvii, pp. 755–6.   [4] Cobbett, vol. xv, pp. 738–9.

[5] *Works*, vol. ii, pp. 153–4.

[6] *Gentleman's Magazine*, vol. xxvi (1756), pp. 432–3, 509–10; vol. xxvii (1757), pp. 29, 30, 58–9. Comparison was made with the Book of Sports.

[7] CJ, vol. xxvii, pp. 717, 719, 724, 726, 733. Nine in all.

[8] Newdigate's diary, 24 February 1757.

[9] But no man was to go more than 6 miles from home, so discretionary power was given to assemble smaller bodies. Cf. 30 Geo. II, cap. 25, ss. 27–8, and the lords' amendments discussed below. Rylands' English MSS., no. 939, items 8, 31–3, 36, contain various alternative drill plans, including a very sensible one to embody the whole force for two weeks' training on its formation.

and read again after the Easter recess.[1] At that very moment an intrigue instigated by Fox and Cumberland led to the dismissal of Pitt and his friends and an attempt to undo the whole revolution of the previous year. Most of the ensuing three months were consumed in the attempts to form an alternative government, ending in a compromise between Pitt and his rivals. The subordinate struggle over the militia bill occupied much the same time and had much the same end.[2] Nor did the one cause the other to be forgotten. On 3 April the king spoke to Hardwicke at the levee and mentioned that the militia bill came on in the lords immediately after the recess, in a way that Hardwicke took to be an intimation to attend.[3]

Newcastle and Hardwicke appear to have decided immediately after the first reading in the commons on a series of amendments designed to render the bill harmless.[4] The numbers of the force to be raised were to be halved, and it was not to be raised by ballot unless it proved impossible to do so by enlisting volunteers. Anyone who did volunteer was to have thereafter the right to carry on any trade in any place in Britain and was not to be removed to his place of settlement under the poor laws unless he required relief. The land tax commissioners were left out of the bill and instead justices of the peace were empowered to assist the deputies. There were various lesser changes[5] and one shattering innovation. The measure was to become a temporary one, lasting only for five years and to the end of the then ensuing session. The great idea now was to let it die a natural death after the excitement that had brought it forth had evaporated.

Proceeding cautiously, the lords considered the bill thrice in committee and on report ordered it to be reprinted, with the amendments in a different type: the third reading was deferred for a week. With the exception of the requirement that volunteers be sought

[1] LJ, vol. xxix, p. 105.

[2] Pitt and Temple were dismissed on 5-6 April. The plan of the new ministry was accepted by the king on 18 June. A. von Ruville, *William Pitt, Earl of Chatham* (English trans., London and New York, 1907), vol. ii, pp. 106-10, 130. Walpole, *George II*, vol. ii, pp. 195-200, 224. The two houses agreed on the text of the militia bill on 8 June.

[3] BM, Add. 32870, ff. 358-9.

[4] There is a copy of the plan in the Hardwicke papers and a summary in the Newcastle papers dated 4 February. Both note the reduction of qualifications announced at the first reading. BM, Add. 32997, ff. 99, 100. Add. 35877, ff. 355-6.

[5] Notably the restoration of the provision that the king was to notify parliament if he called out the militia for service, or to declare his intention in council if parliament was not sitting. Hardwicke said (BM, Add. 32870, ff. 161-2) that this had been left out on report from the bill of 1756 but included in the version circulated in the country and so no doubt was approved by those who had petitioned for a bill. Sir F. Dashwood had already secured an amendment in the commons empowering the king to recall parliament in such a case. Rylands' English MSS., no. 939, items 18-22. Cf. below, p. 372, n. 2.

before a ballot was held and one or two trifling matters, they adopted the whole of the programme described above.[1] They further made the qualifications for officers applicable only to first appointments: any officer might be promoted for good service up to the rank of lieutenant-colonel, without further qualification.[2] The drills they confined to the months of May to October inclusive and the Whitsun meeting was confined to two days.[3]

The bill was sent back to the commons on 9 May.[4] It was now the policy of the authors of the amendments to 'negotiate from strength'. Already on 1 May Newcastle told Hardwicke that he had seen the Marquess of Granby who was glad that the alterations had been made and thought he could get the Townshends to his way of thinking.[5] The commons did indeed give a good deal of ground at this stage, but did not submit entirely. They set up a large committee to deal with the amendments and accepted a great many. They refused, however, to agree to the exclusion of the land tax commissioners. They argued that the justices were too few for the work and that the commissioners were more often resident and had actually been given comparable powers in recent acts to raise men for the regular forces.[6] The promotion of officers without qualification they wished to confine to cases where merit was shown while the militia was on active service, and nobody not qualified to be a captain should be promoted above that rank. They objected to the reward proposed for ex-militiamen as inconsistent with the privileges of corporate towns and having previously been given only to men who had seen actual service.[7] They wished to add March and April to the months when drill was to take place and to restore the days removed from the Whitsun exercise.[8]

[1] LJ, vol. xxix, pp. 124, 131–2, 134, 136–40. See especially, pp. 136–8 and 139, at Press 34, line 35; p. 140, Cl. E. Amendments not carried provided for billeting the militia in Scotland.

[2] Ibid., p. 136, Cl. B.

[3] Ibid., pp. 138–9, at Press 23, lines 7, 8, 15–16; Press 25, line 12.

[4] Ibid., p. 149.

[5] BM, Add. 32871, f. 5. Newcastle wanted a few amendments dropped to facilitate this. It is perhaps significant that the moderate Duke of Bedford managed the conferences between the houses.

[6] For this, see W. R. Ward, 'A History of Land Tax Administration in England, 1692–1798' (Oxford D. Phil. thesis) pp. 655–60.

[7] This provision was copied from an act in favour of soldiers discharged after the previous war. It had rather lost its point with the disappearance of the proposal about volunteers.

[8] The commons' further proceedings are in CJ, vol. xxvii, pp. 898, 903-8, 913–15. They added a clause that there was not to be more than one captain, one lieutenant and one ensign per 80 men. In place of a halving of the number of sergeants they later substituted a quota of one per 20 men (ibid., p. 920; LJ, vol. xxix, p. 176).

The lords accepted most of the modifications to their plan, but they stood firm on the reward for ex-militiamen and the exclusion of land tax commissioners. On this issue they made a full statement of the constitutional objection.

> Acts of Magistracy should not be vested by Act of Parliament in any Set of Men; this being the Executive Part of Government, and undoubtedly, by the Constitution, a peculiar and natural Right of the Crown, which this Practice has doubtless entrenched upon; and the Lords cannot agree, on this Occasion, to countenance another Precedent of that sort.

The commons insisted on restricting the ex-militiamen's privilege to those who had actually served during invasion or insurrection, but on the main outstanding question they gave way.[1]

The final result was thus that the bill became law, but the new force was to be smaller and a little less under popular control than its advocates had wished and it seemed unlikely to have a long life, even supposing that the difficulties of organising it were overcome. This outcome was creditable to the patriotism of the authors of the bill. They showed themselves more concerned for the military than for the political parts of the measure and sacrificed some of the latter to save some of the former. This was the reverse of what their predecessors in the previous century had done and it brought them better luck. But in politics virtue is seldom rewarded for long.

(II) THE ACT OF 1758 AND THE STRUGGLE FOR ENFORCEMENT

The first events after the passage of the new act seemed to show that its opponents had won a total victory. The lieutenancies proceeded to its execution in the summer of 1757 only to find that for the most part the gentry declined to serve as officers and the common people were most unwilling to serve in the ranks. Compulsion was of course available to fill the latter, but the making of lists of those liable to serve was the signal for widespread rioting, especially in the eastern half of the country. These riots will be described elsewhere,[2] but it is here important to note the commonest grievances expressed. One was against 'Digbying',[3] which was most unfairly expected to apply to the militia though it had been excluded by the terms of the act and was very much the work of its enemies. The other important one was

---

[1] LJ, vol. xxix, pp. 170, 173–7, 180, 188 (p. 176 for the quotation and what the lords decided). CJ, vol. xxvii, pp. 917, 919, 920. The lords had proposed to exempt the Tower Hamlets from the bill, but the commons refused to strike out their quota and the lords acquiesced after a division. The Hamlets were left with an organisation under the old acts and a quota under the new. But next year the quota was repealed by 31 Geo. II, cap. 26, ss. 39–41.

[2] Below, pp. 290–302.   [3] Above, p. 122.

that whereas the burden of the old militia had fallen on the land-owners, that of the new would fall mainly on the poor. This was absolutely true and most significant. The independent country gentle-men in parliament had here consulted their own interest, not that of the nation at large, which they prided themselves on representing. Townshend as we have seen expected the new militia to begin training in September 1757. In fact, the most that seems to have been achieved anywhere that autumn was the enrolling of the men, as yet with few officers to command them.

The partisans of the act did not, however, give up the fight. The Townshends made good progress in executing it in Norfolk,[1] despite the opposition of their own father, the Viscount, who was said to have stirred up the mob against them.[2] They claimed that the militia had done well wherever the authorities had seriously tried to imple-ment the act, and that where it had done badly, this was because the lord lieutenants were hostile and had failed to do their duty.[3] How-ever, they recognised that the new act had shown itself imperfect—indeed, its defenders had always said that it was necessarily experi-mental. They therefore began a campaign in two directions, pressing in parliament for the amendment and in the counties for the more vigorous enforcement of the law.

In parliament their position had improved. The new ministry was again one of compromise, based on the reconciliation of Pitt and Newcastle. But Pitt and his friends were much more securely in power than before, especially after his failure to defend Hanover had led to the complete disgrace of Cumberland in October. Joined with them in the ministry were representatives of every faction in British politics. The government accordingly was neutral—even more so than usual—on political issues, which were fought out inside it as well as in parliament. This situation gave the partisans of the militia fruitful opportunities for bargaining.

The Townshends regarded Pitt's agreement with his enemies as a betrayal and had refused to join the ministry.[4] They remained on good terms with him, however, and he remained loyal to the cause of

---

[1] But not until late in 1758 was the Norfolk militia ready for training. *Chatham Correspondence*, vol. i, p. 347. Cf. Appendix A.

[2] Walpole, *George II*, vol. ii, p. 233. The account he gives on p. 232 of the character and effect of the amendments introduced into the bill by Hardwicke and his friends is pure invention. Lord Townshend did not believe that a militia could be tolerable in a trading nation, differing in this from Dean Tucker. HMC, *Town-shend*, p. 376.

[3] *Ibid.*, pp. 394–5. BM, Add. 35351, f. 432.

[4] But Cumberland's disgrace led George to return to the army and to look for advancement there, with the help of Pitt. Townshend, pp. 133, 134, 137–9, 142–4. HMC, *Townshend*, pp. 393–5.

the militia. In cabinet he put the blame for the riot on the lieutenancies, who should have taken more care to explain the act to the people.[1] He seems to have thought that if the opposition was universal the act should not be 'pushed' but that otherwise it should.[2] When parliament met again he defended the scheme but admitted that it had failed. This drew a strong protest from George Townshend, whereupon Pitt more or less retracted and pledged his continued good will.[3]

A few days later (9 December) Townshend moved for leave for a bill to explain the militia act and a large committee was appointed to prepare it. The bill did not receive its first reading until 3 March 1758.[4] On 28 February Townshend had written to Pitt explaining the measure and asking his support. By setting his letter beside the act as passed, we can form a good idea of its intention. Townshend said that the friends of the bill were anxious to avoid giving its enemies a handle to obstruct it either in the lords or in the country. They had therefore kept mainly to explanations and additions. There were firstly attempts to redress the grievances, real or pretended, of the common people, especially that of inequality. Deputies and parish officers were no longer to be exempt from the ballot.[5] Strong penalties were provided for those who obstructed the law or corrupted those executing it.[6] Provision was made for the families of militiamen on active service.[7] Men falling ill during the annual regimental exercise were to be looked after by the parish where it happened.[8] As an incentive to good service, corporals with extra pay were to be appointed from among the privates and vacancies among the sergeants were to be filled from them. Privates' children were to be given preference in the appointment of drummers.[9] Parishes were empowered to escape the ballot by offering volunteers, as Newcastle and Hardwicke had wished in the previous year. But the volunteers were not to be from the class of vagabonds commonly pressed for the army.[10] An extra subdivision meeting of deputies (i.e. at petty-session level) was instituted for the easier hearing of complaints of wrongful inclusion or omission in the lists of men liable for service.[11] The form

[1] He was for punishing the ringleaders. BM, Add. 35417, f. 55.

[2] BM, Add. 32997, f. 257.

[3] BM, Add. 35351, ff. 432–3. I presume the Townshend mentioned is George.

[4] CJ, vol. xxviii, pp. 17, 22, 116.

[5] The letter is in PRO. 30/8, vol. 64, ff. 151–2. The act is 31 Geo. II, cap. 26. For exemptions, see ss. 13–14.

[6] s. 23.   [7] Cf. ss. 27–8.   [8] s. 26.

[9] s. 6. But nothing is said about privates' children.

[10] This part of the letter is obscure. The latter object seems to have been sought by providing (s. 17) that the men were not to be seamen and that a fine was to be paid if they deserted.

[11] s. 11.

of oath, which had proved unintelligible to the common people, was changed.[1]

The other main object of the bill was to prevent the defeat of the law by the failure especially of the lord lieutenants to do their duty. Townshend reminded Pitt that the timetable laid down in the original act had not been kept to and the resulting confusion was an excuse for inaction. It was proposed to shame the lord lieutenants into doing their part by laying down what they had to do so explicitly that they had no honourable way of escape. The bill accomplished this by laying down first that where a ballot had already been held, or all was in readiness for it, the proceedings of the previous year were to stand; otherwise a fresh start was to be made. Where the field officers and captains of a projected battalion had not yet been appointed,[2] the lord lieutenant was to hold a meeting within six weeks or so of the passing of the act and put advertisements in the newspapers inviting all those qualified to attend and offer to serve in the appropriate ranks. If within a further month he had not received offers enough to supply field officers and captains for at least one battalion, he was to suspend all militia proceedings until not later than 25 March 1759, He was then to hold another meeting in the same way.[3] A county was only to receive arms, pay, clothing and so forth for its militia when three-fifths of the required number of officers and men had been appointed and enrolled.[4] To make things easier, certain qualifications were further reduced[5] and provision was made for the filling of vacancies in the ranks.[6]

The bill passed the commons on 14 April.[7] That same day Lord Shaftesbury wrote to Pitt that several peers were ready to oppose it in the lords and warned him that some ministers ought to attend the debate in order to countenance the bill and procure it a majority.[8] Newcastle, indeed, had hoped that the riots would lead to the passing of an amending bill (no doubt of a wrecking kind),[9] and his memoranda show him trying to influence militia proceedings in the commons.[10] In the lords he could be counted on to try harder. But it was now that the general political situation began to be helpful. The most important event of the session of 1757-8 was Pitt's espousal of the

[1] s. 18. For further provisions see part iii, especially chap. xi.
[2] I think it was always assumed that the officers would be appointed before the ballot, but only this act (s. 2) says so. Cf. s. 15.   [3] s. 9.
[4] s. 34. Instead of four-fifths (30 Geo. II, cap. 25, s. 35).
[5] ss. 4, 5; cf. ss. 3, 7, 38.   [6] ss. 19, 20; cf. s. 16.
[7] After five sessions in committee. CJ, vol. xxviii, pp. 150, 164, 169, 176, 178, 179, 181, 194.
[8] PRO. 30/8, vol. 56, f. 1.
[9] BM, Add. 32997, f. 278.
[10] Ibid., ff. 305, 335, 375, 384, 402, 404.

policy of helping Prussia to the limit with subsidies and even by sending token British forces to Germany. He thereby went back on his demands in opposition for the abandonment of Hanover and continental engagements. The second most important event was the Habeas Corpus bill, directed against the expedients by which the judges had tried to reconcile the liberties of the subject with the government's right to press men for the army and navy. The bill, in effect, sought to decide this question in favour of the subject and to the detriment of the recruiting service. It had Pitt's support and was, indeed, the work of his friend Attorney-General Pratt.[1] In becoming a statesman, Pitt was not ceasing to be a popular tribune.

All this helped the militia bill in two ways. Firstly there was the zeal of Pitt for the militia, in which he actually outstripped Townshend. He did not approve of the provision by which no county was to begin training until it had enough field officers and captains for one battalion. He thought the full complement of field officers and half that of captains sufficient and that anything more would play into the hands of unfriendly lord lieutenants. Pitt also favoured, and Townshend opposed, a proposal of Speaker Onslow's that in default of sufficient officers the lord lieutenant should only adjourn proceedings for three months at a time and not until the following year. George Townshend sent—of all people—Lord Royston, Hardwicke's eldest son, to cool him down, which Royston succeeded in doing.[2] It is hard not to see here some disinterested enthusiasm; but hard not to feel that here and with the Habeas Corpus bill, Pitt was trying to atone in the eyes of the country gentlemen for his espousal of the continental policy he had so long opposed.

In the second place, Newcastle and his friends—especially, no doubt, Mansfield and Hardwicke—were determined to throw out the Habeas Corpus bill in the lords, as being both bad law and detrimental to national security. They, too, needed to make atonement, so they finally decided to let the militia bill through. Lord Shaftesbury warned Newcastle that rejecting it would do no good anyway. The existing act would remain in force and its exasperated partisans would press in the counties for its exact execution. It was precisely to spare the lord lieutenants this embarrassment that the new bill had been introduced. Moreover, the lords appeared to have decided the issue already by amending the mutiny bill to make it applicable to the militia if it was called out. It would be inconsistent not to go on in the same way.[3] Newcastle found that Mansfield was against

---

[1] Ruville, vol. ii, pp. 167, 188–91. On the Habeas Corpus bill, cf. Walpole, *George II*, vol. ii, pp. 285–9, 294–302, and Yorke, vol. iii, pp. 1–19.

[2] BM, Add. 35352, ff. 5, 6.

[3] BM, Add. 32879, ff. 319–22. Cf. Add. 32998, ff. 21, 33.

rejecting the bill, and Devonshire and Hardwicke feared 'convulsions' if both popular bills were thrown out at the same time. They therefore proposed to adjourn the third reading of the militia bill until the Habeas Corpus bill had been disposed of. Those who wished to might then oppose it; but some thought passing it the best way of getting the whole thing to drop.[1]

In the event the committee stage of the militia bill in the lords was postponed until the Habeas Corpus bill had been dealt with.[2] On 2 June it was thrown out without a division.[3] Next day Newcastle told Hardwicke that he was now for passing the militia bill: the country would otherwise be thrown into confusion. An attempt to postpone the committee stage again for six weeks, which would have killed the bill, was defeated in the lords without a division and the lords passed the bill with amendments, which the commons accepted. One of these, suggested by Newcastle, empowered the king to forbid the appointment of any person offering to serve as an officer: the significance of this need not be laboured.[4]

In the commons, meanwhile, the government had been driven a step nearer towards countenancing the militia when on 1 May the Chancellor of the Exchequer recommended by royal command that financial provision be made for it. In his letter to Pitt already mentioned, Townshend had said that popular suspicion had been aroused by the absence from the act of 1757 of provision for the militia to be paid. A bill providing the money would allay this anxiety.[5] The commons had appointed a committee to prepare one, but could not have taken action on the estimate which it presented without the Chancellor's recommendation.[6] An act was duly passed appropriating £100,000 to the service of the militia in 1757 and 1758.[7] Thus the friends of the militia had carried their legislative programme: which did not prevent the Duke of Devonshire from hoping at the end of the session that the militia act would not be put in execution.[8]

[1] Sc. from apathy. Sandys was consulted too. Add. 32879, ff. 342, 344. Cf. Add. 32998, ff. 24, 33.
[2] LJ, vol. xxix, pp. 304, 310, 314, 319, 320, 329, 341, 352-3. The lords procured a return of counties issued with arms, etc., under the act of 1757.
[3] As p. 144, n. 1.
[4] LJ, vol. xxix, pp. 355-6, 360, 372, 380. BM, Add. 32880, ff. 311-12, 377. Lord Northumberland drafted the clause which was probably unnecessary, cf. 30 Geo. II, cap. 25, ss. 1, 8. George Grenville's bill about navy pay was another measure grudgingly passed (Walpole, *George II*, vol. ii, pp. 289-90).
[5] Cf. above p. 132 and n. 1.
[6] CJ, vol. xxviii, pp. 21, 218, 221, 226, 228. On the constitutional point see below, p. 171 and n. 3.
[7] 31 Geo. II, cap. 30. Similar acts were passed each year thereafter: see below, pp. 194, 344, 347.
[8] BM, Add. 32880, f. 410.

L

II

To get the law enforced, its partisans set going an agitation in the counties parallel to that in parliament. They had one, and not much more than one, thing to help them. The militia, whatever its merits, was regarded as a patriotic undertaking, the success of which was much to be desired. Anyone, therefore, who wished to shine in national or county politics needed to do everything that could reasonably be expected of him to forward it and avoid giving any grounds for the accusation that any lack of progress was due to his neglect.

A special obligation not to neglect the militia lay upon those ministers of the crown who were also lord lieutenants. They were very conscious that once the militia bills were law it would be dangerous to the authority of government if they were disobeyed. They therefore tried hard to set a good example in this respect and this counter-balanced their dislike of the militia. Newcastle's lieutenancy of Nottinghamshire was an area where he was under no local pressure to do anything. His friends were in control and neither they nor anyone else wished for action. But the Duke was most anxious that the letter at least of the law should be strictly observed. In July 1757 he told John White[1] that he knew he did not like the bill but was sure that he would not want Newcastle to fail in its execution. He urged both the county members and the representatives of the Nottingham-shire boroughs to take the lead in executing the act and make sure that the statutory lieutenancy meetings were held and well attended. He asked for advice whom to appoint as officers and deputies, and contemplated giving deputations to all gentlemen in the county who were qualified, including the tories.[2] His friends bustled about, though they found the act generally disliked and little chance of finding officers.[3] 'Though I heartily wish the Bill to fail,' wrote White, 'and am pretty sure it will I would not have it fail here.'[4] When the riots broke out the Duke was much concerned and said his enemies would not spare him. He vainly urged his friends to get the act executed.[5] In the following summer he was very angry because the first meeting ordered to receive the names of those wishing to be officers was not held because his friends failed to attend. 'I care no

[1] MP for Retford; an old and faithful supporter. Namier, *American Revolution*, pp. 124, 189 and n. 1.
[2] BM, Add. 32872, ff. 19–21, 25, 108–9, 303, 305–7.
[3] *Ibid.*, ff. 110, 129, 188, 190.
[4] *Ibid.*, f. 226. White is actually referring to the *town* of Nottingham—'your Grace being Lieutenant for the County of the Town of Nottingham I would have no Deficiency there'.
[5] *Ibid.*, f. 406. Cf. ff. 397, 478.

more for the Militia than you do,' he told White, 'but I do care for an Act of Parliament, and should be sorry that the Execution of one which belongs to me as Lord Lieutenant should be neglected.'[1] The Duke's friends got to work again and when their efforts had induced only two unimportant whigs, one tory and a 'mad man' to offer to take commissions, Hardwicke told him that he might properly adjourn till Lady Day, 1759.[2] Neither then[3] nor under the pressure of subsequent acts in 1760 and 1762[4] could anything be achieved. Newcastle did his best, but as Job Charlton said, fears of invasion did not operate so strongly in Nottinghamshire as in a maritime county.[5]

Another minister embarrassed with a lieutenancy was Lord Holdernesse, now Secretary of State, who had the North Riding of Yorkshire. In July 1758 he sent his uncle Sir Conyers D'Arcy instructions very like those which Newcastle was giving his friends. By way of apology he said that he had done his best to avoid giving trouble by voting against the bill but it must now be obeyed. D'Arcy set to work, taking care that there should be no grounds for complaint of insufficient notice of the meeting, and produced a much better (or worse) result than in Nottinghamshire. Holdernesse's friends readily offered to take commissions and serve in any rank he pleased. They insisted that D'Arcy take the colonelcy, which he had first held *fifty* years earlier. Others less welcome were there, such as Mr Duncombe, whose conduct in 1745 had not been satisfactory. On account of his wealth and local connections, Holdernesse's friends did not think that he could be refused a commission.[6] Thus his sense of duty could force a lord lieutenant to spur on a measure he disliked and accept in office persons of doubtful political reliability.

In cases like this the acts achieved the political purpose of their sponsors. The independent country gentlemen—tory or otherwise—had an opportunity to gain influence at the expense of those well in with the court. This, of course, caused great alarm. In August 1758 Newcastle complained to Legge that in many counties a spirit of 'folly and faction' was leading to the enforcement, for those reasons only, of a militia act which almost everyone wanted to drop quietly. He pointed especially to Essex, where all the tories had offered to take commissions and nobody else had. Other counties in which he saw the same spirit at work were Surrey, Kent, Devon, Bedfordshire

[1] BM, Add. 32882, f. 289. Cf. ff. 15, 39, 233, 263–4, 287; Add. 32881, ff. 381–2.
[2] BM, Add. 32883, ff. 19, 76, 201, 242, 256–8. Add. 32882, ff. 324, 328, 466.
[3] BM, Add. 32889, ff. 229, 233.
[4] On 1760, numerous letters in BM, Add. 32900–3; on 1762, cf. Add. 32939, ff. 269–70.
[5] BM, Add. 32894, f. 217.
[6] BM, Eg. 3436, ff. 193–202.

and Gloucestershire.[1] But even he did not go as far as Lord Leicester, who reported a rumour that the militia at Southwold were toasting King James III.[2] Newcastle's concern was increased by several of his friends resigning their lieutenancies: Lord Lincoln, his heir, gave up Cambridgeshire.[3] Lord Royston remarked that the new laws would make lieutenancies 'not very acceptable but to those who love a bustle'.[4] Newcastle could not be certain that the vacancy would always go to another friend (as when Royston took Cambridgeshire from Lincoln) and he was himself almost driven to resign the lieutenancy of Middlesex.

Here his opponents subjected him to something approaching a war of nerves. In 1757 he saw to it, as in Nottinghamshire, that everything was done which the law required. He consulted the leading local personalities, especially the county members, and asked their advice on the appointment of deputies.[5] Unfortunately, this led to the filling of the lieutenancy with tories.[6] In 1758 they repaid him ill. The first meeting under the new act produced only a few obscure people willing to be officers, but the clerk called another on his own initiative. To this all the tories came and proceeded to order another, which they urged all gentlemen qualified to be officers to attend, that the county might not appear more backward than the rest. Newcastle was now able to point to his own wisdom in pressing for a clause enabling the king to refuse unwelcome offers of service. But he complained to White that the new system of meetings to receive them, which he regarded as meant to bring further activity to a halt, would result in a tory militia and reproaches to the whigs for lack of patriotism in not joining. 'The Whigs don't like the bill; nor the Tories; But the latter, finding the Whigs don't offer, have in many counties ... all offered.' No 'spring of faction' could produce officers in Nottinghamshire, but Middlesex was different.[7]

However, as Newcastle himself implies, the country gentlemen

[1] BM, Add. 32882, ff. 382–3. Cf. f. 344.

[2] And said that the new Norfolk officers had never shown much enthusiasm for government in peacetime. He quoted Dryden's lines on the militia. BM, Add. 32884, f. 383.

[3] In 1757. BM, Add. 35679, ff. 209, 212, 216, 218–19. Add. 32873, ff. 194–5. Likewise Lord Ashburnham in Sussex (*ibid.*, ff. 248–9, 402, 404; cf. f. 149) and in 1758 Lord Ducie in Gloucestershire, Add. 32883, ff. 440–3. In all these cases the successor was a friend.

[4] BM, Add. 35351, f. 383.

[5] He seems to have been guided by a memorandum by his friend Lord Dupplin. BM, Add. 32872, ff. 35–8. Cf. ff. 166–7; Add. 32997, f. 231. He was warned against two deputies who acted as justices only to protect bawdy houses and the drink trade, Add. 32881, ff. 387–8.

[6] BM, Add. 32882, f. 383.

[7] BM, Add. 32882, ff. 398–9; cf. ff. 247, 344.

were not really eager to undertake the laborious task of raising the militia. They did not therefore effect a political revolution, nor did they compensate for the lack of enthusiasm felt by so many of the lord lieutenants. Newcastle's friends thought that there was little chance of the former, anyway. White advised him not to think of resigning in Middlesex because it would look as if he had quarrelled with the 'New part' of the Administration. All would be well if the offices of profit under the new act were filled by his friends.

> Officers if such be found will have less influence when they find every thing by which any thing can be got, filled without their approbation.

White thought that the crown's power to reject officers was useless, especially in view of the difficulty of replacing them. But he believed that the whole question would again come before parliament, which might then be disposed to admit the dangerousness of 'a Militia constituted as I fear the present must be if it takes place which I yet think impracticable'.[1] Legge agreed that

> should the words Militia or no-Militia ever create as troublesome distinctions in the land as High Church and Low Church it would be very unfortunate. Not that I think it will prove the case, for tho' the immediate fear of invasion raised this spirit in the country yet when the war is over I think there will hardly be zeal enough, or in other words, fear enough left to make officers without pay and keep the country people exercising for 6d. per day, at least to a degree that can distress the country. In some few places it may obtain and make a few Regimts. fit to act with regular troops in case of any sudden emergency and in that there will be no harm. Why won't the Whigs take commissions too, if they did the Tories would soon be outnumbered and the odious distinction avoided of letting the Corps be all of one complexion . . .[2]

Hardwicke acknowledged that in Cambridgeshire there were signs of an agitation to induce the taking of commissions, but he doubted if officers enough would be found to allow the force to be raised. He, too, pressed Newcastle to keep the lieutenancy of Middlesex[3] and events there entirely justified his complacent views. The tories turned out in force for the fatal meeting but none of any consequence offered to serve. One county member was willing to take any commission; the other had gout and did not attend.[4]

Most of the gentry seem indeed, like the ministers, to have done what they thought was due from men in their position and no more.[5]

---

[1] BM, Add. 32883, ff. 19, 20.   [2] BM, Add. 32882, f. 401.
[3] *Ibid.*, ff. 446-7.   [4] BM, Add. 32883, f. 119.
[5] Lord Mansfield reported that in the country areas he had visited there was general indifference and the gentry wished simply to know what the government wanted—to drop the measure or have it executed. BM, Add. 32882, ff. 450-1.

This meant in particular that leading men in the counties, particularly county members, often felt obliged to show their patriotism and set a good example. They therefore associated themselves with the work of raising the militia, but commonly did as little as they decently could. Somersetshire and Cambridgeshire afford particularly good examples of this. The former county was unusual in having a lord lieutenant, Lord Poulett, who was a militia enthusiast and sympathetic to Pitt. In 1757 he nevertheless did little, partly for practical reasons and partly because 'I found the gentlemen of the county at present very averse to it, unwilling to lend much assistance, and the common people outrageously against it, for fear as they called it of being Digby'd abroad.' He thought it 'better not to force things . . . which by and by will be executed very easily . . . for when they find that other counties have taken the lead, they will be ashamed not to follow'.[1] In 1758 he felt that the moment for a big effort had come. He appointed a large number of deputies, being careful to avoid party distinctions.[2] The first meeting for the appointment of officers was a failure: only two gentlemen of the first rank attended and only eight persons offered their services (over forty were required).[3] Poulett responded by presiding in person at the next meeting of the lieutenancy and appealing for volunteers in a rousing speech, which was then printed and circulated through the county. Recalling that 'the whole Kingdom almost', including their own quarter sessions, had clamoured for a militia act, 'obtained at length under the Influence of a Patriot Minister', he asked

> now Ye have the opportunity offered you of having Arms in your own hands, is it possible to believe that a free people, and who mean to be free, will let slip this occasion or take a part counter to the zeal they so lately shewed for it? . . . the principal gentlemen of the county being now assembled, I call upon them previously to any other business, to let me know according to your qualifications in what rank you are willing to serve, and I most earnestly exhort the first gentlemen in the county to serve as officers, for the honour of themselves, of their country, and of this county in particular, To inspire your friends and neighbours with your own examples with a true spirit of honour and patriotism and induce and engage them by accepting the lower commissions (the only point where this act is likely to fail) To promote this essential service to your country, the only means of ever getting rid of a standing army, and of making a military force easy and safe to yourselves.
> . . . Not content with barely doing my duty I have exerted my best

[1] PRO. 30/8, vol. 53, ff. 99–100.
[2] PRO. 30/8, vol. 53, f. 142. (Dated only 2 June but it refers to what is clearly the act of 1758.)
[3] It is interesting that two of those who offered were too shy to join the rest at dinner and one of them had doubts about the sacramental test. *Ibid.*, ff. 101–3.

endeavours in the condition I am in for the carrying this act into execution, and I hope other gentlemen will exert the same endeavours, But if unfortunately it should not meet with the success I expect from it, it will appear publicly to our country and be remembered by our posterity by and thro' whom it failed.[1]

Poulett had already induced the leading men in the county to take the higher commissions, being careful to apportion them in a way that 'must be agreeable to each party and a means of blending them if parties still subsist'. He proposed himself to take the colonelcy of both the projected regiments. The lieutenant-colonels were to be Lord North (whig) and Sir Charles Tynte, one of the county members (tory). The other county member, Prowse, was to be a major. This arrangement was put in jeopardy because Prowse refused the commission proposed for him. Suspecting that he disliked ranking below Tynte, Poulett proposed to switch him with North, who did not mind.

> But on canvassing this matter over privately with Mr. Prowse and some of his friends the first plan was thought best, and it was thought absolutely necessary for his interest not to decline being major, and so it was settled.[2]

Poulett announced these arrangements in his speech at the lieutenancy meeting and promised to be guided in further appointments by the advice of the two lieutenant-colonels. He then called the roll of the deputies, marking those who were absent, and asked those present and all the other gentlemen there in what ranks they would serve.[3] From this time forward things went better and in January 1759 the full complement of officers save three subalterns[4] had been secured.[5]

This story illustrates both the reluctance of the gentry to serve and also the awkwardness of refusing. The spirit of the county in 1758 was thus described by Poulett to Pitt:

> I think the middle rate of people seem much disposed towards carrying the act into execution, the lower rank of people seem afraid only of being sent abroad, They hold an odd language indeed, and talk when they have arms in their hands, of fighting for those who will give them most, so thoroughly debauched is this unfortunate country, but when they are once disciplined they will have other sentiments . . . They will also grow fond of a Militia when they have red coats on their backs, when it becomes a holiday entertainment . . .

[1] For the speech, *ibid.*, ff. 111–12. See too ff. 102, 109–10. He said that the gentry should be compellable to serve as officers on pain of a fine. He cited a recent exploit of the forces of Hesse to prove the value of militia. Pitt's health was drunk at the meeting.

[2] PRO. 30/8, vol. 53, ff. 102–3, 109.   [3] *Ibid.*, f. 112.

[4] I use this term throughout in its eighteenth-century sense of the *two* lowest commissioned ranks: lieutenant and ensign or cornet.

[5] *Ibid.*, ff. 115–16.

As to the gentlemen of the county, one class of them, such as Ld. Ilchester, Egremont, Dodington, Egmont &c. who may be comprehended under the name of Court Whigs, they all seem against it, at least lend no assistance.

The Tories are divided, but those who are for carrying the act into execution are not very forward in lending their assistance towards it.

The Knts. of the Shire are afraid to oppose it, tho' Mr. Prowse is pretty well known to be not much inclined to it. Sir Charles Tynte is but half for it, for my Lady (his better half) is violently against it, but with the Act of Parliament on our side, and the instructions of this County to their members in '56, and with the examples of the neighbouring counties I hope we shall be able to carry it into execution.[1]

Poulett was right in this and also in thinking that the militia might become more popular once it got going. In January 1759 he could report that it had

become the fashion even for those who are not of the elect to learn the manual exercise, and many of the better sort of people, the modern yeomen of these days, have formed themselves into seperate companies, and learnt to do the Prussian exercise very well under the name of Prussian Volunteers.

Another very great advantage has arisen from having planned this Militia in such a proper manner as has in a great measure destroyed all distinction of parties in this county, for none who voluntarily enlist in His Majesty's service and take up arms in his defence can go any longer under any other denomination than friends to this Government. And gentlemen now associate and act together who were very shy lately and scarce knew one another before. Mr. Balch at the head of rigid Dissenters did not scruple travelling to London with Mr. Palmer, member for the university of Oxford, tho' I believe his friends are not entirely pleased with it.[2]

Cambridgeshire, too, was very inactive in 1757. Some tories were appointed deputies, notably Sir Thomas Hatton, his father-in-law Mr Ascham, and Sir John Hynde Cotton, son of a famous old tory leader. They made no trouble, however, and seemed gratified by being given office.[3] The onset of the riots was taken by everyone as a welcome excuse to do nothing further.[4] In 1758 neither whigs nor tories seem to have wished to do anything, but neither side wished the other to secure the credit of raising the militia. The first meeting (27 July) was a ludicrous contest in politeness. Cotton and Hatton asked Lord Royston, the lord lieutenant, if he did not intend to be colonel. Because of an opportune, erroneous but quite sincere[5]

[1] PRO. 30/8, vol. 53, ff. 109–10.   [2] Ibid., ff. 115–16.
[3] BM, Add. 35360, ff. 276–7. Cf. Add. 35351, ff. 396–7, 400.
[4] Ibid., f. 400. Hardwicke (ibid., f. 385) said he disliked riots but wished the popularity of the measure could be tested in that way.
[5] Cf. the end of the letter and BM, Add. 35352, ff. 24, 29.

doubt as to the legality of this, he declined. Royston told his father that

> the two Baronets professed great zeal for the bill, and willingness to take any commission, and that they had rather be Captains than Field Officers, which (by the by) I do not believe. Sir John wished Ld. Granby could be Colonel, and then the scheme would go on with spirit. I told them, I could not take an offer from them but in writing, as directed by the act. They agreed to that, but desired to put off it off (*sic*) till the next meeting, and then we might hear what had been done in other counties.—I thought, there was no harm in closing with the proposal, as it would give us time to prepare our *friends*, and discover more of the real intentions of the *others*. I do not doubt but some of the former will offer to take commissions and I have writ this evening to Ld. Montfort, to beg the favour of his attendance on the 15th. of next month, and that if the others make their offer in form, he would do us the honour to declare his readiness to be *colonel*. I shall then insist on their being explicit, and speaking out, they came now, with no other view, than to see how I should behave, and to give themselves leisure to look about and learn what was done in Suffolk and adjoining Counties . . . I endeavoured to observe a due medium between a *violent zeal*, and a *languid coldness* with regard to this nice and difficult project, and hope I gave them no advantage by anything that fell from me.[1]

Lord Hardwicke approved of what his son had done and thought it important that the baronets desired some action. He considered, however, that such people mostly interfered in the hope of gaining local influence from the distribution of the paid offices and the profit from the pay and clothing.[2] The Yorkes duly saw to it that some of their friends attended the next meeting ready to offer their services if the baronets did so but not otherwise. When the day came Hatton and Cotton offered to be major and captain respectively, and two other tories offered to be captains. Thereupon, Lord Montfort offered to be lieutenant-colonel and seven other whigs offered to be captains. By common consent the colonelcy was left vacant, to be offered to Lord Granby. Hardwicke told Newcastle that as the tories had come forward it had been impossible to do better. He attributed the great change in county feeling since the previous year to the influence of George Townshend, who was a friend of Ascham and through him could reach Hatton.[3]

[1] BM, Add. 35352, ff. 21-2. Cf. ff. 10-11, 14-16. On Montfort see below, pp. 312-13.

[2] *Ibid.*, ff. 24-5. For what it is worth, Horace Walpole says that the tory gentry helped to prejudice the people against the bill in 1757 because they were afraid that the whigs might gain from control of this patronage. *George II*, vol. ii, p. 232.

[3] BM, Add. 32882, ff. 374-8. Cf. Royston, Add. 35352, f. 22: the appointment in Norfolk of 'Lt.-Col. Sir Armyn Woodhouse is enough to make half the Tories in these parts put on the Cockade'.

Humbug was conspicuous in the subsequent proceedings. The tories seem to have thought that enough had been done that year[1] and Hardwicke was ready with legal argument to encourage this view.[2] At the next meeting Cotton proposed the postponement of the next steps until the spring.[3] Enough had been done to ensure that the county contingent was raised: indeed, Royston complained of the weakness of his friends in giving in more names than had been planned.[4] Save in the Isle of Ely the men were levied in the spring of 1759. On 12 July a large meeting was held to organise the regiment attended by sixteen officers in uniform 'who made a very genteel appearance'.[5] But at no stage had there been anything like a demonstration of enthusiasm.

Only modest progress was possible in conditions like these. By the end of June 1759 a force totalling 11,171 private men was under arms, and other units totalling 7320 privates were sufficiently far advanced to have received their arms by the end of the year. Two years' work since the passage of the original act had brought into being half at most of the force of 32,000 there provided for. Some progress had been made with levying some of the remaining men, but the lack of officers made this of no avail.[6] The friends of the militia had worked hard but seemed dispirited by the result. At the meeting in London on 7 April 1759, referred to in the last chapter, George Onslow found that there was 'never less spirit shown'. It did little but resolve on the calling of another meeting the following February, which Onslow predicted would be less well attended.[7]

(III) THE INVASION SCARE OF 1759:
THE MILITIA IN BEING AT LAST

The militia might very well have died the natural death so ardently wished for by Newcastle and his friends had there not been a reappearance of the danger which it had been meant to oppose. By the end of 1758 Britain had got the upper hand in the colonial war. Choiseul, newly arrived in power, hoped to redress the balance by an invasion of her metropolitan territory. He was attracted by the notion that such an attack would halt the British offensive by ruining British credit[8] and after only a few months' activity events seemed to be proving him right. For this he had to thank the divisions in the

[1] *Ibid.*, ff. 41–2.　　[2] *Ibid.*, f. 37.　　[3] *Ibid.*, ff. 57–9.　　[4] *Ibid.*, f. 39.
[5] BM, Add. 35659, f. 30; cf. ff. 22, 24, 28, and Add. 35352, ff. 78–81.
[6] Appendix B. Cf. BM, Add. 35893, f. 243. These totals suppose the units raised to have the full complement of privates, which they often did not.
[7] BM, Add. 32889, ff. 396, 400–1. He thought 130 or so had attended, about a third MPs, the rest mostly unknown to him.
[8] J. S. Corbett, *England in the Seven Years' War* (London, 1907), vol. ii, pp. 3, 4.

British cabinet, which his plans were ideally contrived to exploit. Newcastle and his friends were by now tiring of the war, and of Pitt. Alarmed by the preparations for invasion, they desired the concentration of force at home, to the detriment of Pitt's offensive plans. Pitt, however, made light of the danger and did relatively little to meet it. In April the funds fell ten per cent, and there were mutual recriminations. Newcastle blamed it on the extravagant demands of Pitt and his friends for money. But Holdernesse told Mitchell in Berlin that the trouble began through Newcastle trying to borrow at an unrealistically low rate, and had got worse because he and his friends had encouraged fears of invasion in order to weaken Pitt.[1] On 9 May there was a heated argument in cabinet. Pitt told his colleagues that they had given the alarm and measures must now be agreed upon to quiet it; but for his part he declined to take the danger of invasion seriously. Newcastle and Hardwicke urged on the contrary the reality of the threat. Bedford prudently confined himself to speaking of the danger to Ireland, of which he was now lord lieutenant. Holdernesse said nothing.[2]

It was in this situation that the government found itself obliged to make use of the militia. That this would at least be considered was made inevitable by the shortage of recruits. Already in December 1758 the army was 10,000 below its authorised strength and no attempt was made to remedy this by bringing in a bill to press men for the land service—perhaps because Pitt's supporters would not have liked it.[3] The forces at home were thus not easily able to replace by recruiting the diminution they suffered through Pitt's offensive plans. As early as 19 February ministers had discussed a suggestion that the more forward militia regiments might be used to guard prisoners of war and so release regular troops for more active duties.[4] At the meeting on 9 May Pitt seems to have proposed that a preliminary warning should be given to the lord lieutenants that the services of the militia might be required.[5] In view of his remarks at the meeting, it is likely that his object was simply to restore national morale[6] and to do so in a way that would discomfort those who had lowered it. His military answer to the French preparations seems at that time

---

[1] Cf. BM, Add. 32890, ff. 137–45 and Eg. 3461, ff. 165–8. For this paragraph in general see Corbett, vol. ii, pp. 1–15; Ruville, vol. ii, pp. 216–21, 228–32, 234–5.

[2] BM, Add. 32891, ff. 77–8. My interpretation of Newcastle's rough notes of Pitt's remarks is very slightly different from Corbett's, *loc. cit.*

[3] BM, Add. 32886, ff. 185–6. *Bedford Correspondence*, vol. ii, p. 371.

[4] See BM, Add. 33047, ff. 249–52; Add. 32888, f. 206.

[5] This seems to emerge from a memorandum of the 11th by Newcastle (BM, Add. 32891, f. 86). But the meeting of the 9th is not mentioned, and I am not sure that action was decided on then.

[6] Cf. *Ibid.*, f. 167.

to have consisted of naval precautions, the concentration of troops on the Isle of Wight and the provision of shipping to ensure their mobility.[1] All this was well under way before anything serious was done about the militia. But alarming intelligences multiplied, and in June a dispatch of Choiseul was intercepted giving a full account of an ambitious plan of attack.[2] Even Pitt's nerve seems to have been affected. When the ministers met on 17 May Hardwicke thought him dispirited and on the defensive.[3] When he learned (from Newcastle) the contents of Choiseul's dispatch, Pitt ordered the concentration of forces in camps both in England and Ireland, and seemed eager to have garrison duties taken over by the militia. He told Rigby that the Devon militia was one of their 'sheet anchors'. It was to garrison Plymouth and the king was impatient for it to march 'that the army might better be got together'.[4]

It was after the meeting on 17 May that both Newcastle and Pitt obtained lists of what militia regiments had begun to drill[5] and the ministers started consultations on the form of a royal message to parliament about the militia.[6] This message was presented on 30 May and did not go beyond saying that it might be necessary to embody the militia.[7] On 5 June Pitt sent out a circular to all lord lieutenants, repeating the terms of the message and asking what progress had been made in executing the militia acts.[8] As Hardwicke remarked,[9] this showed that he was adding the militia to his extensive executive responsibilities. But on the 12th Newcastle found him complacent and against drawing out the militia at once, since there were 40,000 regular troops in the British Isles.[10] Newcastle was exasperated by this and told Hardwicke that not more than 30,000 could be assembled for active operations, and if the 'famous' militia was not used to guard prisoners of war that number would be more than halved.[11] By the 17th he had decided to give Pitt a jolt by communicating his startling intelligence, and it was now that Pitt took the plunge.[12] One by one the more forward counties were called upon to mobilise their men.[13]

The friends of the militia now had a splendid chance to make the laggard counties catch up with the leaders. They had already spon-

---

[1] Corbett, vol. ii, pp. 8–17, 21–2.   [2] *Ibid.*, pp. 17–18.
[3] BM, Add. 32891, f. 171; cf. f. 167.
[4] Corbett, vol. ii, pp. 23–4. MSS. of 4th Duke of Bedford, vol. 39, f. 210. BM, Add. 32892, ff. 120–1.
[5] Pitt's is dated 23 May and lists 7491 men; Newcastle's is dated 22 May and lists 9391. PRO. 30/8, vol. 77, f. 189. BM, Add. 33047, f. 258.
[6] BM, Add. 32891, ff. 218, 233, 255, 265, 267–8, 269, 271, 273, 311–14.
[7] CJ, vol. xxviii, p. 600.   [8] SP. 41/30; and in BM, Add. 32891, ff. 423–5.
[9] *Ibid.*, ff. 404–5.   [10] BM, Add. 32892, ff. 26–7, 56.
[11] *Ibid.*, f. 59.   [12] *Ibid.*, ff. 120, 137–8.   [13] Appendix A.

sored a short act [1] perpetuating the arrangement of meetings for the recruitment of officers made in the act of 1758, which had originally been expected to be needed for one year only. When an address was moved in the commons in reply to the royal message of 30 May, the younger Vyner called for a second address asking the king to tell the lord lieutenants to do their duty, which they had neglected. Eventually, Cooke of Middlesex carried an address asking the king to direct them to use the utmost diligence in executing the law. [2] Pitt supported this address, though defending the lord lieutenants, and duly sent out a circular with his other one on 5 June.[3] For the rest of the year indeed, Pitt gave the militia more active support in his ministerial capacity than at any other time. His motives seem to have been a mixture of the political and the strategic. Hardwicke disliked the circular asking for a progress report and said that it would make people think that he was in league with Vyner. But Pitt said it was only to show those of the militia who were called out that they were chosen because the rest were not ready.[4] Horace Walpole thought that Pitt, so far from being in league with the tories, had bullied the reluctant militia officers into taking the field by threatening to have the militia laws repealed if they did not. Though unsupported by evidence, what he says is psychologically quite plausible.[5] But later in the year Bute said that Pitt's support of the militia was only '*par politique*' and complained that Newcastle's opposition to it gave Pitt a 'handle'.[6] Political considerations are to be seen when Pitt praised the militia in the debate on the address at the opening of the session of 1759-60. He said that without it he would have favoured the withdrawal of British troops from Germany.[7] The militia here was used to justify his change of principle on the German question.

Whatever its motives, Pitt's enthusiasm for the militia did no more than reflect a change in national feeling. Ambassador Mitchell was told that 'the Militia, which some time ago was a matter of mirth, or of sham politics with a great many, becomes now to be considered in another light.'[8] Of this, the clearest sign was the review of the

---

[1] 32 Geo. II, cap. 20.

[2] CJ, vol. xxviii, pp. 600–1. *Bedford Correspondence*, vol. ii, pp. 382–3. But the dates do not agree.

[3] SP. 41/30. The younger Vyner had proposed something similar the previous November. Bedford MSS., vol. 38, f. 160.

[4] BM, Add. 32891, ff. 401, 404–5.

[5] *George II*, vol. ii, pp. 356–7. He also says that the tories were 'weaned from their opposition' by the 'silent douceurs' of militia commissions 'without a sudden transition to ministerial employment'.

[6] BM, Add. 32896, f. 303. [7] BM, Add. 32898, f. 224. But cf. ff. 143–4.

[8] BM, Add. 6839, f. 147.

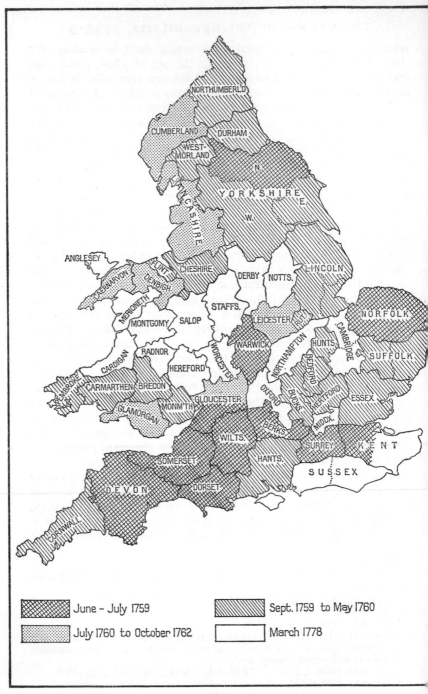

Map showing when the militia raised in each county under the Acts of 1757 and 1762 was first ordered to be embodied for actual service. See further, Appendix A.

Norfolk militia by the king on 17 July 1759. After an enthusiastic welcome by huge crowds of Londoners, they marched past at Kensington. Pitt was present, and wrote in glowing terms to his wife of their good appearance. 'What a charming account of our militia!' she replied, and went on to draw the moral that 'a military figure' could 'be acquired out of the army and without long practice—the true British soul will give the rest'.[1] The *Norwich Mercury* printed a letter which reported that the king had been often heard to 'call out "they are brave fellows", "they are fine fellows", etc.', and that he had asked the name of each officer and taken off his hat to each one as he marched by. The writer claimed, and surely with justice, that this had encouraged the militia in many other counties to offer to serve.[2] The pressure of public opinion in and on the laggard counties steadily mounted, and Newcastle in particular was placed in a more than usually comic position. His fears of invasion had been triumphantly vindicated: 'I *knew* it all along,' he exclaimed in a letter to Ambassador Yorke at the Hague.[3] But the danger had made him reverse his principles and become more eager to raise the militia than Pitt was, while at the same time his enemies did not fail to point out that the militia had not been raised in any county where he presided.[4] A patriotic ballad declared

> We ask not assistance of Hesse and Hanover,
> Nor need we to fetch our own Englishmen over;
> And why should we send for our neighbours the Dutch
> When as many Dutch herrings would serve us as much?
> All over the land they'll find such a stand,
> From our English Militia Men ready at hand,
> Though in Sussex and Middlesex folks are but fiddlesticks,
> While an old fiddlestick has the command.[5]

Newcastle was also bothered by discontent in the City that the militia had not been raised[6] and by a paragraph in the *Evening Post* on the subject of a county's right to protest to the king about the shortcomings of its lord lieutenant.[7]

Newcastle's dislike of the militia was as great as ever. He complained to the king of the political trouble they caused,[8] and told Hardwicke that they would bring destruction on the country. 'It will

---

[1] *Chatham Correspondence*, vol. ii, pp. 5, 6.
[2] See *Ipswich Journal*, 21 July and 4 August 1759.
[3] BM, Add. 32892, f. 230.   [4] See BM, Add. 32893, f. 146.
[5] *Flat Bottom Boats Gone to the Bottom.* Tune, 'Lillabullaro'. BM, Eg. 1719, f. 64. There is also an (inaccurate) list here showing what progress the different counties had made, published in the newspapers at the time.
[6] BM, Add. 32998, f. 318.   [7] BM, Add. 35418, f. 210.
[8] BM, Add. 32893, ff. 102-3, 283.

be a handle against us the next election and will one day or other prove fatal to this constitution.'[1] He and his friends tried everywhere to distract attention from the militia by sponsoring the raising of recruits for the army by public subscription.[2] But the issue could not be evaded, and especially not in Sussex which was a county standing right in the invader's likely path. Here Newcastle thought it essential that his friends should make a serious effort actually to raise the militia. He was frustrated only by their apathy.[3]

Gradually the friends of the militia increased their ascendancy. The royal message of 30 May had prompted the younger Vyner to move for a bill to cancel the suspension of proceedings which had been ordered in the less forward counties and allow the search for officers to begin again forthwith. He failed then to find a seconder.[4] But on the second day of the next session (14 November) leave was given for such a bill, and it received the royal assent only a month later.[5] By a final indignity to Newcastle, the initiative for this bill came from his own county of Middlesex. Here the county members had not at first been eager for action and by their advice Newcastle had suspended further proceedings till March 1760.[6] But when public excitement grew they denied that they had given their assent. As elsewhere, Newcastle proposed a subscription to raise recruits for the army, but the county members agreed to support this only if there were preparatory measures for the raising of the militia.[7] Two lieutenancy meetings were held as a result, and at the second, on 3 October, the deputies resolved to apply to parliament for an act revoking the suspension of proceedings under the militia laws in counties where that had been done. The members for the county and for Westminster were asked to move for such a bill, and Newcastle's help was also to be sought. The deputies agreed to meet again in November and had their proceedings published in four newspapers.[8]

This well-timed demonstration just before parliament met outraged Newcastle[9] and was completely successful. The four members

[1] BM, Add. 35418, f. 206. Cf. Add. 32893, f. 406.

[2] Numerous references especially in BM, Add. 32893–5.

[3] Newcastle was not lieutenant of this county, but was rightly regarded as having the authority thereof in fact. Many references in BM, Add. 32892, from f. 203, and Add. 32893.

[4] *Bedford Correspondence*, vol. ii, p. 384.

[5] 13 December. CJ, vol. xxviii, p. 632; LJ, vol. xxix, p. 559.

[6] BM, Add. 35418, f. 210.

[7] *Ibid.*, ff. 241–2.

[8] Both meetings wished to use part of the subscription for recruiting the militia. PRO. 30/8, vol. 27, ff. 98–9. BM, Add. 33047, f. 277. For the subscription see *ibid.*, ff. 273–6, 279–82, 323–4, and cf. n. 2.

[9] I assume that this is what BM, Add. 32896, f. 300 refers to as 'the impertinence of 13 deputy lieutenants'.

with the assistance of the younger Vyner[1] duly brought in and carried their bill. It required the lord lieutenants of counties where proceedings had been suspended to hold a meeting within a month to receive offers to take commissions. Thereafter, meetings were to be held at monthly intervals until enough officers had been found.[2] Gradually the number of laggard counties diminished until at the end of the war the greater part of the militia had been raised, and only in the midlands and North Wales was there an extensive area of inactivity.[3] Ironically, the Middlesex militia, though raised, had not been embodied for service. It is probable that the difficulties always met with in making the new system work in urban areas had already been encountered.[4]

Thus by 1760 the new militia was at last securely in being. Henceforth the great question was: would it disappear at the end of the war or would its friends succeed in turning it into a permanent institution?

[1] CJ, vol. xxviii, p. 632.   [2] 33 Geo. II, cap. 2.   [3] See Appendix A.
[4] Cf. below, pp. 281-5. See particularly BM, Add. 32900, f. 35; Add. 32915, ff. 304, 366; Add. 32943, ff. 392-4; Add. 33048, f. 15.

VII

1760 – THE FRUSTRATED
COUNTER-ATTACK

I N 1760 the enemies of the militia could do nothing much but
wait for the acts to expire. They managed, however, to inflict two
parliamentary defeats on their opponents on side issues. In the end
the militia benefited from these reverses. They stung Pitt into coming
out publicly in favour of prolonging its life, and by the end of the
year its enemies had as good as decided that it would be impossible
to oppose prolongation outright. In all this George II played an
important part. His support counted for much in the victories won
against the militia, and his death removed the force's staunchest
foe.

The issues over which the friends of the militia were defeated in
1760 were the extension of the new system to Scotland and the payment of the allowances to militiamen's families out of central funds.
There is not room in this work for a full account of the Scottish
militia. It was settled at the Restoration on similar lines to the English,
and it subsequently went through a similar process of degeneration.
A bill just after the Union to assimilate the Scottish militia system
to that of England was the occasion of the last use of the royal veto.[1]
Thereafter the subject attracted little attention.

The invasion scare of 1759 found Scotland in a very exposed
position. The regular force in the country was small, the coastline
to be guarded was long. Merchant ships were captured within sight of
land. The only French force of consequence to reach British
shores made a landing in Scotland. Thurot's small squadron sailed
from Dunkirk in October 1759. After a spell in Scandinavian
waters he landed on Islay in February 1760 to obtain fresh meat. He
then went to Ireland and exacted contributions from Carrickfergus

[1] For the text of the bill see BM, Add. 35891, ff. 242–6. I hope later to write an
account of the Scottish militia of the Restoration.

and Belfast: only after this was his force destroyed off the Isle of Man.[1]

The result was that the militia agitation spread to Scotland. On 26 November 1759 a newspaper advertisement summoned all the justices, heritors and land tax commissioners of the various Scottish shires then in Edinburgh to a meeting on the 30th. The purpose of the meeting was to call for a militia on the English plan. This was not stated in the advertisement but it appears that both the Lord Advocate and the Lord Justice Clerk were given advance notice of it; the latter was covertly rather sympathetic. The meeting appointed an impressive committee to work out a detailed plan: it comprised four peers,[2] six judges,[3] the Lord Provost of Edinburgh, four advocates and a merchant. What it did was to draft a bill by combining the militia acts of 1757 and 1758 and inserting amendments wherever Scottish conditions made this necessary. From Sir William Petty's calculation that Scotland had just over a million inhabitants to England's six, the committee concluded that the Scottish militia should be 6000 strong, that is, about a fifth of the English. This number was apportioned among the counties according to their land tax quotas. The intention was that the privy council should correct both the total and its apportionment when the number of men who could be called on to serve was known.

The plan was published with a commentary in January 1760.[4] Several pamphlets appeared in its support.[5] In October 1759 an Ayrshire county meeting had petitioned the king for the means of self-defence[6] and in April 1760 several counties petitioned parliament.[7] On 4 March 1760 the commons resolved to consider in committee the state of the Scottish militia laws. This was done on the 12th and a bill was ordered to amend them. On its introduction on the 24th it was

[1] Corbett, vol. ii, pp. 47, 88–91. *The Question Relating to a Scots Militia Considered... by a Freeholder* (2nd ed., Edinburgh, 1760), preface and pp. 22–40, where it is noted that the English MPs responsible for the militia bills had asked their Scottish sympathisers to hold back a while so as not to give the other side an extra argument against them. A. Henderson, *Considerations on the Question Relating to the Scots Militia* (2nd ed., Edinburgh, n.d.), pp. 1–7. On fears of Thurot, cf. BM, Eg. 3434, ff. 254–5. Memories of 1745 were also important, see BM, Add. 32903, ff. 398–9.

[2] Lords Errol, Dunmore, Gray and Elibank.

[3] Lords Milton, Stricken, Auchinleck, Nisbet, Coalston and Alemore.

[4] Copies, each with an explanation added in MS of how it had come into being, are in BM, Add. 35891, ff. 217–35 and Eg. 3434, ff. 256–76. Cf. the letter of Charles Airskine, Lord Justice Clerk, *ibid.*, ff. 254–5.

[5] Above, n. 1. The first pamphlet there mentioned was by Alexander ('Jupiter') Carlyle, a leading minister of the kirk; cf. his *Autobiography* (2nd ed., Edinburgh, 1860), pp. 399–401. At BM, Add. 33049, ff. 322–3, is another brief pamphlet.

[6] BM, Eg. 3434, ff. 246–7.

[7] CJ, vol. xxviii, pp. 847, 852, 856, 861–2.

ordered to be printed and the second reading was fixed for 15 April.[1] Its main parliamentary sponsor was Gilbert Elliot of Minto, then a lord of the Admiralty, who had been an adherent of the Grenvilles but was in process of transferring his allegiance to Bute.[2]

Newcastle and Hardwicke were far more resolute in their opposition to a Scottish militia than they proved to be in the case of England. They were not opposed in principle to Englishmen having arms but they considered the laws which then denied them to the Highlanders to be the chief defence against jacobitism. Now of the 6000 men of the projected force, 2491 were to come from the disarmed areas.[3] As for the rest, there was an argument against raising them which seems to have appealed strongly to all Englishmen: most of the cost would have to be borne by England. Comparison of the revenues of the two countries suggested that the proper size for a Scottish militia would be 1000 or less.[4] The principle that the expenditure on the defence of each country should be proportionate to its contribution seems very absurd. But one of the arguments of the Scottish pamphleteers was that a militia would mean employments for the Scottish nobility.[5] It was the prospect of others profiting at their expense which was displeasing to the English.

In 1759 Newcastle and Hardwicke tried to appease the Scots by putting forward their favourite expedient of noblemen's regiments. Certain favoured noblemen were to be made lord lieutenants and were to raise troops for home defence by their personal influence and the assistance of the counties.[6] The regiments raised were included in the annual estimate for the embodied militia instead of in that for the army.[7] They were known as Fencibles, a traditional Scottish term: the name and thing were to be much in vogue in the next two wars as an alternative to straightforward militia augmentation. It was in this form that the old ministerial tradition of a 'select militia' was perpetuated.[8]

The Fencibles did not prevent a militia agitation on this occasion, however. Only two corps were raised in the Highlands in Argyle and Sutherland. None were raised in the Lowlands, and various personal grievances made for trouble.[9] The Duke of Argyle had been worsted

---

[1] CJ, vol. xxviii, pp. 800, 814, 815, 819, 828.   [2] DNB.
[3] BM, Add. 32903, f. 396.   [4] BM, Add. 35891, f. 240; cf. ff. 236–9.
[5] *The Question*, pp. 41–2; cf. Henderson, pp. 1–7.
[6] On the genesis of the plan see BM, Add. 35450, f. 261; Add. 32893, ff. 58, 60.
[7] See, e.g., CJ, vol. xxviii, pp. 638, 946. These estimates originated with the ministers, unlike the annual measure for paying the *unembodied* militia; cf. above, p. 145 and below, p. 347.
[8] Below, pp. 215, 219.
[9] Lauderdale was disappointed of a regiment. BM, Add. 32893, ff. 130, 483–6. Add. 32897, f. 100; Add. 32901, f. 430.

by Bute in several questions of military patronage and seems to have interested himself in the militia as a means of conserving his own influence.[1] It was apparently on his advice that Holdernesse returned a friendly official answer to the Ayrshire petition.[2] Elliot seems to have had strong hopes that most of the ministers would think it best to support him. He discussed his plans with Newcastle before the debate on 4 March, and after it complained of the coldness of the administration.[3]

The first two debates on the question were not encouraging for the opponents of the militia. On 4 March Elliot explained to the commons that the Scottish militia was almost defunct. He praised the English militia and said that while one country was secure the other lived in terror and longed for arms. He claimed that the Highlands were completely subdued, the land being all in loyal hands, and so it would be safe to arm them; indeed, the disarming acts were about to expire. The only militia in being, that of Argyle,[4] had been raised in the Highlands. He urged the need of uniformity in the laws to cement the union of the two countries. He was seconded by Oswald, a treasury lord, and supported by the Townshends, George mildly and Charles violently. Hume Campbell unsuccessfully tried to damp things down by suggesting that all the laws relating to the arming of the Scottish people be reviewed.[5]

On 12 March the commons considered in committee whether anything should be done. Newcastle's younger followers, who looked to the Duke of Devonshire for a lead, were confident that they could carry the question in the negative. They felt sure of a majority among the English members and were encouraged by hearing that Pitt was undecided and by his failure to attend the debate.[6] But to make up for this, Legge and one secretary to the Treasury were for having a bill; the other secretary ostentatiously walked out. Oswald was in the chair,[7] and Hardwicke thought that his attitude throughout did great harm. Charles Yorke seems to have spoken well against the measure, but there was no proper canvass to mobilise the group's full voting strength. Worse still, the mistake was made of attacking the English militia instead of sticking to the special circumstances of Scotland. This brought all the partisans of the English militia down on the Scots' side, and the motion for a bill was carried by a majority con-

[1] BM, Add. 32902, ff. 453–8, 478–9.
[2] BM, Eg. 3434, ff. 250–1, 277–9.
[3] BM, Add. 32902, f. 431. Add. 32903, f. 84.
[4] I.e. the Fencibles.
[5] BM, Add. 35374, ff. 164–5. Charles Townshend had been in Scotland the previous summer and seen its defenceless state.
[6] BM, Add. 32903, ff. 228, 297.
[7] BM, Add. 35360, f. 300. Cf. CJ, vol. xxviii, p. 814.

sisting according to Hardwicke of the Scots, the tories and the enthusiasts for the English militia.[1] Devonshire's friends thought that they had been shamefully let down and refused to do anything more. Hardwicke retorted that 'a few warm young men talking zealously at Arthur's over night' could not carry a question in the commons. The king was very displeased with Newcastle and his friends for not showing more energy, and Newcastle's assurance that the bill would be thrown out or watered down did not satisfy him. Newcastle and the king both thought that Pitt was encouraging projects such as this to divide Newcastle's friends and so strengthen himself and the tories. Newcastle lamented that a body not a sixth part of the house of commons should thus be shown more consideration than the rest.[2]

Newcastle remained full of fight, however. In Charles Yorke he had an able speaker willing to take the lead in the commons and if efforts there failed he was ready to stir up the lords.[3] He, too, had reason to believe that Pitt was uneasy about the proposed bill and at all events in favour of 'drawing the line'—that is, of excluding the Highlands from its operation.[4] Newcastle and his chief ministerial friends discussed the subject over dinner on 20 March and on 3 April they finally decided to try and get the bill thrown out on second reading in the commons.[5] Newcastle at once set on foot a most elaborate canvass. 'I went to work in the old way,' he told his friend Kinnoul, 'practised so often with and by your lordship with success. I summoned avowedly all our friends from every part of the kingdom, and our success more than answered our expectations.'[6] One of those huge lists which were a feature of eighteenth-century parliamentary management was drawn up, showing not only the members to be approached but in each case the person supposed to have influence with the member through whom the approach was to be made.[7] Newcastle wrote many letters to both members and patrons.[8] Devonshire was given the task of negotiating with Henry Fox and his friends,[9] and James West, secretary to the treasury, was sent to canvass other notables.[10] One party leader was not mentioned in the list but was not forgotten. On a hint from Newcastle the king

---

[1] BM, Add. 32903, f. 294.　　[2] Ibid., ff. 294, 296–8.　　[3] Ibid., f. 297.
[4] BM, Add. 35419, f. 172. Add. 32904, f. 343.
[5] BM, Add. 32904, f. 205. Add. 32998, ff. 418–19. Those present on 20 March were Devonshire, Lincoln, Hardwicke, Barrington, Anson, Mansfield, Sir Thomas Robinson, Charles Yorke and Newcastle.
[6] BM, Add. 32907, f. 16. This interesting letter gives a brief account of all the parliamentary events described in this chapter.
[7] BM, Add. 33034, ff. 351–64. Cf. Add. 32904, f. 257.
[8] Such as BM, Add. 32904, ff. 184, 253, 255; cf. ff. 350, 380.
[9] And Gower and Rockingham. Ibid., ff. 205, 259–60, 306.
[10] Ibid., ff. 257, 346.

told 'His little Levée' to attend the debate.[1] One does not have to wait until the reign of George III to find 'king's friends' in the commons.

The debate on 15 April was opened by Sir W. Williams in a misguided speech lashing out against all militias, which he thought bad in England and worse in Scotland. Rose Fuller, by contrast, said that he supported the English militia but was against one for Scotland, where there had been disaffection in every reign since the revolution. Sir Henry Ereskine sought to show that Scotland had a right to a militia and that the time was suitable for establishing one. The younger Thomas Townshend explicitly avoided considering the general pros and cons of a militia and argued simply that it would be unsafe to establish one in Scotland and also unnecessary because there was hope that the war would soon end. Three other speakers[2] thought the measure untimely. Beckford, however, claimed that the fourth article of the Treaty of Union gave the Scots an absolute right to what they asked for. But Vyner, that great militia stalwart, was resolved to oppose the bill unless the whole expense was met by Scotland herself. Here we see the prejudices of the tory country gentleman in fascinating internecine strife.

Oswald next made an old-fashioned speech on the danger of leaving the defence of a free country entirely to a standing army. He was answered by Lord Barrington, and then the Lord Advocate, Robert Dundas, made a much-applauded speech against the bill in which he was able to claim that Midlothian and Fife were against it.[3] Elliot answered him forcefully and attacked 'the Line'. This awkward moment was chosen by Pitt to make a 'confused and unconnected' speech in favour thereof and in defence of the English militia, which he again said had enabled troops to be sent abroad. He ended with the threat that if it incurred 'frowns' from men in power he would be against sending any more. A long speech by Charles Yorke ended the debate. The bill was rejected by 194 votes to 84.[4] Of the Scottish members only Hope Weir of Linlithgowshire joined Dundas in voting against the bill.[5] The episode strikingly demonstrates the independence of MPs at that time. Commonly considered the most servile element in the unreformed house of commons, the Scottish members defied Pitt and Newcastle alike when the interests of their country were at stake. Not that it did any good.

[1] *Ibid.*, f. 344.
[2] Walsingham, Nugent, Lord H. Poulett.
[3] 'Stated the case of his own county and the shire of Fife.' Cf. BM, Add. 32904, f. 388: 'shire of Fife against it'. He sat for Midlothian.
[4] BM, Add. 32904, ff. 392–4. CJ, vol. xxviii, p. 872. Six members pledged to Newcastle were absent. Add. 32905, f. 12.
[5] BM, Add. 35449, ff. 234–5. For attempts to canvass the others, Add. 32904, f. 176.

II

Meanwhile, the friends of the English militia were experiencing a growing discomfiture which the defeat of the Scottish bill helped to make worse. The war had now reached the stage where there were few brilliant victories to be won against France overseas, while the impending collapse of Prussia pointed to the need of unrewarding British exertions on the continent to preserve Hanover. Peace negotiations were tried and failed. The ministers therefore accepted the need for greater efforts in Germany.[1] As 1760 wore on it became increasingly evident that in order to make the army fully available for action there the militia would have to continue embodied for the duration of the war. Service in the militia seems to have filled some of the country gentlemen with martial ardour. Newcastle records a curious conversation in February 1760 between Pitt and Lord Denbigh, the tory colonel of the Warwickshires. Pitt had been refusing to send more troops to Germany to relieve the tottering King of Prussia. Denbigh demurred and said that everybody—meaning no doubt his own friends—was in favour. Pitt was very angry and

> entered into the character of My Lord Denbigh—That he had no knowledge of the sentiments of *those gentlemen*—That indeed *their point* was, to make us depend upon the Militia only—That he'd been for sending troops when the run was against it

and would now oppose it though it was popular.[2] However, the country gentlemen as a body do not seem to have taken kindly to the prolongation of the militia's embodiment. It was felt that the force was being treated more or less as regular troops, in violation of the law and for the sake of undesirable continental measures. The special virtues of the institution—particularly, that men would not be rendered unfit for civil employment by their military service—would be destroyed by lengthy embodiment. Worst of all, instead of the saving of money that had been hoped for, there was heavy additional expense.[3] The Scottish debates publicised these grievances, and one observer thought that the English militia had

> had a thorough roasting, and is scouted out of all credit, as a most ridiculous, expensive, and to the common men (as to morals and industry) ruinous project.[4]

In the all-important matter of finance the family allowances were the sorest point. The militia naturally ceased to be a cheap force when

[1] Corbett, vol. ii, pp. 71–86.
[2] BM, Stowe, vol. 263, ff. 15–16. Cf. O. A. Sherrard, *Lord Chatham: Pitt and the Seven Years' War* (London, 1955), pp. 354–5.
[3] *Reflections Without Doors on What Passes Within* (London, 1760), pp. 7–12, 14–15. BM, Add. 32913, f. 332. HMC, *Matcham*, p. 47. Cf. p. 10, n. 8.
[4] Edmund Pyle to Samuel Kerrich, 26 April (A. Hartshorne, ed., *Memoirs of a Royal Chaplain, 1729–1763* (London, 1905), p. 321) quoted by Sherrard, p. 361.

it was in service all the time, but in some ways it remained cheaper than the army.[1] But the act of 1758 had laid down that when the men were on active service their families should get such relief as was ordered by one justice; the parish overseers of the poor were to pay it and be reimbursed from the county stock.[2] This was a revolutionary humanitarian innovation in the British military system and may be said to represent the victory of the militia riots over the parsimony of the country gentlemen. It tended to make the embodied militia more expensive than an equal number of regular troops. Worse still, this extra expense was not paid for out of general taxation as the militia as a whole now was. Like the old militia, it was a burden falling exclusively on the rates—on the land.

The whole situation was very awkward for Pitt. The continental measures which he supported (however reluctantly) were distasteful to his friends the country gentlemen. The militia, at first a popular distraction, was now becoming distasteful too. By way of atonement he pressed for the redress of the grievance over family allowances. When this proved impossible to achieve he tried to restore the attractiveness of the whole militia question by raising the demand that the new militia be made permanent.[3]

It was in February 1760 that the allowances question came to the fore. Some of the colonels of the regiments of militia that had been called out had held a meeting to discuss the need for extra funds that had arisen in consequence.[4] Lord Shaftesbury presented their conclusions to Newcastle as head of the treasury. The most contentious of them concerned the families: Shaftesbury found it advisable to tell Pitt of this also. It was proposed that this charge should be taken over by the central government. To keep it down, quarter sessions in each county should fix a scale of allowances, as was done in Shaftesbury's own county of Dorset. Shaftesbury explained that the existing system penalised those counties that had been zealous enough to raise the militia and 'people request to be relieved in the matter'. He told Pitt that representations were coming in from all over England, and the question became more urgent every day.[5]

Newcastle and his friends were at first determined that nothing

[1] The officers would not have to be given half-pay after the war and at first £1500 p.a. per battalion was saved on clothing (Add. 35891, f. 236). But cf. below, pp. 344–7.
[2] 31 Geo. II, cap. 26, s. 28.
[3] BM, Add. 32913, ff. 331–2. For the same purpose he helped to promote an act for tightening up the system of landed qualifications for MPs. Walpole, *George II*, vol. ii, pp. 435–7.
[4] Those present at the meeting were Lords Shaftesbury, Orford and Bruce and Messrs. Beckford, Northey, Vyner, Affleck and Bacon.
[5] BM, Add. 33047, ff. 336–8. PRO. 30/8, vol. 56, ff. 25–8. See, too, below, pp. 345–6.

should be done. By the end of March the friends of the militia were preparing a bill to deal with the matter, and Shaftesbury conveyed to Newcastle an offer to drop this if the government put a clause in some other bill by which the counties could claim repayment each year of what they had spent on militiamen's families.[1] Newcastle laid this offer before his friends in the ministry and they advised him to reject it.[2] Pitt angrily reproached Newcastle for this, but Newcastle told Hardwicke that he was bound to be blamed by one side or the other and had made his choice. He was eager in any case to come out publicly against the Scottish bill.[3] No doubt it affected his attitude to the English militia.

But the further development of the Scottish question soon drove Newcastle in the contrary direction. He was anxious to divide the friends of the militia in the two countries, and spoke of Yorkshire being the best barrier to Scotland.[4] Consequently, he became anxious to remedy the grievances of the English militia. The victory of his friends on 15 April frightened him: fierce party conflict was not to his taste and might break up the ministry. He told Rigby that 'these are experiments which must not be tried every day and only when the importance of the question requires it'.[5] To the king he said that the success had been too encouraging for comfort: they must not break with their 'friends'[6]

It was in this situation that Pitt made a strong effort to get satisfaction for the English militia. The commons gave leave for a bill about family allowances on 1 April, Pitt apparently indicating his support.[7] The bill was not presented until 30 April[8] and in the interim there was much bargaining, especially after the Scottish bill had been disposed of. On 18 April Pitt told Barrington the Secretary at War that it was time to decide whether or not to send substantial reinforcements to Germany. He was against it himself unless something was done to keep the militia in good humour by passing the families bill. Barrington passed this on to Newcastle, remarking that clearly the passage of the bill was Pitt's price for agreeing to reinforcements.[9] Newcastle told Hardwicke that unless an expedient could be found the ministry

[1] BM, Add. 32903, ff. 378, 390. Cf. the undated draft clauses, *ibid.*, f. 394; Add. 32999, f. 52; Add. 33035, f. 11.
[2] BM, Add. 32903, f. 392. Same persons present as discussed about the Scottish bill, p. 166, n. 5.
[3] BM, Add. 35419, ff. 184–5.
[4] BM, Add. 32904, f. 388. Rockingham criticised the opponents of the Scottish bill for attacking the English militia as well (*ibid.*, f. 306).
[5] *Ibid.*, ff. 441–2.   [6] BM, Add. 32905, f. 12.
[7] Apparently Lord Strange and Sir F. Dashwood complained that the militia were being kept up to support German measures and would be 'set adrift' when no longer needed for this. BM, Add. 32904, f. 161. CJ, vol. xxviii, p. 853.
[8] *Ibid.*, p. 899. By John Pitt.   [9] BM, Add. 32904, f. 426.

would break up. All he could think of was a parliamentary resolution that the counties would receive reasonable satisfaction when the militia had been discharged.[1] Hardwicke was less alarmed. He said that six weeks before Pitt had shown himself hardly willing to consider sending out reinforcements. Since then the hope of peace had faded and his views had changed: if Newcastle and Devonshire stood firm he would probably give in without conditions. Disharmony would be the result, however, so Hardwicke also favoured an expedient. He thought Newcastle's would not do because it postponed payment and supposed an absolute decision to disband the militia, in place of their existing plan to let it expire. He thought Pitt would 'fly out' at any such overt suggestion. Instead, he suggested that they found out exactly what was in the bill and agreed with as much of it as possible. In return Pitt was to agree to the reinforcements and he and his friends were to promise not to bring in a bill to make the militia perpetual until after the next general election (due in the following year), when the sense of the people would be better known. The existing acts did not expire till the end of the next session but one and by that time, Hardwicke hoped, the war would be over and the great argument for continuing the militia would be gone.[2]

Something now happened which made the bargaining position of the friends of the militia decisively worse—nothing less than the personal intervention of the king. What exactly happened is obscure, but it is clear that he refused to give his approval for the bill's introduction—necessary because it was a money bill.[3] He had already told Newcastle that if a bill to make the militia perpetual was presented to him he would veto it. Newcastle thought that this might deter the bravest from bringing it in.[4] It rather seems as if a knowledge of his intention regarding the lesser measure was enough to make its authors drop the idea of making the families a charge on the land tax.[5] On 23 April Newcastle reported Pitt eager to find an expedient which would make it unnecessary for the king to recommend the bill. Hardwicke, meanwhile, had studied it and produced a proposal for its amendment, to which Pitt agreed.[6] But Pitt also warned Newcastle

---

[1] *Ibid.*, f. 437. A gesture in this direction had already been considered just before the last Scottish debate: Add. 32904, ff. 343–4; cf. ff. 361–3.

[2] BM, Add. 32904, ff. 454–5.

[3] See p. 172, n. 2. On the constitutional point involved see Thomson, *Constitutional History*, p. 205.

[4] BM, Add. 32904, f. 344.

[5] This seems hinted at by Newcastle's memoranda for the king dated 22 April, where the need for the royal recommendation is mentioned, and the dropping of the clause about the land tax is put beside the name of Legge without explanation. BM, Add. 32905, f. 39; cf. f. 47.

[6] Add. 32905, ff. 61–2. Cf. p. 172, n. 1, 4.

that if he knew for certain what he now suspected, that his colleagues intended to avoid a prolongation of the militia laws, he would know what to do next morning; and if a prolonging bill was not introduced next session he would resign and himself second a militia bill in the session thereafter. He was not unfriendly but declared he would no longer amuse the country gentlemen.[1] Caught in a tight corner, he was bound to make a counterstroke.

The decisive moment came in the commons on 25 April. According to Walpole, Lord Strange asked outright if it was true that the bill was delayed because the king would not consent to it. Pitt was obliged to protect the king and yet satisfy his friends. What he said is not altogether clear. Walpole says that he made the excuse that the session was now too far advanced for action.[2] It seems that Vyner asked for an assurance that the militia would be continued and he accordingly came out in favour of a bill for that purpose next session. Newcastle understood that he had spoken only in his private capacity and with a warning of the strength of the opposition likely to be met.[3] Hardwicke had heard a much more alarming version of the pledge from Devonshire. Pitt had declared that if the militia were not continued he would regard the country as undone. He had said that a continuation bill ought to be moved at the very start of the next session, before supply was considered, and promised to second any motion then made.[4]

The day after this debate John Pitt, the main sponsor of the bill, conferred with Hardwicke and accepted a compromise. The counties were to certify their family expenses to the Exchequer each year and be reimbursed by means of a levy on the counties at large. Thus the counties where the militia was not embodied would subsidise the rest.[5] It was now possible to bring in the bill and next day (1 May) Pitt accordingly agreed in cabinet (with some reluctance) to send six

---

[1] BM, Add. 35419, f. 199. The second Earl of Hardwicke noted on this letter that in this reign Pitt made the tories his party; later, when they took up with Bute, he switched to the 'Warm Whigs'.

[2] So far I have followed Walpole, *George II*, vol. ii, pp. 437–8 (where the Scottish bill is also mentioned). He does not give a date but the speech he attributes to Pitt is clearly the same as that referred to in Newcastle's letter next cited. He notes that Speaker Onslow had on an unspecified occasion called the commons' attention to the need for royal approval. Newcastle in his letter says that the Speaker approves of Hardwicke's expedient as being in accordance with the rules of the house. Walpole speaks of the issue as that of militia expenses in general. But most of these, even for the unembodied militia, were already met from central funds.

[3] BM, Add. 35419, ff. 200–1.

[4] BM, Add. 32905, f. 111. Walpole's version is nearer Hardwicke's than Newcastle's.

[5] *Ibid.*, ff. 111–12. I deduce the content of Hardwicke's proposals from the clauses proposed in committee on the bill, cf. below.

battalions to Germany.[1] But the compromise was rejected by the commons. On the second reading of the bill, Sir John Cust said that the proposed method of paying the families was ineffectual and expensive. Thornton thought that it would be better to let such families as required it depend on poor relief. Ongley attacked the militia in general. Cooke said that a heavy charge was to be laid on the land which ought to fall universally: this, of course, was what the bill had been designed to alter, but Hardwicke's alterations made it merely reapportion the burden among the ratepayers. Beckford and Pitt both defended the bill as being the best that could be got. Pitt reaffirmed his preference for relief out of the supplies in general or the land tax but pointed out the danger that army and navy families might be led to demand the same thing. In committee the clause ordering counties to make returns of expenditure to the Treasurer's Remembrancer in the Exchequer was carried, but the clause requiring the Remembrancer to apportion the total among the counties in general was lost, leaving the other as a vestigial appendage.[2] The bill as passed merely fixed a scale of allowances, based on the rate of wages in each locality, and confined them for the future to the families of men balloted and serving in person. All families who were then receiving allowances were, however, to continue to do so. The bill also reduced the establishment of officers, and allowed any officer thereby rendered supernumerary to go on indefinite leave without pay.[3] This was calculated to save money and please those to whom lengthy embodiment was distasteful. The main grievance of the country gentlemen remained unrelieved. After the king's intervention it was impossible to bring in a plan that did anything material for them.

III

Newcastle and his friends had every reason to be pleased with the outcome of the session of 1760, which was a great demonstration of their parliamentary strength.[4] True, Pitt was now publicly pledged to work for the continuation of the militia and the friends of the cause

[1] *Ibid.*, ff. 196, 244. Pitt insisted that the best militia regiments be encamped, 'to make the Face of an army at Home'. Hardwicke thought that this might make the king like the force better.

[2] 33 Geo. II, cap. 22, s. 3. Families were to be paid for by the county for which their men served, irrespective of where they lived (s. 6). For the commons' proceedings, BM, Add. 32905, f. 339; CJ, vol. xxviii, pp. 911, 913, 914, 916–18, 921. It seems that the bill was introduced minus the most controversial clauses, but that everybody knew what these contained.

[3] ss. 1, 2, 7, 10 of the act.

[4] 'our great majority, evident to all the world, when we would exert it, made the remaining business of the session very easy'.—Newcastle to Kinnoull on the Scottish affair, BM, Add. 32907, f. 17.

were encouraged by the approach of a general election. An English pamphleteer said

> that in case any disposition should be made to stave off the next year's intention, such a spirit might arise among Militia Friends, as may make them recommend, support and assist each other in particular counties and places, who might return even a more Militia Parliament than the present.[1]

A Scottish pamphleteer had similar hopes of advancing the plan for a militia there[2] and attempts were made to unseat the only Scottish member who opposed it.[3] The Convention of the Royal Burghs voted thanks to Ereskine, Elliot and Oswald and produced some sort of address to the throne which they annoyed the Duke of Argyle by asking him to present.[4] An attempt was made to have the question discussed by the General Assembly of the Church of Scotland, but soundings revealed that there would be no majority for a violent motion so the question was not brought forward.[5] In 1762 a Poker Club was formed in Edinburgh 'to stir up the fire and spirit of the country'.[6]

But there are signs that neither in England nor in Scotland was the militia agitation at all intense. When a bill for the continuance of the English militia finally appeared in 1762, the Scottish members considered bringing in a bill for their own country and enlisted the extremely lukewarm support of Bute. But nothing came of it.[7] In England there seems to have been only one major attempt to turn the militia to electoral account and that was a failure. In September 1760 the Dean of Lincoln informed Hardwicke that he had seen a letter to the justices of the county from four tory officers of its northern battalion of militia regarding the choice of county members. They said that the officers of the militia had received many letters suggesting that as between them they had a great deal of property and influence, they should consult together on the subject. However, they preferred to leave it to a meeting of the county and urged that one be called. The Dean coupled this with rumours that gentlemen would

---

[1] *Reflections Without Doors*, pp. 18–19. The words are in inverted commas. The pamphlet refers (p. 11) to the promise of a Right Honourable patriot to support a new bill next year, so must have been written after the close of the session just described. It is concerned, however, solely with the question of expense and does not mention prolongation.

[2] *The Question*, pp. 29–32.

[3] Dundas having been made a judge. BM, Add. 35449, ff. 234–5.

[4] BM, Add. 35449, ff. 250, 268–9.   [5] *Ibid.*, ff. 234–5. Add. 32905, f. 335.

[6] P. Hume Brown, *History of Scotland* (Cambridge, 1909), vol. iii, p. 342; citing Henry Mackenzie, *Life of Mr John Home* (Edinburgh, 1822), pp. 26–7.

[7] BM, Add. 32935, ff. 312–13, 328–9, 331–2, 364–5, 392. Add. 35449, ff. 331, 334–5. Add. 35421, f. 219.

stand on the militia interest, both in Lincolnshire and Essex.[1] Hardwicke remarked to Newcastle that Vyner, one of the members for Lincolnshire, was a militia enthusiast, and his son was an officer in the force. No doubt they hoped to drive out the other member for the county, Whichcote, and so end the amicable division of the representation between whig and tory. A newspaper advertisement seemed to confirm the rumour that the same thing was planned in Essex. Hardwicke thought that the officers of the embodied militia, 'confined to live and club together', might fall into the habit of combining for other purposes. He recalled a committee of the commons appointed to look into the abuses of gaols, whose members 'became banded together for factious purposes' for the rest of that parliament.[2]

Newcastle, however, received encouraging news from his relation, Lord Monson, who managed the borough of Lincoln.[3] The disturbers of the county peace—who included a man expelled from Cambridge for seditious activity—had so exasperated the whigs that they were going to put up a second candidate to stand with Whichcote against Vyner.[4] Eventually, one party nominated Vyner and Sir John Thorold, the other Whichcote and Lord Brownlow Bertie. Monson was threatened with opposition in his borough in retaliation for his stand in the county.[5] But the tories soon collapsed. Vyner actually asked for Newcastle's support, saying that he was in no way the cause of dissension.[6] On the completion of his canvass, Whichcote was confident of winning by a large majority.[7] Meanwhile it had become known that there would be no contest in Essex.[8] The militia was not destined to figure as an independent electoral force.[9]

Newcastle and his friends therefore had a good chance of success if they opposed the prolongation of the militia's life. Yet in the end they virtually decided not to fight. The reasons for this decision form a most instructive guide to their political philosophy.

---

[1] BM, Add. 35596, ff. 174–5.

[2] BM, Add. 32912, ff. 299–300, cited by Namier, *American Revolution*, 2nd ed., p. 118; see, too, p. 188. Namier suggests that this refers to the famous committee to which Oglethorpe belonged; interesting, since Oglethorpe was a militia agitator too

[3] Namier, *Structure*, p. 107.

[4] BM, Add. 32912, ff. 281, 326–8. The Dean concluded that the idea had not really come from the militia at all. Add. 35596, ff. 178–9.

[5] BM, Add. 32913, f. 499. Add. 32914, ff. 46–7.

[6] BM, Add. 32914, f. 297. Newcastle's pledges of support to Monson, Bertie and Whichcote are at ff. 191, 193, 195.

[7] BM, Add. 32916, ff. 306–7. For an attempt to arrange a compromise, ff. 220, 302.

[8] BM, Add. 32913, f. 26.

[9] See further, below, pp. 337–8.

Newcastle, at first, was very pugnacious. In August he told Hardwicke that he was determined to oppose Pitt's promised motion for continuance. All their friends agreed with this, and the younger Onslow thought that it could be rejected by as big a majority as the Scottish bill. Accordingly, their friends should be summoned to attend for action on the first day of the session. But the opposing party seemed no less combative, and Devonshire found Temple unconcerned at the prospect of a rift in the ministry.[1] Hardwicke therefore was against a struggle. He did not agree with Onslow and was disturbed by what Temple had said: it was essential that the ministry should not break up while the war continued. If Pitt proposed to make the militia perpetual

> I see no avoiding it, but that it must be withstood. But then all possible endeavours should be used to bring him to some temperament, as suppose to a further term of five years. If that would do, perhaps the King and your friends might give way to it, if the war should be continued another year; for I have met with several persons, enemies to the Militia in general, who have owned themselves convinced that it has been of some use, or convenience, during the war.[2]

Newcastle replied that any continuation looked dangerously like perpetuity. It would not be so bad if it was specifically for the duration of the war. He thought, and Hardwicke agreed, that the best thing would be to wait until the beginning of a new parliament and see if the war was then likely to continue long.[3]

By mid-October Newcastle had almost given up the idea of making the militia a party question. He was furious on learning from Lady Yarmouth, the king's mistress, that Pitt was still determined to raise the issue of continuance. He was angered by Pitt's project of attacking Belleisle, off the mouth of the Loire: he and Hardwicke thought that this was partly a ruse to denude the country of regular troops and make the militia appear indispensable. He was doubtless encouraged by Lady Yarmouth's thinking that the king would never assent to the projected bill. But all he was determined on was individual resistance. To Hardwicke he wrote:

> It is high time for us to come to some joint resolution. For my own part I am so thoroughly convinced that the measure of a National Militia will be the most destructive to our constitution and the liberties of it in many shapes, that no consideration, no advice, no authority, shall or

[1] BM, Add. 32910, f. 130.
[2] BM, Add. 32910, ff. 171–2. He thought co-operation with Pitt in the general election unavoidable. Mansfield said that 'many who are sick of the thing are strongly dipped in the general question'. See *ibid.*, ff. 397–8, 427–31.
[3] *Ibid.*, ff. 232–3. Add. 35419, ff. 266–7. See, too, Add. 35420, f. 65. Add. 32912, ff. 189–90.

can induce me to contribute to the continuance of it one moment longer than the present act of parliament exists. But whether any opposition, or public measure to oppose it, shall be taken, must be left to the opinion of others who think with me as to the measure itself. If I am in the house of lords when it comes up, no consideration shall prevent me from being against it. .... I am far from being very sure that Mr. Pitt may not take this opportunity to go out; pretending that he can't serve if a measure so essential to his system of government and administration is opposed or not suffered to pass. I see the distress the king, the public, and the administration will be in, in that case;

Nevertheless

as to my own conduct *I am determined*; but as to the making it a measure to oppose, that must depend upon the opinions and resolutions of others. I am so much in earnest that if my remaining in business and acting in the manner I must act would have, as I fear it will, a bad effect, I would most willingly go out amicably and content myself with giving my private vote against it. But to be for it, in employment, or not to oppose it if there is any opposition to it, I cannot in conscience submit to. To have an expedition crammed down one's throat one day, and such a measure as this, ten thousand times worse than twenty ridiculous expeditions, is too much for me to swallow.[1]

Even this was too much for Hardwicke. He now favoured a prolongation of the militia laws for two years: partly for the legal reason that there were now men in the militia whose term of service would not expire until after the militia laws did so, partly because many who were 'against this militia in general' thought it

of use during the war. This makes it to be wished that the consideration of continuing it for any length of time should come on after a peace is made, when this temporary argument will not exist.

The king's intention to use his veto 'will not be stood to'; it 'would be a strong measure; His Majesty has never done it; nor has [it] been done in above threescore years'. It was inconsistent with the commendation of the militia in a speech from the throne as lately as 1756 and 'the same reasons which induced the king to submit to that will prevail again, I mean the obtaining support to carry on the war'. There was no real eagerness to oppose a bill in the commons 'unless in some of the warm young men. Several of Your Grace's own friends are really for it'. Newcastle had not always opposed militia legislation and as a lord lieutenant he had helped to execute it: he might be charged with inconsistency if he opposed further legislation and in any case to give a 'private vote' against it

---

[1] BM, Add. 35420, ff. 88–90. Cf. on Belleisle, Add. 32913, ff. 45–54, 67–71; Corbett, vol. ii, pp. 94–101.

in your station would be worst and most unbecoming of all; and to quit your station at present I foresee is impossible.[1]

Newcastle was not eager to take this advice. He was under most disagreeable pressure in the contrary direction from the king, who failed entirely to see why he could not dispose of the projected bill. 'This parliament is the Duke of Newcastle's; he can fling out this bill for the continuance of the militia if he pleases,' he told Lady Yarmouth. To Newcastle he said that 'he would not permit it' and 'You promised me to fling it out.'

'Yes, sir, if I can,' said the Duke, 'but I must have others to join with me.' He 'reasoned a little upon the consequence of losing Mr. Pitt at this time; that made no impression at all'. How, asked Newcastle, were the king's affairs to be carried on? The king 'was pleased to be ungracious, and at last said "this country will be too hot for me after the peace".'

Newcastle's opinion was much the same. The Lincolnshire business and

> the little sparks of opposition rising in counties singly from the militia convince me that the establishment of the militia (and any continuance establishes the principle) would be in time the ruin of the constitution and the immediate destruction of the whig party.

Yet in spite of all this, Newcastle was still in retreat:

> If Mr Pitt would consent that the prolongation should be *only during the war* and *no longer*, possibly we might come into it.[2]

This was, in substance, Hardwicke's view; and Hardwicke once more set out the political arguments in favour of compromise, emphasising both

> the war and the necessity of connecting persons together as much as possible in order to enable the king to make a peace. I would not be understood to be an advocate for *the militia*. Nobody is more strongly against it in principle than I am, and I showed myself so when some others were more tender; and old Horace Walpole found fault with me to his clique for taking the part I did. I mean nothing but His Majesty's ease and the strengthening his hands to close the war and make peace. I hope no great danger will arise to the whig party from a short continuance, so as that the general question may be left open to be determined by a new parliament at a proper time; but if any such danger should arise, they must thank themselves for it, for more whigs have appeared for this measure in the house of commons than tories.[3]

---

[1] BM, Add. 32913, ff. 207–10. Hardwicke noted that Fox was for the militia and would be more so if it was true that he was deserting Cumberland for the young Prince of Wales. He also said that Newcastle had not opposed the militia in the session of 1757–8, which had seemed to him the best time, because the riots had shown it to be unpopular.

[2] BM, Add. 35420, ff. 101–2.   [3] BM, Add. 32913, ff. 253–4.

Newcastle's eventual decision, taken in concert with Devonshire and Mansfield at a meeting on 21 October, was to oppose any bill, but solely on the ground that it was not needed yet and that raising the matter now would create unnecessary 'flame' and 'division' in the ensuing general election. Newcastle's friends were to be warned to attend at the beginning of the session, but were not to be told why. Lord Rockingham and the Duke of Grafton—who were friendly but favoured the militia—were to be specially approached. It was intended that this decision should be communicated to Pitt, a compromise with whom was still hoped for:[1] Newcastle again tried to persuade the king of the need 'to manage him now, to prevent his flying out now'.[2] But the proposed approach to Pitt was forestalled by Lord Temple, who now undertook a similar mission for the other side, revealing that they, too, were not eager for a quarrel. He called on Newcastle and tried to make Pitt's behaviour seem less offensive, holding forth on his difficulties in managing the commons. Newcastle induced him to co-operate in trying to get the question put off for a year.[3]

The trend towards compromise was finally confirmed by the death of the king on 25 October. What the new king and his favourite Bute thought of the militia was and remains something of a mystery. Bute seems to have been hostile to the militia at least down to the spring of 1759 but then to have completely changed.[4] The invasion scare of 1759 was the cause. It led the Prince of Wales to ask the king's leave (which was refused) to take the field against the invader. It also led him to vie with the king in showing favour to the Norfolk militia: he attended the royal review and afterwards met the regiment again in Surrey and gave £100 for distribution among the men. This enthusiasm was not solely due to patriotic zeal. Bute and the Prince wanted to forestall any proposal to bring the Duke of Cumberland out of retirement to organise the national defences.[5] It was not clear if they still favoured the militia a year later.[6] What is certain is that George III lacked his grandfather's implacable hostility to the militia and did not wish his servants to quarrel over it.[7] Henceforth the crown was a force for compromise instead of the reverse.

The immediate effect of George III's accession was that Pitt was induced (or given an excuse) to agree to the plan of shelving the militia question for a year. This was Hardwicke's doing: he was, indeed,

[1] BM, Add. 32999, f. 54.　[2] BM, Add. 32913, ff. 251–2.　[3] *Ibid.*, ff. 331–2.
[4] BM, Add. 32896, f. 303. Add. 32889, f. 348.
[5] Namier, *American Revolution*, pp. 102–4. *Letters From George III to Lord Bute*, pp. 25–8. *Ipswich Journal*, 4 August 1759.
[6] Cumberland said no, Hardwicke yes. BM, Add. 33076, f. 116. Add. 35360, f. 304.
[7] Cf. below, p. 186.

a frequent mediator between Newcastle and Pitt, enjoying the friendship of one and the respect of the other. On 29 October he conferred with Pitt and found that he wished the existing ministry to continue. He then turned to the militia and explained to Pitt that legislation was not immediately necessary for its continuance. Pitt was surprised to learn this and half admitted that he should not have pledged himself as he had done. But he pleaded that he had been obliged to do so because of suspicions that his zeal for the militia had abated. Hardwicke said that Pitt could induce the friends of the militia not to bring in their bill; he could say that they all had a duty to preserve unanimity in order to give a smooth beginning to the new reign. Pitt agreed, except that he doubted if he had influence enough with those concerned. 'I really think I staggered him', Hardwicke told Newcastle, 'and I desired him to try in earnest. That he could do a great deal, if he would set his shoulders to it.'[1]

With the support of Bute,[2] Pitt insisted on a sweetener in the form of a flattering reference to the militia in the new king's first speech to parliament.[3] He then adopted the plan which Hardwicke had suggested, and with success. On 28 November a meeting of 'the Hot ones', as Newcastle called them, decided unanimously after some good-tempered debate not to bring in a militia bill that year. Newcastle was delighted, especially because it 'takes away a handle for heat and opposition at the ensuing general election'.[4] There was a general exchange of congratulations. Pitt congratulated Newcastle on the conduct of his nephews (the Townshends) and Newcastle spoke in glowing terms of Pitt, saying that he had done even more than he had promised. On this rather idiotic note of satisfaction the episode closed.[5]

IV

When a bill to continue the militia at length came before parliament in 1762, Pitt was out of office and the fall of Newcastle was but a few months off. This is, therefore, the best point at which to sum up the part they played in the militia controversy. The support which Pitt gave to the militia cause was of the greatest value but the reasons

[1] BM, Add. 32913, ff. 426–9. Pitt warmly defended the utility of the militia to Hardwicke. Hardwicke was surprised by his pleading lack of influence.

[2] BM, Add. 32914, f. 145. Add. 32999, ff. 70–1. Bute added the reservation 'whatever his private opinions might be', which Hardwicke took to mean that he was pro-militia.

[3] See BM, Add. 32914, ff. 169–72, 189, 211, 213, 275, 279, 281, 304. *Chatham Correspondence*, vol. ii, p. 81.

[4] BM, Add. 32915, ff. 131–2, 138.

[5] *Ibid.*, ff. 134–6, 166, 168, 228, 272. Add. 35423, f. 217. Add. 35596, f. 195. *Chatham Correspondence*, vol. ii, p. 87.

which prompted him to give it are obscure. It must at once be said that the militia was of the greatest use to him politically. Repeatedly he used its progress to justify his change of front on the question of sending troops to Germany. It was a means of reconciling his friends among the country gentlemen to the expense of the war effort, both by satisfying an old political demand of theirs and by giving them a part to play in the war that some of them, such as Lord Denbigh,[1] did not find too distasteful. For all that, there are pointers to the conclusion that Pitt's enthusiasm for the militia was sincere. In the first place, he associated himself not with an empty slogan but with a practical scheme. Horace Walpole (who thought his enthusiasm was feigned) remarked that the speech in which he seconded the motion for enquiry and reform in 1755 showed him to have a great memory for detail and capacity for business, adding 'he had never shone in this light before'.[2] Pitt used the opportunity afforded by the militia bill to escape from sterile opposition and show what he could do as an architect of national defence. This is a sign of merit in an opposition leader, whatever his motive, and was unprecedented in a leading politician interesting himself in the militia. No less striking is the situation in the spring of 1758 when he was apparently more determined than the leading militia enthusiasts to press forward with implementing the new scheme—militia riots notwithstanding.[3] In 1759—partly, it may be, to spite his colleagues—he called the militia into service; this done, he made use of them in his own way, which was agreeable to some country gentlemen but highly disagreeable to a great many and to all old-fashioned militia doctrinaires. It seems fair to conclude that he saw the soundness of the strategic case for a militia and was unable to appreciate the really valid arguments on the other side because they were financial and finance was a subject to which he paid little heed. Perhaps too, like Sir Winston Churchill, he enjoyed seasoning his lofty strategic ideas with a few 'gimmicks'.

Newcastle and his friends dealt with the militia question in a way entirely characteristic of an eighteenth-century 'court party'. Their paramount concern was that 'the king's government should be carried on'. This is particularly obvious in their efforts to enforce the distasteful new militia laws because of the need to inculcate respect for the law as such. But their attitude to legislation was the same. Their great object was to dampen political controversy because it impeded the smooth working of government. They opposed militia bills because they believed them to be dangerous. Yet even when this opposition was successful, they abandoned it whenever it seemed likely to produce a strong feeling of frustrated hostility. They had a majority against the original militia bill in the lords; but they dared not use it

[1] Above, p. 168. [2] *George II*, vol. i, p. 448. [3] Above, p. 144.

more than once for fear of the odium of twice defeating a measure which the commons had unanimously approved. They had at any rate the makings of a majority against the militia in the commons, but they used it decisively only once, over the Scottish militia when their enemies were divided; and only to reflect that such expedients were not for every day. They seemed reasonably confident that the militia was not really popular in the country; but when a general election approached, their aim was to find a compromise which would prevent the matter coming before the electorate as a political issue. In a word, Newcastle and Hardwicke and the rest were of the school of Walpole and felt (rather perhaps than thought) that their position was secure only if the issues on which opinion was divided were kept out of the main stream of politics. To this end they were prepared to compromise with any high-spirited group rather than let it get too discontented. They had patronage and influence at their disposal, but they tacitly acknowledged that they could not fight opinions with it. In the counties and in parliament alike they bowed to the public whim. The weakness of Newcastle's character, of course, made the situation harder for them; but often it was Hardwicke who urged caution on a pugnacious Duke.

It was an essential part of this general picture that after the death of Pelham none of the men capable of undertaking the vital task of being chief ministerial spokesman in the commons was willing to oppose the militia there.[1] Walpole and Henry Pelham had both done so.[2] But Fox and Pitt, Grenville and Charles Townshend were all on the other side. So essentially was Conway, though he was good for some ineffectual wrecking work in committee. It is scarcely relevant to look so far ahead, yet it is worth noting that Lord North actually served in the militia. In Charles Yorke the militia had an able opponent, but his mind was set on other things.[3] It followed that after Pelham's death any ministry, to be viable, had to contain a pro-militia element and be in effect neutral in this controversy.

More generally, the defeat of courtly opposition to the militia represented the triumph of younger generations over the old. The new men were comparatively free from either exaggerated aspirations or exaggerated fears regarding the political effects of the militia. They were seriously interested in the problems of national defence, anxious to make a practical contribution and willing to experiment with open minds until they had found a system that would work. Many of those who helped to make the new militia function had no political after-

---

[1] With the exception of the not very distinguished Dowdeswell, below, pp. 194, 198.

[2] Above, p. 72. For Pelham, cf. Cobbett, vol. xiv, pp. 1118–22.

[3] Advancement in the law; cf. Mansfield.

thoughts at all, but only a sense of patriotic duty. This was very disappointing for some of the older advocates of militia revival, but it strengthened the cause. Hardwicke and Newcastle found that many of their younger friends like Rockingham were in favour of a militia on military grounds and that to oppose its continuance might split their party. Of course, the discomfiture of the old men was capped by the death of the old king. George II shared the fears of his elderly ministers regarding the militia. The young court seems to have been at worst indifferent to it and could rise to enthusiasm.[1] The militia cause accordingly became respectable, almost non-political. It was the new men acting in this spirit who were to carry the bill for the continuation of the militia in 1762.

[1] George III presented colours to the Lancashire militia in 1761 and bestowed on it the title of Royal. Williamson, pp. 101–3. It should, of course, be said that the fiercest opponents of the militia, as well as a large part of its defenders, were to be found among the young men, especially those following the young Duke of Devonshire, who have several times been mentioned in this chapter.

VIII
THE STRUGGLE FOR PERMANENCE, 1761–86

W HEN, after the first general election of the new reign, parliament assembled at the end of 1761, the last chance of avoiding a prolongation of the militia laws had disappeared. The war still showed no signs of ending. Pitt had just resigned over the question of extending hostilities to Spain. George Grenville had taken over the vital post of chief ministerial spokesman in the commons and he was reluctant to give Pitt any opening through which he might recover his old position as leader of a powerful opposition movement among the country gentlemen. White endeavoured to prove to Newcastle that militia legislation ought still to be avoided at all costs. It was necessary to placate the tories and detach them from Pitt by such measures as the choice of a tory speaker.[1] If the militia question came up, nothing could prevent strong whig opposition to continuance and so this strategy would be ruined.[2] But Hardwicke, in a memorandum apparently composed on the occasion of Pitt's retirement, said that it was impracticable to drop the militia during the war, and recalled that the acts would expire at the end of the next session after May 1762.[3] Legislation of some kind was inevitable.

It proved possible to avoid mentioning the subject in the king's speech at the opening of the session. Neither Bute nor Grenville desired it, and a protest from Charles Townshend, now Secretary at War, was overruled: the king and Bute were determined to support Grenville against this potential rival.[4] But Pitt and some others seem to have called attention to the omission and Grenville had to try and

---

[1] Prowse.
[2] BM, Add. 32929, ff. 210–11.
[3] BM, Add. 35420, f. 272. In August, Newcastle had reiterated his personal determination to oppose at least continuance after the war (Add. 32926, f. 353).
[4] BM, Add. 32929, ff. 279, 332–3. *Letters from George III to Lord Bute*, pp. 66–8.

soothe them.[1] On 25 November the parliamentary friends of the militia, to the number of forty or fifty, met at the St Alban's tavern at which it was resolved to move for a bill to make the militia perpetual. Almost all who attended favoured this, including some whom Newcastle had thought of as his friends.[2] Henceforth Newcastle and his adherents strove only to substitute prolongation for a term of years for perpetuity.

It was now that the more moderate partisans of the militia came to the fore and gradually imposed their views on the extremists on either side. Of these the Yorkshire contingent, Lord Rockingham and Sir George Savile, were the most important. Their prominence in both the political and military activities of their important county and their links alike with the gentry and the court gave them a most influential position.[3] Rockingham drew a sharp distinction between those, like himself, who regarded the militia as a 'measure of support', and those who made it an instrument of faction. The former would actually prefer prolongation of the militia laws for a term of years to a 'factious attempt' to make them perpetual.[4] He explained to Newcastle that while the war lasted the militia was certainly of use in enabling the government to employ the regular forces more effectively. Its discontinuance would distress all militia officers now in the house and divide the administration. If Pitt and his friends tried to make political capital out of the situation by pressing the case for perpetuity, the right response would be to propose prolongation for a fairly generous term.[5] Later he expressed the view that the well-disposed would prefer prolongation for five years to perpetuity, so that they could see if the system worked as well in peace as in war; Savile thought that most militia officers favoured 'accepting the longer term'.[6]

Under this pressure, Newcastle and his friends were gradually brought to agree to prolongation not for a short term but for the lengthy period of seven years.[7] This was Lord Shaftesbury's sugges-

[1] BM, Add. 32931, ff. 19, 20. H. Walpole, *Memoirs of the Reign of King George III*, ed. G. F. Russell Barker (London and New York, 1894), vol. i, p. 68.

[2] BM, Add. 32931, ff. 248–9. HMC, *Wood*, p. 180. Wentworth Woodhouse, R. 1–214. Walpole (*George III*, vol. i, p. 68) says that Pitt proposed perpetuity and Charles Townshend opposed it. Newdigate's diary records another meeting at Lord Shaftesbury's on 11 November.

[3] Rockingham was a lord of the bedchamber, lord lieutenant of the West Riding and brigadier-general of its militia. Savile was colonel of a West Riding regiment and a member for the county.

[4] BM, Add. 32931, ff. 390–1.   [5] *Ibid.*, ff. 317–18.

[6] BM, Add. 32932, ff. 306–7.

[7] Their first idea seems to have been three years or the duration of the war if longer (!), BM, Add. 32930, f. 425. After the St Alban's meeting they favoured five years (Add. 32931, ff. 248–9, 299).

tion;[1] the object of it was to adjourn the question of perpetuity until after the next general election. This appealed to Devonshire and also, it seems, to old White.[2] On the other side, likewise, there was a great softening of attitude. The St Alban's meeting apparently set up a committee to draft a bill,[3] and early in December another meeting was held which approved a draft that contained no clause limiting the measure's life.[4] But an explicit motion in favour of perpetuity was opposed by Sir John Philips, who said that it was a matter for the commons to decide. Pitt and Temple defended the bill as it stood and Temple even threatened to vote against it if it was altered. But almost everyone was against them, and so the parliamentary supporters of the bill were never committed to oppose an amendment limiting its duration.[5] The king himself encouraged the trend towards compromise. He was much gratified by the result of the meeting[6] and when George Townshend returned from active service in Germany he asked for his concurrence, declaring his wish that the term of seven years might be unanimously voted. Townshend refused to commit himself, but seemed to be better disposed towards Bute than towards Pitt and did not approve of his brother's insubordination.[7] The king also worked on George Grenville, who was inclined to favour perpetuity for fear of upsetting the militia at a time when a French invasion was again in prospect.[8] He eventually assured Newcastle that Grenville had told him that prolongation for a term of years would be proposed in committee, '"and," says His Majesty, "George will vote for it." '[9] Bute, meanwhile, had been urging his friends to support prolongation; apparently they favoured perpetuity.[10]

The bill was introduced in the commons on 15 December[11] and ordered to be printed. Further proceedings on it were deferred till

[1] *Ibid.*, f. 366: this also records conversations with Sir F. Dashwood and Lord Litchfield and a paper from Legge. Newcastle was negotiating actively with his opponents.

[2] BM, Add. 32932, f. 7.

[3] See Newdigate's diary for 26 November 1761.

[4] Cf. below, p. 191 and n. 2 ; p. 192.

[5] BM, Add. 32932, ff. 82–3.

[6] *Ibid.*, f. 82.

[7] *Letters from George III to Bute*, pp. 73–4.

[8] Walpole, *George III*, vol. i, p. 78.

[9] BM, Add. 32931, f. 410. Add. 32932, f. 87. Newcastle regretted that 'George' would not move the clause himself.

[10] Bedford, too, was for prolongation. BM, Add. 32931, ff. 410, 423. Newcastle curbed extremists on the other side (Add. 32932, f. 176; cf. Kinnoull, f. 168).

[11] CJ, vol. xxix, pp. 87–8. Sedgwick (as n. 7) thinks that the friends of the bill had postponed a decision about perpetuity till Townshend's return: see too references at p. 185, n. 2. But this only occurred on 18 December, when the decision had been taken and the bill introduced. It had certainly been intended that he should introduce it, but Lord Strange did this instead (HMC, *Wood*, p. 180).

after Christmas.[1] Far from being a mere continuing measure, it proposed important changes in the system. This, like the leaving open of the perpetuity question, reflected the influence of the moderates. It was the practical experience of the militia officers and a concern for military efficiency that lay behind most of the amendments and overcame resistance to them. Bute and Newcastle's friends alike seem to have been against any change, but with men like Rockingham on the other side they saw that opposition to it would be dangerous.[2] The most important changes were designed more or less to supersede the ballot as the mode of recruiting the men. The inequity of the ballot as between rich and poor has already been noted, as also the attempts to palliate it. Sir George Savile now reopened the whole question in a pamphlet which is the best exposition of the contrast between the practical militia officer and the politicians.[3] He took as his motto an adaptation of Othello's dying words

> We have done the state some service and they know it
> No more of that—

He declared that the militia as it now existed was

> so very widely differing from what either the friends or the enemies to the first proposition expected to see, that . . . it were no mark of candour in either, to make the sentiments and the passions of two years past the rule and guide of their present opinions.
>
> Forgetting then, that it almost owes its existence, and well nigh its destruction, to popular clamour . . . avoiding, if it be possible, the jealous and untimely notion of a balance against the army of the crown, let a new field be entered into; a field of enquiry, not of contention. Let us see in it simply, a temporary force, confined and pointed to the defence of our country and our king; headed by men of property in the one, and loyalty towards the other. Let us assume too, that there is a something now existing (no matter how produced), which has done important service to this country. Examine what that something is; dissect it while yet alive; fix it, analyse it, secure it. Be it or be it not Militia, see what are its constituent parts; and what is necessary to be done, in order to ensure the having always on occasion that something within our reach.[4]

In accordance with this doctrine, Savile attacked the ballot as 'carrying an Utopian idea of property and patriotism into the ranks'. Compulsory personal service was required of everyone in very extreme emergencies, but usually it was better to raise a smaller force by means of a tax. The ballot in practice was simply a very unfair tax

[1] Cf. BM, Add. 32932, f. 83.   [2] BM, Add. 32931, ff. 410, 423–4.
[3] *An Argument Concerning the Militia*. A note in ink on the British Museum's copy gives Savile as the author and the date as 1762. There is another copy in BM, Add. 35877, ff. 346–54.
[4] Savile, pp. 3, 4. Cf. the rest of pp. 1–6 and 17–19.

and did not ensure that the fittest men were chosen. It might be useful as a means of training all able-bodied men in rotation, but in that case substitutes should not be allowed. The existing militia consisted, in fact, almost entirely of substitutes and this was not a bad thing. Gentlemen did not appear at their best at the head of 'galley slaves'. Yeomen would be a nuisance in the ranks: how could one have a parliamentary elector who had voted for one flogged for drunkenness, especially if one had been encouraging it the day before? 'Let all things be left to the places assigned to them by their nature; and by the wholesome subordination, so essential to all societies.' Personal service was a duty for men of property but the rank and file should be recruited from the lowest class, whose obedience would be ensured by 'every additional bond of neighbourhood and of provincial authority and dependence'.[1] Savile thus abandoned the political aims associated with the militia and drew the logical conclusion from the fact that the militia had not been used only in extreme emergencies but for lengthy service during a foreign war.

Savile proposed that each parish should be empowered to levy a rate and enlist volunteers to the number required. A ballot would only be held if this was not done. Rockingham supported this and used his good offices with Newcastle's group to obviate opposition.[2] The new bill was drafted accordingly.[3] Parish volunteers had of course been sanctioned by the act of 1758, but it was only now that power was given for the levy of a rate, if the inhabitants at a vestry or other meeting authorised it. Among the good effects that this was expected to produce were that parishes would get the men cheaper than individuals could and labourers would not run about the country to evade the ballot. The new device was not made compulsory because if it had been, only a fine could have been levied for non-compliance and what was wanted was men, not money: the payment of fines would embarass the lieutenancy.[4] When a ballot did take place, the

---

[1] *Ibid.*, pp. 6–17. He pointed out that the men and their families appeared to cost nothing, but that was because they were paid for locally. The bounty was £5. 10s.: it had proved no cheaper to hire men for the militia than for the line.

[2] BM, Add. 32931, ff. 390–1. Add. 32932, f. 307.

[3] A useful pamphlet, *Observations on the New Militia Bill now under the Consideration of Parliament, wherein the Material Alterations are pointed out*, was published by the friends of the bill. Reasons are given for the changes proposed. There is a copy in BM, Add. 35877, ff. 332–45. In what follows I shall also cite the relevant sections of the eventual act, 2 Geo. III, cap. 20.

[4] Two justices were to sanction the rate, and anyone who had served in the militia in person or by substitute was exempt. *Observations*, pp. 8, 9; ss. 45–6. For some reason it was hoped that this would put an end to discharging one's obligations by insurance or some other scheme of private subscription. Clauses added in committee made this illegal in most cases. *Observations*, p. 9; ss. 51–3. A printed copy of the bill as it left the committee stage in the commons, distin-

balloted man's position was eased by an amendment to the bill which ordered that when the militia was called out he should receive the sum (not to exceed £5) adjudged to be half the local price of a volunteer.[1] Another easement was that poor men with three legitimate children or more were henceforth exempt from the ballot.[2]

The great drawback of the militia as a means of raising men was that it competed for them with the regular army. At first this had not mattered because unembodied militiamen could still enlist as soldiers. Things changed when the militia began to be called out, and both Temple and Rockingham noted in 1759 that recruiting for the army was suffering.[3] This complaint became common form,[4] and the discharge of the militia was advocated in order to fill the army.[5] The new bill sought to do justice to both services. Militia regiments were forbidden to send out recruiting parties to raise men by beat of drum and a clause added in committee forbade them, when out of the county, to enlist men of any county but their own. Men hired to serve in the militia as volunteers or substitutes might enlist in the line while unembodied, but only if they repaid what they had received on their first enlistment to the overseer of their parish, towards their replacement.[6]

The other really important change made by the bill concerned the drill of the militia in peacetime. Instead of taking place on odd days now and then, this was to occupy either two periods of a fortnight each or one period of twenty-eight days, at the discretion of the lieutenancy. Each regiment or battalion was to assemble in its entirety for these exercises. The system of maintaining discipline by fines was done away with and martial law was to apply, save that there were to be no penalties touching life or limb. The great improvement which this represented and the sound knowledge of military affairs which it suggests in its proposers need no emphasis. The system of training in the militia was brought quite close to that which was used for the conscript element in the Prussian army. Various arguments besides that of superior efficiency were advanced in defence of the proposal. The previous system had often left the men

guishing amendments and additions, is in BM, Add. 35880, ff. 244–74. References to amendments are from this source unless otherwise stated. In 1760 a citizen of York had suggested to George Townshend that the militia should be recruited by the captains of companies from the proceeds of a county rate. He wanted service as officers to be compulsory for those qualified. John Rylands Library, English MSS., no. 939, item 45. Cf. a proposal from a militia officer to Pitt in November 1761, PRO. 30/8, vol. 69, ff. 123–4.

[1] ss. 47–9.   [2] s. 43.
[3] PRO. 30/8, vol. 61, ff. 37–8. BM, Add. 32894, f. 295.
[4] See BM, Add. 32929, f. 389.   [5] BM, Add. 32930, ff. 349–50.
[6] ss. 54–6. *Observations*, pp. 10–12, where the failure to fix a maximum bounty is justified by saying that it would become a minimum.

unable to do their jobs on the day after drill and had forced the officers to stay at home for a large part of the year. The places where the drills would now be held would benefit from having the men quartered there. Under martial law the men would be tried by their officers instead of by the justices, but as the officers were men of property this would make little difference.[1]

Two great questions remained about which debate in the commons was to centre. About the duration of the new act there was now some prospect of agreement. Moderate friends of the bill stood by the plan of extension for seven years. It would give an opportunity to try the scheme in peace and would remove the temptation to repeal the act if the militia encountered a brief spell of unpopularity. In view of the way it had stood up to the fatigues of hard service there was little doubt that it would prove itself by good performance in peacetime training. A short act would suffice to prolong its existence.[2]

The other question related to the counties where the militia had not yet been raised. There was a strong feeling that they should not escape. The proposal was mooted of incorporating the men of counties where officers could not be found into the militia of neighbouring counties. It was pointed out that a new war (with Spain) was just beginning, that the burden of defence should be fairly spread and that even as it was the quotas were uneven.[3] The original text of the bill provided for the calling of meetings in the defaulting counties within a month of its passing to receive offers of service; thereafter there was to be a meeting each month until field officers and captains for one battalion had been got.[4] But in committee on 25 February 1762 Lord Strange carried an amendment. If there were still not enough officers after the second meeting, the lord lieutenant was to certify the fact to a secretary of state, stating the number of men that the county was to find. The king could then either incorporate the men in the militias of other counties or appoint qualified persons from other counties to command them. This amendment was carried by 43 to 26. Newcastle's friends voted against it, but West told the Duke that he had been unable to induce enough of them to stay. He thought that the new clause could be thrown out again on report.[5]

[1] s. 99. *Observations*, pp. 15–18. Other important amendments will be discussed in part iii, since they were not apparently controversial.

[2] *Observations*, pp. 18–23.

[3] Varying from 1 in 17 to 1 in 40. Consequently, labourers were migrating, causing labour shortage in some areas and unemployment in others. *Ibid.*, pp. 23–6, where there is also a good summary of the strategic case for the militia. It was to prevent invasion and rebellion while the army and navy acted abroad.

[4] BM, Add. 35880, f. 248. There was to be an entirely new ballot in these counties and it was only to be held when officers had been found. *Ibid.*, ff. 152–3; s. 42 of the act.

[5] BM, Add. 32880, f. 248. Add. 32935, f. 52 (misdated; cf. CJ, vol. xxix, p. 196).

The bill had received its second reading on 1 February 1762 and there had been seven sessions in committee, one lasting from three till ten and three others ending as late.[1] The session on the 25th was the last and the report was ordered for 1 March. Both sides prepared for battle on that day, both on the question of the defaulting counties and on that of limitation to seven years. George Grenville and Barrington both thought that the report stage was the best time to raise the question of duration; Newcastle was, in consequence, mortified by seeing the bill go through the committee in the form of a perpetual measure and with 'other absurdities'.[2] Stung into action by the 'shameful' defeat of the 25th, he spent the whole of the next day canvassing. He was confident of success and hoped all his friends would see it as a welcome trial of strength.[3] His opponents responded by urging Pitt to make a personal appearance.[4] But again a head-on collision was avoided. Newcastle received pledges of support,[5] but also warnings. Hardwicke wrote an encouraging but restraining letter. He found that some who were no friends to the militia thought that the clause about defaulters could not be thrown out if no alternative proposal was made. Since it was generally agreed that the militia was really necessary for national defence during the war, it must follow that the burden should be shared equally.[6]

When the great day came, it appeared that moderate counsels had been heard on the other side too. Sir Edmund Isham proposed that consideration of the amendments be adjourned and the bill as amended be printed. Charles Townshend, Grenville, Nugent and Rigby all supported this. Lord Strange and John Turner demurred, but they were answered by no less a person than Pitt, supported by Sir Charles Mordaunt. The great length of the bill and the number and complexity of the amendments were good reasons for this proposal.[7] Those who made it urged the need for unity at such a critical time and hoped that some means could be found of preventing division over a measure essential for national defence. Pitt, perhaps in

[1] CJ, vol. xxix, pp. 136, 150, 154, 167, 177, 183, 188, 196. Newdigate's diary sub. 5, 11, 15, 18 February 1762.

[2] BM, Add. 35429, f. 66.   [3] BM, Add. 32935, f. 89.

[4] PRO. 30/8, vol. 18, f. 5; vol. 26, f. 191, where the defaulters' clause is said to be the favourite of George Townshend. During the army estimates debate, Pitt had explained again how 'when I saw America safe, a Militia at home (which if Heaven has blessing in Store for this Country will be made a permanent part of the Constitution) I then consented to send troops to Germany'. BM, Add. 32932, f. 77.

[5] BM, Add. 32935, ff. 105, 121, 123, 125, 127, 131.

[6] BM, Add. 32935, ff. 98–9. Similarly Nugent, f. 129. Lord North (*ibid.*, f. 101) favoured the amendment of the 25th.

[7] Both Bacon and Charles Yorke thought it would take more than a day to get through the amendments. *Ibid.*, f. 119. PRO. 30/8, vol. 18, f. 5.

expiation, added the hope that as the bill came in a permanent measure it would go out so. The house agreed to the postponement without a division.[1]

Proceedings on the bill were resumed on 15 March, by which time a compromise had been devised regarding the defaulting counties. They were to pay £5 a year for every man of their quota.[2] The money was to be levied by quarter sessions, on receipt of a certificate from the lord lieutenant, in the same manner as the county rate. It was to be paid to the exchequer via the treasurers and receivers of the land tax. Raising the militia exonerated the county from the tax for as long as it was raised. It was agreed to recommit the bill in order to study this scheme. There were two sittings in committee, which produced one most significant alteration. The money levied was now to be paid by the exchequer to the counties which had raised the militia and added to the county stock; it was to be shared out in proportion to the militia quotas.[3] This, of course, harked back to the plans of 1760 to relieve the county rates of the expense of the militia families.[4] The whole affair showed Newcastle and his friends once more in retreat; but not they alone. Dempster opposed the whole scheme and accused the defaulting counties and their lord lieutenants of cowardice. Most interestingly it was Charles Townshend who answered him, and he went out of his way to defend the Duke of Devonshire.[5]

On 19 March consideration of the amendments on report was resumed, and the compromise on defaulters finally approved. Charles Yorke proposed the clause limiting the life of the measure to seven years. Barrington and four others supported him; Beckford, Strange, Barré and George Townshend spoke on the other side, but the discussion was quiet and the clause was carried without a division.[6] One more sitting was required to finish the bill, and it seems to have been in this or the previous sitting that George Townshend made what was in effect an appeal from the new friends of the militia to the old. He was concerned with the clause authorising payment of half the price of a volunteer to balloted men when the militia was called out. What aroused his dislike was the proviso that the money should

[1] CJ, vol. xxix, p. 201. BM, Add. 32935, f. 143 (a report by West, who says the house was full and Newcastle's friends present in force).

[2] Newdigate's diary, 15 March 1762.

[3] Cf. ss. 21–7 of the act with BM, Add. 35880, ff. 291–3, which is obviously a first draft. Towns not contributing to the county rate were made liable in this case. See CJ, vol. xxix, pp. 239, 244, 246. For the Newcastle group's efforts to find a compromise, see BM, Add. 32935, ff. 119, 211, 332. Newcastle was optimistic after 15 March, *ibid.*, f. 388. Cf. also Add. 32999, ff. 418–19.

[4] See especially above, pp. 172–3.

[5] BM, Add. 32935, f. 443. Cf. George Townshend's moderation on this issue, f. 247.

[6] *Ibid.*, f. 494 (Barry so spelt). CJ, vol. xxix, pp. 249–50.

not be paid if the man sent to serve (principal or substitute) was discharged by his commanding officer within a month. He said that this was to allow commanding officers to discharge men thought fit by the lieutenancy and put the parishes to fresh expense. This would suggest, unjustly he thought, that militia officers were too keen on smartness and wanted to have only good-looking men. He went on to speak of the great burden about to fall on many counties by the replacement of their original contingent of men, whose time was now expiring. He urged that both the levy-money and the expense of maintaining the families should be repaid to the parishes from the public funds. In conclusion, he bewailed the long embodiment of the militia contrary to the spirit of the original act and the absence of any clause in the present bill to restrain this.[1] This jeremiad shows once more how militia legislation was passing out of the hands of militia zealots into those of men whose main concern was military efficiency.

Newcastle used his influence to smooth the passage of the bill through the lords, and they passed it without amendment.[2] Significantly he congratulated Rockingham on the events of 19 March and added 'you see what you can make us do'. Rockingham in reply said that those who had tried to turn militia extremism to their own advantage had desisted on finding that not all 'comprehended under the name of militia' would join them.[3] These words clearly show the declining importance and usefulness of the militia as an issue in political warfare.

II

Like the act of 1757, the act of 1762 would have borne little fruit had it not been for the continuing efforts of the friends of the militia both in parliament and the counties. Newcastle and his friends had assented to the prolongation of the militia's life because of the needs of the war. By a fine stroke of irony, no sooner had the act been passed than the war ended. This was fatal to Newcastle and his more faithful friends, who went into fruitless opposition because they could not stomach the terms of the peace. It was also dangerous to their old enemies in the militia question. As had been foreseen, the ending of

[1] Rylands' English MSS., no. 939, item 28. This draft speech is headed 'clause P' and addressed to 'Mr. Sp[eake]r.' It must therefore be on report, and seems most probably to refer to Clause P in BM, Add. 35880, f. 273, which became ss. 47–9 of the act. Cf. the typical army view of discipline in Savile's pamphlet: patriotic feeling is less important than obedience and *esprit de corps* taught by attention to minute details like the cock of a hat. For the last session, CJ, vol. xxix, p. 273.

[2] BM, Add. 32936, f. 302, cf. ff. 93, 262. CJ, vol. xxix, p. 296. The king was pleased to hear of the second reading of the bill in the lords (*Letters from George III to Bute*, pp. 88–9).

[3] BM, Add. 32936, ff. 42, 110–11.

O 193

hostilities led to considerable reluctance to go on bearing the burden of a militia. The commons voted their thanks to the militia on its disembodiment at the end of 1762,[1] and for the time being proved willing enough to vote money for peacetime training.[2] But a moment of crisis came with the advent of the Rockingham ministry in 1765. Not only did Newcastle and his friends return to office, but a very hostile Chancellor of the Exchequer appeared in the person of Dowdeswell. He came from Worcestershire, a defaulting county, indifferent to the militia because of its inland situation. It was feared that the new Treasury Board would refuse to sanction any expenditure on training the militia in 1766.[3] Happily for the friends of the militia, the ministers' position in parliament was so weak that they could not afford to quarrel with them. A compromise, involving reduced expenditure, was negotiated by George Onslow, acting for the Treasury of which he was now a junior lord. But in the commons even these cuts were resisted by Lord Strange and Pitt appeared and denounced the ministers for abandoning the militia. The attempt to reduce the peacetime cost of the force was accordingly abandoned.[4] No other such attempt was made until after the next war.

Thus the friends of the militia were able to keep some sort of a hold on parliament. But they had the greatest difficulty in overcoming apathy in the counties. In 1764–5 the commons pessimistically provided only about half the amount of money that would have been required to train the militia had it been at full strength: they proved not pessimistic enough, for none of the money was spent. Militia training was not, in fact, completely in abeyance after disembodiment; other testimony shows that it took place. But it seems likely that even counties which raised the militia failed on the whole to train it properly.[5] Nor was this the worst difficulty. Some counties

[1] CJ, vol. xxix, pp. 393, 417.

[2] In 1763–5 amendments were carried to provide pay for some or all of the officers. CJ, vol. xxix, pp. 496, 542, 900, 919; vol. xxx, p. 240.

[3] Cf., too, below, p. 324, n. 5. re adjutants.

[4] *Chatham Correspondence*, vol. ii, pp. 412–14. PRO. 30/8, vol. 77, ff. 180–1. HMC, *Round*, p. 299. Walpole, *George III*, vol. ii, p. 224. CJ, vol. xxx, pp. 636, 669, 688. Cf. Newdigate's diary, 13, 24 March 1766. For the need of Treasury sanction for militia bills involving expenditure, see above, pp. 145, 171. Walpole says that £15 or £20,000 would have been saved. He asserts that Pitt 'did not care a jot about the militia' and only wanted to remind the ministers of the importance of conciliating him. But about a year before, Pitt had spoken so warmly of the militia to Henry Flood as to induce him to propose a militia bill in Ireland. *Chatham Correspondence*, vol. iii, pp. 1–4.

[5] In 1764–5 £80,000 was voted (CJ, vol. xxix, p. 977; vol. xxx, p. 290); cf. estimates in 1765 and thereafter of £179,766.11s.(*ibid.*,pp. 255,636; vol. xxxi, pp. 141, 556). In 1763 and 1766 £150,000 was voted (CJ, vol. xxix, p. 542; vol. xxx, p. 669). In 1765 and 1766 the house was told that £80,000 remained unspent from the previous session (*ibid.*, pp. 327, 711).

continued to have no militia, for want of officers, and it did not prove at all easy to coerce the defaulters by imposing the new statutory fine.

The coercive provisions inserted in the act of 1762 do seem, it is true, to have worked quite well at first. The leaders of county society had formerly felt obliged to prove their patriotism by a show of zeal in raising the militia. Now they felt obliged to show their devotion to local interests by getting the militia raised and so ensuring that their county did not have to pay a fine. For this reason Rockingham discouraged his friends in the West Riding from retiring from the militia in protest against his dismissal from the lieutenancy in 1762.[1] The same thing preserved the Cambridgeshire militia from death by neglect. Though raised, it had never been mobilised, and in 1761 the officers retired in a body.[2] In July 1762 the deputies postponed the raising of their contingent afresh. But, interestingly, the man who suggested this did not wish the delay to be attributed to him; also, though nobody offered to take a commission, everyone was eager to recommend his neighbour.[3] By January 1763 all was ready for a new ballot, and it became necessary to discover if officers could be found and the militia continued in existence. Sir Thomas Hatton was willing to take a commission and Sir John Cotton was ready to do the same in order to save the county from a fine. But there was a rumour that in Worcestershire they had discovered a means of evading the law. The justices accordingly delayed preparations for the levy of a fine should officers not be found; the deputies for their part failed to attend a meeting advertised for 1 March and so no progress was made in levying the contingent.[4] On 8 April the county became liable for a fine, not having raised its militia within a year of the passing of the act of 1762. In May Lord Royston the lord lieutenant sent a certificate to quarter sessions which showed the need of levying the penalty.[5] But the justices were unwilling to do much towards this till they had found out what other counties did. It was even argued that since the militia had been raised under the previous acts there could be no liability for a fine since the king need not have accepted the resignations of the previous officers.[6]

After 1766 no precise sum was voted; there was a simple order that expenses should be defrayed from the land tax. For training during the 1760s see below, p. 407. Some of it may have been paid for by balances accumulated.

[1] He also wanted them to remain justices to prevent local 'confusion and mischief'. Wentworth Woodhouse, R. 1–344, 368; cf. 760.

[2] Below, p. 305.

[3] BM, Add. 35352, ff. 233, 257, 260. Add. 35680, ff. 40–3, 45.

[4] Montfort was ready to continue. *Ibid.*, ff. 56, 62. Add. 35627, ff. 195–6.

[5] BM, Add. 35679, ff. 423–4. Add. 35680, ff. 68–70.

[6] BM, Add. 35352, ff. 364–5, 388–9. Cf. Add. 35627, ff. 205–6.

In January 1764 quarter sessions took effective steps to raise the militia fine and considered again the prospects of raising the militia. The example of Worcestershire was again brought up, but there was now some eagerness to comply with the law, for fear of having to raise a second year's fine if evasion proved impossible. The leading gentlemen again offered to take commissions—Cotton, it was alleged, only for the sake of popularity. By mid-February the necessary minimum of officers had been found.[1] 'This,' commented Royston, 'was the second Edition of Militia in Cambridgeshire without the least Utility to and some Expense to the Public.'[2]

The system of fines for defaulting counties thus kept the militia at least in nominal existence almost everywhere. But six counties remained for many years in default: Derbyshire, Nottinghamshire, Oxfordshire, Staffordshire, Sussex and Worcestershire.[3] Newcastle's counties remained recalcitrant. He asked old White in 1762 to offer to take a commission in Nottinghamshire because it would not look well if his best friend failed to come forward. But he said that everyone expected the county to prefer paying the fine to raising men, so that White would not have to serve.[4] In Sussex Newcastle's friends had an excuse for inaction in the hostility of the farmers to the militia. (They expected it to intensify the prevailing labour shortage.)[5] Newcastle's friend the Duke of Devonshire was, of course, the leading man in another defaulting county, Derbyshire; on the other hand, the remaining three were traditional strongholds of toryism.

The defaulting counties were a perpetual thorn in the flesh to the friends of the militia. Not only did they provide no men but they paid very little money. The six persistent offenders should have paid in all £17,600 a year.[6] But for the years 1762–8 only £14,144. 12s. 8d. altogether had been paid by 1769;[7] even in 1774 only £16,746. 5s. 3d. had been paid for the years 1762–9.[8] What had happened in Cambridgeshire shows well both the reluctance of the justices to levy the penalty and the damaging effect of reports that any county had evaded the fine with impunity. It was accordingly most important for parliament to keep up the pressure on recalcitrant counties. In 1765 the county

[1] BM, Add. 35680, ff. 75–7, 79, 80, 82–3. Add. 35627, ff. 203–6. On difficulties in raising the fine see Add. 35680, ff. 84, 96–7.

[2] BM, Add. 35680, note on f. 112.

[3] See PRO. 30/8, vol. 77, f. 251.

[4] BM, Add. 32939, ff. 269–70; cf. ff. 376–7.

[5] BM, Add. 32938, ff. 428–9.

[6] For 3520 men, viz. Sussex 800, Notts. 480, the rest 560 each. 2 Geo. III, cap. 20, s. 41.

[7] Notts and Derby for 1766 and 1767, Notts for part of 1763, Sussex for part of 1766. CJ, vol. xxxii, p. 123.

[8] CJ, vol. xxxiv, p. 764.

justices were given special powers to deal with corporate towns outside their jurisdiction which refused to pay their share of the fine. The lieutenancy's obligation to certify the non-raising of the militia to quarter sessions was more precisely expressed.[1] In 1766 there were draconian measures. The lieutenancy was to certify to the clerk of the peace each year either that the militia had been raised or that it had not. The clerk was to lay the certificate before quarter sessions and within fourteen days of its meeting was to certify to the Treasury and to the receiver general of the land tax that he had done so (or that there had been no certificate) and what quarter sessions had done. If the justices had failed to levy the fine, the Barons of the Exchequer were to recover it by distraint from the county treasurer. A clerk of the peace failing to act was liable to a fine of £500 and was to be incapable of holding any office of trust.[2] Such money as was extracted from the defaulting counties mostly came in as a result of this act; but there was not very much of it and in 1767 parliament gave the laggards an extension of time.[3]

The question of how to enforce the militia laws was still unsettled when the time came to consider the larger question of whether to make them perpetual. In 1768 there was a general election, and the new parliament proceeded, as the framers of the act of 1762 had intended, to settle the issue of perpetuity for good. The friends of the militia were determined both to carry perpetuity and to secure a really watertight system of exacting penalties from defaulters. This gave their opponents, especially the representatives of the defaulting counties, a good opportunity to rouse against them the widespread weariness with continued military exertions in time of peace.

The commons established a committee to prepare a militia bill in December 1768, and returns were called for of the state of the militia at the last annual exercise and of militia expenditure and of the fines received from defaulting counties since the act of 1762.[4] The resulting bill was presented to the house by Lord Strange on 14 March 1769 and ordered to be printed. The commons considered it in committee on 20 March, after which it was again printed with the amendments.

---

[1] The clerk of the peace might sometimes act in their place. 5 Geo. III, cap. 36, ss. 1–5. Savile presented this bill, and its third reading in the commons was carried by 32 votes to 6. See CJ, vol. xxx, pp. 404, 422, 424. In 1764 the towns' obligations had been more precisely fixed by 4 Geo. III, cap. 17, ss. 9, 10, and the commons asked the defaulting counties what they had done (CJ, vol. xxix, pp. 775–6, 846, 849, 880, 891).

[2] 6 Geo. III, cap. 30, ss. 20–30. The procedure was modelled on that for counties defaulting in land tax payments.

[3] 7 Geo. III, cap. 15. Cf. p. 196, n. 7.

[4] CJ, vol. xxxii, pp. 117–18, 182, 185, 293.

The report stage did not begin until 12 April.[1] In committee an attempt was made to get rid of the severe penalties on clerks of the peace not taking the action required of them in defaulting counties. No less a person than Sir George Savile supported this, and he also seems to have come out in favour of a further prolongation of the laws for a term of years and against perpetuity. Undaunted, Lord Strange secured the retention of the penalty.[2] New and stiffer penalties were added. The clerk of the peace was to certify the names of the justices present at any quarter sessions which failed to take requisite action to levy penalties and they were to be prosecuted by the Treasury Solicitor, though the act did not specifically lay down what penalty they were to suffer. The Treasury Solicitor was liable to the same severe penalty as the clerk of the peace if he failed to act, and there were also severe penalties on county treasurers and high and petty constables who failed to do their part in collecting the fine. There were, however, inducements as well as penalties. Those who had served as militia officers or who were serving or who offered to serve were exempt from their share of the fine, and the total for which the county was liable was to be reduced by that amount.[3] The property qualifications for subalterns were reduced and so it became easier for counties to find the required number of officers.[4]

The main debate on the bill seems to have taken place on report. The interval before this gave opportunity for canvassing. Dowdeswell tried without success to stir Charles Yorke into action, urging both the case against perpetuity and the dangerous precedent created by the proposal to punish justices. Although their services were voluntary they would here be put on the same footing as parish officers who served by compulsion.[5] The debate saw a curious reversal of roles. Perpetuity was denounced as turning the militia into a standing army which the commons could only abolish with the consent of the lords. The militia was condemned because it consisted of substitutes and officers with little property. Lord John Cavendish (who spoke for Derbyshire as Dowdeswell did for Worcestershire) said that there were not enough officers, that the subalterns were humble people spoiled by being turned into gentlemen and that the men were debauched at the exercises. On the other side it was said that officers would be easier to find once the laws were perpetual and that the

[1] *Ibid.*, pp. 311, 331, 338, 377.

[2] HMC, *Kenyon*, p. 501. Cf. BM, Add. 35430, f. 234.

[3] Local officials were also given allowances towards the expense of collecting the money. The proceeds were henceforth to be disposed of as parliament thought fit, not automatically divided up among the counties which had raised their militia. 9 Geo. III, cap. 42, ss. 17–47.

[4] *Ibid.*, ss. 2–11.

[5] BM, Add. 35430, ff. 232–4.

annual pay bill was a safeguard against the militia becoming a standing army.[1] At length the commons voted in favour of perpetuity by the narrow margin of 84 to 79. The bill was sent to the lords on 18 April more or less in the form its sponsors desired, and it was returned to the commons without amendment.[2] Thus a great controversy ended, quite quietly. No doubt the minds of most members were on other things: it was in these months that Wilkes was expelled from the commons and triumphantly re-elected.

The act of 1769 did something, but not very much, to reduce the number of defaulters. Worcestershire raised its militia in 1770 and Derbyshire in 1773.[3] The rest did nothing. The Duke of Richmond, now lord lieutenant of Sussex, thought it necessary to convene a meeting of the county after the act had passed to consider what to do. Though he disliked the militia he thought it might be wisest now to try and raise it. But his only wish was to do what the county pleased.[4] This it seems was nothing. The defaulters perhaps paid up a shade more readily, but by 1774 only £13,815. 4s. had been paid for the five years since the act was passed—less than what was due for one year.[5] It was the outbreak of the American revolution that finally induced the defaulters to come into line. By 1778 they had raised their contingents and that was the end of the problem.[6]

III

The permanency of the militia laws was never formally called in question after 1769. But after 1783 the militia went through a crisis very similar to that of 1763–9, which forms a sort of epilogue to the debate on perpetuity. Accordingly, it is discussed here, out of its proper chronological position. In both cases there was a strong post-war revulsion against the burden of the militia which almost caused the system to collapse. Although the annual pay bills continued to be passed, it seems that no money was spent on training the militia in the

---

[1] Cobbett, vol. xvi, p. 610. Barré and Lord Beauchamp were apparently the main speakers for perpetuity.

[2] But there was a division in the lords on whether to commit it. Richmond voted against the bill, and so did Rockingham, to Richmond's surprise. Wentworth Woodhouse, R. 1–1180, 1183. Bedford, Grafton, Denbigh and Holdernesse spoke for it; Sandys, Egmont, Suffolk and Bolton against. J. W. Fortescue (ed.), *Correspondence of King George III* (6 vols., London, 1927–8), vol. ii, p. 94. Part of the provisions about the penalties was added on the third reading in the commons. CJ, vol. xxxii, pp. 377, 380–1, 393–4, 444. LJ, vol. xxxii, pp. 345, 354, 371.

[3] PRO. 30/8, vol. 77, f. 251.

[4] BM, Add. 33089, ff. 35–6.

[5] CJ, vol. xxxiv, p. 765.

[6] See Note at the end of the chapter and Appendix A.

years 1783–6.[1] The ministers were eager to save money and repair the war-damaged finances. They did not show any hostility to the militia, but they were discreetly unenthusiastic about providing it with funds. The friends of the militia responded to this emergency by drawing up a comprehensive plan for codifying and amending the militia laws.[2] This was intended to remedy shortcomings which had revealed themselves in the recent war and provide a more economical basis on which the force could continue. In return it was hoped that Pitt could be induced to give official backing when the commons were asked for funds for training. The session which opened in January 1786 witnessed a more or less public process of bargaining for Pitt's support.

On 31 January Mr Marsham told the commons what the friends of the militia had been doing and asked for leave to bring in their bill. Referring to the services of the militia, he contrasted the parliamentary thanks voted them in 1762 with the parliamentary neglect of the force since 1783. He said that three main objections were made against the militia: it was expensive, it impeded the recruiting of the army, and it was burthensome for those who had to find the men. The last two objections were to be met by increasing the term of the men's service from three to five years: this would mean that fewer men would have to be found. As the men were to continue to receive only one set of clothing during their term of service in peacetime there would also be a saving of money. This was to be made greater by reducing the number of sergeants and drummers in permanent pay.[3]

Pitt in reply expressed his goodwill towards the cause of militia reform, but he also said that he would be very pleased if some means could be found of avoiding the expense of annual training. Marsham at once retorted that if there was to be no training there was no point in bringing in the bill at all.[4] Leave was given for the bill to be brought in,[5] and private negotiations took place between Pitt and its sponsors but without result.[6] On 6 February Marsham told the

[1] So Pitt told the commons (Cobbett, vol. xxv, p. 1034). Cf. p. 24, n. 4. In 1783 and 1786 (but not in 1784 and 1785) the estimate presented to the commons provided only for the pay and clothing of the permanent regimental staffs: CJ, vol. xli, p. 903; vol. xxxix, p. 305.

[2] Apparently a meeting was held, as usual, which set up a committee to frame a bill: see Drake's speech, Cobbett, vol. xxv, p. 1246. An abortive attempt was made by Marsham and Orchard to bring in a bill in May 1785 (CJ, vol. xl, p. 905).

[3] Cobbett, vol. xxv, pp. 1028–31. Pye seconded.

[4] Cobbett, vol. xxv, pp. 1031–2. In his opening speech Marsham had said that militia camps were formed as quickly in 1778 as in later war years, which showed the value of peacetime training in making the militia instantly ready for active service.

[5] CJ, vol. xli, p. 158.

[6] It is not clear exactly when. Cobbett, vol. xxv, pp. 1039, 1045.

commons that since Pitt had not made up his mind there was no point in introducing the bill. Pitt replied that

> he saw no reason why the circumstance of one individual member of parliament wishing to withhold his opinion until after a subject of such importance could be debated and argued, should be a means of preventing its coming forward at all.

He chided Marsham for not giving the house the benefit of seeing the plan that had been prepared. Marsham retorted that the minister was evading his responsibilities: the militia was a subject upon which legislation should be prepared by the government and not private persons[1]—an interestingly modern view which no doubt would have greatly shocked the militia stalwarts of an earlier generation.

That the matter did not rest there may very probably be put down to the strong opposition now encountered in the commons by the ministers' own measures for national defence. The most important of these was the Duke of Richmond's plan for fortifying the naval dockyards. This had been debated in the previous session but not carried. Now it was to come up again, and a great battle was in prospect. That all would not go well was suggested by a debate on 8 February when the commons were asked to consider the army estimates. This was opposed, mainly on the grounds that there had not been time enough to study them and that the navy estimate should be considered first. (It was hinted that there was a secret plan to reduce the navy and increase the army.)[2] But Mr Minchin, who opened the debate, based his opposition specifically on the failure to settle the militia. He called attention to rumours of a plan to replace them with some standing troops, remarked that the economy involved was trivial, and invoked both the constitutional reasons for preferring a militia to a standing army and the practical importance of an efficient militia now that our fleets were no longer superior to the combined forces of the Bourbon powers and the Dutch. He was ready to embark on the army estimates if Pitt would come down in favour of the militia bill.[3]

The leaders of the Opposition made the most of this. Sheridan said that it was absurd for Pitt to appear sometimes in his private capacity and sometimes as a minister, adding that when he acted as a private member he was usually beaten.[4] When Pitt—describing himself as 'a

[1] *Ibid.*, pp. 1032–4.
[2] For the debate see *ibid.*, pp. 1034–50. For the fortification question see A. Olson, *The Radical Duke, career and correspondence of Charles Lennox, third Duke of Richmond* (Oxford, 1961), pp. 81–6. In 1785 Pitt had also suffered defeat on the questions of parliamentary reform, Irish free trade and the validity of Fox's election for Westminster.
[3] Cobbett, vol. xxv, pp. 1034–6. Thus, too, Courteney, pp. 1045–6.
[4] As over the Reform Bill of 1785. *Ibid.*, pp. 1038–9.

friend (he might indeed say an hereditary friend) to the militia'—had declined to alter his position, Fox said it was his business as a minister to be properly informed on defence questions and himself bring forward such measures as were necessary.[1] Dundas sought to answer that there was a difference between 'the general plan of defence and a particular regulation' and that Fox had done nothing about the matter when he was minister. Fox rather lamely replied that his peacetime period of office had been too brief for any action to be possible.[2]

The estimates went through on 27 February, but the plan for fortifications was defeated after a long debate by the casting vote of the Speaker.[3] The militia figured only incidentally in this debate,[4] but great play was made with antiquated arguments relating to the political dangers of a standing army—which fortifications were supposed to increase—and it is noteworthy that such militia stalwarts as Bastard and Marsham opposed the bill.[5] Sir William Lemon said that it was ill-timed to propose it when it had not been decided whether or not to have annual exercises of the militia.[6] There seem here to be definite signs that not enough had been done to conciliate the country gentlemen. It is not surprising that on 9 March the commons learned that a compromise had been reached between Pitt and the friends of the militia. They had already deferred to him to the extent of formally introducing their bill on 13 February, and it had been printed and was awaiting committal.[7] Pitt now proposed that only two-thirds of the men balloted should be trained each year. He based himself on the analogy of the regular regiments, which were kept only two-thirds complete in peacetime because it was more necessary to have a full complement of trained officers and NCOs than of trained men. Not everyone liked this. Mr Rolle wanted no training at all because it caused debauchery, and Sir Edward Astley would have preferred two months every second year. But Mr Drake explained that the framers of the bill had approved the proposal and he would therefore support it. The proposal was adopted.[8] The bill seems to have remained con-

[1] *Ibid.*, pp. 1041–2. [2] *Ibid.*, pp. 1047–9. [3] *Ibid.*, pp. 1096–1157.

[4] Bastard said that if they lived in fortifications they would be cut off from their fellow-citizens and turned into a pretorian guard (*ibid.*, p. 1114).

[5] Bastard moved its rejection. He had assembled 2000 men for the defence of Plymouth in 1779 and could not be regarded as indifferent to the needs of national defence. Cf. *ibid.*, p. 1118.

[6] *Ibid.*, p. 1115.

[7] This was originally fixed for 8 March but on the 7th it was put off till the 10th: it looks as if there was intensive last minute bargaining. CJ, vol. xli, pp. 201, 255, 307. In Pitt's papers there is a plan for only *half* the force to be trained: PRO. 30/8, vol. 244, ff. 136–41.

[8] After Sir John Miller had reviewed the history of the militia from the time of the Saxons. Cobbett, vol. xxv, pp. 1244–8.

tentious, for the committee stage was protracted,[1] and on report there was a division on the proposal to restrict the training to two-thirds of the force, which was then carried by 49 votes to 13.[2] The house finished with the bill on 12 June, almost six months after it had been first proposed.[3]

The debate in the lords on second reading gave George Townshend (now a peer and something of an elder statesman) another occasion to lament the way in which the militia system had departed from the ideals of its creators. He complained that the aping of the regulars in standards of drill and in insisting on tall men, together with the bringing in of officers without the legal qualification, had turned the militia into an additional army competing with the line for recruits. The new arrangements for recruitment and training were a move even farther away from the aims of rotation of service and the general diffusion of military training. Reviewing the militia arrangements of France, Spain, Prussia, Hungary and Switzerland, he put forward the aim of interdependence between the services.

> The army, and marines especially, should assist the navy; that whenever there was a propensity in the soldier he might resort to the navy; that the limitation of the militia service might, under like circumstances, feed the army.

The Duke of Richmond sympathised with Townshend's objections, but thought that the militia could not but be 'an army of substitutes'. The Duke of Manchester had attended the private meetings from which the bill had originated and would have preferred the original plan. Earl Stanhope suggested another plan—ballot more men but train fewer at a time.[4] This scheme, worked out in detail, was offered to the house on report and rejected. It would have raised the total strength of the militia to 46,260. The lords made only a few amendments to the bill, but one of them was important. Substitutes were henceforth liable, if the militia was embodied, to serve for the duration of its being so, irrespective of when their term of service would otherwise have expired.[5] This got rid of the extremely tiresome

---

[1] Four sittings in committee—report deferred and the bill printed; recommittal for two more sittings. CJ, vol. xli, pp. 317, 324, 429, 563, 786, 796–7, 847.

[2] *Ibid.*, p. 886. Marsham and Sawbridge were tellers for the noes.

[3] *Ibid.*, p. 895.

[4] Cobbett, vol. xxvi, pp. 136–41. Townshend thought that insisting on rotation would end competition for recruits with the army. There is a plan in Pitt's papers for closer integration of army and militia: PRO. 30/8, vol. 244, ff. 64–77.

[5] LJ, vol. xxxvii, pp. 526, 529–30. For the commons' acceptance, CJ, vol. xli, pp. 924, 927.

necessity of replacing large numbers of men in the middle of a war,[1] but of course it made the militia more like an additional army than ever.

The rescue operation of 1786 was successful and the militia survived the years of peace, although the economies forced upon it made it less well prepared for service than it might otherwise have been when it was next called out in 1792–3.[2] But the experience of the two inter-war periods after 1763 and after 1783 was a portent. It is clear that the new militia, just like the old, depended on local enthusiasm to keep it going and was likely to collapse with the removal of the danger which had called it into being. The friends of the militia had won the battle for perpetuity, but it was essentially a paper victory. After Waterloo the militia was destined to disappear almost without trace for almost forty years.[3]

Note

After there ceased to be any counties in default, the unlevied fines seem to have been tacitly forgotten. In three cases acts of parliament were passed which had the effect of excusing them. In 1793 the two divisions of the county of Sussex petitioned the crown for money levied towards the fines be added to the public stock of the divisions. In the East Division £2097. 10s. 0¾d. had been ordered to be raised under the act of 1767 and the same under the act of 1769. Of these amounts only £886. 12s. 2¾d. and £440. 18s. 11½d. respectively were raised. In the other division the total levied was £882. 2s. 9¼d. That is to say, there had been one attempt after each act to levy the fine for one year and that had failed in each case. The petition was passed to the commons with the recommendation of the Chancellor of the Exchequer and an act, 33 Geo. III, cap. 79, was passed accordingly. The East Division had already petitioned in 1792, but too late in the session for action. (CJ, vol. xlvii, pp. 523, 547, 551–2, 627; vol. xlviii, pp. 263, 429, 774.)

In 1795 Derbyshire and Staffordshire similarly asked that sums raised towards fines should be added to the subscription being raised in each county to recruit extra forces for home defence. This was done by 35 Geo. III, caps. 16 and 60. The sums involved were £8000 in Derbyshire and £3300 in Staffordshire—a somewhat better performance. (CJ, vol. 1, pp. 10–89, 187–8, 226, 342, 354, 358.)

[1] See below, pp. 260–1. In 1779 Lord Beauchamp said that as a result of this the militia was never more than two-thirds complete. Cobbett, vol. xx, pp. 917–18, cf. p. 52. But cf. below, p. 215, n. 2.

[2] See below, p. 374. Under the new arrangements the annual cost of the unembodied militia was £116,137 (CJ, vol. xlii, p. 411), cf. £179,766. 11s. if the whole were trained (above p. 194, n. 5) and £73,278. 5s. for the permanent staff alone in 1786 (CJ, vol. xli, p. 903). The Pay Acts of 1787–9 made a further saving by stipulating that men enrolled before November 1786 and so far not trained should receive neither training nor clothing unless the militia was embodied for actual service. 27 Geo. III, cap. 8, ss. 19, 20. Cf. 28 Geo. III, cap. 11, and 29 Geo. III, cap. 15.

[3] Fortescue, *History*, vol. xi, pp. 43, 98–104, 448; vol. xiii, pp. 22–3.

IX

AN EPILOGUE OF EXPANSION
1775 – 1802

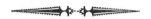

D URING the last quarter of the eighteenth century it was not
often that the militia was in danger of perishing because of the
absence of national danger. In the wars against the American and
French revolutions this was, on the contrary, greater than before.
Accordingly, the nation became more willing to support the militia
and the reliance of the government on it steadily increased. Ministers
continued to make much use of their predecessors' favourite devices,
the Fencibles (descendants of the 'select militia')[1] and bodies of volunteers. But increasingly they sought to enlarge the militia and to turn
it into something more like an army of reserve, from which the regular troops could be recruited. Under ministerial guidance the militia
continued its evolution from a means of limiting the power of the
crown into a mere military expedient without political overtones. To
many this was unwelcome and the opposition of the day could always
arouse hostility to the government on this issue. Ministers, therefore,
never dared to subordinate the militia to the army to the extent that
military necessities required.

The attitude of the Opposition to the militia was affected by the
fact that the core of it was made up of the friends of Rockingham and
later of Fox, who were the political heirs, however tenuously, of
Newcastle and his friends. Their main lines of attack were that
ministers organised the raising of new forces in such a way as to
benefit their own followers, and that they perverted the militia system by departing from the intentions of its creators as to its nature
and purpose. This represented simply the views of the more old-
fashioned of the friends of the militia. But there were also those who
argued that the militia was inherently a bad thing and so of course

[1] Cf. above, pp. 45, 164.

205

found useful by wicked ministers. This definitely harked back to Newcastle and Hardwicke, as did the alternatives most commonly proposed in place of straightforward militia expansion. These comprised the strengthening of the regulars by a more effective system of recruitment and the more intensive development of purely auxiliary bodies for part-time local service. The militia was rightly criticised as a hybrid between these two sorts of force.

I

The opening of the American revolution in 1775 was the moment at which the militia became quite unequivocally the protégé of the ministers, and as such a proper object for opposition attack. About this time there appeared the first signs of that alliance between the mass of the squires and the court which was to constitute the toryism of the early nineteenth century. Alarmed by the activities of the Americans and of the radicals at home, conservative-minded gentry and clergy began to abate their traditional hostility to government. The most striking instance of this was when the University of Oxford chose Lord North as its Chancellor in 1774.[1] In the following year the new trend became visible among the officers of the militia. It seems that disquiet arose in the West Country in consequence of radical propaganda, including numerous invitations to prominent local gentry to take the lead in forming a political association. Addresses of loyalty were promoted as a counterblast, and among others the first regiment of Devonshire militia adopted one promising to do their best when called upon to suppress the domestic enemies of king and constitution.[2] Meanwhile the government was facing the need to send large reinforcements to America. Recruiting from the militia for the army was considered,[3] and in October Lord North was thinking of calling out part of the militia to take over the army's police work at home.[4] On the 30th he introduced a bill in the commons to enable the king to call out the militia should rebellion occur anywhere in his dominions, not merely at home.[5]

Lord Barrington had already proposed such a measure in the commons in 1768, as a response to Wilkite agitation. It had not then had the support of the ministers in general, and it had rapidly succumbed

[1] For the whole subject see Ward, *Georgian Oxford*, chaps. xxv, xxvi, and epilogue.
[2] Cobbett, vol. xviii, pp. 851–2; cf. p. 854, for comparable events in Staffordshire.
[3] *Correspondence of George III*, vol. iii, pp. 215–18, 249, 253.
[4] *Ibid.*, p. 267.
[5] Objection was at once taken to the extension of the crown's powers, *Parliamentary Register* (2nd ed., London, 1802), vol. ii, p. 261.

to the violent attacks of the opposition.[1] Newcastle lived just long enough to urge these on. 'Governing by force,' he wrote,

> seems now to be the point; and as there may be difficulties in doing that by a standing army, they are now attempting to do the same by a militia.[2]

The bill of 1775 was no less strongly attacked by the opposition, on its second reading, as being politically dangerous. Charles Turner, it is true, simply repeated the old argument that militias were a bad thing, anyway.

> The proper men to recruit and supply your troops are the scum and outcast of cities and manufactures; fellows who voluntarily submit to be slaves by an apprenticeship of seven years are the proper persons to be military ones. But to take the honest, sober, industrious fellow from the plough, is doing an essential mischief to the community and laying a double tax. The militia is likewise more expensive than the regulars and therefore the more improper at present.[3]

But the main lines of attack were laid down by Dunning. He accused Colonel Acland, who had presented the militia address, of having acted in improper collusion with Lord North and even allowed him to alter the wording. He went on to claim that the bill completely denatured the militia because the king could now call it out at any time, on the mere apprehension of revolt in some remote dependency, instead of only in great emergencies at home. He was a friend to the militia as it had been but not to this 'monster', and he linked it with the government's objectionable use of foreign mercenaries.[4] Fox underlined the constitutional objection and said that he approved of the militia as a 'succedaneum' to the regulars but this bill turned it into a standing army.[5] Acland refuted Dunning's accusations against himself so completely that Dunning begged his pardon.[6] But Burke argued that the address of the Devonshire militia, as also a recent one from Oxford University, were both objectionable because they came from people who had no business to meddle in politics and were libellous towards members of the opposition.[7]

---

[1] Walpole, *George III*, vol. iii, p. 144. J. Wright (ed.), *Sir Henry Cavendish's Debates of the House of Commons, 1768–71* (2 vols., London, 1841–3), vol. i, pp. 21–6. W. J. Smith (ed.), *The Grenville Papers* (4 vols., London, 1852–3), vol. ii, pp. 297–9.

[2] Wentworth Woodhouse, R. 1–1062–4.

[3] Cobbett, vol. xviii, pp. 846–7. [4] *Ibid.*, pp. 847–9. [5] *Ibid.*, pp. 857–8.

[6] *Ibid.*, pp. 851–3. Acland held a regular as well as a militia commission and served at Saratoga (H. Walrond, *Historical Records of the 1st Devon Militia* (London, 1897), p. 68). His father had wished to raise a corps of regulars to be commanded by the son. North had backed this, saying that he had no political connection with Acland but a favour to him 'will be of considerable political use'. The king refused to allow it. *Correspondence of George III*, vol. iii, pp. 245–51.

[7] Cobbett, vol. xviii, pp. 853–4.

Lord North in reply made light of the constitutional danger and offered to add a clause allowing militia officers to resign if they disliked being called out. The second reading was carried by 259 votes to 50.[1] In committee it was proposed to restrict the life of the measure to the duration of the existing rebellion, in order to lessen the constitutional objection. Sir George Savile said

> there were always two parties in the country; no matter as to their principles: the prince would have it in his power, by this bill, to put the militia under the command of which of those he thought fit.

If there was no rebellion to justify embodiment, he might foment one at a safe distance. Sir Grey Cooper replied that the minister would be obliged to ask the approval of parliament for any call-out. The amendment was lost,[2] but on the third reading an amendment from Savile limiting the bill's duration to seven years was accepted. Fox and Burke renewed their objections all the same, and Acland caused an ugly incident by saying that he was no place-hunter but a gentleman of independent fortune and hinting that this was not true of Fox. The bill was carried by 162 to 26,[3] and in due course became law.[4] No use was ever made of it, though in several counties the officers offered their services.[5]

On the second reading of the bill, Lord Mountstuart had declared that he would take the opportunity to make another attempt to get a militia established in Scotland. Leave to bring in a bill for this purpose was given that very day, 2 November.[6] As in 1760 it was proposed to raise a force of 6000 men.[7] Mountstuart's intervention had stung Dunning into his remarks on mercenary troops already noticed and when the commons came to consider the Scottish bill in March 1776 the opposition attacked it as another step in the denaturing of the militia. On the second reading Townshend began by saying that he was always averse to the increase of any perpetual armed force, as

[1] *Ibid.*, pp. 858–9.

[2] By 140 votes to 55. Thomas Townshend thought that standing armies always started off as militias, but supported the bill to prevent the introduction of foreign mercenaries. *Ibid.*, pp. 859–62.

[3] *Ibid.*, pp. 862–3.

[4] 16 Geo. III, cap. 3.

[5] Glamorganshire, Worcestershire, Essex, Warwickshire: *Calendar of Home Office Papers, 1773–5*, pp. 475, 511. Surrey: J. Davis, *Historical Records of the Second Royal Surrey Militia* (London, 1877), pp. 104–5. The power this act gave of recalling parliament by proclamation if it was used served as an excuse for the ministers' not deferring prorogation in June 1778 (Cobbett, vol. xix, p. 1260). This clause had been suggested by Hartley (*Parl. Reg.*, vol. ii, p. 352).

[6] Cobbett, vol. xviii, p. 847. Cf. p. 1235, on the bill's authorship. CJ, vol. xxxv, p. 419.

[7] Cobbett, vol. xviii, Dempster's speech, p. 1228.

something fatal to liberty wherever it was allowed.[1] Burke also thought that the power of the crown would be undesirably strength- ened.[2] In the final debate on the bill Sawbridge said that the measure carried before Christmas had as good as turned the militia into a standing army, and that the people of Scotland were 'tinctured with notions of despotism' and might, if armed, be 'fit instruments in the hands of a treacherous, tyrannic and unprincipled administration'. He thought that their recent addresses to the throne showed as much.[3]

As in 1760, the opponents of the measure objected not only that Scotland was politically unreliable, but also that she was too poor to pay for her own militia. Mr Grenville calculated that the net revenue of Scotland was £94,945 (much of it already spent on defence) and the peacetime training alone of the proposed militia would cost £34,970 a year.[4] The Scots members were unconvincing in their attempts to refute these financial arguments. They were on stronger ground in claiming that the measure was for the benefit of the king- dom as a whole.[5] Grenville proposed that the cost of the force be met by a special land tax on Scotland, but Lord North (who supported the bill) objected and the proposal was defeated by 67 votes to 54.[6] On the report stage, however, Thomas Townshend moved the rejec- tion of the bill and it was defeated by 112 votes to 93.[7] Although this does not seem to have been mentioned in debate, its popularity can- not have been enhanced by the fact that it was promoted by the son and heir of Lord Bute.

It was not until after Saratoga, when Britain's continental enemies began to take a hand in the war, that the ministers had to make ex- tensive preparations for home defence. In 1778–9 a number of new regular regiments were raised by influential personages or at the ex- pense of large towns and there were subscriptions for raising recruits for the existing regiments of the army. Bodies of volunteers for local service were raised by the same means. In addition to these traditional ministerial measures, the embodiment of the militia was ordered in March 1778, when it became known that France had made an alli- ance with America. In the absence of a militia in Scotland, Fencible Regiments were raised there, to the number eventually of almost 4500 men. In 1778 parliament sanctioned the augmentation of the militia by voluntary enlistment to the extent of one company per battalion. This was a purely permissive measure; but when Spain

---

[1] *Ibid.*, p. 1228. Mountstuart had delayed its introduction in the vain hope of getting a full house to debate it. (*Parl. Reg.*, vol. iii, p. 141).
[2] Cobbett, vol. xviii, p. 1230. [3] *Ibid.*, pp. 1236–7.
[4] *Ibid.*, pp. 1231–2. [5] *Ibid.*, pp. 1230, 1233.
[6] Cobbett, vol. xviii, pp. 1232, 1234. [7] *Ibid.*, p. 1237.

entered the war in June 1779, Lord North proposed to double the strength of the militia by means of a ballot.[1]

The opposition professed themselves willing to help in the defence of the country against France and Spain. But they attacked the ministers' plans as both inefficient and politically obnoxious. They certainly had some justification for the first charge[2] and may well have had a fair amount for the second, though hardly as much as they claimed. In the case of the army, the death of Cumberland had destroyed the most effective means of keeping it out of the clutches of politicians. In his time, expansion had taken place largely by the expansion and division of the old corps.[3] The multiplication of new corps under the auspices of the civilian friends of the ministers naturally made the opposition suspicious. They complained that laymen were promoted at the expense of deserving old officers and that among the laymen the friends of opposition were not given a fair chance to serve.[4] As at other times,[5] the voluntary subscriptions were denounced as unconstitutional. It was thought sinister that they were well supported in areas where the jacobites had been strong.[6]

These questions excited the opposition greatly and were often raised in parliament by them in 1778–80. Only in the light of this can we understand the opposition's attitude to the militia, which was extremely confused. In December 1777 the venerable Chatham recalled that he had been 'a great friend' to the revival of the militia and thought that they should be called out; but he said that he did not know if they were efficient or capable of being made so.[7] The Duke of Richmond thought they were a 'weak defence'[8] and when they had actually been ordered out, Shelburne remarked that the government seemed unable to find the money to pay them. He thought that the king should

> try what could be done with the Whigs. Scotland and Manchester have been tried sufficiently already. The Tories have been applied to and con-

[1] Fortescue, *History*, vol. iii, pp. 245, 287–91. For the mobilising of the militia see Cobbett, vol. xix, pp. 950, 969–70. Fortescue does not distinguish properly between the volunteer corps and the men added to the militia by voluntary enlistment, first sanctioned by 18 Geo. III, cap. 59, ss. 8, 9. On Fencibles see above, p. 164. By ss. 4, 5 of the same act their officers were to rank with those of the militia and, like them, be always capable of sitting in parliament.

[2] As over the poor state of the defences of Plymouth and Portsmouth. A. Temple Patterson, *The Other Armada* (Manchester, 1960), pp. 219–24.

[3] Cf. Cobbett, vol. xxiii, pp. 647–58.

[4] Cobbett, vol. xix, pp. 685–7, 690; vol. xx, pp. 46–53, 1097–8, 1247–8, 1250; vol. xxi, pp. 327–40, 484–5, 488–90.

[5] Above, pp. 117–19; below, p. 219.

[6] Cobbett, vol. xix, pp. 620–2, 633, 685–7, for the last point. For the general question, *ibid.*, pp. 614–44, 684–94. Both sides referred to the debates in 1745.

[7] Cobbett, vol. xix, p. 600.   [8] *Ibid.*, p. 608.

fided in. I do not approve of exclusive distinctions in times of difficulty and danger, nor at any time.'

The ministers should appeal for the help of leading gentlemen everywhere, irrespective of party, offering whatever 'honours and advantages' they could.[1] In a later debate he deplored the lack of regular troops and said that much could be expected of the militia but not that they should 'make head against a numerous veteran army'.[2] It was the ministers (in successive speeches from the throne) who unequivocally praised the militia.[3] But the opposition by no means condemned it for Burke in December 1778 called it 'well disciplined, brave and well-appointed'.[4] What they seem rather to have been saying was that the government could not make it or any part of the defences work properly and the only remedy was to give power, central and local, to themselves.

When Lord North brought in his bill to double the size of the militia in June 1779 the opposition developed on this basis something like a reasoned criticism of the militia system. Coupled with the divisions then almost destroying the ministry, this led to the defeat of the bill's essential provisions. The tone of the debates was not high—they mainly turned on the question of whether Lord North was a traitor and on accusations of naval unpreparedness.[5] But Fox, Burke and other critics consistently declared themselves ready to support, or rather acquiesce in, the bill[6] and it was not mere factiousness that caused it to succumb.

When the bill was introduced on 21 June Fox's firs t reaction was that the men might be got but that officers might not be found so easily. Burke and Thomas Townshend both thought that new regular regiments, able to act on the offensive as well, would be preferable.[7] On the second reading next day Sir George Yonge suggested something entirely different—a return to the old tradition of arming the whole country.[8] Sir Charles Bunbury wanted half the proposed augmentation put on board the fleet. The rest might be added to the existing militia companies, the shortage of junior officers being got over by the promotion of ensigns and sergeants.[9] General Burgoyne wanted to combine the two alternatives that had been suggested in place of a militia augmentation by both raising new regular regiments and giving arms to the 'yeomanry'.[10] It was clear that the opposition

[1] *Ibid.*, pp. 1045–6. [2] *Ibid.*, pp. 1264–5.
[3] See *ibid.*, pp. 1279, 1281; vol. xx, pp. 1021–2, 1024, 1093, 1095.
[4] *Ibid.*, p. 49; cf. p. 50. [5] See *ibid.*, between pp. 915–89.
[6] *Ibid.*, pp. 916, 922, 937, 954, 960–2, 975, 1017.
[7] *Ibid.*, pp. 916, 919, 922. [8] *Ibid.*, pp. 928–9.
[9] *Ibid.*, p. 930. Cf. Onslow, p. 922, and Grenville, p. 955.
[10] *Ibid.*, pp. 931–2.

was inclined to prefer a voluntary to a compulsory levy and they found support on the ministerial side. Earl Nugent was pleased that the opposition seemed ready to help in national defence and he hoped that the traditional expedient of voluntary efforts organised by county meetings would now be adopted.[1] Of course, the opposition favoured the voluntary method in part because they could then exact a political price for their help. Alderman Sawbridge said that the Common Council of London were likely to offer their services on condition that the ministers were removed.[2] Fox raised again the complaint of jobbery in the making of new levies. The Attorney-General was conciliatory. He said that the government thought militia augmentation the fairest expedient, but the voluntary offers of service would probably be accepted.[3] The question was confused by doubts on both sides of the house as to how large a force was needed.[4]

In committee next day (23 June) the house hesitated between augmentation of the forces by ballot and by volunteering, and many suggestions were made for combining the two. The Speaker was against a ballot. So was Sir George Savile, as he always had been. Ministerialists like Nugent and Jenkinson, the Secretary at War, agreed.[5] Pownall, formerly Governor of Massachusetts, praised the American militia, victors of Saratoga, and called for a general arming.[6] But Lord Beauchamp made more impression by proposing a clause allowing volunteer companies to be added to the militia.[7] Lord North vacillated absurdly. After conferring with his colleagues on the treasury bench he prompted Sir Grey Cooper to propose a halving of the suggested augmentation. Dundas expostulated: to allow himself to be overruled was simply to justify charges of incompetence. North thereupon tried to withdraw his suggestion. He also said that the provision for a ballot would only be used if the force could not be got in other ways.[8] On report next day he was accordingly asked not to raise the force at all if the expense could be spared.[9]

[1] *Ibid.*, p. 931. Cf. Gilbert, p. 932.
[2] *Ibid.*, p. 924.   [3] *Ibid.*, pp. 934–6, 941–2.
[4] North said there were 63,000 men in the kingdom and wanted the augmentation only to be on the safe side. Beauchamp said the militia was never more than two-thirds complete because of time-expired men constantly leaving. Colonel Onslow cited Marlborough's opinion that 50,000 were enough for home defence. *Ibid.*, pp. 917–18, 920, 922.
[5] The Speaker recalled the militia riots, some of whose leaders he had prosecuted when Attorney-General. *Ibid.*, pp. 954–5.
[6] *Ibid.*, pp. 955–9.   [7] *Ibid.*, p. 955.
[8] *Ibid.*, p. 959; cf. p. 960. Cooper's amendment was carried, as too was one by Nugent lengthening the bill's life from one year to three. This was welcomed by North, who said he had not ventured to propose it. BM, Add. 35615, ff. 251–2, 255. Cobbett, vol. xx, p. 961.
[9] Cobbett, vol. xx, p. 960.

After this it is not surprising that the augmentation plan should have been virtually killed by the lords—especially as some of the ministers there turned out to be against it. It was attacked as a press bill—a good debating point since it was considered in conjunction with a bill to tighten the press for the navy.[1] Lord lieutenants criticised it sharply in the light of their official experience. The Duke of Richmond's opposition was given weight by his being a professional soldier and point by the fact that his county of Sussex had been a defaulter and had only raised its militia in 1778. He remarked that the ballot had caused riots there and he disliked all the augmentation proposals in the bill, whether by ballot or by volunteers. But he was not against augmentation as such—indeed, he claimed to have suggested it. His complaint was that the militia was becoming too like the army. No corps (save those from inland counties) should be removed from its own county. Local patriotism was the foundation of militia morale and local knowledge of their military usefulness. They should not go to camp and learn 'merely their common evolutions'. The Duke complained of the lack of preparations for driving the country (what we should call a 'scorched-earth' policy) and also wanted the digging of earthworks, in which the Americans excelled. This was what he wanted the militia to do. In committee he said with some justice that a ballot under existing conditions might send up the price of substitutes to the point where it would be cheaper for those liable to pay a fine rather than find a man, thus stultifying the levy. He thought that men should be enlisted for eighteen months only, or chosen by ballot but only embodied when the enemy landed.[2] His criticisms arose out of his efforts to obtain for the regiment of his own reluctant county the privilege of being stationed at home,[3] but that did not mean that they were merely frivolous.

On the motion to go into committee on the bill the Duke of Grafton argued that, like most militia bills, it was so badly drafted that it would not work.[4] The Duke of Manchester said that it would interfere both with the harvest and with ordinary recruiting and might lead to riots.[5] Lord President Gower thought the bill was faulty but could

---

[1] Cobbett, vol. xx, p. 978.

[2] *Ibid.*, pp. 979–85. *Parl. Reg.*, vol. xiii, pp. 566–70. He also complained of the refusal of offers of service, including his own. The bill envisaged the augmentation of each company to 100. Richmond pointed out that the companies were of unequal size, and for this and other reasons the proposed augmentation would be unfairly apportioned: BM, Add. 35615, ff. 255, 258.

[3] For this and the riots see, e.g., WO. 1/1000: Richmond to Barrington, 10 June and 4 August 1778. Cf. above, p. 199. In April 1780 there was an unsuccessful motion in the commons for militia regiments not to be marched an inconvenient distance from their counties. CJ, vol. xxxvii, pp. 800–1.

[4] Cobbett, vol. xx, p. 991.   [5] *Ibid.*, p. 992.

be amended and was sure that more men were needed, though he deprecated the revealing of figures. But Lords Bristol and Townshend urged that priority be given to recruiting the army, and when Lord Amherst the Commander-in-Chief refused to answer Bristol's allegation that the army was 16,000 men short, he moved the rejection of the bill. Townshend said that local corps raised by the gentry among their followers would be more to the point.[1] In committee Gower proposed that counties be allowed to exonerate themselves from the levy by raising recruits for the army. He feared a ballot would not be practicable. Secretary Weymouth wanted volunteer companies only. The Lord Chancellor supported the bill, mainly in the interest of harmony with the commons, and Amherst said that recruiting had been bad and this was the only sure way to get men.[2] This seems to have been the first mention of what would seem the strongest argument in favour of the measure, and it came too late. The clause for an augmentation by ballot was thrown out of the bill by 39 votes to 22.[3]

Back in the commons on 2 July the opposition sought to broaden the question into one of privilege. They contended that the bill was a money bill and the lords had no right to amend it. Ministerial speakers contended that it was not.[4] Fox ably connected this question with those relating to the content of the bill. He said that the commons had backed the plan unanimously, only to find that the ministers in the lords were divided on it and the lord lieutenants found it objectionable. Had 'the idea of contemning aristocracy' made it impossible to consult them first? The bill should be thrown out and a new one brought in. The whole affair showed the ministers to be utterly incapable.[5] North's reply was lame. He lamented that his colleagues disagreed with him and in a phrase reviled by Sir George Yonge he said that he must 'pick up even the crumbs which fell from their lordships' table'. He said that there were many in the commons who were deputy lieutenants or militia officers and could judge if the measure would work: he was sure that in the county of which he was lieutenant[6] it could be executed within a month. He had always been willing to accept an augmentation by volunteers and hoped that those who preferred that method would now try their hardest to make it succeed. The commons eventually decided by 63 votes to 45 to consider the lords' amendments and accepted them by 51 to 23.[7] The ministers now decided to raise 11,000 men for general service, and 2000 for home service only by means of voluntary enlistment.[8] Three

[1] *Ibid.*, pp. 992–5.   [2] *Parl. Reg.*, vol. xiii, pp. 565, 568–71.
[3] Townshend voted with the minority, Gower, Weymouth and Stormont with the majority. *Ibid.*, pp. 571–2.
[4] Cobbett, vol. xx, pp. 1008–13.   [5] *Ibid.*, pp. 1013–15.   [6] Somerset.
[7] Cobbett, vol. xx, pp. 1015–18. The bill became 19 Geo. III, cap. 76.
[8] SP. 41/40, f. 237. WO. 34/116, f. 268.

English Fencible Regiments were formed,[1] and the government abolished the system of 'contingent men' which kept the militia 1400 below its authorised strength.[2] But the volunteer companies of militia raised under the new act never amounted to much.[3] The affair revealed clearly that the ministry was almost disintegrating. The former followers of the Duke of Bedford, led by Gower and Weymouth, were on the point of seceding. They sided against North on the question of the ballot, apparently at the prompting of the Duke of Grafton, and some thought that he had given way in order to placate them.[4] It will also be seen that the house of lords played the same restraining role as it had over the militia bills of 1756–7, though in a rather different political context.

After the debates of 1779 there are signs of a growing feeling that ministers were misusing and perverting the militia. The prolonged embodiment of the force made it costly to keep it complete in men and impossible to ensure that all the officers had the property qualifications required by law.[5] Its augmentation by volunteers, like the other new levies, had a good deal of jobbery about it.[6] Suspicion was also aroused when the Fencible Regiment raised by the Cinque Ports in lieu of militia was given to Lord North's son.[7] In 1780 the dismissal of Lords Carmarthen and Pembroke from their lieutenancies for their political opinions seemed to mark a further step in the destruction of the militia's independence and its assimilation to the army.[8] Lord Shelburne told the lords that this was a new instance of the turning of the militia into an engine of corruption. Lord lieutenants, he said, had always been deemed to hold a balance between

---

[1] Fortescue, *History*, vol. iii, p. 290.

[2] See below, p. 361. But the militia was about 1000 under strength, anyway. SP. 41/28, Jenkinson to Weymouth, 24 July 1779 and enclosure.

[3] Amherst was very pessimistic about the chances of getting men when the use of the ballot had been rejected (WO. 34/116, ff. 110–11). Only fourteen companies had been raised by March 1780 (LJ, vol. xxxvi, pp. 57–8). By the end of 1782 the militia establishment came to 37, 178 rank and file (cf. 30, 840 provided by 2 Geo. III, cap. 20, s. 41), but there were 3009 wanting to complete (WO. 17/1155).

[4] BM, Add. 35615, f. 266. Cf. J. Steven Watson, *The Reign of George III, 1760–1815* (Oxford, 1960), pp. 213, 225.

[5] Cf. below, pp. 246, 305, 317–18.

[6] For an example see *Memoirs of the Anglesea Militia . . . with observations on the evidence . . . against W. Peacocke, late Lieutenant Colonel, sentenced to be cashiered*, etc. (London, 1783).

[7] North was their Warden and he had suggested that they do it because their own special and separate militia organisation had ceased to work. The men were raised in the Ports and his county of Somerset. His son received neither rank nor pay. Cobbett, vol. xxi, pp. 327–9; cf. WO. 34/120, ff. 121–2.

[8] In 1781 the king told North that he would never again appoint as lord lieutenant 'anyone whose sentiments are not cordial with government'. *Correspondence of George III*, vol. v, p. 295.

crown and people.[1] Rockingham said that the purposes of the militia were

> the defence of the kingdom from our foreign enemies and to have that defence composed of men, not immediately dependent upon the crown. This was the original idea on which the militia was first taken up; but if unqualified persons were permitted to serve, merely as mercenaries, for the sake of pay and rank; if substitutes were continued from time to time; and if the lords lieutenants were to be dismissed, merely for their political principles, he, for one, saw no difference between a militia and a standing army: of the two, he was inclined to give the preference to the latter, because they very seldom troubled themselves with parties or politics . . .[2]

It was natural in these circumstances that there should be a resurgence of interest in the old idea of a militia, essentially for local service, based on the general arming of the people. The cry was raised that the Bill of Rights allowed every subject to have arms. The opposition complained that in the formation of volunteer corps for local defence the government had armed only its political friends. Lord George Gordon was especially angry at the refusal of arms to his friends in Scotland and of course saw the hand of popery in it.[3] After the Gordon Riots the Duke of Richmond invoked the same constitutional principle in objecting to Lord Amherst's orders to disarm Londoners who were not in the militia or who had no royal authority to bear arms.[4] In 1781 Sheridan instigated a debate on the police of Westminster largely to protest against the use of the army to preserve order—an argument on parallel lines.[5] In 1781 and 1782 there appeared pamphlets advocating a militia organisation very much like the plans of Toland in 1698 or Martin in 1745. Both spoke of the need for a counterpoise to the standing army, and both regarded the existing militia as an army in all but name, though not necessarily the worse for that.[6] Radicalism was resurgent and anarchical military doctrines came back with it.

[1] Cobbett, vol. xxi, pp. 217–20. He also attacked improper promotions, which involved him in recriminations and a duel (pp. 293–6, 319–27). His motion on this occasion was rejected by 92 to 39. Lord Denbigh pointed out that several lords in opposition had been allowed to keep their lieutenancies (see *ibid.*, pp. 222–8). Rockingham restored the deposed lieutenants in 1782, but to Carmarthen's sorrow himself removed Chesterfield in Buckinghamshire (BM, Add. 27918, f. 68).

[2] Cobbett, vol. xxi, pp. 221–2.

[3] Cobbett, vol. xx, pp. 1107–9, 1178–84. Fortescue, *History*, vol. iii, pp. 288–9, 292.

[4] Ministers said the order was only aimed against suspicious characters. Cobbett, vol. xxi, pp. 726–54.

[5] *Ibid.*, pp. 1305–25.

[6] *Tracts concerning the Ancient and only true legal Means of National Defence by a Free Militia* (2nd ed., London, 1781). *Considerations on Militias and Standing*

When the opposition came to power in 1782 they creditably started on military reforms in accordance with their criticisms of North. Fox on becoming Secretary of State made various ominous remarks about the exposed state of the country and the need for an enquiry to enable the guilty to be punished and reforms to be made.[1] Conway was made Commander-in-Chief and seems to have induced his colleagues to take up at long last his home defence plans of 1757.[2] In May Shelburne sent out detailed suggestions for consideration by the mayors of large towns. Infantry battalions were to be raised in each town, apparently by voluntary enlistment. The officers were to have property qualifications and be appointed on the recommendation of the chief magistrate of the town. There were to be NCOs and an adjutant or town major in permanent pay. The men were to be exercised on Sundays and holidays and in the evenings with arms furnished by the government. They were only to be called into service in the event of invasion or rebellion, when they were to be on much the same footing as the militia. As in 1757, the great advantage claimed for this plan was that it would be easy to collect men for exercise if they lived in one town.[3] Conway also introduced a system (which endured, but only on paper[4]) of attaching each line regiment to a county for recruiting purposes, urging commanding officers to win the co-operation of the local gentry for this work.[5] Finding both the army and the militia very defective in numbers, he favoured the voluntary recruitment of the former from the latter.[6] The Rockingham ministry was thus moving towards the replacement of the now hybrid militia by a more authentic one, coupled with a territorialised army: a synthesis of the best thinking on the subject as revealed in the great militia controversy of twenty years before.

The Shelburne plan was attacked in the commons as putting arms into the hands of people not fit to be trusted with them. The Irish

Armies. With Some Observations on the Plan of Defence Suggested by the Earl of Shelburne . . . (London, 1782). On the existing militia, cf. pp. 47–8 of the former and pp. 22–4 of the latter (the author of which says, p. 27 note, that he followed a plan of 1745).

[1] Cobbett, vol. xxiii, p. 2; cf. vol. xxii, pp. 1353–4, 1415.

[2] That the plan which follows, and that for county regiments, were Conway's is strongly suggested by what Shelburne told the king (*Correspondence of George III*, vol. v, p. 493) and by their similarity to Conway's plans in 1757, above, pp 135–7.

[3] Cobbett, vol. xxiii, pp. 13–14. An act was also passed to give the volunteer corps a firmer legal basis (22 Geo. III, cap. 79).

[4] Cf. below, p. 258.

[5] WO. 3/26, pp. 57–60. Fortescue, *History*, vol. iii, p. 528.

[6] Cobbett, vol. xxiii, pp. 6, 7. Others had proposed this during the war. WO, 34/115, ff. 177–8. PRO. 30/8, vol. 55, ff. 99, 100. The experiment of enlisting men for the army for three years only had been tried. Having to let them out at the end of the war caused considerable difficulties (Fortescue, *History*, vol. iii. p. 499).

Volunteers and the Gordon Rioters were naturally pointed to. Fox replied that the people were loyal, that the Irish example showed how effective a general arming could be, and that had there been such a system here, it would have been a means of checking the riots. He explained that the plan was only a suggestion and the government would be guided by the towns' wishes. He brought out its value in releasing the regular forces for offensive action.[1] Not only his colleagues but supporters of the former ministry like Dundas and Rigby supported him.[2] Emboldened by all this, and alarmed at the increase of danger by Holland's entry into the war, the Scots again tried to establish a militia. Asking leave to bring in a bill, Lord Graham said that

> raising a militia was placing arms in the hands of the middle class of the community, who had little to gain, and much to lose by troubles and commotions. Such men would be a shield to the constitution against the turbulent grasp of democracy, or the encroachments of the crown.

Lord Maitland, seconding, recalled with pleasure that Fox had said 'that nothing was so preposterous as persevering in one opinion, merely for the sake of consistency'.[3] Turner, nevertheless, opposed the motion, calling the militia 'part of our slavery' and proposing that all Britons should learn the use of arms under a new system. But the Secretary at War was neutral and Hartley said that he no longer had the same reason as before to oppose all measures putting power into the hands of ministers.[4] Nevertheless, the bill was killed after its second reading.[5] In the country the Shelburne plan had a very mixed reception.[6] Some thought it dangerous to arm the urban poor;[7] others wanted a simple augmentation of the existing militia.[8] The speedy end of the new ministry and of the war prevented any serious test of the new policy. But Conway's intelligent thinking on military

[1] Cobbett, vol. xxiii, pp. 1–5, 8–10.   [2] *Ibid.*, pp. 5–8, 10–12.

[3] They announced their intention in the debate just mentioned. *Ibid.*, pp. 6, 7, 14–16.

[4] *Ibid.*, p. 16. A Kirkcudbright stewartry meeting declared that they wanted a militia for local defence, not like the English. HO. 42/205, enclosure in Lord Selkirk, 7 June 1782.

[5] The committee stage was postponed three months after an amendment allowing Scots militiamen to enlist in the army was carried against the sponsors of the bill (CJ, vol. xxxviii, p. 1048). According to *Considerations*, p. 66 note, the same happened in 1776: the Scots could not accept this provision unless it was also applied to England.

[6] The answers to the circular are in HO. 42/205.

[7] *Considerations*, pp. iii, 25–6, 46–7. HO. 42/205, Charles McDowell, 28 June; Claud Boswell, 30 June 1782.

[8] *Ibid.*, Lord Poulett, 13 May; Lord Pembroke, 12 May; John Sharp, 14 May; resolutions of the 17th in Edward Coulson, 17 May; A. Clowes, 27 May; enclosure in Geo. Ballard and Richard Royds, 11 May 1782.

organisation suggests that, had he been given the opportunity, he might have proved himself worthy to rank among the tiny band of capable English war ministers.

II

The development of the militia question followed much the same lines in the French Revolutionary as in the American war, but with a happier outcome for ministers. They succeeded where North had failed, in greatly augmenting the militia. They had a little more success than Conway and Shelburne in making the different defensive forces complement one another. But their efforts continued to encounter the traditional objections, and so they could do little towards the creation of a really rational military system.

The mobilisation of the militia began late in 1792, even before the declaration of war.[1] At first there was little danger of invasion and little need to augment the defensive forces. Some (mainly Scottish) Fencible Infantry was raised in 1793–4, however,[2] and in 1794 the counties were invited to raise voluntary subscriptions for home defence. The money was used to augment the militia by voluntary enlistment, finance volunteer corps for local service, and raise county units of Fencible Cavalry. The last were of interest because they were an attempt to give the militia a cavalry arm, lacking since 1757. These county levies were justified by the invasion preparations begun by the Committee of Public Safety, but they roughly coincided with the defection of the Portland whigs to Pitt and served as a useful demonstration of the popularity of ministerial policy. It is not surprising that Fox and those of his followers who remained in opposition revived the complaints of the previous war that such measures were illegal and a piece of jobbery in favour of the ruling party.[3] On this occasion they yielded some 6000 Fencible Cavalry and 5000 militiamen (2700 raised in 1794).[4]

It was at the end of 1796 that the government embarked on a much more ambitious programme, the central feature of which was the

[1] Below, p. 374.
[2] Fortescue, *History*, vol. iv, pp. 943–4. A Scots militia bill was brought in on 17 June 1793, but not proceeded with (CJ, vol. xlviii, pp. 945–6). The Lancashire Volunteers raised by Lord Grey de Wilton seem to have been thought of as militia. When the regiment went to Ireland, it was ruled that they were to have the same privileges as the English militia regiments that went there in 1798. (HO. 50/31, H. Dundas, 4 May 1799 and note). Perhaps this regiment and the Egerton's Fencibles of the previous war (Fortescue, *History*, vol. iii, p. 290) were intended to make up for the relative smallness of Lancashire's militia quota (below, p. 246).
[3] See my article 'The County Fencibles and Militia Augmentation of 1794', *Jol. of the Society for Army Historical Research*, vol. xxxiv (1956), pp. 3–11.
[4] WO. 17/1159. HO. 50/31, return of March 1798.

trebling of the militia. Britain was now isolated, about to lose her last ally, Austria. The government's military advisers, such as David Dundas the Quartermaster-General and Lord Cornwallis the Master-General of the Ordnance, thought that there was a serious prospect of invasion.[1] It was proving impossible to maintain regular forces of the size considered necessary. The strength on the British establishment had been built up, despite considerable casualties, from 35,000 at the start of the war to 130,000 (including Fencibles) in the spring of 1795.[2] The defection of the Dutch made the government think that still larger numbers were required,[3] but it proved impossible to get the men. Heavy colonial commitments brought casualties in excess of recruiting and the army shrunk to a strength of just over 100,000 men in 1797–8; from mid-1795 until early in 1797 there was a deficit of 50,000 on the authorised establishment.[4] The cause of this is obscure. It was partly no doubt that the country had been drained of all who could be induced to enlist in the army.[5] But it seems also that the government was financially too hard pressed to be able to afford the ever-rising bounty demanded by new men. From 1795 it was trying to save money by pruning the army establishment: in the first year £800,000 was saved in this way.[6] One of the economies was a limitation on the size of bounties,[7] and army agents complained that it was becoming harder to get any money issued for recruiting.[8] In March 1797, when the financial problem was at its worst and the country had been forced off gold, the Fencibles were told to cease recruiting entirely because of the difficulty of supplying the army with money.[9]

A cheaper sort of force was needed to augment the home defences and free the regular forces for offensive action.[10] Cornwallis proposed

[1] WO. 30/58, no. 17. WO. 30/64, pp. 1–3, 9–13.

[2] WO. 17/1159–60. Cf. Fortescue, *History*, vol. iv, p. 887. This excludes the Irish and East India Company establishments and foreign mercenaries.

[3] *Annual Register* (1795), p. 165.

[4] As note 2.

[5] For evidence of this in the Highlands see J. M. Bulloch, *Territorial Soldiering in the North East of Scotland during 1759–1814* (Aberdeen, 1914), pp. xlii, xliii.

[6] Cobbett, vol. xxxii, p. 1224. Cf. the reduction in the number of regiments in 1795, Fortescue, *History*, vol. iv, p. 408.

[7] WO. 4/156, p. 375. But the reason given was that high bounties were hindering the recruitment of seamen.

[8] Register House, Edinburgh: Abercairney MSS. 931: H. Donaldson, 11 August 1795.

[9] WO. 4/168, p. 153.

[10] David Dundas wanted 'preparations at hand' sufficient to 'permit the Fleet fully to exert itself at a distance on its own element instead of tying it down to the passive guard of a coast'. WO. 30/64, p. 11. Cf. Pitt in 1795, *Annual Register*, p. 169.

a compulsory levy of men to be trained in their spare time and incorporated in the militia should their services be required. Colonel Anstruther the Deputy Quartermaster-General suggested that the counties be required to enlist volunteers for the army at the rate of half their militia quotas (some 15,000 men).[1] Both these plans for raising forces on the cheap were adopted by the government, who decided that the supplementary militia, as it was christened, should number 60,000. They also decided to strengthen the new militia with bodies of cavalry and sharpshooters. The 'provisional cavalry' was to be raised by a levy of one horse in ten on all those who paid the horse tax and was to number 20,000. Employers of gamekeepers were to find a man each, which was expected to produce 7000 sharpshooters. In both these cases there was a return to the old principle that the levy of the men should be a charge on property owners.

Pitt proceeded cautiously. On 15 October he had a meeting with the friends of the militia in the two houses, to whom the details of some at least of the plans were already known. On at least one important point he made an alteration in accordance with their advice. They thought that it would be impossible to train the new militiamen in their spare time and suggested that a sixth of them at a time should be assembled for twenty days until all had been trained. Pitt presented the plans to the commons on 18 October.[2] The opposition objected that there was no real danger of invasion and that the measures were in the worst French Revolutionary tradition of requisitioning. Ministers were suspected of having some wicked design, and in particular Fox thought the levy of men for the army betokened a foolish desire to renew the offensive.[3] There was truth in this, for Henry Dundas had told Grenville that it would be necessary to come forward with a plan of home defence in order to win support for the war abroad.[4] But in the course of the debates the opposition gradually conceded that the danger of attack was real and they did not oppose the augmentation of the militia.[5] On the other hand they divided the commons on the amendments to the bill for the provisional cavalry[6] and

[1] WO. 30/58, no. 17. BM. Add. 43770, no. 33.

[2] Those at the meeting included Lords Berkeley, Euston, Fortescue, Hertford and Radnor; Colonels Stanley, Sloane, Wodehouse, Steele. Charles Yorke tried to persuade Pitt that the militiamen should be sent to the regiments to be trained. Half the recruits for the regulars were eventually allotted to the navy. BM. Add. 35393, ff. 3, 4. Cobbett, vol. xxxii, pp. 1208–13.

[3] Cobbett, vol. xxxii, pp. 1213–23, 1229–39.

[4] HMC, *Dropmore*, vol. iii, p. 257.

[5] Fox said he would unless the bill was amended, G. Woodfall, *Impartial Report of the Debates . . . in Parliament* (London 1794, etc.), vol. xiii, p. 177. Pitt said nine-tenths of the people believed in the danger, Cobbett, vol. xxxii, p. 1231. See further, *ibid.*, pp. 1237–8, 1247, 1254.

[6] And were beaten by 140 to 30. Cobbett, vol. xxxii, p. 1256.

managed to secure the withdrawal of the gamekeepers' bill which proved unpopular.[1]

The ministers carried the bills incorporating their other plans but they proved to have been so badly drafted that amending bills had at once to be brought in. They also proved so far from popular that there were widespread riots against the militia augmentation, just as in 1757.[2] Fox was emboldened to propose the repeal instead of the amendment of the militia bill. But he did not venture to divide the house. Against evidence of the measure's unpopularity Henry Dundas could now point to conspicuous signs that the French were going to attack. It was 13 December and the attempted landing at Bantry was only a few weeks off.[3]

Even after amendment the government's plans did not all succeed. It remained impossible to find enough men for the regular forces.[4] The provisional cavalry proved difficult to levy and almost impossible to train.[5] It had been raised because there was a general belief in the eighteenth century that cavalry would be especially useful against an invasion because the enemy could bring few horses with them.[6] But in June 1798 the generals told Henry Dundas that they had all the cavalry they could use[7] and eventually the provisional cavalry was wound up.[8] But the supplementary militia was a success. It never reached its full projected strength. In February 1799 Henry Dundas told the commons that the militia forces which had by then been brought into being ought to amount to 106,000, but amounted in fact to 82,000.[9] Even this figure, however, was almost treble the strength of the militia at the start of the war and the augmentation was made after the army had tried and failed to increase its strength. This levy was a milestone in the history of the militia because for the first time it can unequivocally be said that men were brought under arms who would never have joined the regular army.[10] Moreover, by August 1797 David Dundas was able to report that the men had been trained in all counties except Cumberland, Westmorland and Northumber-

---

[1] Woodfall, vol. xiii, pp. 215–16, 223–4, 243. Sheridan said someone must have given Pitt 'in the form of a bill, a bad translation of a German romance'.

[2] See below, pp. 294–5, 297, 301–2.

[3] See Woodfall, vol. xiii, pp. 348–55. The acts were 37 Geo. III, caps. 3, 22 (militia), 6, 23 (cavalry), 4, 5, 24 (recruits for the army).

[4] WO. 30/65, no. 4.

[5] See WO. 1/942, *passim*; National Library of Scotland, Melville Papers, vol. 1048, f. 75.

[6] See, e.g., WO. 30/64, pp. 51–2.

[7] WO. 1/942, f. 255.

[8] Woodfall, vol. xix, p. 270.

[9] *Ibid.*, p. 269. Perhaps because parliament had laid down that the whole militia should not exceed 1 in 6 of those liable to serve. See below, p. 246.

[10] See part iii, chap. x.

land.[1] The new levy was swelled by three local measures. In 1797 the ministers at long last raised the militia of 6000 men that the Scots had so often demanded.[2] In the same year the militia laws were made applicable, with modifications, to the Tower Hamlets and in 1798 to the Stanneries.[3] The City of London militia had already been reformed in this way in 1794, but to little purpose.[4]

When the supplementary militia had first been proposed, Fox and others had accused the ministers of planning to denature it by calling it out for a long period of continuous service, as had been done with the existing militia.[5] The ministers denied this[6] and Sir William Pulteney, one of their supporters, even hailed the new force as a return to the true militia ideal.[7] But the opposition were right at least as to the outcome. In 1797 there were peace negotiations between Britain and France, but they came to nothing, and in October Bonaparte was entrusted with preparations for an invasion on a large scale. Bonaparte gave up the idea of invasion for the time being in February 1798, but preparations continued and resulted in the abortive expedition of Humbert to Ireland that summer.[8] The alarm in Britain was great. Already in August 1797 Huskisson told the Commander-in-Chief's office that Pitt and Dundas thought that the French were probably only prolonging peace negotiations till autumn, when the Channel Fleet would have to go into harbour to refit and the invader would have his chance. They wished to know if the plans which the Duke of York had put before them were going forward, and if other plans, too expensive or alarming for present use, were ready for the moment of danger.[9] David Dundas replied with the account of the supplementary militia and other forces already referred to.[10] By 1798 the time for drastic measures was thought to have come: the supplementary militia was mobilised, half in February and half in April,[11] and by October the Scottish militia had also been mobilised.[12] The opposition did not now question the danger and

---

[1] But the embodied militia was below strength. WO. 30/65, no. 4.

[2] See my article 'The Formation of the Scottish Militia in 1797', *Scottish Historical Review*, vol. xxxiv (1955), pp. 1–18.

[3] 37 Geo. III, caps, 25, 75. 38 Geo. III, cap. 74.

[4] 34 Geo. III, cap. 81. 35 Geo. III, cap. 27. 36 Geo. III, cap. 92. The City and Tower militias remained reserved for local service.

[5] Woodfall, vol. xiii, p. 182, 353.

[6] See especially Pitt's statements, *ibid.*, pp. 181–3. The opposition had sought to limit the life of the bill until early in the next session. Pitt insisted on its being in force for the duration, but said the men would have no more service unless there was an emergency. Cf. below, p. 255.

[7] *Ibid.*, pp. 353–4.

[8] Fortescue, *History*, vol. iv, chap. xxi. E. Desbrière, *Projets et Tentatives de Debarquement aux Iles Britanniques* (Paris, 1900–2), vol. i, chap. v; vol. ii, chap. i.

[9] WO. 30/58, f. 19. [10] As n. 1.

[11] See below, pp. 374–5. [12] As n. 2.

gave little trouble.[1] The year also saw stern measures to improve the finances, notably the introduction of income tax. Both political and financial conditions were thus more favourable than they would have been earlier for this great expansion of the standing forces.

III

At the same time as they decided to embody the supplementary militia, the ministers also began to seek for ways of recruiting the army from the ranks of the militiamen and so make the two forces complementary parts of a single military system.

The raising of the supplementary militia made it harder than ever for the army to get recruits. The deficit was very high in the winter of 1796–7 and in November 1797 the government accepted the position by reducing the establishment.[2] Lord Mulgrave told Windham that the raising of new defensive forces 'put us somewhat in the situation of King James' description of himself in armour: "now I can hurt nobody and nobody can hurt me". '[3] The army was no longer strong enough to provide a 'strategic reserve', as we should say, available for offensive action. In June 1798 the lords were told that no regulars could be sent to reinforce the garrison of Ireland, at grips with rebellion, because it would mean abandoning plans to attack the French coast.[4] In May 1799 Henry Dundas told his colleagues that the army could only get enough men to supply the needs of Ireland and the colonies.[5] Windham thought that the number of men then under arms was the highest that could be got from the existing population.[6] It followed that the army could only be augmented by reducing the militia.

The embodiment of the supplementary militia destroyed the one great advantage it had over an augmentation of the army, that of cheapness. As soon therefore as it was in prospect, consideration was given to plans for assimilating the militia to the army and raising an offensive force from it. In the autumn of 1797 Colonel Anstruther proposed that twenty regiments of the line which had been reduced to 'skeletons' (officers without private men) should recruit from the militia and fencibles. Each should operate in the county to which it had been assigned in 1782 and lord lieutenants and militia colonels would be pressed to help. This should be the beginning of a genuine county basis for all recruiting. Low bounties would be the rule and 18,000 men should be obtainable, 'composed not of the dregs of the

[1] See, e.g., Sheridan's patriotic speech, Cobbett, vol. xxxiii, p. 1424.
[2] WO. 17/1160. WO. 4/170, pp. 27–37 (e.g.), 127.
[3] BM, Add. 37877, f. 4.
[4] HMC, *Dropmore*, vol. iv, p. 237. Cf. Fortescue, *History*, vol. iv, pp. 597–8.
[5] HO. 50/31, Henry Dundas, 1 May 1799. Cf. Fortescue, *History*, vol. iv, p. 601.
[6] HO. 50/31, W. Windham, 27 May 1799.

human race but of robust active men such as form the bulk of the people of Britain'. Anstruther proposed enlistment for five or six years and for service in Europe only, and he seems to have envisaged recruiting largely from the old militia, the gaps in which would then be filled from the supplementary. But it was objected that this was politically impossible, and even Anstruther thought that the colonels of the embodied militia would have to be left free to decide whether their men might be enlisted.[1]

Accordingly attention focused on the supplementary militia, which David Dundas declared in January 1798 was the only source from which the government might hope to get men.[2] It was now discovered that many supplementary militiamen had already joined the army. The Attorney and Solicitor General reported that this was illegal.[3] Now that it had been decided to embody the new militia, the government thought it right in any case to call for legislation allowing men who had left it for the army to stay there and exonerating their parishes from replacing them.[4] The outcome was an act, passed in January 1798, allowing 10,000 men to be enlisted by the army from the supplementary militia. They were to serve in Europe only and for the duration of the war plus six months.[5] A later act legalised all enlistments from the supplementary militia down to 15 May 1798.[6]

The plan was not a success. The lord lieutenants would not co-operate.[7] It is doubtful if many men would have been forthcoming if they had.[8] But at once a new plan emerged, in spontaneous reaction to the growing dangers of invasion and rebellion in Ireland. In May the Marquess of Buckingham (whose view Henry Dundas thought was widely shared) called for legislation to enable up to 10,000 militia to serve in Ireland or on the coast of France. He had consulted his officers and thought he could get his regiment to petition for such a measure.[9] Dundas raised three objections: the 'principles of the militia' would be undermined; the offers would not be really volun-

---

[1] BM, Add. 37877, ff. 182–3, 188. Objection was also taken to the limitation of service to Europe, especially because it was an avowal that overseas service was unpleasant, whereas the army regarded the glamour of it as an inducement to recruits.

[2] HO. 50/31, first undated memorandum. For a plan of December 1797 to recruit from the old and supplementary militia see BM, Add. 37877, f. 197.

[3] WO. 40/9, report of 25 December 1797.

[4] *Annual Register* (1798), p. 217.

[5] 38 Geo. III, cap. 17. For the opposition, Fitzpatrick asked for enlistment for a term of years to be the rule for the whole army and Henry Dundas said that it was being considered. Woodfall, vol. xvi, pp. 464–7.

[6] 38 Geo. III, cap. 55, s. 5.

[7] HMC, *Dropmore*, vol. iv, p. 224.

[8] See below, pp. 269–71.

[9] HMC, *Dropmore*, vol. iv, pp. 218, 222.

tary since anyone not offering would be deemed a coward; the feeling of security required for a resumption of the offensive would be impaired by breaking into the militia, the only force intact for the defence of Britain except the Guards.[1] Buckingham did not then press the point,[2] but on 10 June, having consulted his officers again, he repeated the offer of his regiment and urged the need of sending '10,000 men of all sorts' to Ireland. The government warmed to the idea. He urged them to wait for petitions from the regiments before introducing a bill and wished them luck against obstructive colonels and lord lieutenants.[3]

On 15 June a royal message informed the commons that the officers and men of certain militia regiments had offered to serve in Ireland and asked for legislation to make this possible for a limited time.[4] In the ensuing debate the opposition made the most of the first two grounds of objection mentioned by Dundas. Mr Pierrepont and Sir Lucius Palk declared that despite their disapproval they would go with their regiments if they volunteered; but Sheridan said that this only confirmed that the offers were not truly voluntary. Sir Lucius also urged that the measure might make the country gentlemen unwilling to serve as militia officers. Wilberforce accepted the plan with misgivings. He agreed with the arguments that had been brought against it, but thought that the initiative really had come from the lower ranks of the regiments and that the needs of the government were very great. A hostile amendment was defeated by 118 votes to 47 and a suitable reply was made to the king; a bill was passed accordingly.[5] Twelve thousand men were to be allowed to serve in Ireland, until a month after the end of the next parliamentary session.[6] Considerably more than that seem to have been sent over.[7] At the end of the year Henry Dundas sent a circular to the regiments that had gone asking if they were willing to stay longer.[8] The answer was favourable, and an act was passed in December extending the previous one until a month after the opening of the next session. It was prolonged again the following year.[9] Some progress was made in establishing a regular system of reliefs.[10]

---

[1] HMC, *Dropmore*, vol. iv, pp. 223–4.   [2] HMC, *Dropmore*, vol. iv, p. 227.
[3] *Ibid.*, pp. 231, 235.   [4] Cobbett, vol. xxxiii, p. 1493.
[5] *Ibid.*, pp. 1493–1511.   [6] 38 Geo. III, cap. 66.
[7] On 2 September the Home Office was told that 12,410 men had been ordered to Ireland (HO. 50/8, R. Brownrigg, 2 September 1798 with enclosure). But the Buckinghamshire and Warwickshire regiments had already gone over (R. Holden, *Historical Records of the 3rd and 4th Battalions of the Worcestershire Regiment* (London, 1887), p. 76.)
[8] WO. 6/188, p. 128.
[9] 39 Geo. III, cap. 5. 39 and 40 Geo. III, caps. 9, 15.
[10] WO. 6/188, pp. 156, 168.

The willingness of militia regiments to serve in Ireland declined after 1798,[1] but an important precedent had been set. In 1799 the possibility was discussed of using the Irish militia—which had been revived on English lines in 1793—in Great Britain.[2] The Duke of Montrose foresaw that the Scottish militia would eventually join in the exchanges.[3] The Union with Ireland stimulated this development, and the next war saw the principle established that the three national militias could serve anywhere in the British Isles.[4]

The central problem remained: how to get recruits for offensive action from the militia. Buckingham had at first thought that this, too, might be done by means of voluntary offers by whole regiments, but his own experience in Ireland disenchanted him with the expedient altogether.[5] There remained the possibility of allowing the army to enlist men from the militia. From the autumn of 1798 the formation of the Second Coalition made offensive action easier and the keeping up of very large forces for home defence less necessary. Accordingly, the planners again got busy. General Lord Fielding held a command in the north and had raised a regiment of cavalry in 1794.[6] He had advocated recruiting from the supplementary militia. In September he was arguing that this had been a failure because the militia officers had not been allowed to organise it as they thought fit and because the men had not been allowed a free choice among the regular regiments. The 'jealous suspicion and whymsical temper which is unseparable from the lower classes of this country' made this necessary. The French invasion forces were now partly dispersed, and therefore a third or even a half of the new militia should be disembodied, subject to recall, during the winter. They should be allowed to enlist in any regular regiment: by now they had become used to living without having to work and half of them would readily join the army to perpetuate this happy condition.[7] Fielding was told that there was no intention of disbanding the new militia.[8] He replied that the militia officers might object, but economy was 'a word naturally agreeable to the ears of country gentlemen'—a class which, owing to the unpopularity of the long embodiment, no longer predominated among the

[1] See below, pp. 265–7.

[2] The king thought it would be better to send them to the Channel Islands or America. BM, Add. 40100, ff. 212–14, 220. Sir H. Macannally, *The Irish Militia, 1793–1816* (London, 1949) gives a good account of its subject.

[3] HO. 50/29, Duke of Montrose, 10 September 1798.

[4] Macannally, chap. xvi. J. W. Fortescue, *The County Lieutenancies and the Army, 1803–1814* (London, 1909), pp. 126, 254–5, 257. C. M. Clode, *The Military Forces of the Crown* (London, 1869), vol. i, pp. 300–1.

[5] HO. 50/32: Lord Buckingham, 13 September 1799.

[6] WO. 4/151, p. 338.

[7] HO. 50/44, Lord Fielding, 29 September 1798.

[8] WO. 6/188, p. 125.

officers.[1] Another plan was produced by the Duke of Gloucester, who had been for several years an officer on the central Staff of the army. He wished to raise 20,000 men for the regulars by a ballot, like the militia. They were to serve in Europe only and be discharged at the peace. To help in getting the men, the provisional cavalry and part of the militia would be disbanded. The Duke thought that the militia could never be entirely relied on because its officers had not enough skill.[2]

In February 1799 the ministers decided to wind up the provisional cavalry and also brought in a bill which was apparently intended to stabilise the militia at its existing size and excuse the counties from filling the large deficit in its establishment. But though it passed the commons this bill was eventually dropped.[3] On 1 May Henry Dundas presented to the cabinet a plan combining the suggestions outlined above. He favoured recruitment of the army by ballot, coupled with leave to the people of each county to supply their quota with volunteers from the militia. If this was thought too novel, the army should be allowed to recruit direct from the militia. The men were to serve in Europe only and for five years or until the peace, whichever was the longer. The counties would be placated by a reduction in their militia quotas and the colonels of the militia by restoring their flank companies to their regiments—a sore point which will be explained in a moment. The number of men expected to be got for the army was 28,000.[4]

When the cabinet was consulted, Windham the Secretary at War[5] came out in favour of recruiting both the militia and the army by voluntary enlistment for a term of years. He also wished, however, to reduce the size of the militia very considerably in the hope of providing recruits for the army. He thought that the abolition of the ballot would lead to a fall in the price of recruits.[6] Lord Grenville said that all depended on the lord lieutenants and militia colonels. Whatever scheme they favoured ought to be adopted. A measure which they refused to support would be futile, even if it could be carried in parliament.[7] Dundas took the same view and called a meet-

[1] HO. 50/44, Lord Fielding, 30 October 1798. He thought only half the militia captains were legally qualified.

[2] BM, Add. 37842, ff. 206–14.

[3] Woodfall, vol. xix, pp. 269–73. CJ, vol. liv, pp. 199, 206, 222, 372, 402, 432, 468, 473. The comons had asked on 22 December 1798 to know the size of the militia deficit, *ibid.*, pp. 95, 97. Cf. p. 222 above.

[4] HO. 50/31, memorandum of 1 May 1799.

[5] Since 1794, when Dundas became Secretary of State for War. Dundas took over operational control of the militia from the Home Office in March 1798 (cf. BM, Add. 40102, f. 17).

[6] HO. 50/31, memorandum of 27 May 1799. Cf. HMC, *Dropmore*, vol. iv, p. 85.

[7] HO. 50/31, minute on H. Dundas, 13 May 1799.

ing of lord lieutenants and colonels late in May. The plans were put before them and they were later invited to submit written comments on Dundas' bill.[1]

The ensuing deliberations, both private and parliamentary, showed that, as in previous wars, there was a strong feeling that the militia was being consistently misused. Its lengthy embodiment and great expansion had been felt as a burden. The resulting influx of officers with no property revived fears that the force would lose its constitutional independence. These fears were strengthened by the plans to recruit the army from the militia. But the opponents of this measure were remarkable for their moderation. They did not object to the war, like Fox, or to the size of the forces. They revived the plea for a militia that was less of a hybrid and more unlike the army. But to achieve this, they were prepared to make the militia smaller and the army considerably bigger. They did not entirely oppose the entry of militiamen into the army but wished to disband a large number of them outright, in the hope that they would enlist. What they were determined to prevent was the down-grading of the militia into a recruiting organisation for the army. Unfortunately, this meant that they were an obstacle to any plan for making the different defensive forces complementary.

The complaints voiced in 1799 were not new. The regular forces had long desired to use the militia as a source of manpower and had always been resisted.[2] In 1795 they won a tiny success. The militia contained a certain number of seamen and some of its men had been trained as gunners. These were both types of skilled manpower in short supply.[3] In February 1795 the lord lieutenants were accordingly asked how many seamen there were in their regiments and how best they might be got into the navy.[4] At about the same time a meeting of militia officers agreed to assist the government in the matter of artillerymen. The outcome was a bill to allow the militiamen concerned to volunteer for the navy or artillery. Not more than a tenth of the force were to be allowed to transfer. When it reached the lords it was attacked by Lord Radnor, henceforth one of the government's most inveterate militia critics. He said that he had joined in the offer by the meeting of officers without realising the construction that would be put on it. The bill threatened to turn militia officers into mere drill sergeants for the army: most regiments trained some of their men to be gunners and henceforth these might be taken as soon

---

[1] WO. 6/193, pp. 220, 222.   [2] Below, pp. 264–5.

[3] In the case of the artillery, probably because it was thought necessary to have men at least 5 ft. 7 ins. tall. WO. 4/773, p. 299.

[4] WO. 1/767, f. 47. The army and fencibles were simply told to hand theirs over. WO. 3/13, pp. 150, 184. WO. 3/28, p. 80.

as trained. Allowing certain militiamen an absolute right to ask for their discharge would be subversive of discipline. It was proposed that the militia corps would replace the men they lost by the enlistment of volunteers and this Radnor rightly considered an important and dubious innovation.[1] Among the supporters of the bill were Lord Spencer, who had been a militia officer, Hardwicke, who was one, and old (George) Lord Townshend. But it was opposed by Lord Romney, who as Mr Marsham had introduced the bill of 1786 in the commons, and by Buckingham.[2] The bill was passed and a few recruits were got.[3] But Lord Radnor repeated his objections in a Protest which contained the prophetic words:

> the militia contains a fund for recruiting not only the artillery but every other corps in His Majesty's service, much too good not to be ardently coveted and (however the intention be disclaimed at present) I fear resorted to. . . .[4]

Other complaints that the militia was in danger of losing its true character were heard whenever the shortage of persons properly qualified to be officers became so great that the legislature had to take note of it. In 1795, in order to obtain an adequate number of subalterns, what amounted to a system of half-pay in peacetime was instituted for those ranks. Though devised by the senior officers of the militia, this plan aroused much misgiving.[5] The first supplementary militia act allowed officers from other services to serve therein in a rank not higher than their existing one, in cases where persons legally qualified could not be found. A bill introduced in 1798 would have allowed the government to appoint such officers to all commissions in the supplementary militia left unfilled by the lord lieutenants. Colonel Mitford complained in the commons that the spirit of this bill was quite different from that of earlier militia laws. He did not distrust the ministers but objected to unqualified persons in the senior ranks. Henry Dundas promised to accept any other workable plan. Colonel Bastard said that there were really qualified persons enough. A clause was brought in to allow lord lieutenants to appoint any qualified person who offered within fourteen days of the passing of the bill.[6]

[1] Woodfall, vol. vii, pp. 313–15; cf. p. 320. Radnor did not object to handing over seamen, but thought they should be replaced by an ordinary ballot, the government paying for substitutes. See his letter of 20 February 1795 in HO. 50/23. Cf. below, pp. 262–4.

[2] Woodfall, vol. vii, pp. 316–20.

[3] 463 men joined the artillery and 106 the navy (WO. 4/773, pp. 309–10, 316, 343). The act was 35 Geo. III, cap. 83.

[4] *Annual Register* (1795), p. 152.   [5] See below, p. 321.

[6] The sense of the bill and amendments are conjectural; the final act was so different. Colonel Sloane and, surprisingly, Tarleton of the opposition supported Dundas. Woodfall, vol. xvii, pp. 427–9. Cf. 37 Geo. III, cap. 3, s. 2.

The committee stage in the lords saw an onslaught by Lord Carnarvon on the clause allowing officers of the East India Company's service to enter the militia. He said that the emergency had cooled the ardour of the militia's friends, while its enemies were bent on assimilating it to the army and regarded all differences between the two as due to ignorance and prejudice. He thought that a reduction of the qualifications or even the abolition of the militia preferable to the appointment of unqualified officers and drew a lurid picture of the force under the command of 'Mahometans' and 'Gentoos'. Radnor moved that unqualified persons be not appointed as field officers. This amendment was defeated, but a similar one applying only to commanding officers were carried. Lord Fortescue said that he would revive the defeated amendment and that after the war he would press for the qualifications to be made higher. Lord Sydney (the former Thomas Townshend) did not improve matters by saying that he wished the supplementary militia had been raised as part of the army.[1] The government was evidently impressed by the debate for on report Lord Grenville withdrew the East India clause[2] and the bill ended up totally emasculated.[3]

While this was going on the government quarrelled violently with the militia colonels over the disposal of their flank companies. Each full-sized regiment had two of these, respectively of light infantry and grenadiers, who were the cream of the unit and supposed to be skilled in skirmishing. To make a reality of this supposition they needed to be combined in separate battalions for training and even for action. In April 1798 the Commander-in-Chief ordered the militia flank companies to be detached from their regiments for this purpose and put under the command of regular officers.[4] This caused an outcry, led by Buckingham who said it was illegal. The Attorney and Solicitor General did not agree and the question was put before a meeting of militia colonels. Lord Buckingham thought his views had been misrepresented to the meeting and was angrier than ever.[5] He said he would disobey any order to detach his flank companies and if the question was settled by legislation he would resign.[6] Eventually the scheme was carried through, but only under protest. The government was unwilling to strengthen its position by

---

[1] Woodfall, vol. xvii, pp. 526–36. It was argued that the measure would not affect the old militia, but Carnarvon rightly said that the new and the old militia formed one body, and as the militia hibernated in peacetime, how it was run under emergency conditions was what mattered most.

[2] *Ibid.*, p. 557.

[3] 38 Geo. III, cap. 55. It maintains the existing system of qualifications.

[4] WO. 3/18, pp. 174–82.   [5] HMC, *Dropmore*, vol. iv, p. 177.

[6] *Ibid.*, pp. 177, 179–81. Ministers had thought of so using the contentions clauses in the bill just discussed.

legislation because the debates would reveal wide differences of opinion among militia officers and this might be bad for discipline.[1]

In 1799, therefore, there was every prospect of trouble if the government interfered further with the militia. In February the Duke of Richmond said that recruiting for the army from the militia would produce few men and would further disgust the officers, already upset over the flank companies; a great many would probably resign when peace came.[2] In April Lord Dundas wrote to advocate the enlistment of militiamen, but begged that his views might be kept a secret. Otherwise he would lose all influence with the officers of the regiment he commanded.[3] When it came to the point however, the bulk of the officers rallied to the government. What happened at the May meetings I do not know, but it can perhaps be inferred from certain letters written to Henry Dundas by certain officers who could not attend. Colonel Eliot of Staffordshire said that the proposal was a bitter blow and 'opposition will chatter' but patriotism must come first.[4] Colonel Strutt of Essex thought that regimental commanders should try and induce their men to enter the army. Where they failed, a suitable number of the men should be given furlough without pay to coerce them.[5] Lord Dundas thought that the supplementary men were now used to idleness, and if faced with disbandment and the prospect of having to work, they would enlist.[6] Following no doubt such advice as this, the ministers in June brought in and carried a bill which reduced the militia to 66,000 and allowed militiamen to join the army, up to a maximum figure of a quarter of the new quotas of their counties. Their service was limited to Europe and to five years or the duration of the war plus six months. If a county had not men enough in service equal even to its new quota, one-quarter of the actual strength might volunteer. The king was empowered to disband further portions of the militia (subject to recall) who might also enlist. The work of recruiting was entrusted primarily to the commanders of the militia regiments.[7]

The measure was a great success: 15,712 men joined the army.[8] In consequence, the government decided—not very wisely—to attack Holland, and was soon rewarded by the capture of the Dutch fleet. Henry Dundas, thereupon, convinced his colleagues that it would be

[1] *Ibid.*, p. 169. Cf. p. 228, n. 4. See further, Walrond, pp. 151–3.

[2] HO. 50/30, Duke of Richmond, 24 February 1799.

[3] *Ibid.*, Lord Dundas, 7 April 1799.   [4] *Ibid.*, letter of 14 June 1799.

[5] *Ibid.*, paper endorsed 8 June 1799.

[6] *Ibid.*, letter of 12 June 1799, with enclosure.

[7] 39 Geo. III, cap. 106. For further details see below, pp. 267–8.

[8] The figures of recruits from the militia on this and the next page are from CJ, vol. lxi, p. 636; cited, with mistakes, in G. A. Raikes, *Historical Records of the First Regiment of Militia* (London, 1875), pp. 69–70.

safe to reduce the militia to its original strength in 1793.[1] In October a special session of parliament was held for this purpose. The act then passed allowed the men surplus to the new requirement either to enlist in the army or be disembodied subject to recall.[2] 10,414 men entered the line and the army was further swelled by the disbandment of fencible regiments, many men from which re-enlisted. Early in 1800 the army reached 140,000 men and thus could provide an expeditionary force as well as garrisons. The government had been justified in hoping to have 57,000 infantry available for the offensive.[3] In the summer of 1801 fresh French invasion preparations led to the recall of such disbanded men as had not joined the army. But the French were only bluffing:[4] peace soon followed, the militia was disembodied and a temporary act fixed the peacetime size of the force at the figure of 1793.[5] To the making of peace the men who had left the militia for the army had made an important contribution—the conquest of Egypt.[6]

As the scope of recruiting from the militia widened, increasing reliance was placed on appeals to the self-interest of militia officers. In July 1799 it was decided at Henry Dundas' suggestion that when sixty men from a regiment volunteered, one of their officers might enter the army with them as an ensign.[7] Later, when a whole militia regiment offered to enter the line en bloc,[8] consideration was given to various plans by which militia officers might lead their men into the army. Dundas thought it might be possible for whole companies to go together, and the October act laid down that when eighty men volunteered for the same regiment, officers from their own militia regiment might enter the army and command them as a company. They were to have temporary rank equal to their militia rank and such permanent rank (and half-pay) as the king thought fit.[9] Bucking-

---

[1] HO. 50/32, memo. of 11 September 1799.

[2] Cobbett, vol. xxxiv, pp. 1159, 1183–5. 39 and 40 Geo. III, cap. 1.

[3] HO. 50/51, memo. of 5 September 1799. Cf. WO. 17/1160–1. The raising of the Scots militia made it possible to reduce those Scots fencibles unwilling to serve elsewhere as a unit (WO. 6/131, p. 213). In 1800 almost all the fencible cavalry were got rid of (WO. 6/32, *passim*).

[4] Fortescue, *History*, vol. iv, p. 867.

[5] 42 Geo. III, cap. 12. Woodfall, vol. xxvii, p. 259.

[6] They comprised a tenth of the infantry on the expedition. As they had only engaged for service in Europe they had to be asked to volunteer. Fortescue, *History*, vol. iv, pp. 805–6.

[7] HO. 50/9, Duke of York, 12 July 1799. WO. 6/193, pp. 256–66. Cf. Eliot, 14 June 1799 in HO. 50/30.

[8] HO. 50/38, Eliot, 3 September 1799.

[9] HO. 50/32, Buckingham, 13 September 1799; Dundas, 11 September; Grenville, 8 September. HMC, *Dropmore*, vol. v, pp. 363–4, 381–2. National Library of Scotland, Melville Papers, vol. 1048, f. 169. 39 and 40 Geo. III, cap. 1, ss, 7, 8.

ham and others also pointed out that militia officers would not encourage men to enlist if the consequent reduction of the militia resulted in their own dismissal. Many redundant officers should therefore be kept on.[1] Dundas agreed, and thought that good treatment of the officers should be made conditional on the colonel's co-operation in the levy.[2] The October act allowed the king to retain as many supernumerary militia officers in service as he chose.[3] Buckingham had his own idea of what these officers should do. He proposed that militia regiments should raise recruits by beat of drum at the expense of government and that periodically an equivalent number of men should be induced to transfer from the militia into the line. He was ready himself to recruit men for seven guineas each from government and hoped to supply the army with 300 recruits in a year.[4] He seems to have wished this to be a permanent arrangement.[5] Lord Grenville and Lord Fortescue and many militia officers whom he consulted approved of it, and Henry Dundas was interested.[6] Thus there was, indeed, a strong trend towards turning militia officers into recruiting sergeants and making the militia for them as well as for the men the first step towards service in the army.

Against all this the militia die-hards continually protested. But the protest was often rather oblique. In June 1799, when the commons were considering the first bill, twenty lord lieutenants and senior militia officers met and condemned recruiting from the embodied militia. But they were ready to allow recruiting from the men if they were disembodied first. Dundas responded politely when informed of this resolution but said that the proposed method was too slow.[7] An amendment in the sense of the resolution was defeated in the commons by 37 votes to 4.[8] Colonel Bastard of the East Devonshires offered a compromise: part of the militia should be disembodied and enlistment would be permitted from the rest. Dundas said this might be fitted into the existing scheme.[9] Lord Radnor produced a plan very like Dundas' original one for the raising of a quota of recruits

[1] HO. 50/32, Buckingham, 25 July, 25 August, 13 September 1799.

[2] *Ibid.*, letter of 11 September.

[3] 39 and 40 Geo. III, cap. 1, s. 19.

[4] HO. 50/32, letters of 25 and 29 August 1799. Cf. HMC, *Dropmore*, vol. vi, pp. 413, 425.

[5] *Ibid.*, letter of 13 September.

[6] As notes 2 and 4. One attempt to raise a regiment from the militia was frustrated by the king's refusal to make the raiser a lieutenant-colonel in the army. Castalia, Countess Granville (ed.), *Private Correspondence of Lord Granville Leveson Gower* (London, 1917), vol. i, pp. 269–72. WO. 6/131, pp. 279, 286, 290.

[7] HO. 50/30, Lord Fitzwilliam, 24 June 1799 and enclosure; H. Dundas, 25 June.

[8] CJ, vol. liv, p. 715.

[9] HO. 50/31, papers dated 26 June 1799 and draft letter to Bastard.

from each county, to be coupled with a reduction of the militia.[1] The principle of transferring men from militia to army was accepted.

What seems to have made opposition bitter were provisions in the July act not essential to its main purpose. Deficits in the new quotas were to be filled within three months on pain of a fine of £10 a man on the county or on the area within it particularly in default.[2] Militia recruits were henceforth to receive no pay until they joined the regiment, and if they failed to join they were to be deemed deserters and might be made to serve in the regular army.[3] These provisions, directed against the slackness of the lieutenancies, were resented, and so was the new apportionment of quotas between the counties. This followed the supplementary militia acts in altering the proportion of the levy borne by each county from that fixed in 1786, in accordance with subsequent changes in population.[4] Lord Carnarvon had already complained of this when the lords debated the earlier abortive bill for reducing the size of the militia. He said his own county's quota would be reduced by only two, that of other counties by up to 1500.[5] When the lords considered the July bill in committee the quotas were again much discussed.[6] On report Radnor proposed the rejection of the bill, and all the grievances against the militia system were rehearsed. Radnor spoke of a plan to degrade the militia practised since 1796 and said that all the ministers disliked the force and so did the army officers except the Duke of York. Carnarvon said that a simple reduction would provide the army with more men and the present plan would destroy discipline, drive the gentry out of regiments now reduced to 'dwarfs and invalids' and disgust the country with levies that were followed by the encouragement of desertion at public expense.[7] A Protest by Fitzwilliam, Radnor and Carnarvon went over this ground again. But it went on to complain that the clauses extending the meaning of desertion were a plot to force men into the army and that the new quotas should not have been fixed until the annual lists of men liable for service had been made.[8] Opposition in short was largely directed against the high cost of the militia to the country gentlemen.

Carnarvon developed this line of argument in a paper which sought

---

[1] HO. 50/30, Lord Radnor, 18 June 1799.
[2] 39 Geo. III, cap. 106, ss. 9–14.   [3] *Ibid.*, ss. 16–17.
[4] All this is further explained below, pp. 246, 273–5.
[5] Woodfall, vol. xx, pp. 73–6; cf. pp. 82–4.   [6] *Ibid.*, p. 472.
[7] Radnor proposed that the third reading of the bill be postponed three months. Carnarvon protested at the introduction of important measures late in the session. Woodfall, vol. xx, pp. 475–9.
[8] And that the clauses sanctioning extra allowances for the families of men serving in Ireland (below, p. 269) subverted the financial authority of parliament. Cobbett, vol. xxxiv, pp. 1139–41.

to show that men raised at great expense to the landed interest were now to be seduced from their service at further expense. Parish overseers could not find men as easily as experienced sergeants; the system of fines would cause the latter to offer even higher bounties. The landlords bore a heavy burden from which placemen were exempt and the whole of Scotland largely so.[1] Opposition on these lines was made against the October bill also. Lord Spencer said that Fitzwilliam had shown himself quite crazy on the subject in debate and Carnarvon had declared himself absolved from his allegiance.[2] These two, with Lord Buckinghamshire, signed another protest.[3] There can be little doubt that they were only expressing the normal views of country gentlemen and militia officers. But the bulk of these chose to give preference to what they conceived to be an overriding national interest.

IV

In 1802 a definitive but short-lasting peace was made with France and the government—a new one, under Addington—proceeded to establish what they no doubt hoped would be a definitive scheme of national defence, incorporating all the benefits to be gained from the various experiments made during the war. They undertook the codification of the militia laws. This was itself a change produced by the war. Pitt had refused in 1786 to undertake militia legislation himself,[4] but almost all militia bills from 1793 onwards were ministerial measures. The task fell to Charles Yorke, Secretary at War and a zealous militia officer, though from love of his country rather than of the force as such.[5] In February 1802 he circulated the draft of a bill and received a long memorandum from Lord Pelham, the Home Secretary. Originally composed for Addington the previous September, this again revived the plea that the militia should be made less like the army. Pelham, too, was a zealous militia officer and had served for twenty years—in Sussex, under the Duke of Richmond. It is not surprising that he pressed Richmond's view that each militia unit should be stationed in its own county, or at least near to it. It would then be possible for men who had served out their time in the regiment to rejoin it briefly in emergencies. Large-scale manoeuvres and camping would prepare the regiments for the defence of their own regions. In order to enlarge the supply of men and prevent competition with the army for recruits, they should revert to the ideas of

[1] HO. 50/30, paper dated 8 June 1799.   [2] BM, Add. 41854, f. 190.

[3] Cobbett, vol. xxxiv, pp. 1185–6. Carnarvon had also opposed the first and Radnor the second of the bills allowing the militia to extend their services to Ireland. Woodfall, vol. xvii, pp. 675–6; vol. xviii, pp. 227–8. Buckinghamshire was, of course, not the same person as Buckingham.

[4] See above, p. 201.   [5] See below, p. 310.

the militia as a force only occasionally embodied, which civilians could enter without being turned into professional soldiers. Even in wartime the whole force should only be embodied for two months' training a year, one in the spring and one in autumn. General officers should report on the progress of the training and where this was satisfactory most of the men should be allowed to go home. Pelham had found that in Sussex the supplementary militia had consisted mainly of men serving in person as long as it was thought that the force would only be called out in emergencies. He saw here a way to introduce genuine conscription. The example of Prussia was used to prove that such a system would work.[1]

In March 1802 Pelham produced a variant of his plan by which the militia would consist of 30,000 men liable to prolonged embodiment and 100,000 liable only for service in emergencies, who would receive only the rudiments of training. To lessen competition with the army for recruits, only men over thirty would be accepted as militia substitutes. Militiamen would be allowed to join the army while not embodied. A large part of the militia should be light troops, suited for irregular warfare, and some should be cavalry and take over the maintaining of order from the unreliable volunteer corps.[2]

Pelham had no hope of his ideas being adopted[3] but they are important because it seems that Charles Yorke shared them and tried to realise them as far as he could. After reading Pelham's first paper he told him that he agreed that militia units should be stationed in their own regions and be properly trained by realistic field exercises. He produced a plan for the stationing of the militia accordingly. But he did not think it possible to require it by legislation. He also agreed that the entire militia should only assemble occasionally even in wartime and that as many of the men as possible should normally be left in their civilian occupations. This principle he thought was adhered to in his bill. It had never been so necessary, he further declared, to put the defensive system on a more 'scientific' basis.[4]

Charles Yorke presented his plan to the commons on 13 April 1802. In view of the great increase in the strength of France he considered that the defence of Great Britain would require 30,000 regulars and 70,000 militia; 10,000 of the latter he thought could come from Scotland. To raise and train the whole of this enlarged militia would cost £230,000 a year even in peacetime. He therefore suggested

[1] BM, Add. 33120, ff. 41–52. A brief summary is in Add. 33048, ff. 381–2. Pelham received a detailed account of the Prussian system from Lord Carysfort our ambassador in Berlin, Add. 33109, f. 77, which I take to be that at Add. 33124, ff. 127–31. Cf. for Yorke's bill, n. 4; for Richmond's view, above, p. 213; for Pelham's militia career, below, pp. 310, 398.
[2] BM, Add. 33048, ff. 361–3.   [3] *Ibid.*, f. 366.
[4] BM, Add. 33109, ff. 109–12.

that at first only 9000 in Scotland and 40,000 elsewhere should be raised. The king should be empowered to order the rest to be raised, by a proclamation, when greater danger made it necessary. He suggested that to start with the existing county quotas should be enlarged by a third and provision should be made for them to be revised after some years in the light of the number of men found to be liable for service in each place.[1] The militiamen were to be divided into classes, according to their suitability for military service. (The act as passed established five classes, the first comprising childless men under thirty, the last men with more than one child under fourteen.) The intention was to make it easier to mobilise a part of the militia only, and in that case to call out first the men best able to serve and leaving fewest dependants to be maintained by the parishes. The period of peacetime training was shortened from twenty-eight days to twenty-one, which meant that it would cost no more than if two-thirds of the militia had been exercised as provided by the act of 1786. It was significant, though Yorke did not speak of this, that the bill as passed did not contain explicit provision for fines on defaulting counties. Instead, like the act of July 1799, it imposed fines on counties or localities which did not raise their full quota, at the rate of £10 a man; the lieutenancy was to try and hire recruits with the money. The tacit assumption was that no county would default altogether. Yorke thought it inexpedient to oblige the militia to serve in Ireland (now part of the United Kingdom), but significantly said that he was sure they would offer to serve there if the need arose.[2]

The government's bill made it easier to call out or expand the militia in emergencies and diminish or dismiss it again quickly when the danger was past. The history of the supplementary militia had revealed great possibilities in this direction. The militia could go a little way back towards the original ideal of a temporary, almost a civilian, force. But it was to remain very like the army and for that reason it was most unfortunate that the ministers did not dare to integrate the two forces by perpetuating the system of recruiting militiamen for the line. The plan was accepted in the main by parliament and the debates, though they revealed a wish that the militia should be made far less like the army, would seem also to show that the ministers could not have carried a plan for recruiting the latter force from the former. On the first announcement of the plan Sheridan (professing himself a determined friend of the militia) lamented the unconstitutional way in which it had been broken up and its officers turned into

---

[1] In December 1801 the counties had been asked for returns of men able to serve, to help fix the quotas in the bill. WO. 6/189, pp. 319–21.

[2] Woodfall, vol. xxviii, pp. 390–4. Cf. p. 237, n. 4, and the act, 42 Geo. III, cap. 90. There was a separate act, cap. 91, for Scotland.

'drill sergeants'.[1] On the third reading in the commons, Mr Bryan Cooke said that the bill would make this worse and would over-burden the people and be hard to execute for want of officers. Yorke replied that recent experience suggested that both the officers and men could be got and that the government had no intention of recruit-ing the army from the militia. Should some extraordinary emergency again make this necessary, a special act of parliament would be required.[2]

The bill was strongly attacked on second reading in the house of lords (26 May). It was then introduced by Lord Hobart, Secretary of State for War, who thought the greatly increased length of the French coastline the main justification for increasing the size of the militia. The government thought that this was the cheapest and most consti-tutional way of getting the extra force; the bill of 1756 had provided for a militia of 60,000 and the population had greatly increased since then.[3] Lord Fitzwilliam proposed that the second reading be post-poned three months—equivalent to rejection. He expatiated on the injustice of the levy as between rich and poor, tolerable when the force was of moderate size but not when it was augmented: the price of substitutes had risen from 6 guineas when the system was estab-lished to 17 in 1798. The power of augmentation given to the crown was liable to future abuse by an ill-intentioned sovereign or minister and 'his idea was that . . . something relative to foreign service was in contemplation'.[4] Lord Carnarvon complained of the failure—despite ministers' claims to the contrary—to consult those experienced in militia affairs. He accused the War Office of a long-held design to pervert the militia. It had been intended for use only in emergencies, not to replace the army as the main defensive force. The power to augment was a further departure from this principle because it was at variance with militia's always being ready for instant action. The friends of the militia had resisted the augmentation in 1796 because they thought an enlargement of the army preferable. Augmentation inevitably led to the recruitment of the army from the militia, because it dried up the army's supplies of men. The arguments that had been used against this measure were repeated and Carnarvon tried also to show that the unjust way of levying the militia was a means of burden-ing the land to the relief of placemen and pensioners. He ended by deploring the loss of the militia's local connections, which had made it a 'popular standard' to which volunteers might rally in emergen-cies. In 1779 the men of Devon, rising to defend Plymouth, would not

---

[1] Woodfall, vol. xxviii, pp. 394–5. The bill reached the committee stage on 15 April; was then printed and again committed on 29 April and 17 May. CJ, vol. lvii, pp. 346, 349, 355, 385, 462.
[2] Woodfall, vol. xxix, pp. 280–1. [3] *Ibid.*, pp. 326–7. [4] *Ibid.*, pp. 327–9.

join his own (Wiltshire) regiment but only a corps of their own county.[1] Lord Romney also spoke briefly in support of rejection.[2]

The defenders of the bill were interestingly half-hearted. Lord Buckingham agreed that recruiting the army from the militia had been deplorable but said he had consented to it because he understood it was the only way to get the men. He favoured the bill because it ought to make it unnecessary to raise new corps at the start of a new war and because a large militia was less under crown influence than a large army.[3] Lord Radnor spoke in the same vein as Carnarvon, but ended by saying that in view of the perilous state of the country he would vote for the bill.[4] Lord Pelham, winding up, defended both the transfer of militiamen to the line and the system by which the militia was levied: it was not oppressive to the poor man because he could meet his obligation by joining a club and paying half a guinea. He pointed out that augmentation would be impossible without a parliamentary vote of funds. The second reading was carried by 22 votes to 6.[5] The lords made some important amendments on points of detail.[6] The commons, evidently mindful of their privileges, caused the entries in their journals relating to the lords' militia bill amendments of May 1757 to be read and appointed a strong committee to consider the present ones. Most of them were accepted.[7] Once more the lords had appeared as the main conservative force in the militia question.

The militia act of 1802 made permanent a number of expedients that had been found useful in the 1790s, but it did not really create a rational defensive system composed of several distinct but complementary and mutually supporting types of force. In consequence, the earlier years of the war against Napoleon saw a total absence of policy—or at best a succession of rival policies—in the levying of defensive forces. The confusion only ended in 1808 when Castlereagh, as Secretary of State for War, at last created the system towards which Pelham and Yorke (and Dundas before them) had been groping. A large Local Militia was created, the entirely local service of which made it possible for it to aspire to be a genuinely conscript force. The ordinary militia remained, as the mainstay of home defence; but henceforth it was an essential function of the militia to sup-

---

[1] Woodfall, vol. xxix, pp. 329–39.
[2] *Ibid.*, p. 341.   [3] *Ibid.*, pp. 339–40.   [4] *Ibid.*, pp. 342–3.
[5] *Ibid.*, pp. 343–4. The numbers not recorded in LJ.
[6] *Ibid.*, pp. 385–7. LJ, vol. xliii, pp. 650, 661–3, 666. Lord Berkeley proposed twenty-eight days' training, but Buckingham and Hobart said the men had been in service so long that this was unnecessary.
[7] The committee contained Addington, Yorke, Hawkesbury and all the county members. See CJ, vol. lvii, pp. 551, 582, 592–4, 620–1, 630–1, 645; LJ, vol. xliii, pp. 697, 701–2, 711–12, 722.

ply the army with recruits, and while the war lasted it was the army's main source of men.[1] But we should not suppose that Castlereagh's work could have been done by his predecessors. A great weight of opposition stood in the way, which crumbled only slowly as the perils of the nation became more urgent. Nor was Castlereagh's success long-lasting. As danger declined, obstacles once more appeared to a rational military system and they persisted until danger returned. A century later, on the eve of the First World War, Haldane was again striving to create a rational pattern of defensive forces. Once more there was opposition from the friends of the militia. The only way to overcome it proved to be to abolish the militia altogether.[2]

[1] For a continuation of the story told in this book the reader is referred to Fortescue, *The County Lieutenancies and the Army*, 1803–1814. Published in 1909 it was subsidised by Haldane (preface, p.v.).

[2] J. K. Dunlop, *The Development of the British Army, 1899–1914* (London, 1938), pp. 268–73, 277–84, 290.

PART THREE
The New Militia at Work

X

RAISING THE MEN

How far did the militia system, as it developed between 1757 and 1802, satisfy the political and military needs which had brought it into being? The political story of its creation which has now been told shows that it was a compromise which gave no great satisfaction to anyone. But only a detailed study of the workings of the system can show how far the dissatisfaction was justified and whether anything better could have been done. This task will now be attempted.

The methods of raising men for the militia were the most obviously hybrid part of the system. Falling far short of true conscription, they were yet far more cumbersome than the simple enlistment of recruits for the regular army, which they were accused of wastefully duplicating. Reasons will now be given for believing that the militia nevertheless tapped supplies of men not available to the army. The next chapter will demonstrate the difficulty of introducing a true system of conscription.

(I) WHO BORE THE BURDEN OF THE LEVY?

The militia was not so much a system of conscription as a tax, levied in men, on the manpower of each locality. The number which each county had to furnish was laid down by act of parliament.[1] Thirty-two thousand were called for by the act of 1757, but as we have seen this target was long unattained.[2] Small temporary augmentations resulted from the voluntary enlistment sanctioned in 1779 and 1794.[3] In 1796 the counties were required to raise a supplementary levy of

---

[1] See Appendix B.

[2] Only temporarily indeed by the abolition of contingent men (below, p. 361) and the voluntary augmentation of 1779, since the Tower Hamlets quota of 1160 was struck out in 1758, cf. above, p. 140, n. 1. See 30 Geo. II, cap. 25, s. 16; 2 Geo. III, cap. 20, s. 41; 26 Geo. III, cap. 107, s. 17.

[3] Above, pp. 215, 219.

63,878 men,[1] and more were added by the revival of the militia, about this time, in areas hitherto exempt,[2] raising the theoretical total to over 100,000. After a drastic reduction in 1799–1801 the militia in Great Britain was fixed in 1802 at 51,489, of which 9000 were in Scotland. The king was empowered to order the increase of this number by half as much again.[3]

The earlier militia acts required each county to send an annual return of men eligible for service to the privy council which was to amend the quotas laid down by parliament so that each county contributed the same proportion of its able-bodied manpower to the militia.[4] But the privy council failed to do the job, and in 1796, when returns were asked for to guide the fixing of the supplementary militia quotas, it was found that the burden was very unevenly distributed. The quotas of the supplementary militia were therefore so arranged as to correct the disproportion.[5] Subsequent acts retained the proportion then established,[6] but in 1802 it was laid down that the privy council was to revise the quotas once every ten years, the first occasion to be on or before 25 June 1805.[7]

The proportion of those eligible that might be required for militia service accordingly varied. Some places did better than others. In 1796 it was found that the old militia quotas represented 1 in 8 of the available men in Dorset but only 1 in 43 in Lancashire, 1 in 30 in Cardigan and Carmarthen, and 1 in 28 in Cumberland and the West Riding. In most counties the proportion was from 1 in 12 to 1 in 18.[8] The number of men liable for service in any county might fluctuate unpredictably and tended to fall in wartime. In Northamptonshire between 1762 and 1792 it varied from 15 to 20 times the quota.[9] In Sussex it fell from over 22 times the quota in 1778 to $16\frac{1}{4}$ times in 1782, the figure improving to 17 in 1785.[10] In 1796 parliament established a national maximum of one in six for the old and new levies combined and empowered the lieutenancy of any county where this

[1] 37 Geo. III, cap. 3, s. 3.

[2] Six thousand in Scotland, 2320 for local service from the City and the Tower Hamlets, one in seven of those eligible in the Stanneries. See part ii, chap. vi, p. 235, notes 2–4.

[3] For 1799–1801, cf. above, pp. 232–3. For 1802: 42 Geo. III, cap. 90, ss. 19, 146; cap. 91.

[4] 30 Geo. II, cap. 25, s. 18. 31 Geo. II, cap. 31, s. 21. 2 Geo. III, cap. 20, s. 74, 26 Geo. III, cap. 107, s. 50.

[5] Cobbett, vol. xxxii, p. 1210.

[6] Cf. above pp. 235, 238.

[7] 42 Geo. III, cap. 90, ss. 37–9.

[8] PRO. 30/8, vol. 244, ff. 92–3, 96–7 (no returns for eight counties).

[9] Northamptonshire RO.: X. 269, items 11–12.

[10] East Sussex RO.: LCG/EW.1.

proportion was found to have been exceeded to discharge the extra men.[1]

The acts empowered the county lieutenancies to levy their quotas by imposing an obligation of service on the proper number of men. Those who might be called upon comprised at first the bulk of able-bodied men between eighteen and fifty years of age. In 1762 the upper age limit was reduced to forty-five and poor men with three children or more born in wedlock were excused; from 1786 one legitimate child sufficed to exempt a poor man, who was also to be excused if he was less than 5 ft. 4 in. tall. A lengthening list of special categories of people were exempt: peers, officers of the army and militia, members of the English universities, clergy (including dissenting teachers and preachers), articled clerks, apprentices, seafaring men, regular soldiers below commissioned rank, Thames watermen, workers in the royal dockyards and arsenals, former militia officers who had served four years and members of volunteer corps. For the augmentation of 1796 exemption was extended to those serving in the old militia but withdrawn from peers, non-resident members of universities, persons entering volunteer corps after 20 October 1796 and poor men with up to three children;[2] a child, moreover, had to be under ten or infirm to count towards exemption. The minimum height was lowered to 5 ft. 2 ins. The act of 1802 undid these provisions of 1796; the volunteers had recovered their exemption in 1799.[3]

For assessing and exacting the burden of service the lieutenancies used what was in effect the ordinary machinery of local government. The general and subdivision meetings which directed the work were simply military equivalents of quarter and petty or local sessions respectively; justices of the peace could attend and do most of the business provided at least one deputy lieutenant was present. The orders of the meetings were executed by the civil officers of parish and hundred. The militia acts laid down a routine to be followed, which always remained much the same though no two acts are identical. In 1757 a general meeting was required to be held on the first Tuesday in

[1] 37 Geo. III, cap. 22, s. 15. Note that parishes situated in two counties were deemed to belong to the one where the church lay, and some were appropriated to particular counties by name. 30 Geo. II, cap. 25, ss. 59–63. 2 Geo. III, cap. 20, ss. 132–8. 26 Geo. III, cap. 107, ss. 33, 107–8. 42 Geo. III, cap. 90, ss. 48, 151–2.

[2] Cf. below, p. 290 and n. 4.

[3] The regular soldiers and Thames watermen were added in 1758, and the last three in 1778, 1786 and 1794 respectively. Deputy lieutenants, parish officers and persons mustered to *defend* the dockyards were at first exempt. 30 Geo. II, cap. 25, ss. 11, 19, 69. 31 Geo. II, cap. 26, ss. 12–14. 2 Geo. III, cap. 20, ss. 42–3. 18 Geo. III, cap. 59, ss. 16–17. 26 Geo. III, cap. 107, ss. 22, 27, 37. 34 Geo. III, cap. 31, s. 5. 37 Geo. III, cap. 3, s. 18; cap. 22, s. 9. 39 Geo. III, caps. 14, 35. 42 Geo. III, cap. 90, ss. 26, 43.

June each year and order the chief constable of each hundred to produce a list of all the men within his jurisdiction who were of an age to
serve and not in one of the exempt categories, noting to which parish
they belonged and those who were physically unfit. The chief constables in turn were to require the parish constables to supply them
with lists from which such a list could be compiled, affixing a copy of
the parish list on the door of the parish church on the Sunday before
the return had to be made. When the returns were before them, the
general meeting was to apportion the county quota among the
hundreds in proportion to the number of men liable for service in
each. It was also to divide the county into subdivisions, in each of
which a meeting was to be held at once. The high constables had
there to produce copies of their lists and complaints were to be heard
from those who considered themselves wrongfully included in the
lists, or that others were wrongfully left out. Next, the meeting was to
apportion the hundredal quotas among the parishes and hold a ballot
in which the proper number of men in each parish was chosen to
serve. Lastly, it was to appoint another meeting within three weeks
and require the high constables to direct the petty constables to give
the men seven days' notice at their homes to appear at it. From 1758
it was an additional, earlier subdivision meeting which received the
lists and heard complaints before passing them on, corrected, to the
general meeting for fixing the hundredal quotas. From 1762 the fixing
of the parish quotas and the holding of a ballot took place at two
separate subdivision meetings, with three weeks between them, instead of one. From 1762 also the first general meeting was to be on
the last Tuesday in May or October; from 1786, October was specified.[1] The same procedure was followed for the augmentation of 1796
and laid down for the augmentation which the king was empowered
to make in 1802.[2]

At local as at national level, the burden was not very evenly shared.
The arithmetic of fixing and keeping the quotas of the different
hundreds and parishes exactly proportionate to their manpower was
not always easy. From 1758 the lieutenancies had explicit power to
alter the quotas fixed for each hundred and subdivision meetings
might where convenient combine parishes and establish a joint quota
for them.[3] Most complicated arrangements might result from trying
to do justice by this means. In Sussex each village was commonly

[1] Other parish officers might be used in default of constables; from 1802 a
deputy might be appointed if the constable was a quaker. 30 Geo. II, cap. 25,
s. 19. 2 Geo. III, cap. 20, ss. 42, 57, 65–6. 26 Geo. III, cap. 107, ss. 18, 20, 22, 24.
42 Geo. III, cap. 90, ss. 21, 25, 33.

[2] 42 Geo. III, cap. 90, s. 146. Cf. 37 Geo. III, caps. 3, 22.

[3] 31 Geo. II, cap. 26, ss. 16, 22. 2 Geo. III, cap. 20, ss. 44, 75. 26 Geo. III,
cap. 107, ss. 23, 28. 42 Geo. III, cap. 90, ss. 34–5.

given a quota, but those whose fair share should have included a fraction were combined in groups in respect of the fractions in excess of their quotas.[1] The heaviness of the burden on those who had to bear it fluctuated according to the number of exemptions allowed. These could be very numerous: in Sussex in 1803 there were 9630 men of the right age who were exempt and 14,102 who remained liable.[2] It was, therefore, of great importance that the system of exemptions should be fairly administered and this did not always prove easy. Many people did not bother to claim their exemptions until they were chosen in the ballot.[3] This was tolerated though illegal: the clerk to the Cornish general meetings once suggested to the Home Office that they be made to pay a small fine.[4] Of course the quotas of their localities would have been fixed on the assumption that they could be included in the total of those liable for service. Similarly, the totals were swelled by the listing of itinerant workers in several counties.[5] Some claims for exemption were fraudulent: bogus apprenticeship caused enough trouble to be specifically dealt with in the act of 1762. Subdivision meetings were empowered to investigate suspicious indentures and if they turned out to be a sham, to fine the 'master' £10 and compel the 'apprentice' to serve on the first vacancy.[6]

Claims for exemption because of physical unfitness seem to have been very haphazardly decided. In Dorset the clerk to the general meetings took it upon himself to simplify proceedings by striking out those who were undersized. In 1801 he removed 750 names from the total of 11,593 on the lists. This apparently led to parliament fixing the county's quota lower than it would otherwise have been.[7] In 1796 a Cambridgeshire subdivision meeting heard eighty appeals, of which eighteen succeeded on the grounds of short stature and eleven because of the applicants' children (including one unborn child). The rest claimed to suffer from various physical disabilities, often of a sort hard to prove completely, such as lameness in the legs and arms. Some claims were accepted, some rejected and in some cases a medical certificate was asked for. How justly the deputies dealt it is hard to say, but the man with a hare lip whose appeal failed was doubtless

[1] Thus, in 1794, Ardingly and Crawley found respectively two and one men; but each ought to have found a fraction of a man in addition and so they were required to find one man more between them. East Sussex RO.: LLM/E.1.

[2] *Ibid.*, LCG/EW. 1.   [3] There are many examples in *ibid.*, LLM/E. 1.

[4] HO. 50/30, C. Rushleigh, 21 June 1799.

[5] BM, Add. 35693, ff. 167–70. They could only be made to serve in one: 32 Geo. II, cap. 20, s. 5. 2 Geo. III, cap. 20, s. 94. 18 Geo. III, cap. 59, s. 22. 26 Geo. III, cap. 107, s. 32. 42 Geo. III, cap. 90, s. 47.

[6] 2 Geo. III, cap. 20, s. 73. 26 Geo. III, cap. 107, s. 34. 42 Geo. III, cap. 90, s. 34.

[7] BM, Add. 33108, ff. 24–5. Cf. HO. 50/33, Lord Rivers, 27 October; Duke of Portland, 19 December 1799.

envious of the man who was excused because he had been knocked on the nose, while the three one-eyed men who were not excused seem hardly treated. In all, twenty-one appeals were rejected.[1] Two interesting cases occurred when the supplementary militia was levied in Sussex. In July 1797 the deputies at Lewes ordered the replacement of a man who had lost the top of his right forefinger: this looks very like a profitable piece of self-mutilation. In June 1798 it was shown that a man who had been discharged as over-age was not 47, as he had said, but 43.[2] Mistakes about age and fitness were, of course, even harder to avoid then than now.

Haphazard though the system was, the only serious criticism it seems to have aroused was when exemption was extended to volunteer corps. Those concerned with the militia disliked this greatly. The Duke of Northumberland refused to support and Lord Bateman opposed the formation of volunteer corps in the counties of which they were lord lieutenant, because they would damage the militia.[3] An officer of the Surrey militia who tried to discover why the county had been unable to raise its full quota of men reported that the volunteers were mainly just a way to escape the ballot.[4] In 1796 a volunteer corps was formed at Swansea by a not very reputable character and it was thought that the men had joined to escape service in the supplementary militia. But the law wisely denied exemption from the new levy to those who became volunteers after 20 October, and so the Swansea men were refused it.[5] The defence of the volunteers' privilege in this matter was usually that they spent as much or more on their equipment than they would have had to do to avoid personal service in the militia.[6] This was probably true of middle-class corps. But in the course of the war there was a growth of volunteer corps comprising members mainly of the working class, who did not pay their own expenses. They usually had to engage to serve a fair distance from home if required, but even so they had something of a soft option.[7]

[1] BM, Add. 35667, ff. 108–9.

[2] East Sussex RO.: LLM/E.2, sub 1 July 1797; 23 June 1798.

[3] HO. 50/341, Duke of Northumberland, 9 March 1797. HO. 50/43, Lord Bateman, 30 July 1798. HO. 50/44, Lord Bateman, 3 September, 22 November and cf. J. Mathews, 12 August 1798. WO. 6/199, p. 288.

[4] HO. 50/30, T. B. Sewell, 9 March 1799.

[5] HO. 50/335, T. Morgan, 9 November 1796; J. Beavan, received 17 December 1796. HO. 50/387, f. 353. HO. 50/55, W. Jones, 7 March 1797. Cf. HO. 50/27, Deputies of Swansea, 21 January 1797; 37 Geo. III, cap. 3, s.18.

[6] See HO. 50/44. J. Longley, etc., 24 August 1798. HO. 50/40, A. Aubert, 1 March, 1798.

[7] C. Sebag-Montefiore, *A History of the Volunteer Forces* (London, 1908), pp. 192–200, 211–14, brings out the distinction. Cf. my article 'The Volunteer Movement as an Anti-Revolutionary Force, 1793–1801', *English Historical Review*, vol. lxxi (1956), pp. 607–9.

The act of 1757 required certain individuals to be chosen to serve by ballot, but did not require them to serve personally. If they did not, they had to produce a substitute, who needed to be approved by three deputies. In either case, the 'principal' was excused from being chosen to serve again until it was his turn by rotation. He had the third alternative of paying a fine of £10, but in that case he was automatically appointed to serve again next time. Quakers, however, were to have substitutes hired for them by the subdivision meeting, which was to recover the cost from them by distraint. In 1758 it was similarly laid down that the £10 fines were to be used to get substitutes for those who paid them, and also that substitutes were henceforth to have privileges at first reserved to men serving in person: exemption from service in parish offices, from being pressed for the army, and from the 'statute work' (on the roads). No militiaman might be sent to serve abroad. Militiamen had to serve for three years, save that any who were 35 or over were entitled to be discharged after two.[1] From 1786 the term of service was five years, and substitutes who were embodied for service when their term expired had now to serve until disembodiment.[2] In 1782 those paying the fine were given the same freedom from further ballots as those who found a man.[3] From 1786 they were made to take their chance in succeeding ballots and from 1802 so were those who had found a substitute.[4] The arrangements for the supplementary militia were mostly the same as in the act of 1786. But the men's term of service was to be the duration of the war plus one month and the fine for not providing a man was £15, which conferred exemption for five years.[5]

From 1758 there were means of avoiding a ballot altogether. The first arrangement was that churchwardens or overseers might produce volunteers at the ballot meeting towards filling the quota of their parish. They had to be approved by the deputies; if they failed to appear to be sworn, whoever had produced them was fined £10.[6] From 1762 such levies had to be approved by a meeting of the in-

---

[1] A militiaman moving to another parish served the rest of his term for it, on the first vacancy (after 1762, only if it contributed to another regiment). 30 Geo. II, cap. 25, ss. 19–26, 51. 31 Geo. II, cap. 26, ss. 24, 29. 2 Geo. III, cap. 20, ss. 42, 57, 67–71, 76, 78–9, 87, 93. 18 Geo. III, cap. 59, s. 15 obliged Quakers to produce a certificate of their being so, a requirement made stiffer in 1802. See further, 26 Geo. III, cap. 107, ss. 35–6, 51, 96, 130–1; 42 Geo. III, cap. 90, ss. 50–1, 66, 112, 174–5.

[2] 26 Geo. III, cap. 107, s. 24. 42 Geo. III, cap. 90, s. 41.

[3] 22 Geo. III, cap. 62, s. 1.

[4] 26 Geo. III, cap. 107, s. 26. 42 Geo. III, cap. 90, ss. 43, 45.

[5] Principals who had chosen to serve might obtain their discharge later by finding a substitute. 37 Geo. III, cap. 3, ss. 6, 7, 9, 16.

[6] Volunteers ready trained and equipped might also add themselves to the militia when it went on service (till 1786: next n.). 31 Geo. III, cap. 26, ss. 17, 36.

habitants and be financed by a rate, sanctioned by the justices.[1] For the augmentation of 1796, a ballot might be postponed for five days if volunteers amounting to two-thirds of the quota had come forward. The bounty from the parish was not to exceed 4 guineas. Later, it was provided that volunteers might offer themselves to the deputies, who were to fix the amount of their bounty and allot them to any parish willing to pay it.[2]

Parishes often made use of these statutory powers. When the Bedfordshire militia was raised in 1760, Lord Tavistock found that most places made the attempt, paying 6 to 10 guineas for men.[3] In Kettering subdivision in 1763 four villages (out of some thirty) produced a volunteer each and avoided a ballot.[4] But more important as a rule was collective effort of a less official kind. Sometimes the wealthier inhabitants of a district subscribed to hire substitutes for their poorer neighbours. In December 1759 the magistrates and gentlemen of Norwich announced that they would pay for substitutes for poor married men.[5] In 1797 the extension of the militia to Scotland was palliated by the raising of subscriptions, mainly among the gentry, to hire substitutes for the poor, and the Duke of Buccleuch declared this to be the normal English practice.[6] Actually, another arrangement was probably commoner: a subscription by all those in a parish liable to serve to indemnify those of them who were unlucky in the ballot. In 1760 such a scheme was started in Middlesex and commended to the public on the grounds that the expense would be trifling, that the honour of the subscribers would be engaged to provide good substitutes and that the scheme was much approved by some persons of high rank.[7] From Atherton in Lancashire there survives a rough paper (unfortunately without date) the phrasing of which suggests an uneducated writer, by which 166 men engage to subscribe 7s. each,

[1] Those serving in person or by substitute were exempt. From 1786, maximum bounty of £6. 2 Geo. III, cap. 20, ss. 45–6, 88, 120. 26 Geo. III, cap. 107, ss. 36, 42. 42 Geo. III, cap. 90, ss. 42, 51.

[2] 37 Geo. III, cap. 3, ss. 10–13. 37 Geo. III, cap. 22, ss. 10–12. The privy council might authorise further postponement of a ballot. Men balloted for or serving in the old militia were exempt from service in the new; but not, it seems, the reverse unless they served personally. 37 Geo. III, cap. 3, s. 18; cap. 22, s. 13. Cf. PRO. 30/8, vol. 241, f. 22.

[3] MSS. of fourth Duke of Bedford, vol. xli, ff. 10, 40 bis.

[4] Northamptonshire RO.: X. 266, item 4.

[5] The substitutes were to be single and the intention was clearly to escape the charge of the families. *Ipswich Journal*, 15 December, 1759, quoting *Norwich Mercury*, 8 December.

[6] See my article 'The Formation of the Scottish Militia in 1797', *Scottish Historical Review*, vol. xxxiv (1955), p. 13; R. C. Dudgeon, *History of the Edinburgh or Queen's Own Regiment of Light Infantry Militia* (Edinburgh and London 1882), Appendix iii.

[7] *Ipswich Journal*, 26 January 1760.

yielding (after deduction of 2s. 'paid for warming') £58. If none of the subscribers were chosen in the ballot the money would be refunded. If it proved insufficient for the hire of substitutes, the balloted men had no further claim on the subscribers.[1] It is likely that the formation of these 'clubs' was encouraged by the parish authorities. At Sutterton in Lincolnshire in 1783 a vestry meeting decided that everyone liable to serve in the militia should pay 5s. to the constables and that if this was not enough to 'higher men that is drawn' the rest of the expense was to be met out of the rates.[2]

The 'clubs' were in effect a crude form of insurance. In 1762 insuring against the ballot, except by subscriptions confined to one parish, was forbidden.[3] But this prohibition lapsed in 1786 and there were many instances of commercial insurance schemes. In January 1762 a single issue of the *Ipswich Journal* carried three insurance offers. One was by a Colchester bookseller named Keymer, in partnership with one Seaber, whose 'Essex militia insurance office' had agents throughout the county. A second came from a Colchester draper named Duke and an Ipswich bookseller named Shawe, who had thirty-three local agents. They advertised not only for subscriptions but for substitutes and accused Keymer of pirating their own proposals, first made five months before. Both concerns claimed the patronage of the officers of the Essex militia. The third offer was made by a partnership of a 'gentleman', two farmers and a grocer, who were ready to hire a substitute or pay the fine for anyone balloted for the Suffolk or Norfolk militia. The premium was 10s. 6d.[4] In 1780 a Devonshire firm offered for a 12s. premium to pay 5 guineas towards hiring a substitute.[5] In the nineties an army officer reported that the postmaster of Salisbury (who was also the printer of the local paper) sold the prospectus of an insurance society.[6] In 1795 a 'Militia Society' advertised in the Worcester newspaper its willingness to get a substitute for anyone drawn in the ensuing year. The premium was 5s. 6d. There were agents in Evesham and Kidderminster, and customers could also send their subscription through their newsagent.[7]

From 1762 the private efforts—individual or collective—of poor men to escape personal service were subsidised from public funds. They were to receive from the parish the sum (not to exceed £5) ad-

[1] Lancashire RO.: PR. 1700.
[2] Lincolnshire RO: Sutterton Parish Records, Highways Account Book, 14. A.1.
[3] On pain of £100. But a principal might employ anyone to find a substitute for him. 2 Geo. III, cap. 20, ss. 51–3.
[4] *Ipswich Journal*, 16 January 1762.
[5] Walrond, p. 83.
[6] BM, Add. 37874, f. 249.
[7] Holden, pp. 60–1.

judged by the subdivision meeting to be half the price of a volunteer.[1] Finding this amount seems to have been unpopular with the rate-payers. Writing of conditions in North Wales, Thomas Pennant complained that those who contributed were as poor as those who received the allowance, the only result of which was to send up the price of recruits. He thought that these payments should never be made where the cost of recruiting was borne by a club.[2] In 1799 some Cornish yeomen complained that because those who had been balloted were exempt from the rate, the burden of finding £5 for each man balloted threatened to ruin the rest.[3] There was much argument about whether the supplementary militiamen should receive the allowance. One of the acts of 1796 empowered the deputies to fix its amount, but did not say if the new men were to receive it.[4] In Lancashire the deputies paid the money and then found themselves involved in a legal dispute.[5] The Sussex lieutenancy ruled that the men were not entitled to the bounty until the militia were ordered out for actual service.[6] When the supplementary militia was embodied, parliament laid down that the allowance was only to be given to men balloted after embodiment.[7] The act of 1802 made the Sussex ruling the law for the whole militia.[8] No doubt the idea was that when the force was not embodied it was not expensive to get men.

The development of the law on the raising of militiamen can be summed up by saying that the principle of obligatory personal service receded farther and farther into the background. Every facility and encouragement was given for the discharge of the obligation by some means of voluntary enlistment, and few balloted men seem to have had to serve in person save by their own free will. In one division of Cambridgeshire a deputy was astonished after the ballot for the supplementary militia to find that many who could ill afford it were paying 10 guineas for a substitute without a murmur.[9] The element of conscription that remained in the law was there as a penal sanction, to oblige those liable for service to make the painful effort of hunting for recruits.

In 1786 a poor man was defined as one not worth £500. From 1778 a church-warden failing to pay was to be fined £10 (from 1786, £5). 2 Geo. III, cap. 20, ss. 47, 49. 19 Geo. III, cap. 72, s. 14. 26 Geo. III, cap. 107, s. 41.

[2] T. Pennant, *Free Thoughts on the Miltia Laws* (London, 1781), pp. 19, 20. He said that the allowance was usually 4 guineas and it raised bounties from 4 to 10–12 guineas.

[3] HO. 50/32, letter of 29 July 1799.   [4] 37 Geo. III, cap. 22, s. 14.

[5] Lancashire RO.: LM 1/1, ff. 29, 31; HO. 50/30, T. Bayley, 11 February 1798.

[6] East Sussex RO.: LCG/EW. 2, sub. 11 March 1797.

[7] 38 Geo. III, cap. 18, ss. 3, 6.

[8] 42 Geo. III, cap. 90, s. 122.

[9] BM, Add. 35667, f. 193.

1. George Townshend.

2. 1745, as the Militia Enthusiasts saw it.

(II) WHO SERVED IN THE MILITIA?

The militia idealists had dreamed of a citizen army in which men of property would be willing to serve. The only times when there seems to have been any chance of this was when it appeared that the force would not be embodied for any length of time: 1757–9 in the case of the old militia, 1796–7 in the case of the supplementary. At Doncaster in 1757 sixteen 'gentlemen' volunteered to serve for the town in order to show their willingness to stand in the ranks with the common people and their belief both that the militia was useful and that it would not be sent abroad.[1] The Dorset regiment was said to contain fifty volunteers, most of whom were gentlemen,[2] and Major Pitt said that some of his men had no wish to receive a clothing allowance from the government and would gladly give their share towards the general expenses of the regiment.[3] In Leicestershire fifty men of considerable property came forward as volunteers in 1759, though few of the wealthier gentry were then willing to serve as officers.[4] The patriotic enthusiasm which led such men to serve in person had the same effect—helped by a few judicious pourboires—on humbler folk.[5] Volunteers often appeared in considerable numbers in advance of the ballot[6] and their enrolment was made the occasion of patriotic demonstrations. In 1757 thirteen men at Dartford assembled at a public house belonging to one of them and marched in a body to the enrolment, a drum and two French horns at their head playing patriotic and martial airs. They returned to their starting point in the same fashion after the meeting and spent the evening drinking patriotic toasts.[7]

The supplementary militia was at first expected only to serve occasionally: the government pledged itself to the Duke of Richmond in the strongest terms not to call it out unless invasion was immediately in prospect.[8] Accordingly, there were hopes that men of substance would serve in person. Richmond wished the supplementary men in Sussex to be added to the existing regiment when called out in 1798

[1] Widely reported in the press: e.g. *Cambridge Journal*, 29 October 1757; *Kentish Post*, 5 November 1757.

[2] *Ipswich Journal*, 4 August 1759.

[3] One seems to have been a J.P. WO. 1/978, ff. 545–7.

[4] HMC, *Rutland*, vol. ii, p. 200.

[5] Forty-four men sworn at Stratton received 1s. pay and 1s. to drink the king's health (*Kentish Post*, 30 November 1757). Twenty-three men sworn at Cromer (mostly principals it seems) got 1s. and a cockade (*Gloucester Journal*, 22 November 1757).

[6] At Bristol in 1758, over eighty for fifty vacancies (*ibid.*, 12 September, 1758). Cf. Cambridge in 1759 (*Ipswich Journal*, 19 May 1759).

[7] *Cambridge Journal*, 29 October 1757. Cf. Marylebone (*Kentish Post*, 5 November 1757).

[8] HO. 43/8, p. 333.

because the better sort among them liked to know beforehand who was to command them.[1] The citizens of Westminster petitioned the lieutenancy to have the supplementary militia trained locally so as to encourage men of substance to serve.[2] It is unlikely that many better-off men chose to serve even then. Of 123 supplementary militiamen enrolled for the Lewes subdivision only 35 were principals and only 12 of these could sign their names.[3] But Thomas Pelham discovered that in Sussex the working-men balloted had mostly chosen to serve in person, and farmers who were drawn sent their favourite workmen to serve for them and so benefit by a bounty. Later, the prospect of lengthy service made many principals apply to leave the force and serve by substitute.[4]

Special occasions apart, the militiamen were neither persons of substance nor impelled to join by patriotic enthusiasm. They were poor men who joined for the pay or for other purely personal reasons, like recruits for the army. Principals serving for themselves were very much in a minority. Answers to a War Office circular of 1793 showed that most of the men were substitutes.[5] Returns of this period show 143 principals out of 560 in the Leicestershire militia, 69 out of 216 in Monmouth[6] and 11 out of 477 in West Middlesex.[7] The Nottinghams had only 14 principals and in Worcestershire the substitutes outnumbered them by 6 to 1.[8] In 1768 and 1771 the North Lincolnshire battalion contained about 50 principals.[9] In 1778 it was estimated that there were 60 out of the 460 then in the Cambridgeshires, and when a ballot was held in the county in 1779 Sir Thomas Hatton thought that not 20 of the 353 men to be chosen would serve in person.[10]

From the few records which survive it would seem that principals and substitutes alike were mostly manual workers and that most of both groups were illiterate.[11] Some of the serving principals must have

[1] HO. 50/38, Duke of Richmond, 6 March 1798. But in Lincolnshire a separate regiment was wanted: HO. 50/27, Brigg subdivision resolutions, 8 February, 1797.

[2] BM, Add. 43770, f. 17.

[3] But only twenty-four of the rest could, so the principals were more literate than the others, East Sussex RO.: LLE/2/E.1.

[4] BM, Add. 33120, ff. 50–1.

[5] WO. 4/770, pp. 21, 72. Unfortunately the answers themselves have mostly not survived.

[6] HO. 50/19, returns of 30 December 1792 and 1 January 1793.

[7] *Ibid.*, general return, January 1793.

[8] *Ibid.*, E. J. Gould, 29 January; Lord Coventry, 6 February 1793.

[9] I.e. at two successive renewals of the regiment. Lincolnshire RO.: Ancaster Lieutenancy Papers, 2 Anc. 9: 59, 61.

[10] BM, Add. 35626, f. 41. Add. 35660, f. 130.

[11] See Note at the end of the chapter. In Lewes subdivision the substitutes enrolled in 1788–93 were more literate than the principals: 39 out of 88 as against 4 out of 14 could sign their names. East Sussex RO.: LLE/1/E. 1 (two rolls).

been men with an inclination to enlist who chanced to be balloted: one in the Lancashire militia said that he was an old soldier who had served at Gibraltar.[1] Others were the only true conscripts in the force—men so poor and unfortunate that they could take advantage of none of the ways of evading personal service. From 1782 there was explicit provision that men who could neither find a substitute nor pay a fine were to be made to serve,[2] and this was occasionally done. [3] There was perhaps only one sign of respectability among either principals or substitutes: a surprising number were parliamentary electors. These had a statutory right to have leave of absence when there was an election,[4] and the number claiming this privilege at the dissolution in 1780 was quite embarrassing to the authorities. For some of the regiments the figures have survived, as follows:

Corps	Officers	Men	Corps	Officers	Men
Northants.	7	31	Berkshire	43	8
Montgomery	8	10	Dorset	3	15
East Riding	15	45	Leicester	19†	300
Gloucester	25	100	South Lincoln	All ranks, 59	
Denbigh	9	43	Sussex		
Derby	13	28	Nottingham	35	144
West Kent	24	28	Northumberland		
Cardigan	3	42*			

* plus say seventy on the march.   † plus twenty-two NCOs.

But these totals must contain a good many artful dodgers.[5] Some in the Somersets simply went off to 'potwalloper' boroughs to achieve a residence qualification. General Haviland thought this unfair, and he tried to restrict leave as much as he could in the regiments under his command. He had heard that the dissolution might be so sudden that men from the remoter counties would not be able to get home in time to vote, and he tried to stop the Leicestershire men going on those grounds.[6]

It can be seen why the militia was so readily accused of taking recruits from the army. Yet there was a difference between militiamen

[1] HO. 50/35, W. Smith, 5 July 1799, enclosed in R. Brownrigg, 11 do.

[2] 19 Geo. III, cap. 72, s. 22. 26 Geo. III, cap. 107, s. 26. 42 Geo. III, cap. 90, s. 45.

[3] I have found three cases of this, all in Sussex. East Sussex RO.: LPM/E. 1, ff. 51–2, sub. 8 February 1794; LLM/E.1, sub. 5 March 1796. LLE/2/E.1, roll of supplementary militiamen, sub. Southover.

[4] 30 Geo. II, cap. 25, s. 41. 2 Geo. III, cap. 20, s. 111. 26 Geo. III, cap. 107, s. 129. 42 Geo. III, cap. 90 s. 173.

[5] The figures are from WO. 34/167, ff. 12, 14, 39, 43, 91, 95. Cf. the Herefords, f. 97, where only one officer asked leave, and Sir George Savile's regiment, f. 72, where there were only two freeholders besides the officers.

[6] WO. 34/166, f. 293. WO. 34/167, ff. 44–5.

and soldiers, connected not with the sort of person they were but with the way in which they were recruited. The trend of the law was away from conscription, but also towards making the militia a truly territorial force. Recruiting was to be done by the parish, or by individual principals helped by parish funds, and the recruits if possible were to be local men. From 1786 they had to be from the county for which they were to serve or an adjoining one.[1] For the supplementary militia they had to be from the same county.[2] In 1802 they were required to be from the same county or from the parish or place adjoining that for which they were to serve, whether in the same county or not.[3]

If law and reality were at one in this matter, the result would be a force very different from the army. Regular regiments at this time drew their recruits from those places in which their officers had friends or influence. These were commonly scattered. A Lieutenant Cameron raising a company of regulars in 1793 had seven recruiting parties in the Fen counties, where he was assisted by the 'first people', others in London, Essex and Suffolk, and three under relatives in the Highlands.[4] When Thomas Graham of Balgowan in Perthshire raised the 90th foot in 1794 he called it after his county and received financial help from the Burgh of Perth.[5] But he also got men from Leicestershire and Shropshire,[6] from Lancashire and Cheshire and other industrial areas and from a London crimp.[7] Assigning each foot regiment to a county in 1782[8] does not seem to have altered the situation. The 22nd (Cheshires) had five recruiting parties in its county in November 1796 and only one outside, but in June 1797 there were three in the county and seven outside ranging from Glasgow to Norwich and Bristol. This recruiting pattern persisted more or less through 1798–9.[9] The 49th (Hertfordshires) had one to four parties in its county from July 1796 to December 1797, but there were usually other parties in Scotland, the West Riding and Gloucestershire or South Wales.[10] Of just over 1000 recruits joining the 53rd (Shropshires) in 1755–9 only 38 were from its own and 97 from adjoining counties.[11] For 633 men joining the 14th (Bedfordshires) the figures were 55 and 28.[12]

The army, moreover, attracted men from industry and especially from the big towns rather than from agriculture. A Dr Kerr of Northampton, who sometimes busied himself with recruiting to aid

[1] 26 Geo. III, cap. 107, s. 24.   [2] 37 Geo. III, cap. 3, s. 7.
[3] 42 Geo. III, cap. 90, s. 41.   [4] WO. 1/1057, f. 107.
[5] National Library of Scotland, Lyndoch Papers: vol. 3595, f. 126.
[6] *Ibid.*, ff. 88, 118, 153.   [7] *Ibid.*, ff. 116, 150, 155, 164.
[8] See above, p. 217. Note that these affiliations were not the same as the later ones introduced by Cardwell.
[9] WO. 17/124.   [10] WO. 17/162.   [11] WO. 25/412.   [12] WO. 25/337.

the military career of his son, said in 1794 that he lived in 'perhaps the worst recruiting town in England as we have no manufactory of consequence'. He had been obliged to send (significantly) the sergeant-major of the local militia to Birmingham to make up the number of men he wanted.[1] That town and its environs were spoken of by a local magistrate as 'this populous and trading part of the country (the grand nursery for soldiers and sailors)'.[2] The official recruiting instructions of 1796 recognised the situation by requiring each regiment to recruit in its own county, but giving them permission also to send parties to any of the manufacturing towns of England and Wales (and to Scotland and Ireland).[3] Of course it was partly just that there were more people there; but it seems that it took the unsettling character of town life and employment to make the average man consider enlisting in the army.[4]

If, therefore, the militia was a genuine territorial force, with each township contributing a few men, it might fairly claim that it complemented rather than duplicated the recruiting effort of the army, by drawing on the manpower of the nation more uniformly and bringing in a higher proportion of country people than the regulars could attract. As country people were commonly supposed to be both physically and morally superior to the town workers, this might be something well worth doing. Now there is evidence enough to show that the militia really was a territorial force, as the law required. Many men in it, it is true, served for counties other than their own. The accounts of family allowances kept by the county treasurer of Middlesex in the nineties show that men with families living in the county were serving in the militias of twenty-seven other counties while men from thirty-four other counties were serving in the Middlesex militia.[5] But the greater part of the militiamen who entered the army in 1799 seem previously to have been serving for their own counties. Of 723 men from a dozen different militia regiments who joined the 82nd foot all but 191 had been born in the county for which they had been serving, and half the remainder were serving for counties adjacent to their own.[6] Of 739 men joining the first battalion

---

[1] Lyndoch Papers, vol. 3595, f. 102.   [2] WO. 1/1088, f. 287.

[3] *Regulations and Instructions for Carrying on the Recruiting Service for H.M. Forces Stationed Abroad* (20 March 1796), Art. I.

[4] Cf. E. Halévy, *Histoire du Peuple Anglais au 19e Siècle* (2nd ed., Paris, 1913), vol. i, pp. 173–4. Highlanders were often enlisted by Highland regiments in London and Glasgow, not at home: see WO. 27/82, return of April 1799. In 1804 General Craig reported that high wages impeded recruiting, and Sir John Moore said that only a recession would materially increase the supply of men (WO. 1/902, ff. 87, 115). But recruiting tended to be bad in harvest months and best in the months following. See, e.g., WO. 25/279, 307, 337.

[5] Middlesex RO.: Militia Records, item 56.   [6] WO. 25/489.

of the 52nd from the regiments of some twenty counties only 223 had been serving for counties other than their own and again half of these had been serving for adjacent counties.[1]

In the American war the position would seem to have been the same. Until 1786 the men were entitled to their discharge at the end of the normal term, even if the regiment was embodied. This was obviously inconvenient in wartime, and so from 1778 commanding officers were empowered to ask their men, some months before their time expired, whether they were willing to re-engage and for what bounty. They had then to inform the subdivision meetings of the county of these particulars, and the deputies had forthwith to hold ballots and try and induce those on whom the lot fell to engage the men then serving as substitutes at the stipulated price.[2] It was the operation of this system that strongly demonstrated the territorial character of the militia regiments: the men would not re-enlist unless the regiment was first sent to its own county and they were given a rest at home with their friends. The North Devons in 1778 were no farther from home than Falmouth but few of the time-expired men would rejoin—most said that 'they will go home to make their own bargains'.[3] Precisely the same was said of the Flintshire battalion, and its removal to a distance as soon as it had been re-raised was asked for, lest the men be tempted to stray home.[4] The Glamorgan men found service in England very disagreeable, owing to the difference in customs and language. In the autumn of 1778 they were determined not to re-engage when their time expired the following summer and Lord Mountstuart could only suggest that they be offered two months at home in exchange for re-enlisting.[5] Colonel Caldecot asked that the North Lincolnshires be stationed near home in 1780 and given furloughs; otherwise few would re-enlist in the autumn.[6] The Glou-

---

[1] WO. 25/405.

[2] Cf. above p. 252. In 1781-2 deputies had to be told also who refused to re-engage and replace them before their time was up. The act of 1786 permitted such replacement, and also allowed commanding officers to enlist time-expired men as parish volunteers. 18 Geo. III, cap. 59, ss. 1, 2. 19 Geo. III, cap. 72, s. 21. 21 Geo. III, cap. 18. 22 Geo. III, cap. 6. Cf. 26 Geo. III, cap. 107, ss. 40, 46; 42 Geo. III, cap. 90, ss. 60, 123-5.

[3] WO. 1/1000, Lt.-Col. Geo. Buck, 13 July 1778. Cf. Walrond, p. 92.

[4] Ibid., Sir R. Mostyn, 10 July; Major R. Hughes, 21 July 1778. In this and other cases it was urged that the officers were needed in the county to help in recruiting, either to see that good men were got or because they included the most active of the deputies: cf. WO. 34/138, f. 55. WO. 34/150, ff. 303-4, 369; WO. 34/155, f. 150; WO. 34/165, f. 245.

[5] WO. 34/146 (i), ff. 57-8. One hundred and fifty eventually re-enlisted (WO. 34/150, f. 369).

[6] WO. 34/156 (i), ff. 49-50. The other Lincolnshire regiment was refused this, as a bad precedent. Ibid. (ii), ff. 328-9. WO. 34/157, ff. 17-18.

cestershires in 1781 refused to re-engage before they got home, and the same was expected of Sir George Savile's men in 1779.[1] As time-expired men had a statutory right to be dismissed in time to reach their county by the end of their term, the men were in a strong position.[2]

It is likely that the supplementary militia was even more a territorial levy than the rest.[3] In 1797 the officer in charge of the training of the new men in Cambridgeshire was anxious that it should be done at a central rendezvous and not in the divisions for which the men served. In the latter case they would be laughed at by their friends for their awkwardness, discipline would suffer because they would be able to go home in the evenings and officers punishing them would incur the 'risque of being knocked on the head by old women and their families—I assure you I fear those viragos . . . more than I do the invasion of the French'.[4] In 1799 Lord Fitzwilliam asked that equal numbers be disembodied from each of the West Riding regiments. Each was recruited from a particular area, which would gain the advantage of extra labour if its own regiment alone were reduced.[5] As will be explained later, militia regiments were usually stationed outside their own counties when embodied, because the men's ties with the people of their own county might make them take the wrong side in civil disturbances: to be stationed at home was always a privilege eagerly sought.[6]

Against all this must be set certain signs that within each county recruiting for the militia tended to be concentrated in the same places and in similar hands as recruiting for the army. Little evidence survives as to how the men were found, and no doubt this is because it often happened in a spontaneous way, by a balloted man finding someone ready to serve among his acquaintances or even his relatives.[7] But there was some sort of trade in substitutes. It was some-

---

[1] WO. 34/139, ff. 193–4. WO. 34/145, ff. 428–9. But some Middlesex men re-engaged in 1778 without going home (*ibid.*, ff. 401–2).

[2] 2 Geo. III, cap. 20, s. 64. Cf. WO. 34/158, f. 242. The regiments had been raised at different times—and the men in each of them sometimes in different years—and so not all had to be replaced at once. But 1778 and 1781 were peak years. I do not know how many normally re-engaged in peacetime: few seem to have in Lincolnshire in 1771 (Lincolnshire RO., 2 Anc. 9, nos. 59, 61).

[3] In Lewes subdivision the supplementary men comprised 35 principals, 30 substitutes serving for their own parishes and 58 other substitutes. For the 'old' men enlisted in 1788–9 the figures were 14, 12 and 76. East Sussex RO., LLE/1/E.1; LLE/2/E.1.

[4] BM, Add. 35667, f. 130.

[5] HO. 50/39, Lord Fitzwilliam, 22 November 1799.

[6] See below, p. 402.

[7] Occasionally enrolments show substitutes with the same surnames as their principals.

times possible to hire them at fairs, just as servants could be.[1] The organisers of insurance schemes sometimes provided them. When the Northamptonshires were first raised in 1762, most of the men were found by an insurer named Cook.[2] A gentleman of Oundle raised volunteers to the number needed for the supplementary militia thereby employing James Rippener, 'a most worthless Fellow, artful and sensible, with a Tongue that will lead a Regiment anyway'. Powerful for good or ill, he was in 1798 very loyal, but half a crown or a pot of ale could make him otherwise.[3] In 1778 Richard and Jeremiah Page, of Stetchworth, Cambridgeshire, were chosen in the ballot. They went to the Cock Inn at Barnwell to look for substitutes and employed one Holland to find two. He accordingly sent one to the Cock, who undertook himself to find another. Two others balloted at the same time employed two of the militia sergeants to find men for them, and Soame Jenyns records a subdivision meeting at which the only recruits appearing were two vagrants brought by a sergeant. He thought that they would desert and that the sergeant—who had received at least a guinea each for them—could then earn more money by finding replacements.[4]

Many instances besides this last show that the militia authorities were themselves drawn into the recruiting trade. In the nineties most of the parishes in the Linton subdivision of Cambridgeshire had subscriptions to raise volunteers, but it was the subdivision clerk who found the men. The deputies approved of this since balloted men could hardly wander around the county searching for substitutes and were not good judges of who was fit to serve. The clerk expected something for his trouble but only a little: in raising a batch of nineteen men he had only made 3 guineas![5] A good many of those balloted preferred from the outset to pay fines, and in wartime the proportion increased as the cost of recruits went up.[6] Sometimes the civil authorities tried to find men with this money. In 1758 the Cambridgeshire clerk of the general meetings had 600 copies of a recruiting poster distributed through the high constables.[7] In 1781 the clerk in the Isle of Ely was busy finding men.[8] But increasingly the work

[1] Northamptonshire RO., X. 270, item 6: W. Walcott, two letters of 21 May 1798.

[2] C. A. Markham, *History of the Northamptonshire and Rutland Militia* (London, 1924), pp. 7, 9.

[3] As n. 1.

[4] BM, Add. 35659, ff. 321, 323, 367. On 'bawdy Barnwell', cf. below, chap. v, p. 399.

[5] BM, Add. 35663, f. 76.

[6] £200 was paid at the initial levy in Middlesex (*Ipswich Journal*, 22 March 1760). Cf. below, pp. 276–7.

[7] BM, Add. 35659, f. 3.   [8] BM, Add. 35661, f. 150.

was done by the militia officers. Even in 1759 the men required for the Ryedale division of the North Riding were raised by the officers of the company concerned, who collected 2s. 6d. from each man liable to stand the ballot.[1] It was the officers who found the men for the Sussex militia when it was first raised in 1778[2] and in Cambridgeshire one deputy was then encouraging the payment of 5 guineas a man to the officers of the regiment for the filling of vacancies.[3] In the same county in 1781 the adjutant was asked to raise seventeen men with the fines that had been paid and Hale Wortham (captain and magistrate) found recruits for all the penalties in his subdivision.[4]

Regimental recruiting was used more for the replacement of casual ties than for the initial levy. In 1796 the Marquess of Buckingham offered to raise the whole Buckinghamshire supplementary militia by voluntary enlistment, and said that some militia officers whom he had consulted said that it could not be done in any other way. The government decided that this would be illegal.[5] But Buckingham replaced all the county's casual vacancies by this means, mainly at his own expense: after 1798 the whole machinery of the ballot fell into disuse there.[6] In Cambridgeshire in 1796 a general meeting apportioned the county's deficit of men among the parishes and in view of the scarcity of substitutes advised everyone to pay a fine and let the regiment find the men.[7] A memorandum sent to Henry Dundas about 1799 declared that this had become the general practice.[8]

Regiments recruited mainly in their own counties. The Duke of Richmond and the Marquess of Buckingham thought that theirs could not achieve much anywhere else[9] and when the Hertfordshires were short of men in 1778 the sergeant-major was sent back to the county to find recruits.[10] Since the principal officers would come from the county it was natural that that should be the unit's main recruiting ground.[11] From 1762 militia corps were forbidden by law to send

---

[1] R. B. Turton, *History of the North York Militia* (Leeds, 1907), pp. 179–80.

[2] WO. 1/1000, Duke of Richmond, 4 August 1778.

[3] BM, Add. 35659, f. 315.

[4] BM, Add. 35661, ff. 78, 104. Cf. Add. 35681, ff. 313–14.

[5] BM, Add. 41851, f. 49. HMC, *Dropmore*, vol. iii, pp. 143–4. HO. 50/26, Lord Buckingham, 30 November 1796. HO. 43/8, pp. 120, 146.

[6] BM, Add. 33108, ff. 16–17.   [7] BM, Add. 35667, f. 47.   [8] In HO. 50/30.

[9] BM, Add. 42058, f. 46, and as n. 2.

[10] WO. 1/1000, Lord Cranborne, 20 December 1778. Cf. Staffordshire in 1796: William Salt Library, Stafford: SMS. 478, W. Sneyd, 16 June 1796.

[11] Lt.-Col. Ward thought that the Cambridgeshires needed to go home to recruit, because the recruits needed the stimulus of a rousing send-off from their friends. BM, Add. 35660, f. 136. In peacetime it was awkward to have men from outside the county because of the difficulty of getting them to the annual training. In 1777 the Cambridgeshire training was cancelled and there was no fund to pay those who had come from a distance for it. BM, Add. 35659, f. 222.

out recruiting parties as regular regiments did and to enlist men who did not belong to their own county. But the latter provision disappeared in 1786 and seems never to have been effective.[1] In 1793 the North Riding regiment reported that they could raise men in Newcastle,[2] and in 1781 the Cambridgeshires wanted to have the proceeds of fines sent to them so that they could pick up any recruits they came across.[3] Recruiting parties crept in when the militia was augmented by volunteers, and were sanctioned in 1795 for the replacement of the men then allowed to join the army and navy.[4] The recruiting methods of militia regiments had thus a tendency to get more like those of the army.

One characteristic of militiamen should especially warn us against making too much of the difference between them and regular soldiers due to their mode of recruitment. The towns and industrial areas were over-represented among them, as they were among the regulars. In 1780 Lord Beauchamp said that nine-tenths of the Warwickshire regiment came from the towns of Birmingham and Coventry,[5] and in 1793 it was asserted that Warwickshire supplied half the militiamen in each of the adjoining counties.[6] On a smaller scale, fifty-one out of eighty-seven substitutes enrolled for Northampton subdivision in 1766 came from the town of Northampton itself.[7]

Thus its territorial character only goes a little way towards clearing the militia of the charge of poaching recruits from the army. Positive evidence is needed that some at least of those who joined the militia would not have been willing to join the regular forces. This is provided by the history of the efforts to get militiamen to enter the army and to extend their services to Ireland.

(III) WHAT MILITIAMEN WOULD ENTER THE ARMY?

The recruitment by the army even of unembodied militiamen had always been objected to by the militia authorities, if only because of the trouble it caused.[8] From 1762 volunteers and substitutes could

[1] 2 Geo. III, cap. 20, ss. 55–6. 26 Geo. III, cap. 107, s. 48. 42 Geo. III, cap. 90, s. 65. 20 Geo. III, cap. 44, s. 4, made enlistments of men from another county invalid if made *after* 14 May 1780.

[2] WO. 68/205, item vii.

[3] BM, Add. 35661, f. 104.

[4] 35 Geo. III, cap. 83, s. 4. The Cambridgeshires had five recruiting parties in 1794 (BM, Add. 35664, ff. 276, 309).

[5] WO. 34/165, f. 245.

[6] HO. 50/19, Sir C. Willoughby, 2 February 1793.

[7] Northamptonshire ¦RO., X. 266, item 11. The rolls preserved in this Office show that some men came from Warwickshire, but nothing like a half.

[8] Examples from 1759: WO. 1/978, ff. 619–23. WO. 1/979, J. A. Affleck, 17 August, 1759. WO. 1/980, ff. 359–62.

only enter the army if they repaid the bounty they had been given for joining the militia, and from 1767 it was illegal to enlist a militiaman to serve in any other force.[1] Until the nineties the only thing that was sometimes encouraged was the enlisting by the army of militiamen whose time had expired.[2] In 1798 and 1799, however, there were great efforts to recruit first from the supplementary and then from the whole militia. At the same time the militiamen had a chance to show their willingness to undertake overseas service like the army by offering to serve in Ireland.[3]

It speaks well for the militia that a good many of them were induced to go to Ireland in the hour of need. But the efforts to make them go and stay there show also their great reluctance to embark on foreign service. A good many of the men in the regiments that volunteered refused to join in the offer and had to be left behind.[4] Some regiments showed little interest: only half the East Suffolk would go.[5] At the end of 1798 the regiments that had gone over in the autumn were asked if they were willing to stay on in 1799. Six were willing to stay indefinitely, but seven more fixed dates for their return ranging from the end of March to the beginning of June.[6] To keep it in mind that they were British militia the South Lincolnshire regiment limited their offer to a period of six months and made their colonel promise that they should stay no longer save of their own free will.[7] As 1799 wore on the reluctance to stay increased. The Cambridgeshires asked to be home by Christmas.[8] The Oxfordshires also refused to remain, though some impression was later made on them by threats and by lavish supplies of ale.[9]

For, as the parliamentary opposition had feared, both threats and bribes were used to stimulate and prolong these 'voluntary' offers of service—which makes the recalcitrance of the men the more striking.

[1] Enlisting in another corps of militia and regulars joining the militia were other things legislated against. 2 Geo. III, cap. 20, s. 54. 4 Geo. III, cap. 17, s. 4. 5 Geo. III, cap. 36, s. 6. 7 Geo. III, cap. 17, s. 18. 9 Geo. III, cap. 42, s. 48. 26 Geo. III, cap. 107, s. 47. 42 Geo. III, cap. 90, s. 64.

[2] In 1778 the War Office asked the counties to excuse men who had enlisted when their time had almost expired, but this was not always agreed to: BM, Add. 35659, f. 258. WO. 34/144, f. 259. WO. 1/1000, Maj. Daniel, 1 June 1778. In 1783 Capt. Hill of the 5th (Northumberland) and Lt.-Col. Irving of the 47th (Lancashire) regiment tried to recruit from the militia of those counties (WO. 1/1019, ff. 343–6, 637–8, 647–9, 651–4).

[3] Throughout this section, cf. above, pp. 224–36.

[4] See, e.g., WO. 3/19, p. 309.

[5] HO. 50/8, Sir C. Grey, 4 September 1799.

[6] HO. 50/30, paper of December 1798.

[7] HO. 50/30, H. Sibthorpe, 3 December 1798.

[8] HO. 50/32, Sir E. Nightingale, 24 September 1799. BM, Add. 35672, ff. 279, 288.

[9] As n. 8.

Lord Rolle found the South Devon regiment unwilling to follow him on board ship. He paraded them and asked each man why he would not go, correcting their misconceptions and hearing grievances. When this suasion by their colonel had induced a good number to embark, he suggested a spell of really hard duty for the rest and said that they must at any rate be moved before the taunts of the regular soldiers in their barracks led to a fight.[1] In the Lancashire regiment there was a shortage of new clothing and so the men who were going to Ireland set upon the rest and stripped them almost naked. The officers apparently did nothing to interfere.[2] The Warwickshire and Buckinghamshire regiments were the first to go to Ireland, and at the end of 1798 they were the most eager to get home. The Marquess of Buckingham thought that this was because Lord Hertford had allowed the Warwickshires too much licence. His own regiment at first refused to stay.[3] But he used his influence to such effect that they apologised for behaviour insulting to their colours, their guns[4] and himself and agreed to stay until April. 'Lord Hertford has allowed the Warwick to run riot and they tainted ours till they found me more sturdy than his lordship' was his summing up.[5] Lord Hertford's brother managed to bring the Warwicks also into line.[6]

Many things helped to make Irish service odious to the militia. Their duties were disagreeable: garrison duty in a country largely hostile to British rule. They suffered outrages like the murder of three men of the Worcestershire in their beds,[7] and things were made worse by a serious outbreak of fever.[8] Their enthusiasm waned when the French failed to appear in force, and they thought that there should be a fair system of reliefs, to share out the burden.[9] They resented the fact that certain of their allowances were lower in Ireland than at home, as also the stoppage of $6\frac{1}{2}d$. a day towards the cost of their transport, and sometimes the discomfort of the ships in which they had to travel.[10] There were fears that their families would not be properly looked after in their absence: the government had to pay a

---

[1] HO. 50/8, Lord Rolle, 30 and 31 August 1798.   [2] Williamson, pp. 150–1.

[3] HMC, *Dropmore*, vol. iv, pp. 410, 503; cf. pp. 368, 397, 402.

[4] Presented to the regiment by county subscription.

[5] HMC, *Dropmore*, vol. iv, p. 412. HO. 50/30, Lord Buckingham, 13 December 1798 and enclosure.

[6] *Ibid.*, Lord Hertford, 25 December 1798. HMC, *Dropmore*, vol. iv, pp. 369, 412.

[7] Holden, p. 85.

[8] HMC, *Dropmore*, vol. iv, p. 369; BM, Add. 41851, ff. 140, 146, 154.

[9] HO. 50/33, Lord Rolle, 24 May 1799. HMC, *Dropmore*, vol. iv, pp. 343. 351, 352, 369, 397.

[10] HO. 50/33: Lord Rolle, 14 and 19 November; H. Dundas, 22 and 30 November 1798. Cf. HO. 50/8, Lord Rolle, 30 August 1798; HO. 50/30, H. Sloane, 29 January 1799.

special allowance to the families of men who went.[1] Above all, there was a simple desire to get home. The Oxfordshires eventually offered to stay until Christmas 1799, but were eager to be stationed near their own county after that and see their families.[2] This favour was granted in the case of the Bedfordshires,[3] and it is important to note that it was desired even more ardently by the officers than by the men.[4]

As for the recruitment of militiamen for the army, the first thing that can be seen is that it could not usually be done with success by army officers but only by the militia officers themselves. The enlistment of men from the supplementary militia when it was called out in 1798 was entrusted mainly to the army. Eleven regiments were assigned the task, and were each assigned certain counties and a target figure in each. They were to send one captain and two subalterns for every 130 men they hoped to get, together with all the NCOs they could spare, to recruit at the places where the men were being assembled. The bounty was to be 7 guineas, with 1 guinea to anyone who found a recruit.[5] The lord lieutenants were instructed to help in every way.[6] But they seem to have disliked the army's interference with their force. The Duke of Richmond said that his officers had tried to help the 55th foot, but were disgusted at the way that the best men were weeded out and the militia left with the refuse. Those who had enlisted were mostly drunk and were sorry afterwards.[7] The measure was a failure and Henry Dundas thought that it was because the lord lieutenants had not exerted themselves.[8]

In 1799 on the other hand the work of recruiting was left to the militia officers. In July the commanding officer of each unit was to explain the scheme to the men on three successive days after roll call. In October he was required to explain it to them within a month. As already remarked, the officers in general were encouraged to help by the promise of commissions.[9] Army recruiters were not far off in

---

[1] Below, p. 269. Cf. p. 266, n. 10, last letter, and assurances given in Bedfordshire, J. M. Burgoyne, *Records of the Bedfordshire Militia* (London, 1884), p. 42.

[2] HO. 50/37, Lord C. Spenser, 16 October 1799.

[3] HO. 50/32, F. Moore, 19 September and 28 October 1799.

[4] Cf. below, p. 305.

[5] HO. 50/7 circular of 23 January 1798 and schedules.

[6] HO. 50/31 draft circulars of January 1798.

[7] HO. 50/38, Duke of Richmond, 6 March 1798. There were complaints that recruiting continued when men were actually marching to their regiments, that they failed to repay money advanced them as militiamen, and that unauthorised regiments joined in the recruiting. WO. 3/18, pp. 79, 107. WO. 4/825, p. 74. WO. 6/197, p. 76. HO. 50/35, Lord Derby, 24 March 1798.

[8] HMC, *Dropmore*, vol. iv, p. 224.

[9] In August commanding officers of regiments where few recruits had appeared were asked to explain the scheme three more times. Militia deserters were pardoned if they entered the army. WO. 6/193, pp. 256–70. For July, WO. 6/188,

July. Lord Lonsdale suspected that they had plied the Cumberlands with beer.[1] The East Norfolks reported, even before the act passed, that a recruiting party had come to ingratiate itself and corrupt the men.[2] Lord Radnor was infuriated when a regular officer was sent to explain the scheme to his men in his absence.[3] But the regulars were warned in October to leave the work to the militia officers and in no case to take any action at all until the act came into force.[4]

A few commanding officers were obstructive. Lord Buckinghamshire gave orders that the better men in his regiment should not be allowed to leave.[5] Lord Rolle denounced the scheme to his regiment in a speech replied to by his lieutenant-colonel, refused to recommend one of his officers for a regular commission as a reward for getting recruits, and neglected to sign the men's discharges.[6] But on the whole even opponents of the scheme like Lord Radnor co-operated loyally in its execution, and the militia officers must be given a good share of credit for its success. It cannot be said that they were nicer in their methods than the regulars. Some seeking army rank wished to bring recruits from regiments other than their own, which was not allowed.[7] Colonel Bastard remitted punishments to encourage volunteering and his men were personally canvassed by their officers. After a time, he asked if he might cease because discipline was deteriorating.[8] 'We had a dreadful scene of riot and confusion for these ten days,' said the commander of the 5th Lancashire regiment, 'and the regiment was completely disorganised—I don't think anything will restore the militia during the present war.'[9] Large bounties to be consumed in drink were the way to success, and when Pitt and Dundas reviewed a force formed out of these men on Barham Downs they found them still so drunk that they could manage no more than a disorderly *feu de joie*.[10]

pp. 269–75; 39 Geo. III, cap. 106, ss. 18, 23–4. For October, 39 and 40 Geo. III, cap. 1, ss. 6–11.

[1] HO. 50/33, Lord Lonsdale, 29 August 1799.

[2] HO. 50/36, J. Wodehouse, 11 June 1799.

[3] HO. 50/32, Lord Radnor, 17 July 1799

[4] WO. 3/19, p. 438, WO. 3/20, pp. 291, 427, 435.

[5] HO. 50/35, Lord Buckinghamshire, 1 September 1799.

[6] Walrond, pp. 169–71. HO. 50/33, W. Elford, 24 August, 3, 12 and 27 September 1799, and enclosures. 39 and 40 Geo. III, cap. 1, ss. 10–11 allowed commanding officers to refuse discharges to musicians and armourers and to appeal to the local G.O.C. against the discharge of any other man.

[7] HO. 50/33, J. Boggis, 17 November 1799. WO. 6/189, p. 22.

[8] HO. 50/33, Col. Bastard, 27 July 1799.   [9] Lancashire RO., LC. 5, f. 26.

[10] Fortescue, *History*, vol. iv, pp. 658–9. Officially the bounty was 10 guineas, and the men were paid as little as possible of it before they reached their new units: 39 Geo. III, cap. 106, s. 23; 39 and 40 Geo. III, cap. 1, s. 5; cf. WO. 3/20, pp. 26, 434. By ss. 21–2 and 2–4 of the respective acts the men could choose their unit from a number specified by the king, but the militia was asked in October to help the regiments that had been unsuccessful in July; WO. 6/188, pp. 330.

Recruiting from the militia, then, had to be done by militia officers. The other important thing that can be seen from all the experiments of 1798–9 is that the supplementary militiamen were much less willing to extend their service than the rest. Few men could be got in 1798, even when the lord lieutenant did co-operate and, like Lord Milford and Lord Lonsdale, give an extra bounty out of his own pocket.[1] Henry Dundas said that in July 1799 the supplementary men had been much less willing to volunteer than the others, and whenever a regiment supplied few recruits in that year it commonly turned out to consist largely of supplementary men.[2] Many of these men had likewise been unwilling to accompany their regiments to Ireland.[3]

It was natural that the supplementary militia, raised when the army had exhausted the supply of men willing to join it, and at first not intended for more than temporary service,[4] should contain many men not eager to enter the army. Beyond this, only one precise reason for their reluctance can be documented: a high proportion of them were family men. In 1786 it was laid down that substitutes were not to have more than one child.[5] For the supplementary militia, this rule was waived.[6] Now regular soldiers as a class were unmarried—though there were many exceptions—and there was no system of family allowances in the army. The families of militiamen on the other hand were entitled to allowances by law.[7] In May 1799 Henry Dundas proposed that the families of men who transferred to the army should continue to receive their allowances at the expense of the central government, and that for the whole army there should henceforth be a system of pensions for the widows of men who died in the service. He thought that this would encourage recruiting and said that the soldiers were jealous of the provision made for sailors' families by private subscription.[8] In 1798 the central government had decided to contribute to the maintenance of the families of militiamen going to Ireland.[9] But Dundas' colleagues were against family

---

[1] HO. 50/7, R. Brownrigg, 19 March 1798, cf. return of 24 July 1798, HO. 50/37. HO. 50/33, Lord Lonsdale, 18 March 1798. Cf. HO. 50/32, Lord Stamford, 7 June 1798 and enclosures; WO. 6/188, p. 64. Probably most of those willing to join had enlisted before embodiment, cf. above, p. 225.

[2] HO. 50/32, H. Dundas, 11 September 1799. WO. 6/188, pp. 300, 302.

[3] HO. 50/8, O. Nicholls, 8 September 1798.

[4] Cf. above, pp. 223, 255.

[5] 26 Geo. III, cap. 107, s. 24. 42 Geo. III, cap. 90, s. 41.

[6] 37 Geo. III, cap. 3, s. 8.

[7] Below, pp. 287–90.

[8] HO. 50/31, H. Dundas, 13 May 1799.

[9] Adding 8d. a week per wife and child under 10 to the normal allowance. WO. 6/169, pp. 99, 142. HO. 50/31, W. Windham to Lord C. Spencer, 8 December 1798. Cf. 39 Geo. III, cap. 106, ss. 36–8.

allowances in the army, though Windham liked the idea of pensions.[1]

Recruitment from the supplementary militiamen suffered accordingly. Those in the Norfolk regiments were said to be unwilling to enlist because most of them were married.[2] The Lincolnshire men were thought to be held back by the want of family allowances in the army. [3] The 4th Devonshires were in their own county and the men were with their families and did not wish to leave.[4]

The success of army recruiting from the militia was due to the large number of men who entered from the portion of the force raised before the augmentation of 1796. Some of these may indeed be regarded as men whom the militia had 'stolen' from the army. But not all: the general impression was that long service rendered men unfit for civil life, so that when offered the choice of disembodiment or enlistment in the army they would choose the latter. Many of the West Somersetshires, for instance, were expected to enlist after disembodiment, since they would not care for 'hard labour and poor living' after 'better fare and an easier and more idle life'.[5] Surviving figures suggest that the longer a man had been in the militia, the more likely he was to join the army. Of 723 men who joined the 82nd foot, 248 had served for less than two years, but 360 had served for more than four.[6] Of 739 men going to the 52nd (1st battalion), only 56 had served as little as two years, and 149 had served more than ten.[7] A person with experience of recruiting in the West Riding thought that even the supplementary militia had been 'soldiers long enough to like *it* and to *dislike* work'[8] but it seems on the contrary that the new men were eager to return to civil life and benefit from the current industrial boom. Colonel Patten of the 5th Lancashires thought that his men would prefer disembodiment to joining the army because the demand for labour in Manchester was such that they could earn 10 guineas in a few weeks.[9] There was a similar report from the

[1] HO. 50/31, W. Windham, 27 May 1799. Cf. Spencer's and Grenville's minutes on Dundas memorandum. Spencer said that only the families of sailors killed in action were provided for.

[2] HO. 50/36, R. Harvey, 25 August 1799.

[3] HO. 50/35, Lord Buckinghamshire, 30 August 1799.

[4] HO. 50/33, Sir B. Wray, 30 August 1799.

[5] HO. 50/38, J. K. Tynte, 22 October 1799; cf. W. Elford, 13 October, in HO. 50/33 and H. Maister, 22 October, in HO. 50/39.

[6] WO. 25/489.   [7] WO. 25/405.

[8] HO. 50/39, 'A.C.', 3 September 1799. It should be said that Col. Eliot of Staffordshire thought that the supplementary men would be less likely to enlist in 1799 than in 1798, when they had experienced only the good side of soldiering— trying on uniforms and drinking the bounties (HO. 50/30, F. P. Eliot, 14 June 1799).

[9] HO. 50/35, P. Patten, 28 August 1799, printed by J. G. Rawstorne, *An Account of the Regiments of Royal Lancashire Militia, 1759 to 1870* (Lancaster, 1874), pp. 186–7.

3. The Recruiting Serjeant. One of George Townshend's Caricatures, 1757.
From left to right: Lord Winchelsea, Bubb Dodington, Lord Sandwich, Welbore Ellis, Henry Fox and the Duke of Cumberland. (The ships are bringing foreign mercenaries.)

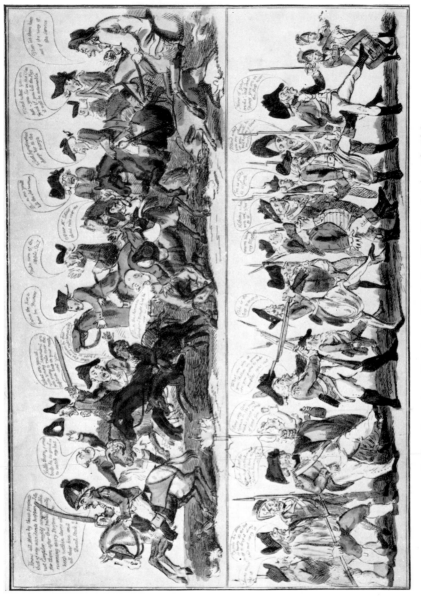

4. Supplementary Cavalry and Infantry. The New Levies of 1796.

youngest West Riding regiment, with the interesting addition that when the scheme for joining the army had been announced the men's families had swarmed in from all over the Riding to dissuade them from transferring.[1] It was men long accustomed to military life, and who perhaps had forgotten their trades, who were uninterested in such opportunities. It clearly follows that they might not have been as willing to join the army before their lengthy experience of military service as they were in 1799.[2]

It seems fair, therefore, to conclude that the recruiting machinery of the militia, cumbersome and absurd though it was, could bring under arms many men who would not have entered the army. It had help, especially from the country gentlemen, which the army did not always receive in the same degree. This enabled it in particular to tap the rural areas, where men were unwilling to cut themselves off from their roots by joining a regular regiment with no local ties and serving mainly overseas. Many who joined the militia remained reluctant to leave their own country and were not disposed to stay under arms for ever. On the other hand, there were many who gradually became used to military life, to the point where they became unfitted for anything else. They were willing, therefore, to transfer to the army in order to maintain their livelihood. The militia, therefore, was in a position to supply the army with men that the army could not get for itself. It is undoubtedly true that there was a great deal of wasteful competition between them for men. But if the army was allowed to recruit from the militia even it would be a gainer in the end.

Note

Trades of Men Sworn to Serve for Different Subdivisions in Northampton-shire.

Northampton, 1763.

Principals: 12 labourers, 4 servants, 4 cordwainers, 3 weavers, a victualler, a 'snedmaker', a shopkeeper, a gardener, a woolcomber, a currier, a mason, a millwright: total 31.

Substitutes: 21 labourers, 18 weavers, 18 cordwainers, 17 stocking weavers, 12 woolcombers, 7 servants, 5 tailors, 30 of other trades, including 2 or 3 each of masons, glaziers, gardeners, husbandmen, blacksmiths, carpenters and breeches-makers: total 128.

[1] HO. 50/39, G. Cooke, 28 August 1799.
[2] Cf. in 1779 Lt.-Col. Ward's advice about how to induce the men of the Cambridgeshire to re-enlist. They should be allowed to spend some time in the county before they were due for release, to give them and their friends time to tire of each other. Then 'having been long used to a life of dissipation—and their money all gone—they will take on again upon easier terms'. BM, Add. 35660, f. 136.

Northampton, 1766.

Principals: 9 labourers, 9 servants, 3 weavers, 3 shoemakers, a carpenter, a shepherd, a blacksmith, a woolcomber, a gardener, a victualler, a brazier, a 'tradesman': total 32.

Substitutes: 24 labourers, 24 weavers, 6 woolcombers, 6 masons, 5 cordwainers, one unknown, 22 others, including 2 or 3 each of tailors, nailers, carpenters, mat-makers, blacksmiths: total 88.

Brackley, 1787.

Principals: 4 labourers, a schoolmaster, a servant, a currier, a weaver: total 8.

Substitutes: 23 weavers, 19 labourers, 11 more weavers of particular materials, 5 servants, 4 cordwainers, 4 woolcombers, 3 tailors, 2 servants, 10 others, including a 'dealer' and a 'yeoman': total 81.

Sources: Northamptonshire RO., X.266, items 9 and 11; X.268.

XI

THE OBSTACLES
TO REAL CONSCRIPTION

THE militia's recruiting system was cumbersome, its yield at best was not great and it was constantly threatening to fall short of the statutory target. The supplementary militia was never anywhere near complete[1] and in wartime the older part of the force had a steadily mounting deficit. When the militia was embodied there was naturally a certain wastage by death, disease and desertion. In 1758 it had been laid down that vacancies caused by death, enlistment in the army, discharge for a proper reason or promotion to the rank of sergeant were to be filled by a fresh ballot, even in the case of a substitute.[2] But in 1795, for instance, a return in March showed that 53 corps were together short of 1207 men and the Home Office sent out a circular urging the speedy completion of 17 of them, each more than 25 short.[3] In April 1796 the deficit in the entire force was 1832 (the effective strength was 35,333), and appropriate orders were again given.[4] In 1799 a memorandum sent to Henry Dundas said that deputies had sometimes failed to do anything about vacancies for three or four years,[5] and in July a system of penalties was brought in. Deficits in the reduced quotas then fixed had to be filled within three months of certificates being sent by commanding officers to the lieutenancy of the numbers actually serving. In default of this, quarter sessions was to levy £10 a man by county rate; where it was only

---

[1] See above, pp. 222, 228.

[2] Corporals counted as part of the quota. 31 Geo. II, cap. 26, ss. 19–20. From 1762 commanding officers might grant discharges while the militia was embodied. 2 Geo. III, cap. 20, ss. 59–63. Deputies were given power in these acts to speed the filling of vacancies by holding extra meetings: cf. 18 Geo. III, cap. 14; 19 Geo. III, cap. 72, ss. 23–4. Cf. 26 Geo. III, cap. 107, ss. 38–9; 42 Geo. III, cap. 90, ss. 55–6.

[3] HO. 50/23, return of 1 March and circular of 16 March 1795.

[4] HO. 50/25, return of 18 April 1796. HO. 51/148, p. 314.

[5] In HO. 50/30, headed '1799: Remarks on the Militia Bill'.

certain places in the county that had failed to provide men they alone were to pay. The money was to be available to the deputies for three months for the hiring of volunteers and any then left was to be paid to the receiver general of the land tax. These arrangements were perpetuated in 1802.[1]

The growing scarcity of men lying behind these deficits made itself felt in various other ways. Competition for recruits encouraged desertion: men would enlist with several different corps in succession. Even in peacetime, in 1788, Colonel Maister of the East Riding said that there was reason to believe that substitutes often served in several regiments.[2] This was especially likely to happen in the militia because of the delay in bringing the men under the control of their officers. At the final subdivision meeting to which the men on whom the lot had fallen were summoned, the persons who were actually to serve were sworn and enrolled; from 1758 a copy of the roll had to be sent to the lord lieutenant within fourteen days.[3] But in peacetime they then disappeared until the time of exercise; if the militia was embodied, they had to make their own way to their regiment. In 1778 an act declared that men were deserting as soon as they received their money. The law allowed them to be sent to prison for six months, but this merely corrupted their morals and threw their families on the parish. So thenceforth they suffered military punishment if caught, and had to serve in the militia for three years (from 1786 five years) from that day. The county was to replace any deserter not caught within three months, but the man replaced was still to serve if captured.[4]

In the supplementary militia non-appearance was at first only punished by a fine of £5 or three months in prison.[5] But in 1798 the penalties obtaining in the rest of the force were applied to it, and it was finally laid down that if the supplementary men who had not joined their units were not caught within two months they were to be replaced— in the case of substitutes, by the principal.[6] In 1799 substitutes and volunteers who failed to join were made liable to the full penalties for desertion in the mutiny act and might be sentenced to

---

[1] 39 Geo. III, cap. 106, ss. 3–14. 42 Geo. III, cap. 90, ss. 59, 158–63.

[2] BM, Add. 28063, ff. 160–1.

[3] The form of oath was altered in 1758. 30 Geo. II, cap. 25, s. 19. 31 Geo. II, cap. 26, ss. 15, 18. 2 Geo. III, cap. 20, s. 70. 26 Geo. III, cap. 107, s. 49. 42 Geo. III, cap. 90, s. 36.

[4] 18 Geo. III, cap. 59, ss. 12–14. By 19 Geo. III, cap. 72, s. 11 persons taking a bounty and not appearing to be sworn had to return it, and (as in the army) pay £1 damages, on pain of fourteen days' imprisonment. Cf. 26 Geo. III, cap. 107, ss. 44, 83–4; 42 Geo. III, cap. 90, s. 62.

[5] 37 Geo. III, cap. 3, ss. 19–21, 23.

[6] 38 Geo. III, cap. 18, ss. 3, 6, 10, 14. 39 Geo. III, cap. 44, ss. 4, 5.

serve in the regular army. Pay was only to start when they reached their unit (subject to an allowance for the time of marching to it and for any necessary delay in their arrival.[1]) No doubt this was the result of a complaint to Henry Dundas that deputies or their clerks were allowing newly raised men to delay their departure from home for a month or more although they were paid from the day of enrolment.[2] The act of 1802 perpetuated these arrangements and also required that when the militia was embodied half the recruit's bounty should be paid in the first instance to his regiment, and put towards the hire of a replacement if he deserted or was found unfit to serve.[3]

For recruits of poor quality were a further result of scarcity. Much friction resulted between regiments and deputies. Even in 1778 Lord Orford, on the assembly of his Norfolk regiment for service, dismissed twenty 'misshapen, underlimbed, distempered' men and told the deputies to send only 'sizeable, able-bodied' ones.[4] The Cambridgeshire commandant complained in 1779 that the substitutes from Wisbech hundred were the worst he had ever seen and he gathered that little trouble had been taken at the meetings.[5] In the nineties the Cambridge regiment frequently quarrelled with the deputies about the fitness of men. An inspecting general was shown some whom the deputies would not discharge, though the regiment considered them unfit. He agreed that they were so, remarking especially on two who were lame and one with a growth on his neck.[6] One recruit was sent back at once with an expression of astonishment that he had been passed by an experienced deputy.[7] One parish flatly refused to replace a discharged man and got two deputies (apparently by false pretences) to sign a letter saying so.[8] When some supplementary militia joined the regiment, twenty-six at once proved to be unfit.[9] It was largely to avoid this sort of thing that regiments tried to take over the recruiting themselves.

In fairness it should be said that the authorities were sometimes accused of being too fastidious. Thomas Pennant warned the men of North Wales that magistrates sometimes refused a fit substitute because he was physically inferior to his principal, and would take a

[1] 39 Geo. III, cap. 106, ss. 16–17.

[2] HO. 50/30, F. Glanville, 28 March 1799.

[3] 42 Geo. III, cap. 90, ss. 63, 118, 119, 127. By 26 Geo. III, cap. 107, s. 45 a single deputy or justice might enforce the payment of a promised bounty.

[4] WO. 1/1000, Lord Orford, 20 April 1778.

[5] BM, Add. 35660, f. 120.

[6] BM, Add. 35670, ff. 308, 324. Cf. Add. 35669, f. 266. 26 Geo. III, cap. 107, s. 38 required confirmation of the commanding officer's discharges by the deputies.

[7] BM, Add. 35669, f. 240.

[8] BM, Add. 35670, ff. 119, 130.

[9] BM, Add. 35669, f. 262. The Suffolk men were better and the writer concluded that the deputies there were more zealous.

man as a substitute for one principal whom they had refused when offered by another.[1] In Cambridgeshire there was a great uproar in 1778 because the regiment refused good men offered to them and insisted on recruiting for themselves at a higher cost to the principals. A civilian employed by a parish to raise men was threatened by a sergeant, who said he would get his recruits rejected.[2] A further anomaly, reported by Lord Hardwicke in 1798, was that parishes were reluctant to send good-looking men to serve because they were more likely to be promoted and need replacement. Hardwicke suggested that the cost of replacing promoted men should be borne by the county as a whole.[3] In 1799 the law was amended accordingly.[4] In 1802 the deputies were required to have recruits examined by a surgeon before they were enrolled.[5] This must have done something to reduce disputes, as must the establishment in 1764 of a minimum height of 5 ft. 4 in. for substitutes and volunteers as well as for principals.[6] It should further be said that militiamen as a class seem to have been of rather good physique.[7]

The most obvious symptom of the shortage of recruits was the rise in bounties. Parliament gave some idea of what it thought should be paid by limiting the bounty for parochial volunteers to £6 and the allowance of half the price of a volunteer to poor principals to £5.[8] But in 1795 the Worcestershires were offering 15 guineas for men, which was the most that even regular regiments were allowed to give.[9] About the same time twenty-one volunteers raised for the Cambridgeshires cost from £7 to £19.12s., but all but four cost over £13.[10] In the West Riding a recruit had cost 1 guinea at most in 1757. In 1762 the price was £7, in 1782 £10 and in 1796 over £16.[11] The result was, as Lord Hardwicke explained in 1798, that the £10 penalty, which in peacetime was much higher than the price of a recruit, became the cheaper of the two—a fact recognised by making the penalty £15 in the case of the supplementary militia.[12] Balloted men paid the money

---

[1] Pennant, pp. 10–15.

[2] BM, Add. 35659, ff. 321, 323–4, 341, 362, 367; cf. 401.

[3] HO. 50/313, Lord Hardwicke, 5 February 1798.

[4] 39 Geo. III, cap. 106, ss. 19, 20. 42 Geo. III, cap. 90, s. 58. In 1799 but not in 1802 this provision applied in cases of death or discharge too.

[5] 42 Geo. III, cap. 90, s. 52.

[6] 5 ft. 2 in. for the supplementary militia. 4 Geo. III, cap. 17, s. 3; cf. above, p. 247.

[7] See, e.g., MSS. of fourth Duke of Bedford, vol. xli, f. 98; WO. 1/1000, Duke of Richmond, 4 August 1778.

[8] Above, p. 252, n. 1; pp. 253–4.

[9] Holden, p. 60. Cf. WO. 4/156, p. 427.

[10] BM, Add. 35666, f. 92.

[11] Wentworth Woodhouse, Y. 23: T. Bolland, 2 May 1802.

[12] HO. 50/313, Lord Hardwicke, 5 February 1798.

instead of finding a recruit. In 1794 Lord Radnor found that in Berkshire the fines paid did not provide enough money to hire the necessary men and asked the Home Office if he might make up for this by holding several ballots for each vacancy.[1] This situation may have done something to lessen the competition of the militia with the army for men by limiting what it was worth while for balloted men to pay.[2] But it was liable to leave the county or the regiment with a balance in cash and no recruits.[3]

The shortcomings of the system are so obvious that it is worth considering why more was not attempted in the direction of compulsory personal service. Each war down to the American saw pressing for the army, mainly of vagabonds;[4] but nothing more systematic received very serious consideration. From the workings of the militia system it is easy to see why not and what were the obstacles to real conscription.

(I) ADMINISTRATIVE, ESPECIALLY IN URBAN AREAS

The militia's recruiting methods could hardly be better than the organisation which carried them out, and eighteenth–century local government was always cumbrous and lax. It proved very difficult to find active magistrates enough to hold the meetings required to execute the laws. For most purposes the quorum of a general meeting was the lieutenant and two deputies or three deputies, and for a sub-division meeting three deputies. But from the outset up to two deputies in the latter quorum might be replaced by justices.[5] The concern of parliament at first was virtually to dictate the appointment of deputies by fixing a high qualification and requiring twenty to be appointed in each county or as many as were qualified.[6] (The king, it is true, retained the appointment of lieutenants and could disallow the deputies they appointed[7] or require their

---

[1] HO. 50/22, Lord Radnor, 16 October 1794. The Duke of Grafton seems to have assumed he might do this in 1779, WO. 34/152, f. 285.

[2] Cf. BM, Add. 43770, f. 33.

[3] Cf. memo. in HO. 50/30. In 1800 Colonel Colby of the Pembrokeshire militia was charged before a court-martial with failing to replace two men who had entered the regular forces in 1795. It was found that this was so, but he had not embezzled the money provided for it. HO. 50/37, Sir Charles Morgan, 26 April 1800.

[4] Clode, vol. ii, pp. 10–19.

[5] For the meeting discharging a proportion of the officers (below, p. 304) the lieutenant and four deputies or five deputies had to attend.

[6] The qualification was the same as for a colonel, cf. below, p. 340. 30 Geo. II, cap. 25, s. 3. 2 Geo. III, cap. 20, s. 5. 26 Geo. III, cap. 107, s. 4, 42 Geo. III, cap. 90, s. 5.

[7] 30 Geo. II, cap. 25, ss. 1, 2. 2 Geo. III, cap. 20, ss. 1, 3, 4. 26 Geo. III, cap. 107, ss. 1, 3. 42 Geo. III, cap. 90, ss. 2, 4. Deputies' appointments were not in-

removal.[1]) But in 1758 it was necessary to allow the appointment of persons with only half the qualification if the number could not other wise be made up to twenty,[2] and in 1769 the qualification was halved: henceforth it was £200 a year in land or being heir to twice that amount, which even so was twice the qualification of a justice.[3] From 1778 it proved necessary to allow two deputies, or one deputy and a justice, to do acts for which three had hitherto been required.[4] In the hope of ensuring that there would always be enough persons ready to act, deputies were appointed in large numbers wherever possible and entirely lost their former exclusive character. After the act of 1757, fifteen counties soon had forty or more and three of these had over 100.[5] After the supplementary militia acts there were further massive appointments.[6]

In spite of this there were complaints that deputies were too few.[7] Meetings were commonly conducted by the statutory minimum of magistrates.[8] In the earlier years two dutiful ones might often meet only to find their pains in vain for want of a third.[9] From 1759 the general meeting might alter the times and places of subdivision meetings, and subdivision clerks were given power to appoint another meeting when a quorum did not attend.[10] From 1778 there was a similar provision respecting general meetings.[11]

validated by the death of the lieutenant (s. 71 of first act). From 1762 the king might appoint three deputies to act in place of a lieutenant absent abroad, and in 1764 he was empowered by this means to dispense with a lieutenant entirely. 2 Geo. III, cap. 20, s. 2. 4 Geo. III, cap. 17, s. 2. 5 Geo. III, cap. 36, ss. 2, 3. 20 Geo. III, cap. 44, s. 5. 26 Geo. III, cap. 107, s. 2. 42 Geo. III, cap. 90, s. 3.

[1] 30 Geo. II, cap. 25, s. 8. 2 Geo. III, cap. 20, s. 14. 42 Geo. III, cap. 90, s. 17. Omitted in 1786, see below, p. 334.

[2] 31 Geo. II, cap. 26, s. 5. 2 Geo. III, cap. 20, s. 9.

[3] 9 Geo. III, cap. 42, ss. 2, 3, 7. 26 Geo. III, cap. 107, s. 5. 42 Geo. III, cap. 90, s. 6. Cf. 5 Geo. III, cap. 18.

[4] 18 Geo. III, cap. 59, s. 11. 24 Geo. III, sess. 1, cap. 13, s. 15. 26 Geo. III, cap. 107, s. 19 (but cf. s. 23, five at the general meeting required to alter hundredal quotas). 42 Geo. III, cap. 90, s. 22, cf. s. 40.

[5] See SP. 44/190, pp. 281, 285, 287, 291, 294, 297, 302, 305, 309, 321, 351, 356, 394, 478, 511; SP. 44/191, pp. 51, 95, 128, 140, 232.

[6] See, e.g., HO. 51/10, pp. 142, 187, 224.

[7] HO. 50/24, Deputies of Flint, 16 November 1796 (misdated 1795).

[8] Usually for instance in the Forest Division of Berkshire in 1786–95 (BM, Add. 34303) or at Sussex general meetings in 1782–96. (East Sussex RO., LCG/EW.1).

[9] See, e.g., BM, Add. 35659, f. 6; Add. 35680, f. 23.

[10] 32 Geo. II, cap. 20, ss. 2–4. 2 Geo. III, cap. 20, ss. 65, 92. 26 Geo. III, cap. 107, s. 21. 42 Geo. III, cap. 90, s. 24. 19 Geo. III, cap. 72, s. 19 required subdivision clerks to give notice of meetings to all deputies in the division.

[11] 18 Geo. III, cap. 59, s. 23. 26 Geo. III, cap. 107, s. 18. 42 Geo. III, cap. 90, s. 21. In 1767 a Cambridgeshire general meeting had three present as required, but not all at one time. BM, Add. 35659, f. 118.

It was only in 1758 that parliament empowered each lord lieutenant to appoint a clerk of the general meetings and the deputies in each subdivision to appoint (by majority vote if necessary) a subdivision clerk.[1] The annual pay acts provided that the former should receive 5 guineas for each meeting he attended and the latter one, paid by the receiver general of the land tax.[2] The clerks had a great deal of work to do in the compiling of lists and rolls, and it was probably they who did the arithmetic involved in working out the local quotas.[3] They had to have the meetings advertised[4] and try and find deputies to attend them; as we have seen, they were often involved in finding men as well.[5] Their fees were an insufficient reward for this; they sometimes supplemented them by charging fees for drawing the officers' commissions, but this could be unpopular.[6] They put in bills for their expenses, but this was of doubtful legality.[7] It is not surprising that pluralism and bad clerical work sometimes resulted. The clerk of the Bedfordshire general meetings in 1798 was also clerk of two subdivisions comprising two-thirds of the county.[8] The Cambridgeshire regiment complained that in 1795, two years after embodiment, they had still not been sent a roll showing what men should be serving with the regiment, and the adjutant accordingly could not say which parishes were in default.[9]

Sometimes magistrates were obstructive, and they were encouraged in this by the complexity, bad drafting and frequent alteration of the militia laws, which seem to have been as difficult for contemporaries to grasp and explain as they have been for the writer, and are, alas, likely to be for the reader of this book.[10] In 1796 the deputies of Northumberland felt unable to execute the supplementary militia act because the annual lists of men liable to serve had been made before they knew of it and did not contain information now needed for determining exemptions. The act did not empower them to call for new lists. The Home Secretary, the Duke of Portland, criticised their lack

---

[1] 31 Geo. II, cap. 26, s. 8. 2 Geo. III, cap. 20, s. 90. 26 Geo. III, cap. 107, s. 16. 42 Geo. III, cap. 90, s. 18.

[2] See 31 Geo. II, cap. 30, ss. 5, 6, 9.

[3] See BM, Add. 35680, f. 10; Add. 35659, ff. 15, 17–18.

[4] See BM, Add. 35662, ff. 283–4, 289.

[5] Above, p. 262.

[6] See BM, Add. 35661, f. 112; Add. 35663, ff. 207–8; Add. 35664, f. 27.

[7] See BM, Add. 35662, ff. 67, 69.

[8] Bedfordshire RO., Quarter Sessions Rolls, 17, f. 103.

[9] BM, Add. 35665, f. 407.

[10] Note that proceedings of lieutenancies were not removable by certiorari, and from 1778 a measure of indemnity was extended to justices and civil officers executing their orders. 30 Geo. II, cap. 25, s. 58. 2 Geo. III, cap. 20, s. 131. 18 Geo. III, cap. 59, s. 28. 26 Geo. III, cap. 107, ss. 127, 133. 42 Geo. III, cap. 90, ss. 171, 177. Cf. 37 Geo. III, cap. 22, s. 19.

of initiative when they wrote to him about it and referred them to the amending act.[1] They refused to do anything till June 1797, six months after the levy had been made everywhere else. A strong protest by Portland to the Duke of Northumberland[2] at length drove them to act, but nothing much was accomplished till the end of the year.[3]

Trouble occurred particularly where the unit of administration was small. It was then harder than ever to find men enough to do the work. From the outset the Welsh and certain small or poor English counties had special low qualifications established for deputies and officers, to make it easier to find enough of them. Two deputies, moreover, were to have the same powers there as three elsewhere.[4] In addition to these cases, there were certain places with a tradition of militia autonomy which was respected by the acts and where a determination to preserve local rights often aggravated the trouble caused by shortages of magistrates and officers. Towns which were counties of themselves and had such traditional rights had their own lieutenancy. The deputies were appointed by the lieutenant or chief magistrate of the town and had to have £300 a year in land or £5000 in personal estate (both figures were halved in 1769). The county lieutenancy fixed the quota of the town and the men belonged to the county unit, but otherwise the town lieutenancy was autonomous.[5] An instance of municipal obstructiveness comes from Cambridge in 1782. The chief constable failed to give notice to the petty constables to return lists of men liable to serve. Fortunately this was discovered and orders were eventually given through another channel. The chief

[1] HO. 50/27, Duke of Northumberland, 17 February 1797, and enclosures.

[2] HO. 51/10, p. 371.

[3] HO. 50/28, Duke of Northumberland, 28 June, 21 November and 4 December 1797, and enclosures. He was contemptuous of his deputies, and angry with Portland for having answered their query in the first place. See his and Portland's letters of 20–21 February 1797 in HO. 50/27.

[4] The qualification was land worth £300 a year or being heir to land worth £500; from 1769, £150 and £300 were the amounts. Cumberland, Huntingdon, Monmouth, Westmorland and Rutland were the English counties. 30 Geo. II, cap. 25, s. 52. 31 Geo. II, cap. 26, s. 38. 2 Geo. III, cap. 20, ss. 8, 91. 9 Geo. III, cap. 42, s. 6. 26 Geo. III, cap. 107, s. 6. 42 Geo. III, cap. 90, s. 7.

[5] From 1762 real and personal estate could be counted together. 30 Geo. II, cap. 25, s. 55. 2 Geo. III, cap. 20, s. 11. 9 Geo. III, cap. 42, s. 9. 26 Geo. III, cap. 107, s. 8. 42 Geo. III, cap. 90, s. 9. What towns were covered is nowhere specified in the acts. In specifying quotas they name, along with their counties, Berwick, Canterbury, Carmarthen, Chester, Coventry, Exeter, Gloucester, Haverfordwest, Hull, Lincoln, Litchfield, Newcastle, Norwich, Nottingham, Poole, Southampton, Worcester, York. The law was specifically applied to Berwick by 31 Geo. II, cap. 26, s. 42; 2 Geo. III, cap. 20, s. 126; 26 Geo. III, cap. 107, s. 105; 42 Geo. III, cap. 90, s. 149. That Newcastle was affected was once denied, HO. 51/8, p. 203.

constable said that a gentleman had advised him that he need not act and was prepared if necessary to indemnify him.[1]

The Isle of Wight enjoyed a rather similar position to a borough and from 1762 its militia was reserved for the defence of the island. It is significant that when the rest of Hampshire raised its militia in 1759 the island failed to do so.[2] The Isle of Purbeck, in Dorset, at first had a similar position but soon lost it.[3] The Isle of Ely acquired a special status by sheer obstruction. There was hardly anybody there with a deputy's qualification, and in 1757–9 it was almost impossible to get anything done there: political resentments and doubts about the law held back almost everyone who might have acted.[4] A special scale of qualifications for deputies and officers in the Isle had to be established and it was varied several times, evidently because the danger of a shortage persisted.[5]

The worst trouble of all, however, was naturally where the whole system of local government was in danger of breaking down: in the new or rapidly expanding urban areas. The big towns provided more than their fair share of voluntary recruits, but it was very hard to make their inhabitants submit to a compulsory levy. Even a town no bigger than Brighton could cause trouble: in 1794 it was found that there were only ten men serving for it instead of the proper number of thirty-three.[6] In Birmingham there seems as a rule to have been no making of lists or ballot. The county fixed the town's quota under the act of 1786 at 109 men and this number of volunteers was raised at the expense of the parish rates.[7] The second supplementary militia act ordered the townspeople to make a special return of men liable to serve there to the privy council, which was itself to fix their quota.[8]

The real black spots were Middlesex, Surrey and Lancashire. The Middlesex regiments were the worst in the militia. In August 1793 the Western regiment and in November 1798 the Eastern was re-

---

[1] Perhaps he was a quaker. BM, Add. 35626, ff. 230–1. For powers to compel the attendance of officers, and penalties for false returns see 31 Geo. II, cap. 26, ss. 16, 22; 2 Geo. III, cap. 20, ss. 71–2; 26 Geo. III, cap. 107, ss. 30–31; 42 Geo. III, cap. 90, ss. 31–2.

[2] 30 Geo. II, cap. 25, s. 53. 2 Geo. III, cap. 20, s. 127. 26 Geo. III, cap. 107, s. 106. 42 Geo. III, cap. 90, s. 150. Cf. PRO. 30/8, vol. 244, ff. 82–3.

[3] 30 Geo. II, cap. 25, s. 54. 31 Geo. II, cap. 26, s. 43.

[4] BM, Add. 35659, ff. 3, 5, 7, 8, 11, 13, 24, 28, 30, 31, 35, 37.

[5] 32 Geo. II, cap. 20, s. 7. 33 Geo. II, cap. 22, s. 14. 2 Geo. III, cap. 20, s. 10. 9 Geo. III, cap. 42, s. 8. 26 Geo. III, cap. 107, s. 7. 42 Geo. III, cap. 90, s. 8. Cf. BM, Add. 35680, ff. 64–5; Add. 35383, ff. 273–4. Legislation was also needed because the Rapes of Sussex and Lathes of Kent were the best divisions for militia purposes, but did not coincide with the hundred and parish boundaries. 19 Geo. III, cap. 72, s. 25. 26 Geo. III, cap. 107, s. 115. 42 Geo. III, cap. 90, s. 156.

[6] East Sussex R.O., LLM/E.1, sub. 22 February 1794.

[7] HO. 50/25, Lord Warwick, 23 August 1796.   [8] 37 Geo. III, cap. 22, s. 16.

ported ninety short of the numbers it was supposed to have had at the start of the war. On the latter occasion Colonel Lord Mansfield further said that he had only received 120 supplementary men instead of over 700, and half of them were unfit. No rolls of men supposed to be serving had been received from the deputies during the war, so he did not know who was entitled to the bounty for long service.[1] In 1799 the Westminster regiment was 745 men short. There were only five satisfactory officers and only eighty of the privates were fit for service: the youngest of these was sixty![2] In the same year the first Surrey regiment was described as a poor one, with poor senior officers.[3]

Until 1796 Lancashire had little trouble because her quota was small in relation to her population.[4] But in 1796 her contingent was so augmented that instead of one regiment there were five and after the reduction of 1799 there were still three.[5] Troubles at once appeared: in November 1798 the fifth regiment was 600 short and the War Office considered it useless.[6]

The first source of the trouble was the huge amount of work involved in organising a ballot.[7] In Middlesex in the nineties a Mr Stables was clerk both to the general meetings and to the subdivisions of Westminster, Holborn and Finsbury. For the supplementary militia these supplied 4987 of the county quota of 5820.[8] For the ballot Stables had to supply lists and tickets to the numbers respectively of 25,801; 23,311; and 9310 in the three subdivisions. Repeated extra ballots were held to replace men who absconded: 53 in Stables' area in 1797, 21 in 1798, 42 in 1799. In the latter year Stables had to attend 137 meetings in Holborn alone. In 1798 new lists and tickets had to be made. The number of men chosen to serve was seldom under 100 at a meeting, usually over 200, often over 400.[9] Each of these men had to be summoned to appear by a constable, and in 1798 the number of summonses in the parish of St Giles in the Fields reached the remarkable total of 2901.[10] It is clear from the surviving accounts that each parish had to have several constables. Another

[1] HO. 50/2, Gen. Johnston, 1 August, in Lord Amherst, 6 August 1793. HO. 50/36, Lord Mansfield, 18 November 1798. WO. 6/188, p. 134.

[2] HO. 50/9, Lord C. Somerset, 26 July 1799; return of 24 July 1799.

[3] Inactive lieutenant-colonel. One major undesirable, the other too old. WO. 27/82, A. Ross, 18 March 1799.

[4] Above, p. 219, n. 2; p. 246.

[5] WO. 17/1159–60.

[6] HO. 50/35, Lord Derby, 11 November 1798, and enclosure.

[7] HO. 50/23, Lord Titchfield, 23 March 1795. HO. 50/36, the same, 22 November 1798.

[8] Middlesex R.O., Militia Records, bundle 96, ii: undated paper.

[9] Ibid., Bundles 16, 96, ii.

[10] Middlesex Militia Records, bundle 16.

task of the pluralist Stables was to make a roll for the use of the regiments and inform them of the progress made. We do not know what help he had, but he noted that making a roll of the force for Henry Dundas was a very troublesome business.[1]

In Lancashire, too, the amount of clerical work was impressive. An alphabetical roll of the men serving for the county in 1799 covered seventy-six sheets and the charge for making it was £7. 12s.[2] The shortcomings of the personnel were conspicuous in this county in the nineties. The clerk of the general meetings was past his work for some years before his replacement in 1798 by a younger man.[3] There were no deputies in the Warrington subdivision while the militia was embodied because they were all officers.[4] In 1792 the constables of Blackburn and Rossendale left several hundred men off the lists who ought to have been on.[5] In 1798 it was found that no return had yet been made of men liable for service in the supplementary militia of Preston. The general meeting eventually got one, but considered it so defective that an enquiry was ordered at which the corporation, the vicar and the justices of the town were invited to attend.[6] The apportionment of the supplementary militia quotas had to be done three times because returns of men liable in various subdivisions turned out to be defective. At Liverpool the deputies twice rejected the lists presented to them as defective: as a result the number reported liable for service increased from 3000 to 4800.[7]

The other main source of trouble was the ease with which men could abscond in urban areas. When the first training of the Middlesex supplementary militia was held, only 70 came out of 485 summoned.[8] When that force was first partially embodied, only 300 men appeared out of 1000 summoned in the Borough subdivision of Surrey.[9] The Croydon subdivision raised 500 men for the supplementary militia at a cost of over £5000. But in 1798 the third county regiment was 860 men short, and Croydon was called on for 200 more, expected to cost another £2000.[10] Nathaniel Conant, one of the stipendiary magistrates, estimated that 3000 men deserted from the Middlesex militia in the years 1793–9 and pointed out how easy it

[1] *Ibid.*, Stable's bill for executing supplementary militia acts, sub. 26 June 1798.
[2] Lancashire R.O., LM. 1/1, f. 127.
[3] HO. 50/35, Lord Derby, 21 November 1798.
[4] Lancashire R.O., LC. 4, f. 35. [5] *Ibid.*, LC. 2, ff. 13–14.
[6] *Ibid.*, LM. 1/1, ff. 56, 61. Cf. HO. 50/35, printed paper of 20 July 1798.
[7] Lancashire R.O., LM. 1/1, ff. 19–23. The clerk said that even the first total was a record.
[8] HO. 50/28, Lord Titchfield, 6 November 1797. He said those that came were a poor lot.
[9] HO. 50/38, Lord Onslow, 26 March 1798.
[10] HO. 50/38, G. Shepley, etc., 24 November 1798. They wanted to put their provisional cavalry into the militia.

was since the inhabitants of the urban districts, especially the poorer ones, were not personally known to each other as they were in the country. Men would hire themselves out as substitutes many times over: Conant thought the Irish were the worst.[1] In 1799 Lord Titchfield, the lord lieutenant, said that it would be hopeless to disband any of the Middlesex militia with the idea of recalling them later: they would never be seen again.[2] In Lancashire it was the same. When the supplementary men were first trained, 250 men were absent from the body trained at Wigan alone.[3] In Liverpool and Manchester seamen often engaged to serve as substitutes and before they could be sent to their units went off again to sea.[4]

Energetic steps were eventually taken to put things right. In July 1798 a special general meeting was held in Lancashire and found that the total deficit was 1255, of which 412 were men who had enlisted in the line and did not have to be replaced, but 549 had deserted or were not to be found. The meeting ordered a number of measures. Subdivision clerks were to track down deserters. Proper certificates were to be got of men who had joined the army. Fortnightly medical certificates were required for thirty-one men reported too ill to join. There was to be a drive against defaulting constables and insufficient returns. New men were to be apportioned between the regiments by ballot. The three senior supplementary regiments together were only 161 short and Lord Derby hoped that they at least could be speedily completed.[5] The new clerk of the general meetings expected the lieutenancy to order the stationing of an officer at Preston to collect recruits before they could desert.[6] In November he thought that the deficit was down to 237: the fifth and last regiment then had 371 rank and file.[7] By July 1799 it had 476 privates, and as it bore the whole reduction of the county quota by enlistment in the army in 1798 this probably means that the deficit had disappeared.[8]

Surrey, like Lancashire, held an important meeting in the summer of 1798. Some improvement resulted, though in 1801 the Second Regiment was still 144 short.[9] But in May 1799 Lord Titchfield re-

[1] HO. 50/36, Lord Titchfield, 22 May 1799, and enclosure.
[2] The same, 23 October 1799.
[3] HO. 50/313, W. Banks, 3 January 1798.
[4] HO. 50/317, Lord Derby, 10 September 1798. HO. 50/35, Lord Derby, 7 November 1798.
[5] HO. 50/35, printed paper, 20 July 1798; Lord Derby, 23 July. Rawstorne, pp. 169–73.
[6] Lancashire R.O., LC. 14/1, letter of 15 October 1798.
[7] Lancashire R.O., LC. 14/1, letter of 18 November 1798.
[8] HO. 50/35, return of 2 July 1799 (deducting 111 men detached from the first regiment). It had been meant to have 900 men, and at least 412 had joined the army.
[9] HO. 50/38, Lord Onslow, 7 November 1798. WO. 6/189, pp. 242–3.

ported that the militia laws would never work in Middlesex and presented a report by Conant, already referred to, which included a draft bill, with annotations by himself. Principals, whose substitutes deserted before joining, were to be liable to take their chance in a fresh ballot, but balloted men could gain complete exemption by paying a sum, not exceeding 10 guineas, adjudged to be the price of a volunteer. With this money the regiment was to raise recruits, rendering account to the county. The census of men liable to serve was to be done by the constables requiring householders, under penalty, to return lists of the appropriate members of their households.[1] This draft bill was duly presented to parliament and carried with little change. It was made applicable to Middlesex and Surrey.[2] Introducing it in the commons, Lord Titchfield said that £45,000 had been spent on raising the supplementary militia in Middlesex, but only 1700 men had been got out of the quota of 5820 and a third of these had deserted.[3] His bill represented the virtual abandonment of the pretence that the militia was a conscript force. In debate, Colonel Wood said that it would be a good thing to extend its application to the whole country.[4] This would have been a counsel of despair indeed, but one part of it was incorporated into the general act of 1802: henceforth it was the householders, on the requisition of the constables, who provided the material for the lists of men liable to serve.[5]

In view of all this it seems unlikely that the existing administrative system could have operated a real and systematic plan of conscription. In particular, the increased numbers involved would have made every county to some extent like Middlesex or Lancashire. In time of acute danger there might have been zeal enough to carry through a *levée en masse*, but it would have been a hazardous thing to attempt at any other time.

(II) ECONOMIC, ESPECIALLY THE COST OF THE FAMILIES

There was reason, anyway, to believe that the number of men under arms, at the end of the century at least, was the most that the country could afford. There were some signs that a labour shortage was resulting. In September 1801 the Duke of Richmond said that as there were no manufactures in Sussex all recruits there had been taken

[1] As p. 284, n. 1.
[2] 39 Geo. III, cap. 90. Recruits were assigned as substitutes to those who paid fines, to entitle their families to allowances. Certified quakers did not have to make lists. Its application to Surrey was objected to, Woodfall, vol. xx, p. 335. There was an attempt to extend it to Kent, CJ vol. liv, p. 683.
[3] Woodfall, vol. xx, pp. 281–2.
[4] Woodfall, vol. xx, p. 282.
[5] 42 Geo. III, cap. 90, ss. 26–9.

from the plough and the shortage of labour was a serious grievance. There was now a large potato harvest to be got in, and many hands were wanted to thresh the corn (which might help to bring down its price) and for the carting and spreading of dung. A detachment of the county regiment had been sent home to harvest and he induced the Duke of York to let it stay a month longer for work on the farms, as also the men disembodied in 1799 but now recalled. Needless to say, he commended Pelham's plan of letting militiamen work for most of the year, on the model of the Prussian army.[1] In 1798 there was a complaint in Northamptonshire against the embodiment of the second half of the supplementary militia. The expense of their families and the difficulty of getting in the hay and corn harvest would be much felt in all midland counties.[2]

More important was the prevalence of the opinion that military service corrupted the poor and made them unfit for civil occupations. This had been an argument against having a militia in the first place,[3] it was thought to account for the success in getting militiamen to join the army,[4] and it led to considerable fears of the social damage that a militia might do. The poet Cowper complained that

> . . . universal soldiership has stabb'd
> The heart of merit in the meaner class

and that 'the clown, the child of nature, without guile' after his 'three years of heroship' in the militia 'returns indignant to the slighted plough' and thereafter is 'a pest where he was useful once'.[5] Some pains were taken to prevent this happening. As a warning to some Cambridgeshire men due for discharge in 1779, a magistrate proposed that the corps should attend a public hanging. In 1782 he said that they were 'a very reprobate set of men and swear every sentence they utter'.[6] Lord Tavistock was concerned that his regiment was disembodied in December 1762, a 'dead' time of the year for finding work, and he arranged that those who could not find any should be employed on the Bedford estates. He told his father the Duke that he had always tried to preserve the morals of his men and not make them bad citizens by making them good soldiers, and their orderly behaviour to the end made him think that he had succeeded. Most of them he expected to return to their old trades.[7] At the end of the next war Lord Salisbury similarly employed 200 of the disembodied Hert-

[1] BM, Add. 33108, ff. 26–7. Cf. Add. 33107, f. 228.
[2] Northamptonshire R.O., X. 270, item 6.
[3] Above, pp. 108–9.
[4] Above, pp. 270–1.
[5] 'The Task', book iv, quoted by Holden, p. 48.
[6] BM, Add. 35626, ff. 77, 244.
[7] MSS. of fourth Duke of Bedford, vol. xlvi, f. 194.

fordshire militia on the improvements being made at Hatfield.[1] Militiamen who had served their full term were given the statutory encouragement of being allowed to set up in any trade in any corporate town except Oxford and Cambridge.[2] A memorandum of 1799 suggested that those militiamen who had been in service for several years should be given furloughs without pay, batches being let out for six months at a time. This would enable them to recover lost habits of industry and feelings of duty towards their families.[3]

Most important of all was the fact that the number of men under arms could not be greatly increased without bringing in many more men with families: this was recognised by allowing substitutes with any number of children in the supplementary militia.[4] It will be recalled that to make the militia more popular with the poor, embodied militiamen's families were accorded allowances in 1758, but that the resulting expense was very unpopular with the gentry. This was a dilemma that could never be resolved. In 1760 the allowances were confined to the families of principals, though the families of other men then serving were not to lose it. One day's wage a week at the local rate was to be paid for the wife and for each lawful child under ten up to the number of three. One extra allowance was payable if there were more than five children. Parishes paying these allowances were reimbursed by the county and if the man concerned was serving for another county, the treasurer thereof in turn was to be called on for repayment.[5] These arrangements were confirmed in 1762, but in 1778–9 it was found necessary to do something once more for the families of substitutes and volunteers. The cost (at first half the cost) of relieving them if they became chargeable was to be repaid to the parish, at first by the county but from 1779 by the parish for which the man served. If the parishes were in different counties the transaction went through the county treasurers as before.[6]

[1] BM, Add. 35626, ff. 290–1.

[2] Like members of the regular forces. 24 Geo. III, sess. 2, cap. 6. 42 Geo. III, cap. 69. At first only those who were married and served during invasion or rebellion were so privileged: 30 Geo. II, cap. 25, s. 25; 2 Geo. III, cap. 20, s. 79; 26 Geo. III, cap. 107, s. 131; 42 Geo. III, cap. 90, s. 175. 3 Geo. III, cap. 8 is ambiguous. Provision was made for militiamen to recover wages from former civil employers by 2 Geo. III, cap. 20, s. 49; 26 Geo. III, cap. 107, s. 43; 42 Geo. III, cap. 90, s. 61. From 1796 employers did not have to pay them for time spent at peace-time training, cf. 37 Geo. III, cap. 3, ss. 22–3. Buckingham said that in 1783 his men were eager for the certificates allowing them to set up in trade (HMC, *Dropmore*, vol. ii, p. 327).

[3] HO. 50/30, Anonymous, 24 February 1799.

[4] Above, p. 269.

[5] Special provision for places not contributing to county rate. See 31 Geo. II, cap. 26, s. 28; 33 Geo. II, cap. 22, ss. 1–6; and above, pp. 168–73.

[6] 18 Geo. III, cap. 59, ss. 24–5. 19 Geo. III, cap. 72, ss. 1–5. Cf. 2 Geo. III, cap. 20, ss. 81–6.

The act of 1786 made no provision for families at all. But in December 1792, when the force was again embodied, a meeting of senior militia officers called Henry Dundas' attention to the subject and he promised to bring in a bill.[1] The question of whether to include the substitutes proved so contentious that it was brought before the cabinet.[2] Lord Euston had reported from Suffolk that men would be disinclined to serve if the relief of their families was left to the discretion of the magistrates, and from other counties there were reports of neglect of families by magistrates and murmurings among the men.[3] So substitutes were included in the bill, though Dundas said with no more than literal accuracy that it did not fix the amounts which their families were to receive.[4] An allowance of one day's labour at the local rate was granted to each wife and to *every* lawful child under ten, unless they followed the regiment.[5] The provision was later extended for the first time to the families of NCOs.[6] Volunteers if raised in addition to the statutory quota were at first not included, but it seems that for long this was not realised. In 1797, however, the overseers of Birmingham reported that the treasurers of the many counties which the town had supplied with recruits had stopped paying.[7] In Kidderminster the poor rate rose from £70 to £100 a year as a result and the demand arose for legislation.[8] Although it was objected that they would be saddled with an unlimited liability, the counties in 1799 were required to pay for allowances to these volunteers' families.[9] It will be seen that the effect of all this legislation was partly just to shift the burden of maintaining certain poor families from some parishes on to others,[10] but partly also to ensure that certain families had allowances as of right instead of casual relief.

When the militia was first raised the enthusiasm of the moment seems to have caused local authorities to interpret the law generously. The Guardians of the Poor at Norwich established a committee to receive applications from the families in July 1759, and instructed it to be liberal. They were not to be 'deemed as Parochial Poor, but that the Allowances to them shall be adequate to their several occasions'.[11] (!) In Kent, meanwhile, the justices were giving a handsome

[1] HO. 51/8, p. 208. [2] *Ibid.*, p. 222.
[3] HO. 50/19, Lord Euston, 13 January 1793; Lord Rolle, 6 January 1792 (*sic*); C. Sisted, 10 January 1793; Lord Cork, 28 January 1793.
[4] HO. 51/8, p. 350. [5] 33 Geo. III, cap. 8.
[6] Later acts on the subject were 34 Geo. III, cap. 47; 35 Geo. III, cap. 81; 36 Geo. III, cap. 114.
[7] HO. 50/30, undated memorandum on the case. HO. 50/28, W. Price, 13 June 1797 and enclosure. WO. 4/774, p. 337.
[8] HO. 50/39, W. Lygon, 26 December 1798. HO. 50/30, A. Onslow, 26 May and 27 June 1799.
[9] 39 Geo. III, cap. 106, s. 15. Cf. WO. 4/774, pp. 337-9.
[10] Cf. n. 4. [11] *Ipswich Journal*, 7 July 1759.

allowance to the families, which caused great satisfaction.[1] But prudence soon set in. In October 1759 a Suffolk general meeting ordered divisional meetings of justices to fix rates for family allowances, preserving uniformity by informing each other of their decisions.[2] This was the method followed for fixing allowances under the various acts from 1760 onwards,[3] and its purpose was restrictive.[4] In 1778 the chairman of Cambridgeshire quarter sessions admonished those responsible to look after militia families and regard it as a duty. But one of his brother justices thought that those not in their place of settlement could be passed back thereto as vagrant. The chairman himself thought that in future only unmarried men should be accepted as substitutes, though he despairingly remarked that they could not be prevented from marrying afterwards.[5] In 1779 he said that the militia was a great burden and that time-expired men who had families should not be re-enlisted.[6] The cost of the Cambridgeshire families at this time was over £700 and a county rate had to be ordered that was something like double the normal maximum.[7] Things were made worse by substitutes concealing at the time of being hired that they had families, and by counties and parishes that ought to have reimbursed the county treasurer failing to do so.[8]

It is not surprising that in 1793 the Marquess of Buckingham said that the allowances to militia families were the heaviest burden for the farmers in the American war. He thought that there should at least be a limit of 5s. a week on what each family could receive as of right.[9] Sir Charles Willoughby, chairman of Oxfordshire quarter sessions, also spoke in 1793 of the burden on the poorer farmers, and the need to conciliate them for political reasons. Egged on by their officers, men were demanding 2s. a week for a wife, even when the parish offered to find her work and supplement her earnings. Interestingly, Sir Charles complained of the political power of militia officers and lord lieutenants, whom he blamed for promoting these expensive measures.[10] Various dodges were tried in the nineties to get the burden down. There was an unsuccessful attempt to confine

[1] *Ibid.*, 14 July 1759.

[2] Rates then agreed were: wife, 2s. a week; children under 10, 1s.; children aged 10–14, 6d.; maternity benefit, 4s. a week for three weeks and 2s. to the midwife. *Ibid.*, 20 and 27 October 1759; cf. 10 November.

[3] See, e.g., *Ibid.*, 21 June, 19 and 26 July 1760; HO. 50/20, E. Bastard, 25 October 1793, and enclosure.

[4] Cf. Shaftesbury, above, p. 169.

[5] BM, Add. 35659, f. 299.   [6] BM, Add. 35626, ff. 78–9.

[7] BM, Add. 35660, f. 130. Add. 35629, ff. 7, 8. Add. 35681, ff. 122–4.

[8] £185. 9s. 8d. was owing in December 1781. BM, Add. 35662, ff. 5, 13. Add. 35626, ff. 244–5, 273.

[9] HO. 50/19, Lord Buckingham, 13 January 1793.

[10] *Ibid.*, Sir C. Willoughby, 2 February 1793.

U

allowances to children born before the father had entered the service.[1] The right of families to receive allowances when the regiment was stationed in the county was challenged: the law officers in 1799 concluded that the families were in the right.[2]

Militiamen's families then were felt to be a troublesome burden, and there was no eagerness to bring family men under arms in either the army[3] or the militia, except in serious emergencies. In 1796 the government had to give up the idea of making men with large families stand the ballot for the supplementary militia,[4] and from 1799 new measures were adopted to keep down the number of family men in service. When part of the militia was dismissed in that year the government asked that men with large families should, along with the physically unfit, be the first to be let out.[5] The act of 1802 divided militiamen into classes and envisaged the calling out of the family men last. There were to be five classes: childless men under thirty, older childless men, those with no children under fourteen, those with only one such child, and those with more. When only a part of the force was called out, the men in the earlier classes were to go first. If a fraction of a class had to be taken to get the required number, a ballot was to be held; but those not chosen by the ballot, if they had no children under fourteen and were themselves thirty-five or less, might offer to go in place of others.[6] The absence from the act of any provision for families suggests that it was hoped as a rule to dispense with the service of the hindmost classes. If married men were on the whole not to be included, plans for general military service at once became less worthwhile: especially as an exemption for the married might unduly encourage the growth of population.

(III) POLITICAL: THE MILITIA RIOTS

For the overwhelming bulk of Englishmen military service was profoundly distasteful, and when it seemed likely that they could not personally escape it they forcibly resisted the execution of the law. Both the militia act of 1757 and the supplementary militia acts of 1796 provoked rioting on a nation-wide scale. These disturbances were mainly due to a misunderstanding of the law. There was little

[1] HO. 51/9, p. 64. Cf. WO. 4/774, p. 431.

[2] HO. 50/30, J. Mitford, W. Grant, 19 July 1799.

[3] Cf. above, pp. 269–70.

[4] Sir William Young moved an amendment to the supplementary militia bill exempting men with more than two children. Pitt tried without success to get the figure raised to three. Sheridan added the qualification that they must be under ten years old. Woodfall, vol. xiii, p. 191; cf. pp. 182–3.

[5] WO. 6/188, p. 222.

[6] 42 Geo. III, cap. 90, ss. 54, 129, 132, 134, 136, 141, and Schedule E.

trouble once it was understood that real conscription was not to be introduced. But the riots were a warning against any rapid move towards universal military training.

Militia riots followed a common pattern. They were set off by the making of the lists of men liable for service by the parish constables. The men of the village would then rise in order to seize and destroy the lists and thus stop the execution of the act. Sometimes they took them from the parish constables, but sometimes they did not manage to lay hands on them until they had reached the constables of the hundreds or the deputy lieutenants. In that case, seizing the lists often involved outrages against the houses and persons of the deputies and the forcible breaking up of their meetings. Because the outbreak of the riots resulted directly from the execution of the acts, they were roughly simultaneous everywhere. This, of course, made them more alarming.[1]

Both in 1757 and in 1796 the disturbances were at their worst around the Humber, and more serious in the eastern than in the western half of the country. In 1757 the riots took place in late August and early September. The East Riding was particularly disturbed. The lieutenancy meeting to take action on the lists had been fixed for Saturday, September 17. A week before this, mobs began threatening the chief constables of Holdernesse and also some of the gentry who lived there.[2] On Monday the 12th a mob assembled near Beverley and made the chief constable give up the lists in his possession. They then invaded the town and threatened to burn it down. After beginning to demolish a house, they were induced to leave by some gentlemen who gave the men of each township a guinea or two for drink.[3] On the 13th, men from forty townships descended on the house of Sir Henry Willoughby, high sheriff of Yorkshire, at Birdsall, armed with guns, scythes and clubs. They forced him to promise not to take part in the execution of the act and to ask the lord lieutenant if he insisted on its continued application. They promised to be quiet until his answer was received, but threatened to pull down all the gentlemen's houses if it was unfavourable. They seized the lists from the constables and threatened retribution on their houses and persons if others were made. They visited the houses of several other gentlemen, and everywhere the men of each township had to be given money for drink before they would go away. Sir Edmund Anderson they found away from home. His wife bravely parleyed with them in the courtyard, but could not prevent them invading the house and

[1] Riots of exactly the same kind resulted from the Scottish militia act of 1797. See my article 'The Formation of the Scottish Militia in 1797', *Scottish Historical Review*, vol. xxxiv (1955), pp. 3–6, 10–13.
[2] BM, Add. 32874, ff. 61–3.   [3] *Ibid.*, f. 124.

pillaging the larder. She did manage to keep them out of the cellar, placing her back against the door, and in this position kept them at bay for some time until her husband returned and pacified them. The outrages continued next day: the house of the bishop of Carlisle's brother narrowly escaped destruction through his being absent when the mob came. Several magistrates had to promise to have nothing more to do with the militia act and at last, on the 15th, the lord lieutenant, Lord Irwin, issued a sort of proclamation ordering no lists to be returned, pending instructions from the king.[1]

On the same day the hard-pressed sheriff had to face another rising, this time in the North Riding. Its purpose was to prevent a meeting of deputies in York for the receiving of lists from the Wapentake of Bulmer. Mobs first visited the houses of several magistrates, and perhaps for this reason no deputies attended the meeting. The mob which had gone on to York nevertheless destroyed the inn where it was to have taken place and also another one. Such lists as had been brought by constables for the meeting were seized. To restore quiet, Willoughby and the Lord Mayor of York told the mob that they would try and prevent further lieutenancy meetings.[2] The magistrates seem to have been completely terrorised and abandoned their next meeting, planned for the 20th at Thirsk.[3] The Riding remained disturbed, particularly in the region of Whitby.[4] The West Riding also seethed with discontent, and the constables did their work with difficulty.[5] But here resolute action prevented a serious outbreak. A mob assembled in Sheffield and was expected to descend on the lord lieutenant, Lord Rockingham, at Wentworth Woodhouse and demand the surrender of the lists. But Rockingham prepared to resist them by arming his tenants and servants and they did not disturb him. He was asked by the deputies at Leeds to sanction the giving up of the lists, but dissuaded them from doing it. Two bodies of men appeared at the meeting of deputies at Doncaster, but they were induced to go home.[6]

Yorkshire was the worst but not the first county affected. In Lincolnshire the second meeting of the lieutenancy under the act, fixed for 6 September, had to be given up because of the disturbances.

---

[1] BM, Add. 32874, ff. 46–7, 61–2, 64–5, 88, 90–1, 121–2. BM, Eg. 3436, ff. 137–8. Lincolnshire R.O.: Anderson MSS, 5/2: 1, f. 28.

[2] *Kentish Post*, 24–28 September 1757. BM, Eg. 3436, ff. 133–4, 137. BM, Add. 32874, ff. 66–7.

[3] The mob threatened to return in greater numbers. BM, Add. 32874, f. 69. BM, Eg. 3426, ff. 134, 136, 143–5.

[4] BM, Add. 32874, ff. 444–6. *Kentish Post*, 24–28 September, 15–19 October 1757. Cf. BM, Eg. 3436, ff. 162–3.

[5] BM, Add. 32873, f. 445.

[6] BM, Add. 32874, ff. 264–5, 270–3.

There was a general rising for the seizing of lists, the townships round Lincoln taking the initiative. The gentry were visited and contributions levied: Lawrence Monk of Cainby had to tour the villages round him and persuade each one not to attack his house. One party he met on the road, and had to entertain them at home. A township belonging to the Duke of Ancaster, the lord lieutenant, was threatened with burning but the tenantry rallied to its defence.[1] In Nottinghamshire widespread intimidation of constables began at the end of August. Fifty lists were seized, and in two divisions none were made at all. The Duke of Newcastle's friends had some success in quieting the people, and the bulk of the returns safely reached the meeting of the county lieutenancy on 5 September.[2] But then a mob invaded the meeting, well armed with clubs, and seized the lot. Sir George Savile was collared and Lord Robert Sutton nearly stifled.[3] In Derbyshire the lists were seized, though the people were quiet thereafter.[4]

Farther south, too, there was trouble. On 30 August there was a rising in the eastern division of Bedfordshire. The magistrates assembled to conduct the ballot at Biggleswade were told that a thousand men were coming to murder them and promptly fled. The mob visited their houses levying contributions, took the lists from the inn where the meeting was to have been held, and broke its windows.[5] Next day the Gamlingay district of Cambridgeshire rose and took the lists from the high constable.[6] On 5 September Hertfordshire joined in. At Berkhamstead the magistrates argued with a mob for several hours, but finally had to adjourn and surrender the lists. At Hertford the meeting was apparently undisturbed, but the people threatened to pull down the magistrates' houses if they did any more.[7] At Royston the magistrates did not venture to meet, but this did not save them from visits at home. They had to give money for drink and promise to take no further part in executing the militia act.[8] There was further trouble in Bedfordshire,[9] and on the 8th a mob visited several gentlemen in southern Cambridgeshire in a vain search for the

[1] *Ibid.*, ff. 157–60.

[2] BM, Add. 32873, ff. 311, 313, 341, 345–7. BM, Add. 32874, f. 127. *Kentish Post*, 3–7 September 1757.

[3] BM, Add. 32874, ff. 125, 127. Add. 32873, ff. 556–7. *Ipswich Journal*, 17 September 1757.

[4] BM, Add. 32874, f. 70. *Kentish Post*, 8–12 October 1757.

[5] *Bedford Correspondence*, vol. ii, p. 267. *Chatham Correspondence*, vol. i, p. 261.

[6] BM, Add. 32873, f. 470. Add. 35351, f. 400. The county meeting next day was able to adjourn until October because there were no returns from Gamlingay and Ely.

[7] PRO. 30/8, vol. 77, ff. 168, 172–3.

[8] *Ibid.*, ff. 176–8. BM, Add. 32873, ff. 510–11. Add. 35353, f. 222.

[9] BM, Add. 32873, ff. 510–11. Add. 35351, ff. 402–3.

one who had the lists. Lord Hardwicke expected a visit from them at Wimple his country seat. They did not come, however: it was said that they realised he was an opponent of the act.[1] Other counties disturbed were Northamptonshire,[2] Huntingdonshire,[3] Norfolk[4] and Middlesex.[5] In some places the riots were occasioned by a later stage in the proceedings, the meetings for the swearing in of the men chosen to serve. This was the case in Gloucestershire[6] and also at Sevenoaks in Kent, where the meeting was broken up and Lord George Sackville was besieged in Knowle Park. The mob was eventually driven off by the servants under the command of Captain John Smith, Lord George's ADC.[7]

In 1796 the riots took place mainly in November and the area worst affected was Lindsey, the northern part of Lincolnshire. News of the new levy led to attacks on the routine meetings for receiving lists under the act of 1786. None could be held at the proper time. At Lincoln and Gainsborough this was simply because the deputies failed to attend.[8] But at Caistor the deputies were forced to adjourn by a mob of 500 men, who seized the lists from the constables. The Horncastle meeting was, unfortunately, held on 5 November—Guy Fawkes' Day and market day—and there were a lot of young men in the town. Pickets were set up on all the roads, and the constables coming to hand in the lists were made to give them up. Those objecting were lifted up by the ears until they complied. The mob then assembled where the meeting was to be held and the deputies adjourned to avoid a riot.[9] These disturbances caused the postponement of the meeting to have been held at Alford.[10] A mob assembled, nevertheless, and proceeded to levy 5s. from every person of property in the area. It was peaceably done, but the vicar feared the worst when night came and the men started drinking.[11] Money had also been demanded at Horncastle.[12]

Farther south a mob tried to interrupt proceedings at Boston, but were frustrated by the Yeomanry.[13] At Norwich the mob disturbed a

---

[1] Further, he was not lord lieutenant and his son, who was, was not there. One magistrate, Wortham, cravenly revealed that the county clerk had the lists. BM, Add. 32874, ff. 3, 4. Add. 35351, ff. 417–19. Add. 35353, f. 222.

[2] PRO. 30/8, vol. 39, f. 28. BM, Add. 32874, f. 146.

[3] BM, Add. 35351, f. 412.   [4] Above, p. 141.

[5] *Kentish Post*, October 22–6.   [6] *Ibid.*, 19–23 November.

[7] *Ibid.*, 8–12 October.

[8] HO. 50/26, C. Tatham, 1 November 1796.

[9] *Ibid.*, C. Tatham, 1 November 1796; M. Tomlin, 4 November 1796; T. Coltman, 5 and 7 November 1796; Sir J. Banks, 7 November 1796.

[10] *Ibid.*, T. Coltman, 5 and 9 November 1796.

[11] *Ibid.*, T. Coltman, F. Wilson and J. Anderson, 9 November 1796.

[12] *Ibid.*, Sir J. Banks, 11 November 1796.

[13] *Ibid.*, Mayor of Boston, etc., 10 November ; T. Wilson, 18 November 1796.

Norfolk general meeting on 15 November. They clustered round the carriages of Lord Townshend and his deputies, and would not let them enter the courthouse until a public session was promised.[1] Once inside, the leaders of the mob were given abstracts of the act and it was explained to the people. The leaders, however, kept the meeting in an uproar and the lieutenancy at length retired and did its business in an inn.[2] At Lalingford, in what was thought the most turbulent part of the county, a meeting to receive lists was stopped by the mob.[3] In Northamptonshire there was a noisy demonstration in the county town and the mob invaded the room where the meeting was being held. But the deputies managed to save the lists, disperse the mob without military help and finish their business.[4] At Wellingborough there was a riot which was put down by a speech from one of the magistrates and the arrival of the Yeomanry.[5] At Kettering the subdivision meeting was forced to adjourn and the lists were destroyed.[6] Meetings were also interrupted and lists destroyed at Wing in Buckinghamshire,[7] at Oswestry,[8] at Barmouth,[9] and at Ulverstone in Lancashire.[10] There were signs of unrest in Cambridgeshire,[11] Warwickshire and Gloucestershire.[12] At Penrith it was the ballot that was interrupted, later on, in December. A mob seized all the records and burned them, and the deputies had to disperse to prevent the firing of the building in which they met.[13]

The risings of 1757 and 1796, extensive though they were, subsided very quickly and seem to have had no serious after-effects. The upper class rallied energetically in defence of its authority. True, in 1757 Hardwicke thought that the militia act could not be enforced, even by the use of troops, if those balloted refused to take the oath: they would be too many to prosecute. He and Newcastle and their friends further regarded the riots as making the amendment of the law inevitable.[14] But even the opponents of the act were anxious to crush resistance to it and enforce respect for the law.[15] The friends of the

[1] BM, Add. 35667, ff. 130, 133, 136.
[2] HO. 50/26, Lord Townshend, 17 November 1796, with resolutions.
[3] *Ibid.*, R. J. Buxton, 25 November; Lord Townshend, 27 November 1796.
[4] *Ibid.*, Lord Northampton, 13 November 1796.
[5] *Ibid.*, Lord Northampton, 11 November 1796, and enclosure.
[6] *Ibid.*
[7] *Ibid.*, Lord Buckingham, 25 November and 13 December 1796.
[8] *Ibid.*, Lord Clive and J. Mytton, etc., 3 December 1796.
[9] *Ibid.*, E. Corbet, 23 November 1796.   [10] HO. 43/8, p. 470.
[11] HO. 50/331, Lord Hardwicke, 24 November 1796.
[12] HO. 50/26, Lord Warwick, 6 December, Lord Berkeley, 18 December 1796.
[13] *Ibid.*, Sir W. Lowther, 22 December 1796.
[14] BM, Add. 35353, ff. 223, 227. Add. 32997, f. 278. Add. 32873, f. 471. Add. 32874, f. 356.
[15] BM, Add. 32874, f. 146. Cf. above, pp. 146–7; PRO. 30/8, vol. 77, f. 176.

militia, as remarked elsewhere, attributed the whole business to sabotage by the other side.[1] Pitt made light of it and said that Potter, one of his supporters, had spoken to a mob in Bedfordshire and easily satisfied them (this seems to have been untrue).[2] No objection was therefore made to sending out regular troops to crush resistance to what had been meant to be in part an anti-militarist measure.[3] The troops seem easily to have accomplished their mission. At Northampton a mob was charged by cavalry and suffered severely.[4] On the other hand at Royston a captain of the Blues managed to make the rioters go away by simply showing them his men and making a speech.[5]

Sometimes the spontaneous action of the citizens made it less necessary to use troops. After the big riot at York the Lord Mayor at once beat the townsfolk to arms and two days later a body of 500 of them was organised to mount guard. Much the same was done at Leeds.[6] Lord Rockingham thought that the country should be organised in defence of the law and the ministers encouraged him to do this in the West Riding. He accordingly set about the revivial of the sheriff's posse.[7] Lord Irwin, on the other hand, was much criticised for his lack of vigour in face of the East Riding rioters. He eventually called a meeting of the gentry to organise the restoration of order, but Rockingham declared that it had been a failure: Irwin did not dare to hold it inside the Riding or to attend in person, and so he got no support.[8] Even in the West Riding, however, the presence of troops was thought necessary to give the magistrates courage enough to punish the rioters.[9] It proved hard to get them arrested, and there were fears that juries could not be found to convict them.[10] Eventually, some of the ringleaders were seized and punished. Those in Yorkshire were tried by a special commission of oyer and terminer. Two were sentenced to death and one actually executed.[11] The gentry's

---

[1] Above, p. 141.

[2] BM, Add. 35353, ff. 227, 231. Cf. PRO. 30/8, vol. 53, ff. 65–6; *Chatham Correspondence*, vol. i, p. 259–61.

[3] See, e.g., BM, Add. 35595, ff. 86, 90, 92; Add. 35605, ff. 236, 237; SP. 44/189, p. 432.

[4] *Kentish Post*, 12–15 October 1757.

[5] BM, Add. 32874, f. 4.

[6] Wentworth Woodhouse, R. 1–101. *Kentish Post*, 24–28 September 1757. BM, Add. 32874, f. 222–3.

[7] BM, Add. 32874, ff. 265, 270–2, 327–9, 332, 403–4, 421–3, 440–1. Wentworth Woodhouse, R. 1–102, 104, etc.

[8] BM, Add. 32875, ff. 330–1. BM, Eg. 3436, ff. 155, 156, 160–1, 164–5.

[9] BM, Add. 32874, ff. 304–5, 328, 421–2, 425.

[10] *Ibid.*, f. 425. Add. 32875, f. 331. BM, Eg. 3436, ff. 154, 157.

[11] See, e.g., *ibid.*, ff. 141–2, 164–5, 171, 185–7; BM, Add. 32874, f. 467; Add. 32875, ff. 155–6, 411; Raikes, pp. 19, 20.

almost complete lack of zeal in carrying out the militia act[1] and the care now taken to explain it to the people[2] and to amend it[3] must have done much to lessen tension and complete the work of pacification.

Repression in 1796 was much more vigorous and speedy and the execution of the law was not interrupted. Troops were sent down[4] and lord lieutenants were instructed to hold large meetings of deputies and others to enforce the law, which everyone of any weight or influence should be got to attend.[5] The ringleaders were to be arrested as soon as it could be done without fear of their release by the mob.[6] In Lindsey the lead was taken by Coltman, chairman of quarter sessions, and Sir Joseph Banks, President of the Royal Society. They duly arranged meetings and were helped by the presence of Ellison, one of the members for Lincoln.[7] When the troops arrived, a series of night raids was made to catch the ringleaders, some of whom fled.[8] Three men were sent under guard to Lincoln, and informations taken before the justices were sent to the government with a view to prosecution at the expense of the Treasury.[9] On 19 November Ellison reported that all was quiet, though the farm servants were still restless and the troops were therefore still needed.[10]

In Norfolk a second general meeting was held without incident. The magistrates of Norwich, who had been supine on the first occasion, pledged their assistance. Special constables were sworn in. An imposing body of troops was drawn up before the castle. The mob contented themselves with burning Pitt and Windham in effigy.[11] In Northamptonshire troops attended the next meetings in all the subdivisions, at the request of the magistrates. One deputy named Wodhall objected to this, and subsequently resigned. He refused to billet the soldiers at Thorpe, but some farmers gave them shelter and thus, it was thought, prevented a riot.[12] Ensuing meetings in Buckinghamshire were successfully protected by the Yeomanry, who also

---

[1] The Cambridgeshire meeting, adjourned from 1 September to 13 October (above, p. 293, n. 6), was further adjourned to 29 December: BM, Add. 32875, f. 39. Cf. above, p. 154.
[2] Below, pp. 301–2.
[3] Above, pp. 142–3.
[4] HO. 51/150, pp. 41, 45, 47, 49.
[5] HO. 43/8, pp. 110, 121, 141, 163, 172.
[6] Cf. HO. 50/26, draft to Coltman, 10 November 1796.
[7] HO. 50/26, Sir J. Banks, 11 November 1796.
[8] *Ibid.*, Coltman, 14 November 1796; Banks do.
[9] *Ibid.*, Banks, 14 November, Coltman, 13, 25 and 28 November 1796.
[10] *Ibid.*, R. Ellison, 19 November 1796.
[11] *Ibid.*, Lord Townshend, 20 and 24 November 1796.
[12] *Ibid.*, J. C. Villiers, 5 December 1796; M. Wodhull, 3 December, sent on by Lord Northampton, 9 December, 1796.

chased and caught some of the troublemakers. (The people of Cheddington fought a rearguard action with them to allow two to escape.) Prosecutions were again planned at the expense of the Treasury.[1]

Militia riots were not confined to the two years discussed above and were always a possibility to be reckoned with. Kent was disturbed four times between 1757 and 1759[2] and there was trouble in Huntingdonshire in 1759 and 1761.[3] The act of 1769 was fairly soon followed by disturbances in Buckinghamshire and Denbighshire.[4] There were riots in Sussex in 1778 and Merionethshire in 1779,[5] consequent on mobilisation. Some riots at Gateshead, Morpeth and Hexham in 1761 led to the mobilised militia itself being used against the populace to enforce militia recruiting. At the last place the mob advanced to the points of the militia's bayonets and after lengthy parleyings they were fired on and driven back with great loss of life. There were twenty dead at least and many wounded.[6] But serious though such incidents might be, they were too sporadic to be really dangerous.

What was more significant than the riots themselves was the motives of the rioters—the attitude to military service which the riots revealed. In 1757 the commonest reason for them was the fear of being forced to serve, and especially of being forced to serve abroad. In Nottinghamshire men said that they would rather be hanged in England than scalped in America.[7] There was a general admission that the trouble here arose from the enlistment of men for the army in 1756, who were then sent abroad contrary to their expectation.[8] Some Lincolnshire men, on being told that the militia act laid down that they were not to go abroad, said that they had been promised the same a year before and had been deceived; now they would trust nobody.[9] The Duke of Ancaster protested that he had not enlisted men with this limitation of service,[10] but Lord Dupplin said that whether there had been a stipulation or not, most people had expected the recruits of 1756 not to go abroad.[11] Lord Hardwicke also

[1] *Ibid.*, Lord Buckingham, 17 and 18 December 1796.

[2] SP. 41/30, Lewis Watson etc., 18 July 1759.

[3] *Ibid.*, Lord Mandeville, 28 June 1759. *Calendar of Home Office Papers, 1760–5*, p. 22, no. 92.

[4] *Calendar of Home Office Papers, 1766–9*, p. 477, no. 1230; *1770–2*, p. 21, no. 69.

[5] Above, p. 213, n. 3. WO. 1/1005, f. 927.

[6] BM, Eg. 3436, ff. 381–2. *Calendar of Home Office Papers, 1760–5*, p. 26, nos. 107–8. *Ipswich Journal*, 14 and 21 March 1761. Turton, pp. 43–6.

[7] BM, Add. 32873, f. 311.

[8] See further, Add. 32874, f. 265; Add. 35679, f. 230–1. Cf. PRO. 30/8, vol. 53, f.66.

[9] BM, Add. 32874, f. 159.　　[10] *Ibid.*, f. 158.　　[11] BM, Add. 32873, f. 445.

thought there had been a breach of faith.[1] One of the regiments raised in 1756 was sent back to Yorkshire, whence the men came, so that their friends could see that they had not been ill-treated.[2]

The absence of provision for pay in the militia act was another cause of trouble in 1757.[3] This was a mere misunderstanding: for various reasons it had seemed desirable to have separate legislation about pay.[4] More notable was the objection that army rates of pay (6d. a day for a private) were not enough. One leaflet circulating in Yorkshire claimed that the deputies had prevented some arrangement for augmenting the pay to 1s. 6d. a day because it would cause jealousy among the private soldiers of the army.[5] Another thing sometimes objected to was the actual making of lists of the male population: in Nottinghamshire this was identified with David's sin of numbering the people.[6]

The foregoing objections could all be dismissed as due to misunderstanding or prejudice, but there was another which was perfectly well founded. The previous militia had been a burden on property, but the new one, selecting men by lot from among the able-bodied, fell on rich and poor alike and might easily bear more heavily on a poor man than on his rich neighbour. It seems that Newcastle's friend White had warned the commons that this would cause trouble.[7] Hardwicke also claimed to have foreseen ill consequence. He aptly compared the change in the law to the Restoration bargain by which the feudal burdens borne mainly by the rich were abolished, and the king compensated by an excise on beer and ale drunk mainly by the poor.[8] Bitter class feeling was aroused by the new system of ballots. It was said that gentlemen kept poor men alive only to fight for them.[9] Nor was it only the poor who were indignant. The farmers were said to be encouraging resistance.[10] In the East Riding some constables appeared at the head of the mob.[11] Lord Royston found that both the middle and the lower sort disliked the act, and that after the riots the people triumphed at having beaten the nobility.[12] Feelings like this caused the whole act to be viewed as an upper-class plot and reminded middle and lower class alike of other grievances against their rulers. A threatening letter sent to two Lincolnshire justices is virtua-

---

[1] BM, Add. 35353, ff. 223–4.   [2] BM, Add. 32875, f. 156.
[3] BM, Add. 35353, f. 223.   [4] Above, p. 132 and n. 1.
[5] BM, Add. 32874, f. 274. Cf. ff. 158, 265; PRO. 30/8, vol. 53, f. 66.
[6] BM, Add. 32874, f. 46. Add. 32873, f. 311.
[7] BM, Add. 32874, f. 265.   [8] BM, Add. 35353, f. 224.
[9] BM, Add. 32874, f. 158. Cf. Add. 32873, f. 311.
[10] BM, Add. 35351, f. 409. Cf. Add. 35679, ff. 228–9; *Chatham Correspondence*, vol. i, p. 259.
[11] BM, Add. 32874, f. 46. Cf. BM, Eg. 3436, f. 152.
[12] BM, Add. 35351, ff. 412, 415.

ally a middle-class political manifesto. It begins by threatening to destroy all gentlemen's houses if the making of lists is ordered: if they want men they should hire them 'by the assistance of your long green purses'. If a poor man is drawn, the letter goes on to ask, 'which of you buntin-ars'd coated fellows will maintain his family?' But then the letter turns to other grievances: high parish expenditure and the failure of landlords to abate rents after the previous year's bad harvest.

> If the Just-Asses and the other start up Officers that buys a Commission for a Trifle and sells his Nation to make his Fortune when he comes abroad, and throws Thousands of Poor men's lives away about it, such men as those sho'd behave well to their tennants at home: Then they would have the Countreyes Goodwill, for 'tis the Farmers that maintains both the Poor and such as they too . . .[1]

The connecting of the militia with other grievances and attempts to exploit it politically were a good deal noticed in Yorkshire. There were rumours of a levelling scheme—talk of the gentry having been long enough in possession of their estates. There were also more immediate economic grievances. Mills with 'French stones' were objected to. One was destroyed at Sheffield by the mob which was thought to be going to attack Lord Rockingham.[2] An attack on Sir Rowland Winn's mill in the same district was feared.[3] In the Whitby area a militia riot was followed by another against the millers. They had been buying corn at a good price from the farmers, with the result that very little was coming on to the local retail market. The first riot was quelled with fair words and promises, but a second one ended in the forcible seizure of some flour by the mob.[4] The restriction of corn exports was one of the measures proposed by the Yorkshire authorities to restore peace.[5] There had been considerable corn riots the previous year also.[6] Charles Yorke thought the militia grievance only a pretext for 'disorder in a time of scarcity, dissatisfaction and general relaxation of government'.[7] There was at least one clear case of jacobites attempting to exploit the situation. A poster was put up one night at Halifax which listed the grounds for objecting to the militia and called on the people to 'remember your legal and native king' and be ready to 'arise and act like men', so that 'your blood and labour be no more devoted to the service of any but your own

[1] BM, Add. 32874, ff. 161–2.
[2] *Ibid.*, ff. 222, 270–1.
[3] Enclosures and game associations were also mentioned, *Ibid.*, f. 265.
[4] *Ibid.*, ff. 425, 426, 444–6. *Kentish Post*, 15–19 October 1757.
[5] BM, Add. 32875, ff. 285–6, 411.
[6] *Gentlemen's Magazine*, vol. xxvi (1756), pp. 408, 447–8. BM, Add. 27538, f. 474. Wentworth Woodhouse, R. 1–79, 80.
[7] BM, Add. 35353, f. 227.

country'.[1] There were several reports that catholics were active in stirring up riots.[2]

In 1796 all this was repeated on a smaller scale. The people were set against the act by misleading rumours: that they would be sent to the East Indies,[3] that hiring substitutes would cost 2 or 3 guineas to every man liable to be balloted.[4] Behind the riots lay a certain amount of intelligence and organisation. Before the affray at Horncastle in Lindsey, the Crier of Spilsby had gone about reading a notice that the young men going thither were resolved neither to pay nor to serve. There were Sunday meetings in the village churchyards.[5] The rioters both at Horncastle and Alford wore blue ribbons.[6] It was the radicals who now tried to make political capital out of the disturbances. At Nottingham a radically inclined Friendly Society held a meeting to consider either opposition to or infiltration of the new force. There were rumours of a Pistol Club, and loyal citizens were terrorised by shots fired into their houses.[7]

To some extent this popular hostility to the militia could be overcome by explanation and argument. A number of manifestoes on the subject were published by lieutenancies or inserted by individuals in newspapers. They mainly concentrated on removing misunderstandings regarding the law. In 1757 it was explained that there was no possibility of service overseas, that the amount of service to be required at home was limited, that pay and clothing would certainly be provided, and that there were certain advantages to be gained by serving, such as exemption from service as a peace officer.[8] In 1796 there were explanations on similar lines.[9] In 1757 there was also an attempt to put across the general case in favour of the militia. Hardwicke thought that the people would never understand the 'train of political arguments' behind the act.[10] It could, however, be pointed

---

[1] BM, Add. 32874, ff. 274–5. BM, Eg. 3436, ff. 155, 159.

[2] *Ibid.*, ff. 152–3. But the report here that a gentleman was not harmed because he was a Roman Catholic may mean only that as he was not a magistrate there was no point in attacking him. See also Lincolnshire R.O., Anderson MSS. 5/2, f. 28.

[3] HO. 50/26, Lord Warwick, 6 December 1796.

[4] *Ibid.*, Sir J. Banks, 7 November 1796.

[5] *Ibid.*, T. Coltman, 7 November 1796. Cf. for 1757, Wentworth Woodhouse R. 1–98.

[6] HO. 50/26, T. Coltman, 7 November; J. Andrews, 9 November 1796.

[7] *Ibid.*, Lord Newark, 22 November 1796, and enclosures. HO. 50/6, p. 227.

[8] *Gloucester Journal*, 13 September, 11 and 25 October, and 8 November; *Ipswich Journal*, 13 September; *Cambridge Journal*, 17 September 1757.

[9] HO. 50/27, R. Ellison, 9 February 1797, and enclosures. Holden, p. 66. In both years explanations were translated into Welsh: *Gloucester Journal*, 4 October 1757. HO. 50/26, Lord Bulkeley, 13 December 1796.

[10] BM, Add. 32874, f. 147.

out that the militia was a traditional institution, not meant for 'romantic' foreign wars but for home defence;[1] that the militia might shorten the war by releasing the army to attack the French;[2] and that the alternative would be a larger army and perhaps conscription, which would be worse.[3]

Whatever the success of these apologetics it seems evident—from their very tenor, from the recurrence of riots and from the course of legislation—that popular hostility to military service was not got rid of. Attempts to move towards it were felt as a grievance and were apt unseasonably to remind the people that they had other grievances as well. The arming of the manhood of the nation at large by a régime which was fairly liberal and yet not democratic was bound to be a delicate operation. The aversion of the people to being armed gave their rulers a salutory early warning of this, and only under extreme pressure from Napoleon did they make a half-hearted attempt.[4] Thus for political no less for economic and administrative reasons it was not possible to advance to a true system of national military training from the quaint simulacrum of it that was the militia.

[1] *Gloucester Journal*, 27 September 1757.
[2] Said at least in the following year (*ibid.*, 5 and 12, September 1758).
[3] *Ibid.*, 8 November 1757; cf. *Cambridge Journal*, 10 September 1757.
[4] See especially Fortescue, *County Lieutenancies*, pp. 202–219.

XII

THE OFFICERS

WHEN the men had been raised, the law required the lieutenancy to form them into units appropriate to the size of the county quota. The act of 1757 delimited the size of these in a negative way, suggesting a fear that too many officers might be appointed. There were to be not more than one captain, lieutenant and ensign for every eighty private men, and regiments were to consist of at least seven companies of at least forty men. If a county had men enough for more than twelve such companies it was to have more than one regiment; where there were fewer than seven companies, they were to form a battalion. A regiment could have three field officers (colonel, lieutenant-colonel and major), but a battalion could only have one, exclusive of the lord lieutenant.[1] By 1760 it was realised that the real problem was to prevent the number of officers from sinking too low, and the more detailed regulations in an act of that year reflect this. Companies were to consist of from sixty to eighty men and were to have a captain, lieutenant and ensign. Regiments might contain from eight to twelve such companies and were to have three field officers. Where there were from five to eight companies to be regimented, they were to form a battalion under a lieutenant-colonel and a major. Three to five companies might similarly form a battalion under a lieutenant-colonel only. When a county had only one or two companies they were to remain independent, but the king was empowered to combine such small contingents in order to form a battalion.[2] Unfortunately this was seldom done.[3] From 1786 each regiment had to have a company of light infantry and one of

[1] 30 Geo. II, cap. 25, ss. 17, 27, 29.

[2] 33 Geo. II, cap. 22, ss. 7, 10. Cf. 31 Geo. II, cap. 26, s. 13; 2 Geo. III, cap. 20, ss. 28–9, 95–7 (by s. 97 a major might be appointed to command the smaller type of battalion).

[3] The only case I have found is the incorporation of the Brecon companies in the Monmouth corps in 1793. The Duke of Beaufort was lord lieutenant of both counties. WO. 4/770, pp. 304. 308–10.

grenadiers, while in a battalion of more than five companies, one company was to be one or the other.[1] In 1802 the maximum permissible size of a company was increased to 120: companies with ninety privates or more were now to have an additional lieutenant, regiments of 800 privates or more an additional major. A corps was to have three field officers if it comprised 480 privates or more and two field officers if it had more than three companies. The number of captains was increased by ending the practice whereby field officers were captains of companies as well.[2]

Under this system the average English county down to 1797 had one or two regiments; Middlesex and the West Riding three each; and most Welsh and a few English counties very small units indeed. The formation of the supplementary militia on the same plan meant additional units in many counties for a time: Lancashire, Middlesex and the West Riding had five regiments each.[3]

The officers for these corps were appointed by the lord lieutenants, but their choice was restricted by the system of property qualifications. The authors of the earlier militia acts had intended that the militia should be commanded by men of property, and that as far as possible all men of property should take their turn. Until 1802 the acts provided that up to a third of the officers in each county must retire every four (later five) years if others duly qualified offered to serve in their place.[4] But the willingness of men of property to serve was greatly reduced once it became the practice to embody the militia for the duration of each war. Many who could undertake local and temporary service could not afford to neglect their private affairs and become to all intents and purposes regular soldiers for years on end. Already in 1760 a number of officers took advantage of the permission given by the act of that year to any who were superfluous to the new requirements to retire.[5] In 1761 officers in Somerset were eager to resign because—or so they said—they doubted the legality of the royal proclamation declaring that commissions granted under George II were to remain valid in the new reign. Some thought that it amounted to giving them new commissions, not under the militia

[1] The subalterns in such companies were both to be lieutenants. 26 Geo. III, cap. 107, ss. 53–4.

[2] Additional officers had already been sanctioned by 38 Geo. III, cap. 55, s. 1; 39, 40 Geo. III, cap. 1, s. 19. A unit of three companies was to be called a corps, one of four to seven companies a battalion. The king might order the appointment of extra officers if he wished any of the militia trained as artillery, and he was empowered to depart from the letter of the act in cases not provided for. 42 Geo. III, cap. 90, ss. 68–71.

[3] See Appendix B.

[4] 30 Geo. II, cap. 25, s. 13. 2 Geo. III, cap. 20, ss. 30–1. 26 Geo. III, cap. 107, s. 15.

[5] WO. 4/759, pp. 95–110. Cf. 33 Geo. II, cap. 22, s. 10.

laws, and obliging those who held them to serve wherever and for as long as the king saw fit.[1] In Cambridgeshire a similar doubt seems to have been started by the lord lieutenant himself, and the officers seized the opportunity to retire in a body and not accept new commissions. Sir John Hynde Cotton said that the original plan had not included either lengthy embodiment or service outside the county, and business in London made constant attendance impossible for him. He felt that the decline of enthusiasm for the militia in the county justified his resigning.[2] In 1804 (not for the first time) the Duke of Richmond complained of the stationing of militia corps away from their homes, and said that it would ruin the force by obliging the more respectable officers to retire.[3] The unwillingness of the officers to be away from home too long was an important obstacle to the sending of English militia corps to Ireland. In Lord Rolle's Devonshire regiment, which went over in 1798, many of the officers became so anxious about their private affairs that they threatened to resign if any attempt was made to keep the regiment away after the following Midsummer.[4] The whole grievance was best expressed by some officers of the Berkshire Provisional Cavalry, when it was proposed that their regiment should volunteer for overseas service. They complained at being

> pressed to extend our services beyond our abilities or inclinations by adopting a line of life which ought to have commenced at an earlier period when we might have secured an interest in the Profession if such had been our object.[5]

Of course, in peacetime this objection to service did not exist, but on the other hand the need to serve was less apparent in the absence of national danger. In 1785 Colonel Maister of the East Riding regiment said that if the peacetime trainings were resumed his own and many other corps would be found to have lost many of the officers who had been serving at the end of the American war. He thought that they could only be replaced by men of rather inferior social rank, and was therefore in favour of not assembling the militia again until another war broke out, when the gentry and the old officers would again be willing to serve.[6] Thornton said much the same in 1769, lamenting also that even the richer gentry were unwilling to go on once pay ceased.[7]

[1] *Calendar of Home Office Papers, 1760–5*, pp. 73–4, no. 344. PRO. 30/8, vol. 53, ff. 140, 149–50.
[2] BM, Add. 35659, ff. 61, 63, 69, 70, 72. Cf. Add. 35352, ff. 163, 172–3.
[3] BM, Add. 33112, ff. 176–8. Cf. above, p. 213.
[4] HO. 50/33, Lord Rolle, 17 March and 24 May 1799.
[5] WO. 1/942, f. 575. [6] BM, Add. 28060, ff. 237–8.
[7] Wentworth Woodhouse, R. 1–1187.

There was accordingly a permanent shortage of qualified officers, overcome with difficulty for the higher ranks and altogether impossible to overcome in the case of the subalterns because the class from which they were supposed to come was ceasing to exist. As Colonel Ward complained that Cambridgeshire 'does not abound with the better sort of yeomen', whose younger sons would do for ensigns.[1] Parliament bowed to the realities of the situation by gradually watering down the system of qualifications.[2] From the outset it was necessary to have a different and lower set for Wales and the smaller English counties,[3] and yet another set for boroughs having their own lieutenancy.[4] Peers and their heirs were allowed to serve without further qualification, although from 1769 they were only allowed to do so in the militias of the counties where they resided.[5] In 1769 the difficulty of finding lieutenants and ensigns led to their qualifications being halved and to the introduction of new ways of qualifying: in compensation, the qualifications of the senior officers were increased. From 1769 until 1786 and again from 1802 the usual stipulation that half the qualifying property must be in the county where the officer served was waived in the case of the two junior ranks.[6] For the supplementary militia it was laid down that if properly qualified persons could not be found, officers and former officers from any service might be appointed, but not with a rank higher than that which they already held.[7]

The filling of the higher ranks was made a little easier by allowing officers already in the militia to be promoted to a rank higher than

[1] BM, Add. 35660, f. 263.

[2] For the figures see Note at the end of the chapter. For the qualifications generally applicable see 30 Geo. II, cap. 25, s. 3; 2 Geo. III, cap. 20, s. 5; 9 Geo. III, cap. 42, ss. 2, 3; 26 Geo. III, cap. 107, s. 5; 42 Geo. III, cap. 90, s. 6. Leaseholds and property in reversion could count towards a qualification in certain cases: 30 Geo. II, cap. 25, s. 4; 31 Geo. II, cap. 26, s. 4; 2 Geo. III, cap. 20, ss. 6, 7; 9 Geo. III, cap. 42, ss. 4, 5; 26 Geo. III, cap. 107, ss. 9, 10; 42 Geo. III, cap. 90, ss. 10–11.

[3] Viz. Cumberland, Huntingdon, Monmouth, Rutland, Westmorland. 30 Geo. II, cap. 25, s. 52; 2 Geo. III, cap. 20, ss. 8, 91; 9 Geo. III, cap. 42, s. 9; 26 Geo. III, cap. 107, s. 6; 42 Geo. III, cap. 90, s. 7. The Isle of Ely had a scale of its own, and so at first did the Isle of Purbeck. For references see above, p. 281, notes 3 and 5.

[4] 30 Geo. II, cap. 25, s. 55. 2 Geo. III, cap. 20, s. 11. 9 Geo. III, cap. 42, s. 9. 26 Geo. III, cap. 107, s. 8. 42 Geo. III, cap. 90, s. 9.

[5] 30 Geo. II, cap. 25, s. 11. 2 Geo. III, cap. 20, s. 18. 9 Geo. III, cap. 42, s. 16. 26 Geo. III, cap. 107, s. 14. 42 Geo. III, cap. 90, s. 14. The lord lieutenant could always take personal command of the militia, but he could not command more than one unit nor draw pay beyond the rank proper for the commanding officer of a unit of that size. 33 Geo. II, cap. 22, ss. 8, 9. 2 Geo. III, cap. 20, ss. 28–9. 26 Geo. III, cap. 107, s. 55. 42 Geo. III, cap. 90, s. 72.

[6] The process began in 1762. See notes 2–4 above.

[7] 37 Geo. III, cap. 3, s. 2.

that for which they possessed a qualification. From 1757 until 1786 meritorious service during actual invasion or rebellion might be rewarded by promotion in such cases.[1] From 1778 a lieutenant-colonel who had served five years in command of a battalion could be made a colonel. When a county contingent consisted of two companies the eldest captain was from 1778 to have the brevet rank of major, and when it consisted of four companies a second field officer might be appointed by brevet. From 1786 there could be a third where the companies numbered six.[2] Until 1802 lieutenants could advance to the intermediate rank of captain-lieutenant, with effective command of a company, though for a time they needed a captain's qualification.[3] A final way by which the system of qualifications was relaxed was by the occasional inclusion of deputy lieutenants and militia officers in the acts commonly passed each year to indemnify those who had omitted to qualify themselves for the offices which they held.[4]

Militia officers, like all others, were subject to religious tests designed to exclude any who were not members of the Church of England.[5] The difficulties encountered in raising the supplementary militia led to an attempt to remove the religious disabilities in respect of that force. For some reason this was a question in which Yorkshire was particularly interested. It first arose in regard to the men, who had to swear that they were protestants. On behalf of the deputies of the West Riding, Lord Hawke wrote to the Home Secretary pointing out the unfairness of this to catholics who wished to serve in person.[6] The greivance was also aired by Sheridan in the commons, and at the end of 1796 the law was amended accordingly.[7] In the fol-

[1] But not above the rank of lieutenant-colonel and a captain's qualification required for promotion to that rank. 30 Geo. II, cap. 25, ss. 5, 6. 2 Geo. III, cap. 20, s. 12.

[2] 18 Geo. III, cap. 59, ss. 3, 6, 21. 26 Geo. III, cap. 107, ss. 57–8. Slight alteration by 42 Geo. III, cap. 90, ss. 73-4. I am not sure about the meaning of these clauses. When qualifications were raised, existing officers were not disqualified. From 1798 their seniority was preserved if they changed regiment. 9 Geo. III, cap. 42, s. 11. 38 Geo. III, cap. 55, ss. 2, 3. 42 Geo. III, cap. 90, ss. 15, 75; cf. s. 16.

[3] 19 Geo. III, cap. 72, s. 6. 26 Geo. III, cap. 107, s. 59. The captain-lieutenant was in charge of the regimental or battalion commander's company. From 1786 units of fewer than six companies were not allowed to have one and the reorganisation of 1802 made them unnecessary. By warrant of 26 March 1778 (in SP. 41/32) they were to rank as captains.

[4] See, e.g., 31 Geo. II, cap. 9; 33 Geo. II, cap. 29; 1 Geo. III, cap. 12; 2 Geo. III, cap. 23; 3 Geo. III, cap. 5; 4 Geo. III, cap. 31; and below, p. 309.

[5] They had to take the necessary oaths, etc., within six months of appointment. 30 Geo. II, cap. 25, s. 9. 2 Geo. III, cap. 20, s. 15. 26 Geo. III, cap. 107, s. 13. 42 Geo. III, cap. 90, s. 13.

[6] HO. 50/26, Lord Hawke, 10 December 1796.

[7] Woodfall, vol. xiii, pp. 183–4. 37 Geo. III, cap. 22, s. 2. Applied to the whole militia by 42 Geo. III, cap. 90, s. 41.

lowing year Wilberforce and Lascelles, the members for Yorkshire, introduced a bill to allow catholics to become officers in the supplementary militia and provisional cavalry. It was passed by the commons, with the addition of a clause extending the same relief to protestant dissenters.[1] In the lords its main defender was the Duke of Norfolk, a protestant member of a mainly catholic family and at that time lord lieutenant of the West Riding.[2] He and Lord Hawke argued that those to be relieved were thoroughly loyal, and that it was absurd to allow poor catholics to serve while debarring catholic gentlemen.[3] Among the speakers on the other side, the bishop of Rochester said that the catholics were certainly loyal, but 'he did not know what a Protestant Dissenter was at this time of day'. The term had come to cover the wildest heresies, and in any case history had shown the dissenters to be incurably seditious.[4] Lord Sydney and the bishop of Bristol were careful to dissociate themselves from this argument: they thought any religion better than none at all. The Lord Chancellor, too, thought that the bill was not a real breach in the Test and Corporation Acts since it only applied to a purely temporary force. But he was against it because it was stirring up undesirable controversy. The bill was rejected by 23 votes to 6—mainly on the ground that it was the thin end of a dangerous wedge.[5] In spite of this both catholic and dissenting officers are to be found in the militia. Richard and Edward Huddleston for instance, members of a well-known catholic family, were captains in the Cambridgeshires in the nineties. In 1799 Richard was promoted major and thereupon thanked the lord lieutenant for ignoring his religion, 'a favourable circumstance I should not have met with in every regiment'.[6] The religious test was apparently ignored if local sentiment did not support it.

Parliament clung to the religious tests and refused to sanction a further relaxing of qualifications in 1798.[7] There was also a tightening of the system of registering qualifications. These had to be filed with the clerk of the peace within six months of appointment, on pain of a fine of £200 for a field officer or deputy and £100 for other officers. At first enforcement was left to the common informer.[8] But when

---

[1] CJ, vol. lii, pp. 596, 611, 674, 681, 689, 701.

[2] Removed in 1798 for drinking to 'the majesty of the people'. DNB.

[3] Woodfall, vol. xv, pp. 558–60, 564.   [4] *Ibid.*, pp. 556–8.

[5] *Ibid.*, pp. 560–7. Cf. Sheridan's attack on the tests in 1794, *ibid.*, vol. iv, pp. 159–166.

[6] See my note on 'Roman Catholics holding Military Commissions in 1798', *English Historical Review*, vol. lxx (1955), pp. 428–32, especially p. 431, n. 1. On dissenters, below, p. 431. No doubt toleration increased as time went on.

[7] Above, pp. 230–1.

[8] 30 Geo. II, cap. 25, ss. 9, 10, 57. 2 Geo. III, cap. 20, ss. 15–16.

some qualifications were lowered in 1769, clerks of the peace were required to send an annual return of all those filed with them to a secretary of state.[1] From 1779 militia commissions had to be gazetted like those of the army and the lord lieutenant had to be informed when the qualification was filed. If he received no such certificate, he was to advertise the commission as vacant.[2] At length, in 1786, the obvious step was taken of requiring qualifications both to be certified to the lord lieutenant before the commission was granted and stated in the body of the commission itself. But very significantly this provision was not applied to lieutenants and ensigns.[3] In 1795 Pitt said that experience had shown that the system of qualifications could not be applied to subalterns and claimed that the public's real security lay in the qualifications of the captains.[4] Yet even with the higher ranks parliament could not bring itself to be really firm. Both in 1780 and 1787 there were special measures of indemnity for those who had failed to comply in time with the more stringent rules established in the previous year. The indemnity of 1787 was renewed each year from 1789.[5]

II

Even with a relaxed system of qualifications it was very hard for the lord lieutenants to keep their establishment of officers complete, and almost impossible to ensure that the officers were fit for their job. For the ranks of captain and above, the most natural source of supply was to be found in the sons of noblemen and wealthy gentlemen, who had neither to care for an estate nor earn a living. The Duke of Richmond was approached in 1804 by a young man whose father's income had just been greatly augmented, to about £2000 a year. The son felt that this entitled him to give up trying to become a lawyer,

---

[1] 9 Geo. III, cap. 42, ss. 13–15. In 1770 the commons asked for a return of all militia officers then serving: CJ, vol. xxxiii, pp. 42, 228.

[2] 19 Geo. III, cap. 72, ss. 8–10. Cf. 18 Geo. III, cap. 59, s. 27. In 1780 the commons ordered a return of qualifications filed since the act of 1779, CJ, vol. xxxvii, pp. 718–19, 764; cf. LJ, vol. xxxv, pp. 780–1. Lord Radnor proposed a further bill on the subject in 1781, LJ, vol. xxxvi, pp. 224, 242. Cf. Parl. Reg., vol. xiv, p. 192; vol. xv, pp. 78–9.

[3] 26 Geo. III, cap. 107, ss. 11–13. 42 Geo. III, cap. 90, ss. 12–13. There was a rumpus in 1798 about the delays and extra expense in gazetting the many supplementary militia officers. Lincolnshire RO., Lindsey Records, Box 2: W. Wickham, circular of 26 April 1798; Ellis to Brackenbury, 24 April 1799. Lancashire RO., LC. 4, ff. 113a, 164 sq.

[4] Woodfall, vol. vi, pp. 287–9.

[5] 20 Geo. III, cap. 8. 27 Geo. III, cap. 8, s. 18. Cf. annual indemnity acts from 1789. Cf. Wentworth Woodhouse, Y.23: W. Brooke, 28 February 1798 that West Riding qualifications seldom if ever sent to the clerk of the peace in the Duke of Norfolk's time.

but he did not wish to be idle and so asked for a captaincy in the militia.[1] Young men like this were sometimes full of martial enthusiasm. In 1760 the Marquess of Tavistock, appointed by his father the Duke of Bedford to raise and command the Bedfordshire militia, confessed that he was 'militia mad . . . you don't know how dangerous it was to let me loose'.[2] His parents (significantly) suspected that this only meant that he was developing a taste for low company. He denied this indignantly and spoke again of

> my ruling passion in life, I mean my rage for everything that has connection with a Military life—I own the prevelency of it and confess it to be a madness.[3]

In 1762 he could still say that 'my old hobby horse has entirely distanced all the new ones', and when the regiment was due to be disbanded at the end of the year he wished to have a painting done of four or five of the men in uniform:

> (like every other lover) I cannot part with my favourite mistress my regiment without desiring to have her picture.[4]

In the American war Thomas Pelham, later to be second Earl of Chichester, told his family that he took much pleasure in the militia service and felt not a little vain at the good appearance made by the Sussex regiment when it was left for a time under his command.[5]

Sometimes it was patriotic zeal rather than military enthusiasm which stirred the young men. On the approach of war in 1792 Charles Yorke, the later Secretary at War, took a captaincy in the Cambridgeshire militia, of which his brother the third Earl of Hardwicke was colonel, because, in effect, as one of the county members he felt that he should set an example.[6] When the war came he encouraged his brother to 'consider the business of the Regiment *now* as your principal and indeed sole occupation'. 'I did not come into this d——d Regiment for amusement,' he said, but only to help the colonel and the service; and he promised to stay till the war ended 'if all the Devils in Hell were in it'.[7] Of course, with such men as these a narrower patriotism weighed heavily: they had to serve the county of which they were the political leaders and save it from the burden and disgrace of a fine for not raising the militia. As already explained,[8] it was this above all which induced some of the large landed proprietors to enter the higher ranks of the militia and provide a stiffening to the young and often inexperienced members of their class who more readily served there.

[1] BM, Add. 33112, ff. 178–9.
[2] MSS. of fourth Duke of Bedford, vol. xli, f. 98.   [3] *Ibid.*, f. 172.
[4] *Ibid.*, vol. xlv, f. 206; vol. xlvi, f. 108.   [5] BM, Add. 33128, ff. 45, 47–8.
[6] BM, Add. 35392, ff. 248–9; cf. ff. 251–2, 257–61.   [7] *Ibid.*, ff. 310, 325.
[8] See especially above, pp. 147, 149–54, 195–6.

The militia officers afford some shining examples of devoted public service. After the disembodiment of his men Lt.-Col. Bramstow of the Essex supplementary militia tried to arrange to serve in the old militia in case of invasion as a simple captain-lieutenant.[1] In 1802 Lord Essex said that he had taken command of the Herefordshires because of his disgust at the corrupt practices allowed by his predecessor, Lord Bateman.[2] But even in the relatively respectable higher ranks there was much that was deplorable. Young men of the better class often proved unfit for responsible posts. They were commonly unused to hard work and to the complicated financial dealings which even the command of a company then entailed. Captain Parker served without scandal in the Cambridgeshires while his father lived,[3] but went to pieces after his death, which plunged the family into a suit in chancery. In October 1796 he had to ask his colonel to pay some bills.[4] Threatened with a court of enquiry into his accounts with his men, he fled to Jersey in February 1797. It was found that he owed the corps £60, largely as a result of making away with money stopped from his men's pay to pay for leggings.[5] He also left a servant unpaid, a mistress unprovided for, and numerous civilian creditors who demanded payment from his commanding officer.[6] He begged his superiors to help him because he had the offer of a 'mercantile' post if he could settle with his creditors, and his brother had spent the family fortune in horse racing. But the lieutenant-colonel said that he could not write well enough—or be trusted enough—to be a clerk and that he was shamefully ungrateful to his brother, who had embarrassed his own finances to help him.[7]

This sort of thing might not have mattered much if the supply of qualified persons willing to serve had been large. In fact, it was so small that anyone remotely suitable had to be taken on, and officers had to be retained who had shown themselves, or had become, unfit for the work. In 1804 the Duke of Richmond was obliged to retain the colonelcy of the Sussex despite his advanced age, and to beg Thomas Pelham to stay on as lieutenant-colonel, though he was now a peer and a minister and could only contribute his 'name and occasional superintendence'.[8] In 1759 Soame Jenyns thought that a young

---

[1] BM, Add. 33107, ff. 336–8.   [2] BM, Add. 33110, ff. 314–15.

[3] For over a decade, having transferred from the Surrey militia in 1782. His father had property in both counties but sold that in Cambridgeshire in 1785. BM, Add. 35661, ff. 252, 273–5, 278, 298. Add. 35662, ff. 138, 190.

[4] BM, Add. 35667, ff. 76, 92.

[5] BM, Add. 35667, ff. 265, 269, 275, 277. Add. 35669, ff. 81, 85, 131, 133. He does not say that his father is dead, but only alludes to him once, as his 'poor father', while often mentioning his mother and brother.

[6] BM, Add. 35667, ff. 309, 346. Add. 35668, ff. 180–96.

[7] BM, Add. 35669, ff. 81, 131.   [8] BM, Add. 33112, ff. 176–8.

man who wanted to be a captain in the Isle of Ely would 'add military dignity to the corps' though he only had one arm.[1] At the age of seventy-five, Thomas Sockwell could look back on thirty years' service with the Westminster regiment, during which he had risen to the rank of major and found himself finally the commanding officer because the colonel and lieutenant-colonel had both died.[2]

For many years Cambridgeshire had to put up with most undesirable men at the head of its corps because no satisfactory candidate appeared. From 1759 until the American war the commandant was Lord Montfort, a political ally of Hardwicke. He and his father had been the managers of the whig interest in the county and borough of Cambridge, and he had represented the borough in parliament. On succeeding to the title in 1755 he found his estate very much encumbered and successfully asked for a secret service pension.[3] His conduct thereafter seems to have been calculated neither to restore his finances nor to win the respect of his neighbours. Even in 1762 Lord Royston declared that his behaviour was impossible, and serving under him in the militia went against the grain with most people.[4] In 1775 he was obliged to flee from his creditors to Paris, but clung to the command of the militia because he could use its patronage to reward dependants and because there was now a prospect of war service and so of pay.[5] No gentleman would serve under him,[6] and so there were not enough officers to enable the militia to be embodied for service.[7] When at length the militia was ordered to be embodied, in 1778, he was induced to resign. Complaining that this meant a loss to him of five or six hundred pounds, he made Hardwicke[8] use his influence to get promotion in the army for his son and tried also to secure the agency of the militia for a dependent.[9] Hardwicke seems to have been uneasy at his removal, but Sir John Hynde Cotton told him that if there was no precedent for turning a peer out of a commission there was also none for such a peer having one. He had sold all his property in the county and had no qualification.[10] He

[1] BM, Add. 35659, f. 32.

[2] Undaunted, he asked for the colonelcy. See his memorial and letter dated 3 April 1788 in HO. 50/17.

[3] Namier, *Structure of Politics*, pp. 205, 223, 450, n. 3.

[4] BM, Add. 35352, f. 257.

[5] Cf. BM, Add. 35659, f. 154 and f. 260.

[6] *Ibid.*, ff. 156, 175. Soame Jenyns heard that his wife 'was gone quite off' and had been seen at the theatre 'with the most common w—— in the boxes'. BM, Add. 35631, f. 142.

[7] As note 5 (draft on back).

[8] The second earl, previously Lord Royston.

[9] BM, Add. 35659, ff. 260, 266, 270, 272, 277, 334.

[10] As a peer he had only to hire a house (cf. p. 306), but Cotton thought that this would conform to the letter but not the spirit of the law.

had made the militia contemptible whenever he was with it and if he stayed it would become so in the eyes of the whole kingdom.[1]

Thomas Watson Ward, who had been found to replace him, was an improvement only in the short run. At first active in reforming the regiment, he seems steadily to have gone to pieces during the American war. Regarding himself, as he said, as a kind of father of a family, he tried to avoid taking sides in the furious quarrels which raged among the officers.[2] This want of firmness seems to have made the situation much worse. Anonymous letters told Hardwicke that the regiment was well disciplined but badly governed; that Ward should be told to be sober and attend to the dignity of his rank; that he cared only for profit and neglected regimental business.[3] Philip Yorke (Hardwicke's nephew and heir) confirmed these charges and said that Ward was a 'good humoured singular man with little delicacy or sense of honor in his composition'.[4] Hardwicke and Sir Thomas Hatton both believed that he wanted weight, and in 1780 Hatton heard that the regimental funds were badly managed.[5] In 1781 Lord Amherst, the Commander-in-Chief, thought that Ward would have to be removed,[6] and an officer joining the regiment from the army was horrified at the lack of 'internal management' and said he had never known officers so dissatisfied with their commander, under whom everyone must appear either a peculator or an ignoramus.[7] In 1782 Ward went too far. He displaced the regimental agent in favour of his brother-in-law, a linen-draper in Cheapside, having no other way of paying a debt to him. He was forced to retract by a meeting of officers instigated by Hardwicke, who henceforth was determined to get rid of him.[8] This was eventually done by making Philip Yorke colonel over his head (he was only lieutenant-colonel commandant).[9] He seems never to have resigned, but his finances had been deteriorating all the

[1] BM, Add. 35659, f. 261.

[2] See, e.g., BM, Add. 35660, ff. 10, 15, 39, 112. Properly speaking it was a battalion.

[3] *Ibid.*, f. 2. Add. 35661, f. 30. The first does not name Ward, but cannot mean anyone else.

[4] BM, Add. 35379, ff. 240–1.   [5] BM, Add. 35681, ff. 316–17.

[6] BM, Add. 35380, ff. 48–9.

[7] BM, Add. 35661, ff. 129, 140. He put his complaints before a meeting of the officers, and Ward virtually admitted his incompetence but would do nothing. But cf. Add. 35380, ff. 128–9.

[8] BM, Add. 35661, ff. 162, 170, 172, 174, 176, 181, 187, 189–90, 193, 195, 198. Add. 35380, ff. 159, 162–5, 167–9, 177. Add. 35619, f. 45. But in 1778 Hardwicke had illegally forced his own nominee on Ward. Add. 35659, ff. 280, 284, 290. For regimental agents, see below, p. 344.

[9] This was only possible when the act of 1786 allowed corps of only six companies to have three field officers. BM, Add. 35380, ff. 178, 180–4. Add. 35382, ff. 309, 314–15. Add. 35383, ff. 2, 5. Add. 35681, f. 386. Cf. Add. 35662, f. 123; Add. 35383, f. 252; Add. 35380, f. 186.

time [1] and eventually he had to sell his property and was no longer qualified to act.[2]

Hatton had earlier summed up Ward's case when he wrote that the main business of a militia commandant was not to exercise the battalion (which Ward could do), but to make the service easy for those public spirited enough to give up their time to it and to keep a good grip on the business side.[3] Hardwicke, too, was very right in remarking that the militia was a vexation unless the lord lieutenant could command it himself or get a friend or relation to do so.[4] The charitable truth is that Ward was put up with because he was the only person who could be found until Philip Yorke was old enough.

If the higher ranks were not always suitably filled, the lieutenants and ensigns were frankly a disgrace. There was only one really copious source of supply: needy individuals in search of a living and youths of impecunious family who wanted a military career on the cheap. A commission in the militia, unlike one in the army, did not have to be bought. Those who could not afford the army joined the militia in the hope of somehow contriving a transfer. Thus the militia laws, designed to ensure that only men of property became officers, had just the opposite effect. As early as 1760 it was reported that many of the West Riding subalterns had entered the army.[5] In 1762 Edward Gibbon wrote in his journal that the prospect of demobilisation pleased 'the few men of property' in the Hampshire regiment in which he was captain, but caused only

> grief to our young adventurers who either having no home or nothing to do at home, looked upon the disembodying of the Militia like the breaking of a regiment of regulars.[6]

Much the same was being said twenty years later in Cambridgeshire. Militia officers were mostly 'distressed idle young men' who had lost their money or never had any and had entered the militia for that reason.[7] Sir Thomas Hatton pitied them at the close of the American war, fearing that many would find 'a strange alteration'.[8] For, of course, the disembodied peacetime militia did not provide such people with a living. It tended, therefore, to be impossible to find subalterns in peacetime at all.[9]

[1] BM, Add. 35682, ff. 81, 367. Add. 35684, ff. 148–9.
[2] A successor was appointed in 1792. Add. 35383, f. 274. Add. 35624, ff. 217–18, 235–6.
[3] BM, Add. 35661, ff. 200, 206.   [4] BM, Add. 35380, f. 159.
[5] BM, Eg. 3436, f. 366. But cf. *ibid.*, ff. 342–3, for a propertied North Riding subaltern with military ambitions.
[6] D. M. Low (ed.), *Gibbon's Journal to January 28, 1783* (London, 1929), p. 133.
[7] BM, Add. 35693, ff. 494–5.   [8] BM, Add. 35682, f. 11.
[9] The Cambridgeshire subalterns seem to have disappeared in a body at the peace of 1783. Cf. BM, Add. 35661, f. 301, and Add. 35663, f. 58.

A poor man need not be a bad one. Gibbon speaks kindly of one young aspirant, a cabinet-maker who had become eager for a military career.[1] But as a class the militia subalterns leave a bad impression. Gibbon spoke of being 'chained down to company I dispised' and described the atmosphere of his regiment thus:

> a great deal of noise and no conversation, a great many people and no society, a most excessive familiarity and no friendship; in a word the usual scene, only I think we are not so quarrelsome as we used to be.[2]

When a young officer was sent away from the regiment to avoid being put in prison for debt, Gibbon thought it the 'unhappy but necessary effect of our deviation from our first principles and instead of men of property taking raw boys without a shilling'.[3] When the Cambridgeshires were embodied in 1792 they were so short of subalterns that Charles Yorke said that they must wink at qualifications and if possible get officers from the half-pay.[4] In this way the vacancies were quickly filled,[5] but Yorke soon began to fear that they might be sacrificing quality to quantity[6] and so it proved. Nine subalterns, in an establishment of sixteen including the captain-lieutenant, had left by the spring of 1794.[7] Hatton, a younger son of Sir Thomas, was socially a great catch, but resigned after a long spell of only partly authorised absence.[8] Amiel had served ten years in the army and soon returned to it.[9] Addison resigned in a huff[10] and Manby proved a permanent invalid.[11]

The rest all departed in less creditable ways. Rowning was accused of assaulting a girl and thrown into gaol protesting his innocence. He had already been briefly imprisoned because of his behaviour while incapably drunk in a private house: he seems then to have made a successful appeal to Lord Hardwicke's[12] clemency by saying that he had only his character to live by.[13] Long departed without fuss but under a cloud,[14] Wray resigned after a mysterious transaction concerning a horse.[15] Chester died in debt, kept out of prison by Hard-

[1] *Journal*, pp. 128, 132.
[2] *Ibid.*, p. 133. J. E. Norton (ed.), *The Letters of Edward Gibbon* (London, 1956), vol. i, p. 128.
[3] *Journal*, pp. 189, 190.   [4] BM, Add. 35392, ff. 268, 272–3.
[5] See BM, Add. 35663, f. 58.   [6] BM, Add. 35392, f. 280.
[7] Not counting two resigned and replaced at the outset, Add. 35663, ff. 48, 70. By March 1793 there were fifteen subalterns including the captain-lieutenant and staff officers. As n. 5.
[8] BM, Add. 35392, ff. 274–5. Add. 35663, ff. 239, 307–9.
[9] BM, Add. 35392, ff. 294, 305–6, 309. Add. 35664, f. 40.
[10] *Ibid.*, f. 11.
[11] Add. 35663, ff. 201, 286. Add. 35664, ff. 13, 28, 65, 342.
[12] Philip Yorke, now third Earl.
[13] BM, Add. 35663, ff. 146, 148, 150, 169, 171–2, 307.
[14] *Ibid.*, ff. 156, 167, 194.   [15] *Ibid.*, ff. 247, 249.

wicke's generosity.[1] Finally, there was Fell, 'that strange, trouble-some ci-devant lieutenant-colonel'. He had retired from the East Essex at the end of the previous war with that rank, after twenty-four years in the regiment, and had been thirty-six years all told in the militia. He proved a 'totting old fellow' quite unfit for duty and was with some difficulty induced to leave. He asked Hardwicke to get him a captaincy of invalids.[2] The regiment continued to be plagued in this sort of way, and in 1798 Lt.-Col. Nightingale said that with two officers in prison for debt and another likely to follow they would make but a poor figure.[3]

Constant efforts were made in Cambridgeshire to find more respectable subalterns but with little success. Things were, of course, at their worst under Montfort. At the end of his period of command it was said that the officers were mostly without the education necessary for an officer and a gentleman,[4] and that none of the subalterns had a legal qualification. One subaltern was an innkeeper, another a breeches maker and a third had said that he would be glad to be a nobleman's butler. Apparently the others were much the same.[5] Hardwicke thought that nothing could be done except to make good appointments as vacancies occurred.[6] By 1780 this policy had produced only four subalterns with pretensions to gentility (exclusive of those who had come and gone). Hall was unexceptionable—of good family and six feet tall.[7] Freeman was at least the nephew of a clergyman and studied fencing and the manual exercise before joining.[8] Jennings was not from the county or a landed family, but he was personable and enthusiastic: Ward liked him and vouched for his being well off.[9] Cotton was the son and heir of a deceased grocer and tallow-chandler in Cambridge.[10] Four more of the subalterns' commissions had had to be given to the adjutant, the quartermaster and the two surgeons[11] and two were vacant. Two of the old subalterns still remained: the innkeeper and Rooke, the would-be butler.[12] Once possessing a qualification, he had refused to resign in 1777, although it had lapsed;[13] nor did he do so when imprisoned for debt in 1778.[14] Poverty forced him to it at the end of the war, but Hardwicke told him to wait and see what provision parliament made for subalterns and gave him £50. In 1786 he was 'under the Delamay' of asking help

---

[1] BM, Add. 35664, ff. 1, 3, 18, 64, 102.
[2] *Ibid.*, ff. 58, 94, 96, 98, 245.   [3] BM, Add. 35670, f. 393.
[4] BM, Add. 35659, f. 175.   [5] *Ibid.*, f. 275.
[6] *Ibid.*, f. 280.   [7] BM, Add. 35660, ff. 222, 227.
[8] *Ibid.*, ff. 287, 323. Cf. Add. 35681, f. 269.
[9] BM, Add. 35660, ff. 93, 234, 243, 245, 247.
[10] *Ibid.*, ff. 138, 140, 144.   [11] Cf. the next section of this chapter.
[12] See BM, Add. 35660, f. 347.   [13] BM, Add. 35659, f. 195.
[14] BM, Add. 35660, ff. 47, 52.

again. He said he had been eighteen years in the 'Ridgment'. He wanted a job, preferably in the farming line in which he had been brought up.[1] Perhaps he was a disappearing small landowner!

Ward said that Cambridgeshire did not produce the right sort of person for the junior commissioned ranks and so the right thing to do was to look for proper gentlemen from other counties.[2] But much of the trouble with subalterns came from taking strangers to the county whose credentials were hard to confirm.[3] In 1779 Ward was much puzzled by an applicant named Check. It was suspicious that he had tried and failed to enter the army; also that he had left the Buckinghamshire militia, whose colonel could not or would not remember him. But he made a good personal impression and his sister was married to a respectable tradesman in Newmarket, said to have £50 a year in land.[4] In 1798 Lord Hardwicke was sent a testimonial purporting to be from Lord Cork and found it impossible to establish whether it was in his handwriting or not. [5] Reporting that a new officer was an incorrigible Yahoo, Lt.-Col. Nightingale said that if he ever proposed the appointment of another person without prior enquiry into his conduct he would go on water-gruel for a year.[6]

The Cambridgeshire regiment was admittedly below average, but there is reason to think that its subalterns were not much so. In 1778 Hardwicke said that even in counties where many leading gentlemen served in the militia there were few good subalterns.[7] Ward thought that other counties did not require their subalterns to be qualified and that few had a qualification in their own county.[8] The Militia Lists, published by the War Office as a companion to the Army Lists when the militia was embodied, make it very clear that all was not well with the subalterns. In May 1779 there should have been over 900 of them, but in fact there were under 800 and the deficiency remained close to 100 throughout the American war. Of those serving in 1779 the ensigns seem almost all to have entered the service in 1778 and the great bulk of lieutenants had also received their commissions in that year. Even after generous allowance for promotion and transfer to the army,[9] it remains clear that when the militia was embodied in 1778

---

[1] BM, Add. 35662, ff. 77–8, 125.　　[2] BM, Add. 35661, f. 92; cf. f. 96.

[3] Even when a man from the Isle of Ely with a legal qualification was appointed, Ward complained that nobody had made sure that his appearance was satisfactory. *Ibid.*, ff. 117–19, 122.

[4] BM, Add. 35660, ff. 157, 160, 167, 171.

[5] BM, Add. 35670, ff. 398–9.　　[6] BM, Add. 35667, f. 220.

[7] BM, Add. 35659, f. 280.

[8] BM, Add. 35660, f. 243. Add. 35661, ff. 92, 96. But in 1781 he was briefly afraid of a stricter enforcement of the law, *ibid.*, f. 13.

[9] Hardwicke was annoyed when this took place without his permission. BM, Add. 35660, ff. 220–2, 226, 231. Add. 35681, f. 159.

a staggering number of subalterns' commissions were either vacant
or held by men who had hastily to be got rid of. In each of the two
years following May 1779 over 200 subalterns left the service; in
1781–2 over 100. Allowing again for transfers to the army, it remains
clear that a great number of unsuitable people were constantly being
given commissions in the effort to fill the lower commissioned ranks,
and that things were only a little better towards the end of the war
than at the beginning.[1]

With the formation of the supplementary militia the hunt for officers became fiercer still. Again it is unlikely that many subalterns
were found until the force was actually embodied for service in 1798:
it is interesting that by then commission brokers were trying to exploit the huge new market in militia officers. These men's normal
business was the trade in army commissions resulting from the purchase system and their honesty was highly suspect.[2] Now in 1798 a
Captain Smith wrote to Hardwicke recommending two men for commissions, and in each case naming another officer as a referee. One
of these could not be found and the other did not know the applicant
well enough to be relied on. Hardwicke's agent said that Smith had
been chief clerk in a firm of army commission brokers now defunct;
how he got a living or whether he really was a captain he did not
know. He thought that Smith and his referees might be in league,
sharing the fees.[3]

Respectable subalterns did exist, even in the supplementary militia. In Lancashire it was necessary to advertise in order to fill the
many vacancies at the time of the call-out in 1798, but a general meeting recommended that in the first instance only those with a legal
qualification should be taken.[4] They seem to have been right to do so,
for quite a number of qualified candidates appeared.[5] Lord Derby
was able to reject some applicants who seem quite acceptable by
Cambridgeshire standards. One of these was a former corporal in the
Guards who had left and become a sergeant in the Volunteers at
Manchester. Despite a testimonial from several Volunteer officers he
was told that his station in life precluded his appointment unless one
of the militia colonels particularly recommended him.[6] Another was
the son of one of Lord Derby's tenants, who held lands worth £300
a year. He had received a classical education at Manchester Grammar
School and served five years as a militia private, being given some
administrative tasks because of his 'scholarship.' He, too, was referred

[1] See below, p. 319, n. 2.
[2] Fortescue, *History*, vol. iv, p. 213.
[3] BM, Add. 35670, ff. 397, 401, 404, 414, 416–17.
[4] Lancashire RO., LC. 4, f. 32.
[5] E.g. *ibid.*, ff. 24, 29, 34, 48, 65.
[6] *Ibid.*, ff. 72, 79, 80.

5. A Militia Meeting. Magistrates Organize Recruiting.

6. Battalion Officer, Bucks Militia, 1793.

to the colonels.[1] Perhaps the gravity of the national danger was now inducing more men of property to serve.

There can be no doubt, all the same, that the junior ranks gave very much more trouble than the senior. The comparison comes out unmistakably in the Militia Lists for the years of the American war. True, a great deal of purging and filling up of the higher ranks must have taken place when the militia was called out in 1778. Half the majors and captains and a third of the colonels and lieutenant-colonels who were serving a year later had been appointed since or just before the call-out was ordered. But there were very few changes among the field officers after 1780. Among the captains there was a wastage rate of some sixty a year (in an establishment of over 300), but this declined in 1781-2 and there was never any failure to keep any of these upper ranks full.[2] The impression given by the changes in the

[1] His militia service had displeased his school and he badly needed a job. *Ibid.*, ff. 81, 89, 98-9. Lord Derby increasingly made it a rule to make no appointment without the colonel's recommendation. *Ibid.*, ff. 58, 111, 257. His care did not save him from the *faux pas* of appointing a 'graceless youth of fifteen', who turned out not to have his father's permission. The angry father not only insisted on his son's resignation but refused to pay the fee for his commission. *Ibid.*, ff. 144-6.

[2] *List of the Officers of the Several Regiments and Corps of Militia Embodied the 26th of March 1778*, dated War Office, 14 May 1779, and similar lists dated 31 May 1780, 31 May 1781 and 31 March 1782. The lists contain a great many obvious mistakes and the information in them is not complete. I do not claim that any of the figures I have arrived at by collating them are more than approximately correct, and I have accordingly kept the statements in the text vague. For the sake of their interest, I give here some of the figures that I have compiled.

Officers serving in May 1779

| Rank and Establishment | Commissions dated: | | | Vacant |
	1778-9	Earlier	Unknown	
Colonel, 55	12	36	2	0
Lieutenant-Colonel, 49	13	27	6	3
Major, 62	22	29	10	1
Captain, 333	116	168	38	11
Lieutenant, 559	251	157	120	31
Ensign, 413	182	16	97	118

(Many dates of commissions are wanting in the list of 1779, but to be found in later lists: they mostly turn out to be recent.)

| Rank | Vacancies (establishments in brackets) | | | Officers Leaving the Service | | |
	1780	1781	1782	1779-80	1780-1	1781-2
Captain	6 (359)	7 (368)	9 (370)	60	62	35
Lieutenant	40 (615)	35 (633)	28 (635)	202	133	72
Ensign	83 (451)	76 (453)	85 (455)	44	77	48

As the list of 1782 was issued in March instead of May the figure for officers leaving in 1781-2 is not strictly comparable with the others. There were fifty new appointments among the field officers in 1779-80, thirty-eight being promotions. For 1780 to 1782 the figures were thirty-six and twenty-four. There were never more than the three vacancies in these ranks shown in 1779.

law regarding qualifications is thus confirmed by what we know of
the officers: it was possible though not easy to fill the senior ranks
with men who were at any rate good enough to be kept a fair time.
With the captains the system began to break down, while a constant
search among inferior material failed to produce enough subalterns
and, as we have seen, a great many of those who were appointed had
speedily to be got rid of.

III

The partial abandonment of the system of qualifications led naturally
to a greater use of professional soldiers to officer the militia and parliament eventually came to treat the junior militia officers as professionals rather than amateurs. Even the act of 1757 had required the
militia to include some professional soldiers. The king was to appoint
an army officer as adjutant to each militia unit and also one sergeant
from the regulars for every twenty men. These all received pay and
did duty when the militia was not embodied for service or training.[1]
When the militia came to be called out, the government on its own
authority allowed each unit to appoint a quartermaster and a surgeon.[2] In peacetime each regiment and battalion had a clerk, who was
analogous to a quartermaster.[3] The act of 1802 required the appointment of both quartermasters and surgeons even in peacetime and laid
down what had always been the obvious and accepted thing—that the
surgeon should have a proper professional qualification and that the
quartermaster should be a regular soldier.[4] For neither was there any
question of a property qualification. Almost from the start the practice developed of using these 'staff officers' to fill vacancies in the
lower commissioned ranks. From 1760 adjutants were allowed to
hold a subaltern's commission as well without qualification, and
from 1786 they might be appointed captain by brevet if they had
served five years as a lieutenant either in the militia or in the line.[5] In
1778 similar appointments of surgeons, quartermasters and battalion
clerks[6] were recognised by a provision that they were not to hold a
second commission *above* that of lieutenant, even though they had a

[1] 30 Geo. II, cap. 25, s. 14, and as n. 4. Cf. p. 326, n. 3.

[2] WO. 4/757, pp. 60, 62.   [3] Below, p. 344.

[4] 42 Geo. III, cap. 90, ss. 78–9. There was only to be a quartermaster if the
corps was 360 strong and service in the embodied militia qualified an applicant. A
corps of one company was not to have a surgeon.

[5] Till 1802, only in a corps of six companies. In 1802 five years' service in
embodied militia or line was made the qualification for being an adjutant and so
all might be captains. 33 Geo. II, cap. 22, s. 11. 2 Geo. III, cap. 20, s. 33. 9 Geo.
III, cap. 42, s. 10. 26 Geo. III, cap. 107, s. 60. 42 Geo. III, cap. 90, s. 77. Applied
to additional adjutants by 38 Geo. III, cap. 55, s. 4.

[6] 18 Geo. III, cap. 59, s. 7. 26 Geo. III, cap. 107, s. 62. 42 Geo. III, cap. 90,
s. 81. From 1786 a battalion clerk might be made captain-lieutenant.

qualification. Militia surgeons had only 4s. a day compared with 10s. in the army, and so had a strong claim to a second commission. Nevertheless in 1802 surgeons and quartermasters were forbidden to hold a second commission, though the latter might be promoted to be subalterns.[1] Another staff officer had by then appeared—the paymaster.[2]

The shortage of officers in 1778 already noticed led to a more positive effort to bring regular soldiers into the militia. Since 1762 anyone giving up his half-pay to enter the militia had been entitled to have it restored on leaving that service. Now a strong inducement was given to unemployed army officers to come in by allowing such of them as took subaltern's commissions to retain their half-pay in addition to their full militia pay. In 1779 this provision was extended to the adjutants, quartermasters and surgeons.[3] In the next war the shortage of officers produced an even more drastic step. From 1795 lieutenants and ensigns were entitled to allowances in peacetime, when disembodied, of £25 and £20 a year respectively. This was conditional on their remaining in their corps and attending the annual exercise. It was not to be given to anyone on the half-pay list, but it was to be in addition to any other allowance, such as pay during the time of training.[4] This measure was brought forward by the government on the advice of the friends of the militia, but in spite of this the opposition attacked it as assimilating the militia to the army by introducing a system of half-pay for the former. They seem to have been basically right, although it was truly said in reply that the allowance ceased if the officer left the regiment and did not therefore amount to half-pay, which was a right enjoyed for life. Wilberforce curiously said that the subalterns,

men of inferior fortunes, were by their rank as officers, and the habit of associating with persons of superior fortune, drawn into expenses,

[1] As p. 344. On surgeons, cf. WO. 26/37, pp. 99–102, and WO. 4/770, pp. 424–5.
[2] From 1798 (see below, p. 365). He was allowed by implication in 42 Geo. III, cap. 90, s. 81 to hold another commission.
[3] 2 Geo. III, cap. 20, s. 35. 18 Geo. III, cap. 59, s. 10. 19 Geo. III, cap. 72, ss. 15–16. 26 Geo. III, cap. 107, s. 63. 42 Geo. III, cap. 90, s. 82. But the clause of 1762 disappeared in 1786 so that the entry of senior army officers into the militia was discouraged; cf. the raising of the qualifications for the higher ranks in 1769 when the others were lowered. Walpole says that a meeting of lord lieutenants in April 1778 rejected a ministerial plan to complete the militia officers from the half-pay. *Journal of The Reign of George III, 1771–83* (ed. J. Doran, London, 1859), vol. ii, p. 252.
[4] 35 Geo. III, cap. 35. 36 Geo. III, cap. 116. 37 Geo. III, cap. 116. 38 Geo. III, cap. 70. 39 Geo. III, cap. 103. 39 and 40 Geo. III, cap. 75. 41 Geo. III, cap. 56. 42 Geo. III, cap. 55. The measure was a temporary one, annually renewed. The number of lieutenants who might benefit was limited according to the size of the unit. From 1764 the annual Pay Acts (see below, p. 344) provided pay for captains and subalterns but not field officers at the annual peacetime training.

which might not, in every instance, be suitable to their private income. It was equitable, therefore, that they should receive some compensation for the inconvenience to which they were necessarily subjected in the public service.[1]

A further application of this principle was the payment from 1799 of gratuities to officers on demobilisation.[2]

As already noticed, army officers were allowed to serve in the supplementary militia without further qualification, and in 1797 lord lieutenants were advised to supply the deficiency of subalterns in the supplementary militia by employing subalterns on the half pay list. This, too, was a suggestion by the friends of the militia, and they also proposed another measure that was thought too drastic: the completion of the old militia from subalterns on full pay not otherwise employed.[3] By the end of the century, therefore, it was accepted that a fair number of army officers would be needed in the militia, that they should have special incentives to enter and that militia subalterns not drawn from the army should have similar financial prospects to those from the half-pay. Not only did this mean the abandonment of the principle of a property qualification but it also meant (as in other instances) that a system designed to save expense was tending to become more costly than the system of pay for the army.

Professional soldiers were a valuable reinforcement in point of numbers. But were they equal to the task of making the militia proficient in its military duties and compensating for the ignorance of the non-professional officers? This was the purpose for which they had been brought into the militia in the first place. In any eighteenth-century regiment it was the adjutant who commonly bore the main burden both of internal management and the direction of the training. By requiring the adjutant to be a professional soldier and giving him the help of some sergeants from the army, the authors of the act of 1757 hoped to secure a minimum of proficiency in each unit of militia.

Dormant in peacetime and unlikely to see action in war, the militia was ill-placed to attract from the army experienced and able officers capable of undertaking this heavy task. It was far more likely to get (besides novices awaiting better things) the incapable, the infirm[4] and

---

[1] Woodfall, vol. vi, pp. 284–91. Cf. BM, Add. 35665, ff. 243–8. Against the wishes of the friends of the militia, the government refused to make officers ineligible who transferred to the fencibles and later returned to the militia. Woodfall, vol. vii, pp. 1 and 2. An attempt was made to get the pay of army subalterns correspondingly increased. *Ibid.*, pp. 322–3.   [2] Below, p. 377.

[3] HO. 50/6, ff. 303–5, 337, 341, 381–5. Cf. p. 323, n. 2; BM, Add. 35393, ff. 3, 4.

[4] John Day entered the Cambridgeshires as a lieutenant in 1778. Aged 52, he was the oldest lieutenant on the half-pay list. He proved useless and resigned on not getting the quartermastership, for which he had been intended. BM, Add. 35659, ff. 236, 264, 290, 293.

the malcontent.[1] The army officers who came in added far more noticeably to the quantity than they did to the quality of those in command. There were, however, a certain number of proficient regular soldiers who had special reasons for wishing to serve in the militia. These might with luck suffice to give a unit a 'backbone' of professional competence.

Two types can be distinguished which may have included a fair proportion of the officers in question, although it is hard to be sure.[2] First there were officers who left the army because they had inherited an estate or expected to do so, but retained their interest in military affairs. This accounted especially for regular soldiers being sometimes found in the higher ranks of the militia.[3] But it was also operative lower down. Lieutenant Corfield of the 33rd took the adjutancy of one of the Somerset regiments in 1760 because he had married a young lady of considerable fortune and his friends thought that he ought in consequence to leave the army.[4] Exactly similar circumstances brought Captain Charles Wale to the adjutancy of the Cambridgeshire militia in 1793. His prospective father-in-law was prepared to make a settlement if he left the army. His own father was ready to do the same on his marriage, and Wale, who was a younger son, feared that unless this took place soon there would be nothing left to settle. In this way the undeserving Cambridgeshires acquired a really able officer, destined later to rise to the rank of general and be knighted for his services. In three years he improved the regiment out of all recognition. But he found it very galling to be constantly under the command of officers far less experienced than himself; when his financial position became better through the death of his brother, he resigned. He later came back as major of the supplementary militia, and returned to the army in consequence of the plan for recruiting the regulars from the militia already described.[5]

Second, there were deserving men without fortune or much education who achieved promotion from the ranks. For them, junior commissioned rank was the climax, not the beginning, of a career. The fact

---

[1] Like Anthony Tolver (below, pp. 328–31) or Richard Bendishe, who served briefly as a captain in the Cambridgeshires after leaving the army in disgust and failing to get back on satisfactory terms. BM, Add. 35660, ff. 261–5, 268, 273, 275, 279, 281, 307, 316, 328–9. Cf. Add. 35380, ff. 128–9.

[2] Cf. Ensign Spooner of the 47th who wanted to enter the militia as a captain in 1780 because most of his regiment had been taken prisoner and he would be little employed till they were released. WO. 1/1009, f. 1019.

[3] E.g. the Duke of Richmond in Sussex. Cf. Lt.-Col. Gibbs of the East Suffolk (WO. 1/1007, f. 507) and Lt.-Col. Gladwin of the Derbyshire (WO. 1/1015, letter of 17 July 1782).

[4] PRO. 30/8, vol. 53, ff. 130–1. Cf. SP. 41/31, Lord Poulett, 24 March, and enclosure, and 2 April 1760.

[5] BM, Add. 35663, ff. 136, 141, 154. Add. 35667, f. 249. DNB.

that service in the militia was professionally something of a dead-end was not likely to worry them; indeed, they might find it rather attractive, since it put them in touch with influential magnates able to provide for their declining years. Some of them must have been of the highest value. In 1759 a Lieutenant Day was recommended to the Cambridgeshires as a quartermaster. He had been a drill sergeant in the Grenadier Guards and had served in Flanders under George Townshend himself, who thought him second to none in 'learning' young recruits. He had just returned from the capture of Guadaloupe.[1] After the American war, William Hannan of the Coldstreams sought the adjutancy of the West Essex. He had served thirty-one years in his regiment, twenty-eight of them as an NCO. For five years he had been senior sergeant-major in the Brigade of Guards and also had experience of duty as regimental clerk and quartermaster-sergeant. He said that no one who had reached his rank had ever failed to get promotion.[2]

The Cambridgeshires acquired a treasure in Robert Mann, recommended to them in 1793 by Lord Mulgrave. He had been eighteen years in the army, and for most of that time had been a sergeant and kept the accounts of Mulgrave's company. Starting as quartermaster with a subaltern's commission, he succeeded Wale as adjutant and became captain by brevet. He was also considered for, but not given, the captain-lieutenancy. Each promotion he modestly regarded as a favour beyond his deserts, and of the last proposal ventured only to say that it would enable him to do more for his mother (aged 80) and the education of his 'small' family of four children. The regimental correspondence through the years shows him to have been a model of unostentatious diligence and efficiency.[3]

The usefulness of such men was unfortunately often diminished by the length of time for which many of them served. They must often have been quite unfit for duty in their last years.[4] This reflects the lack of proper provision for retirement. From 1766 adjutants of corps that were discontinued were entitled to an allowance till the ensuing March.[5] But they were not always entitled to half-pay, and do not seem to have been allowed to sell their army commissions on entering the militia,[6] nor to sell their adjutancies to their successors. Precarious

---

[1] BM, Add. 35659, f. 46. I do not know if this was the Day of p. 322, n. 4.

[2] HO. 50/17, undated memorials to Lord Waldegrave and Lord Sydney (ennobled and Secretary of State, 1783).

[3] BM, Add. 35692, ff. 290–1. Add. 35664, f. 48. Add. 35669, ff. 96, 116. Add. 35670, ff. 362, 377, 380. Cf. Add. 35671, ff. 114, 120. There are many references to his work in Add. 35663 and the ensuing volumes.

[4] See the printed Militia Lists cited earlier.   [5] 6 Geo. III, cap. 30, ss. 17–18.

[6] Richardson of the Cambridgeshires apparently resigned outright, and his army commission was given to someone else some time later. He had no claim to

alternatives were devised. In Cambridgeshire, Anthony Tolver had to pay a pension to Richardson his predecessor—who after forty-five years' service (twenty in commissioned rank) found it hard to believe that his enforced retirement was due to his state of health and not to Lord Hardwicke's displeasure or wish to serve a relation.[1] In the East Riding Adjutant Raines was not allowed to sell in 1778, but instead received an annuity from Hudson, his successor. Hudson, in turn, was not allowed to sell, and received nothing from his successor, Martin, who continued the pension to Raines but at a reduced rate. Colonel Maister said that he would have felt entitled to recommend the appointment of Martin even if he had been unable to pay a pension at all. This case apparently led the lord lieutenant, the Duke of Leeds, to press for a change in the law.[2] In consequence, from 1793 adjutants who had served for thirty years (fifteen of which had to have been in the militia) were entitled to a pension of 6s. a day.[3] But this did not help Anthony Tolver when he was induced to surrender his adjutancy to Wale in 1793 partly by hopes of the new allowance. His service proved to be a few months' short of what was required to qualify him. By making a great deal of trouble in the regiment, he had managed to get a lump sum in cash and an annuity of £50 for his wife from Wale. With this and his half-pay as a lieutenant in the army he had to be content.[4]

To compensate for their scarcity, the competent professionals among the militia officers needed the help of proficient sergeants, able to do a good deal both of the training and the administration. It might be expected that good men could be got in plenty from the line for this purpose, just as they were for the commissioned ranks, by the prospect of a comfortable billet for life and of as much promotion as they could get anywhere.[5] The quality of the sergeants entering the militia at its first formation is attested by the reluctance with which the army let many of them go. The Secretary at War pro-

any pay by virtue of his army rank. BM, Add. 35605, f. 86. Corfield (above, p. 323) was not allowed to sell, but apparently that was because he was not considered to have bought his first army commission. Of course, one could not sell outright without forfeiting half-pay, but one would normally get a financial consideration for creating a vacancy.

[1] BM, Add. 35659, ff. 177, 181, 190.

[2] BM, Eg. 3505, R. Hudson, 6 May 1795, and enclosure; H. Maister, 12 May 1795.

[3] 33 Geo. III, cap. 19, s. 18.

[4] BM, Add. 35663, ff. 184, 214, 229, 240, 257, 283, 320, 322. Add. 35664, ff. 9–85, *passim*. Add. 35666, ff. 48–51, 65–7, 86. Add. 35668, ff. 1, 3, 30, 77, 79, 91, 115–16.

[5] In 1793 Charles Yorke wished for a time to make the Cambridgeshire sergeant-major, who seemed a 'discreet, grave man', quartermaster. BM, Add. 35692, f. 284.

tested to Pitt in 1761 against giving the Lancashire militia the best recruiting sergeant in the 66th.[1] Some surviving lists of men transferred in 1759–60 show that out of some 220 individuals over half had served for more than ten years, while at the same time less than half were over forty and very few were over fifty.[2] This suggests the right combination of experience and vigour.

But good sergeants were in short supply. This, too, is suggested by the complaints of regular regiments losing any, and it is also shown by the development of militia legislation on the subject. In 1758 promotion of militia privates to the rank of sergeant (or corporal) was sanctioned. From 1762 sergeants brought in from the army were required only to have served one year in the regulars (three had at first been insisted on). A chance of betterment was given them by the formal sanction of something that seems, in fact, always to have been done: the appointment of a sergeant-major from among the sergeants in each battalion or regiment. In 1778 the system of pensions was improved. Originally men brought in from the army had been promised the same chance of winning a Chelsea pension as if they had stayed in it, and pensioners who entered the militia were to recover their pension when they again retired. Henceforth, sergeants were, with certain exceptions, entitled to a pension after fifteen years' service, and pensioners becoming sergeants were to keep their pension in addition to their pay.[3] In 1799 sergeant-majors and sergeants rendered superfluous by the reduction were granted an allowance until their services were again required. Adjutants and surgeons' mates then reduced were also provided for.[4]

All this pointed to a greater use of non-regulars and pensioners. Such was the desire of the army. Lt.-Col. Mompesson of the 8th foot, plagued in 1759 with demands for men he was unwilling to spare, told the Secretary at War that elderly privates and out-pensioners

[1] *Calendar of Home Office Papers, 1760–5*, p. 19, no. 74.

[2] SP. 41/30–1, *passim*. I have found a record of the age of 234 and the length of service of 224 individuals: the two lists almost but not quite coincide. Men who had been privates or corporals in the army outnumber those who had been sergeants.

[3] From 1802 out-pensioners also might continue to receive pensions while serving. Only in 1758 was the appointment of corporals and drummers legally sanctioned. Cf. above, p. 142. From 1786 corporals were in permanent pay and there were one sergeant and one corporal per twenty men during embodiment: one of each per thirty men, otherwise. Sergeants demoted for misconduct had to serve a term in the ranks. Innkeepers might not be sergeants. 30 Geo.II, cap. 25, ss. 14–15. 31 Geo. II, cap. 26, s. 6. 2 Geo. III, cap. 20, ss. 36–9. 18 Geo. III, cap. 59, ss. 18–19. 26 Geo. III, cap. 107, ss. 64, 67. 42 Geo. III, cap. 90, ss. 83, 86. By 2 Geo. III, cap. 20, s. 76, sergeants were given the privileges of privates (above, p. 251).

[4] Adjutants 3*s.*, sergeant-majors 1*s.* per day, sergeants 2*s.* 6*d.* a week. 39 and 40 Geo. III, cap. 44. 41 Geo. III, cap. 55. Cf. below, p. 377.

were the thing to use.[1] The Secretary himself urged, though did not insist, that invalids (i.e. old soldiers reserved for garrison duty) should be employed in preference to younger men.[2] Militia regiments seem often to have done what was wanted. Sir Richard Grosvenor, asking for three men from the army, justified himself by saying that he had supplied himself as far as possible from the invalids and out-pensioners.[3] In 1778 the Duke of Richmond had to raise the Sussex militia from scratch, and yet did not ask for any men from the army in view of the shortage there.[4] As a regular soldier he doubtless sympathised with the army's difficulties.

Pensioners, at all events, might do well enough if carefully selected. Because of the early age of many enlistments, they were often quite young and fit.[5] Unfortunately appointments, from whatever source, seem often to have been unwisely or improperly made. The act of 1757 vested the appointment of adjutants and sergeants in the king; but the internal promotions allowed in the later acts were to be made by the regimental officers,[6] and in practice it was left from the first to the militia regiments to choose the men they wished to have from the army and ask for their transfer. The choice was often influenced by the fact that the militia officers had friends to gratify. Lt.-Col. Mompesson said that there were many in his regiment born in Devonshire (where they were then stationed) who got their friends to ask the militia officers to appoint them. These officers applied for their discharge forthwith, without enquiring into their suitability. One man asked for had been demoted and sentenced to 200 lashes for embezzlement. A better man had been offered in his place but had been refused. Mompesson suspected that militia officers were more interested in the appearance than in the merit of the men.[7] A common complaint was that the militia had asked for a man who was a tolerable soldier but would not make a good sergeant in a new regiment.[8]

[1] WO. 1/979, letter of 9 February 1759. [2] WO. 1/980, ff. 779–80.

[3] WO. 1/979, letter of 5 September 1759. For similar instances see *ibid.*, Sir J. Lowther, 18 August 1759; WO. 1/980, ff. 97, 101–2, 105–6, 543–6.

[4] WO. 1/1000, letter of 27 July 1778.

[5] One pensioner who served in the militia was described as a stout fellow aged 46. WO. 1/980, f. 546.

[6] The sergeant-major and drum-major were appointed by the commanding officer. Till 1802 the captains appointed the rest with his sanction, the procedure for dismissals being the reverse. From 1802 he controlled all appointments and dismissals. 26 Geo. III, cap. 107, s. 65; 42 Geo. III, cap. 90, s. 84; and as p. 326, n. 2.

[7] WO. 1/979, letters of 9 February, 5 March and 12 and 21 May 1759.

[8] See *ibid.*, Lord Ancram, 2 August 1759. But capable officers like Stanley in Lancashire and Thornton in Yorkshire asked for such men, and said in response to objections that they had tried them out and found them satisfactory. WO. 1/980, ff. 587–90, 689–90.

Not surprisingly, some very improper appointments of sergeants were made by Lord Montfort in Cambridgeshire. Tolver, who became adjutant after Montfort's flight to Paris, found that he had displaced five sergeants to make jobs for musicians, and that five more were his servants.[1] Others had been appointed at the request of the corporation of Cambridge—obviously to support Montfort's electoral interest. They appear to have regarded their posts as sinecures. When Tolver forced them to do duty—it will be recalled that they, like himself, were in permanent pay—he received a threatening anonymous letter.[2] Small wonder that soon after the embodiment of the regiment for service in 1778 Tolver told the sergeants and drummers that 'not a single man of you from the first to the last knows his duty'.[3] Thus in the non-commissioned as well as in the higher ranks professional competence was conspicuous by its rarity.

IV

Irrespective of the merits of the persons concerned, the social diversity so apparent among the officers was a source of weakness. It made for divisions within militia units destructive of efficiency and morale. When the Cambridgeshires were mobilised in 1778, a virtual class war broke out among the officers. A number of gentlemen were induced to join after the departure of Montfort, the most important being the son and heir of Sir John Cotton, who became major. He was eager for a purge of all the older officers who were not gentlemen, and began his career with a letter to Hardwicke denouncing the subalterns and their lowly origins in unmeasured terms. Hardwicke wrote a soothing reply, warning him not to rush things. He favoured the gradual reformation of the subalterns as vacancies occurred and did not wish the regiment to become a clique.[4] The new and old officers formed, indeed, two rival parties. The social basis of the division is suggested by the fact that the officers ceased to mess together because it was too expensive for the subalterns, even with a subscription graded according to rank.[5]

The toughest opponent of the newcomers was one who, like them, had been brought in to make the regiment more efficient. Lieutenant Anthony Tolver, the adjutant, had entered the army as a surgeon in 1748 and held regular commissions since 1756.[6] He came to Cambridgeshire in 1776 with a good recommendation[7] and proved a very

[1] BM, Add. 35659, f. 191.   [2] *Ibid.*, ff. 191, 228, 230. BM, Add. 35681, f. 100.
[3] See BM, Add. 35659, ff. 356, 394.
[4] BM, Add. 35659, ff. 275, 280. New appointments, *ibid.*, ff. 282, 284, 289, 290, 293, 311, 317.
[5] BM, Add. 35660, ff. 17, 31.   [6] BM, Add. 35668, f. 30.
[7] BM, Add. 35659, ff. 175–7.

capable man.[1] But he was also extremely quarrelsome and this failing, which had caused his expulsion from several regular regiments,[2] was to spoil his chances in the militia as well. Originally appointed because he was both efficient and a gentleman,[3] he had been active in purging the unfit.[4] But he opposed equally the claims of social rank not combined with ability or experience.

As early as July 1778, Cotton and Tolver quarrelled. Cotton tried to make Tolver report all the commandant's orders to the other field officer, himself. Tolver declined and Cotton accepted his statement that this was not the custom of the army. However, Cotton claimed that Tolver's answer had been insultingly worded, that he had said that he was 'as much of a gentleman as yourself and as independent' and had complained of such treatment of an old soldier by one so ignorant. Both complained to higher authority, and Tolver declared that Cotton had 'an ungovernable temper' and was interested only in 'parade and vanities'. He threatened to resign if he was not supported.[5] Things were made worse when Tolver, on parade, berated the sergeants and drummers for their ignorance, and by his declaring that 'the best regiments are formed by the stick and by God by the stick shall you be formed, gentlemen'. Cotton took some of this as meant for himself.[6] He placed Tolver under arrest, whereupon he was himself placed under arrest by Lt.-Col. Ward. Cotton then released Tolver, who at first refused to leave arrest and demanded a trial but later relented. Ward, however, refused to release Cotton, who put himself badly in the wrong by breaking arrest.[7] A small mutiny now took place among the men,[8] and compromise became essential. The affair ended with apologies all round and Lord Amherst, the Commander-in-Chief, agreed to pardon Cotton because a court-martial would have menaced the discipline of the regiment.[9]

Cotton was soon involved in another quarrel, this time with Lieutenant Simson, in civil life a small tradesman of dubious character.[10] Cotton accused him of stealing his servant's stockings and called him a villain and a rascal at the head of the regiment. Simson was taken from duty at the request of the officers, and some days later sought to save his honour and employment by publicly insulting

---

[1] Below, p. 331.   [2] BM, Add. 35660, ff. 59, 108, 205.   [3] As p. 328, n. 7.
[4] See above, p. 328 and e.g. BM, Add. 35659, ff. 195, 205–7.
[5] BM, Add. 35659, ff. 348–55. Cf. what follows. A friend of Cotton's corroborated the charge, but Ward, who was present, did not hear the words.
[6] *Ibid.*, f. 356; cf. f. 375.   [7] *Ibid.*, ff. 357, 359, 360, 375; cf. ff. 369, 371.
[8] *Ibid.*, ff. 369, 371.
[9] *Ibid.*, ff. 375, 379, 381, 383–4, 387. Dr Smith the rector of Yarmouth, where the regiment was stationed, went to London to intercede with Amherst. He was an old army chaplain.
[10] BM, Add. 35660, f. 32.

Cotton in the same terms.[1] After some sort of scuffle both were arrested, and each asked for a court-martial on the other. A general court-martial was accordingly held which found both guilty but suspended Simson from service for two years and Cotton for only a week. On seeing the evidence, the king pardoned Cotton but ordered Simson to be dismissed, so that Cotton ended in triumph.[2] The party character of the affray had earlier been shown when five of the newer officers asked Lord Hardwicke to order an enquiry, adding that they were sure that Cotton would clear himself.[3] The elder Cotton believed that there were one or two officers who wanted no gentlemen in the regiment and therefore stirred up these quarrels because they knew that 'officers of better fashion' would offer to resign if implicated.[4]

The next phase in the conflict was the frustration of Tolver's desire for the captain lieutenancy. Cotton had wished from the start to give this to a young gentleman named Holworthy, but had given way before the objections of the lieutenants and of Ward.[5] Holworthy agreed to join as a lieutenant. But in September 1778 he again asked for the higher rank, saying that he had come in with that in view and it would satisfy the gentlemen of the county with whom he had to serve. Eventually he got his way.[6] Ward sympathised with Tolver's pretensions at first, but later he noted that they might be against the law and that it was essential to stop gentlemen of property resigning from the corps.[7] There was a plan to console him with the quartermastership.[8] Tolver's relations with the other officers, however, were now very bad. They accused him of wishing to keep them as ignorant as possible in order to maximise his own authority. He did not consider it his duty to train the officers as well as the men, and refused to conduct the exercise if there was an officer superior to himself present. The officers contemplated asking for his removal, but Sir Thomas Hatton had them to dinner on Boxing Day 1778 and induced them not to do so.[9] But Ward told Tolver that to avoid more disharmony in the regiment he was not to have the quartermastership and advised him to try and get on better terms with the other officers.[10]

[1] *Ibid.*, ff. 1, 11, 23.

[2] *Ibid.*, ff. 1, 6, 10, 13, 16, 25–9, 39, 41–2, 53, 55, 57–8. Amherst thought both should have resigned. Cotton had to make a public apology. The president of the court was Sir John Wodehouse, whom Cotton had turned to as a friend in the previous affair.

[3] BM, Add. 35660, f. 21.　　　[4] *Ibid.*, f. 20.

[5] BM, Add. 35659, ff. 319–20, 325, 330, 332, 344, 346, 348.

[6] BM, Add. 35660, ff. 48, 74.　　　[7] *Ibid.*, f. 61; cf. f. 15 and Add. 35659, f. 387.

[8] He had just lost most of his possessions in a fire. BM, Add. 35660, ff. 85–6, 95, 97–8, 103.　　　[9] *Ibid.*, ff. 59, 77, 99, 108.

[10] *Ibid.*, ff. 109, 112. Amherst told Hardwicke (f. 111) that it was, indeed, no part of an adjutant's duty to instruct young officers, but he usually did so when the officers were on good terms.

Tolver's discomfiture reflects the steady weakening of Ward in face of pressure by the newer officers. At first he had strongly resented their 'correspondence' and complained that 'Wilkes and liberty is got amongst us'.[1] Regarding the affair of the arrests he asked where discipline would be if younger members of noble families did not obey orders; when Hardwicke spoke of Cotton's powerful position in the county he replied stoutly that innocence must be protected and discipline maintained.[2] But the Simson affair unnerved him. He made it worse by staying neutral.[3] He needed to keep Holworthy in the corps so as to have a real gentleman ready to take over Cotton's company in the event of his removal.[4] He continued to praise Tolver and said that it had been

> always my desire and wish to gain credit under Mr. Tolver by raising in Good Form a Militia that was ridiculed by the whole Kingdom.

He continued to complain of the wilfulness of the younger generation. But he now said that he wanted to safeguard Hardwicke's interest in the county.[5] He gradually ceased to press Tolver's claims and they ceased to be friends.[6]

Tolver took his final disappointment badly, demanding in vain to know his accusers.

> I now know indeed, an Exertion that would establish friendship and reputation in the Army may lose a man in the Militia. . . . If it be imagined the regiment has passed its infant state and can now go alone, the Ungrateful Thought, perhaps, is premature . . . In States, my Lord, disorder does not often originate in the lower orders—in Regiments the evil is traced upwards. It does not exist, or shall ever begin, in me . . .

He scorned the idea 'that the office of an Adjutant is incompatible with a Gentleman or that I undertook the employment *merely* for bread'.[7] But his financial position did not allow him to take the gentlemanly course of resigning. In August 1779 he told Hardwicke that his original objects had been honour or profit. He had lost sight of the former and as a married man was bound to consider the latter.[8] He continued for the rest of his life to agitate, with varying success, for promotion or financial relief, and to regard himself as a cruelly wronged man.[9]

---

[1] BM, Add. 35659, f. 348.   [2] *Ibid.*, f. 369.
[3] BM, Add. 35660, ff. 15, 39.   [4] Cf. *Ibid.*, f. 15.
[5] *Ibid.*, f. 50. Add. 35659, f. 387. Cf. Hatton's good opinion of Tolver, Add. 35660, f. 99.
[6] BM, Add. 35660, ff. 52, 122, 205.
[7] *Ibid.*, f. 116. Sir John Cotton was later to have the 'ungrateful thought' (*ibid.*, f. 238).
[8] *Ibid.*, f. 203.
[9] He might have got the captain lieutenancy in 1780 but for the raising of the legal qualification. *Ibid.*, ff. 273, 303, 306. See above, p. 325.

In 1778, then, the regiment was dominated by a party of the younger gentry. But it was not always to be so. Despite endless warnings, Cotton's behaviour remained impossible. He gradually forfeited all sympathy.[1] In October 1780 he again quarrelled with Tolver and placed him under arrest. As before, Tolver asked for a trial and Ward said that this would be the fourth court-martial that Cotton had figured in, each one disgracing them more. The General commanding the camp where they were thought changes indispensable, and at length a meeting of the officers asked that Cotton should be removed. On his father's advice he resigned.[2] There was talk of bringing in an outsider to replace him; but the officers met again and asked Hardwicke not to do so.[3] This amounted to a vote against the gentry and in favour of the claims of long service. The officers clearly desired the appointment of the eldest captain, William Stevenson who was a poor man but had been in the militia for many years.[4] Hardwicke was angry at the interference of the officers and asked Amherst if Ward would not be justified in arresting the lot! Amherst prudently demurred.[5] Sir John Cotton had already told Hardwicke to ignore the demands of a body who had 'been the Contempt and Laughter of all others wherever they have been', and Ward called their second meeting 'gunpowder treason day' and again spoke of 'Wilkes and liberty'.[6] But, unfortunately, Hardwicke had already offered the majority to Stevenson in expectation of a refusal and it was now accepted.[7] The officers' change of attitude probably betokened a growth of *esprit de corps*, resulting from service together during the wartime embodiment. Their spell in camp was probably important in this for here they were at last induced to mess together.[8]

These Cambridgeshire quarrels—which continued to rage until 1782[9]—show that there was always likely to be a tension between the claims of wealth, of professional competence and of simple long service. This made it harder than ever for a lord lieutenant to maintain his complement of officers, because of the constant need to adjust rival claims.[10]

[1] Cf. BM, Add. 35660, ff. 59, 65.

[2] *Ibid.*, ff. 336, 341–2, 345–7, 353, 357. For the third court-martial see ff. 291, 336–7, 339, 345. Cf. Add. 35681, f. 315.

[3] BM, Add. 35660, f. 363. Cf. ff. 349, 358, 361 for plans to bring in outsiders.

[4] His father had been wealthy but he had lost his fortune, buying with the last of it a commission in a new regular regiment, soon disbanded. *Ibid.*, f. 351.

[5] *Ibid.*, ff. 365, 367, 368.   [6] *Ibid.*, ff. 378, 384, 386. Add. 35681, f. 315.

[7] BM, Add. 35660, ff. 361, 367, 370.

[8] *Ibid.*, f. 172. Cf. f. 205.

[9] Tolver soon quarrelled with Stevenson (*ibid.*, f. 393) and in 1781 two captains were cashiered for attacking Stevenson and Ward in an anonymous letter to Hardwicke (Add. 35661, ff. 30, 63, 65, 70–2).

[10] For a good example see BM, Add. 33112, ff. 178–81.

V

The militia officers then were an unsatisfactory body from the professional point of view, and yet fell far short of the original intention that they should be independent men of property. In spite of this it is fair to say that the system achieved the political objects of its inventors, though in a roundabout way. Their aim had been to make the officers independent of the government, so as to ensure that the force would never allow itself to be used for unconstitutional purposes. They also wished to restrict the number of jobs which ministers could dispose of in order to win political support. They wanted, in short, to deprive the crown of control of militia patronage and in this they succeeded.

The central authorities were very unwilling to take any initiative in the appointment of militia officers, either directly or through their nominees, the lord lieutenants. Their reluctance to interfere comes out very clearly in a curious affair in Suffolk. In 1787 Captain Walter Waring of that county's East Regiment quarrelled with Colonel Edward Goate over the demotion of a corporal. The question arose from the reduction of the peacetime establishment of NCOs by the act of 1786: both officers claimed the last word in deciding who was to be demoted.[1] Waring took counsel's opinion, and both sides appealed to the lord lieutenant, the Duke of Grafton. Waring resigned, but the quarrel dragged on and in 1789 Waring offered to serve as a captain in the West Regiment instead. Goate protested that acceptance of this offer would be a reflection on himself and prejudicial to discipline. Grafton was so perplexed that he referred the whole matter to the Home Secretary, William Grenville, and suggested that the original subject of the quarrel be referred to the law officers of the crown and the disciplinary aspect to a committee of general officers. Grenville referred the whole thing to Gould, the Judge-Advocate General, who came down on the whole on Waring's side and suggested means for a reconciliation. But Grenville insisted that Grafton must decide what was to be done and refused to give any ruling about Waring's appointment or even undertake the invidious task of sending Gould's report to Goate. Grafton said that he had promised both parties not to interfere; that it was his duty to transmit all offers of service by legally qualified persons; and that for thirty years he had, as lord lieutenant, passed on every offer of service to which there was no legal or notorious objection, the person being in many cases not

---

[1] Cf. p. 326, n. 3, and p. 327, n. 6. Goate claimed to be following the long-observed practice of the Suffolk militia. Waring accused him of using NCO's places to provide for musicians whom he ought to have paid out of his own pocket.

known to him. In this entirely formal sense he was prepared to recommend the appointment of Waring.[1]

The central authorities were equally unwilling to take the initiative in displacing officers open to objection. The power to do so was actually allowed to lapse in 1786 and was restored, on Pitt's initiative, only in 1795.[2] It was used occasionally, but only in extreme cases. When, for instance, the militia was embodied for service in 1778, one of the general officers sent to enquire into its efficiency reported the North Devon regiment unfit for service. Lord Poulett the lord lieutenant advised the supersession of the field officers and the government agreed.[3] Lt.-Col. Buck declared himself 'hurt in the nicest point' by his dismissal and went so far as to memorialise the king. The government, in the person of Gould, took the line that in such matters the judgment of the lord lieutenant had to be relied on, and that if Buck had asked for a court-martial he would probably have been allowed that chance to clear himself.[4] It was, indeed, only after conviction by court-martial that officers were commonly removed by royal order.

There was an effective sanction to restrict the latitude of the government and the lord lieutenants in the matter of appointments. To overcome the great difficulty of finding men of property legally qualified for and willing to serve in the higher ranks, it was essential for the lord lieutenant to cultivate the good will of the whole county. The gentry for their part did not fail to take advantage of this. Collective pressure was applied when the lord lieutenant was felt not to have done the right thing. Cambridgeshire is a good example, although what was objected to there was the failure to remove bad officers, not mistaken appointments. From 1776 the unfitness of Lord Montfort for the command and the consequent refusal of the gentry to serve under him threatened to end in the non-raising of the militia and the imposition of a fine on the county.[5] Lord Hardwicke tried to get some to serve in 1776–7 but in vain. Sir John Cotton thought that the militia must 'hobble on in that disrespectful manner it has hitherto done' or they must pay (or evade) the fine: 'if we are drove to this dis-

---

[1] HO. 50/17, Grafton to Grenville, 4, 19 and 25 August 1789, with enclosures; Grenville to Grafton, 14, 23 and ? August 1789, with enclosure.

[2] Woodfall, vol. vii, p. 67. CJ, vol. l, p. 463. 35 Geo. III, cap. 83, s. 8. 42 Geo. III, cap. 90, s. 17. Cf. 30 Geo. II, cap. 25, s. 8; 2 Geo. III, cap. 20, s. 14.

[3] SP. 41/32, Weymouth to Poulett, 30 July and 6 August 1778; Poulett to Weymouth, received 29 July, 3 July (mistake for August) 1778 and 4 January 1779. WO. 1/1000, Poulett to Barrington, 11 July 1778.

[4] SP. 41/32, Gould to Harris, 14 November 1778, and enclosures. WO. 1/1000. Buck to Barrington, 16 August and 11 December 1778, and enclosures. For the final compromise solution see Walrond, pp. 67–8.

[5] Cf. p. 312, above.

7. Grenadier Private, Bucks Militia, 1793.

8. A Trip to Coxheath. Visiting the Militia in Camp.

honour, no one can blame your Lordship and which I have already declared often and often'.[1] But this tone changed when the government called out the militia in 1778, and the deputies met on 9 April to organise the assembling of the men. In the name of the meeting Cotton wrote to Hardwicke complaining of the failure to remove Montfort, and saying that until this was done there would be neither deputies nor officers. The deputies who had gone to the meeting decided, in fact, to attend no more until Montfort was removed, while Cotton's son and at least one other gentleman were prepared to be officers if he resigned. Faced with this strike action, Hardwicke had little option but to ask for Montfort's resignation—which as it happens he had nerved himself to do a day or two earlier.[2]

In 1787 the lieutenancy made a very similar protest, this time to the effect that the bulk of the officers (names were mentioned) were not legally qualified.[3] Nor was it only at county level that such protests were made. In 1778 the corporation of Leicester protested because their Recorder, who was major of the county militia and had served for eighteen years, had been passed over for the lieutenant colonelcy.[4]

A much more common form of pressure came from the regimental officers themselves. Quarrelsome though they were, they often took a united stand on questions of appointment and promotion. Sometimes it was directed to the exclusion of plebeians and professionals. In 1768 the officers of one of the Suffolk battalions demanded the resignation of an ensign who had become an innkeeper.[5] The unfortunate Lt.-Col. Buck was especially mortified because he had been superseded by a regular officer, Captain Kelly, whom he believed to be without legal qualification. He managed to get almost all his officers to sign a petition asking for his own retention. The lord lieutenant brushed this aside, saying that Kelly had sworn to his qualification, that he was improving the discipline of the regiment out of all recognition, and that the officers preferred Buck because he had given them an easy time.[6] It was otherwise in Cambridgeshire when in 1764

[1] BM, Add. 35659, f. 172. The statutory training took place in 1776 despite the shortage of officers. In 1777 it was postponed because of smallpox. See, too, *ibid.*, ff. 160, 195–207; Add. 35631, ff. 151–2; Add. 35681, f. 98.

[2] BM, Add. 35659, ff. 250, 253, 255, 257. Hardwicke had written to Montfort on the 5th (*ibid.*, f. 260).

[3] Not immediately important. The decision (above, p. 204, n. 2) to train no men enrolled before November 1786 meant inactivity in Cambridgeshire till 1788. BM, Add. 35662, ff. 170–1; cf. ff. 172–3, 175, 180, 184, 192.

[4] WO. 1/1000, John Coleman, Mayor, and ten aldermen, 29 July 1778.

[5] SP. 41/32, Lord Maynard, 10 May 1768.

[6] Buck was also angry because Lord Hinton, the lord lieutenant's heir, had been preferred to him for the colonelcy; but Poulett said that the old colonel, whom it was wished to remove, would resign to nobody else. WO. 1/1000, G. Buck, 11 December 1778, and enclosures. SP. 41/32, Lord Poulett, 4 January 1779.

Thomas Nightingale, a captain on half-pay, offered to come into the militia with the same rank. This would have involved his ranking above the three existing captains, and they said that rather than accept this they would resign. Nightingale had no wish to rank above them, but feared the displeasure of his brother officers of the army if he did not uphold the pretensions of his rank, and so himself resigned.[1]

More often it was the principle of filling vacancies by promotion by seniority that was upheld. When, in 1762, Sir Francis Dashwood resigned from the colonelcy of the Buckinghamshire militia on becoming Chancellor of the Exchequer, he urged both publicly and privately that 'the succession should go in the regiment', and his place was taken by the next in command—John Wilkes.[2] On this issue the lord lieutenants seem to have been more inclined to make a stand. In 1779 the officers of the North Gloucestershires intervened in a body on behalf of their senior lieutenant, Crauford, and went so far as to petition the king. Crauford had been in the corps from its inception, was popular with all ranks, and had several times waived his claims to promotion so that gentlemen of property might be brought in as captains. He was felt to deserve the vacant captain lieutenancy, but the lord lieutenant, Lord Berkeley, refused to give it to him. The other officers claimed that Berkeley, with whom they had long been at odds, hoped to drive them all into resignation.[3] In 1802 Thomas Pelham thought that lord lieutenants needed to be restrained from departing from the rule of promotion by seniority. He had known a major driven out of a regiment by the promotion of a captain over his head, because he refused to sign a false muster. But Pelham pointed out that the result of such proceedings was a shortage of respectable officers.[4]

The political consequence of these county and regimental susceptibilities was that lord lieutenants had, as a rule, to avoid partisan appointments. In 1786 the Duke of Richmond promoted Thomas Pelham from the majority to the lieutenant colonelcy of the Sussex regiment, even though they were political opponents at the time. He declared that in militia appointments he was determined to be guided by what was best for the public service.[5] In 1761 Lord Poulett strove to break up the party political groupings among the Somerset officers. Not only were they bad for discipline but they seem to have threat-

[1] BM, Add. 35659, ff. 78–9, 83, 85. Cf. Add. 35361, ff. 108, 110, 112.

[2] BM, Add. 30867, ff. 178–9. BM, Eg. 2136, ff. 45, 49.

[3] SP. 41/28, Lord Amherst, 20 October 1779, with enclosures; cf. his letter of 7 August 1778. SP. 41/33, Colonel Blackwell, 13 and 17 October 1779, and an undated memorial to the king.

[4] BM, Add. 33048, f. 362.

[5] BM, Add. 33100, ff. 106, 108.

ened him with the loss of the services of a prospective lieutenant-colonel.[1] In 1781 Dashwood (now Lord Le Despencer) could not decide whether to give the Buckinghamshire colonelcy to a political friend, Lord Chesterfield, or to Lord Temple, who was the better officer. He consulted Lord North, who was no less embarrassed.[2]

The removal of officers on political grounds had also, if possible, to be avoided. This can be clearly seen in the case of John Cartwright, radical reformer and for many years major in the Nottinghamshire militia. He was several times passed over for the lieutenant-colonelcy, in spite of some sort of promise to the regiment that all appointments should go by seniority. It was fairly evidently the intention to drive him out altogether. But he refused to resign except in circumstances that would put his enemies clearly in the wrong,[3] and it proved difficult to dismiss him. When he was first passed over, the officers met and protested, adding significantly that no officer should be dismissed without a court of enquiry.[4] Two officers who were successively appointed lieutenant-colonel over his head soon left the regiment and so did two others who were eligible to be so.[5] If Cartwright is to be believed, the slackness of his senior colleagues made him indispensable in the running of the regiment for much of the American war.[6] It was in peacetime (1791) that his removal was ventured on, by an improper use of the requirement in the Militia Act that a proportion of the officers should retire every five years.[7] It is worth noting that it was only during or after demobilisation in 1762-3 that Wilkes was removed from his militia colonelcy and Rockingham from his lieutenancy.[8]

The militia was preserved from entanglement in the governmental system of patronage, but there was clearly a danger that, as some of its enemies had always predicted, it would become a formidable political force in its own right. The collective protests of the officers pointed that way and so did the jobbery practised by some of the local controllers of patronage. Few, no doubt, were as bad as Lord Montfort; but even Lord Rockingham was accused in 1760 of not making a man a colonel because he was a friend of Lord Holder-

---

[1] *Calendar of Home Office Papers, 1760-5*, p. 92, no. 412.

[2] *George III, Correspondence*, vol. v, p. 140.

[3] *A Letter to the Duke of Newcastle, Lord Lieutenant of the County of Nottingham ... Respecting his Grace's Conduct in the Disposal of Commissions in the Militia ... By Major Cartwright* (London, 1792), pp. 1, 2, 51.

[4] *Ibid.*, pp. 159-64.

[5] Viz. Cooper (*ibid.*, pp. 10, 163) and Sherbrooke (pp. 18-19, 25).

[6] *Ibid.*, pp. 26-7.

[7] *Ibid.*, pp. 49-52. The procedure required by the act was not observed and two field officers were removed instead of one (pp. 59-75).

[8] DNB, cf. above, p. 195.

nesse.[1] Then, too, there were a surprising number of parliamentary electors in the militia, and this could be useful when a militia officer stood for his county.[2] It was also not unknown for a militia regiment stationed near a parliamentary borough to intervene in its elections.[3] The militia officers and the lieutenancies were always strongly represented in the two houses of parliament and the parliamentary friends of the militia constituted, as we have seen, a powerful 'lobby'.[4] In 1789 a Militia Club was founded which seems to have been intended to give this institutional form. It was open initially to all field officers and captains, to lord lieutenants and to MPs well disposed towards the militia. From February 1790 officers of any rank were to be eligible, but new members other than MPs had to be elected by ballot. The club was to hold three meetings a year, in February, March and April: that is, during the parliamentary session.[5]

However, there seems to be no case of the militia officers taking any important political step collectively in anything but militia concerns.[6] There were good reasons why this should be so. Formed according to the wishes of the county, the militia officers everywhere were likely simply to represent the balance of forces among their county's leading families and not therefore to be a distinct political grouping.[7] Had all the leading men been officers, a militia regiment might often have gained importance by voicing the opinion of the county, as quarter sessions or the grand jury at the assizes often did. But as we have seen, few leading men could be got to serve—it was probably more usual to have them represented by their sons—and the bulk of the officers were socially undistinguished. This made the militia unimportant compared with other county assemblies. The many quarrels within regiments of course diminished their political importance still further.

In devious ways then, the militia achieved the political goal of its inventors. It was to the army what county constituencies were to rotten boroughs: the first in each of these pairs was relatively free

---

[1] BM, Eg. 3436, ff. 330–1. Cf. a case in 1780, BM, Add. 38213, ff. 282–3.

[2] Such as Thomas Pelham, BM, Add. 33108, f. 50. Cf. above, p. 257.

[3] E.g. BM, Add. 33108, ff. 176–7. Lord Darlington was reported in 1806 to be putting up two officers of his militia regiment for one of his boroughs. HMC, *Lonsdale*, p. 215.

[4] The list of field officers of militia printed in the *Royal Kalendar* for 1795, p. 289, contains eighteen British peers and, I think, eighteen MPs (cf. the list beginning, p. 55). What looks like a list of militia officers in parliament to be canvassed is at BM, Add. 35665, f. 247.

[5] BM, Add. 35662, f. 249.

[6] Robinson feared they might when the state of the defences of Plymouth was debated in 1779. *George III, Correspondence*, vol. iv, p. 491.

[7] On the balancing of political and social forces in the militia at its first formation see above, pp. 147–54.

from the influences of plutocracy and government patronage dominant in the second. There was jobbery in the militia just as there was in county elections, and in both the truly independent freeholder was conspicuous by his rarity: but this did not invalidate the general picture. To gain this result, however, a heavy price had to be paid in military efficiency. The officers were the achilles heel of the militia. The men were satisfactory material, and in wartime at least they were not too badly trained.[1] But they were so badly led that it is doubtful if they could have faced seasoned troops with any hope of success. A militia regiment was commonly like the sepoy regiments of the same period, whose efficiency depended on the British NCOs attached to them and the two or three junior British officers in command at the top. A militia regiment, likewise, would contain a few capable professional soldiers, commissioned or otherwise, backed by a few enthusiastic or conscientious amateurs, especially in the higher ranks. But the bulk of the officers were likely to be raw or disreputable or too old or absent and there would probably be some vacancies. The efficient minority could keep things going only up to a point. It must again be said, however, that the British army in the eighteenth century was not much better. As a class its officers were slothful and ignorant. Active service abroad brought out their good qualities, but regiments long in garrison at home seem often to have been no better than the militia.[2] It is not easy to see how good officers could have been found in any quantity for a force intended solely for home defence.

[1] Cf. chaps. i, vi.
[2] Cf. on army officers, etc., E. Robson in *New Cambridge Modern History*, vol. vii, pp. 185–7; Fortescue, *History*, vol. iii, pp. 524–6. Cf. above, p. 103.

Note
Legal Qualifications of Militia Officers

The following table shows the amount of property needed as a qualification for the different ranks at different dates. The entries for each rank are alternative. For references see p. 306.

Rank		Possessor of Land Worth p.a. £	Heir to Land Worth p.a. £	Son of Owner of Land Worth p.a. £	Possessor of Personal Estate Worth £	Son of Owner of Personal Estate £	Possessor of Real and Personal Estate Worth £	Son of Owner of Real and Personal Estate Worth £
Colonel	1757	400	800					
	1769	1000	2000					
Lt.-Col.	1757	300	600					
	1769	600	1200					
Major	1757	300	600					
	1769	200	400	600				
	1802	400	800					
Captain	1757	200	400	600				
	1769	200	400	600				
Lieut.	1757	100		200				
	1769	50		100	1000	2000	2000	3000
Ensign	1757	50		100				
	1769	20*		50*	500	1000	1000	1500

Welsh and smaller English counties

Rank		Possessor of Land Worth p.a. £	Heir to Land Worth p.a. £	Son of Owner of Land Worth p.a. £	Possessor of Personal Estate Worth £	Son of Owner of Personal Estate £	Possessor of Real and Personal Estate Worth £	Son of Owner of Real and Personal Estate Worth £
Colonel	1757	300	500					
	1769	600	1200					
Lt.-Col.	1757	200	400					
	1769	400	800					
Major	1757	200	400					
	1769	150		300				
	1802	200	400					
Captain	1757	150		300				
	1769	150		300				
Lieut.	1757	100		200				
	1762	70		200				
	1769	30		60	600	1200	1200	2400
Ensign	1757	50		100				
	1762	20		50				
	1769	20		30	300	600	600	1200

Cities and Corporate Towns with own Lieutenancy

Rank		Possessor of Land Worth p.a. £	Heir to Land Worth p.a. £	Son of Owner of Land Worth p.a. £	Possessor of Personal Estate Worth £	Son of Owner of Personal Estate £	Possessor of Real and Personal Estate Worth £	Son of Owner of Real and Personal Estate Worth £
Field-Officers	1757	300			5000			
	1769	300			5000		5000*	
Captain	1757	150			2500			
	1769	150			2500		2500*	
Lieut.	1757	50			750			
	1769	30			750			
Ensign	1757	50			750			
	1769	20			400			

* From 1762.

XIII

PAY, CLOTHING AND
EQUIPMENT

THE authors of the act of 1757 had intended the militia to be
as different from the army in its internal organisation as it
was in the provenance of its officers and men. While it was disembodied, assembling only occasionally for training, the militia necessarily was rather unlike the army. But during its lengthy embodi-
ments for wartime service the militia was in much the same situation
as the regular forces, and experience showed that it had to be run in
much the same way. A full and satisfactory account of how this was
done could only be given by paying as much attention to the army as
to the militia. Accordingly, only a brief sketch is attempted in this
chapter and the next, emphasis being placed on such points of difference as there were between militia and regulars. A final chapter
considers in rather more detail the standard of military proficiency
which the militia achieved.

Paying and equipping any military unit in the eighteenth century
was largely a business venture on the part of the officers. They received funds from the government and supplied themselves and their
men with what they needed, making a profit if they could. Any attempt
to describe the system is complicated by the need to ask who gained
from it and how much.

Some items of equipment were, indeed, supplied by the government from its own stores. When the militia of a county was first
raised and its formation reported to the government,[1] arms and
accoutrements were issued for the NCOs and men, together with
colours and drums. A ration of ammunition was also issued for training.[2] When the militia was called out for service, it was customary to

[1] Three-fifths (originally four-fifths) of the officers and men had to be recruited
before arms or pay could be issued. 30 Geo. II, cap. 25, s. 35. 31 Geo. II, cap. 26,
s. 34. 2 Geo. III, cap. 20, s. 107.

[2] In the American war the issue was as follows: *Each corps*: silk colours, oil-
skin cases baize-lined. *Each private and corporal*: short musket, bayonet and scab-

341

issue knapsacks in addition to what had already been provided.[1] When a militia corps was ordered to camp, tents were issued for the NCOs and men, and on some occasions the other equipment required was issued as well.[2] A militia regiment in wartime would normally have with it two small field-guns.[3] But these were normally only lent to it, sometimes just for the summer, and were often in the care of gunners from the regular artillery.[4]

But even when the government supplied the equipment, the regimental officers were involved in financial dealings and anxieties. They had to see to and pay for the repair, storage and transport of what they received, and the replacement of certain items when they wore out.[5] Other items were supposed to be replaced by the government, but the regiment was often in trouble because they wore out too quickly or were defective to start with. The standard issue of arms and accoutrements was supposed to last at least twelve years.[6] Even after that replacements were tardy, partly because of wartime shortages.[7] The arms of the Buckinghamshires in 1781 had been in use for sixteen years.[8] The Duke of Chandos complained in 1778 that his cartouche boxes were eighteen years old and no longer waterproof.[9] But often the arms wore out before they were twelve years old. In 1781 a reviewing general found 220 muskets unfit for service in the

bard, steel rammer, leather sling, cartouche box with belt and frog, brushes and wires, small hanger with brass hilt and scabbard, leather waistbelt, iron wiping rods and worms. *Each sergeant*: halberd, large hanger, belt, scabbard, leather waistbelt. *Each drummer*: drum with carriage and case, waistbelt, small hanger with brass hilt and scabbard (a large one for the drum major), leather powder bag, turnscrews, formers, a musket complete. Ammunition consisted of powder, ball, flints and sheets of paper for making cartridges. WO. 34/111, ff. 105–6.

[1] E.g. (1759) WO. 4/757, pp. 1, 2; cf. WO. 30/8, vol. 77, f. 182; (1778) WO. 4/762, pp. 33, 45, 65; (1793) WO. 4/771, pp. 81, 153, 188.

[2] E.g. in 1781 when the ministers decided how many men were to camp some time before they decided which regiments so to employ. They ordered the equipment themselves to save time. WO. 4/767, pp. 76–7, 86–7. Cf. WO. 4/766, pp. 63–4; WO. 4/772, pp. 214–17. For tents see WO. 4/758, p. 284, and generally each spring in this series of volumes. The knapsacks and camp equipment were supplied by the remarkable firm of Trotter, which ended as a government department (S. G. P. Ward, *Wellington's Headquarters* (Oxford, 1957), pp. 14–15).

[3] From 1802 extra militia officers might be appointed to command these if they were manned by militiamen. 42 Geo. III, cap. 90, s. 69.

[4] Inconveniently, the terms of the militia laws made it impossible for militia officers to court-martial regular artillerymen under their command (WO. 4/767, p. 297; WO. 4/774, p. 383) and for militiamen trained as gunners to be paid otherwise than as infantrymen (WO. 4/773, pp. 266–7). In 1778 and 1780 the Ordnance sent representatives round the regimental quarters to see if the guns were being properly looked after. (WO. 34/146 (ii), f. 321; WO. 34/162, f. 177; cf. WO. 34/158, ff. 114–5.

[5] All this is discussed at length later in the chapter, pp. 361–2.

[6] As p. 341, n. 2.   [7] WO. 34/114, f. 140.   [8] WO. 34/140, f. 8.

[9] WO. 1/1000, Duke of Chandos, 8 July 1778.

Montgomeryshire corps which had been issued in 1775.[1] Those of the Cornish were bad in 1779 though issued in 1770: £300 was spent on repairing them.[2] Sometimes the fault was clearly with the supplier: wartime scarcities meant bad quality as well. The arms supplied for drilling the Cambridgeshire supplementary militia in 1797 often had springs and locks which broke. [3] A reviewing general in 1782 said that the arms of the corps which he had inspected, even those delivered during the current year, had such bad locks and soft hammers that many of the troops would have been unable to fire in actual combat.[4] At other times, however, the Board of Ordnance accused the militia of failing to keep the arms in proper repair,[5] and with much justice: in 1781 the East Devons were found to have 229 arms unserviceable but repairable.[6] In 1792 the Duke of Richmond, then Master General of the Ordnance, proposed a new arrangment for both army and militia which fixed more clearly the extent of the officers' financial risk on this head. Arms reported unfit were to be examined by a general officer assisted by a gunsmith, who were to decide if they could be repaired and if they had become bad by neglect. In the latter case the captains were to bear the cost of making them good, and a regiment whose arms did not last for twelve years was to pay for replacing them.[7]

II

Paying and equipping the militia, then, was mainly a matter of financial relationships. Even within each unit the purchasing of the requisite goods and services was decentralised. Each officer and man was ex-

---

[1] WO. 1/1013, ff. 211–12, 215.
[2] The regiment claimed they had been issued in 1760. WO. 34/121, ff. 133–8, cf. WO. 34/117, ff. 134–7.
[3] BM, Add. 35667, f. 251.
[4] WO. 27/50, f. 25. The review returns in this volume show that almost all units had had new arms since embodiment in 1778. Yet there are more complaints of bad arms than in the 1778 review returns: see WO. 27/40, which also shows that most of the arms replaced during embodiment must have been less than twelve years old.
[5] SP. 41/39, H. S. Conway, etc., 19 March 1771, and enclosure. The period of renewal seems then to have been ten years. Initial issues of arms had by then totalled 28, 266 stand and cost £72,490. 10s. Replacements had cost £18,397. 14s. 7d.
[6] Walrond, p. 95.
[7] HO. 50/367, Duke of Richmond, 29 December 1792. There was a similar problem with ammunition, of which, in the American war, each regiment was supposed to carry sixty rounds a man. It tended to be used up in practice firing and spoilt in the constant process of changing quarters and could not then be replaced. WO. 34/138, f. 167. WO. 34/155, ff. 37, 193. WO. 34/166, f. 18. In 1793 it was agreed that regiments were to order fresh supplies through generals commanding districts. WO. 4/771, pp. 374–6.

pected to provide certain things, for himself or for others, and each had a corresponding claim on the available funds. Money was issued to the corps in the form of pay and allowances for various purposes, but to some extent it was possible to divert money issued for one purpose to another for which the allowance was insufficient. The private men received only a little of their pay in the form of money to spend as they chose; the officers tended to have something to spend besides their pay. Many had a chance to make a profit; all ran the risk of loss or suffering through insufficient funds.

When the militia was disembodied, the channel through which funds reached each unit was the battalion clerk.[1] He drew the money from the county's receiver general of the land tax, and because of the considerable sums passing through his hands he was required to give security to the lord lieutenant.[2] When the militia was embodied there ceased to be a battalion clerk and the colonel or equivalent officer of each unit was required to appoint an agent, as was the practice in the army. The agent had to give security to the colonel and received 6d. in the pound from the clothing money and a stoppage from the officers' pay. The source on which he drew for funds was the Paymaster General in London.[3] Not only was he the banker of the corps but he was also their principal instrument in haggling with the War Office and other government departments for more money and supplies. He needed, therefore, to be resident in London and a businessman or government official was usually appointed.

Of the different headings under which the militia received and spent money, those comprising the clothing will first be considered because it was chiefly the profits made here that covered the deficits incurred elsewhere. For the unembodied militia both pay and clothing were provided by an annual act, drafted by a committee of the house of commons without any interference from ministers.[4] Originally (1758) a guinea was allowed for clothing each private and drummer and £2. 10s. for each sergeant.[5] From 1760 the rates were 30s. for a

---

[1] He was appointed by the lord lieutenant until 1762; thereafter by the commanding officer, none to be appointed in a unit of less than two companies. 30 Geo. II, cap. 25, ss. 27, 29. 2 Geo. III, cap. 20, ss. 36, 98. 26 Geo. III, cap. 107, s. 61. 42 Geo. III, cap. 90, s. 80.

[2] 31 Geo. II, cap. 30, ss. 6, 10, and the subsequent annual pay acts. On clerks' shortcomings see Ward, thesis, p. 664.

[3] The law did not require the appointment of an agent till 1762 but the War Office took it for granted when embodiment began in 1759. 2 Geo. III, cap. 20, s. 119. 26 Geo. III, cap. 107, s. 100. 42 Geo. III, cap. 90, s. 120. Cf. WO. 4/757, pp. 27, 61; on emoluments, WO. 4/771, pp. 153–4.

[4] Except to recommend that provision be made, cf. above, pp. 145, 194. Acts were regularly passed, even in years when the militia was embodied and so otherwise provided for. See Clode, vol. i, p. 43.

[5] 31 Geo. II, cap. 30, s. 2. Corporals were not separately provided for.

private, £2 for a drummer and £3. 10s. for a sergeant.[1] From 1762 it was laid down that the sergeants and drummers, being always in pay, were to be reclothed each year, while unembodied privates were to receive only one set of clothing during their term of service.[2]

These provisions reflect the old idea that the militia was to be a cheap force simply equipped. The original allowance for a private in particular seems to have been enough only for a coat, perhaps a hat and some oddments, but not enough for shirts or breeches.[3] One pamphleteer was able to make heavy jokes about giving the men an extra weapon in the rear and imitating the breechless victors of Agincourt.[4] More would clearly be needed if the militia was to be embodied for any length of time. Already in 1758 it was laid down that on being embodied for actual service each man was to have a guinea, to be spent on the provision of 'necessaries', that is, on extra items of equipment and clothing.[5] This 'marching guinea' was an army usage and when embodiment began in 1759 the militia colonels soon began to clamour for the full army clothing allowance. This took the form of 2d. a day deducted at source from the pay of each man, and Lord Poulett and Lord Romney asked that an amount equal to the annual total of such 'stoppages' be issued in respect of their regiments.[6] The Secretary at War thought this impossible because the militia would then be better paid than the army, but he was willing to give some temporary relief until the matter could be settled by parliament.[7] In October 1759 it was decided to give the embodied militia the difference between what they had already received for clothing and what they would have received if they had been part of the army. This was computed at £2. 4s. 7d. for each sergeant, and £1. 0s. 5d. for each private, corporal and drummer, the latter inclusive of provision already made for a pair of gaiters. Each man was to receive a waistcoat, breeches, shirt, roller and a pair of shoes and stockings. With what was left of the new allowance the regiments were to repair their

---

[1] 33 Geo. II, cap. 24, s. 1. 2 Geo. III, cap. 35, s. 1 added an extra £1 for each sergeant-major and drum major. The allowances had already been raised by 32 Geo. II, cap. 21, ss. 1, 2, regiments already clothed receiving a supplement.

[2] Viz. three years till 1786 and thereafter five. 2 Geo. III, cap. 35, s. 1, and subsequent pay acts (the earlier ones simply provided for those not clothed before). From 1786 the sergeants and drummers were clothed biennially. 26 Geo. III, cap. 107, s. 64. 42 Geo. III, cap. 90, s. 83.

[3] WO. 1/980, ff. 327–8. Cf. PRO. 30/8, vol. 53, ff. 130–1.

[4] See p. 14 of the *Letter from a Militia Man to his Colonel* more fully discussed below, pp. 405–6.

[5] 31 Geo. II, cap. 26, s. 27. 33 Geo. II, cap. 24, s. 12. 2 Geo. III, cap. 20, s. 122. 26 Geo. III, cap. 107, s. 101. 42 Geo. III, cap. 90, s. 121.

[6] WO. 1/980, ff. 200, 327, 367.

[7] WO. 4/757, pp. 146, 161; cf. WO. 1/980, f. 330.

old clothing or buy new as they saw fit, and were to expect nothing more.[1]

The officers were not satisfied. George Pitt reported that the Dorset clothing could not last beyond the winter, though of good quality and well mended.[2] Lord Poulett claimed that the militia had received, excluding gaiters, only £2. 3s. 11d. a man, whereas the army stoppage yielded £3. 0s. 10d. a year. His men were so ragged that it would be best to wait and see what parliament did, meanwhile repairing the old coats and buying hats, breeches and shoes. In January 1760 the Secretary at War advised the Treasury, on the basis of reports by inspecting generals, that the regiments then embodied would need new coats and hats. The government was further urged by meetings of important militia personages to give the men the 'full pay' of a regular private (i.e. including the stoppage). But Poulett admitted that clothing a regular soldier really cost only 32s., and Newcastle was told on behalf of the meetings that the essential requirement for 1760 was 30s. for each private, and proportionately more for the other ranks. A minute on this paper declared this not unreasonable for regiments whose clothing was worn out.[3] As remarked already, the friends of the militia applied this scale in the act for clothing the unembodied militia in 1760. The government decided to give the embodied militia the same allowances as in that act.[4] The colonels evidently continued their agitation, for the embodied militia was treated more generously in 1761 and 1762. Like the army, it was given funds for a completely new set of clothing each year and the rate of the allowance was equal to what had been issued in 1760 *plus* the supplementary allowance made in October 1759.[5]

When the militia was embodied in 1778, they were at once given the same allowances as in October 1759 to supplement their peacetime clothing.[6] At the end of the year, after discussion and complaint, it

[1] WO. 4/757, pp. 221–9, 238, cf. 289. NCO's had to pay for their gaiters, *ibid.*, p. 261. A roller was a piece of wood used in forming the soldier's pigtail.

[2] WO. 1/980, ff. 261–2.

[3] For the meetings, WO. 1/980, ff. 265–6; BM, Add. 33047, ff. 336–8. Cf. above, p. 169. For Poulett, WO. 1/980, ff. 237–42; WO. 4/757, p. 322; PRO. 30/8, vol. 53, ff. 130–1. He had provided new waistcoats and intended to convert the old hats into nightcaps for guard duty. For the Secretary at War, WO. 4/758, pp. 139–40.

[4] WO. 4/758, pp. 227–8. 35s. for a corporal. Cf. above, pp. 343–4.

[5] Not quite exactly: sergeants £5. 14s. 7d., drummers £3. 0s. 5d., corporals £2. 15s. 5d., privates £2. 5s. 7d. WO. 4/759, p. 302. J. Davis *Historical Records of the Second Royal Surrey Militia* (London, 1877), p. 90.

[6] WO. 4/762, p. 8. The peacetime clothing then in use, however old, was expected to last the year (*ibid.*, p. 78). If new peacetime clothing was due in 1778, however, the corps was to draw on their county receiver general and buy it; likewise in 1793. WO. 4/763, p. 36. WO. 4/770, pp. 321–2.

was decided that in 1779 they were to receive an amount equal to the peacetime allowance plus the supplementary allowance, that is to say £5. 14s. 7d. for each sergeant, £3. 0s. 5d. for each drummer and £2. 10s. 5d. for each corporal and private.[1] They received the same each year during the war,[2] and also each year of the war following.[3] With the supplementary militia an attempt was made to return to simplicity. The men were to have a jacket, waistcoat, pantaloons and a cap with a feather at a total cost of 25s. 9d., and the sergeants were not to have a special uniform.[4] But when the supplementaries were embodied they were given the same clothing provision as the rest of the militia.[5] It should be noticed that from the start it was tacitly conceded that the ministers must decide on the allowances to be made to the militia during embodiment. The pay and clothing of the embodied militia were accordingly provided not by a special act but according to estimates presented to parliament by the Secretary at War, like those for the army.[6] The militia, however, differed from the army in receiving a separate allowance for clothing, instead of issues of pay from which the clothing money was technically a stoppage.

This allowance provided each man with one coat, hat, waistcoat, shirt and pair of breeches, stockings and shoes. No overcoat was so provided: the militia were expected at first to follow the custom of the army and provide watchcoats for sentries by means of stoppages from the men's pay.[7] From 1793 militia corps received a half-yearly allowance of 6d. per NCO and private to buy watchcoats,[8] but this seems

[1] WO. 4/763, p. 286.

[2] CJ, vol. xxvii, pp. 24, 479; vol. xxxviii, pp. 39,608. But the 1779 estimate was finally as p. 346, n. 5.

[3] At embodiment, 1792–3, the third of the men who had not been trained and so had not been clothed (cf. above, p. 202) were given the peace-time clothing allowance by the government, and an allowance for necessaries was paid of 19s. 6d. for sergeants and 17s. for the rest. WO. 4/770, pp. 74–5, 78–9, 81–5, 130–1. A complete reclothing of the militia was ordered for Midsummer 1793 and annually thereafter. WO. 4/771, pp. 104–7. WO. 4/772, pp. 142-4. WO. 4/773, pp. 153–4. WO. 4/774, pp. 54–7, 298–9. See further below re 1798–1802; also as in n. 6.

[4] WO. 4/824, pp. 3, 4. Small expenses in making the sergeants' clothing a little different from the rest were allowed, *ibid.*, p. 183. The lord lieutenants were asked to see to the supply of this clothing. Some declined, and it was then ordered by the War Office from whatever firm supplied the embodied militia of that county. *Ibid.*, pp. 23–5, 31, 32, 35.

[5] See especially WO. 4/825, p. 186. The first half, called out in February 1798, received some items of clothing to tide them over till the new clothing for 1798 was provided. The rest of the supplementary men were embodied just before that time and did not need a stopgap allowance. WO. 4/775, pp. 480–1.

[6] See CJ, indices s.v. 'estimates'.

[7] WO. 1/980, f. 250. WO. 4/758, p. 53.

[8] *Certain Rules and Orders to be Observed by the Embodied Militia* (London, 1792), p. 18.

to have left the men worse off than those of the army. There the expense fell on the man, but each man got a coat to himself, which was his own property. A militia corps would only have a few, perhaps not even enough for the numbers required at any time to be on guard.[1] In 1801 it was decided that both in the army and in the militia every man was to receive a greatcoat, but the government soon decided that as the militia was about to be disembodied, no greatcoats need be supplied to it.[2]

To provide the men with a change of underwear and other clothing beyond the basic issue, various funds existed. The 'marching guinea' paid to recruits has already been mentioned. From 1786 men were entitled to another guinea after five years' service in the embodied militia—i.e. when they would have been entitled to discharge had it been disembodied.[3] In 1793 the government decided to pay 2 guineas to those men who were almost due for discharge when they were called up, and 2 guineas thereafter to each man after five years' service.[4] From 1778 the men of the embodied militia were entitled to 'poundage' (6s. 1d. every half year),[5] and from 1792 to an extra annual allowance of 13s. 2½d.[6] Lastly there was the possibility of further stoppages from the men's pay. During peacetime training, privates and corporals were liable from 1764 to stoppages of up to 6d. a day to pay for 'necessaries' and also for the repair of arms damaged by their carlessness and if need be, the relief of their families.[7] During embodiment the custom of the army gave commanding officers a very free hand in imposing stoppages. In 1759 the East Suffolks were almost proud of having only one stoppage, of 5d. a week for 'small clothing'.[8] In 1792, however, a royal warrant limited the amount of stoppages from pay and poundage together to £3. 5s. 5d. a year. From these the soldier was expected to provide himself with a pair of gaiters and of stockings, two shirts, two pairs of gloves

[1] Charles James, *A Comprehensive View of the Interior Œconomy of Infantry Regiments upon the British Establishment, Particularly in the Militia* (London, 1798), pp. 15–25; cf. 34–5.

[2] They were to be paid for without an increase of expense: the watch-coat allowance was discontinued, and 1s. 10d. had lately been saved by giving the men coats without lapels. WO. 4/777, p. 373. WO. 4/778, p. 225. Fortescue, *History*, vol. iv, p. 902.

[3] 26 Geo. III, cap. 107, s. 102. 42 Geo. III, cap. 90, s. 126.

[4] WO. 4/770, pp. 72–3, 76–7, 79–81, 83–4.

[5] In the army this was a refund of 1d. in the £ from gross pay, which had formerly been deducted from the clothing stoppage to pay for Chelsea Hospital. In the militia it took the form of a special allowance. WO. 4/763, p. 152. *Certain Rules and Orders*, pp. 19–20.

[6] *Ibid.*, p. 19.

[7] 4 Geo. III, cap. 17, s. 7. 26 Geo. III, cap. 107, s. 87. Reduced to 4d. in 1802: 42 Geo. III, cap. 90, s. 96.

[8] WO. 1/979, T. Vernon, 25 October 1759.

and a foraging cap, replacing them as they wore out. He had to supply various other articles too, notably combs, clothes-brushes, pipeclay and the like, and to pay for washing and shoe repairs. Certain articles commonly paid for by stoppages were henceforth to be supplied to him gratis, including a second pair of breeches.[1] In 1797 the amount of stoppages was increased to £3. 16s. 1½d. and the men thereafter paid for the breeches themselves.[2]

Commanding officers enjoyed a wide discretion in the spending o᾽ the various clothing funds, and from this arose suspicions of profiteering, complaints by the men that they had been cheated and sometimes serious inadequacy in what was supplied. One sore point was the disposal of the old clothes when new ones were issued. The law was that after a full term of disembodied service a man's clothes were his own property. When the militia was embodied, each man was re-clothed annually and his old clothes were to be disposed of as his commanding officer thought fit.[3] When embodiment ceased at the end of a war, it was usual to make a present to the men of the clothes in wear.[4] At other times, however, it was usual to make the men con-continue to use their old clothing, storing the new and keeping it for special occasions. Thus in March 1795 the men of the Cambridgeshires wore their new clothes (ordered in 1794) only on Sundays, and otherwise wore the suit of 1793, with the coats made into jackets by cutting off the tails, and a well-polished forage cap. Many still had the clothing of 1792 and used it to work in.[5] In October 1798 the frugal lieutenant-colonel of this regiment ordered that the clothing of 1797 was to be worn on Sundays only.[6] In January 1799 he had to order the general use of that clothing for parades, but the clothing of 1796 was still to be carefully kept. It was to be inspected every week, and any man parting with his old coat without permission was to be confined to barracks until it was replaced. The old clothes of the supplementary militiamen who had joined the regiment could no longer be worn but were to be used for mending.[7] This sort of thing was

[1] Fortescue, *History*, vol. iii, p. 522; cf. WO. 4/770, p. 231. I assume the articles to be supplied gratis listed in Fortescue correspond roughly to what was meant to be supplied by the allowances mentioned in *Certain Rules and Orders*, p. 18. Fortescue (*op. cit.*, p. 521) supposes the refunding of poundage to begin in 1792, but cf. p. 348 and n. 5.

[2] WO. 26/37, pp. 130, 133.

[3] 31 Geo. II, cap. 26, s. 25. 33 Geo. II, cap. 24, s. 14. 2 Geo. III, cap. 20, s. 80. But these provisions were not repeated in later acts.

[4] WO. 4/761, pp. 273–6. WO. 4/768, p. 350. WO. 4/779, pp. 18–20. In 1802 some men received cash in lieu of clothes due to be issued. The men demobilised in 1799, received their clothes and new shoes, shirt and stockings or a cash equivalent. WO. 4/776, pp. 310–11, 318.

[5] BM, Add. 35665, f. 418.   [6] BM, Add. 35670, f. 323.

[7] BM, Add. 35671, f. 9.

approved army practice and obviously sensible up to a point. But the men regarded their old clothes as their own property. It was a grievance that they had to wear them out in order to preserve the new clothes, belonging to their colonel,[1] whose financial position was thereby improved.[2]

This grievance related mainly to the uniform suit and hat. As for the other items of clothing, there was a long-standing grievance over the shirt, stockings and shoes issued as part of the annual clothing. They were often of such poor quality as to be useless, and sometimes none were issued at all but a small sum of money was given instead. The soldier was obliged, thereby, to depend for his 'half mountings'[3] mainly on his allowances and stoppages.[4] In 1795 there was a major scandal when Colonel Cawthorne of the Westminster Regiment of Middlesex militia was cashiered for offences partly of this kind.[5] The watchcoat allowance, insufficient though it was, seems not always to have been fully used for its proper purpose.[6] Stoppages from pay and the allowances to the men might also be misappropriated, as when a sergeant of the Cambridgeshires collected a stoppage of 1d. a week per man for pipeclay and hair powder, but only once gave them a 1d. worth of the articles in return.[7]

Perhaps a more serious cause of embarrassment all round was that as each commanding officer decided what articles were to be bought it was difficult to satisfy the men that they were getting their money's worth. In 1779 some of the East Devons twice mobbed their colonel in camp because they had not received their 'half mountings'. They were rebuked but apparently not punished.[8] In 1794 the Cambridgeshires were supplied with a pair of trousers and a pair of flannel drawers instead of breeches and black gaiters, to be paid for by their pay and allowances. Private John Pittom refused to sign his subsequent pay accounts on the grounds that the articles supplied were not worth what was charged for them, that more was being

[1] James, pp. 47–51. By army custom the clothes belonged to the men a year after they were or should have been issued. WO. 4/776, pp. 243–4.

[2] As also by 'clothing' non-existent men, James, pp. 68–77.

[3] The usual term for articles of clothing other than the uniform. A distinction was made between 'half mountings' renewed regularly out of allowances and 'necessaries' renewed when they wore out, by stoppages. Stocks and gaiters were among the latter. WO. 4/778, pp. 143, 298.

[4] James, pp. 36–44. He quotes Cuthbertson, a standard authority on regimental administration, to the same effect.

[5] Ibid., p. 43 note. Woodfall, vol. xii, pp. 14–15, 192, 329–50, for his expulsion from the commons.

[6] James, pp. 24–5, 101. He claims one regiment had over £76 unspent in three years.

[7] The men were long afraid to complain. BM, Add. 35665, ff. 302, 313, 317.

[8] Walrond, p. 75.

stopped from his pay than the regulations allowed and that his drawers did not fit him. Adjutant Wale said that it had become very common to buy trousers, and it was really a saving to the men. Pittom, he thought, was only making trouble in the hope of getting his discharge.[1] No doubt Wale was right; but one may sympathise with illiterate privates suddenly called on to give up several shillings for some item of clothing they had hitherto managed without.

However the grievances of the men were matched to some extent by the tribulations of the colonels in dealing with the government and the firms which supplied the clothing. The former might cause them financial loss by altering the pattern of the uniform. A great deal of latitude was left to the colonel in this matter, but general regulations were made from time to time.[2] In 1798 coats without lapels were ordered, but the news did not reach the clothier of the Cambridgeshire until he had 500 coats of the old pattern ready for 1799.[3] In 1802 the Sussex militia still had 395 of the old-pattern coats unused in store, but could not use them unless they could get special permission to have 203 more made, so that the whole regiment could be issued with coats of the same pattern. As old-pattern coats cost more than new, the regimental accounts might be challenged.[4] In November 1801 the First West Riding Regiment was ordered to cease wearing scarlet coats. But in consequence of a private assurance from the Duke of York, 400 yards of cloth had already been dyed scarlet on the regiment's account. Eventually the regiment got permission to wear scarlet another year, but had to change the pattern of its looping.[5]

Regiments might also be caught out by changes in the numbers on their establishment. In 1799 colonels were ordered to provide new clothing only for the reduced numbers established by the act of July.[6] But it was soon known that a further reduction was in contemplation, and the War Office was unable to get an indication from the Secretary of State as to how large it would be. Some regiments did nothing

[1] BM, Add. 35665, ff. 292, 333, 418. Add. 35666, f. 7. The sum in dispute was 7s. 8d.

[2] For instance, WO. 4/774, pp. 54–5. Cf. WO. 4/764, p. 84.

[3] The Duke of York wished greatcoats to be supplied with the money saved, though this did not become a regulation till later (p. 348, n. 5). It was expected to take four years to recover the cost of the greatcoats in this way. BM, Add. 35670, f. 199. Add. 35671, ff. 173, 255.

[4] BM, Add. 33110, f. 156.

[5] Northamptonshire R.O., Fitzwilliam MSS., Box 1415: Fitzwilliam to Brownrigg, 13 November 1801, and enclosures; Brownrigg to Fitzwilliam, 15 November 1801; cf. W. Wynyard and H. Calvert, 20 November, and Duke of York, 18 September 1801.

[6] WO. 4/776, p. 73.

about new clothing.[1] Those that provided it were encouraged to hope that it would be paid for.[2] Eventually what had been provided was paid for, but any surplus to the new requirement was regarded as public stores and had to be used towards the reclothing of 1800.[3] In 1801 there was another bothersome change in regulations, the shifting of the time at which new clothing had to be provided from Midsummer to Christmas. Some regiments had already ordered their clothing for the usual time before they heard of the change.[4]

The relations of regiments with their suppliers were commonly a source of profit through the prices charged for the different items being less than the official allowance for them. But prices and quality varied greatly, according to the firm employed and the state of the market. A regiment could easily suffer loss and vexation. In 1760 the clothing of the East Riding regiment cost 32s. a man (more than the allowance for reclothing that year), and was not satisfactory in quality. Other regiments had paid only 28s. In 1761 the East Ridings wrote to a number of different makers and were determined to do better.[5] In the French Revolutionary war, the Cambridgeshires constantly strove for a better deal with the clothiers. In 1793 they were being supplied by the big London firm of Duberly, subcontracting for Fisher, a local banker. Fisher claimed to be interested only in the honour of the connection and that he did not make £20 a time from a reclothing. Lord Hardwicke thought that he made more like £90 in 1793 and was dissatisfied with his associate.[6] The coats supplied by Duberly in 1793 were only half lined. He claimed that he needed to make every possible saving in order to keep his price within the official allowance. Cloth was so dear (because of the high prices given by the French!) that his profit had vanished. He managed to convince the regiment that half lining was common in the militia, but agreed that coarse lining material made heavy cloth sit in wrinkles. Eventually, glazed material was sent down to the regiment to line the armpits.[7] Another complaint was that the clothes were not well

---

[1] Such as Lord Fitzwilliam's. He badgered the government on this question, perhaps because he opposed the recruiting of the army from the militia. WO 4/776, pp. 138, 195. Northamptonshire R.O., Fitzwilliam MSS., Box 1415: Fitzwilliam to Secretary at War, 12 September 1799; Rolleston and Hammond, 20 September.

[2] Cf. WO. 4/776, pp. 409, 414.   [3] *Ibid.*, p. 333. WO. 4/777, pp. 108–9.

[4] There was an allowance for a few items of clothing to cover the half-year. WO. 4/777, pp. 368–9, 372–4, 387, 394, 402–3. The re-embodied men got some of the clothing saved from 1799. Because of approaching disembodiment, new clothing was not issued in December 1801, another special allowance was made instead. WO. 4/778, pp. 3, 4, 225, 340–1.

[5] HMC, *Du Cane*, p. 225.

[6] BM, Add. 35663, f. 130. Add. 35664, ff. 144, 224.

[7] BM, Add. 35663, f. 159. Add. 35392, f. 344.

enough sewn. Duberly admitted this and said that the work was done by women, who had not the necessary strength.[1]

For the next reclothing (Midsummer 1793[2]) Hardwicke turned to another big London firm, Pearce and Sons,[3] but had the same trouble as before. When they sent the clothing to the regiment in September the makers remarked that the heavy demand and the scarcity of cloth had caused a decline in quality, but they were sure that the clothing would not shrink and expected prices to be lower and quality better another year.[4] The regiment at once sent the clothing back. Again the coats were only half lined, and the waistcoats and breeches not lined at all. Pearce claimed that Hardwicke had agreed to this and said that lining was often omitted in the militia, though it was compulsory in the army. They remarked that it was no use lining coat-sleeves, because the men always tore the lining out. Another complaint was that the collars and cuffs of the coats were the wrong size and not uniform. The makers replied that it was hard to get uniformity because the work was done by the lowest sort of people.[5] Pearce supplied the regiment till 1796, but there were constant disputes. The pattern submitted in 1794 was returned and Pearce was told to do better in colour and quality.[6] The coats and breeches of 1795 were fully lined, but in 1796 Pearce again tried to dispense with sleeve linings, although the officers found them useful in protecting the sleeves from wear.[7] There was further argument about the sewing, which Pearce maintained was as good as it could be for 1s. 9d. a suit.[8]

For clothing the supplementary militia it was decided to employ Fisher and Duberly again, and the clothing of the old militia was restored to them as well.[9] But the regiment interfered more actively than before in the procurement of its clothing. This had never really been in the hands of a single supplier. Both Pearce and Duberly subcontracted for hats,[10] and the regiment had sometimes bought items separately, like feathers and gaiters.[11] In 1797 Hardwicke decided to

[1] BM, Add. 35663, f. 165.

[2] The clothing supplied by Duberly in 1793 was that for the third of the men not previously trained or clothed, cf. above, p. 347, n. 3, and the last peacetime clothing for the rest, BM, Add. 35664, f. 144.

[3] Recommended by the East Kent. BM, Add. 35663, f. 117.

[4] BM, Add. 35663, ff. 281–2.   [5] Ibid., ff. 289, 291, 296.

[6] BM, Add. 35664, f. 320.

[7] Ibid., f. 343. All the other corps stationed in Norwich had them.

[8] BM, Add. 35667, ff. 164, 196.

[9] Ibid., ff. 156, 164, 177, 196, and BM, Add. 35668, ff. 57, 83.

[10] Pearce's hatter, Oliphant, continued to be employed in place of Duberly's hatter, Wagner, after 1796, although he did not give satisfaction. BM, Add. 35670, ff. 50, 161. Add. 35672, f. 207. Cf. Add. 35663, f. 286; Add. 35392, f. 327; Add. 35665, ff. 164–5.

[11] See BM, Add. 35663, ff. 196, 305; Add. 35664, f. 88.

buy cloth for the uniforms direct from the Leeds firm of York and Sheepshanks and give it to Duberly to make up. Duberly at first said that the whole arrangement was out of his line and he could give no estimate. He also thought the proposed cloth too fine and not hard wearing enough. At length he agreed to take it at 5s. 6d. a yard and make it up at 5s. 6d. a man.[1] There was trouble because Sheepshanks did not make the same allowance as Duberly's usual suppliers for the shrinkage of the cloth. Sheepshanks also annoyed Duberly by suspecting him of using other cloth than that which he had sent.[2] Duberly's bill was very large, and he failed to credit the full amount of cloth that he had received from Sheepshanks.[3] This was sorted out and Duberly was given a large sum from which Sheepshanks also was to be paid.[4] But that firm objected to receiving money through Duberly and said that they had tendered at the lowest price and expected to pay no bonuses, however customary. They complained that there were too many fees in transactions between merchants and peers and added that they were in no hurry for their money, which perhaps explains why they eventually got their way.[5] Despite its prickly character, the arrangement seems to have lasted for the rest of the war.

The regiment did not relieve itself of all trouble by employing contractors for the clothing. A great deal of fitting and altering had to be done when it arrived. The system was apparently to inform the contractor how tall each man was and thus obtain a uniform roughly proportionate to his size,[6] which could be altered to fit better. The bad sewing of the uniforms already noted had, moreover, often to be replaced,[7] and it was common for the regiment to make the buttonholes.[8] To pay for these alterations up to 2s. 6d. a man a year might be levied by stoppages.[9] They represented quite a big undertaking: in November 1793 the tailors of the Cambridgeshires had moved into

[1] BM, Add. 35668, ff. 119–21, 138, 141, 143, 154–5. About 1⅞ yds. were required per man.

[2] Ibid., ff. 222, 232, 234, 239, 241.

[3] Quartermaster Mann did not think his charges excessive. BM, Add. 35670, ff. 109, 111, 140.

[4] Ibid., ff. 142, 146.   [5] Ibid., ff. 147, 159, 165, 322.

[6] Duberley in 1788 sent down clothing in sizes from 5 ft. 5 ins. to 5 ft. 10 ins., an inch between each size and the 5 ft. 7 ins. to 9 ins. sizes divided into large and normal. In 1797 he asked for a size roll. BM, Add. 35662, f. 236; cf. Add. 35668, f. 155. A man who offered to supply the regiment in 1798 proposed to avoid the expense of remaking by measuring every man. Add. 35696, ff. 256–7.

[7] BM, Add. 35663, f. 165.   [8] Ibid., f. 291. Add. 35668, f. 234.

[9] WO. 4/772, pp. 92–3. Colonel Cawthorne was restrained in 1794 from charging the men more than the actual cost, WO. 4/772, p. 240. James says (p. 69, note) that this fund was often improperly used for converting and mending old clothes.

Huntingdon town hall and were working up to eight o'clock every evening.[1] It is not surprising to find this regiment having thoughts of manufacturing clothing for itself. In 1794 Adjutant Wale proposed that they buy cloth and do the whole job, hiring a master tailor and giving him the rank of sergeant or corporal. It would be worth the loss of an effective NCO to get a good man.[2] In 1797 some of the cloth bought from York and Sheepshanks was made up at the regiment into clothing for the band,[3] and in 1798 not only was it proposed to do this but all the breeches for the year were made at the regiment under the direction of Quartermaster Mann.[4] Under half (by value) of the cloth supplied by York and Sheepshanks in 1798 was made up by Duberly.[5] In October the regiment was seeking to hire a skilled master tailor full time, and a regular scale of charges for work by regimental tailors was posted in the officers' mess.[6]

The less the use made of a single big contractor, the more chance there was for more junior officers to share in the work and profit of clothing. It was the colonel or equivalent officer who was responsible for the whole,[7] but he might choose to farm part of it out. When the Cambridgeshires received some extra clothing on their call-out in 1793, Tolver, the adjutant, was allowed to supply them. Hardwicke later acknowledged that this was improper, or at least against custom, and he maintained that Tolver had not been authorised to take any profit beyond an indemnification for supplying the goods on credit.[8] Tolver claimed that Hardwicke had originally given the contract to Fisher, who had offered him 5 per cent to deliver the articles. He thought that he deserved the entire profit because of his superior knowledge of the business, and claimed that Hardwicke and Fisher had agreed.[9] He therefore allowed himself nearly 5 per cent on the shirts and 15 per cent on the shoes supplied, besides receiving 5 per cent discount from the supplier.[10] He later claimed that he had overcharged for the shoes by mistake,[11] and eventually was made to refund almost £50.[12] He had employed one Prater as his supplier, apparently

[1] BM, Add. 35664, f. 75.   [2] *Ibid.*, f. 193.
[3] BM, Add. 35668, f. 154. Add. 35669, f. 209. Cf. Add. 35670, f. 323.
[4] BM, Add. 35670, ff. 50, 104, 109, 413. Cf. Add. 35674, f. 184.
[5] See BM, Add. 35670, ff. 312–13; Add. 35672, f. 270.
[6] BM, Add. 35670, ff. 319–20.
[7] The commanding officer if the colonel, etc., was abroad (WO. 4/774, p. 324) or before 1794 the agent (WO. 4/772, pp. 359–60).
[8] BM, Add. 35664, f. 398. Add. 35665, f. 60. Cf. Add. 35664, f. 272.
[9] BM, Add. 35664, f. 394. Cf. Add. 35663, f. 38.
[10] BM, Add. 35665, ff. 6, 64: Tolver paid 5s. 3d. for shirts and was allowed 5s. 6d. He paid 5s. 3d. a pair for shoes and was allowed 6s.
[11] *Ibid.*, f. 24.
[12] *Ibid.*, ff. 107, 112, 117, 119; cf. ff. 62–4. This affair was mixed up with other disputes about accounts touched on below.

a personal acquaintance.[1] In 1794 Quartermaster Mann was entrusted with the procurement of gaiters for the regiment from a man named Clarke.[2] Mann did not do too well out of this, for he had trouble in recovering the cost from the officers and men to whom the gaiters were issued. He was too shy to dun the officers, and some left the regiment without paying. The men were put under stoppages, but Captain Parker made away with what his men had paid when he quit the regiment. Half the amount due to Clarke was still outstanding in 1797. Clarke, who was going bankrupt, then secured payment after complaining to Hardwicke.[3]

It is hard to come to any general conclusion about either the quality of militia clothing or the amount of the profit made from it. Inspecting generals sometimes found regiments very ill-clad. In 1798 an enquiry had to be ordered into the bad quality of the clothing supplied by the colonel of the South Middlesex. Blame was found to attach mainly to the clothiers (Gilpin and Davenport), who were told to send a bale of what they had supplied for inspection by the Army Clothing Board.[4] Fraser the accoutrement-maker was also asked to justify himself, which he seems to have been able to do.[5] In 1800 the colonel of the North Lincolnshires was told to remedy the many deficiencies in the clothing and equipment of his corps reported by the inspecting general.[6] In January 1802 Lord Mansfield had to be told to go at once to the East Middlesex regiment of which he was colonel and put the men in clothing applicable to the service of a British soldier. The trouble here seems to have been reluctance to spend anything on reclothing when the militia was about to be disembodied.[7] When the militia were embodied at the start of a war, their clothing likewise was often bad at first.[8] On the other hand, the surviving review returns of 1778 and 1782 contain few complaints about the clothing, although there are a good many about the arms and

---

[1] He stayed at his house (*ibid.*, f. 48), and Prater was reluctant to provide evidence against him (*ibid.*, ff. 16, 18, 112, 115).

[2] BM, Add. 35664, f. 88; but cf. f. 90.

[3] £122 odd had been outstanding, out of £242 odd. Parker's company owed £27 odd. BM, Add. 35667, ff. 286, 350, 358. Add. 35668, f. 47. Cf. above, p. 311.

[4] A bale that had been opened was mistakenly sent instead of an unopened one. The Adjutant General said that the militia clothing allowance was now larger than that for the army: £2. 10s. 5d. for a private instead of £2. 5s. 11⅜d. This was because poundage (p. 348, n. 5), etc., was not a charge on the clothing fund in the militia. WO. 3/19, pp. 117–18, 137, 212–13, 238–9, 266.

[5] *Ibid.*, p. 302.   [6] WO. 3/22, p. 343.

[7] WO. 3/34, pp. 318, 345, 351. WO. 4/778, p. 373.

[8] On 1759, cf. pp. 345–6. For examples in 1778, WO. 34/146 (ii), ff. 355–6; WO. 34/147, f. 210. For supplementary militia ragged after call-out, BM, Add. 35670, f. 137.

accoutrements.[1] This should probably be seen as negative evidence that militia clothing did not fall much below the not very high standard set: Harry Calvert, Adjutant General at the end of the century, wrote that the clothing of the militia was dependent on the county and the colonel, and inspecting generals could only see that the men had the articles to which they were entitled and that they were of good quality.[2] There is more positive evidence that the men were ill-paid than that they were ill-clad.[3]

As to profits made from clothing, all that can be done is to give some specimen figures. Lord Fitzwilliam as colonel of the First West Riding Militia from 1798 had an active balance on his clothing account of £771. 19s. for 1798, £123. 12s. 3d. for 1799 and £535. 5s. 2½d. for 1800–2.[4] Lord Hardwicke seems to have lost money on re-clothing the Cambridgeshires in 1793,[5] but from 1794 his account as colonel with the regimental agent (mainly concerned with clothing) was in a healthy state, and he was able to draw £172. 17s. 10½d. out of it in 1797 and £303. 1s. 8d. in 1798.[6] In his contemporary study of the clothing question, Charles James printed the clothing accounts of an unnamed militia regiment, showing active balances of over £400 for each of the three years 1793–5.[7]

There seems little doubt that with prudent management, and in spite of the risks involved, a substantial income was forthcoming from the clothing. But that is not to say that the colonels benefited personally. The official doctrine was that the clothing allowance in the militia was not designed to yield a profit at all.[8] Colonels commonly applied their balances to meeting expenses borne by themselves and their officers for which the official allowances were insufficient. Anything left over was often devoted to comforts and frills for the corps for which the government would not pay—the maintenance, for instance, of a regimental band. Some colonels, however, hung on to their profits, at the expense of their officers and men. For them the militia was a lucrative employment indeed.[9]

---

[1] WO. 27/40, 50.

[2] WO. 3/19, pp. 152–3.

[3] See below, pp. 367–9; cf. the increasing of their allowances, pp. 348–9. From 1792 there was an allowance for the wear on clothes caused by long marches escorting deserters. Fortescue, *History*, vol. iii, pp. 520–2 *Certain Rules*, pp. 20–1.

[4] Accounts in Northamptonshire R.O., Fitzwilliam MSS., Box 1415.

[5] BM, Add. 35664, f. 163.

[6] BM, Add. 35666, ff. 334, 354. Add. 35669, ff. 98, 127–9 (balances paid to Biddulph and Cox).

[7] James, pp. 98–101. For this writer, see the DNB.

[8] WO. 4/774, p. 324.

[9] James, pp. 53–4, 93–7. He remarks on the discontent caused by men being treated better in one corps than another.

III

The expenses at regimental level which might eat up the colonel's income from clothing comprised first of all the making good of deficiencies in articles supplied by the government. The annual allowance for reclothing was officially regarded as sufficient to meet the cost of replacing accoutrements that wore out before a new issue was due,[1] and also the extra cost if the colonel desired buff accoutrements instead of the standard issue of tan leather. In that case he was given an allowance equal in value to the standard issue and bought accoutrements himself at whatever price he chose.[2] The clothing and equipment acquired by the regiment had, of course, to be stored and transported, and this was another source of expense. When the militia was not embodied, the arrangement at first was that captains of companies were to store their arms and clothing under the care of some proper person in chests provided by the churchwardens of the place. The lord lieutenant or the colonel could order the seizure of the arms should the safety of the kingdom require it.[3] In 1786 these last were directly entrusted with the proper storage of the whole,[4] and it was laid down that a third of the sergeants and drummers in permanent pay should always be at the place where the arms were kept, under the command of the adjutant.[5] Tolver of the Cambridgeshires was duly established at Ely, in a house rented from the regiment at £10 a year.[6] He had originally wished to have the armoury in his house,[7] but in 1790 a storeroom was still being rented. An armourer was employed for £12 a year. The expense apparently fell on the contingent fund provided in the annual pay act.[8] In 1802, however, parliament empowered the lieutenancies to hire or erect storehouses at the expense of the county rate.[9] In this way the militia of each county

[1] WO. 4/775, pp. 69, 70, cf. pp. 361–2. Knapsacks had to be replaced every six years by the regiment, which might impose a stoppage of 1s. a year per man. Ibid., pp. 374–7. Cf. WO. 4/774, p. 209; WO. 4/765, pp. 262–3.

[2] See further, WO. 4/774, pp. 206–7; WO. 4/762, p. 14.

[3] The muskets were to be marked with an M. and the county, and there were penalties for soldiers or keepers concerned in their embezzlement. 30 Geo. II, cap. 25, ss. 32–4, 36–7, 40, 42. 2 Geo. III, cap. 20, ss. 104, 106, 108–110, 112.

[4] 26 Geo. III, cap. 107, ss. 85–6, 90. 42 Geo. III, cap. 90, ss. 101–2.

[5] And were to be subject to martial law. The sergeant-major or a sergeant was to command in the absence of the adjutant. 26 Geo. III, cap. 107, ss. 88, 91–2. 42 Geo. III, cap. 90, ss. 103–4, 107–8. Cf. for earlier arrangements for punishing offenders among them, 4 Geo. III, cap. 17, s. 8; 7 Geo. III, cap. 17, ss. 19–25.

[6] BM, Add. 35662, f. 250.

[7] BM, Add. 35659, f. 186. He had then (1777) lived in Cambridge.

[8] BM, Add. 35662, ff. 246, 250, 279. In 1792 a man who had served at Gibraltar was appointed (ibid., f. 285). The regiment also hired an exercise ground (Add. 35391, ff. 236–7).

[9] 42 Geo. III, cap. 90, s. 106.

acquired a permanent headquarters and depot, a thing which the nomadic regiments of the line entirely lacked.

When embodied, the militia too were nomadic. Each corps was allowed to charge the consequent expenses of transport and storage in a contingent account, the actual amount of which was paid to it after scrutiny at the War Office. Postage,[1] stationery and the cost of fire and candle for guards were also borne on this account, as well as such incidental expenses as the Secretary at War chose to sanction. There was an official specially appointed for the work of going through these accounts, and in deciding what to allow he was governed strictly by rules and precedents. Unusual cases were referred to the Secretary at War.[2] There were constant disputes between the War Office and regiments refusing to accept its rulings. The accounts of 1778–9 were particularly troublesome. It seems that the regimental agents that had been appointed on embodiment in 1778 were often inexperienced, and had failed to find out the rules and precedents and inform the regiments of them. They may also have failed to advance money to the regiments to pay the contingent expenses until the bills were allowed: they were supposed to do this and take £5 per cent for it. Things were made worse by the official concerned having a long illness, which delayed the scrutiny of the accounts.[3] The Secretary at War was sorry for the inexperienced militia officers, but he felt that his main duty was to protect public funds and that he could not usually allow unprecedented items of expenditure. There had long been a printed paper explaining what the rules were, but the agents had evidently failed to send copies to the regiments.[4] At the next embodiment in 1792 this was remedied: the government sent out a booklet containing the rules respecting contingent accounts and many other matters relating to pay and allowances.[5]

Regimental transport was mostly provided by the pressing of wagons by the order of justices along the route. The mutiny act (in peacetime the militia act) sanctioned this, and required that no wagon was to go above a day's journey or carry more than 30 cwt. They had to be supplied complete with drivers and draught animals, and were paid for at the rate of 1s. a mile for a five-horse wagon or a six-ox wain and 9d. for a four-horse cart.[6] The War Office allowed enough

[1] Letters received, that is. Letters written by soldiers went at a reduced rate. For an abuse of this privilege see WO. 4/775, pp. 217–18.

[2] WO. 4/764, pp. 229–30.

[3] WO. 4/765, pp. 62–6; cf. pp. 83, 94; WO. 4/764, p. 310.

[4] WO. 4/767, pp. 355–8.

[5] *Certain Rules and Orders*, already cited: a first draft dating from 1791 is at WO. 4/769, pp. 235–55.

[6] Counties were empowered to pay expenses beyond the statutory allowance by those whose wagons were pressed. See, e.g., 37 Geo. III, cap. 33, ss. 47–51. Cf. 2

money for each company to have one wagon on the march: 1s. a mile per company. There was also £10 a year for the carriage of ammunition, and the actual expense of bringing clothes and equipment from the supplier to the regiment was also paid.[1] These were probably the most contentious items in the contingent accounts. Regiments demanded in particular more money for the carriage of ammunition,[2] and for moving tents and camping equipment. This last was mainly the responsibility of company commanders, as will be explained, but regiments were sometimes allowed extra funds for doing it, especially when leaving camp in the autumn.[3] The War Office probably did well to be vigilant on this head. Thomas Pelham complained in 1795 that few regiments used less than double the number of wagons officially approved of and commonly pressed as many as they could afford.[4] Complaints sometimes arose, too, that wagons had not been paid for or had been overloaded.[5] A more legitimate way of keeping expenditure below the allowance was to hire water transport. In 1795 the Cambridgeshires moved part of the men and baggage from Harwich to Ipswich by wherry at the same cost as two wagons. Later the regimental baggage was sent from Harwich to Yarmouth for about £15.[6] A disadvantage of this method was encountered by the Westmorlands when some new arms being sent to them by sea were captured by the enemy. In the usual manner of the age, they were recovered by paying a ransom.[7]

In 1792 the allowances for postage, stationery, guardrooms and storerooms was £36 a year for a large corps and £24 for smaller ones. All but the smallest corps had 6d. a day for fire and candle for the guards.[8] Allowances under these heads caused some trouble, but

Geo. III, cap. 20, ss. 123–4; 26 Geo. III, cap. 107, s. 80; 42 Geo. III, cap. 90, s. 95. (30 Geo. III, cap. 25, ss. 49–50 applied only in invasion or rebellion.)

[1] *Certain Rules*, pp. 22–3. The expense of warrants for pressing wagons was also paid. Detachments smaller than a company were allowed 9d. a day in 1792.

[2] WO. 4/766, p. 489; WO. 4/767, pp. 227–8; WO. 4/771, p. 329, are examples. The £10 for carrying ammunition was an old-established allowance, and in 1780 the Secretary at War consulted Lord Amherst because of the number of requests for more: WO. 4/766, p. 255; cf. WO. 4/765, p. 218. The War Office computed from its own marching orders the mileage that each regiment had covered. WO. 4/769, pp. 23–5.

[3] See WO. 4/765, p. 122; WO. 4/772, pp. 348–9; WO. 4/773, p. 107. Extra baggage was allowed for by weight. WO. 4/775, p. 192.

[4] BM, Add. 33120, f. 16.

[5] WO. 4/766, pp. 396–7, 432, 433, 435. WO. 4/774, pp. 411–13. WO. 1/1017, ff. 429–30.

[6] BM, Add. 35666, ff. 31, 201–2.

[7] WO. 34/137, ff. 148–9.

[8] *Certain Rules*, pp. 22–3. Small corps were those under 360 privates. The totals include an *extra* postage allowance of £6 or £4.

relatively less than over transport.[1] The arrangements made were no doubt economical. They were not always satisfactory in other respects: there were complaints, for instance, of gunpowder stored in ordinary cellars in the middle of towns, to the danger of the inhabitants.[2]

Some expenses fell by custom not on the regiment but on the company commanders, who comprised not only the captains but also the colonel and other field officers, who till 1802 each had a company. In the army these were long defrayed by an allowance of 'contingent men'—that is, each captain was allowed to keep his company short of its full complement to the extent of one man in twenty-five, but to draw for his own use the pay of these non-existent men. In 1759 the Secretary at War seems at first to have intended that captains' expenses should be included in the regimented contingency bills.[3] But almost at once it was decided to introduce 'contingent men' into the militia. For the time being these 'men' were born on the establishment as supernumeraries. But the militia units were told to let their strength decline, by leaving vacancies unfilled, by a number equal to that of the 'contingent men' to which they were entitled.[4] The militia potentates meeting in the winter of 1760 claimed that their allowance was smaller than that of the army, which they said was one in twenty. But they were apparently satisfied once the allowance was calculated by battalion not by company, so that fractions of twenty-five could be allowed for.[5] The main expenses covered by the 'contingent men' were the maintenance of a hospital, and the repair and care of arms and accoutrements. The system was revived in 1778,[6] but in 1779 the government, its major plans of augmentation having failed, decided to fill up the vacancies caused by 'contingent men'.[7] The captains received the same amount as an allowance, which continued to be paid from the 'non-effective pay' as before, while there was any available.[8]

---

[1] The 6*d.* guards allowance was a long standing one, cf. WO. 4/765, p. 385; WO. 4/766, p. 256. The other allowances were new, and in 1793 the Secretary at War said they had been introduced both to consolidate and check the increasingly generous treatment of claims under these heads in the previous war. WO. 4/770, pp. 422–3, 426–7.

[2] WO. 1/1004, J. H. Ley, 14 August 1779; cf. SP. 41/33, N. Tredcroft, 12 August, and C. Gullet, 20 August 1779. WO. 1/1012, ff. 249–50.

[3] WO. 1/980, ff. 195–6. WO. 4/757, pp. 150, 315.

[4] WO. 4/758, pp. 70, 86. Cf. WO. 1/979, Sir J. Cust, 16 December, and Sir R. Mostyn, 27 December 1759.

[5] WO. 1/980, f. 265. BM, Add. 33047, ff. 336–7.   [6] WO. 4/762, pp. 9, 10.

[7] WO. 4/764, pp. 266–86. Lord Rockingham challenged the legality of this, WO. 4/765, pp. 4, 29, 30, 96–7.

[8] WO. 4/765, pp. 93–6, 100–2. 'Non-effective pay' (in the case of officers 'vacant pay') was the part of the money issued for the pay of a corps not used because the corps was below full strength. It remained in the hands of the agent. Note that the system of 'contingent men' increased the colonel's profits from clothing.

From 1792 the captains were relieved of the expense of hospitals and given a straightforward allowance ranging from £38. 5s. for a company of fifty men or fewer to £56. 10s. if there were more than seventy-five.[1] They were thought officially to be £20 better off as a result.[2] There was also a separate allowance for the articles needed to clean the arms and accoutrements: brushes, pickers, turnscrews, worms, brickdust, emery and oil. Actual expenditure on these up to 1s. 4½d. a man per half year was to be repaid.[3] According to Charles James, much of this money stuck to the colonels' hands and the men might have to supply themselves.[4]

There was an entirely different arrangement when the militia was disembodied. Starting again in 1759, the annual pay acts provided a straightforward allowance of 5d. a man a month. The captains were to receive and account for it, and any surplus was to be disposed of by a vote of the field officers and captains of the corps.[5] In 1763 the allowance was increased to 6d., a penny of which was for hospital expenses during the annual exercise.[6] From 1769 the commandant of the unit disposed of the hospital allowance and was to order what was necessary from the rest for the repair and carriage of arms.[7]

An expense falling particularly on company commanders but also on the rest of the officers was the provision and transport of camping equipment. Officers had to provide their own tents, though in 1759 and 1778 they were called out at such short notice that the government provided them instead. They were also expected to provide bat horses to carry the tents, and to cover their camping expenses they received bat, baggage and forage money.[8] Originally, company commanders were expected to transport their men's tents, and for this they received £10 bat money and sometimes another £10 for a horse to carry blankets. They also received £7. 10s. baggage money in respect of their own effects.[9] These allowances appear not to have been enough. In 1778 it was computed that each company required three horses to move its tents and baggage,[10] and in 1794 the War Office declared that the sum formerly allowed for buying a horse was insufficient.[11] Accordingly, in 1793 the company commanders were relieved of the expense of transporting their men's tents, losing their allowance of bat money. Subalterns, who had hitherto received

[1] *Certain Rules*, pp. 14–15. [2] WO. 4/771, pp. 467–8.
[3] *Certain Rules*, p. 18. [4] James, pp. 3–7, 55.
[5] 32 Geo. II, cap. 21, ss. 1, 5. [6] 3 Geo. III, cap. 10, ss. 1, 4.
[7] 9 Geo. III, sess. 2, cap. 40, ss. 1, 5, 6.
[8] See WO. 4/757, pp. 152, 266; WO. 4/762, pp. 176, 180; and e.g. WO. 4/770, pp. 361–2, 376–7; WO. 4/771, pp. 38–40.
[9] WO. 4/771, pp. 181–4. Cf. WO. 4/767, p. 289 (where I suppose the baggage money is for the two subalterns), and pp. 41–2.
[10] WO. 3/26, p. 4. [11] WO. 4/772, p. 215.

£6. 5s. for baggage and forage money together, were now to get double.[1] In 1794 it was laid down that each field officer and captain was to have one horse, subalterns were to have one between two and the surgeon was to have one for the medicine chest. Eighteen guineas was allowed for the purchase of each of these horses.[2] Through all these changes, forage money for the company commanders remained fixed at £27. 10s. for a colonel, diminishing by £5 a rank down to £12. 10s. for a captain.[3] From 1794 subalterns and staff officers received 8 guineas forage money.[4] This allowance was supposed to feed the horses for 100 days. Sometimes the government required the officers to keep their horses throughout the year, in which case more forage money was issued.[5] On other occasions the horses were ordered to be sold,[6] and then the officers had to be given money to buy more when they next camped.[7] All the changes made in this complicated system in 1793–4 point strongly to its having borne hard on the officers in earlier years.

Such were the main expenses of the officers officially recognised by the bestowal of an allowance to meet them. (The special cases of the surgeon and paymaster will be considered later.) Though even contingent accounts afforded occasional chances of profit, there was much more chance of loss. As the next chapter will show, a host of minor emergencies occurred in the life of every unit and all too often the War Office left the officers to foot the bill. They are found paying for a wondrous variety of things, ranging from the funerals of men who died while on service (unaccountably not paid for out of public funds)[8] to the five patent British artificial filtering stones bought for the Cambridgeshires in 1793.[9] To defray such expenses (normally placed on what was called the stockpurse account) there was first whatever the colonel chose to allow from his clothing profits. When the Cambridgeshires were embodied in 1778, Lt.-Col. Ward the commandant renounced his entire profit, and it was apparently because of this that the field officers and captains could decide to buy buff belts for 100 guineas and musical instruments, caps and other articles for a further 50.[10] Some of the fines levied under the militia acts went to the regimental funds,[11] and when regiments took to recruiting the

[1] Likewise staff officers. WO. 4/771, pp. 181–4.

[2] WO. 4/772, pp. 214–16.   [3] As n. 2 and p. 362, n. 9.   [4] As n. 2.

[5] They belonged to the company. WO. 4/763, p. 255. WO. 4/765, pp. 74–5.

[6] WO. 4/766, p. 127. WO. 4/767, pp. 299, 300; cf. 397. WO. 4/772, p. 137.

[7] I fancy that the baggage money was otherwise expected to last three years, cf. WO. 4/774, p. 266. The Duke of Grafton and Lt.-Col. Bruce tried to get more money for their subalterns in 1778; WO. 4/763, pp. 190–1.

[8] WO. 4/765, pp. 122, 308. WO. 4/772, pp. 247–8.

[9] BM, Add. 35663, f. 193.   [10] BM, Add. 35660, ff. 174, 176.

[11] 4 Geo. III, cap. 17, s. 8. 30 Geo. II, cap. 25, s. 56. 2 Geo. III, cap. 20, ss. 55, 128. 26 Geo. III, cap. 107, s. 132. 42 Geo. III, cap. 90, s. 176.

fines to pay for this swelled the stockpurse and might yield a profit.[1]
The colonel's pay, failing all else, might be called on to fill the remaining gap, and likewise that of the other senior officers. But as the
Duke of Grafton remarked in 1778, even the colonel might not
always find it convenient to give up his pay,[2] and none of the field
officers received any pay at all during the peacetime exercises.[3] Field
officers and captains might often find themselves drawing on their
private means. That they were hard hit in the American war is
suggested by their pertinacity at its end in trying to get £20 each from
the 'non-effective' fund. Since 1766 captains in the army had been
allowed this in any year when the 'non-effective' pay[4] of their companies would yield it after the deduction of £5 a man wanting to
complete. But in the army the 'non-effective' fund financed recruiting
and this allowance was really a reward for success in that field. In the
militia this was not the case, and so the request for an allowance
there was refused. The field officers and captains were so angry that
they held a meeting and resolved to raise a fund and sue the colonels
and agents.[5]

IV

The picture of loss and gain is distorted by the curious system of
issuing and accounting for funds then prevalent, which it is simplest
to discuss separately. Money was sometimes issued before it was
needed and might yield a profit in the interim. The agents received a
good deal in advance on various accounts and it proved hard to make
them disgorge any that was not used. The settlement of accounts between the regiments and the governments took so long, anyway, that
the agents had a good excuse to sit tight. The accounts for the American war were not finally cleared up till 1798.[6] From 1787 the Secretary at War was pressing agents to pay in part of their balances,[7] but

---

[1] See BM, Add. 35669, ff. 107, 109. Cf. Northamptonshire R.O., Brooke of
Oakley MSS, B.2, pp. 81–2 (replacement of men buying their discharges).

[2] He remarks that a board of enquiry at Coxheath Camp in 1778 found that
there was no surplus from the clothing allowance. WO. 34/156 (i), pp. 495–6.

[3] Nor did the subalterns till 1763, nor the captains till 1764. The daily rates
were: captain 7s. 6d.; lieutenant, 3s. 6d.; ensigns 3s. From 1758 adjutants (in
permanent pay) had received 6s. a day. See 31 Geo. II, cap. 30, s. 3; 3 Geo. III,
cap. 10, s. 6; 4 Geo. III, cap. 30, s. 6; and the other pay acts. For the pay of the
regular infantry which the militia received in wartime, see Fortescue, *History*,
vol. ii, pp. 613–14; vol. iv, p. 937. But the adjutant's pay was only 4s. a day
when embodied, unless he was given a second commission. WO. 4/760, pp. 108,
110–13. BM, Add. 35669, f. 68. Cf. WO. 26/37, pp. 101–2.

[4] Cf. p. 361, n. 8.

[5] Because the militia was legally entitled to the same pay as the line. WO.
1/1020, ff. 857–64. WO. 4/768, pp. 406–9. WO. 4/769, pp. 7, 218. Cf. WO. 4/766,
pp. 293–4.

[6] WO. 4/769, *passim*.   [7] *Ibid.*, pp. 148, 154, 158–60, 162–3, 170, 184–7, etc.

little had been paid in by 1793. The sum owed to the public by agents and officers in 1789 was some £57,000.[1] One agent, at least, had used his share to settle a private debt.[2]

Within each militia unit there were comparable advantages for those concerned with the issue of pay. During disembodiment, the battalion clerk drew it four months in advance for those in permanent pay, and most of it passed through the hands of the captains, who received it two months in advance.[3] In wartime, all but the smallest units had a paymaster. He was appointed either by the commanding officer or by the field officers and captains jointly, and whoever appointed him was responsible for his good conduct.[4] For long paid by a stoppage from the pay of his unit,[5] he received instead from 1792 an allowance ranging from £35 to £120 a year according to its size.[6] This appointment was always held by one of the ordinary officers. From 1797 paymasters in the army were given a more independent position, held no other appointment and had to find securities.[7] In the militia they had to continue to hold a regimental commission, so that they could be used on courts-martial. But henceforth, commanding officers were to give no orders to the paymaster respecting the discharge of his duties as such, nor could he be dismissed save by royal order or the sentence of a court-martial. Field officers and captains ceased to be responsible as such for the regimental accounts, and in consequence no longer had part of their pay kept back under the heading of 'arrears' to cover undischarged debts. This responsibility passed, in fact, to the paymaster, who accordingly was required to enter into a bond of £1000 and find two sureties of £500. In recompense he was given a new allowance, sufficient to bring his pay up to 15s. a day.[8] From the paymaster, money passed to

[1] *Ibid.*, pp. 208–13, 275–7. Cf. similar bad conduct by battalion clerks in peace, above, p. 344, n. 2.

[2] *Ibid.*, pp. 172–4.

[3] Independent companies had no battalion clerk. His salary was £50 p.a., and he had to give a bond for half the amount normally issued to him. See the annual pay acts. From 1766 the receiver general paid the clothing bill direct: 6 Geo. III, cap. 30, s. 17.

[4] *Certain Rules*, p. 7. Cf. WO. 4/758, p. 243; WO. 4/772, p. 361.

[5] See, e.g., WO. 4/768, p. 344. In the American war the surgeon and paymaster together received 2d.ʾa week per sergeant, ¾d. per corporal and musician, and ½d. per private. Walrond, pp. 108–9.

[6] *Certain Rules*, p. 16.

[7] Fortescue, *History*, vol. iv, pp. 898–9; cf. p. 937, n. 2.

[8] Staff officers were henceforth not to be paymasters. The paymaster became responsible for musters (i.e. seeing there were no fictitious men on the books). His accounts had to be confirmed by the adjutant and commanding officer. Very small corps got a paymaster for the first time. HO. 50/388, printed circulars to commandants of militia corps, 5 December 1797 (with accompanying papers) and 25 January 1798; unprinted do., 9 February 1798.

the men (or their creditors) through a pay sergeant in each company. These, too, had their chance of profit, for example by paying the men in base coin obtained on terms favourable to themselves.[1]

But there was a serious chance of loss as well as of profit from the issue of money. The War Office ordered expenditure, but it was from other departments that the money came and they were often very slow in issuing it.[2] Expenditure on necessary items could hardly be delayed, and so somebody had to bear a charge for deferred payment. Money for the annual reclothing was regularly issued a year or so after it had been ordered.[3] The clothing money for 1795 was issued in May 1796—mostly in exchequer bills at a 5 per cent discount which the government promised to make good.[4] The Cambridgeshires were at once pressed for payment by Pearce, then their clothier, who said that they had suffered badly by the delay, money being very tight in the commercial world.[5] The agent paid them at once, but only in July did the issue of the previous year's camp allowance and the compensation for the 5 per cent discount enable him even to think of paying the hatter.[6] In April 1798 six clothiers complained to Pitt that half the clothing of 1796 and all that of 1797 was unpaid for. They had already provided most of the current year's clothing, but they could not fulfil their contracts unless another half-year's money was forthcoming.[7] Sometimes the clothiers passed on their loss to the regiments by charging interest on their bills: the Lancashires had to pay over £300 on the bills for reclothing in 1781 and 1782.[8]

Most of the pay had necessarily to be issued on time, but a comparable difficulty here was that it was issued in London and no charge was allowed for remitting it to wherever the corps was stationed.[9] The War Office liked (but would not urge) revenue departments with local balances to supply cash.[10] At worst, banknotes cut in two to guard against theft could be sent through the post.[11]

The difficulties that the junior ranks might get into by the non-arrival of funds are exemplified by Sergeant Watts of the Cambridgeshires, who complained to Lord Hardwicke in November 1798 that he had paid £30 for the year's breeches for his company out of his own pocket. He asked for a refund, to give him a working balance.

[1] WO. 4/774, pp. 120, 124, 129. Markham, p. 43.
[2] WO. 4/759, p. 3. WO. 4/777, p. 65.
[3] See, e.g., BM, Add. 35668, f. 60; Add. 35670, ff. 92, 95.
[4] BM, Add. 35666, f. 349.   [5] *Ibid.*, f. 351; cf. f. 14.
[6] BM, Add. 35667, ff. 1, 12.   [7] PRO. 30/8, vol. 241, f. 144.
[8] Lancashire R.O., Derby Muniments, DDK. 1741, item 5. The War Office denied that this happened, WO. 4/777, pp. 402–3. Cf. BM, Add. 33110, f. 156.
[9] WO. 4/759, pp. 273, 276.
[10] WO. 4/767, p. 197. WO. 4/776, p. 262.
[11] *Ibid.* Cf. WO. 4/825, p. 236.

The pay for the company often arrived late and if he had no reserve he had to pay the men with money intended for the butcher and baker. As the tradesmen had lost money by sergeants deserting, they were very eager for prompt payment and it was undesirable to put them off. Watts owed money, in any case, for more breeches, which he could not pay till he received the money for an issue of panta-loons.[1] Happily this came by January 1799 and yielded a profit, which was passed on to the men by buying rosettes and hair leathers at 7*d*. and selling them at 4*d*.[2]

Senior officers had a more aristocratic way with creditors than was possible for Watts. Sir Nicholas Carew, colonel of the Surrey militia, once received a complaint from one of his officers that he had failed after five weeks to return some bills sent him for signature. An account for £15 for stockings was owed to a poor man who had borrowed the sum two or three times over and in defence of his credit now threatened to arrest the writer. The ruin of the regiment's credit and greater expense than necessary were likely to be the conse-quences.[3] A series of bills from 1778–80 were left unpaid by the West-morlands, and Sir James Lowther dismissed complaints and said that those who presented them could go to law if they thought they had a case.[4] But financial malpractices of one kind or another were the natural result of the system. There were both windfall gains and windfall losses, and both in their way were equally demoralising.

V

One thing more must be considered in striking a balance. Against the possible gains of field officers and captains must be set the claims on their charity resulting from the crying insufficiency of the pay of the lower ranks. The army rates of pay which applied to the embodied militia did not change for a century after the Revolution. Officers and men alike had normally to pay for their food and lodging, as will be explained in the next chapter. The cost of living rose in the wars of the later eighteenth century, and the pay of the men, diminished by the deductions mentioned above, became increasingly insufficient for this.[5] There were constant attempts to improve it. The militia acts themselves provided a higher rate of pay for the peacetime exercises, though this had to cover all sorts of expenses that might be spread

[1] BM, Add. 35670, f. 363.
[2] BM, Add. 35671, f. 37.
[3] BM, Add. 29599, ff. 443–4.
[4] He may have been in the right; but he produces no refutation, as he does against other charges presented at the same time. WO. 34/137, ff. 150–1; cf. else-where in ff. 144–58.
[5] See notably Fortescue, *History*, vol. ii, pp. 613–14; vol. iii, pp. 515–23.

over a man's pay for a longer period when he was embodied.[1] The extra allowances for clothing have already been noticed. From 1768 NCOs and privates in barracks received an allowance towards the cost of their bread: the government paid the excess if the standard loaf cost more than 5*d*. The militia benefited from this when they were next called out.[2] In 1792, NCOs and men both in barracks and in quarters were ordered to be given bread at the public charge to the value of 10½*d*. a week each,[3] and the amount that they had to pay towards the cost of their food was limited to 3*s*. a day.[4] In 1795 the price of meat over 4½*d*. a lb. and of bread over 5*d*. a loaf was ordered to be defrayed by the government,[5] and the other extra allowances for food and clothing that had been given over the years were consolidated into a single one, to be accounted for monthly with each man.[6] The private's daily emolument had now risen from the traditional 6*d*. to 10*d*. In 1797, warned by the naval mutinies, the government added a further 2*d*. The men were not to have to spend more than 4*s*. a week on food, and a further allowance was to be made when bread rose above 1¼*d*. and meat above 6*d*. a lb. They had to contribute 1*s*. 6*d*. a week towards 'necessaries' and were to receive 1*s*. 6*d*. a week (less the cost of cleaning materials and washing) in cash.[7]

The fortunes of the subalterns were similar. Though paid more than the men, they had the extra burdens of living like gentlemen[8] and buying expensive uniforms. Lieutenant Cheveley of the West Essex paid £15. 12*s*. 5*d*. for his original outfit in 1759 and at least £52. 12*s*. 6¼*d*. more in 1759–61. His gross pay was only just over £85 a year.[9] Officers also suffered certain deductions from their pay from

[1] Privates and corporals received respectively 1*s*. and 1*s*. 6*d*. a day during exercise. Sergeants received 1*s*. and drummers 6*d*. a day all the year round. From 1762 the privates and corporals received pay for the number of days they were away from home. See the pay acts. From 1786 corporals were in permanent pay at 8*d*. a day, and from 1802 this was increased to 1*s*. 2*d*., sergeants getting 1*s*. 6*d*. and drummers 1*s*. 26 Geo. III, cap. 107, s. 64. 42 Geo. III, cap. 90, s. 83.

[2] WO. 4/763, p. 85. WO. 4/768, p. 2. An analogous system obtained in camp, WO. 4/764, pp. 176–7.

[3] They were only to receive it for the time that they were actually present with their unit. *Certain Rules*, p. 17.

[4] Fortescue, *History*, vol. iii, p. 522.   [5] WO. 4/773, pp. 207–9.

[6] *Ibid.*, pp. 389–90. The allowance for necessaries had previously to be accounted for every two months, the captain paying the balance to the man. WO. 4/771, p. 138.

[7] WO. 26/37, pp. 113, 129–33. The 1795 allowance for bread and meat was computed at 1¾*d*. a day. The men now received this in cash, but had to pay for their food to the amount stated. For necessaries see p. 348. See Fortescue, *History*, vol. iv, pp. 897–8, 935, 937.

[8] Above, pp. 321–2.

[9] G. O. Rickword, 'Military Gleanings from the Cheveley Papers', *Jol. of Society for Army Historical Research*, vol. xl (1962), pp. 129–32.

which the men were free, notably for the support of Chelsea Hospital,[1] and in the form of the 'arrears' already mentioned.[2] They received these arrears in the end, but the subalterns' arrears for the American war were still not fully paid in 1785[3] and those for 1796 were unpaid in 1798.[4] Such were the subalterns' sufferings that in 1797 they were allowed to participate in the general increase of pay given to the lower ranks. Arrears and certain stoppages were abolished in their case[5] and they were given an 'allowance' of 1s. a day—in fact, a pay raise.[6]

Governmental relief for the lower ranks was little and late. The senior officers had often to come to the relief of their men,[7] and might even have to subsidise the subalterns. In the West Essex during the Seven Years' War the subalterns' pay was augmented, by means of a subscription among the other officers, to the extent of 10s. a week for a lieutenant and 12s. 6d. for an ensign.[8] So although by the nineties the profits of militia colonels had risen high enough to cause complaint in parliament,[9] there were never wanting hardships elsewhere in the system to which a conscientious colonel would apply his gains. Complaint arose not because too much was spent on the militia but because not all colonels did so use their profits. The blame for this must rest largely with parliament, which was curiously unwilling to be strict with militia officers. It was only from 1781 that the militia were liable even to be regularly mustered by Commissaries of Musters, to ensure that fictitious men were not borne on the books.[10] But when a lieutenant of militia was cashiered for doing this in 1781, Lt.-Gen. Parker remarked that the militia did not see this offence in the same light as did the army. He pointed out also that the trial revealed that it was the practice of the militia to draw pay for the full establishment of a corps, however incomplete it was.[11] The patriotism of some generous noblemen and gentlemen at the head of the force did not make up for the lack of a strong professional ethos running

[1] *Ibid.*, p. 129. Cf. WO. 4/762, p. 98.   [2] Above, p. 365.
[3] WO. 4/769, p. 48.   [4] WO. 4/825, p. 294.
[5] Arrears were generally abolished soon afterwards. Above, p. 365.
[6] WO. 4/774, pp. 343–4. Cf. on the equally penurious army subalterns Fortescue, *History*, vol. iii, pp. 520–2; vol. iv, p. 898.
[7] See, e.g., below, p. 401.
[8] Rickword, *loc. cit.*, p. 127.
[9] In 1796 General Smith, Sheridan and Bastard (a militia officer) proposed a bill to regulate militia stockpurses. CJ, vol. li, p. 689. In 1799 there were complaints in the commons about militia clothing profits and Colonel Stanley said many officers wished the government would take over the job. Woodfall, vol. xx, pp. 270–1.
[10] WO. 4/767, pp. 171, 178. For the system, *Certain Rules*, pp. 7–14; cf. above, p. 365, n. 8. In 1770 a clause had been put in the pay act to prevent the issue of pay for non-effective sergeants and drummers. 10 Geo. III, cap. 9, s. 5.
[11] WO. 34/137, ff. 201, 293–5. WO. 34/138, f. 32.

through it. The business side of the militia stood in need of a great deal more effective supervision than it got.

Note: Regimental Bands

These were not part of the standard equipment of an eighteenth-century regiment. The militia acts provided only for two drummers per company and a drum major (in 1786 this was reduced in peacetime to one drummer per company, but the grenadier and light infantry companies were to have an extra drummer each, both in peace and war).[1] But a band was increasingly felt to be desirable and thus became one of the things which colonels commonly wished—or were expected—to finance out of their regimental profits. This was recognised in the militia act of 1786, which empowered either the lord lieutenant or the commanding officer to appoint supernumerary drummers at their own expense to serve as musicians.[2] In 1781 Lt.-Col. Ward told Lord Hardwicke that the Cambridgeshires proposed to spend £60 on new players and instruments and asked for a donation. He recalled that Hardwicke had said that they should have a good band and in view of his generous past donations was ashamed to ask for more. But music masters were expensive.[3]

From the military point of view, the band seems indeed to have been an expensive nuisance. Musicians were borne on the regimental books as privates and even NCOs, reducing the effective strength. Thomas Pelham in 1802 thought that the misapplication of pay to set up a band should be specifically declared by law to be a false muster.[4] The bandsmen were not easily kept in order, especially perhaps because they were often foreigners. In 1794 Johann Gottfried Lehmann became bandmaster of the Cambridgeshires, in consequence of a recommendation to Lord Hardwicke by an oboeist in the Guards' Regiment at Hanover.[5] In 1796 he was in trouble for playing without leave at a private house. He then said that he did not consider himself under military discipline. He complained, too, that his pay was in arrears, that it was too small to justify his doing much work for the regiment, and that the expense of his journey from Hanover had not been refunded. As he spoke no English and the commanding officer no German, the situation was not easy![6] In 1798 there was trouble when the band were asked to function as (apparently) a string ensemble at the officers' ball. They said that they had no instruments and were generally obstructive. Their object was to exact a gratuity. Lehmann took their part.[7] Rather surprisingly he volunteered to go with the corps to Ireland. He eventually asked for his discharge on the ground that his constitution had been impaired by too much exertion on wind instruments.[8]

In 1796 the Cambridgeshires had eighteen drummers and eight additional

[1] 31 Geo. II, cap. 26, s. 6. 2 Geo. III, cap. 20, s. 38. 26 Geo. III, cap. 107, s. 64. 42 Geo. III, cap. 90, s. 83.

[2] 26 Geo. III, cap. 107, s. 66. 42 Geo. III, cap. 90, s. 85.

[3] BM, Add. 35661, f. 88.   [4] BM, Add. 33048, f. 362.

[5] BM, Add. 35665, f. 39.   [6] BM, Add. 35667, f. 31.

[7] BM, Add. 35670, f. 202.   [8] BM, Add. 35674, f. 193.

drummers. The band consisted of the latter plus seven of the former.[1] In April 1797 the 'additional music' comprised a sergeant, a corporal, and five privates.[2] As to the music played, a bill sent to the First West Riding Regiment in 1798 shows that they had bought a number of marches and dances, two songs and a larghetto and divertimentos by Mozart.[3] The Berkshire militia had its own regimental march, commissioned for it in 1792 by that noted militia enthusiast Lord Radnor;[4] no doubt other examples might be found.

[1] BM, Add. 35667, f. 6.
[2] BM, Add. 35668, f. 18.
[3] Northamptonshire R.O., Fitzwilliam MSS., Box 1415: account of F. Eley for purchases on 6 April and 2 July 1798.
[4] Emma E. Thoyts, *History of the Royal Berkshire Militia* (Reading, 1897), p. 127, and illustration facing.

XIV

THE ROUTINE OF LIFE
DURING SERVICE

ONE of the most important and original features of the militia organisation was its capacity to summon from civil life a large body of trained men living scattered all over the country and return them to their homes to await a fresh call when their services were no longer needed. It was the petty constable in each parish, acting on orders from the lieutenancy received through the constable of the hundred, who had to summon the men. For training meetings during disembodiment he had, till 1796, merely to post a notice on the church door.[1] But from 1762 each man had to be given notice of a call out for actual service in writing at his usual place of abode.[2] Despite the shortcomings of the old system of local government, this system seems to have worked well enough.

The royal order to embody the militia of a county for service was sent to the lord lieutenant, and as a rule he was allowed to decide where they were to assemble.[3] If he did his job properly, he had a busy time informing everyone required to take action. Acknowledging the orders for calling out in 1759, Lord Shaftesbury said that he had been writing all day and could scarcely see.[4] Lord Poulett on that occasion circularised the receiver general of the land tax, the company commanders and the adjutants and battalion clerks of the two

[1] The acts of 1796 and 1802 prescribed notice to each man in writing. 30 Geo. II, cap. 25, s. 27. 2 Geo. III, cap. 20, s. 103. 26 Geo. III, cap. 107, s. 69. 42 Geo. III, cap. 90, s. 129. 37 Geo. III, cap. 3, s. 27.

[2] 2 Geo. III, cap. 20, s. 116. 26 Geo. III, cap. 107, s. 98. 37 Geo. III, cap. 3, ss. 32, 35. 42 Geo. III, cap. 90, s. 114. 30 Geo. II, cap. 25, s. 45 lays down no method. From 1786 the king had to summon parliament if it was not sitting when he called out the militia. Before then it was optional. 30 Geo. II, cap. 25, s. 46. 2 Geo. III, cap. 20, s. 117. 26 Geo. III, cap. 107, s. 97. 37 Geo. III, cap. 3, s. 34. 42 Geo. III, cap. 90, s. 113.

[3] WO. 4/758, pp. 180–3. WO. 4/762, pp. 6, 7. But cf. the orders for 1759–60 in WO. 4/757–8, where the place of assembly is laid down.

[4] WO. 1/980, f. 521.

Somerset battalions.[1] Because the militia was still so inexperienced in 1759, the government sent a regular officer to each regiment, to show the officers how it should be run.[2] This help was generally very welcome,[3] although Lord Poulett felt obliged to decline it at the outset in Somerset because he thought it might lead the men to fear that they would be forced into the army.[4] In Lincolnshire, Lord Scarborough suggested an officer for this duty who was a native of the county.[5] In 1778 the militia was considered experienced enough to manage without help of this kind, and a regular officer was not sent unless one was asked for.[6] All the corps were reviewed soon after embodiment, to find out how proficient they were.[7]

The inexperience of the first regiments called out in 1759 led them at once into trouble because they did not know how to collect their pay. At first they were not told officially of the need to appoint an agent.[8] The Duke of Bedford failed to appoint one to his Devonshire regiment. The local receiver general was willing to advance money, but this was not allowed. There was a small mutiny through want of pay before things were put right.[9] Poulett reported almost at once a serious want of pay and asked to be allowed to draw on the receiver general.[10] Pay was issued to the agents as from the date of the order for embodiment, but the men were supposed to be paid only from the date of their leaving their homes. Unfortunately, it was only from November 1759 that regiments were told this on embodiment.[11] In Somerset the captains had paid their men from the earlier date and stood to lose about £20 each. The men seem to have expected pay only from when they actually left home, two days before assembling, but the paymaster had indiscreetly revealed how much money was in the agent's hands.[12] In Essex, too, there was danger of hardship. The men had only just been dismissed from training when they were called out, many had left for winter work outside the county and had the expense of a return journey. Many, too, had been induced to train daily when the call-out order first became known, in the ex-

---

[1] *Ibid.*, ff. 159-60.

[2] See call-out orders in WO. 4/757-8.

[3] See WO. 1/979, C. Duroure, 6 July; W. Aston, 6 October, 5 and 15 November; H. Holmes, 11 November 1759. Cf. WO. 1/980, ff. 245, 246, 381, 540.

[4] WO. 1/980, ff. 163-4, 173-4, 187-8.

[5] WO. 1/980, ff. 607-8.

[6] WO. 4/762, pp. 10-11.   [7] *Ibid.*, pp. 63-4, 70-1.

[8] See, however, WO. 4/757, pp. 133, 185-8.

[9] WO. 1/979, C. Duroure, 19 and 22 July; J. Duke, 17 July 1759. WO. 1/980, ff. 167, 203, 775. WO. 1/978, f. 531.

[10] WO. 1/978, ff. 533-4, 536. Cf. PRO. 30/8, vol. 53, f. 121.

[11] See WO. 4/757, pp. 296-300.

[12] WO. 1/980, ff. 199, 202, 209-10. Cf. other cases, ff. 195-6, 381. Dorset (f.517) got it right.

pectation of pay.[1] The Secretary at War was prepared to count time away from home before marching as part of the march, but for the rest referred the officers to the Attorney and Solicitor General or parliament.[2] The friends of the militia pressed the point with the Treasury that winter[3] and the pay act of 1760 finally established that men were to be paid from the date of the warrant for embodiment.[4]

From 1786 the system of mobilisation and the way it was used grew increasingly complicated. The decision to train only two-thirds of the men in peacetime made it necessary to have a means of choosing those to be trained. In 1786 it was decided to do this by assembling all the men enrolled to serve and selecting two-thirds of the number by ballot. These then received training each year. The others were simply sent home, but could be used to fill vacancies occurring among the trainees and might themselves volunteer to replace men upon whom the lot had fallen.[5] In 1792 the government applied this principle in mobilisation. At first only the counties on or near the south or east coasts were called on for men,[6] and they were called on only for those that had been trained. Later the rest were called out,[7] and also the men of the remaining counties, the government gradually working westward across the country to Wales.[8] The calling out of the supplementary militia in 1798 followed the same pattern. A special act was passed requiring all the men to assemble, whereupon half of them were to be chosen by ballot for embodiment.[9] Again the rest were called out soon afterwards, in April.[10] In 1799 the militia was reduced to its former strength, but the men then released were recalled in 1801. The act of 1802, with its arrangement of classes already described, facilitated the calling out and dismissal of the militia a part at a time.[11]

Among the problems encountered in the later mobilisations was that of men's time expiring just as they were called out. In 1778 such men still had an absolute right to discharge, and nothing could

[1] WO. 1/978, ff. 63–4. They left the county to teach agricultural skills. Cf. Hertfordshire, WO. 1/980, ff. 595–6; WO. 4/757, p. 303.

[2] WO. 1/978, f. 66. WO. 1/980, ff. 213–15. WO. 4/758, pp. 20–1.

[3] BM, Add. 33047, f. 336.

[4] 33 Geo. II, cap. 24, s. 15.

[5] 26 Geo. III, cap. 107, ss. 69–77.   [6] HO. 51/8, pp. 148, 157.

[7] *Ibid.*, p. 176.

[8] HO. 51/8, *passim.* Mobilisation took from December 1792 to May 1793.

[9] Again men might volunteer in place of those on whom the lot fell. 38 Geo. III, cap. 18, ss. 1, 2, 4, 5, 7–9, 11, 14. Those who were chosen were to be kept at the rendezvous for some days while efforts were made to make them volunteer for the line: HO. 50/31, draft circulars of January 1798.

[10] WO. 6/188, pp. 1–9. Sanctioned by 38 Geo. III, cap. 18, ss. 15–16.

[11] Above, p. 290. If a fraction of a class was required for service the ballot was used. 42 Geo. III, cap. 90, ss. 129–41.

be done beyond asking them to stay.[1] In 1792–3 they might in theory have been made to serve, but in fact the lieutenancies were allowed to do as they pleased.[2] The Buckinghamshire regiment was invited to re-enlist, but those who declined were replaced by a ballot.[3] In Lincolnshire there was a complaint that men who had failed to appear had been replaced by ballot, but those who had come had been made to serve.[4] The system of training only two-thirds of the force introduced in 1786 seems to have impeded mobilisation because in practice only two-thirds of the proper number of men seems to have been raised. The establishment of NCOs had, moreover, been proportionately reduced, and had now to be re-expanded. This took time, and meanwhile efficiency suffered.[5]

In 1798 and 1801 the task was mainly to collect men in their own county and send them to join an existing county unit stationed, as a rule, a fair way away. Sir David Dundas, the Quartermaster General had originally proposed that a third of the supplementary militia be embodied for some months, then be replaced by another third and so on. But he stressed the difficulties of moving 20,000 men about the country in all directions at once and this plan was never tried.[6] The work to be done in calling out half the force under the special act of 1798 was very complicated, though the government tried to make it easier by sending out both advance instructions and copies of the proposed bill.[7] An amending bill had to be passed immediately after the first one, to give ten days more for executing it.[8] There was a shortage of officers and NCOs to take charge of the men. This meant among other things that they had to march in larger bodies than was customary, to the inconvenience of the towns where they were billeted.[9] Such of the men as were formed into entirely new regiments were the worst provided for. Their needs were met in part by sending NCOs and suitable privates from the existing regiments to be NCOs in the new ones.[10] This problem did not exist on the recall in 1801 of the men let out in 1799. Officers and NCOs additional to the reduced

---

[1] See WO. 34/144, ff. 212–13, 221, 228, 230, 234; WO. 34/145, f. 343. The militia was asked not to claim men who had joined the army, WO. 4/762, pp. 36–7.

[2] WO. 4/774, p. 54.

[3] HO. 50/19, Marquess of Buckingham, 13 January 1793. HO. 51/8, pp. 195–6.

[4] HO. 50/20, Anon., 12 May 1793.

[5] BM, Add. 33108, f. 93. 26 Geo. III, cap. 107, s. 64; cf. BM, Add. 35663, f. 68. But Fortescue is quite wrong in implying (*History*, vol. iv, p. 83) that the militia had to be raised again from scratch.

[6] HO. 50/31, three papers, the last dated 3 December 1797.

[7] HO. 50/313, draft circular of February 1798; cf. HO. 50/31, Sir D. Dundas, 26 January 1798.

[8] 38 Geo. III, cap. 19.   [9] WO. 4/775, p. 135.

[10] Recruits from the new regiments were given in exchange. HO. 50/31, Sir W. Fawcett, 22 and 26 February; R. Brownrigg, 24 February 1798.

establishment of 1799 had been retained in service and others, pensioned off, were now recalled. It was easy for each regiment to send a party to its county to collect its men.[1] These, however, might have melted away and ceased to be within reach of the county authorities. In Lancashire and perhaps elsewhere, it was necessary to ballot for new men to replace those in reserve who could not be found.[2]

Disembodiment was a much simpler and smoother affair than calling the men out, especially because it could all be done by the regiment without the aid of the lieutenancy. Normally each regiment was marched to its own county, and the men were then sent off with fourteen days' pay and the clothes they stood up in. They were forbidden to travel armed or in parties of more than three. They had to be accounted with for all their pay and allowances before they left. The arms had to be placed in store in the manner provided by the militia acts.[3] This all seems to have been done without excessive trouble, though in 1762 the Cumberland militia was demobilised in error before the official order arrived,[4] while in Somerset both officers and men departed so precipitately that it was hard to get the accounts settled.[5] In 1799 the partial demobilisation brought problems of its own. It will be recalled that it took place in conjunction with enlistment for the army and was done in two phases: the county quotas were reduced by a quarter in July, and the new quotas were reduced by three-fifths in October. On the first occasion the government asked that men who were unfit or had large families be chosen for discharge and these were not subject to recall.[6] In October the men let out were subject to recall, and so it was laid down that the volunteers raised for the augmentation of 1794 were to be retained. These could not legally have been ordered to rejoin.[7]

In the larger counties with several regiments—some of which now

---

[1] No new corps had to be formed. Existing companies were augmented to eighty rank and file, and new ones formed where necessary. WO. 6/193, pp. 356–7. Cf. WO. 4/778, pp. 1–4; above, p. 326, and below, p. 377.

[2] The law officers seem to have thought that this was legal only to replace men lost after re-embodiment. Disembodied men were liable to be balloted to fill vacancies among those still serving. WO. 6/189, pp. 218–19, 262–5, 287–8. Lancashire R.O., Derby muniments, DDK. 1741, no. 5.

[3] For 1762, WO. 4/761, pp. 273–6. For 1783, WO. 4/768, pp. 350–2. For 1802, WO. 4/778, pp. 488–90; WO. 4/779, pp. 17–26. Cf. above, p. 358. The men were allowed to keep their knapsacks. In 1802 supernumerary NCOs and drummers and those not entirely fit were directed to be discharged.

[4] *Calendar of Home Office Papers, 1760–5*, pp. 212, 260, 262, 264, 266, 289; cf. p. 205.

[5] WO. 1/985, ff. 679–83.

[6] WO. 6/188, p. 222. Cf. above, p. 290.

[7] WO. 4/776, pp. 310–11, 316–19, 325. It is not clear whether men of the 'old' militia who had served five years could be made to rejoin. BM, Add. 33107, f. 294. Cf. 39 and 40 Geo. II, cap. 1, s. 18.

ceased to exist—the lord lieutenant had to co-ordinate the work. This was a harassing task. In Lancashire Lord Derby feared in the earlier reduction that too many men would be discharged through lack of co-ordination and that the county would refuse to fill the deficit.[1] On the second occasion two of his regiments were disbanded, and he ordered them to send equal numbers of their men to each of the other three regiments. The men to be let out were chosen from these aggregates.[2] This was to make sure that each regiment got its fair share of good men but even so, one regiment complained. Accordingly the men sent to another regiment were marched to it, having already participated in one disbandment.[3] Lord Fitzwilliam decided to adopt Derby's plan in the West Riding, and also to disband family men first and then men serving as principals. The rest were to be chosen by lot.[4]

The gratuities to the men were much as on other occasions but there was a new departure in the provision for officers. NCOs and second adjutants rendered supernumerary might be kept on or pensioned. Other supernumerary staff officers who were also subalterns might be kept on in that capacity. A certain number of the field officers, captains and subalterns rendered supernumerary also might be kept on. Captains and subalterns who were not kept were given a gratuity of six months' pay and field officers might in exceptional cases be given the same. It was left to the lord lieutenant and commanding officer to recommend what officers and NCOs were to be kept or pensioned.[5] As already noted, these rewards and bounties were essentially a recompense to the officers for helping in the recruitment of the army from the militia. But they did serve to make remobilisation easier,[6] and perhaps that is why something similar was done on demobilisation in 1802. Subalterns and staff officers then received a gratuity of two months' pay.[7]

II

When embodied, a militia corps might find itself stationed in quarters, in barracks or in camp. The last two the militia entered as a rule only when embodied for actual service. The purpose of the camps was to concentrate troops in large bodies, both to make their

[1] HO. 50/35, Lord Derby, 25 August 1799.
[2] *Ibid.*, Lord Derby, 13 and 15 November 1799, Rawstorne, pp. 192–3.
[3] HO. 50/35, Lord Derby, endorsed December 1799. Rawstorne, pp. 196–7.
[4] WO. 6/189, pp. 6–9, 28–9.
[5] When a regiment's complement of field officers was reduced, those remaining retained their existing rank, but sometimes had only the pay of a lower one. WO. 4/776, pp. 310–29. Cf. above, p. 326.
[6] Cf. above, pp. 234, 376.
[7] Adjutants, one month. WO. 4/779, p. 17.

training more efficient and so that they should be ready to oppose invasions. Camps assembled in the spring and dispersed in the autumn (when the weather became too bad for invasion to be attempted). The biggest concentration of troops was naturally round London, and the most important camp sites were Coxheath near Maidstone, Danbury near Chelmsford and Warley near Brentwood. Forces posted here blocked the two main routes, through Kent and Essex, by which an enemy might be expected to approach the capital.[1] Other camps were mostly found near important naval bases and ports—Plymouth, Yarmouth, the Tyne.[2] Barracks, too, were mostly found in such places, often in conjunction either with fortifications or with depots for prisoners of war. A few of the last, with barracks attached were however inland—at Winchester and later at Norman Cross. In camp or barracks a regiment was often under a good deal of supervision. The militia acts empowered the king to put the militia, when embodied for service, under the command of general officers.[3] At important bases like Plymouth and Portsmouth there was normally a general in command of the garrison, while a camp was almost always under the command of a general officer with quite a large staff.[4] Elsewhere in wartime the militia was usually subject to the command of the general officers commanding the military districts into which it was customary to divide the country.[5] But regiments in quarters were left very much to their own devices, their strongest link with higher authority being usually the correspondence (mainly financial) with the Secretary at War.

It was in quarters that a militia corps was most commonly to be found. They were provided by the compulsory billeting of the troops in public houses and other 'licensed premises'. The procedure was laid down in the mutiny acts, which the militia acts extended in this instance to cover the militia's peacetime training. During embodiment, the militia received from the Secretary at War the marching orders which told them where to go. On the production of the order, the mayor or constable or other chief officer of each place to which

[1] In 1761 Charles Townshend showed Newdigate a plan for 27,000 men to be stationed round the capital. Newdigate's diary, 28 July 1761.

[2] See, e.g., lists at BM, Add. 35661, f. 147; Add. 35662, f. 24.

[3] 30 Geo. II, cap. 25, s. 45. 2 Geo. III, cap. 20, s. 116. 26 Geo. III, cap. 107, s. 95. 42 Geo. III, cap. 90, s. 111.

[4] Anything from one to three general officers if the camp was large. In 1779 camp commandants had two ADCs and other generals on this service one. Regimental officers were appointed majors of brigade. WO. 3/26, pp. 2, 3, 27–8; cf. pp. 47–9.

[5] See, e.g., orders for returns to them in BM, Add. 35664, f. 304; Add. 35665, f. 146.

troops were sent had to allocate them among the houses obliged to receive them.[1]

This system gave rise to a constant altercation between the inn-keepers and the regiments in which the Secretary at War had to mediate. Their interests were diametrically opposed. The innkeepers wanted the troops to be spread as thinly as possible. Commanding officers wanted concentration. This made it easier to train the men, and was especially important when they were newly embodied. In 1759 Sir John Cust's Lincolnshire batallion was sent to Manchester, Stockport, Macclesfield and Knutsford. Some men were later sent on to Warrington when he found that they were having to sleep three or four in a bed. His regiment was therefore unable to train together, and he would have preferred them all to have been sent to Chester.[2] The Berkshire militia had been destined for Marlborough and Devizes. but Sir Willoughby Aston was so eager to drill them together for a little that on his own authority he put them all in the latter town for a few days, and managed to induce both the men and the townspeople on whom they were billeted to support this inconvenience.[3] In December 1778 Lord Cranborne was faced with the problem of training a Hertfordshire corps newly re-raised on the expiry of the previous men's time and now dispersed in eight different places in Kent, which threatened to become twelve. He pleaded for concentration in four and said that as things were, the officers could not even keep order and prevent 'moroding'.[4] The quarters of the West Middlesex were ordered to be enlarged at this time, and the colonel protested that already they were so dispersed that he could not be responsible for their discipline and 'oeconomy'. Thirty-two men were absent with leave because there were no quarters for them, forty could not be given medical care and one detachment had to march three or four miles each time there was a parade.[5]

Set against such complaints were the pleas of overburdened inn-keepers. The indigent publicans of Beverley were saddled with the Cumberlands and others beside in May 1780. Some houses had as many as thirty-six men. The mayor thought three companies should be moved, and suggested quarters for four within a day's march.[6] King's Lynn in November 1781 wanted the removal of one of its four companies of Huntingdonshire militia. The depression of trade and the increase of poor rates due to the pressing of seamen was said

[1] A J.P. could be appealed to when a chief officer was recalcitrant. See, e.g., 37 Geo. III, cap. 33, s. 31. Cf. 30 Geo. II, cap. 25, s. 48; 2 Geo. III, cap. 20, s. 100; 26 Geo. III, cap. 107, s. 78; 42 Geo. III, cap. 90, s. 94.

[2] WO. 1/979, Sir J. Cust, 1 and 8 December 1759.

[3] WO. 1/979, Sir W. Aston, 14, 15 and 29 September 1759.

[4] WO. 1/1000, Lord Cranborne, 9, 10 and 14 November 1778, and enclosures.

[5] *Ibid.*, G. J. Cooke, 2 December 1778.   [6] WO. 1/1008, ff. 1167–8.

to be causing houses to shut. The commanding officer retorted that there were seventy-one houses for 280 men, and many towns of the same size had three times the burden.[1] Some places on the main lines of communication were perpetually overcrowded. Doncaster had many troops passing through along the Great North Road and so objected when five companies of militia were put there. Fifty houses were available for them but twelve were very small and the larger houses had each to have nine officers and twenty-three men.[2]

The cases of particular individuals often seem very hard. In 1780 the principal inn in Whitehaven had so many men put in it that the landlord had to hire lodgings elsewhere for them. He would otherwise have had no room for ordinary guests. The cost was equal to his rent in the previous year.[3] Two small alehouses in Gatton, whose normal burden was two men, suddenly found themselves each with seven soldiers and their wives.[4] The Chequers, Maresfield, Sussex, had its complement doubled in January 1780, owing to the bankruptcy of another inn and the discovery that a third was technically not in a place on the route of the Shropshire company concerned. The landlord had to turn away ordinary customers and even hire accommodation for some of his family when they were all at home.[5]

The temporary removal of troops was requested on some occasions. An act of 1735 had made it obligatory during parliamentary elections, and it was always done during the assizes.[6] In April 1779 the publicans of Reigate said they could not accommodate the court and suitors at the ensuing quarter sessions unless the Middlesex militia was removed for four days and this was done.[7] In 1782 Guildford asked for the militia to be removed for the races, and Lord Temple requested the clearing of Newport Pagnell for a horse fair.[8]

In their complaints to the Secretary at War, the militia was assisted by the political influence which many of the senior officers had, while the innkeepers appealed to the local magistrates and MPs. These last often seem to have been remarkably conscientious in trying to do justice between the two sides. A Kentish justice, asking relief for his locality, said that he had been trying to keep the publicans quiet, but complaints were now so just and frequent that he had to do something for them.[9] William Baker, MP for Hertford, was appealed to in 1781 because the town had been given more than its fair share of the West Essex regiment. Before taking action he consulted the lieutenant-colonel, and then put forward what he took to

[1] WO. 1/1013, ff. 25–32.   [2] WO. 1/1008, f. 41.   [3] WO. 1/1009, f. 367.
[4] WO. 1/1016, Lord Newhaven, undated.   [5] WO. 1/1009, ff. 493–8.
[6] For the removal of militia units during elections see WO. 4/759, pp. 304–5.
[7] WO. 1/1006, f. 223.   [8] WO. 1/1017, ff. 341–6.
[9] WO. 1/1009, f. 1137.

be a fairer arrangement.[1] The Secretary at War seems likewise always to have done his best to be fair, and heard every complaint patiently. In 1780, and perhaps in other years, he tried to satisfy both sides by relieving the publicans as much as possible in the winter, and then bringing the troops closer together when the better weather came and there was more opportunity for training.[2]

The system of quartering gave rise to all sorts of unpleasant incidents between soldiers and civilians. Publicans tried to dodge their obligations. A party of the Glamorganshires, seeking billets after a hard march at Newport in Gloucestershire, were refused them because the publicans argued that the place was not explicitly mentioned in the route for the march. A prosecution took place, but the local justices refused to convict.[3] In 1779 the innkeepers of Stevenage, to keep their houses free for ordinary guests, hired empty houses for the troops that were very ill-supplied with beds and blankets. Some men had to sleep in stables on straw. In this case a justice was found who fined one innkeeper 40s. and threatened to take away his licence. He said that the trouble had been caused by the activity of seditious lawyers.[4] The presence of the troops might be irksome to others than their hosts. Two inhabitants of Sunderland were annoyed by a sentry box placed outside the lodgings of Major Cooper of the Cumberlands. They assaulted the sentry and successfully indicted the Major for a nuisance, though they did not contest his appeal.[5] The Herefordshires gave offence at Penryn by parading in the street in front of the church, which was the place which had customarily been used by the local Volunteers.[6]

Occasionally hostility resulted in actual fighting. The annual peace-time exercise of the Cambridgeshires in May 1774 ended with a riot in the county town. On Friday the 27th Lord Montfort, the commanding officer, went to a parade on Market Hill to give orders for the handing in of arms and uniforms. By his own account, some members of the university who had vainly tried to put him in the wrong were determined to insult him. A crowd of them collected round him on the Hill, isolating him from his own men. He ordered these to come over to him, but on coming into contact with the crowd they halted in confusion. Montfort was knocked down in the gutter several times, whereat some of the bystanders urged the soldiers to protect him. A fight accordingly began and soon the whole regiment, except the grenadiers, ran on the crowd. Some used the butts of their muskets and some at least fixed bayonets. They chased the crowd down Pump Lane towards St Mary's and inflicted several casualties. Lord Montfort was accused of various outrages during

[1] WO. 1/1010, ff. 201–4.   [2] WO. 4/765, p. 332.   [3] WO. 1/1008, ff. 49–60.
[4] WO. 1/1009, ff. 505–7.   [5] WO. 34/155, ff. 351–2.   [6] WO. 34/138, ff. 257–8.

the pursuit: he had urinated on a scholar of Emmanuel; to someone complaining of being seized by the throat he had said 'what of that? Do you look on yourself as a gentleman?' At length Montfort dismissed his men and told the guard to keep their door locked. Next day the Vice-Chancellor ordered all college gates to be shut and got Montfort to dismiss the regiment at once instead of on Monday as planned.[1] Thus ended what was really a glorified town and gown riot, for Montfort, as already explained, was not only a preposterous individual, but was also closely connected with the corporation.[2]

Despite much friction, it is remarkable how often the relations between troops and townspeople were cordial. The people of Norwich were very satisfied with the Cambridgeshires in November 1795, though significantly declaring that they had never seen the like before. This was the more remarkable as the town was reputed to be seditious,[3] and Adjutant Wale was consequently inclined to wish that the men were less 'peaceably inclined' towards the inhabitants.[4] But there the troops were in barracks. It is more noteworthy that the Cambridgeshires received the thanks of the corporation of Huntingdon in May 1794 for their good behaviour in quarters during the winter.[5] Of course, well-behaved troops might be welcome as a means of keeping out others who were not. The mayor of King's Lynn was anxious in 1780 to get back some of the East Essex who had behaved well there the previous winter.[6] Lord Shaftesbury in 1763 said that Dorchester and Forthington would hold more militia (for the peacetime exercise) than they would regulars: the militia were paid better and spent more.[7]

But as the size of the land forces increased, the burden on the publicans became intolerable, particularly in coastal counties like Kent and Sussex, where troops had to be massed to face invasion. Publicans began to go on strike, taking down their signs and giving up their licences. In July 1793 the arrival of the Surrey militia led to a strike of all the publicans round Rye and Winchelsea. The mayor and inhabitants of Rye found temporary quarters for the men, but the government was much alarmed and the Prime Minister himself took note of the affair. The mayor of Rye was told that it would endanger national security if the innkeepers escaped unpunished and they should not be allowed to renew their licences. It was pointed out that a good many barracks had been built in the area to lessen the burden of billeting as much as possible.[8] The magistrates were duly

[1] BM, Add. 35659, ff. 132, 135, 137, 140, 142, 148. This account is based on evidence from both sides, which seems to tally quite well.
[2] Above, pp. 312–3, 328.   [3] BM, Add. 35666, ff. 190, 205, 210.
[4] Ibid., f. 199.   [5] BM, Add. 35664, f. 339.   [6] WO. 1/1007, f. 73.
[7] WO. 1/981, Lord Shaftesbury, 22 April 1763.
[8] WO. 4/771, pp. 263–7, 278–80.

severe, but the publicans humbly admitted themselves in the wrong and their licences were then restored.[1] There had already been incidents of this kind in the area in 1779–80,[2] and there were others in the course of 1793–4.[3] Nor were they unknown elsewhere.[4] At length, in 1794, the government empowered commanding officers, when they found the licensed houses overcrowded, to hire barns or other accommodation and to pay the publicans a reasonable price for the provisions which they were obliged to furnish under the mutiny act.[5] It was about this time that there began an extensive building of barracks which eventually superseded the use of quarters.[6]

The earliest barracks cannot as a rule have been regarded by the troops as an improvement on billets. Those in Winchester in the American war were in two parts of the town about a mile apart. Hyde Barracks comprised mainly an old malt house, divided into three stories of which the lowest was only 5 ft. 9 in. high and had no floor but the bare earth, full of holes and often muddy. The middle storey had an even lower ceiling and the top one was a mere loft, stifling in summer and very cold in winter. It was intersected by beams $2\frac{1}{2}$ ft. above the floor which were precariously crossed by step-ladders. The staircases were outside and were slippery and dirty in wet weather. The drainage was bad, and the cooking had to be done in the dormitories. The men slept two to a bed,[7] and the beds were packed so tight that it was often impossible to make them. A surgeon in 1779 thought things might be made better by fitting ventilators and windows that opened. But the Duke of Richmond thought in 1781 that two of the three stories should be virtually done away with. Kingsgate the other barrack was simply some disconnected buildings in a street. In the officers' quarters in 1779 subalterns and staff officers (except the surgeon) were two to a room. Sergeants enjoyed the distinction of a bed each.[8]

Sometimes it was the situation of the barracks that was at fault. Hilsea Barracks at Portsmouth were a veritable deathtrap. They were low-lying and surrounded by salt springs.[9] In 1779 stagnant

---

[1] *Ibid.*, pp. 297, 314.

[2] WO. 34/120, f. 148. WO. 34/121, f. 38. WO. 1/1009, f. 1096.

[3] WO. 4/771, pp. 491–4. WO. 4/772, pp. 1, 2, 4–8, 40, 57, 484–5, 492–4, 499, 500. WO. 4/773, pp. 63–4.

[4] E.g. WO. 1/1007, ff. 1047–50; WO. 1/1008, f. 81.

[5] WO. 4/772, pp. 477–8. WO. 4/773, pp. 17–19, 24, 229–31, 245. Cf. the refusal of relief to publicans claiming it as of right, pp. 45, 47, 56.

[6] Fortescue, *History*, vol. iv, pp. 903–7.

[7] Cf. three to a bed in 1796: William Salt Library, Stafford, SMS. 478, E. Disbrowe, 6 November 1796.

[8] WO. 34/134, ff. 101–3, 109. WO. 34/116, ff. 77–80. Cf. WO. 34/153 (i), ff. 167–8, 298–9.

[9] PRO. 30/8, vol. 19, f. 63.

water covered most of one side of the buildings and only one of the two pumps produced water fit to drink. It was said that better drains would make the place healthy, but a government surgeon admitted that everyone thereabouts was subject to intermittent fevers.[1] Here, too, subalterns often had to 'double up', and in 1780 this irritated those of the Berkshires almost to the point of resignation.[2] There was a long history of militia discontent with Hilsea. Lord Orford's Norfolk regiment was sent there on its first call-out in 1759. It found the place infected with smallpox. Fresh from isolated villages, the men readily succumbed to it and were soon a prey also to dysentery and typhus. Casualties were severe and convalescence long for those who did not die. Orford said afterwards that no other regiment would endure Hilsea so long[3] and he was not far wrong. The Warwickshires succeeded the Norfolks in October 1759. To protect them from infection, the barracks were whitewashed, the bedding cleaned and tarred rope burned in every room. Colonel Lord Denbigh, however, insisted on completely fresh bedding, and it was also agreed that all the Norfolk men should be got out before their successors arrived. Unfortunately, most of the Warwickshires had moved in before these conditions were complied with, and a case of smallpox appeared almost at once. Denbigh (who was a friend of Barrington, the Secretary at War) got the regiment taken away again.[4] The Wiltshires in the following year also sought to avoid Hilsea while in 1779 the desire of the Cornish to leave Portsmouth was put down to a fear of being sent there.[5]

There was a barrack master in charge of each barracks, whose business it was to keep the buildings in good repair and properly furnished. He also had to supply coal and candles for heating, cooking and lighting. In 1792 the coal ration was $1\frac{3}{4}$ to $3\frac{1}{4}$ bushels a week per twelve men according to the season, and the corresponding candle ration $\frac{3}{4}$ to $1\frac{1}{4}$ lb. There was an extra allowance for guardrooms during the winter months. Each man was issued with a spoon, a small bowl and a trencher (of wood), and there was also supposed to be a supply of cooking utensils.[6] But quite often the barrack master

[1] WO. 34/157, f. 133.   [2] WO. 34/166, ff. 11–12.

[3] WO. 1/980, ff. 85, 89–92, 793–6. PRO. 30/8, vol. 68, f. 15. WO. 4/757, p. 214. The flux and putrid fever were what the men were said to have.

[4] When they had first been told they were going there, there had been cries of 'no barracks'. Newdigate's diary, 6–21 October 1759. WO. 1/979, Lord Denbigh, 7, 17, 19, 20 and 22 October, and H. Holmes, 22 October 1759. WO. 1/980, ff. 575–6. WO. 4/757, pp. 215–16, 235–7, 259–62.

[5] PRO. 30/8, vol. 19, f. 63. WO. 34/156 (ii), ff. 527–8. Cf. WO. 34/120, ff. 150–1; WO. 34/121, ff. 39, 40.

[6] There was a candlestick, bellows, etc., per twelve men. Certain Rules, pp. 29, 30; cf. WO. 4/771, pp. 318–20, and BM, Add. 33059, ff. 214, 239–40. The last reference shows the beds furnished with bolsters, blankets and rugs. In the Ameri-

failed in his duty. Regiments had themselves to supply coal, candles and utensils,[1] and even get buildings repaired.[2] On the other hand they, too, were often at fault, and incurred large bills for breakages.[3]

Barracks, all in all, do not seem to have been popular. They were made less attractive still by their association with the task of guarding prisoners of war. In 1759 General Holmes, commanding at Portsmouth, attributed the fuss about Hilsea made by the Warwickshires to their desire for an excuse to escape guard duty.[4] The Buckinghamshires were very irked by their stay in Portsmouth in 1795–6, and the Marquess of Buckingham objected strongly when it was proposed to send them to a similar station in Bristol. In 1800 when they were ordered to the great prison camp at Norman Cross, he lamented their being sent to the worst quarter, the unhealthiest place and the heaviest duty in England.[5]

In the warmer months, the sending of troops to camp provided a further alternative to quartering them. A suitable piece of ground had first to be secured, and this was commonly done by the General locally in command, who would strike a bargain with its owner.[6] Next, the ground plan of the camp had to be laid out. When the Warwickshires camped at Warley in 1761, Major Newdigate brought the first division to the neighbouring town of Brentwood and then conferred on the site with Captain Brown, a Deputy Quartermaster General, who had made a rough plan. Next day the lines were paced and measured, and the 'streets' in which the tents were to stand were accurately plotted. Enough progress was made to allow the first division to camp, leaving the town free for the rest of the regiment, who then camped the next day.[7] Pioneers and tools[8] had usually to be supplied by the regiments for preparing the ground. In 1794 each regiment going to Danbury had to send a subaltern and thirty men, making 120 men in all.[9]

The normal issue of tents by the government was one for the sergeants of each company, one for the quarter- and rear-guard of

---

can war the ration per company of sixty was from 12½ to 20 bushels of coal, and from 5 to 7½ lb. of candles a week. WO. 4/767, pp. 152–3.

[1] WO. 4/771, pp. 318–20; cf. pp. 36–7, 74.

[2] Ibid., p. 78. Cf. BM, Add. 35665, ff. 147, 152, 157.

[3] The Sussex at Rumsey, November 1795–June 1796: £79. 3s. 9d. BM, Add. 33059, ff. 214, 239–40.

[4] WO. 1/979, H. Holmes, 22 October 1759.

[5] BM, Add. 41851, ff. 45–6, 173–4; Add. 42058, ff. 46–7.

[6] See, e.g., WO. 34/164, ff. 107–8; WO. 34/123, ff. 8–10; WO. 34/124, ff. 248–52.

[7] Newdigate's diary, 30–1 July, and 1 August 1761.

[8] In 1793 Trotter's supplied a hatchet, saw, leather apron and cap for £2 the set. BM, Add. 35663, f. 128.

[9] But one regiment had their ground prepared for them. BM, Add. 35665, f. 208. Cf. Add. 35666, f. 78.

each company, and one for every five men of the corporals, drummers and privates.[1] These tents were of the oblong sort with a pole along the ridge.[2] They were not entirely satisfactory. Thomas Pelham pointed out in 1795 that they were not the type used in foreign service and needed a great many carts to move them. Round tents, in which the men slept in hammocks, would be more portable and convenient.[3] In February 1797 it was laid down that troops actually marching against an enemy were to use round tents able to hold sixteen infantry or twelve cavalry. A regiment of foot was consequently expected to make do on active service with at most four wagons for its tents and four days' supply of bread.[4] Round tents seem to have been coming into use for ordinary camping as well.[5]

Other camping equipment, provided usually by the regiment,[6] included bell tents for storing the arms, camp colours, drum cases and powder bags. In 1793 each man had to have a wooden canteen with straps and a haversack; each tent a hatchet and a tin kettle in a bag.[7] Within the tents the men were normally expected to sleep on straw, but there was a growing tendency to give them blankets. It appears that in 1778 two blankets per tent were issued to start with and a third in the autumn when it got colder.[8] Issues in subsequent years followed the same pattern.[9] Regiments sometimes had to give up their blankets on leaving camp,[10] but sometimes they were allowed to keep them. In this way the West Kents acquired a stock of four blankets per tent: they received three in 1778 and two more in 1779, of which they later had to give back one.[11] Generals commanding camps had often to press for more blankets. In May 1781 Lord Adam Gordon said that they were indispensable, especially at his camp near Newcastle, because there was a local shortage of straw.[12] In

---

[1] WO. 4/764, p. 216. WO. 4/770, ff. 361–2. WO. 4/771, pp. 308–9.

[2] WO. 1/1015, Thos. Tydd, 30 March 1782 with list, enclosed in W. Haviland, 5 April. Cf. WO. 1/1011, return of camp equipage, 29 August 1781.

[3] BM, Add. 33120, ff. 13–15, 20. Cf. Add. 33048, f. 337.

[4] BM, Add. 35667, f. 279.

[5] WO. 4/772, pp. 246–7. Cf. WO. 4/775, p. 85.

[6] Above, p. 342. The allowance to the regiment for providing it was increased in 1793 because of rising prices, WO. 4/771, p. 285. For prices in 1778 see WO. 34/110, f. 140.

[7] In 1778 instead of the wooden canteen there had been a tin water-flask with strings. WO. 4/771, pp. 35–6. Cf. WO. 4/762, p. 177; WO. 34/110, f. 137.

[8] WO. 4/762, p. 177. Cf. WO. 4/764, p. 318.

[9] See WO. 4/765, pp. 136–7, 139–41, 184; WO. 4/767, pp. 248–54; WO. 3/26, p. 40.

[10] WO. 1/1011, P. Gill, 27 June 1781.

[11] WO. 1/1014, Memo. of 11 July 1782.

[12] He was sent extra blankets only in August. WO. 1/1011, ff. 121–4, 129–34, 153–8, 161–78, 186. Cf. the similar request in his letters of 14, 16 and 25 August 1782, in WO. 1/1015.

the next war there seems again to have been a blanket ration of three per tent,[1] but in 1795 it was decided to give every man two blankets to himself.[2] How the previous ration of two or three per tent had been shared out among five men is not clear.

When the camps broke up, tents and other equipment were stored until the regiment needed them again and the regiment made good any loss or damage.[3] In 1794 the troops were allowed to leave the camps standing, and the dismantling and packing was done by Trotter's.[4] The government replaced the tents when they wore out and the regiments were allowed to regard the old ones as their own property and use them for such purposes as enlarging the hospitals and housing the men's families.[5]

Officers normally provided their own tents, which were often large and elaborate.[6] Sir Roger Newdigate's tent in 1761 was floored with boards and equipped with a bureau, table and chairs. His wife followed him to camp, and so he also hired lodgings at Brentwood[7] and slept there a good deal; in spite of this he had a severe attack of rheumatism.[8] When Thomas Pelham camped in 1780, he set his family to work finding bed and table linen. He proposed to use a bed he had had in Spain and sent his father to look at a new sort of camp table and see if it was any use.[9] In October he kept out the cold by a good fire in his tent and a high straw hedge round its windward side to screen it from the weather.[10] The former seems to have been a common arrangement, although chimneys were virtuously avoided by Ward of the Cambridgeshires who said that they 'tendered' those using them.[11]

A camp, when everything had been got into order, was a very fine spectacle. In 1778 Coxheath stretched for $3\frac{1}{2}$ miles and held 15,000–17,000 troops. It was divided into two wings, with a regular regiment at each extremity. The tents were drawn up in a formation analogous to a regiment on parade. The front rank consisted of the tents of the quarter-guard, each regiment posting its guard in the centre of its

[1] WO. 4/773, p. 155.　　　　　　　[2] *Ibid.*, p. 227.
[3] See, e.g., WO. 1/1015, W. Haviland, 5 April and 19 March 1782, and enclosures; cf. his letter of 21 October 1781 in WO. 1/1011.
[4] WO. 3/28, pp. 64–5.
[5] See, e.g., BM, Add. 35664, f. 330 (but cf. f. 339); WO. 4/772, p. 279; WO. 4/774, p. 391. In 1783 what was in use was sometimes sold for the benefit of the public, WO. 4/768, pp. 357–60. Tents too worn to be any use were sometimes sold for the benefit of the regiments: 2128 fetched £106. 8s. at Maidstone in 1779. WO. 34/158, ff. 217–18.
[6] Cf. above, p. 362. In 1778 the government supplied some with horsemen's tents. WO. 4/762, p. 177.
[7] Newdigate's diary, 1, 3 and 5 August 1761.
[8] See *ibid.*, 13, 18–20 and 26 August.　　　[9] BM, Add. 33128, ff. 56–8.
[10] *Ibid.*, f. 68.　　　　　　　[11] BM, Add. 35660, f. 229.

portion of the line. Next came the privates' tents, fourteen deep, each company occupying a whole file from front to rear. Behind these were the officers' tents, or rather marquees. Each company had two: one for the captain and one for the two subalterns. The field officers, however, had their tents in yet another rank: those of each regiment were pitched together in the centre of its portion of the line, with the colonel's in the middle. This last often comprised two or three marquees one behind the other, each forming a room with floors and carpets and the whole surrounded by gravel walks. Behind all this again were wooden kitchens and temporary stables. Each regiment was separated from the next by a space in which stood two guns. Right at the rear were turf huts for wives and families, and all round the heath were the booths of sutlers—civilian tradesmen, many of whom had come down from London.[1]

Warley Camp in 1778 was rather less impressive. The common on which it stood was smaller than Coxheath, the ground was not level and it was covered with wood and furze, some of which had to be cleared. The 11,000 men there (nine militia and three regular regiments) had pitched their tents in two oblongs, set at an angle to each other. There was a separate park for the artillery. The tents were less regularly arranged, the marquees were only floored with turf, the booths were shabby. To make matters worse, the East Riding regiment complained of the want of provisions and looked half starved.[2] One of its officers said that Warley was damnation on earth.[3]

III

No less important than shelter for the men was the provision of food and medical care. Food was supplied either by publicans or by contract or by shopping in the ordinary retail market. Most of the cost in each case was met by the men from their pay. Troops on the march had by law to be fed by the persons with whom they were billeted, in return for a fixed payment which for infantry amounted to 1s. a day for an officer and 4d. for a ranker. When the troops were in quarters but not on the move, the publican had the option of providing them with food in the same way or supplying (without payment) candles, vinegar, salt, a fire, cooking and eating utensils, and up to five pints of small beer or cider per man per day. For the rest, the troops fended for themselves.[4] The publicans appear always

[1] BM, Add. 35659, f. 392. Cf. the plans, etc., in BM, Add. 15532–3.
[2] BM, Add. 35660, f. 4. These descriptions of the two camps come from an acquaintance of Lord Hardwicke who visited them.
[3] HMC, *Du Cane*, p. 239.
[4] See, e.g., 37 Geo. III, cap. 33, ss. 42–4.

to have opted for the latter system when they could,[1] and must indeed have found it very onerous to feed the troops at statutory rates in times of scarcity. From 1795 annual acts were passed for their relief, raising the statutory rates and providing payment for the articles hitherto supplied free instead of food.[2]

Contracting was naturally commonest in camps and barracks, where a large body concentrated in one place had to be supplied. For the camps, it was usual for the Treasury to make contracts for bread, fuel and forage.[3] In 1778 each camp had a Resident Commissary from the Treasury, assisted by one of the officers, to see to the supplies. The regiments sent in returns of how much bread was wanted and the Assistant Commissary told the contractor, who ordered it to be baked. After every fourth delivery the regimental quartermasters received money from the officers responsible for paying companies, and met the Assistant Commissary and the contractor to settle accounts. The bread ration in 1778 was a 6-lb. wholemeal wheat loaf every four days (or half that amount every two days) for which each man paid 5d. Servants and women were allowed to buy bread at the same price.[4] The men, however, disliked wholemeal bread, and in some camps they were therefore given a lighter loaf, from which some of the bran had been removed. In 1779 the Treasury proposed to do this everywhere, but eventually it was decided to keep the original weight and charge the men 4⅝d.[5]

The forage ration was 18 lb. of hay and 8 lb. of oats a day to each horse. This cost 6d., but infantry corps were given free rations for the number of horses they were allowed to have.[6] The ration of firewood in 1778 was 15 lb. a day per tent, normally delivered every four days. There was also an issue of straw for bedding every eight days. Two trusses of 36 lb. each were issued for each tent on the first occasion, one truss on the second and the third, then two on the

---

[1] They tended to refuse provisions to troops reaching the end of a march, arguing that they were then in quarters. Some Surrey officers refused provisions in Rochester in 1780 spoke of consulting the Speaker and Dunning (both eminent lawyers) on the state of the law. WO. 1/1009, ff. 531–2.

[2] 10d. for full board for a ranker, 2d. for articles in lieu (from 1800, 1s. 4d. and ½d.) per day. 35 Geo. III, cap. 64, ss. 1, 2. Cf. especially 39 and 40 Geo. III, cap. 39, ss. 1, 2.

[3] A draft advertisement for tenders in 1780 is at WO. 34/124, f. 150.

[4] There was a complicated system of returns designed to prevent fraud. Regimental returns were on honour. Contractors might charge for delivering bread. They were not to give money in lieu of goods, and regiments were to refuse to receive articles deficient in quality. WO. 3/26, ff. 3–15, cf. ff. 21–8.

[5] See further WO. 34/114, ff. 51, 64, 81. WO. 34/110, f. 187 looks very much as if it is the copy of the Treasury Minute there referred to, though it is dated 1778.

[6] In 1778, a colonel 11, a lieutenant-colonel 9, a major 7, a captain 5, a subaltern or staff officer 1; surgeons, 1 extra. Cf. chap. iv, p. 25.

fourth and so on.[1] Straw and firewood were also paid for by the government.[2] Many succumbed to the temptation of drawing more than they were entitled to. In 1779 the regulations were accordingly more detailed. General officers were to set an example by drawing forage for effective horses only. Officers who were commissaries were to have forage for one horse more than their normal entitlement, 'providing that horse doth exist'.[3] In spite of this, William Roy, the Deputy Quartermaster General, reported that there was even more overdrawing of forage rations in 1779 than in 1778. In June 1779 Lt.-Gen. Parker talked very seriously to the commanding officers of the four regular regiments under his command at Warley and hoped that a a result they would draw for effective numbers only.[4]

When the government took to paying for or subsidising the bread of the men in quarters and barracks, contracting was encouraged in order to keep down the cost. In 1779 commanding officers in barracks were told to invite tenders for bread of the same quality as that issued in camp and accept the lowest.[5] In 1800, with the idea of reducing the consumption of flour, the government itself made a large contract for supplying bread of camp quality to troops not in camp.[6] Until 1800, when they were given 1d. a day 'beer money' instead, men in barracks got a beer ration just as they did from their host in quarters. Sometimes the regiments contracted for this, sometimes the barrack authorities, the regiments supervising its issue.[7] From 1795 the government subsidised the soldier's meat and required part of the bread allowance to be spent on meat and vegetables (again to save flour).[8] The authorities were increasing their interference in provisioning.

But retail trading continued to meet most of the soldiers' needs. Proper contractors could not always be found. When the Oxfordshires invited tenders for bread at Dover in 1779, the baker who had hitherto supplied the garrison finally agreed to continue at 6d. a loaf, but would not enter into a contract lest prices rise.[9] When the Cambridgeshires reached Norwich in October 1795 they had great

---

[1] As p. 389, n. 4.

[2] In 1778 the items contracted for to supply the camps cost £83,046. 8s. 8¾d., of which the regiments paid £22,626. 13s. 3¼d. WO. 34/148, ff. 72–3.

[3] WO. 3/26, ff. 21–8.   [4] WO. 34/115, ff. 101–2. WO. 34/123, ff. 88–9.

[5] WO. 4/764, pp. 176–7.

[6] There were complaints about the quality of the bread: both that it was too good and that it was too bad. WO. 4/777, p. 160; cf. pp. 79, 104–5.

[7] At Yarmouth in 1795–6 each man got three pints a day; at Colchester five pints of small beer. There was much complaint of short measure. BM, Add. 33109, ff. 106–8. Add. 35667, ff. 27–9. Add. 35669, ff. 12–14, 42. For regimental contracts and 'beer money', Walrond, pp. 125, 180.

[8] WO. 4/773, p. 347–8. Cf. above, p. 368.

[9] WO. 1/1005, ff. 821–4. Cf. WO. 4/766, pp. 454, 498–9.

difficulty in settling with suppliers who were not extortionate. The cheapest meat that was at all good was 5d. a lb. in carcase, and this they had to take. Adjutant Wale complained that the butchers raised their prices whenever they saw soldiers. For bread they invited tenders from two local bakers and another who had supplied them in camp. But meanwhile the men supplied themselves and had a penny a day added to their pay. The sergeant-major was sent round the bakers to find out the level of prices. Eventually the regiment settled for a 6 lb. loaf at 1s., each man to receive one every four days and pay 6d.[1] When they briefly moved to Yarmouth they found things worse: 9d. for a 4 lb. loaf and meat at 5¼d. a lb. The South Lincoln-shires, stationed there, were allowing the men to buy their own meat, giving them 5d. a lb. with which to do so.[2] Earlier in the year the Nottinghams had secured permission to give their men cash instead of bread because the regiment was too dispersed to be supplied by contract.[3]

Even in camp, the role of contracting was limited. Official con-tractors were not always reliable. In August 1779 Lt.-Gen. Peirson found that the bread supplied at Coxheath was bad. The East Riding regiment found a third of each delivery unusable. A month later the camp was short of wood and straw and Peirson warned the contractor that the penalty provided in the contract would be levied.[4] Sometimes bulk buying by regiments supplemented the official contracts. Lord Orford seems to have supplied his Norfolk regiment when they camped by themselves under his command in 1779 and 1780. In 1779, 102 head of cattle were bought for £813. 12s. 2d. In 1780 the regiment got through 70 bullocks and 170 sheep in 20 weeks.[5] But retail buying was again the more usual supplement. Sometimes parties were sent to buy in a near-by market. On 29 October 1794, for instance, the Lancashires sent to Brighton, near which they were encamped, a large contingent comprising a captain, two subalterns, an NCO per company and two men per tent.[6] The privates might even be told to see that the sergeants bought food of the right quality and price.[7] In addition, the shopkeepers came to the camp. In 1781 Lt.-Gen. Haviland established a market for the camp at Roborough Down,

[1] BM, Add. 35666, ff. 195, 197, 199, 205.   [2] Ibid., f. 227.

[3] WO. 4/773, p. 197.   [4] WO. 34/118, f. 145. WO. 34/154, f. 306.

[5] The meat was sold to the men, but in 1779 the offal and the profit from the sale of hides and tallow were distributed among them to the value of £64. 9s. 3d., the quartermaster giving up his perquisites. WO. 34/124, ff. 115–17. WO. 34/127, ff. 151.

[6] Lancashire R.O., Captain Farrington's Order Book, 28 October 1794; cf. 31 October.

[7] William Salt Library, Stafford, 429 (i): Lord Bagot's Order Book, 26 April, 1799.

outside Plymouth, where plenty of beef, mutton, butter, milk and vegetables were available at reasonable prices. He thought that this would prevent marauding, and be better than sending parties to market because it was hard to keep these in order.[1] At Warley Camp in 1779 no less than 128 booths sprang up in the rear to supply ale, beer and spirits. There were also officially recognised sutlers' booths within the lines. It was suggested that there should be a system of licensing, operated by the camp commandant and local justices in conjunction, to keep down drunkenness.[2] In 1778 hawkers went round the camp crying beans, peas, cabbages, hot puddings and pies.[3] Sutlers were found in barracks as well, appointed by the barrack authorities to run a canteen. An order of 1797 gave these official sutlers a monopoly of sales in barracks and forbade tippling in the barrack rooms.[4]

Cooking the food was another mainly decentralised activity. The tenor of the barrack regulations was that men should be divided into messes of twelve, each of which had a fuel ration and implements with which to prepare the food.[5] In camp, arrangements were often similar. When the Northamptonshires camped at Dartford in 1780, the rule was established that a drum beat for dinner at noon. The men then brought the food which they had prepared into the 'streets' between the tents to be inspected by an officer. He had to report which tents were messing regularly and which were not messing.[6] Sometimes there was more centralisation. The Sussex militia fed its men in camp in 1796 on a scientific plan. Grates and some special boilers devised by Count Rumford[7] were bought and the regiment was divided into two groups of three companies, each with a boiler. Some of the men were trained as cooks and served in rotation, receiving 1s. for eight days' service, less fines for justified complaints. The pay sergeants of the companies took it in turns to have charge of the boiler and buy whatever the season would furnish in the way of vegetables. Besides the part of the bread allowance officially set aside for this, they spent whatever the commanding officer chose to make the men contribute. Meat was apparently bought in some other way, for the individual messes brought their

[1] WO. 34/135, ff. 243–6.

[2] The number of booths proved too great for the trade and many were abandoned. WO. 1/1009, ff. 807–9, 1343–50. It was customary for sutlers to sell ale without being required to have a licence. WO. 4/773, pp. 407–8.

[3] Holden, pp. 34–5.   [4] WO. 3/31, pp. 8, 9.

[5] Pot, frying-pan, gridiron, ladle, hooks, etc., and a new broom each month. WO. 4/771, pp. 318–20.

[6] Northamptonshire R.O., Brooke of Oakley MSS., B. 162, Captain Supple's Order Book, 16 July 1780.

[7] An American loyalist who ended in the service of Bavaria. See DNB.

shares to the boiler each in its own bag, and in these the meat was cooked. Each man had meat and vegetables at mid-day and a pint and a half of broth for supper. There was a very great saving of fuel.[1] Centralised cooking was found in barracks also: in 1796–7 the Cambridgeshires had from eight to sixteen men assigned to cooking.[2]

Officers were naturally freer to make their own arrangements about eating but they normally tried to have a mess, financed by subscription.[3] In quarters this would be organised by the inns where they were staying. At the peacetime exercises of the Cambridgeshires in 1788–92 the officers seem to have quartered and messed in two or three inns each time and handed over a subscription to the adjutant to pay for the whole. Captains gave the whole of the pay they received during the exercise, lieutenants a half and ensigns 2 guineas.[4] In camp the officers engaged a sutler.[5] When the Cambridgeshires camped outside Landguard Fort in 1795 they were lucky enough to be able to use the old canteen in the fort for a mess. Their sutler supplied a daily dinner with small beer for 1s. 6d. and port at 3s. a bottle. These items were covered by a subscription. A supper of cold meat, bread and cheese and beer was to be available for those who wanted it at a charge of 6d.; likewise breakfast at 8d. (eggs or cold meat 1s.) and dinner à la carte at an extra charge. The regiment provided cutlery, table linen and a good deal of kitchen equipment. Two rooms were in use, as mess and drawing-room, and there was a civilian waiter and a mess-man from the regiment.[6]

Preserving the health of the men, about which something must now be said, was a hard task. The worst problem was probably presented by newly embodied or re-recruited regiments, whose men often lacked resistance to common infections because they had spent their lives in isolated villages, little exposed to them. This was the case when the Norfolks were stricken in Hilsea in 1759.[7] In May 1779 the South Lincolnshires tried to avoid being sent to Poole, where putrid fever (i.e. typhus) had been introduced by the crew of a captured French ship. The surgeon of the corps stressed that his men were 'fresh' and therefore vulnerable.[8] In another case, the inhabitants of a place

---

[1] BM, Add. 33059, ff. 233–8, 248, cf. ff. 213–14.

[2] BM, Add. 35667, f. 9. Add. 35668, f. 18.

[3] See above, pp. 328, 332.

[4] BM, Add. 35662, ff. 234–5, 246, 279. Tolver complained in 1792 of improper charges such as a dinner drum which never sounded, and 'snaps' sent into the field but neither snapped nor seen. *Ibid.*, f. 285.

[5] Sutlers were apparently allowed rations of firewood and forage in proportion to the size and number of corps they served. WO. 3/26, pp. 8, 24–5.

[6] BM, Add. 35666, ff. 25, 80. Hardwicke ordered a large amount of cutlery and crockery for the mess in 1793. Apparently the officers helped to pay for it. BM, Add. 35663, f. 151.

[7] Above, p. 384.   [8] WO. 1/1002, Ben. Bromhead, 23 May 1779.

where smallpox was prevalent asked for the removal of a regiment, half of whose men had not had it, lest their presence make the epidemic worse.[1] But even a seasoned regiment might fear being sent to certain unhealthy places. The Cambridgeshires were disgusted at being sent to the Isle of Ely for the winter of 1781–2. Captain Bendishe reported that there had been so many deaths lately that the graveyard where he was looked like a mound of turned earth. He felt sure to die if he stayed and two men did die within a month. The men in general were sickly. The trouble seems to have been temporary, due to the dryness of the season.[2] When the corps went back there the following year the Fens were under water, and the commanding officer thought the place healthy and said that there were more old people there than anywhere else he knew.[3]

Camps were probably healthier than quarters, or barracks such as Hilsea, but the men's health suffered from the government's tendency to keep camps together till late in the year. On 14 November 1779 Lt.-Gen. Haviland reported from Plymouth that the hills were covered with snow, it had snowed, hailed and rained all day, the ground was wet and spongy and the tents rotten. The troops were very uncomfortable and the number of sick was increasing.[4] On the same day, Lt.-Gen. Parker reported from Warley that high winds and bad weather during the night had damaged the tents extensively. Cold and snow had made the camp so uncomfortable that he had ordered an extra truss of straw for each tent and he expected an increase of sickness.[5] In 1759 William Beckford complained to Pitt as early as 18 September that a man a day was falling sick in his Wiltshire regiment and a Secretary at War living comfortably at home seemed to have forgotten that they were lying on the cold ground. He twice renewed his complaint and urged that the undoubted benefit to regimental efficiency of hard duty should be generalised by rotation.[6]

As noticed already, each militia corps on embodiment was allowed to appoint a surgeon to care for its men.[7] He was provided with a chest of medicines by the Apothecary General.[8] Hospital expenses were originally paid by the captains out of the money from their 'contingent men',[9] but there was an allowance of £7. 10s. a month

[1] WO. 4/758, p. 81.
[2] BM, Add. 35661, ff. 127–8, 142–3; cf. ff. 132, 149, 152–5.
[3] BM, Add. 35662, f. 12. Cf. Add. 35661, f. 208.   [4] WO. 34/157, ff. 260–1.
[5] WO. 34/157, ff. 265–6. Another problem in camp was to find good drinking water. See WO. 34/133, f. 130; WO. 34/134, ff. 16–17, 79, 125.
[6] PRO. 30/8, vol. 19, ff. 51–6.   [7] Above, p. 320.
[8] See, e.g., WO. 4/757, pp. 154, 156–7, 282; WO. 4/762, p. 170.
[9] Sometimes the War Office sanctioned a grant in addition. WO. 4/758, p. 171. Cf. WO. 4/761, pp. 118, 176.

for a hospital when the regiment was in camp,[1] and from 1778 there was one of £30 a year for the maintenance of a hospital in quarters.[2] Surgeons also received the proceeds of a stoppage from the men's pay,[3] but in 1792 this was done away with and instead they received an allowance, inclusive of that for the hospital, which was £30 a year for corps of 180 or less and rose for larger corps to a maximum of £120 for those of 500 men and upwards.[4] The provision thus made was not always adequate: no subject occupies more space in the Secretary at War's correspondence with the militia than the demands of surgeons for more money and regiments for more surgeons.

A single surgeon was not enough for a large corps, especially if its quarters were dispersed. In 1759 the surgeon of the Hertfordshires had a round of 36 miles.[5] There were constant requests for leave to appoint a surgeon's mate. At first they were all refused but soon large corps were allowed to appoint them on a temporary basis.[6] After the embodiment of the supplementary militia, corps over 1000 strong were even allowed two.[7] In default of this, civilian doctors were sometimes called in,[8] and sometimes the officers did the job themselves. In September 1759 Sir Roger Newdigate dosed two men of his company who had fevers with James' Powder and had the satisfaction of seeing them recover.[9] A difficulty of another kind was that any serious epidemic was likely to prove a bad thing financially for the surgeon. Early in 1779 a detachment of the West Kent at Weymouth and Poole encountered the outbreak of typhus already mentioned. It carried off most of the prisoners they were guarding and many civilians. The regimental surgeon was able to save all but six of the 200 soldiers who caught it, but he had to employ two local doctors, buy a good deal of port wine and expensive medicines, and hire extra nurses. He ended out of pocket to the extent of £185 and appealed for relief to his colonel, who in turn appealed to the Commander-in-Chief.[10]

[1] See, e.g., WO. 4/762, pp. 266–7. The militia also got this allowance in 1759 before they had any 'contingent men'. WO. 4/757, pp. 263–4, 266, 280; cf. p. 311. On 'contingent men' see above, p. 361.

[2] WO. 4/762, p. 288.

[3] In 1759 it was $\frac{1}{2}d$. a man a week. WO. 1/979, T. Vernon, 25 October 1759.

[4] *Certain Rules*, pp. 15–18.   [5] WO. 1/979, Lord Cowper, 25 November 1759.

[6] See, e.g., WO. 4/758, pp. 111, 125, 153, 241; WO. 4/770, pp. 28–9, 95, 98, 100. For an early refusal, WO. 1/980, f. 196; WO. 4/757, p. 149.

[7] WO. 4/775, pp. 460, 485. WO. 4/776, p. 24.

[8] E.g. BM, Add. 35660, ff. 248–54. There are signs that the trouble here was low spirits due to homesickness. There were several quarrels about the size of civilian doctors' bills, e.g. WO. 4/759, pp. 291, 294; WO. 4/767, pp. 191–3, 220–2, 232.

[9] Newdigate's diary, 22–25 September 1759.

[10] WO. 34/119, f. 190. WO. 34/157, ff. 340, 344–5.

In camp the surgeon was further assisted by the provision of an extra medicine chest,[1] hospital tent and extra bedding. There was also a general hospital for the whole camp,[2] used especially for the isolation of infectious diseases like smallpox. These last were sometimes not adequate. In 1778 both Warley and Coxheath had one, situated in a house, with a staff of two or three. But in the previous war there had been half a dozen such hospitals and a large staff, since part of the force at home was destined for foreign service.[3] In 1779 Coxheath had only a barn for smallpox cases, able to hold thirty, and no staff save the regimental surgeons. The outbreak of a 'low, bilious autumnal fever' in September found the camp unprepared. Donald Munro, Physician to the Army, advised that blankets and staff be sent down for the establishment of isolation hospitals at a distance from the camp—in barns at first if need be. Lt.-Gen. Peirson, the camp commandant, put the sickness down to the troops overloading their stomachs with nuts and thought it would soon be over. But over 600 of the men had it, and forty-two died.[4]

It was clearly desirable that those men who had not been exposed to it should be inoculated against smallpox. This was a further source of trouble and expense for the surgeon, and indeed for the regiment as a whole. In 1779 the Duke of Richmond found that 390 men in his newly formed Sussex corps required inoculation. Those treated were ill for three weeks and had to be housed in an isolation hospital. The Duke was, fortunately, able to use a house of his own for this, but it only took sixty at a time. It took from May to August to work through the regiment.[5] This sort of thing might not be welcome where the regiment was quartered. The corporation of Devizes protested violently, invoking their MP, when the Wiltshires tried to set up a hospital for inoculation near by. The corps was prevented from hiring a house.[6] To meet the expense the War Office was originally willing to allow the surgeon a guinea a man.[7] But in 1780 this was suspended after 1 May because infection was spread by inoculated men coming to camp.[8] In the next war, the War Office argued that the surgeon would save money by inoculation in the long run and so he ought to

[1] Cf. WO. 4/764, p. 126.
[2] All camp hospitals had allowances of forage, fuel, etc. WO. 3/26, pp. 26, 32. WO. 4/771, pp. 34, 79, 176–8, 211–14, 294.
[3] WO. 34/114, ff. 119–23.
[4] To disinfect the camp, Peirson moved it for a few days, burned the straw and turned over the earth. WO. 34/118, ff. 116–18, 145. WO. 34/121, ff. 207–9.
[5] WO. 34/115, ff. 80–1. WO. 34/154, f. 412. One hundred of the Hertfordshires needed inoculation in 1781. WO. 34/139, f. 140.
[6] WO. 34/113, ff. 151–2, 154–8.
[7] See, e.g., WO. 4/763, pp. 225, 246; WO. 4/764, pp. 11, 12, 16, 24.
[8] WO. 3/26, p. 40.

pay for it. In some cases, however, they were willing to pay 5s. a man.[1]

The spiritual health of the men received far less organised care than the physical. A full-time chaplain was sanctioned only in camp.[2] At other times the troops attended the local parish church. The clergyman might receive a fee in certain cases, such as when he had to hold a 'second sitting' because of the extra numbers.[3]

IV

Before we turn from the logistics of the militia to their military activities, it is worth stressing that these left them with a fair amount of leisure. For the officers, regimental life could with luck become an agreeable holiday. Sir Roger Newdigate's stay at Salisbury with the Warwickshires from August to October 1759 sounds far from irksome. He took lodgings at a staymaker's for a guinea a week and his wife joined him. Attendance at drill occupied him in the early morning each day and sometimes part of the afternoon. But he had plenty of time to make and receive calls and moved in very good society. Besides the Bishop and the Dean there were Lord Feversham, Lord Folkestone and other notables locally resident, while the officers of the regiment, Lord Denbigh at their head, were a very respectable body. Newdigate also found time for various excursions—to Winchester, Fonthill, Longleat and Stonehenge. He read a number of books, among them *Candide* and Clarendon's *History of the Great Rebellion*. The officers gave two balls, and a cathedral city offered the further pleasure of good music.[4] The ensuing winter in the depths of Hampshire seems to have been very tedious, but at Southampton in the spring of 1760 there were fishing, boating and visits from Colonel Berkeley, the Duke of Beaufort and others. At Winchester that summer the large militia garrison produced a brilliant social gathering. There was a review by the Duke of York, at which Newdigate kissed hands, and several balls. Newdigate seems to have been kept rather busy by the number of guards to be mounted, but he attended many plays and concerts.[5] Worcester in the summer of 1762 he seems also to have found a pleasant social centre.[6] Leicester the previous summer was duller, but Newdigate was nearer home there.[7]

[1] See WO. 4/770, pp. 232–3, 365–6, 421–2; WO. 4/772, pp. 167, 299, 301.

[2] See WO. 4/759, p. 12; WO. 4/762, p. 285; WO. 4/770, pp. 28–9. He was paid 6s. 8d. a day. For exceptions to the rule see WO. 4/761, p. 53; WO. 4/766, p. 174.

[3] *Ibid.* WO. 4/764, p. 197. The allowance for a chaplain in camp ceased on the establishment of a chaplain general's department in 1796. WO. 4/774, pp. 216–17, 241–2.

[4] Newdigate's diary, August–October 1759.

[5] *Ibid.*, January–September 1760.   [6] *Ibid.*, June–August 1762.

[7] *Ibid.*, June–July 1761.

The experiences of Thomas Pelham in the next war were those of a young man, only 23 in 1779 and still dependent on an allowance from his father.[1] The Sussex militia in which he was a captain spent that summer at Shoreham and Brighton, and by his own account he found it very pleasant.[2] As the heir of an important local magnate he did not lack hospitality. There seems to have been a ball every week, and his family frequently tempted him home.[3] The regiment spent the autumn and winter at Exeter, which Pelham (who soon become major) did not altogether like. His servant died and the replacement proved sickly and incompetent.[4] He did not enjoy the dinner which the corporation gave the officers to mark the election of a mayor. He looked forward to the return of local families from the sea-coast and the beginning of regular assemblies. But a little later he said that there were only two families worth knowing—the Dean's and the Bampfyldes. After his friend Lt.-Col. Hay had left in November he was very lonely.[5] But he seems to have managed two tours through Devonshire, with visits to leading families (the second was delayed by the appearance of the enemy fleet off the coast).[6]

The summer of 1780 Pelham passed at Ranmer Camp near Dorking. He declared himself busy—too much so to be bored—but managed to visit his family and also the Sussex assizes and, apparently, the races. He concerned himself, too, with the general election both in Sussex and Surrey, being returned a member himself for the former county.[7] In 1781 he was at Winchester and had very heavy duty, including the mustering of the regiment and the training of recruits. He missed the Sussex assizes and had to forego a tour in Yorkshire. But he got home occasionally, and made various excursions—to Stratfieldsaye, to the Bishop's residence at Farnham and to Portsmouth to see a ship launched, a thing he had never seen before. In the town there was a club to belong to and various entertainments. The races were especially brilliant because of a great ball given by one of the county members.[8]

Patricians like Pelham or Newdigate could be expected to travel anyway, but for some of the junior officers of inferior class the

[1] BM, Add. 33128, ff. 3, 23–5, 31, 40, 45. Newdigate was 40 in 1759.
[2] BM, Add. 33128, f. 4.   [3] *Ibid.*, ff. 6, 7, 10–12, 16–17, 20–7.
[4] *Ibid.*, ff. 33, 35–6, 41, 43–4, 46–8.   [5] *Ibid.*, ff. 39, 41–2, 45.
[6] *Ibid.*, ff. 33–4, 37–40, 42.
[7] *Ibid.*, ff. 53-4, 59–69. Militia camps could be social centres of some brilliance in their own right. In 1778 Lord Cholmondeley gave a dinner in his marquee at Coxheath to the Duke of Grafton, the Duke and Duchess of Devonshire and other notables. The one inn on the heath and those in nearby Maidstone were thronged with visitors to the camp. BM, Add. 35659, f. 392.
[8] BM, Add. 33128, ff. 72–8. In 1782 he entered the Rockingham ministry and was seldom with the regiment, *ibid.*, ff. 83–9.

wanderings of the militia must have been a unique and fascinating experience. John Cobbald, 'yeoman', was three years an ensign in the Suffolk militia. A diary has survived of his first march out of the county to Leicester at the end of 1759, when he was just over 30. Each place he passed received a shrewd and earthy appraisal. At Cambridge he admired King's chapel and Clare hall, but also noted the village of 'Bawdy Barnwell, consisting of good-natured girls for the use of the colleges'. At Kettering he found hogs' 'shite' soap and cows' fire: the poor washed with one and burned the other. Market Harborough was a pretty town and their fuel was pit coal, as it was in Leicester. That town had good houses, but only one good church. The sights included 'John of Gaunt's Kitchen', where the size of the old suits of armour proved that there were giants in former times. The inhabitants were prosperous, but kept few carriages because they were 20 or 30 miles from any other town of note and so stayed at home. Meat was coarse there, but bread and cheese superb. From Leicester in February 1760 Cobbald went on an excusion to Derby, where he saw the silk mills, and Matlock, where he found

> the country so wild and romantick that 'tis beyond Description for when God Form'd the world he left all the odd pieces in Derbyshire.

Wherever the regiment went, the local gentry entertained the officers lavishly and sent them venison, hams and the like. At Leicester the mayor gave them a supper on their arrival, at which seventy sat down and passed a 'joyous night'.[1] Such were the militia officers' campaigns; the annual peacetime training, likewise, was a good excuse for balls and dinners.[2]

In the case of the men, the main sign that they had time to spare from their duties is that they were often able to have civilian jobs as well. In December 1794 the Lancashires at Canterbury were given permission to work to the number of five men per company at a time —each man was allowed to work for a week. Company commanders were to recommend men for the privilege every Saturday.[3] Even at a temporary halt on their march to Salisbury in 1759, the men of the Warwickshires were given permission to engage in harvesting. Unfortunately it rained, and they were unable to do so. In 1761 Newdigate employed some men from the regiment (then stationed quite

---

[1] *Notes and Queries*, vol. 193 (1948), pp. 422–5. Documents in the possession of Charles Partridge, Stowmarket.

[2] Markham, pp. 11–12.

[3] A sixth man was added later, but without being excused parades etc. Farrington's Order Book, 10 and 25 December 1794. Cf. the Staffordshires in 1799, Bagot's Order Book, 24 May.

near his home) to make a road, and next year he used some to level the ground north of his house.[1]

The government itself employed soldiers as labourers. An order of 1778 laid down that making entrenchments and posts, clearing ground and mending roads for the march of troops were a part of ordinary duty, which soldiers could be required to do without extra pay. But if they were called on to build forts or other public works, they were to be paid 9d. a day for ordinary labour and 1s. 3d. if they chanced to be skilled masons, carpenters or artificers.[2] At Portsmouth in 1778 the officers of the Buckinghamshires and Huntingdonshires objected to the militia doing that sort of work. They contended that it was degrading and improper for a citizen force intended for emergency use only. But the real objection seems to have been that supervision involved a lot of work for the officers.[3] In 1781 the Huntingdons were eager to work, and they and other militia corps were commended for their proficiency.[4]

Like the officers, the men sometimes had their families with them, but they were there on sufferance and must have had a thin time. The mutiny act specifically forbade the requisitioning of billets for them,[5] but they are found living in both barracks and billets[6] as well as lodgings,[7] and since the men had largely to look after themselves, the presence of some women was not unwelcome.[8] In camp the need for washerwomen led to some degree of official provision for soldiers' wives, though the number allowed to go there was limited. In 1779, for instance, each corps in camp was allowed wood and straw for three women per company (wives or hired washerwomen). They were only to share in the three first deliveries of fresh straw for beddings; after that they were to use what the men had finished with.[9] Soldiers' wives provided for themselves as best they could from their own earnings and the leavings from their husbands' pay, but sometimes they were in need of charity from the officers. At Christmas 1794

[1] Newdigate's diary, 30–31 July 1759; 11 May and 17–18 June 1761; 7 May 1762.

[2] WO. 3/26, pp. 15–16.

[3] This is the best sense I can make of WO. 34/111, ff. 108–12; WO. 34/122, . 95; WO. 34/144, f. 46; WO. 34/145, ff. 256–7.

[4] WO. 34/138, ff. 106–7. Cf. WO. 34/154, f. 282.

[5] E.g. 37 Geo. III, cap. 33, s. 45.

[6] See, e.g., above p. 380; Farrington's Order Book, 7 January 1795.

[7] Bagot's Order Book, 27 May 1799.

[8] It was important and not always easy to make the men keep themselves clean. Regimental orders of the Lancashires at Canterbury in 1795 require men in hospital to keep neat and clean, men to sleep separately each in his own blanket, blankets to be beaten twice a week, shirts to be changed twice a week and when going on guard. Ibid., 31 January, and 2, 9, 10 and 13 February 1795.

[9] WO. 3/26, pp. 22, 32, 33.

Colonel Pelham of the Sussex ordered meat and bread for the women and children of his own company, and he allowed a bushel of coals and three issues of broth each week to those who seemed in distress during the frost.[1] In November 1795 the wives following the Cambridgeshires were given twenty-four pairs of blankets.[2]

Less desirable women were, of course, to be found in the company of the soldiers. In 1795 Lord Townshend had to warn the regiments going into camp to keep down the number of women with them and see that they were all respectable. Profligacy in the huts at the rear of the camp led to indiscipline and marauding.[3] No sooner had the Warwickshires left their home county in 1759 than they were reported in need of a surgeon through being 'somewhat gallant'.[4] Sick lists of the Cambridgeshires for September to December 1797 show venereal cases, reaching double figures every time but two, to have been the commonest complaint.[5] For the other pleasures of the soldiers there is testimony mainly in the form of the efforts by the authorities to suppress them. At Warley in 1778, for instance, an attempt to establish a billiard table at the rear of one regiment was reported to the commandant. He 'of course' forbade it, and warned regimental commanders to take care that nothing of the sort took place near the camp. They were to discourage gaming of every kind among both officers and men and if sutlers allowed it in their huts, these were to be pulled down.[6]

An important consequence of the relatively light load of duty on the militia was that even when embodied the officers and men were able to spend a fair amount of time at home. The authorities seem at first to have thought of compensating the militia for lengthy embodiment by allowing them to spend the winter near their families. In October 1760 most of the militia regiments were ordered to return to their own counties.[7] Later, this was done only sparingly and became a coveted privilege. Stationing at home seems to have been bad for discipline. The Warwickshires, for instance, were home for

[1] BM, Add. 33101, ff. 154–6.
[2] BM, Add. 35666, f. 216. In 1800 four companies of this regiment had with them nine children and twenty-six women. BM, Add. 35673, ff. 120–4.
[3] BM, Add. 35666 f. 29; cf. Walrond, p. 96.
[4] WO. 1/979, Lord Denbigh, 29 July 1759. Regimental standing orders required them to pay 5s. for their cure. 'The Warwickshire Militia in 1759'. *Jol. of the Society for Army Historical Research*, vol. xi (1932), pp. 83–9 (p. 84, order no. 12).
[5] But there were few cases left by February 1798; this instance need not be regarded as typical. BM, Add. 35668, between ff. 244–74; Add. 35669, between ff. 6–63; cf. between ff. 190–237.
[6] Markham, p. 19. Cf. Walrond, pp. 85–6, 103 and the Warwickshire orders (n. 5), no. 7.
[7] WO. 4/759, p. 171. The West Kents never left their own county in 1759–62. Bonhote, pp. 109–10.

the winter of 1760–1 and a good many men were given furloughs. On the day that they were to leave the county, Sir Roger Newdigate's division paraded late and many were drunk. The first day's march was very disagreeable.[1] Another objection to stationing regiments at home was that in the event of riots the troops could not be relied on to fire on the mob: this would be likely to contain a good many of their friends and relations. In 1781 some inhabitants of Manchester asked for the removal thence of the Lancashire militia. There was unemployment among the 'smallware weavers', who enjoyed popular support, and riots were likely. The 'known attachment' of the Lancashires to their 'neighbours and connexions' made it probable that they would take the wrong side.[2]

But if the regiments could not be sent home *en bloc*, it was possible to be generous with leave of absence for the officers and furloughs for the men.[3] At harvest time it seems to have been a national necessity for soldiers to be released to join in the work. In October 1795 there was an order for as many men as possible to be allowed to join in the threshing.[4] In 1796 a third of the men were allowed to harvest, but were not to go more than a day's march from their unit.[5] In 1798 the embodiment of the supplementary militia meant that fewer men were left on the land. A third of the 'old' militia were, perhaps for this reason, allowed to have furloughs of up to six weeks at harvest time. One hundred and two of the Cambridgeshires were given leave and eighty-three of them went back to their own county —no doubt to their own homes, for they went to forty-four different places.[6]

In winter there was seldom much likelihood of invasion and so officers and men could readily be spared. At the end of 1759 it was decided that all the men were to have thirty days' furlough, ten men per company to be absent at a time.[7] In the winter of 1780–1 a third of the officers were allowed to be absent.[8] In that of 1793–4 a third of the NCOs and privates might be on furlough at a time. Of the officers, only one field officer, a third of the captains and one subaltern per company had to be present in most units, and proportion-

---

[1] Newdigate's diary, 11 October 1760 to 24 April 1761.

[2] Maj.-Gen. Style, locally in command, agreed. WO. 34/137, ff. 118–19, 124.

[3] This was the terminology always used in this period.

[4] BM, Add. 35666, f. 195.

[5] WO. 3/29, pp. 70–1. In 1795 Generals commanding districts had been allowed to release as many as they saw fit. WO. 3/28, p. 113.

[6] BM, Add. 35670, ff. 214, 233, 252. In 1801 the Duke of York rebuked some men who asked such high wages that the farmers forwent their labour. WO. 3/24, p. 142.

[7] Newdigate's diary, 13 November 1759.

[8] BM, Add. 35661, f. 18.

ately fewer in very small corps. In both case this was subject to there always being officers and men present sufficient for the duty with which the corps was entrusted.[1] Sometimes there was danger even in winter, and then the arrangement was less generous. In 1797–8, when Bonaparte was preparing invasion at the head of the Army of England, the Duke of York required half the field officers and captains and two-thirds of the subalterns to be always present, with all leave to end by 14 March. All officers were to leave their addresses with the adjutants. Furloughs were to be given sparingly and only to the deserving.[2] Even so, all ranks might look forward to quite a considerable prospect of release. These arrangements were not peculiar to the militia. As a rule, the regular forces at home were treated in the same way. But there was a means here of preserving something of the original character of the militia as a force liable only to temporary embodiment. The men were not completely cut off from civilian life and work, and to that extent could more readily return thereto at the end of the war. The officers had time to attend to their private affairs: this, no doubt, is why it never became completely impossible to officer the force with men of property.

[1] WO. 4/772, pp. 73–6.
[2] WO. 3/31, pp. 54–6. BM. Add. 35668, f. 275.

XV

HOW EFFICIENT WAS THE MILITIA?

T HE militia's housekeeping and convivial arrangements did no more than provide a setting for its real work. Officers and men had to make themselves proficient as soldiers, and had in wartime to undertake their fair share of the tasks for which military force was required. How far did they succeed in these undertakings?

I

The formal military training which the militia received appears as a rule to have been adequate and to have taught them as much about the art of war as they could have been expected to learn before going into action. This did not amount to much in those days: the conscripts of Frederick the Great or Napoleon were considered ready for active service after being trained for only a month or two.[1] The militia's task here was accordingly limited. The basic elements of training were the manual exercise (i.e. arms drill), the firings and the practice of marching and evolutions—the rapid alteration of a unit's formation from line to column or square and back. These parade-ground movements were then the basis of the actual motions made on the battlefield. The firings comprised the various ways of firing volleys in close formation, including changes in formation by which men who had fired could be replaced at the front by men who had not. There would also be some target practice. The more advanced forms of training involved the use in the field of what had been learned on the parade ground—as when a unit formed column to pass through a narrow defile and then rapidly changed back into line at the far end, to engage an enemy supposed near at hand. For the more ambitious there were mock battles and practice in scouting. The more senior officers needed further to study the choosing of positions and the skilful movement of troops about the field.

[1] Shanahan, pp. 43–4. G. Lefebvre, *Napoleon* (Paris, 4th ed. 1953), ff. 198–9.

The amateur atmosphere and low standards of the British army[1] eased in a way the task of the militia in attaining the standard of proficiency expected of them. Until 1792 there was not even an official drill book: each regiment had its own rules. Some degree of uniformity was preserved by the existence of certain authoritative textbooks such as Bland's *Military Discipline* and by the official regulations for reviews described below. But many divergencies of detail remained, and it was often difficult for two or more regiments to act together in the field.

The militia seemed likely at first to take advantage of this latitude by adopting a system of drill peculiar to itself, simpler and less centred on achieving parade-ground smartness than that of the army. There was a good case for this as long as the militia was expected to serve only now and then. The Norfolk militia, thanks to George Townshend's expert knowledge, took the field with a drill book of their own, which was eventually printed as an example to others.[2] Dorset and Somerset likewise produced simplified schemes of drill,[3] and the West Kent also had its own manual (by Edward Fage, the adjutant), which took in the more advanced parts of training, like field days. Kent also assisted its tyro officers by producing a set of cards with the words of command printed on them.[4]

From the outset, however, this trend towards distinctness met with opposition. A Wiltshire officer published a pamphlet calling for uniformity in drill with the army. Major Young spoke with the authority of a former colonel of colonial militia. He said that within the army the variations were only small and there was an officially recognised drill book not two years old, which meant that the militia did not need to depart from established custom in order to keep up to date. Corps that did so laid themselves open to the suspicion of wishing, for political reasons, to maintain a gulf between the militia and the army. Whatever the Wiltshire militia did, they should at least adopt an existing system and not invent a new one.[5] As for simplification, Young denied outright that it was a good idea. Only the 'pride of ornament and parade' could stir the imagination of the uneducated and make 'the dread of an artificial shame' prevail over the fear of death. 'The Genius of Knight-Errantry,' he added, 'is nearly related

[1] Cf. above, p. 339, n. 2.

[2] MS in Towshend Papers, BM, Add. 41142. Printed as *New Military Instructions from the Militia* (1760).

[3] *A Letter from a Militia Man to his Colonel; Representing the Inconveniences that may Attend a Deviation from the Regular Establish'd Exercise of the Army*, pp. 4, 5.

[4] MSS. of Fourth Duke of Bedford, vol. xxxix, f. 140. Bonhote, pp. 83–8.

[5] *Letter from a Militia Man*, pp. 1–4, 9, 10. He says (p. 1) he has been appointed major by Lord Pembroke, who was lord lieutenant of Wiltshire. An ink note on the British Museum copy says the pamphlet is by Mr Young.

to the Spirit of Soldiery.'[1] He therefore objected to the Dorset system (and parts of the Norfolk) as being without 'grace and ornament'. He also denied that the movements in the newly invented systems were really more natural or easy to make: for instance, the Norfolks had reduced priming and loading from nineteen movements to nine, but only because some movements had been counted as one instead of several.[2]

Sensible militia officers seem to have accepted at least the need for uniformity. Lord Tavistock at the outset was anxious to have the Dorset system adopted in Devon because the militia of the two counties would almost certainly have to act together.[3] The uniform system at length introduced for the land forces in 1792 was interestingly defended by the militia officers at Danbury Camp in 1794. When the general in command proposed to make some departures from it, they very sensibly said that with amateur officers and NCOs not of the best, they must have an invariable rule and their chance of improvement in camp would be wasted if they had first to unlearn what they already knew. Lord Amherst upheld their objection.[4] Not all officers were so wedded to uniformity, especially in earlier days. But at no time did the militia as a body have a system of training really distinct from that of the army.

The training which a militia unit received was pretty thorough when it could be sent to camp for several months, but a good deal less so at other times, whether in peace or war. Peacetime training needed to be good enough to ensure the efficiency of the militia as a reserve force, able to be called into service at a moment's warning. This was the only accomplishment of the militia not shared by the army, and it therefore played a large part in giving the militia its value for the defence of the nation. Not everyone set great store by it, however, and as we have seen, the friends of the militia did not always find it easy to get money voted for peacetime training.[5] Nor were good results likely to come from the original system by which the men drilled in small groups on odd days during the warmer months and a regiment could only be exercised as a whole for two or three days a year.[6] Remarkable zeal alone could overcome the difficulties of this arrangement, as when Lord Shaftesbury drilled the Dorsets for twelve hours a day in Easter week 1759 (to his own complete exhaustion) although the law prescribed a maximum of six hours a day.[7]

---

[1] *Letter from a Militia Man*, pp. 12–13.   [2] *Ibid.*, pp. 4–10.
[3] As p. 405, n. 4.   [4] BM, Add. 35664, ff. 378, 380, 384, 386, 393.
[5] See above, pp. 194, 200–3.
[6] 30 Geo. II, cap. 25, ss. 27–30.
[7] WO. 30/8, vol. 56, ff. 13–14. Cf. 31 Geo. II, cap. 26, s. 32.

From 1762, however, the unembodied militia received twenty-eight days' continuous drill a year. To save money only two-thirds of the force was trained each year from 1786 and this economy was got rid of in 1802 only by reducing the period of training to twenty-one days.[1] But with these limitations there was now a firm opportunity for serious work and ambitious programmes could be adopted. The meeting of the West Essex in 1764 concluded with a mock battle and a display of Indian methods of bush fighting in a part of the ground where there were gravel pits and hedges.[2] In 1763 the Warwickshires were able on 2 June (ten days after assembly) to go through the entire manual exercise and the movements prescribed for reviews, fire volleys and charge. This was repeated on the 4th. On the 7th and 8th there were field days, the second on the rough ground of a common where columns and squares were formed and defiles passed, the whole ending with a volley and a charge. On the 16th and 17th there was an extensive practice of firings (sixteen rounds fired on the second day), and on the 18th a very comprehensive exercise closed the meeting.[3]

These were regiments which had recently been embodied and not all reached their standard. The Cambridgeshires had evaded embodiment in the Seven Years' War, had nearly ceased to exist thereafter, and in 1764 only just managed to assemble in time to avoid a fine on the county.[4] In that and succeeding years there were many vacancies,[5] and though the men seem as a rule to have been well behaved,[6] in 1776 Tolver complained of their 'obstinate unmilitary spirit'.[7] The improvement of the regiment once Philip Yorke had taken it over[8] was such as to elicit the praise of the bishop of Ely for their performance at the exercise of 1792.[9] But when soon afterwards they were embodied, Tolver found the officers inadequate and the sergeants able to do little by themselves. A bayonet charge ended

[1] 2 Geo. III, cap. 20, s. 99. 26 Geo. III, cap. 107, ss. 68–77. 42 Geo. III, cap. 90, ss. 87–91. Also the reduction of the peacetime establishment of NCOs was retained in 1802 (above, p. 326, n. 3). The act of 1762 permitted two exercise periods of fourteen days each. The act of 1802 empowered the king to excuse training if a unit had been recently disembodied, and allowed training in bodies as small as two companies of sixty privates (smaller of course where the county quota was smaller).

[2] BM, Add. 30012, f. 240 (*Public Advertiser*, 16 October 1764).

[3] Dismissal on the 20th. Newdigate's diary, 1763, dates cited.

[4] BM, Add. 35659, ff. 77, 81, 87, 91, 93. Cf. above, pp. 195–6.

[5] Never more than 430 rank and file present out of 480. *Ibid.*, ff. 93, 101, 103, 111, 124.

[6] *Ibid.*, ff. 104, 117, 120, 124, 126, 132.

[7] *Ibid.*, ff. 183, 195, 213.

[8] Above, pp. 313–14.

[9] BM, Add. 35391, ff. 232–3.

in confusion, and drill seems only to have been possible in open order.[1] Charles Yorke said that Lt.-Col. Wortham had 'infinite self-sufficiency' and 'not a single military idea in his head'. He made '*sad, sad* work' at field days and disgraced the regiment in the sight of the officers of the Huntingdonshires.[2] How common such ineptitude was it is hard to say. There seems no doubt that training was seriously neglected in the first few years after disembodiment in 1763, and 1783. A Scottish officer in the French service, reporting to Choiseul in 1768 on the possibilities of a surprise invasion of England, had a poor view of the militia. He had watched one regiment vainly trying to learn how to form line.[3] But when the militia was called out in 1778, general officers were sent to inspect the regiments and report if they were fit for service[4] and they mostly replied in the affirmative. Of thirty-three units for which reports survive, mostly inspected a month or so after embodiment, only eight were found to be notably lacking in training, and in four cases this was because they consisted wholly or largely of new recruits.[5] Three or four regiments with few or bad officers were nevertheless adequately trained, and so were a like number with numerous recruits. The Huntingdons were commended for their rapid training of their new men and some units were warmly praised: the 'steadiness and attention' of the South Lincolnshires 'would have done credit to any corps whatever'.[6]

The initial training of the supplementary militia raised in 1796 was on the same lines as that of the ordinary militia in peacetime. The lieutenancies were required to train the new men for twenty days as soon as possible. They could divide their contingent into several sections and drill them separately. Clothing and arms were to be supplied as they thought necessary,[7] but at this stage there was an attempt to avoid the expense and trouble of a fully fledged regimental organisation. As far as possible the men were to be trained by the

---

[1] BM, Add. 35663, ff. 71, 129.   [2] BM, Add. 35392, f. 319.

[3] Mary C. Morison, 'The Duc de Choiseul and the Invasion of England 1768–70', *Transactions of the Royal Historical Society*, 3rd series, vol. iv (1910), Grant of Blairfindy's report, p. 91. Cf. above, pp. 194, 199, 200.

[4] WO. 34/110, ff. 169–70; cf. ff. 85–6, 89–91, 163–4. The same was done in 1793: WO. 3/11, p. 107.

[5] WO. 27/40. It is not entirely easy to interpret these laconic reports, but the ones I take to be firmly unfavourable in this respect are East and West Middlesex, West Norfolk, Rutland, North Lincolnshire, East Norfolk, Radnor and the East Riding: the last four consisted of recruits and the West Middlesex also contained many. (Reports are in alphabetical order).

[6] *Ibid*. The regiments with few or bad officers were the Westminster, Northumberland, East Suffolk and perhaps the Leicester. The quotation is f. 51.

[7] 37 Geo. III, cap. 3, ss. 25, 29. WO. 4/824, p. 1. Training was expected to cost £177,600 (CJ, vol. lii, p. 208). Of course the contingents were mostly much bigger than those of the existing militia.

officers and NCOs of the existing militia, though additional officers might be appointed.[1] The amending act allowed the use of Chelsea pensioners[2] and regular officers and NCOs, temporarily redundant through the dearth of regular recruits, could also be used.[3] The lieutenancies duly made arrangements and reported them to the government: February, March and April 1797 were the months when most of the training was done.[4] The supply of instructors was a considerable burden on the embodied militia, especially as this was the season when officers expected to be allowed a spell at home. Lord Bateman feared that any officer sent on training duty would use the occasion merely as an excuse to take some leave.[5] Absenteeism among those to be trained was also a problem.[6] But Charles Yorke seems to have been right in supposing that the men would quickly learn how to 'load and fire well and to walk straight and firm . . . all that is required of a foot soldier to know'.[7] Wale found the first division in Cambridgeshire very willing and made good progress despite falls of snow. Some of the men became desirous of joining the embodied militia and Wale thought the whole body fit enough to be added to fully trained units without inconvenience. Only one man absconded and the main problem arising (with subsequent divisions) was lack of specie for pay.[8] In August 1797 General Dundas was able to tell the government that in all but three counties the supplementaries were not only raised but trained.[9]

When these men were embodied in 1798, those who were added to the existing regiments nevertheless presented their receivers with a problem in digestion. The Cambridgeshires were quite pleased with what they got and one Suffolk regiment ventured to put their recruits in with the rest at a review. But this proved a mistake. The recruits did well enough in squads, but not when the regiment formed line.[10] As for the Cambridgeshire recruits, they came on well in camp at Harwich, but hard work was still required afterwards when the regiment reached Chelmsford barracks. The adjutant drilled all the companies individually once a week in order to pick out the awkward men, who were then ordered extra drill.[11]

When the militia was embodied, the opportunities for training were obviously much increased, but they remained severely limited for

[1] 37 Geo. III, cap. 3, s. 26.   [2] 37 Geo. III, cap. 22, s. 6.
[3] WO. 3/17, pp. 96–7.   [4] WO. 4/824, pp. 50–184.
[5] HO. 50/26, letter of 31 December 1796.
[6] Lord Radnor (HO. 50/28: 5 April 1797) was not sure how to punish or if need be replace them.
[7] BM, Add. 35393, f. 4.
[8] BM, Add. 35667, ff. 233, 239, 241, 243, 247, 317, 321, 333.
[9] WO. 30/65, f. 4.   [10] BM, Add. 35669, f. 306.
[11] BM, Add. 35670, ff. 99, 308.

most of the time by the other duties which had to be done and by the dispersion of units in quarters.[1] Finding a suitable training ground cannot always have been easy. When the Warwickshires reached the Southampton district at the end of 1759, the portion quartered at Romsey used first a close belonging to the mayor, then a meadow, then the churchyard.[2] In 1793 the Secretary at War agreed to meet a charge of a guinea incurred by the East Norfolks in hiring a ground at Colchester, and 16s. 6d. for the like at Chelmsford. But he complained of their failure to get his permission first, and he refused to meet a charge stated by the Shropshires.[3]

The vicissitudes that training might undergo in quarters are well shown in the history of the Cambridgeshires from 1793 to 1796. At their first quarter in Sudbury the companies at headquarters were some time getting a place for drill, but eventually found a field (with a respectful audience of mechanics) and later a small market place.[4] The regiment was rather scattered, and Tolver lamented this and thought that they would not be fit for service for some time.[5] Wale, however, when he took over the adjutancy, thought the men's drill very satisfactory despite the inefficiency of the sergeants.[6] In March 1794 it proved possible to get six of the eight companies concentrated at St Ives (Huntingdonshire) and hold some field days. Later, six companies were together at Huntingdon and trained every day on the racecourse, which did not prevent Wale thinking them the worst regiment but one when they reached Danbury Camp.[7] After a profitable summer there, they spent the winter of 1794–5 in Landguard Fort and Harwich, where only occasional drill was possible. Wale said that drill was useless if it was not regular, and confined the men to the manual exercise.[8] By contrast there seems to have been no interruption of training during the following winter, spent in Norwich barracks, and in April 1796 Wale was able to say that both the behaviour and the drill of the corps were good.[9]

But it was only in camp that the embodied militia could expect to reach a really high standard of proficiency. Here they were concentrated in large bodies under the command of experienced regular officers and could devote almost their whole attention to training.

---

[1] As noted above, pp. 379, 381.

[2] Newdigate's diary, 28–30 October and 1 and 5 November 1759.

[3] WO. 4/771, pp. 114, 237–8. Other cases, pp. 50, 370, 382, 482, 494–5.

[4] BM, Add. 35663, ff. 85, 92.

[5] Ibid., f. 97. He and Major Nightingale were very much fatigued by drilling cf. ff. 105, 107.

[6] BM, Add. 35664, f. 88.   [7] Ibid., ff. 230, 241, 243, 355.

[8] BM, Add. 35665, f. 175.

[9] BM, Add. 35666, f. 329. He had been using a field for drill, but now that the grass was growing would have to move to Mussell Heath.

The coming together of a number of regiments enabled the officers especially to benefit by competition and comparing notes. It was particularly valuable for militia regiments when they could be stationed together with regiments of the army and so learn, as one camp commandant put it, 'the minutiae and forms of service, some of which they had no means of coming at'.[1] In camp, too, it was possible to have exercises on a grand scale, with several regiments acting together, and this both called for and made possible the achievement of uniformity in systems of training and standards of achievement. The first steps towards a uniform system of drill for the whole army were the instructions issued each year to ensure that regiments training together in camp followed the same rules. These were sometimes the work of individual camp commandants, sometimes of the Commander-in-Chief. By the holding of reviews it was possible to discover if the rules were being followed and the prescribed lessons properly learned and so the camp became a regular military academy, with a syllabus and a pass examination.[2] The regulations laid down by the Duke of York for the camps in 1795 show the system fully developed. The material of the syllabus was now, of course, provided by the official drill book of 1792, which was everywhere to be followed without deviation. Every Monday and Friday each unit was to exercise separately, practising the part of the exercise which the commanding officer or the camp commandant thought that it did least well. On Tuesdays and Saturdays there were to be brigade exercises under major generals, and on Wednesdays the camp commandant was to exercise the whole body. When an exercise was well done the troops were not to be kept too long under arms, and Thursday was to be a day of rest except for corps that had behaved badly that week or were in some way below standard. On Sunday the troops had of course to attend divine service.[3]

A further great advantage of training in camp was its realism. Lt.-Gen. Parker told Lord Amherst in 1779 that his aim would be to fit the troops in his camp for real service by making them exercise in brigades, taking them into rough and difficult country, and teaching them to fire by divisions and not in the formal and intricate manner of the parade ground. Three weeks later he was able to take his whole

[1] WO. 27/40, f. 251.

[2] C. James, *Universal Military Dictionary* (4th ed., London, 1816), s.v. 'Exercise', p. 210. Review Regulations will be found in WO. 3/26, pp. 12–14, 29–32, cf. pp. 183–4. In 1779 General Fawcett asked for printed copies of the last one for the instruction of two very backward militia corps stationed in Lancashire. WO. 34/157, f. 94.

[3] Some generals had to be tactfully reminded of the need for uniformity. WO. 3/28, pp. 89–91. Cf. WO. 3/14, pp. 82–3, and earlier WO. 3/11, pp. 140–1, 161–2, and above, p. 406.

force (save the backward Cambridgeshires) to exercise together on a common, and reported that they did well for a first attempt and after a few more days' practice would be in good order for service.[1] Haviland, at Plymouth in 1781, marched seven regiments for a mile in two columns and formed line, to get them used to acting together. He thought they did such manoeuvres as the weather allowed very well and had the field officers to dinner.[2] Marching and camping in field conditions was another thing practised. Peirson made the six corps at Dartford Camp in 1780 march to Gravesend and cross to Tilbury one day, taking with them their tents and twelve wagons with entrenching tools but leaving their heavy baggage behind. They took a dinner cooked the previous day in their haversacks and were issued with grog on the other side. They started off at 3 a.m. and some of them did not get back till 1 a.m. next day.[3] In 1781 Peirson made both wings of Coxheath Camp go on similar marches, pitching and striking their tents before the return home, and said that they did it as quickly as it could be done, save that in loading the pack-horses they lacked the skill that could only come from long experience.[4]

Camp conditions were particularly well suited to the training of light infantry, that is, of men intended to fight in irregular formation as skirmishers, especially in rough country. Interest in light infantry grew steadily in the later eighteenth century, especially because of the wars in America; British regular and militia battalions came as a rule to have one company of light infantry and another of grenadiers, which in practice did the same work.[5] These 'flank companies' usually contained the pick of the officers and men, but they did not always receive the appropriate special training. In camp this was often remedied by collecting all the flank companies into temporary battalions and training them separately under specially appointed field officers.[6] (From this developed the idea of special centres for training light infantry, the hostility to which on constitutional grounds has already been noticed.[7]) The light infantry at Coxheath one year were in training twice a day, and were said to be very expert and to be able to bear much fatigue. Though not tall, the men were very robust and active. One display they gave consisted of evolutions, in open order and mostly at the double, which took them a mile from the spectators and into apparent confusion. Then a horn sounded and to the amazement of those watching they at once formed two

---

[1] WO. 34/154, ff. 150, 589.   [2] WO. 34/137, ff. 240–1.
[3] WO. 34/126, ff. 144–5, 153, 156. Half the force were regulars.
[4] WO. 34/154, f. 80.   [5] Cf. above, pp. 303–4.
[6] See, e.g., WO. 34/153 (i), f. 256; WO. 3/29, pp. 137–9.
[7] See above, pp. 231–2.

columns facing each other like enemies about to engage.[1] 'Scouting' seems to have been part of the programme for everyone at Coxheath in 1778, for 4000 or 5000 men were so engaged twice a week.[2]

The standard of marksmanship in eighteenth-century armies was poor, thanks both to the weapons and the type of training, with its emphasis on precisely timed volleys. In camp, efforts were made to improve it by target practice and by practice in rapid loading and firing.[3] Peirson in 1780 complained that the 160,000 loose ball with which he had been issued would only last a week. He asked for 1,000,000 and expected to use more.[4] In 1798 the Cambridgeshires had fifty men trained as marksmen while in camp. It proved rather hard to find anywhere for them to continue practice afterwards.[5]

The effect of camp on individual regiments was striking. The Cambridgeshires were several times redeemed by it from uselessness. In 1779 they had just been re-raised and Lt.-Col. Ward complained that the men were a sleepier sort than those of other counties and lacked emulation. Because almost all were illiterate it was hard to recruit NCOs from them. They were put under Lt.-Gen. Parker at Warley Camp, and he turned out to be a Cambridgeshire man and was very helpful. He lent them some Irish sergeants from other regiments whose efforts, together with the diligence of the field officers, produced a remarkable improvement. The camp was twice visited by Lord Amherst and whereas the Cambridgeshire could do little but march past on the first occasion, on the second it could perform all the movements ordered and many more.[6] In 1782 the regiment was again full of new recruits. It camped at Hopton Warren, near Yarmouth, and again managed to do rather more at the end than was expected of it, to the surprise of the General.[7]

In 1794 as we have seen the regiment arrived in Danbury Camp in poor shape, but Wale had the skill to make full use of a camp's advantages. The regiment was divided into a proficient and an 'awkward' division, the former drilling twice a day under Wale himself, the latter three times a day under NCOs. Ten dumb-bells were bought and the men were kept working on them all day to improve their physical condition, of which Wale thought poorly. Wale believed, however, that the regiment was made of good material and

---

[1] BM, Add. 30012, f. 242 (*St James' Chronicle*, sub. Coxheath, 19 August). The display lasted two hours.
[2] BM, Add. 35659, f. 392. [3] WO. 34/154, ff. 150, 362.
[4] WO. 34/126, f. 194. He was apparently getting tools to make or salvage balls.
[5] BM, Add. 35670, ff. 99, 308.
[6] BM, Add. 35660, ff. 181–3, 187–9, 196, 214, 217, 229. Hardwicke gave Parker some venison. None of the units seem to have done much at the first review.
[7] BM, Add. 35661, ff. 237, 266, 277, 286, 296, 309. Add. 35662, f. 4. More venison.

said that a month would make a great difference. When the camp broke up, General Johnston's congratulations proved him right.[1]

During the American war, the West Norfolks seem to have benefited greatly from camp, even though it was only by themselves and under their own officers. Their colonel, Lord Orford was unfortunately subjects to fits of insanity.[2] But he had the good qualities of this defect and was enterprising and enthusiastic. At Aldeburgh in 1778 they staged a 'Noumachia', a mock battle at sea. A ship anchored about a league out had to be attacked. The regiment was divided in four, each division in four boats ten yards apart and the divisions twenty yards apart. Commands were given by hoisting flags. They first practised forming their boats in column and line and firing volleys from them. Then they rowed out to the ship, formed a circle round her, fired two volleys and boarded with fixed bayonets. A prize of half a crown was offered for the first boat to board.[3] This was their most spectacular achievement, but there are signs of good, steady work in each of the next three campaigns. All the evolutions prescribed in Amherst's instructions were practised and more besides: Orford had his own cards printed showing the movements to be made and the rules to be observed.[4] Inspecting the regiment at the end of 1778, Maj.-Gen. Warde reported that 'they must have been a great deal manoeuvred and likely to be ready and attentive to orders in the noise and confusion of service'. He complained, though, that they 'are not a *very* highly finished parade regiment'.[5]

Orford was keen on marksmanship and his regiment (about 600 strong) used some 14,000 rounds each camping season in target practice.[6] The result was considered most praiseworthy,[7] though it hardly seems impressive now. Once in 1780 the regiment, firing at a target *en masse*, made 130 hits out of 600 shots. They next fired from a height at a target 100 yards away and scored only 80. One company which always won the shooting competitions was suspected of loading with two balls instead of one, and Orford tried experiments to determine if this was a good idea. A target at 80 yards received 203 hits when half the regiment fired at it loaded with two balls, and only 64 when the other half fired, loaded with only one. On another occasion a target at 140 yards received 57 and 51 hits respectively.[8]

[1] BM, Add. 35664, f. 355. Add. 35665, f. 143.

[2] See the many references to this in the correspondence of his uncle, Horace Walpole.

[3] WO. 1/1000, Lord Orford, 28 June 1778, and enclosure.

[4] WO. 34/114, ff. 125–6, 128. WO. 34/125, ff. 10–11. WO. 34/154, ff. 459, 599.

[5] WO. 27/40, f. 101.   [6] WO. 34/133, ff. 115–16.   [7] WO. 27/50, f. 127.

[8] The target was 2 ft. broad and seems to have been the same length as the division firing at it. WO. 34/165, f. 207. WO. 34/166, ff. 132–3, 227–8. Cf. WO. 34/114, f. 127.

Reviews in camp have been mentioned as constituting a sort of pass examination, ensuring a minimum standard of proficiency. Regiments which did not go to camp were also inspected at intervals and by this means the authorities sought to keep a check both on their military proficiency and on the soundness of their internal management. In 1798 the Duke of York made this branch of military administration, as he made so many others, more systematic. General officers in command of military districts were required to send in half-yearly reports on each regiment under their command, covering the state of drill and discipline, the equipment, accounts and other regimental records, the hospital and messing arrangments and any courts-martial that had been held. Cases of persons receiving pay without doing duty were to be reported and there was to be an assessment of the abilities of the regimental commander, to guide the Duke in the selection of officers for higher posts.[1]

On the strictly military side, what went on at a well-conducted review can be seen from two by Lord Amherst at Warley Camp. For that in August 1778, the seven militia and one regular regiments paraded at 6 a.m. for preliminary inspection by their own officers. At 8 a.m. a flag was hoisted on the camp commandant's tent and the whole body stood to arms. At 8.45 Lord Amherst arrived, accompanied by a crowd of notables, ADCs and so forth, and was received with a salute of nineteen guns. He passed along the whole line while arms were presented, with his hat off and bowing to each company. The camp commandant then took the whole body through the manual, firings and march past. This was followed by a skirmish and the men, after reforming, were dismissed some time after 2 p.m.[2] In September 1793 Amherst arrived during a heavy shower and as the troops were wet he thought it best not to inspect them but put them in motion at once. They marched past in slow and then in quick time. They then went through an advance in battle order, forming line from column, firing, forming column again and moving forward a little, and then repeating the whole in a different way. Advancing under fire was also demonstrated, and at one point the troops were formed in two lines, alternately firing and passing through each other. The whole ended with a charge and a general salute. Lord Amherst professed himself very satisfied with what he had seen.[3]

Reviews were the main guarantee of the militia's standard of efficiency and review reports are our most direct means of finding out what that standard was. For both reasons it is important to know if inspections were efficiently done. It must be said at once that the

[1] WO. 3/19, pp. 111–14. This, of course, was meant primarily for the army.
[2] BM, Add. 30012, f. 242 (*St James' Chronicle*, sub. Warley Common).
[3] WO. 3/11, pp. 168–9.

surviving reports arouse misgivings. They are very brief and there is more than a hint that parade-ground smartness was too readily accepted as proof of efficiency. Under the heading 'Officers' it is quite common to find only the remark 'Good appearance. Salute well.'[1] But as can be seen elsewhere, inspecting generals were frequently outspoken about the bad state of equipment, and there are also plenty of cases where they complain about the state of a unit's discipline.[2] When a regiment was in quarters it was sometimes not possible to arrange for them to do much in the field during the review,[3] but normally they went through quite an extensive programme before the reviewing general, and criticisms on this head also are by no means uncommon. The Glamorganshires in 1781 were reported to look well and be fit for service, but to be below average in training owing to long dispersal in quarters. Movements were slow, the men aimed too high when firing volleys, the officers looked unmilitary and the NCOs were too old. On the other hand the drums and fifes were well played.[4] The Bedfords in 1780 deviated slightly from the rules that had been established—a fault easy to correct.[5] The Denbighshires in 1779 were fine men and quite proficient, although they had had little chance to train together. The pauses between the movements in the manual exercise were too long, which the commanding officer promised to correct.[6]

There seem to be grounds enough for believing that the reviews were tolerably thorough. It is, therefore, a significant point in the militia's favour that it came quite well out of this test. As already remarked, the reports of 1778 mostly show the newly embodied regiments fit to take up their work.[7] By the end of 1782, when the force had had the benefit of some years' continuous service, the picture was even better. Reports on thirty-eight units survive from that time and a bare half-dozen are seriously criticised on the score of defective training, three being small units trained as artillery, which in consequence had forgotten their training as infantry.[8] Generals in command of camps commonly believed that their charges had reached a high pitch of efficiency by the end of the 'campaign'. Townshend remarked in 1782 that despite bad weather his regiments had become

> as steady in their firings and manoeuvres and as correct to the time, as
> I believe any other, and in their manoeuvres in the field, such as taking

[1] See in general the earlier volumes of WO. 27.
[2] See above, pp. 342–3, and below, pp. 417, 422.
[3] WO. 27/50, f. 31, e.g.   [4] WO. 34/196, ff. 120-9.
[5] WO. 34/126, ff. 206–7.   [6] WO. 34/120, f. 52.   [7] Above, p. 408.
[8] The Carnarvon, Radnor and Rutland Corps. The East Suffolk and North Lincolnshire seem to have been indifferent; also the Leicestershire, which however, like several others, had many recruits. WO. 27/50.

possession or defending posts and positions, passing woods and defiles, and acting against each other as the ground required, the officers were emulous to improve and the men the same.[1]

II

The militia then were tolerably proficient in military exercises. Unfortunately, they were much more shaky when it came to discipline and morale. Some regiments, it is true, were found by camp commandants to be good in these respects too. Maj.-Gen. Warde in 1778 said that the 1st West Riding regiment 'appeared to have an Esprit de Corps, which would (I think) be of service to them on trying occasions'.[2] Lord Adam Gordon in 1782 said that the East Riding regiment

> are complete masters of their business and it would be a happiness to have Colonel Maister and the East York under one's command on actual service.[3]

But quite a few review reports complain of bad discipline even when a regiment was well drilled.[4]

When the revival of the militia first began, there were high hopes of the standard of discipline that might be expected from an army of patriotic citizens. Even the rather blimpish Major Young hoped to rouse the lower sort, now sunk in luxury, to martial exertion and make every village a nursery of soldiers. He wished the militia to behave so well that men of all classes would be eager to join. The men were to be taught to think of themselves as gentlemen and the officers were to win their affection by 'easy address' and by giving them employment and protection in civil life.[5]

This spirit was never extinct in the militia. It can be seen in a document produced some time during the American war, apparently for the instruction of the sergeants of the Sussex militia. Sergeants must present a shining example to their men and teach them the sentiments which a soldier should feel. Patriotism is the only proper motive for taking up arms and it is never too late to insist that a good soldier must be the best of citizens. He should be generous to the conquered and kind to the unfortunate. The honour of the colours should be sacred to him. Desertion and bad conduct presage coward-

---

[1] WO. 27/50, f. 169. Cf. n. 2, 3. Haviland staged a mock attack on the defences of Plymouth in January 1780 in which the militia did well. WO. 34/122, f. 113.

[2] WO. 27/40, f. 251.   [3] WO. 27/50, f. 192.

[4] See WO. 27/50, ff. 15, 31, 117; and f. 180 where the objection is to the regiment's 'private economy'.

[5] He thought the militia officers, since they served out of pure patriotism, as deserving as those of the army. *Letter from a Militia Man to his Colonel*, pp. 10–13.

ice in the field, for a soldier must dread death less than misbehaviour before his officers. Because the regiment bears the name of Sussex, the whole county will share in its honour or its disgrace.[1] A curious incident in 1796 seems to be a token of good regimental spirit, based on harmony between officers and men. Some robberies had been committed in Norwich by men in uniform and the local general had issued an order putting the blame on the garrison. But the robbers turned out to be civilians and after their trial Lt.-Cols. Nightingale and Hutton of the Cambridgeshire and the West Kent (the two regiments in the town) put an advertisement in the papers declaring that the honour of their men had been vindicated. As a result, when Nightingale next appeared at evening parade, the men gave him three hearty cheers.[2]

But militiamen did not in the end turn out to be superior in character and social origin to the rank and file of the regular army, and consequently the maintenance of discipline was as hard in the 'constitutional' as in the 'mercenary' force. Law-breaking was rampant in both forces. Men deserted in shoals. When a man deserted from the Cambridgeshires in 1796, Nightingale at once issued handbills offering 2 guineas reward for his capture, as a deterrent.[3] Drunkenness, the universal failing of the age, was naturally rampant. The increase in pay in 1797 was displeasing to the military authorities because it increased the amount that the men could spend on drink. The Cambridgeshires were sternly warned against temptation, but even so the consequences were such that Wale thought it best to mount guard in the mornings instead of in the evenings, to avoid having to punish men who had been drunk off duty.[4] Pilfering and bad behaviour towards civilians was a great nuisance, especially in camp. In 1780 things at Tiptree Camp were so bad that a meeting of representatives of the surrounding parishes decided to prosecute offenders at public expense, offering rewards for evidence leading to conviction. Lt.-Gen. Parker told Amherst that the camp was surrounded by outposts and sentinels so numerous that had the NCOs done their duty nobody would have been able to get out at night. But significantly he went on that Amherst knew as well as he did how lax militia regiments were in their observance of orders and internal discipline.[5] In 1800 four men of the Cambridgeshires were courtmartialled for poaching. They were acquitted, but it was fairly clear

[1] BM, Add. 33048, ff. 350–1.
[2] BM, Add. 35666, ff. 329, 338, 340.
[3] BM, Add. 35667, f. 23.
[4] BM, Add. 35668, ff. 210, 215. Cf. Add. 35667, f. 342.
[5] Parker was thanked by the meeting for helping to arrest four men accused of burglary. He complained at the number of officers absent to vote in elections. WO. 34/127, ff. 101–2.

that they had been gathering pease and they were sentenced to 200 lashes for being out of bounds. They were pardoned at the request of the owner of the land concerned.[1]

Worse than the actual crimes, of which only three especially common classes have been mentioned, was the chronic state of insubordination which constantly threatened to overturn discipline altogether. Officers seem to have felt themselves to be on the edge of a volcano. When the Cambridgeshires were at Landguard Fort in the winter of 1794–5 Captain Huddleston, in temporary command, received an anonymous letter relating apparently to the meat supply. He gave it out in orders that the sender would be punished if caught and that no anonymous complaints were received, though complaints properly made would receive attention. He told the acting sergeant-major to make discreet enquiries. When Wale next came to the Fort he induced Huddleston to offer 5 guineas reward for the discovery of the offender. Both officers thought that some 'old growsers' in the regiment were responsible, and resolved to keep strict discipline, especially among these and punished the least offence. The men were to be made to work hard and told that it was because of their mutinous spirit. The governor of the fort soon after reprieved a man court-martialled for insolence and Wale feared that any sign of weakness would set off a mutiny. Lord Hardwicke in later regimental orders said he was sure that most of the men were properly grateful to their officers; but he doubled the 5 guinea reward.[2]

To keep the militia in order, recourse was had to the harsh system of punishments then in force for the army. At first it was only when they were embodied that the militia were subject to the mutiny act. Discipline at peacetime exercises was to be maintained by a system of fines levied by the justices. But from 1762, martial law was applicable here too, save that there were to be no punishments extending to 'life and limb'. Only in 1786, however, was martial law extended to NCOs in permanent pay at times when the militia was not embodied. Courts-martial had to be composed of militia officers only, which sometimes led to difficulties in organising them.[3] Lesser offences,

[1] BM, Add. 35674, f. 147.

[2] The local butcher was overcharging and bad weather hindered his supersession by supplies ferried over from Harwich. BM, Add. 35665, ff. 206, 320, 323. The regiment was very annoyed by the governor's claiming the right to pardon men regimentally condemned. *Ibid.*, between ff. 344–69.

[3] 30 Geo. II, cap. 25, ss. 36–40, 45, 47. 2 Geo. III, cap. 20, ss. 99, 116, 121. 4 Geo. III, cap. 17, s. 8 (system of penalties extended to drummers). 7 Geo. III, cap. 17, ss. 19–25 (punishment of NCOs disembodied: desertion to be punishable by martial law). 26 Geo. III, cap. 107, ss. 68, 88, 95, 98–9. 42 Geo. III, cap. 90, ss. 89, 103, 111, 115–16. By s. 104, officers might sometimes be summoned to attend courts-martial without pay during disembodiment. From 1762 non-attendance at drill counted as desertion, but was punished by a justice. There was

including all those in peacetime, were tried by regimental courts-martial, appointed by the commanding officer and with sentences subject to his confirmation. More serious offences were tried by general court-martial, appointed by some higher authority. Here, too, there was a power to revise the sentences, but there was no regular system of appeals.[1]

These powers were fully used. In the North Yorkshire Militia, more than thirty men were punished by order of regimental courts-martial in 1793–4. Almost all were flogged, the sentences varying from 50 to 300 strokes. Absence without leave was the main offence, mostly in mild forms like returning late to quarters. The remaining offences were either pilfering or various forms of disorderly behaviour. It is fair to add that sentences were often reduced and a fair number of men were acquitted.[2]

The severity of martial law was useless unless regimental life was well organised. The scattering of troops in quarters made this very difficult. Newdigate noted that the captains should visit their men's quarters at least once a week and the subalterns twice; the major should tour the quarters of the whole regiment frequently, to keep his subordinates up to the mark.[3] This sort of remote control was not always enough. Charles Yorke's company of the Cambridge-shires was in some disorder in the spring of 1793. One subaltern was long either absent or sick; the other was conscientious but too diffident to be a good disciplinarian. The men in consequence ran up debts at the local public houses and one of them—though it can hardly be called a breach of discipline—ate a jackdaw alive, presumably for a bet.[4]

In barracks or in camp it was possible to have a much stricter way of life. At Winchester in 1799 there was a set of rules not only for the men of the Staffordshires but also for the women in barracks. Each company had to provide four men each day for cleaning. Urine tubs were to be regularly emptied. The men were to leave the dormitories at 6 a.m. each day and they were not to be used either for cleaning equipment or for the sale of provisions by the women.[5]

a penalty for aiding desertion and, from the act of 1767, special machinery for catching deserters and sending them to their regiments. See further 26 Geo. III, cap. 107, ss. 82, 92–4; 42 Geo. III, cap. 90, ss. 99, 108–10, 131; and above, pp. 274–5.

[1] For possibilities of appeal in exceptional cases see WO. 4/760, p. 20; *Calendar of Home Office Papers, 1760–5*, p. 309, no. 1018.

[2] WO. 68/195, Court-Martial Book of the North Yorkshire Militia, 1793–1806. In the East Devons, minor offences were sometimes dealt with informally by a court made up of privates and presided over by a sergeant, the commanding officer reviewing the sentence. Walrond, p. 131.

[3] Newdigate's diary, 1759, note at end.

[4] BM, Add. 35392, f. 319.   [5] Bagot's Order Book, 22 May 1799.

When the Lancashires reached Canterbury Barracks in November 1794, a regular routine was at once established. Lights were to be out at 9 p.m. and any man leaving his barrack after that save to visit the 'necessary' was to be punished. The roll was called twice a day, and the sergeant doing this in each company was to enter any man absent after 'lights out' and would be punished if any man was seen outside and he failed to report him. One NCO was to sleep in each room and be responsible for any disorders in it. Each company was to be visited in the evening by one of its officers, and it was soon laid down that he should not go round till after 9 p.m., so that he could see that all the lights were out and receive a return of absentees.[1] Parades were frequent and regular: twice a day normally, at 10 a.m. and 3.30 p.m. On Sundays there was church parade, the roll being called both before and after it. The men had to move from quarters to parade and from regimental to company drill in regular formation under the command of an officer. There were regular inspections of arms and necessaries.[2] The commanding officer was rewarded for his care by being able on 9 January to commend the men for their good behaviour; he did not fail to warn them against spoiling their record when their arrears were paid.[3]

To enforce these arrangements there was an officer of the day and a guard consisting of a subaltern, sergeant, corporal, drummer and twenty-four privates, all of them changed each day. The officer of the guard had to patrol the town each evening after 'lights out' and arrest any soldier found in the streets or in a public house.[4] This was the usual system. At Colchester barracks in 1797–8 the Cambridgeshires had to join with other regiments in mounting a very extensive guard. On 19 November 1797 there was a main guard with sixty-nine privates under a captain and a rear-guard with forty-five under a subaltern. They mounted respectively twenty-two and thirteen sentries by day and twenty-three and twelve at night. They had various prisoners in custody for such offences as drunkenness, insulting sergeants and bringing bad women into barracks. The tasks of this guard included reporting articles broken, mounting guard over the kitchen of the officers' mess and preventing asses entering barracks. (Baskets with goods to be sold were likewise not allowed to stand inside the barrack gates).[5] As for the officer of the day, his duties when the regiment was at Ipswich in 1800 included attending roll-call at dinner-time, seeing that the messing arrangements worked, and enforcing cleanliness and especially the opening of windows.[6]

[1] Farrington's Order Book, 21, 23 and 30 November 1794.
[2] *Ibid.*, 14, 20 and 24 November 1794, and *passim.*
[3] *Ibid.*, 9 January 1795.   [4] Farrington, 30 November 1794, and *passim.*
[5] BM. Add. 35669, ff. 20, 22, 24, 37, 62, 232–4.   [6] BM, Add. 35674, f. 113.

At camp, likewise, there was an elaborate system of guards, of which a field officer of the day, provided by each of the regiments in turn, was in charge.[1] At Warley in 1779 there were three of them: a colonel who made 'grand rounds' and reported in the morning to a Major General of the Day, and a lieutenant-colonel and a major who made 'visiting rounds'. The guards there were a quarter-guard and a picket, to which each regiment contributed men. The picket was formed at sunset and the men served for twenty-four hours, during which they were always ready to oppose a surprise attack and never undressed. Ordered out by officers at different hours of the night, they searched the huts in the rear for soldiers who should have been in their tents.[2] At Coxheath in 1778 about a quarter of the men— some 4000—were on guard every night: an extensive system of outposts round the camp both checked desertion and gave practice in guarding against surprises.[3]

By these means a regular routine was enforced, which at Warley in 1779 began at daybreak. The men were up before five and after roll-call they drilled until eight. At nine there was breakfast and the relief of the quarter-guard. The 'marked men' drilled from 10.30 till 11.45. There was a roll-call at noon to prevent rambling and then dinner and at 4.30 another exercise. The day seems to have ended at sunset, as it did at Coxheath, where the firing of a gun gave notice that nobody was allowed out of camp.[4] One morning in 1781, Maj.-Gen. Rainsford, suspecting that some officers were sleeping in quarters with their families without his leave, turned out the whole force at Harwich Camp at reveille without warning. He was pleased to find that the line was formed in order and silence in a quarter of an hour. Only a few officers were absent, and they were put 'in arrest' but released on making a proper apology.[5]

But a good system of regulations was no use without officers capable of enforcing them and here was the ineradicable flaw in the militia, as has already been explained. Officers were insufficient both in numbers and professional competence. On mobilisation in 1778 the Leicestershire had only two subalterns and the lieutenant-colonel was not expected to join,[6] while the officers of the West Norfolk were described as not well chosen, and the adjutant had been incapacitated by a stroke.[7] As for the Westminster battalion, its officers were mostly old and apparently ignorant: during parade they fell to the rear and left it to the sergeants to give orders.[8]

---

[1] Farrington, October 1794, *passim*.
[2] BM, Add. 35660, f. 210.   [3] BM, Add. 35659, f. 392.
[4] BM, Add. 35660, f. 210. Cf. Add. 35659, f. 392.
[5] WO. 34/137, ff. 113–14.   [6] WO. 27/40, f. 46.
[7] *Ibid.*, f. 96.   [8] *Ibid.*, f. 67.

Officers, furthermore, were often ill-behaved. Absence without leave was frequent. Major Cooper, commanding the Cumberlands in 1781, rushed off to London on urgent family business though he had been refused leave and though he had military zeal enough to wish to provide for all his six sons in the army and navy. He was put under arrest on his return.[1] An anonymous letter of December 1778 reported that the major of the Denbighshires had been absent since June, the colonel since September; one captain had never joined and the other, who had never been away above two weeks, was an MP and had to attend parliament.[2] Lieutenant Baillie of the Anglesey was given leave in November 1779 and simply disappeared.[3] In September 1780 Captain Apreece, in temporary command of the Huntingdons, absented himself from Tiptree Camp because his wife was dangerously ill, and prolonged his absence for reasons which had the air of having been thought up afterwards. Lt.-Gen. Parker said he deserved a court-martial, but would in fact be simply kept some time in arrest. He reported the affair to Amherst to give him an idea of the quality of the officers.[4] In 1798 it was found that no field officer had been present with either the Cumberlands or the Westmorlands since the call-out in 1793.[5]

It must in fairness be said that things were little better in the army, and the Duke of York launched a campaign to improve attendance in both services. In the spring of 1797 he was displeased with the slowness with which officers returned from winter leave and the leniency which general officers showed them. In the case of regulars and fencibles he ordered that successors to those remaining absent should be recommended to him.[6] In 1800 and 1801 the War Office was told to stop the pay of various officers until they had returned to duty or justified their absence.[7] Lt.-Col. Brettell of the West Middlesex was one officer caught out at this time. On his then asking for leave, enquiry was made and it was found that he had not attended for several years. He was given leave for two months and then resigned.[8]

Officers were also perpetually quarrelling among themselves. Sometimes there was physical violence. Seven or eight Essex officers got drunk and had a fight at Danbury Camp in 1780 in full view of the men. There were arrests, a duel and apparently some resignations as a result, but no court-martial.[9] A Norfolk captain in 1781 went up to another in the mess room and said 'Boo!' in his ear. On doing

[1] WO. 34/138, ff. 59, 60, 209.   [2] WO. 34/146 (ii), f. 246.
[3] WO. 34/163, f. 50.   [4] WO. 34/167, f. 51.
[5] HO. 50/7, W. Grinfield, 3 February 1798.
[6] WO. 3/31, pp. 21, 29, 44–5.
[7] WO. 3/32, pp. 353, 393. WO. 3/33, pp. 9, 37, 106, 385, 566, etc.
[8] WO. 3/22, pp. 253, 342, 367, 534.   [9] WO. 34/165, f. 246.

it a second time he received a blow on the side of his face and both officers ended under arrest. The joker was got rid of, it seems, without fuss as he had been intending to leave soon, anyway, in order to enter the church![1] A little earlier, three Hampshire subalterns had been involved in a fight which began in the streets of Beaconsfield and ended, after a journey through the night on horseback, in the streets of High Wycombe.[2] No less tiresome were the constant courts-martial in which officers brought charges against each other. In 1801 Major Senhouse of the Cumberland sought to have his adjutant court-martialled after a long quarrel between them, in the course of which the major forced the adjutant to put an order reflecting on his own character in the regimental order book, only to be met by the insertion of a letter of expostulation to the Secretary at War in the regimental letter book. Senhouse scraped together all the charges he could, some old and one for which the adjutant had already been officially rebuked. The Duke of York objected to this practice as calculated to subvert regimental harmony.[3] He made the same objection in 1800 when the officers of the Pembrokeshire brought some charges against their colonel.[4] Superiors, be it noted, as well as inferiors might be accused: in 1799 a Norfolk major was restrained from doing both at once, by prosecuting both his colonel and his adjutant.[5]

Financial irregularities by officers have already been spoken of and were only the worst instances of a tendency to slack administration.[6] Of course not all officers were bad, but there was a constant trickle of dismissals and enforced resignations.[7] This sort of thing was doubly harmful. A bad example was set and necessary business went undone.

Even conscientious officers might undermine discipline by denying the right of senior officers to command them. The king was empowered to put the militia under the command of general officers, but it was common to claim that they could not be put under the command of army officers of lower rank.[8] In the early days some militia colonels had been given the rank of brigadier general,[9] and two at least of these, Sir James Lowther and Lord Darlington, considered them-

[1] WO. 34/131, ff. 58–9.
[2] WO. 34/128, ff. 57–8.
[3] WO. 3/33, pp. 435–6, 466–8, 534–6.
[4] WO. 3/32, pp. 173, 191–3, 217–18, 239.
[5] WO. 3/21, pp. 92–3.
[6] Such as failure to make proper returns, e.g. WO. 3/17, pp. 43, 54.
[7] E.g., WO. 3/32, pp. 4, 5; WO. 3/33, pp. 581, 589, 592; WO. 3/21, pp. 327, 332, 366, 396. NCOs, too, behaved badly: for an example see WO. 34/141, ff. 128–31.
[8] See, e.g., WO. 34/165, ff. 29-32, 129; WO. 34/126, f. 297, cf. WO. 34/166, f. 306 and WO. 34/167, f. 24.
[9] Including Rockingham and Shaftesbury. See WO. 1/980, ff. 353, 455–6, 515, 526, 541–2; WO. 4/757, p. 6; WO. 3/18, p. 81.

selves absolved thereby from having to ask for leave of absence.[1] Militia officers who also held regular commissions sometimes claimed to command army officers junior to themselves. The most famous case was that of the Duke of Richmond, who held general rank. A board of army officers considered his claim in 1779 and ruled that army rank was in abeyance as long as its holder served in the militia.[2] Richmond also blocked a sensible plan for settling an order of precedence among militia regiments—necessary in order to determine who should command when detachments of several militia regiments served together. In 1778 a meeting of lord lieutenants proposed that the county units should rank according to their first date of being called out under the current laws. But this would have made Sussex rank last and Richmond objected to the favouring of those who had adopted a 'raw and undigested revival' above those who had prudently waited until twenty years and twelve acts of parliament had improved it. Precedence had to be settled each year by drawing lots until 1795, when it was settled by lot for the duration of the current war.[3]

The social eminence of some of the militia colonels seems to have made it harder for general officers to insist that their regiments maintain a proper standard of discipline. When the Dorsetshire were sent to Plymouth in 1759, Governor Duroure humbly promised to do his best for them and said he would think it an honour if he could win the esteem of Lord Shaftesbury.[4] When he found the Devonshire officers dissatisfied with their quarters, he asked that all his orders be sanctioned by the Secretary at War, to give them a better chance of being obeyed and remove suspicions of partiality. When there was trouble over pay and quarters, he complained that the officers had gone over his head and failed to take his advice.[5] Onslow, his successor, was more ready to exert his authority, but was not always readily obeyed. Some Devon men sent out on escort duty were given leave to visit their families and failed to rejoin the detachment, returning to Plymouth on their own. Onslow was having trouble with straggling in such parties and he ordered these men to be confined as an example. Colonel Sir John Rogers came to intercede

---

[1] Lowther was a bad officer, but Darlington was a good one. WO. 34/156 (i), ff. 243–5, cf. WO. 34/157, f. 77.

[2] See WO. 3/16, pp. 90–1.

[3] WO. 34/110, ff. 93–5. WO. 34/111, ff. 46–56. WO. 34/124, ff. 33–6. Lots were first drawn in 1760 to settle precedence locally: WO. 4/758, pp. 311–16; cf. BM, Add. 35660, ff. 310, 314; Add. 35661, f. 25; on 1795, WO. 3/28, p. 116. Some corps still had not drawn in 1799 (WO. 3/19, pp. 218, 396). See W. Y. Baldry, 'Order of Precedence of Militia Regiments', *Jol. of Society of Army Historical Research*, vol. xv (1936), pp. 5–16.   [4] WO. 1/979, letter of 24 June.

[5] *Ibid.*, letters of 6, 8, 17, 20 and 22 July.

for them and said he thought it hard, whereat Onslow on his own confession lost his temper and threatened to arrest Rogers. Sir John replied that he was a country gentleman doing a patriotic duty and not an ordinary soldier. He obeyed the order, but appealed through Pitt to Ligonier the Commander-in-Chief. Onslow complained of misrepresentation and looked forward gloomily to trouble in parliament. But, significantly, Ligonier (who had already warned Onslow to keep his temper) said that the service of the militia was much wanted and the country gentlemen must be kept in good humour.[1]

The consequence of all this was perpetual disorder in the militia, ranging from mutiny to mere absence of discipline. As early as 1759 there was a mutiny in the Duke of Bedford's Devon regiment, stationed at Plymouth. On 24 August one of its sergeants was imprisoned for selling ale in St George's Square, contrary to orders. That evening some of the men assembled and declared that no militiaman should suffer confinement. They went to demand the release of the prisoner and when the guard refused them admittance they threw stones, and one of them was arrested. The others fetched their arms and fired several rounds at the guard, next attacking the barrack gate with their hangers. Only then did the guard open fire, wounding three and driving them off. Next morning they returned without arms and asked for the release of the man who had been seized, which the officer in command thought it prudent to allow.[2] Nothing more happened, but Onslow reported that the militia could not be depended on and their officers could not control them.[3] The matter came before the cabinet and Pitt and Ligonier ordered examples to be made. In defence of his men, Bedford said that mutinies were not unknown among raw regular regiments. It was also the case that the rest of the militia in the garrison stood firm, including those guarding the prisoner.[4] The morale of Bedford's regiment had been visibly lower than that of the other Devon regiments even before the mutiny,[5] perhaps because its colonel was an absentee politician.

In the next war (1780) there was again an affray at Plymouth, resulting from a quarrel between some Somerset and Brecon men in a disorderly house in Dock. One night the Somersets took arms and tried to force the lines, where their rivals were quartered. The 97th foot was ordered to stop them and there was fighting in which ten men were wounded and one killed. The Somersets continued to vow vengeance and it was thought necessary to remove them to a camp

---

[1] WO. 30/8, vol. 77, ff. 193-203.
[2] WO. 1/980, ff. 775-8. BM, Eg. 3444, ff. 246-7.   [3] *Ibid.*, f. 244.
[4] *Ibid.*, ff. 242, 246. See, too, MSS. of Fourth Duke of Bedford, vol. xl, ff. 50, 54, 66; *Bedford Correspondence*, vol. ii, pp. 385-6.
[5] One colonel had thought of asking for their segregation. WO. 1/980, ff. 775-8.

outside the town. Lt.-Gen. Haviland said that the trouble was that the officers screened the men rather than punish them. The lieutenant-colonel and the major could be depended on, but that was no use when the colonel was present.[1] At about the same time there was a fight in Tiptree Camp between the Cumberland and Radnor corps which threatened to draw in the rest. Lt.-Gen. Parker called a meeting of commanding officers and complained of the want of discipline and inattention to orders in many units. He said that it was essential for the officers to set a good example and do their own duty properly.[2] When the Warwickshires joined him, he said that they performed well in the field and their shortcomings were mostly confined to or caused by the officers; poor internal discipline he found to be a failing of all militia corps.[3]

At the opening of the war against revolutionary France, reports were reaching the Marquess of Buckingham of something even more serious—political disaffection in the corps from the industrial areas. The Duke of Norfolk had told the house of lords that there were so many 'manufacturers and Sheffield men' in the West Riding militia that it was 'upon a different footing' from the rest and he was glad to preserve quiet by turning a blind eye to breaches of discipline. A music master serving there but formerly in Buckingham's regiment confirmed this and said that many of the men had 'little books' from Sheffield. Captain Badcock, who had been sent to muster regiments in the north, said much the same, and also that the Nottinghamshires were very undisciplined and had got some of the writings of their major, Cartwright, from a Nottingham club. One of Buckingham's sergeants confirmed this report, and from a similar source came word that the Warwickshires had been mutinous at the exercise of 1791 and had had 'little books' given them; also that the Westminsters, who were the refuse of London, were supplied with 'little books' and had officers little better than the men.[4]

Whatever the truth of these reports, the militia seems to have been loyal enough in the war that ensued. In several regiments the men replied to seditious handbills by loyal addresses or offering a reward for the capture of the authors.[5] But less political disorders continued. In April 1795 the Oxfordshires mutinied against the high price of

[1] One of the wounded men died. The ringleaders were court-martialled. WO. 34/123, ff. 215–16. WO. 34/126, ff. 220, 250. WO. 34/127, f. 187. WO. 34/166, f. 215.

[2] WO. 34/123, ff. 217–18. Cf. the pilfering at Tiptree, p. 418.

[3] WO. 34/166, f. 295. For a mutiny in the Derbyshires in 1778, see WO. 1/1000, Charles Gould, 24 July 1778.

[4] It took ten of the twenty-eight days to collect and disperse the West Riding men for the annual exercise. HMC, *Dropmore*, vol. ii, pp. 344–5.

[5] E.g. Bonhote, pp. 161–3; Holden, p. 69; Walrond, pp. 147–9.

THE NEW MILITIA AT WORK

food, seizing grain and selling it cheaply to the poor.[1] The Cambridgeshires met some ill-disciplined regiments in their wanderings. The Huntingdons were their neighbours at Warley in 1793, and there was much resentment because the Cambridge men had to keep strict order in the evenings and retire to their tents at 8 or 9 p.m. but the Huntingdons did not. There was a riot, suppressed with difficulty.[2] Late in 1795 the Huntingdons were in Yarmouth Barracks with the South Lincolnshires whose colonel, Sibthorpe, commanded the whole and was very strict. He imposed a curfew because of the men's depredations in the town, whereupon the Huntingdons rioted and devastated their quarters. For a time it looked as though they would have to be put down by force, but in the end they were simply sent away and the Cambridgeshires took their place. Wale and Nightingale complained bitterly at having to move into the devastated barracks and feared that the men would bear a grudge against the Huntingdon 'banditti', whose sole object had been to get more comfortable quarters.[3]

The Huntingdons' version of this affair was that they had been corrupted by the South Lincolns, and the Cambridge officers were the more happy at being able to escape from them fairly soon.[4] They met the South Lincolns again, however, on guard over prisoners of war at Norman Cross, in Huntingdonshire, in the spring of 1797 and found them to be indeed a bad regiment. Nightingale said that the 'Major and Majoribus' of the regiment were, respectively, mostly absent and an 'old woman'.[5] Hardwicke found that the colonel and lieutenant-colonel both lived in the village of Stilton, some miles off, and there was often no field officer with the regiment. Proper order was not kept, the sentries left their arms in the boxes and ran errands for the prisoners, the guards were changed without formality and with laughing and talking. The Cambridge men were constantly ridiculed by those of Lincoln for their good behaviour and were becoming infected. Nightingale declared that the Lincolns were beneath contempt and more to be feared by friends than by foes.[6] The authorities set down General Bowyer to take command, after which things seem to have improved. A Lincolnshire sergeant was publicly degraded and punished for conniving at a prisoner's escape.[7] The

---

[1] WO. 1/1088, f. 133.

[2] Coming from neighbouring counties, the men knew each other well. Lord Hardwicke tried to prevent their being put together in 1795. BM, Add. 35666, ff. 18–19.

[3] *Ibid.*, ff. 214, 217, 223, 225–7, 229, 232, 234, 236. Quarters in this barracks were very cramped.

[4] *Ibid.*   [5] BM, Add. 35668, f. 39.

[6] *Ibid.*, ff. 89, 99.

[7] *Ibid.*, f. 159. See, too, ff. 94, 106, 140, 148.

Cambridgeshires were plagued with drunkenness due to the increase in pay, and they disobeyed an order forbidding them to take outside work.[1] But their discipline in general stood the strain and the Duke of York refused Hardwicke's request that they be moved. He said that he had given them this difficult assignment because their discipline was good. Bowyer, however, thought that both regiments should have gone elsewhere. They were near home, and in consequence debauched by visits from their friends.[2]

Once again it is necessary to emphasise that the army was no shining example to the militia. Haviland said in 1781 that the militia under his command in that campaign had behaved well and the regulars had behaved less well.[3] A big fight at Stowmarket Barracks in 1801 between militiamen and some regular soldiers was acknowledged by all to have been the regulars' fault and Nightingale thought it most unfair that the militia as well as the regulars should have received a reproof.[4] But this does not make less true or generally applicable the view which Haviland expressed in 1780:

> Upon the whole my opinion of the Militia Corps is that they learn their exercise and go through their manoeuvres well, but subordination is much wanted in many of them; which I look upon to be the most material part of discipline.[5]

III

The conclusive test of the militia's efficiency would have been a full-scale engagement with a real enemy. In default of this, it is instructive to consider how well they performed such humbler military tasks as were allotted to them, not for practice, but in earnest.

The most important of these was the guarding of prisoners of war. By taking this over, the militia freed regular troops for more active service abroad. The prisoners were mostly sailors and they were the responsibility of the Admiralty. They tended to be kept at or near naval bases, in makeshift accommodation. Only in 1797 was a prison camp built at the more suitable inland site of Norman Cross; Dartmoor and Perth prisons were opened only in 1809 and 1812.[6] While

---

[1] An extra roll-call was imposed as punishment for the latter. A man who suggested that they should not attend was sentenced to 300 lashes. *Ibid.*, ff. 210, 215. On the drunkenness see above, p. 418.

[2] *Ibid.*, ff. 161–2.

[3] WO. 34/136, ff. 221–2. WO. 34/137, ff. 313–14. Parker similarly found at the start of his camp in 1780 that his one regular regiment was less forward in training than most of the militia regiments. WO. 34/126, ff. 131–2.

[4] BM, Add. 35674, ff. 296–9, 304.

[5] WO. 34/128, ff. 28–9.

[6] For the whole subject see T. J. Walker, *The Depot for Prisoners of War at Norman Cross, Huntingdonshire, 1796 to 1816* (London 1913).

the prisoners were near the coast, it was an anxious task seeing that they neither escaped nor attempted to sabotage the bases.[1]

Standing orders issued by Lt.-Gen. Monckton at Portsmouth during the American war give an idea of the work to be done. The guard was naturally to be most vigilant at night, when extra sentries were to be posted and relieved each hour, a corporal and two privates going the rounds half an hour after each relief. 'Lights out' for the prisoners was at 10 p.m., and after that, sentries were to report any light or sound. They were to challenge everyone after nightfall. But it was no less important that unauthorised persons should be kept out in the day-time, for experience seemed to show that it was by such outsiders that escapes were organised. Tradesmen were allowed to attend every weekday from nine till three to sell the prisoners anything not prohibited. But everyone except employees of the Agent in charge of the prisoners needed a pass to get inside. Prisoners were not to be allowed to communicate with strangers. The guard was not to interfere in the administration of the prison, but it was to look out for abuses because these might lead to disorder. Any complaints to the Agent were to be made in writing by the officer of the guard, who had, of course, also to keep a careful watch on his own men, going the rounds frequently at night, seeing that they were sober and inspecting their arms and ammunition.[2]

The arrangements for guards were not perfect. In 1779 Sir George Savile's West Riding regiment was on guard at Liverpool. The prisoners were almost equal in numbers to the regiment and seem to have been in quarters and not under lock and key. There were also pressed men on the ships in harbour who needed watching and various alarms arose of which something is said below. The regiment consisted mainly of new recruits and the heavy guard duty retarded their training. The prisoners were disorderly and a sentry was obliged to shoot one.[3] In Plymouth that same year some prisoners escaped by digging a tunnel into the garden of a public house, whence they could easily escape because of the crowd of people going in and out. The Somerset and Cornish militia were on guard at the prison with the 13th foot. They had a difficult time because the weather was very bad

[1] The Admiralty was worried in 1762: *Calendar of Home Office Papers, 1760–5,* p. 188, no. 613; p. 190, no. 621. Cobbald (*loc. cit.*) found prisoners inland at Derby.

[2] WO. 1/1009, ff. 1519–22. These orders were apparently the basis of those issued by royal authority in the next war, WO. 4/770, pp. 374, 380. The prisoners might send out parties to shop for them and might have strong beer but not spirits. Unrest had resulted from punishing them in the 'black hole' and from bad behaviour by turnkeys.

[3] WO. 1/1003, ff. 171–4. WO. 1/1004, ff. 227–30. The sentry was exonerated by a (?coroner's) jury and so doubtless acted in self-defence.

(it was January) and there had been no proper provision of guard-houses and lamps. After the escape the dockyard commissioner ordered that patrols should go round outside the walls as well as sentries within, to ensure a proper watch. What was less creditable to the militia was that the Cornish regiment consisted mainly of untrained men and, worse still, the Somersets were politically suspect. Many of the officers were dissenters and did duty on the American prisoners with reluctance. The regiment was removed from Plymouth soon afterwards at the commanding officer's request.[1]

Against this can be set occasions when the militia showed itself alert and efficient. On 25 June 1781 Lieutenant Barwick of the East Essex mounted guard at the old prison, Yarmouth, from which a man had lately escaped. He discovered that some prisoners had filed off their fetters and ordered a search of their cell. A large hole was discovered under the stairs. He placed a guard there and augmented the sentinels on the gates, sending a warning to the mayor.[2] In May 1779 Captain Waterhouse, commanding the Surrey militia at Gosport, discovered that the prisoners were digging a tunnel. A Walloon prisoner, moreover, reported a plot to overpower the guard. Thirteen prisoners were closely confined as a result and the guard was increased from sixty to ninety, with a picket ready to turn out. As there were 1500 prisoners there, unsuitably housed in a former seamen's hospital, it was well that the discovery was made.[3] In May 1762, twenty-four prisoners got out of the King's House at Winchester through a large drain. The Buckinghamshires were on guard that day, with John Wilkes in command. One of the sentries spotted the men as they were making off, challenged and fired. Two were wounded and only four managed to get away into the fields. It was a dark night and the turnkeys had failed to light the lamps at the proper time, but the regiment exerted itself and those who got away seem to have been retaken.[4]

Another important task which the militia was expected partly to take over from the regulars was the suppression of riots. The most spectacular action of this kind in which they were engaged was the Gordon Riots of 1780. More important still, perhaps, was the part which some regiments played in the policing of Ireland from 1798. But in these cases the militia were acting in conjunction with regulars

[1] WO. 34/112, ff. 182–3. WO. 34/113, ff. 80–1. WO. 34/150, f. 230. Cf. the bad behaviour of the Somersets, above, pp. 426–7.

[2] WO. 34/134, f. 175. The prisoners had grievances.

[3] WO. 1/1005, ff. 455–8. WO. 34/114, f. 147.

[4] BM, Eg. 2136, ff. 29, 30. Of course the militia had sometimes to escort prisoners on the march. This was usually done in relays, the prisoners being passed from regiment to regiment across the country. See, e.g., WO. 4/771, pp. 221, 228–9, 246–7.

and volunteers. What they could do on their own is perhaps better shown in the machine-breaking riots in Lancashire in 1779. It was late on 3 October that Sir George Savile, whose regiment had all too much to do in Liverpool as we have seen, received an urgent request for help from Wigan. He at once sent 200 men there, who marched the twenty-six miles in eight hours and arrived at 6 a.m. Half the regiment remained in Liverpool and 100 men went to Prescott under Savile's command, to be ready to reinforce either detachment if it got into difficulties. The riots spread to other centres and were soon estimated to involve 4000 men with sixty-five guns. Savile brought his reserve to Wigan, and then took the 200 men first sent there to Chorley. Arriving too late to prevent the destruction of a mill, he went on to Preston.[1] On the 7th, 100 men had to be sent at top speed from Liverpool to Stockport. Fortunately the Denbighshire militia responded to appeals from Savile and the mayor of Liverpool and three companies were sent there from Chester to replace the men who had left.[2]

After this the riots seem to have become a sort of guerrilla war, with mobs assembling on the moors and the regiments split in detachments in pursuit. The magistrates had no great confidence in the militia and Savile, too, was anxious for them to be relieved by regulars and get back to training. He thought the magistrates supine and was bothered (like the authorities in London at the time of the Gordon Riots) by the uncertain state of the law regarding the use of troops against rioters. But his corps met no resistance and took a number of prisoners. Regular troops were sent in and by the end of the month quiet had been restored.[3]

Some miscellaneous examples may be given of other disturbances where the militia was called in. Early in 1783 there were disturbances in the Berwick district because of the shortage of corn: the Cumberland and Northumberland militia helped to keep order.[4] In 1780 the 'no popery' agitation disturbed Lancaster to the extent of some unauthorised military drilling among the young men, the hoisting of the American flag and the cursing of the king. Fifty men of the Glamorganshires preserved the peace, behaving well under serious provocation, and Lieutenant Jenkins, their commander, seems to have shown considerable skill in restoring quiet.[5] In 1781 there were

[1] WO. 1/1003, ff. 183–202, 211.
[2] WO. 1/1003, ff. 203, 207, 215–22, 227–30, 251–4.
[3] *Ibid.*, ff. 231–4, 247–50, 255–8. Cf. f. 192; WO. 34/119, ff. 81–4; HMC, *Foljambe*, pp. 152–3. Fawcett, sent to investigate, thought the seriousness of the disturbances had been exaggerated. WO. 34/119, ff. 136–8, 172–3. WO. 1/1003, ff. 353 *et seq.*
[4] WO. 1/1018, ff. 15–18; W. Dent, 14 February 1783.
[5] WO. 1/1007, ff. 968–71. WO. 1/1008, ff. 719–20, 723–6.

dangerous disturbances among the inmates of Carlisle prison, and a party of the Westmorlands were called in and stayed for the best part of a month.[1]

A frequent task of the militia was chasing smugglers. In 1779 Lord Orford's Norfolk regiment, camped at Aldeburgh, sent a party four miles up the coast on the news that a cutter was landing goods there. They arrived too late to intercept the landing, but found thirty 'half anchors' of spirits cleverly hidden away in a cave by the sea. A party was left camped on the spot to prevent more landings. A little later a landing was made at Dunwich, and twenty militiamen mounted on baggage horses chased the smugglers forty miles in four hours. They did not catch them but one had to drop his load, which included a letter giving details of the next run. Again a detachment was sent to camp at the landing point, for a cutter was hovering there, waiting its chance. Lord Orford remarked that the clergy, lawyers and doctors of the area were all smugglers and in Aldeburgh itself every inhabitant was one except the parson.[2] In 1778 a detachment camped at Southwold had actually to fight a battle with smugglers, for a 12-gun cutter tried to make a landing under cover of a bombardment. Reinforcements came in and all the goods were seized.[3] Many other examples could be given of action against smugglers, not all of course so exciting.[4] Police work of this kind seems to have been within the militia's capacity. But as already noticed, the precaution was taken of stationing militiamen as far as possible outside their own counties, so that they would never be called on to fight their friends and relations.[5]

The militia, finally, seem to have done useful work in the protection of the coast. Most of this involved no more than tedious vigilance. When the Lancashires were sent to Dover Castle in 1795 they were required to maintain elaborate precautions for the defence of the fortifications. The guards and picket in the castle, changed at 10 a.m. each day, numbered over 100 men; those in the outer forts, over 80. On an alarm, the sentries at all gates were to be doubled. The picket were to sleep in one room in their clothes, and they and each company in the garrison had precise instructions as to the position they were to take up in the event of an attack. They were to practise moving into those positions and it was also laid down by what route they were to retire if the attack became overwhelming. To keep the regiment in fighting trim there were two parades a day, and a

[1] WO. 1/1013, ff. 85, 109.
[2] WO. 34/154, f. 513. WO. 34/155, ff. 201–2. WO. 34/156 (i), f. 35.
[3] WO. 1/1000, K. Gobbet, 18 July 1778.
[4] See, e.g., WO. 1/1016, R. Jones, 7 April 1782; WO. 1/1017, ff. 591–5; WO. 4/770, p. 352; WO. 4/771, pp. 387–8; WO. 4/772, pp. 41–2.
[5] Above, p. 402.

field day once a week, while thirty men were told off to learn the use of the great guns in the fort. From the outer forts, sentries were posted all along the beach to prevent surprise. At night they were relieved every two hours. They had to call 'all's well' along the line every half-hour, and a patrol visited them all an hour after each relief.[1]

The tribulations of sentry-go by the water's edge are to be seen in the case of the Shropshires, on guard at Gravesend in the winter of 1778–9. The sentries were exposed to severe weather and high tides. Just after the New Year a sentry had to leave his post when the water reached his knees and in order to get ashore had to leave his clothes behind. Two sentry boxes on the Tilbury side were washed away, to the consternation of the watchers on the other shore, but the men inside were saved by the exertions of a sergeant. Thereafter the commanding officer was given some discretion in the posting of guards. and the sentry boxes were protected against the inclement weather by being mounted on swivels. The chief engineer at Chatham told the regiment that mounting guard in such a place was a post of honour.[2]

More exciting than guard duty were occasions when the militia had to rush to the coast to beat off a raid by an enemy warship. In August 1779 a detachment of the Huntingdons at Alnwick heard the sound of guns and were told that there were French frigates off the coast at Alnmouth near by. They reached the threatened spot just over two hours after the first alarm, sending word to the commanding officer of the regiment who soon had all his men in motion. It turned out that two frigates had attacked a whaler off the coast, but when others had come up they had sailed away. Lord Adam Gordon, the general locally in command, thought the whole affair a silly alarm.[3] In June 1781 a company of the West Norfolks at Patrington in Holdernesse was told that a lug-sail privateer had driven two brigs ashore at Holmpton, five miles away, and would take them off at high tide. An ensign and twelve men set off, covered the distance in forty minutes and took position on a cliff. The privateer, said to be only 40 yards offshore, sent out two boats to attack them and bombarded them with grape and double-headed shot, to which they replied with small arms. When the rest of the company arrived, the lugger withdrew and the militia took possession of the brigs.[4]

This was about as near as the reformed English militia ever got to coming to grips with an enemy. What would have happened if

[1] Farrington, 15, 24 and 26 March, and 4 April 1795. Cf. WO. 34/117, f. 228, similar arrangements in 1779.

[2] WO. 34/112, ff. 77–8, 100–5, 126.

[3] WO. 34/117, ff. 85–7. Cf. a false alarm, WO. 1/1000, R. J. Price, 22 October 1778.

[4] WO. 34/134, f. 99. The privateer managed to take two other ships farther out. The militia alerted the navy.

contact had really been established? A few guesses on this subject seem to follow rather naturally from the foregoing analysis. The militia was fairly well trained, but not in general very well led. It seems unlikely, therefore, that it would have shown up well had there been a massive invasion at short notice. But things might have been different if the first attack had not been overwhelming and the militia had had a chance to recover its breath: if, let us say, the Irish rebellion of 1798 had built up slowly into a full-scale campaign. Not only would such a situation have given the militia all-important battle experience but it would have brought at last the possibility of an adequate supply of good officers. If the militia had been involved in real fighting, on which the safety of the nation depended, then both the country gentlemen and the more talented army officers would have been much more willing to serve in it—and also much more willing to forget their mutual jealousies. Then at last the men would have had the leadership which they needed and would have been able to make the good showing in the field of which they were undoubtedly capable.

CONCLUSION

T HE story of the militia from the Restoration to the advent of Napoleon has now been told. Personal intrigues and administrative details have bulked large in the telling and it may seem daring to seek for a pattern in such a tangle. But certain general remarks suggest themselves regarding the development both of British political life and of the nation's military resources as revealed in the history of this one institution.

Politically, the story of the militia shows first how, for at least a century after the Civil War, the continued existence of a viable national executive government was endangered by disputes about the extent of its powers. In retrospect it appears that the Restoration did at least decide that the government was to be monarchical and that the king was to have sole command of the armed forces. After 1689, parliamentary regulation, by mutiny acts and the control of expenditure, overlaid but did not supersede royal executive authority. But in the agitations for militia reform, especially under Charles II and William III, it was this very thing that was attacked. To abolish the standing forces, arm the freeholders and restrict royal freedom in the choice of military commanders—this was republicanism and anarchy brought in by the back door. The national government would have ceased to control the armed forces of the state: neither the king nor any other central authority would have had the means to enforce obedience to their commands in the country. It is not surprising that Charles II vetoed the militia bill of 1678, modest though it was.

The more radical militia schemes probably had little chance of adoption after 1700. But the act finally passed in 1757 was a more moderate move in the same direction. The system of property qualifications for deputies and officers, the requirement that a minimum number of deputies should be appointed if so many persons qualified could be found, the provision that officers should periodically retire in favour of other qualified persons offering to serve—all these pointed to a force controlled by the notables of each county rather than by the freely chosen agents of the king. Another pointer in the same direction was the proposal to entrust the execution of the militia laws in part to the commissioners of the land tax, for these were nominees of the house of commons, not of the sovereign. This proposal was successfully resisted in the house of lords on the grounds that it would unduly strengthen the 'democratic' part of the constitution[1] and that 'acts of magistracy' should be vested in the crown.[2]

The militia act of 1757 and the way that land tax commissioners were appointed were only two indications of a strong tendency to strip the crown of its executive functions and vest them either in parliamentary nominees or in independent local bodies.[3] It was the many independent country gentlemen in parliament, with their inveterate suspicion of the Court and all it stood for, who gave strength to this trend. Of the general political ideas which lay behind it, the story of the militia tells us much. The militia reformers were mainly whiggish in their political views—some of them deists and admirers of republics. Some, indeed, were nominal tories, but as a rule they were not tory in the sense of being warm champions of royal authority. When tories in this stricter sense took up the militia question, they did so half-heartedly, to embarrass the government of the day.[4] But though the friends of the militia were not really tories they certainly were backward-looking. They admired the old feudal nobility and the old yeomanry—independent of the crown and able to maintain that independence because they were armed. This was the state of things that they hoped to restore by militia legislation. This harking back to a golden age was, of course, a characteristic feature of all English radical movements alike in the seventeenth and in the eighteenth centuries. It gave them perhaps an appeal to the country gentry and to the countryside at large which they would not otherwise have had. It carried with it the danger that radical successes would reduce England to the condition of the Polish republic.

But the country gentlemen never wished to go to such lengths. Fundamentally loyal to the state and the crown, they felt obliged to support ministers in parliament whenever their measures were shown to be in the national interest.[5] Because of this, an equilibrium was

---

[1] Above, p. 131.   [2] Above, p. 140.

[3] This was favoured not only by country gentlemen but also by mercantile interests jealous of London. Examples are the unsuccessful attempt to set up a board of trade under parliamentary control in 1696 (R. M. Lees, 'Parliament and the Proposals for a Council of Trade, 1695–6,' *English Historical Review*, vol. liv (1939), pp. 38–66) and parliamentary assignment of ships of the fleet to convoy duty (see, e.g., J. H. Owen, *The War at Sea under Queen Anne* (Cambridge 1938), Appendix F.)

[4] Above, pp. 97–8.

[5] For the political attitudes of the independent country gentlemen see Sir L. Namier, 'Country Gentlemen in Parliament, 1750–84', and 'Monarchy and the Party System', now conveniently accessible in *Crossroads of Power* (London,

gradually established. The government lost much of its authority in church affairs and local government, but it retained control of the armed forces and had power enough to see that the taxes were collected. Very gradually in the course of the eighteenth century the question of the extent of the executive's powers ceased to be a live issue. Increasingly it was the influence and not the power of the crown that came under attack. The use of royal patronage for political purposes had long been complained of. From this controversy there developed campaigns for the reform of the representative system and some demand for greater parliamentary control over the appointment and dismissal of ministers. The king and the court therefore continued under fire, but the existence of the governmental machine was no longer threatened.[1]

The story of the militia affords a good deal of evidence as to when this transition from one political era to the next took place and why the old issue died, making room for the emergence of new ones. The militia agitation of the 1750s was one of the last in which what was at stake was the formal extent of the powers of the crown.[2] Already the challenge to royal authority was weak by comparison, say, with the closing years of King William's reign. The revival of the militia was recommended as a counterpoise to, not a substitute for, the standing army. It was advocated not only for political reasons but as essential to national defence. Hostility to the crown was disclaimed, and the act of 1757 subjected the militia, when mobilised for service, to the authority of royal generals and the full rigour of martial law. The main political effect of this measure was to set a limit to the growth of royal military patronage,[3] and thus the agitation ended as an attack on the influence rather than the power of the crown.

In the course of George III's reign, interest in keeping the militia independent of royal influence diminished. Protests, it is true, were regularly made when the government was suspected of trying to

1962), pp. 30–45, 213–34. Although it is and was customary to apply the term 'country gentlemen' to one particular segment of the house of commons, I think that there is no doubt that the interests and prejudices which they embodied were powerfully represented in other parts of the house also: cf. J. B. Owen, *Pelhams*, pp. 41–2, 49, 50, 56, 59–65, on the independent spirit and willingness to oppose ministers shown by the generality of members, even 'courtly' ones, in the Walpole-Pelham era.

[1] Even in 1784, with Pitt in office against the wishes of the then house of commons, the passage of the mutiny bill was not challenged, though admittedly Fox was losing ground already at that time. J. Steven Watson, *The Reign of George III, 1760–1815* (Oxford, 1960), p. 270.

[2] Another was the question of the legality of general warrants raised by Wilkes. Note that in Wilkes' later adventures his ostensible enemy was the house of commons not the king.

[3] Above, pp. 333–9.

destroy the separate identity of the militia or of packing the ranks of its officers with ministerial nominees.[1] But there was relatively little objection to the embodiment of the force for the duration of successive wars, although this destroyed the quasi-civilian character which its designers, despite their concern for military effectiveness, had hoped that it would retain. It was the country gentlemen in the militia themselves who asked for wider royal powers to mobilise it in 1775.[2] It was likewise the friends of the militia in parliament who urged a reluctant minister to assume responsibility for militia legislation in 1786:[3] an earlier generation would almost certainly have resented direct ministerial interference in the making of militia bills. In the 1790s the increasing professionalisation of the junior commissioned ranks of the militia, the increase in its size and the transfer of militiamen to the regular forces all aroused misgivings. They were all rightly thought to portend the degeneration of the militia into a mere recruiting and training department of the army. But the opponents of these measures were half-hearted and in the end they commonly gave up.[4]

What mainly lay behind this was the growth of a certain identity of view between the government and the bulk of the country gentlemen. There were various reasons for this. First, the danger of invasion grew fairly constantly, from war to war, from 1739 to 1802 and was fairly consistently associated with revolutionary threats (jacobite or jacobin) to the position of the gentry. This made them see the need of a strong and well-armed government. Second, the militia was a good billet for some at least of these same gentry, giving them local consequence, and in some cases profit. Now it is clear enough from the events of 1760, 1766 and 1786[5] that it was difficult if not impossible to get funds voted for the militia if the ministry was hostile. This gave the ministers a hold over all those interested in the militia's continuance. Third, the financial aspect of the militia led to something of a rift between the country gentlemen and the bulk of the nation for whom they commonly claimed to speak. The militia had been designed to lessen the burden of taxes on the gentry, but it was itself felt as a burden by poorer men who had to stand the ballot, subscribe towards the hiring of recruits and pay rates for the relief of militiamen's families. If the militia riots were spectacular rather than significant, quieter grumbling about the militia down the years may have been more important. The gentry were beginning to side with the government against the other tax-

[1] See above pp. 215–16.   [2] Above, pp. 206–8.
[3] Above, p. 201.
[4] E.g. Radnor in 1802: above p. 240.
[5] Above, pp. 171–3, 194, 199–203.

payers instead of with the other taxpayers against the government.[1]

There was a deeper reason why the quarrels over the militia died down—the palpable obsolescence of the backward-looking radical ideas which had inspired the militia's revival. Rapid social change made it hard for even the most resolute backwoodsman to go on taking them seriously. As opponents of the militia agitation had never tired of pointing out, the ideal of a citizen army, with men of property filling the ranks, had been made incapable of realisation by the development of a capitalist economy. The middle class of business-men and farmers-for-profit needed to devote their entire attention to business and could not take time off for fighting. That was possible only in a community of poor subsistence-farmers. The upper class, likewise, no longer regarded war as its profession, and was not eager to sacrifice time and money to military pursuits.[2] Even the skilled artisan could not be spared from his trade (he might forget it). Save for a privileged body of sportsmen, the people had ceased to have arms. Consequently, the militia could never be made very unlike the army. The rank and file of both were recruited from the lowest class. Only a few of the gentry could ever be induced to serve as militia officers. This being so, it was hard to work up much horror against some degree of assimilation of the two forces. One ideal only of the old militia champions received some practical expression. They had hoped by militia legislation to encourage patriotism and disinterested public service. Now the later part of the eighteenth century saw a heightening in all sorts of ways of the sense of public duty among the upper class.[3] The militia agitation may have helped to encourage this, and the revived militia certainly did give some members of the upper class an opportunity for public service which they would not other-wise have had. But the patriotism evident in some of the senior militia officers was not an anti-governmental sentiment.

Besides illuminating the changes in the character of the central issues in politics, the story of the militia is helpful in measuring the temperature and atmosphere in which political life was carried on. The militia established under the Restoration acts belonged to a

[1] Cf. R. A. C. Parker, 'Direct Taxation on the Coke Estates in the Eighteenth Century'. *English Historical Review*, vol. lxxi (1956), pp. 247–8. The mediation of the lords between ministers and commons on several occasions may have helped to produce a consensus of opinion on the militia.

[2] In the backward Scottish Highlands, farmers were still willing to leave the land and fight, and landlords made financial sacrifices to encourage them to do so. J. M. Bulloch, *Territorial Soldiering in the North East of Scotland during 1759–1814* (Aberdeen, 1914), pp. 210, 212, 221. Of course they too looked for profit, but from military service itself.

[3] E.g. there was more feeling against sinecures and laxity in accounting for public money.

world of bitter political and religious animosities, where any party quarrel was an incipient civil war and those in power always tried— though not always very systematically—to suppress their opponents by force. The decline of the old militia was a sign that things were changing. Men were not only ceasing to possess weapons but also trying more and more to live amicably with those with whom they differed in politics or religion. Though there continued to be forcible suppression of radical upsurges from below, the ruling class at least was living a civilised political life.

The resulting changes in political attitudes can be seen very clearly in the wrangles about the militia from 1756 to 1762. For the older generation—Newcastle, George II and their equivalents on the other side—the question was one of life and death. Not only did it involve the fundamental issue of the balance of powers in the state but its settlement in the wrong way might mean bloodshed and chaos. For younger men, most notably Rockingham and Sir George Savile, it was evident that such dreadful issues now belonged to the past. They were anxious to close that part of the debate for good, so that the militia could be looked at in a purely empirical way. Their standpoint was utilitarian: how could the national interest most efficiently be served? They point forward to a time when political divisions would be not about the nature of the state but about the best practical means of ensuring the wellbeing of the people.

II

The armed forces of a nation are only as efficient as its political conditions allow. How efficient those of eighteenth-century Britain were allowed to be can in part be seen from the story of the militia. Uncertain relations between executive and legislature were a constant hindrance to sound planning. What those in control of the government seem to have wanted from first to last was a body of reservists recruited by voluntary enlistment, able cheaply to bolster national defence in emergencies and perhaps make offensive action easier. Parliament repeatedly rejected schemes of this kind as tending unduly to strengthen the crown. Eventually the political situation seems to have destroyed even the will of ministers to bring plans forward. In the middle years of the eighteenth century they might have carried one had they chosen a proper moment. But the mere defence of their authority, coupled with routine business, took up all their attention and resources. They lived from hand to mouth. They lacked the expert staff required for preparing comprehensive plans in advance. As the conduct of Newcastle and Hardwicke in the militia question shows, they were so concerned to preserve the existence of the executive that they cared little in the last resort what it was made to do. A firm and consistent line of policy could only come if parliament took the initiative.

In parliament there was a certain amount of utopian enthusiasm for a citizen army and a consciousness of national danger, at first small but growing. Because of this it was possible, both in 1660–2 and in 1757, to get measures enacted that represented a compromise between what ministers would have liked and what parliament desired. On the earlier occasion what resulted was an irregular force, useful for police work but not for much else. It was given a fairly elaborate organisation in the hope of making it into something more like an army. But for want of funds and enthusiasm, this organisation failed in its purpose and was more of an encumbrance than a help. Something simpler, akin to the Volunteer Movement of Napoleonic times, would have harmonised better with the real character of the Restoration militia.

The events of 1744–6 and 1756 produced a new, strong feeling of national danger, and in consequence the force established in 1757 was much more useful to the government and turned out to be readily convertible into a supplement to the regular army. The militia still had many military shortcomings, resulting from parliamentary jealousy of the crown. But it may fairly be argued that its military usefulness now outweighed them. It enabled a body of men to be recruited, trained and made available for service whenever required, without the need, to pay them when they were not required. Only by harnessing the machinery of local government to military purposes was this possible. The army had no administrative system for dealing with reservists: it was the militia alone which had even the rudiments of a regimental depot in the recruiting area of each corps. Now it is unlikely that the country gentlemen would have been willing or even able to do for the army what they did for the militia, which was in some tenuous way the property of the counties. The separate existence of the militia had therefore to be tolerated, with the drawbacks that army and militia competed for recruits and militiamen could not be put into the army or sent abroad. On the other hand, there is reason to believe that many men in rural areas entered the militia who would never have joined the army. Further, by taking over the burden of home defence, the militia released regular troops and even some naval forces for service abroad. It was, nevertheless, a great step forward when the political obstacles to recruiting the line from the militia were at last overcome. Men who would not have joined the army at once could then be accustomed to military life in the militia and afterwards induced to transfer. The first real move towards this system was made in 1799.

The militia in theory was raised by assigning men to military service by ballot. In fact, it consisted mostly of substitutes and volunteers, hired by parishes or balloted individuals. The machinery of the ballot was cumbersome and it may well be asked if it could not simply have been dispensed with, as it was in the nineteenth century.[1] But it was probably essential to retain it if the local authorities were to be obliged to furnish quotas of men. If they had had no power to do anything but enlist recruits, they might simply have paid fines instead. The threat of conscription was an incentive to them to take their recruiting work seriously. What almost certainly was a mistake was to apply the system in urban areas like Middlesex. It was here that the regulars did most of their recruiting, and the militia both competed with them and failed in its own task because so many of its recruits deserted. It would have been better to have exempted such places from contributing to the militia on condition that they helped to get men for the army.

A final drawback of the separate existence of the militia was that the men were under the command mainly of amateur officers, whose general standard of efficiency was low. This again was part of the price to be paid if local gentry were to undertake recruiting and to bring under arms the men of the rural areas. These countrymen, moreover, needed to be sure that gentlemen from their district would command them on service and look after them. The dubious quality of the officers makes it rather doubtful if the militia would have behaved well in the face of an enemy in the field. However, there is no reason to believe that a different sort of force would have been better led. The officers in the army were themselves deplorably unprofessional in the main. Any attempt, of whatever kind, to expand the number of men under arms was bound to be handicapped by the shortage of well-trained officers to take command. The militia contained a small nucleus of professional soldiers and enthusiasts. Thanks to them, there is little doubt that militia units usually reached a tolerable standard of technical proficiency. Parliament proved increasingly willing to encourage the use of regular officers in the militia, especially in the lower ranks where men of property seldom wished to serve. No doubt the best way of promoting efficiency would have been to make a spell in the militia a regular stage in every army officer's career. No doubt also, a larger supply of good officers, both from the army and from the gentry, would have been forthcoming had invasion ever taken place.

The militia of the eighteenth century represents two related military tendencies: it was an attempt both to create a reserve formation for home defence and to use an obligation of military

[1] Fortescue, *History*, vol. xi, pp. 103–4, 448; vol. xiii, pp. 22–3.

service on the citizen as the basis for recruiting. Political factors made it impossible to introduce true conscription and necessary to keep the militia distinct from the army, which led to various inconveniences. On the other hand, the national dangers which led to the revival of the militia were not so acute that its shortcomings led to any national disaster. It may fairly be claimed that the militia was an expedient proportioned to the extent of the danger to be met. It is not true that the danger was imaginary and the militia superfluous; at the same time there were good reasons for avoiding revolutionary measures like full conscription. The economic burden that this would represent was reason enough in itself for caution. The militia laid the foundation in various ways for a truly conscript force. It was recruited on a truly territorial basis, each regiment from a particular area. In this it was very different from the regular regiments of the time and pointed the way forward. It caused the authorities to begin facing the social problems arising from conscription, notably by the provision of allowances for militiamen's families. As the national danger increased, parliament showed itself increasingly willing to move towards real conscription by increasing the levy and tying the militia more closely to the army.

Had the national danger continued to increase, instead of coming abruptly to an end in 1815, there can be little doubt that militia and army together would have gradually evolved into a conscript army of the modern type. Instead of being forgotten, the militia would be revered as the true ancestor of this citizen army and yet another example of how British institutions 'broaden down from precedent to precedent'.[1] As it is, the militia is perhaps an example of something else: the genius of the English governing class for self preservation. From the prejudices of the gentry which parliament incorporated in the militia acts there resulted inefficiency of every kind. But when danger threatened, the gentry abated its prejudices in proportion and a stronger national effort resulted, just sufficient to meet the danger. From the example of the militia it can be seen how the British state in the eighteenth century, ramshackle though it was, proved itself strong in adversity and often victorious against its foes both at home and abroad.

[1] There was also, of course, a long tradition of pressing men for the army, just as they were pressed for the navy. This again was done by local magistrates and in the eighteenth century it was always sanctioned by act of parliament. But there was no attempt to build this into a regular system and it was discontinued after 1779: perhaps because it was applied mainly to vagabonds and was blatantly conscription applied to the lower classes only. Clode, vol. ii, pp. 10, 18–19, 48.

APPENDICES

A. DATES OF THE FIRST FORMATION AND
EMBODIMENT OF THE MILITIA IN EACH
COUNTY , 1758–78

B. MILITIA QUOTAS OF EACH COUNTY AND
UNITS INTO WHICH FORMED, 1757–1802

C. MPs AT A MEETING OF FRIENDS OF
THE MILITIA, APRIL 1759

INDEX

APPENDIX A

DATES OF THE FIRST FORMATION AND EMBODIMENT OF THE MILITIA IN EACH COUNTY, 1758–78.

County	First formation (date of first issue of arms)[1]	First embodied for actual service (date of Secretary at War's orders thereon)[2]
Dorset	27 August 1758	21 June 1759
Norfolk	7 October 1758	24 June 1759
Wiltshire	8 November 1758	21 June 1759
Kent, West Regt.	20 November 1758	23 June 1759
Devon	5 December 1758	23 June 1759
Hertford	5 March 1759	11 October 1759
Somerset	22 March 1759	4 July 1759
Warwick	28 March 1759	7 July 1759
Surrey	18 April 1759	6 July 1759
Suffolk	27 April 1759	16 October 1759
Gloucester, South Bn.	15 May 1759	27 July 1759
Lincoln, North Regt.	28 May 1759	1 November 1759
South Regt.	17 July 1759	1 November 1759
Berkshire	6 June 1759	26 July 1759
Essex	23 June 1759	1 November 1759
Carmarthen	3 July 1759	8 December 1759
North Riding, Yorks.	4 July 1759	3 July 1759
West Riding, Yorks.: 2 battalions	21 August 1759	6 September 1759
3rd battalion	29 August 1759	6 September 1759
Huntingdon	22 August 1759	22 October 1759
Cambridge	3 September 1759	31 March 1778
Pembroke	7 September 1759	15 December 1759
Hampshire, North Bn.	?14 September 1759	15 December 1759
South Bn.	? 3 October 1759	12 May 1760[3]
Cheshire	18 September 1759	1 November 1759
Flint	3 October 1759	8 December 1759
Buckingham	31 October 1759	14 May 1760
Rutland	27 November 1759	15 December 1759
Westmorland	29 November 1759	28 December 1759
Northumberland	?29 November 1759[4]	29 January 1760
Monmouth	1 December 1759[5]	21 March 1760
East Riding, Yorks.	3 December 1759[6]	8 January 1760
Brecon	6 December 1759[6]	29 January 1760

447

Kent, East Regt.	25 February 1760[1]	31 March 1778
Durham	12 August 1759[2]	27 February 1760
Bedford	25 February 1760[1]	7 March 1760
Cornwall	18 March 1760[1]	29 April 1760
Leicester	19 April 1760[2]	9 July 1760
Denbigh	8 May 1760[3]	18 July 1760
Cumberland	20 June 1760[1]	4 August 1760
Lancashire	18 July 1760[1]	23 December 1760
Glamorgan	January 1760[1]	20 January 1761
Middlesex	7, 12 August 1760[1]	31 March 1778
Gloucester, North Bn.	22 August 1760[1]	9 April 1761
Bristol		25 June 1762
Carnarvon	28 August 1762[3]	5 October 1762
Hereford	7 September 1762[4]	31 March 1778
Cardigan	1 October 1762[3]	31 March 1778
Anglesey	19 November 1762[3]	31 March 1778
Shropshire	December 1762[3]	31 March 1778
Merioneth	25 January 1763[3]	31 March 1778
Radnor	21 February 1763[3]	31 March 1778
Northampton	14 April 1763[3]	31 March 1778
Montgomery	11 May 1763[3]	31 March 1778
Worcester	6 October 1770[3]	31 March 1778
Derby	4 September 1773[5]	31 March 1778
Nottingham	14 November 1775[3]	31 March 1778
Stafford	7 February 1777[3]	31 March 1778
Sussex	29 June 1778[3]	31 March 1778 (sic)
Oxford	31 July 1778[3]	31 March 1778 (sic)

[1] By 31 Geo. II, cap. 26, s. 34, the government was only to issue arms on receiving a certificate that three-fifths of the men of a unit had been enrolled and the same proportion of officers appointed. Unless otherwise stated, the dates in this column are those of issue from the Tower of London, from a list dated 29 November 1759, BM, Add. 35893, f. 243.

[2] These are in WO. 4/757–762. They are cited in preference to the formal warrants for embodiment by the Secretary of State, because they are more informative.

[3] I think that the Isle of Wight company was first embodied in 1778.

[4] The list of 29 November cited in n. 1, says the arms for this county are 'ready'.

[5] Secretary of State's order for issue of arms, SP., bundle 144.

[6] Certificate by lord lieutenant, three-fifths complete. *Ibid.*; SP. 41/30.

[1] Certificate by lord lieutenant, three-fifths complete, SP. 41/30. Gloucestershire, date of reception. Glamorgan, see WO. 34/112, f. 106.

[2] Like report that officers complete, SP. 41/30.

[3] Secretary of State's order for issue of arms, HO. 51/2, 3; SP. 44/193, 199. Shropshire, day omitted. Cf. undated list, SP. 41/32.

[4] As n. 3. But there is a certificate as n. 1 dated 21 November 1760.

[5] Lord George Cavendish reported three-fifths of the officers obtained, HO. 51/4, pp. 60–1.

APPENDIX B

MILITIA QUOTAS OF EACH COUNTY AND UNITS INTO WHICH FORMED, 1757–1802

County	No. of Men to be Found[1]			No. of Regiments, Battalions and Corps in:	
	In 1757–96	Extra, in 1796–99	In 1802	1779[2]	1799[3]
Bedford	400	254	317	1††	1
Berkshire	560	749	561	1*	1
Buckingham	560	662	599	1*	1
Cambridge	480	646	481	1	1
Cheshire	560	1460	885	1*	2
Cornwall	640	828	647	1*	2
Cumberland	320	1180	615	1††	1
Derby	560	1666	939	1*	1
Devon	1600	1694	1512	3*†	4
Dorset	640	185	411	1*	1
Durham	400	800	492	1	1
Essex	960	1756	1244	2*	3
Gloucester	960	1757	1163	2(1*)	2
Hereford	480	662	520	1*	1
Hertford	560	500	480	1*	1
Huntingdon	320	0	159	1††	1
Kent	960	1873	1296	2*	3
Lancashire	800	5160	2439	1*	5
Leicester	560	928	643	1*	1
Lincoln	1200	2140	1368	2*	3
Middlesex	1600	5820	3038	3*	5
Monmouth	240	360	280	1	1
Norfolk	960	1992	1209	2*	3
Northampton	640	1128	724	1*	2
Northumberland	560	824	649	1*	2
Nottingham	480	896	564	1*	1
Oxford	560	852	603	1*	1
Rutland	120	80	83	1	1
Shropshire	640	1558	991	1*	2
Somerset	840	2960	1556	1*†	3
Southampton	960	847	850	3§	3
Stafford	560	2095	1133	1*	3
Suffolk	960	1470	1042	2*	2
Surrey	800	2460	1336	1*†	3
Sussex	800	1160	803	1*	2
Warwick	640	900	853	1*	1
Westmorland	240	350	243	1††	1

GG   449

Wiltshire	800	1049	917	1*	2
Worcester	560	825	616	1*	2
York, West Riding	1240	4694	2429	2*†	5
North „	720	1360	911	1*†	2
East „	400	861	564	1	1
Wales.					
Anglesey	80	320	128	1**	3
Brecon	160	340	204	1	incorporated with Monmouth
Cardigan	120	474	244	1	1
Carmarthen	200	790	405	1	1
Carnarvon	80	176	128	1**	1
Denbigh	280	420	344	1	1
Flint	120	311	201	1	1
Glamorgan	360	622	403	1	1
Merioneth	80	174	121	1**	1
Montgomery	240	259	279	1	1
Pembroke	160	331	201	1	1
Radnor	120	220	140	1	1

[1] 30 Geo. II, cap. 25, s. 16. 2 Geo. III, cap. 20, s. 41. 26 Geo. III, cap. 107, s. 17. 37 Geo. III, cap. 3, s. 3. 42 Geo. III, cap. 90, s. 19. For levies made or projected in Scotland, the City of London, the Tower Hamlets and the Stanneries, see above, pp. 215, 219. For small voluntary augmentations see above, p. 245, n. 2; p. 246, n. 2. The quotas fixed by the acts were exclusive of sergeants and commissioned and warrant officers. In 1802 the king was empowered to increase the quotas then fixed by a half if he saw fit (42 Geo. III, cap. 90, s. 146).

[2] CJ, vol. xxxvii, p. 23. *List of the Officers of the several Regiments and Corps of Militia*, 14 May 1779. These figures are given as a specimen of how the militia was organised while the quotas were as fixed in 1757. Comparison with CJ, vol. xxix, p. 33, shows that the part of the militia embodied in 1762 was organised much as is shown in this column: alterations between 1762 and 1779 have been noted.

* denotes a regiment, i.e. a corps with three field officers and at least eight companies.

** denotes an independent company.

†† denotes a corps with less than eight companies, but which had three field officers because the lord lieutenant served as colonel.

§ Hampshire had two regiments plus an independent company in the Isle of Wight. In 1762 this was not counted separately.

Corps with none of the foregoing symbols against them consisted of from two to seven companies and had either one or two field officers.

† denotes a county that had one corps more in 1762 than in 1779.

[3] CJ, vol. liv, p. 22. This column shows how the militia was organised during the short time that the entire supplementary militia was embodied.

APPENDIX C

MPs AT A MEETING OF FRIENDS OF THE MILITIA, APRIL 1759

This meeting, in London on 7 April, was the subject of a report by George Onslow which reached the Duke of Newcastle via James West (BM, Add. 32889, ff. 394, 396, 400–1). He said that there were about 130 people present, among whom he identified 51 MPs: 23 tories and 22 whigs. He shows their party affiliations by a W. or a T. He said that there were other members present whom he did not know, and also noted the presence of six lord lieutenants: Lords Bateman, Cholmondeley, Pembroke, Shaftesbury and Temple and Mr Price.

I have retained Onslow's order and spelling, adding Christian names (in brackets) where wanting, constituencies and some biographical details. The number of electors in the larger boroughs concerned is given in brackets. The members about whom nothing further is said appear to have been ordinary country squires. For this further information I am indebted to Sir Lewis Namier and John Brooke, *The House of Commons, 1754–90* (London, 1964) and to the guidance kindly given me by Mr Brooke personally.

Name	Whig or Tory	Constituency	Remarks
(Charles) Amcotts	T	Boston	Former jacobite.
Sir Willoughby Aston	T	Nottingham (2000)	
(Sir) Nic. Baily	W	Anglesey	Supporter of Frederick, Prince of Wales.
(Richard) Barry	T	Wigan	Former jacobite. Son of Fourth Lord Barrymore.
Sir Walter Blackett	T	Newcastle (2000)	
(William) Bouverie	T	Salisbury	Son of Lord Folkestone. A small but independent electorate.
(John) Bullock	W	Maldon (800)	Chosen with tory support but sought favour of Newcastle and Bedford.
(Thomas) Chester	T	Gloucestershire	
(George) Cooke	T	Middlesex	Chief Protonotary, Court of Common Pleas. Supported Pitt.

451

Sir William Coddrington	W	Beverley (1000)	West Indian interests.
Sir J. H. Cotton	T	Marlborough	See pp. 152–4.
Sir John Cust	W	Grantham	Clerk of the household to Frederick, Prince of Wales and his widow, but left her because of Bute.
Sir Francis Dashwood	W	New Romney	Supporter of Bute Militia pamphleteer.
(Robert) Fairfax	W	Kent	Supported by Duke of Dorset. Impecunious, financially supported by Pelham and Newcastle
Adml. (Thomas) Frankland	W	Thirsk	Thought to be pro-Newcastle.
John Fuller	W	Tregony	Supported by government in election of 1754, but troublesome.
Rose Fuller	W	Romney	West Indian interests and strong whig principles.
(Sambrooke) Freeman	W	Pontefract	Described as a country gentleman supporting government.
James Grenville	W	Buckingham	Brother of Temple, brother-in-law of William Pitt.
(William) Harvey	W	Essex	Connected with Bute but approached Newcastle for favours.
(Alexander) Hume	W	Steyning	Merchant; sometime director of East India Company.
(George) Jennings	W	Whitchurch	Country gentleman friendly to Newcastle
Sir Robert Long	T	Wiltshire	
(Richard) Lowndes	T	Buckinghamshire	

Lord Malpas	W	Bramber	Served at Fontenoy and in the '45. Son of Lord Cholmondeley. Grandson of Sir R. Walpole, pensioner.
(James M.) Molyneux	W	Haslemere	Sided against Newcastle, 1755.
Lord North	W	Banbury	Appointed a lord of the Treasury, 1759.
Sir Roger Newdigate	T	Oxford University	Independent and conservative, an eminent representative of tory traditions.
(William) Northey	T	Calne	Supported Downe's motion to arm the nation, March 1756 (p. 128). Made a lord of the Bedchamber by Geo. III, 1760.
George Onslow	W	Rye	Son of the Speaker, nephew of Newcastle, dismissed for supporting him in 1762.
Sir John Philips	T	Petersfield	An ex-jacobite who became a supporter of Pitt and later of Bute.
George Pitt	T	Dorset	Made a lord of the Bedchamber by Geo. III, 1760.
John Pitt	T	Dorchester	Took office with his cousin W. Pitt, 1756.
(Thomas) Prowse	T	Somerset	See above, pp. 151, 152, 184, n. 1.
(Henry) Pye	T	Berkshire	
(Isaac) Rebow	W	Colchester (1500)	The Rebows an old town, not landed, family, which often provided a member for the borough.
Sir William Stanhope	W	Buckinghamshire	Brother of Lord Chesterfield.
(Alexander) Thistlethwaite	W	Hampshire	

Sir Charles Tynte	T	Somerset	See above, pp. 151–2.
(William) Thornton	W	York (2500)	Rockingham's candidate. See above, chap. v.
(Arthur) Vansittart	T	Berkshire	
(Robert) Vyner	T	Lincolnshire	Above, pp. 124, 167, 172, 175.
(Robert) Vyner jun.	T	Okehampton	As last. Duke of Bedford's candidate but independent all the same.
(John) Rolle Walter	T	Exeter (1500)	
(Charles) Whitworth	W	Minehead	Relative of Newcastle. Pensioner. Deputy Governor of Tilbury.

INDEX

Individual militia corps are indexed under their respective counties

455

Aston, Sir Willoughby, M.P., 70, 379, 451
Atherton, 252
Atkinson, Captain Robert, plotter, 39–40
Atkyns, Sir Robert, 4 n.1, 13, 69
Augusta, Princess of Wales, mother of George III, 121, 452
Austria, 104, 107, 220; Croats, 101; Hungarians, 97 n.5, 107, 203
Ayrshire, 163, 165
Axminster, 54

Bacon, Edward, M.P., 109 n.4, 191 n.7
Baggage, movement of, 16, 87, 266, 359–60, 362, 386, 389 n.6, 390, 412; *see also* camp: tents
Baillie, Lt., 423
Baily, Sir Nic., M.P., 451
Baker, William, M.P., 380
Balch, Mr, Somerset dissenter, 152
Ballot, recruitment of militia by, 113, 128–9, 138, 143, 187–8, 190 n.4, 195, 212–15; abolition proposed, 228; appeals relating to, 142, 248–50, 279; burthensome, 200; discontinued, 263; householders to make lists, 285; insuring against, 188 n.4, 240, 252, 253 n.3, 254, 262; liability to, exemptions, 131, 142, 189, 210, 247–8, 250, 252 n.2; penalties for false returns, obstruction, 142, 249, 281 n.1, 284; utility, 443
Balloted men, allowance to, 189, 192–3, 253, 254, 276; paying fine, 129, 213, 251, 262, 276–7; serving in person, 237, 251, 254–7, 261 n.3, 377; minimum height, 247
Bamfield, Thomas, M.P., 11
Banbury, 453
Bands, regimental; *see* drummers
Banks, Sir Joseph, President of Royal Society, 297
Bantry, 222
Barham Downs, 268

Barmouth, 295
Barnard, Sir John, 125 n.4, 134
Barnet, 42
Barnstaple, 21, 66
Barnwell, 262, 399
Barracks, militia in, 266, 377–8, 382–5, 392, 400, 410, 420–1
Barré, Isaac, 192, 199 n.1
Barrington, William Wildman, Viscount, Secretary at War, 113, 115 n.2, 134, 135 n.1, 166 n.5, 167, 170, 191–2, 206, 346, 361, 374, 384, 425
Barry, Richard, M.P., 451
Barwick, Lieutenant Mark A., 431
Bastard, Colonel John P., M.P., 202, 230, 234, 268, 369 n.9
Bateman, John, Viscount, 250, 311, 409, 451
Bath, 55
Bath, John Grenville, Earl of, 41
Beachy Head, battle of, and invasion scare, 53, 73 n.5, 88, 112
Beaconsfield, 424
Beauchamp, Francis Seymour-Conway, Viscount, 199 n.1, 212, 264
Beaufort, Henry Somerset, 1st Duke of and Marquess of Worcester, previously Lord Herbert, 36, 37 n.1, 38, 59, 82
Beaufort, Harry Somerset, 3rd Duke of, 5
Beaufort, Henry Somerset, 5th Duke of, 303 n.3, 397
Beckford, William, M.P., 135, 167, 169 n.4, 173, 192, 394
Bedford, 35
Bedford, John Russell, 4th Duke of, 124, 133, 155, 186 n.10, 199 n.2, 215, 286, 310, 373, 426, 451, 454
Bedford, Wriothesley Russell, 2nd Duke of, 38 n.5
Bedfordshire, 35, 38 n.5, 124, 147, 252, 258, 267, 279, 293, 296, 310, 416, 448, 449
Bedloe, William, 80
Belasyse, Sir Rowland, 70
Belfast, 163